The New World Reader

THE
New World
Reader

Thinking and Writing
about the Global Community

Gilbert H. Muller

La Guardia Community College
City University of New York

Houghton Mifflin Company
Boston   New York

Publisher: Patricia Coryell
Executive Editor: Suzanne Phelps Weir
Development Manager: Sarah Helyar Smith
Editorial Assistant: Anne Leung
Senior Project Editor: Bob Greiner
Editorial Assistant: Trinity Peacock-Broyles
Manufacturing Manager: Marie Barnes
Senior Marketing Manager: Cindy Graff Cohen

Cover art: Photo of an Iraqi market scene, 1993, by Peter Turnley

Printed in the U.S.A.

Library of Congress Catalog Number: 2003110132

ISBN: 0-618-39594-6

1 2 3 4 5 6 7 8 9-QUF-08 07 06 05 04

Brief Contents

Contents

1 │ Thinking, Reading, and Writing About the New Global Era   1

4 | Global Relationships: Are Sex and Gender Roles Changing? 117

PHOTO ESSAY

5 | The Challenge of Globalization: What Are the Consequences? 161

6 | Culture Wars: Whose Culture Is It, Anyway? 211

9 | The Digital Revolution: Will It Bring Us Together?   345

"At least since World War II, American strategic interests in the Middle East have been, first, to ensure supplies of oil and, second, to guarantee at enormous cost the strength and domination of Israel over its neighbors."

Rhetorical Contents

Illustration

Comparison and Contrast

Definition

Classification

Process Analysis

Causal Analysis

Argument and Persuasion

Culture or Conflict?: Images of Globalization

Preface

> *We live in a world of transformations, affecting almost every aspect of what we do. For better or worse, we are being propelled into a global order that no one fully understands, but which is making its effects felt upon all of us.*
>
> —Anthony Giddens

The New World Reader presents provocative essays about contemporary global issues and challenges. The book provides students with the resources needed to think and write in ways that foster varieties of global understanding and citizenship. Especially since the terrorist attacks of September 11, 2001, and subsequent interventions in Afghanistan and Iraq, students have been challenged to reconsider and reflect upon the relationship between America and its place in the world. Salman Rushdie observes that the West has met the "rest," and the writers in this text deal with this reality as well as those global forces that increasingly shape our lives. These writers from a variety of backgrounds and perspectives reveal that globalization is *the* big story, the most pressing issue of our times.

Students using *The New World Reader* will find interconnected chapters and selections dealing with such strategic global questions as the changing demographics of the United States, the impact of September 11th on individuals as well as entire populations, the nature of globalization, the clash of cultures and civilizations, the changing roles of women and men in the global arena, the Internet revolution, and the state of the global environment. Challenged by such well-known contemporary thinkers and writers as Richard Rodriguez, Amy Tan, Francis Fukuyama, Esther Dyson, Barbara Kingsolver, Arthur Schlesinger, Jr., and Edward Said, today's students will be encouraged to come to grips with a world that, in Anthony Giddens's words, is now subject to complex and often mystifying transformations.

This book demonstrates that critical thinking about our new global century begins when students consider unfamiliar perspectives and arguments, when they are open to new global ideas and perceptions. Put differently, this text combines and encourages intercultural and transnational inquiry. As such, the design of the anthology encourages students to ask not only who they are in this society but also who they are in the world. Many of the diversity themes that teachers of college writing find especially productive and stimulating—gender and sexuality, race and ethnicity, class and cultural orientation—lend themselves to these issues of local and global perception. The selections in the text present a tapestry of diversity in both a local and a global light, moving from personalized encounters with cultures to analytical and argumentative treatment of topics. Students are provided the opportunity to move across cultures and continents, interrogating and assessing authors' insights into our evolving transnational society.

The writers in *The New World Reader* present keen emotional and intellectual insights into our new global era. Most of the essays are relatively brief and provocative and serve as models for the types of personal, analytical, and argumentative papers that college composition teachers ask their students to write. Many of the essays were written after September 11, 2001, and most since 1990. (George Orwell is one necessary exception.) Drawn from a wide variety of authorial backgrounds and sources, and offering diverse angles of opinion and perspectives, the readings in this text lend themselves to thoughtful responses, class debate, small-group discussion, and online research. Some of the longer essays—for example, Jamaica Kincaid on the nature of colonialism and Anthony Giddens on the meaning of globalization—orient students to those forms of academic discourse that they will encounter in the humanities and social sciences. With introductions to chapters and writers, previewing questions, a three-part apparatus following each essay, a casebook on the Middle East, three appendices offering guidelines on conducting research in the global era and defining rhetorical and global terms, and extensive Web resources, *The New World Reader* can serve as the core text in composition courses.

Features

Lively Selections in Chapters That Challenge Our Understanding of Ourselves and Others

The New World Reader presents seventy-four essays in ten interrelated chapters and a casebook. The first chapter introduces students to the challenges of thinking, reading, and writing about their place in the new global era. Nine subsequent chapters, each consisting of seven essays that move from personal and op-ed pieces to more complex selections, focus on key aspects of our increasingly globalized culture, presenting ideas and themes that radiate through the text. A casebook concludes the text with essays that provide insight on the Middle East and how its peoples perceive the West.

Chapter 1. Thinking, Reading, and Writing About the New Global Era. This concise introductory chapter offers guidelines for students as they think, read, and write about key issues in post–September 11th America and the world. Clear thinking about the "new world order" involves a knowledge of both what has gone before and what lies ahead, as well as mastery of the analytical and cognitive skills at the heart of the reading and writing processes. Three brief essays permit students to practice their critical thinking, reading, and writing skills. Columnist Nicholas D. Kristof discusses the changing world of relationships in "Love and Race." Writer and college professor Ray Gonzalez in "The Ladybugs" tells of his return to the classroom in the wake of September 11. And journalist Patricia Leigh-Brown offers fresh insights into how young Muslim women cope with prom night in the United States.

Chapter 2. New American Mosaic: Are We Becoming a Universal Nation? Presenting compelling insights into the new American demographics, writers N. Scott Momaday, Richard Rodriguez, and others stress the ways both native and "fourth wave" patterns of acculturation are changing the face of the American nation while fostering a greater appreciation of other cultures. The chapter introduces students to the idea that globalization is not only "out there" but also "here."

Chapter 3. Speaking in Tongues: Does Language Unify or Divide? Presenting essays by Amy Tan, James Baldwin, and other well-known writers, this chapter explores the varied ways in which language forms identity and cultural relationships in our increasingly polyglot world.

Chapter 4. Global Relationships: Are Sex and Gender Roles Changing? Across the globe, the perception of gender and the larger struggle for human rights vary in the amount of change they are undergoing. Ellen Goodman argues for justice for women, while Richard Rodriguez offers a revealing appreciation of his sexual orientation and changing family values. The last essay, by Barbara Ehrenreich and Annette Fuentes, "Life on the Global Assembly Line," is a contemporary classic, detailing the exploitation of women in factories overseas.

Chapter 5. The Challenge of Globalization: What Are the Consequences? The debate over globalization, whether framed in economic, political, environmental, or cultural terms, serves increasingly to define our lives in the twenty-first century. Essays by Thomas L. Friedman, Jamaica Kincaid, Anthony Giddens, and others argue the benefits and dangers of globalization.

Chapter 6. Culture Wars: Whose Culture Is It, Anyway? This chapter examines the impact of popular American culture on the nation and on the world. From McDonald's to Hollywood to MTV, the new American landscape has had a global impact. Among writers offering critical appraisals of the contemporary culture wars are Henry Louis Gates, Jr., Mario Vargas Llosa, and Ellen Goodman.

Chapter 7. The Clash of Civilizations: Is Conflict Avoidable? Building on the issues raised in the first six chapters, this unit offers a critical examination of the clash-of-civilizations debate. A classic essay by George Orwell, "Shooting an Elephant," alerts students to the fact that today's global conflicts do not spring spontaneously from September 11th but rather have deep historical and political antecedents.

Chapter 8. The Age of Terror: What Is the Just Response? The essays in this chapter, written by such prominent writers as Barbara Kingsolver and Anna Quindlen, focus on the cataclysmic events of September 11 and how these attacks have altered the ways Americans perceive their relationship to the rest of the world.

Chapter 9. The Digital Revolution: Will It Bring Us Together? The role of information technology in globalization preoccupies numerous contemporary writers including Thomas L. Friedman and Esther Dyson. The essays in this chapter focus on the "digital divide," the potential for technology to increase literacy and opportunity, and whether or not information technology can be a force for global understanding.

Chapter 10. The Fate of the Earth: Can We Preserve the Global Environment? From global warming to weapons of mass destruction, the Earth's ecology faces major challenges. Essays by Rachel Carson, Annie Dillard, Andy Rooney, Francis Fukuyama, and others offer insights into how we might save the environment—and the world—for future generations.

A Casebook on the Contemporary Middle East: Why Does It Matter? Eight essays by writers of Middle Eastern background offer provocative insights into a region that arguably is the most consequential and compelling for today's college students. Representing diverse backgrounds and perspectives, these writers, including Edward Said, Amos Oz, and Azar Nafisi, examine such issues as the Arab-Israeli conflict, the fate of Afghanistan, and the roles of women in traditional societies. A full introduction and apparatus following each essay offer students the opportunity to build on basic knowledge of the region and formulate responses to the ways these indigenous writers see their region and the West's relationship to it. Photographs capture some of the complexities of the region as its peoples cope with the forces of globalization.

Three Distinctive Appendices

Appendix A. Conducting Research in the New Global Era. This unit provides students with cutting-edge, practical information on the kinds of research skills they are expected to acquire during their college careers. The appendix stresses the new world of information technology that increasingly guides research and offers extensive guidelines on locating and evaluating print and online sources. Containing an annotated student research paper on the impact of ecotourism, this appendix draws information from the newest 2003 MLA guidelines on conducting research.

Appendix B. Glossary of Rhetorical Terms. Concise definitions of dozens of key rhetorical terms provide a handy reference for students.

Appendix C. Glossary of Globalization Terms. This appendix makes the vocabulary of globalization, drawn from political science, history, economics, and other disciplines, accessible to students.

A Second Table of Contents by Rhetorical Mode

This rhetorical table of contents adds flexibility for teachers who prefer to organize their syllabus around such traditional forms as narration and description, comparison and contrast, process and causal analysis, and argumentation and persuasion.

Consistent Editorial Apparatus with a Sequenced Approach to Exercises

The New World Reader provides brief introductions to all chapters, highlighting the central issues raised by the writers in each section. All readings contain substantial author headnotes followed by a prereading question. Following each essay, three carefully sequenced sets totaling ten questions provide students with the opportunity to respond to the form and content of the text in ways that promote reading, writing, discussion, group work, and Internet exploration.

- **Before Reading.** One question asks students to think about their current understanding or interpretation of an event or a condition.
- **Thinking About the Essay.** Five questions build on the student's ability to comprehend how the writer's ideas develop through essential rhetorical and stylistic techniques.
- **Responding in Writing.** Three writing activities reflect and expand the questions in the first section, offering opportunities for students to write personal, analytical, and argumentative responses to the text.
- **Networking.** Two questions encourage small-group and Internet work. One question promotes collaborative learning. The other question provides practice in the use of Internet and library sources to conduct deeper exploration and research into issues raised by the author.

Exciting Visual Materials

Students today need to read and analyze visual as well as written texts. *The New World Reader* both integrates photographs, art work, cartoons, graphs, and maps into the chapters and casebook and features an exclusively visual, four-color essay devoted to examining the question of "Culture or Conflict?" These illustrations add a visual dimension to aid students' comprehension of the issues raised by written texts. All visual materials offer questions for informed response and analysis.

Interactive Website

Houghton Mifflin offers dynamic student and instructor websites for this book. The websites include prompts for chapters and essays, answers to questions, additional questions and activities, sample student essays, interactive guidelines for grammar and writing, links to other sites, visual and music portfolios, and additional resources for students and teachers. Much of the instructor's material will also be available in the Instructor's Resource Manual. Go to *http://college.hmco.com/english*.

Instructor's Resource Manual

The Instructor's Resource Manual for *The New World Reader* provides new as well as experienced teachers with suggested reading sequences, additional assignments, resources (both print and online) for further information and research, and possible responses for all activities in the student text. In addition, the IRM discusses classroom management issues unique to the teaching and discussion of challenging, controversial material in the composition classroom.

Acknowledgments

This book is the result of very special relationships—and considerable serendipity—among friends, collaborators, reviewers, and supporters. I was first alerted to the possibility of developing a global reader by my good friend and former colleague John Chaffee, an acclaimed author and specialist in critical thinking and philosophy. To John I offer my gratitude for his faith in an old friend.

Serving as matchmaker, John introduced me to Suzanne Phelps Weir, the executive editor of English at Houghton Mifflin, and she and I began a conversation and collaboration that proceeded rapidly to a proposal, sample chapters, reviews, and a manuscript that was revised and polished by numerous professional hands. Suzanne is any author's dream executive editor; she likes and nourishes writers, and I wish to express my appreciation for her kindness and commitment to this project.

I learned long ago that any college text is only as good as the editorial staff developing it, and here there are several special people who saved me much grief, improved the book, and prevented me from sounding at times like a turgid academician. First and foremost, I thank my development editor, Meg Botteon, whose light touch can be detected in virtually every section of *The New World Reader*. Meg has been more than a development editor. In fact, she has been a partner and collaborator, and I'm deeply grateful for her keen intellect, common sense, and good and gracious humor.

Supporting Meg have been other members of the Houghton Mifflin family who have taken more than ordinary interest in this project. To Sarah

Helyar Smith, development manager, I offer deep appreciation for her ability to keep everything on a very fast track. To Bob Greiner, the senior project editor, I express thanks for his expertise and his promise to buy me a Mexican meal in Boston if I hit all targets in the production schedule. To the crack copyeditor, Mary Anne Stewart, I express my pleasure and sheer amazement at her knowledge and ability to improve a text right down to the smallest detail.

I also thank my friend and agent, John Wright, who negotiated the contract for this book. Finally, I express love and gratitude to my wife, Laleh, a specialist in international relations and the Middle East, who offered support and advice as the design for this book evolved.

Several reviewers wrote detailed appraisals of the manuscript, recommendations for changes and improvements, praise and cautionary advice, and their collective wisdom informs this book. Thanks go to the following:

> Cathryn Amdahl, Harrisburg Area Community College
> Sandra L. Clark, University of Wyoming
> John Dailey, New Jersey City University
> Stephen F. Evans, University of Kansas
> Eileen Ferretti, Kingsborough Community College
> Len Gougeon, University of Scranton
> Tim Gustafson, University of Minnesota
> Jeff Henderson, Kalamazoo Valley Community College
> Pearlie Peters, Rider University
> Avantika Rohatgi, Butler University
> Renee Schlueter, Kirkwood Community College
> Henry Schwarz, Georgetown University
> Micheline M. Soong, Hawai'i Pacific University
> Mark Wiley, California State University, Long Beach
> Rosemary Winslow, Catholic University
> Randall J. VanderMey, Westmont College
> William Vaughn, Central Missouri State University
> Julie Yen, California State University, Sacramento

Gilbert Muller

The New World Reader

Thinking, Reading, and Writing About the New Global Era

T he events of September 11, 2001, revealed the impact of global events on our lives. With the collapse of the World Trade towers and the bombing of the Pentagon on 9/11, Americans had to think anew about their relationship to the rest of the world. Global trends that had been developing slowly over the previous decade—the end of the **cold war,** the spread of worldwide communications networks, the "clash of civiliza-tions," **terrorism** in many regions and continents, environmental chal-lenges, and **transnational** population shifts—suddenly came into sharp, sometimes uncomfortable focus. Isolated by two oceans and seemingly immune to some of the world's more disastrous events (just as they had been prior to the bombing of Pearl Harbor in 1941), Americans had to reexamine their complex global fate. Regardless of what we choose to call it—the new world order, the post–cold war world, the age of **globaliza-tion,** the age of terror—we have entered a new era.

But what sort of new era is in the process of formation? The historian Francis Fukuyama, who has an essay in this book, has observed that Americans often confuse their national needs with universal ones. Another writer who appears in this anthology, *New York Times* corre-spondent Thomas Friedman, suggests that we have to pay attention to the "super-story." This super-story involves all the trends of globalization—among them world trade, the formation of transnational economic and political alignments, and the spread of **information technology,** right down to new dating and marriage patterns—that are altering national and international behavior. Clear thinking about these issues requires an understanding of what has gone before (some knowledge of history helps) as well as a willingness to think critically about the proper role of the United States as the dominant power in the world today.

Colleen Kelly, center, is a nurse from New York City whose brother William died in the September 11, 2001, attacks on the World Trade Center. She later traveled to Iraq as a member of the group Peaceful Tomorrows, all of whose members are relatives of people killed on September 11. In this photograph, she is at a Baghdad shelter to meet with the relatives of Iraqis killed by allied strikes on a Baghdad bomb shelter during the first Gulf War in 1991.

Thinking About the Image

1. Think about the composition of this image. Who is in the center? What, or whom, surrounds the central character? What story does this composition tell?

2. What do you think the group Peaceful Tomorrows represents? Do you think they have any hope of achieving their mission? Why, or why not?

3. If you were a reporter holding one of those microphones, what questions would you want to ask Colleen Kelly? What would you want to ask the Iraqi children?

4. Why are there no Iraqi girls in this picture?

We live today in what some call the post–cold war era, which came about with the collapse of the Berlin Wall and in its aftermath the collapse of the Soviet Union. But the collapse of the Twin Towers was a different sort of moment, an instant in time etched in the minds of an entire generation. At that moment, we were connected to one another, in the United States and around the world, as never before. We have to find ways to manage change and minimize disruptive events if all of us are to reap the benefits of this new global era.

Critical Thinking

Are you ready for the brave new world of the twenty-first century, the new global era? Do you know enough about *globalization*—the interplay of cultures, societies, economies, and political systems—that is changing your world? Assuredly you will study this new era in various courses, prepare for careers in it, sit next to people from around the world in your classes, and perhaps even marry into it. The three thousand people from around the world who died in the World Trade Center disaster were working, collaborating, and living in this new world. Among the dead were civilians and citizens from sixty-two countries, including 250 Indians, 200 Pakistanis, 200 Britons, and 23 Japanese. Sadly, there were other individuals—call them terrorists—who felt threatened by the new international order represented by the 9/11 victims.

Your success in college hinges in part on your ability to make choices based on knowledge, experience, and careful reflection about the new world order. You will have to think critically about the global contexts that influence you and your nation. *Critical thinking* is clear thinking: it is a type of mental practice in which you respond to issues logically and, for the purposes of this course, deal with texts and the meanings they generate among class members. Often you will have to *rethink* your opinions, beliefs, and attitudes, and this too is a hallmark of critical thinking—the willingness to discard weak ideas or biased opinions for more mature or simply more logical intellectual opinions. For example, how do you define a *terrorist*? Why would Americans define a terrorist as anyone who takes the lives of innocent civilians, while others around the world view such individuals not as terrorists but as freedom fighters or defenders of the faith? Such questions do not admit easy or facile responses. They require deep and complex thought, for we live in a complex world.

To work effectively with the readings in this text, which deal with varieties of global experience, you need to develop a repertoire of critical thinking skills. In all likelihood, you have come to college possessing many of these skills. But it is important to refine, strengthen, and expand these skills to achieve a degree of authority over any given body of knowledge. How then do you think critically—in other words study and interpret—any given text? How do you look closely at the ideas of writers and evaluate them? How do you respond critically in writing? Having a repertoire of critical thinking skills creates the foundation for being a critical reader and writer.

Every writer in this textbook had a project much like the projects that you will develop: to articulate clearly and convincingly a key idea or nucleus of related ideas about an aspect of human experience—whether in the United States or elsewhere. They developed their ideas by using the repertoire of critical thinking skills—which for our purposes we can associate with key rhetorical strategies. **Rhetoric** is the art of writing or speaking, often to convince an audience about a particular issue. **Rhetorical strategies** are the key patterns that writers employ in this effort to clarify ideas and opinions. We divide these patterns into three major groups: *narration* and *description;* *exposition* (consisting of definition, comparison and contrast, illustration, process analysis, causal analysis, and classification); and *argument* and *persuasion.* These are not just the classic patterns of rhetoric but also powerful ways of thinking about and understanding our world.

Research demonstrates that different people think most effectively in different ways, or **cognitive styles.** You might like to argue—hopefully not in the style of *Crossfire* or *Hardball*—where viewpoints often are reduced simplistically to positions on the political "right" or "left"—but rather with reasonableness and respect. Or you might be great at telling a story to make a point. Or perhaps you have a talent for analyzing global events. All writing reflects one or more of those cognitive styles that we see reflected in narration and description, exposition, and argumentation. You can gain control over your reading and writing practices by selecting from among these major rhetorical strategies or thinking styles.

Narration and Description

Narration can be briefly described as telling a story, and **description** as the use of vivid **sensory detail**—sight, sound, smell, taste, touch—to convey either a specific or an overall impression. Although narration and description are not always treated in studies of reasoning, the truth of the matter is that it is foolish not to consider these strategies as aspects of the thinking process. The study of narration and description reveals that this type of thinking can produce authority in college writing.

Some composition theorists actually believe that narration and description, relying as they do on the creation of a personal **voice**—your personal voice—is the gateway to successful student writing. For example, Where were you on 9/11? How did you feel? What was your response? How did you get through the day and the aftermath? If you were answering these questions in an essay, you would need to employ a special kind of thinking and reflection, one in which you get in touch with your feelings and find vivid ways to express and make sense of them. It would be useless to say that you are not engaged in reasoning because you would employ narration and description—perhaps even insert **visual texts** downloaded from the Web—to arrive at your personal form of truth about the event. In all likelihood, you would also state or imply a **thesis** (a main idea) and even other generalizations about the event that go beyond pure narration or description; in fact, the vast majority of essays, while they might reflect one or two dominant rhetorical patterns or styles of organizational thought, tend to reveal mixed patterns or approaches to the writing process.

Consider the way the famous novelist, poet, and essayist John A. Williams begins a piece entitled "September 11, 2001":

I saw the second plane.

My wife, Lori, had deserted the radio in the kitchen of our house in Teaneck, New Jersey, having heard something about an explosion in one of the World Trade Center buildings and was now standing before the TV set in the sitting room where I joined her.

The plane circled slowly past the north tower, then, dipping a wing, turned to ram into the south tower three-quarters of the way from its top. The jet disintegrated in a raging bright-orange inferno that billowed out and up against a sun-streaked blue sky, merging with the whirling orange-brown clouds boiling out of the north tower. At that instant I knew I wouldn't be driving Lori into Manhattan for her dental appointment.

—From *September 11, 2001: American Writers Respond*

Here Williams employs narrative and descriptive skills we see at the outset of his essay to set the stage for personal reflections on the role of the United States in the world. Of course, we would expect a novelist to call up his unique storytelling skills to convey his ideas. He uses narration and description to create a sense of immediacy within the text.

Exposition

Exposition is a relatively broad term that defines a type of writing in which you explain or convey information about a subject. Expository writing is the form of writing that in all likelihood you will be required to produce in college courses. In an expository essay, you set forth facts and ideas—in other words, detailed explanations—to support a thesis, or main idea. As a form of critical thinking, expository writing provides a way of clarifying many of the cultural, political, and economic forces that mold global events today.

To produce effective expository essays, you need to develop skill and fluency in the use of several key rhetorical strategies, among them *definition, comparison* and *contrast, illustration, causal analysis, process analysis,* and *classification.* The use of any one or several of the patterns will dictate your approach to a given topic or problem, and the effective application of these strategies will help to create an authoritative voice, for the readers of your expository essay will see that you are using these rhetorical patterns to think consistently about a body of information and present it coherently. Once again, you employ specific reasoning abilities to make sense of your world.

When you consider the international events that increasingly shape both local and personal life—indeed, that are shaping your identity—it is clear that you must think critically about the best way to approach these events. The way you are able to reason about events, the perspectives you may develop on a particular problem, will inform your understanding of the subject and your ability to convey this understanding in writing.

Think about a term that already has been introduced and that you will encounter in numerous essays in this collection—*globalization.* This is one of the many terms that you will have to look at closely as you come to an understanding of the global forces shaping lives, identities, **cultures,** and civilizations in the twenty-first century. How might you unravel the significance of this word, gain authority over it, explore its relevance to various texts that you will read, and ultimately express your understanding of it in writing?

To start, *definition* of a complex term like *globalization* might be in order. (Definitions for many of the key terms relating to globalization appear in Appendix C.) As a way of thinking about a subject, **definition** is a statement about what a word or phrase means. It is always useful to be able to state this meaning in one or two sentences, as we have already done earlier in this chapter—"the interplay of cultures, societies, economies, and political systems" in the world today. But entire books have been and are being written about globalization, for it is a complex and controversial subject. We call these longer explanations **extended definitions,** which typically rely on other rhetorical strategies to expand the field of understanding. Finally, you might very well have a highly personal understanding of a term like *globalization.* Perhaps you have witnessed or read about workers in overseas factories producing Nikes for a few cents a day and consequently have mixed feelings about the Nikes you are wearing today. In this instance, *globalization* has a special meaning for you, and we term this special meaning a **stipulative definition** because it is colored highly by your experience. Remember, as with all discussions of rhetorical strategies, you are developing and polishing critical thinking skills. With definition, you are taking abstract ideas and making them comprehensible and concrete.

A second way to approach *globalization* would be through comparative thinking. **Comparison** and **contrast** is a cognitive process wherein you consider the similarities and differences of things. Imagine that your instructor asks you to write an essay entitled "Two Ways of Looking at Globalization." The title itself suggests that you have to employ a comparative method to explain and analyze this phenomenon. You would need a thesis to unify this comparative approach, and three or four key points of comparison and/or contrast to support it. The purpose of comparison and contrast is usually to state a preference for one thing over the other or to judge which one is superior. For example, if you maintain that globalization is about inclusion while those opposing globalization define it as a new form of colonialism or exploitation, you are evaluating and judging two positions.

Any approach to a subject requires a thoughtful and accurate use of **illustration**—that is, the use of examples to support an idea. Illustration, which we also call **exemplification,** enables you to make abstract ideas concrete. Normally several examples or one key extended example serves to illustrate your main and minor ideas about a subject. If, for example, you want to demonstrate that globalization is a trend that will foster understanding among nations and peoples, you would have to provide facts, statistics, examples, details drawn from personal experience, testimonials, and expert opinions to support your position. Illustration is the bedrock of virtually all ways of thinking, reading, and writing about a topic. Whether telling a story, explaining a topic, or arguing a point (which we deal with in the next section), illustration provides the evidence required to produce a powerful text. Illustration teaches the value of using the information of others—typically the texts of others—in order to build a structure for your own paper.

Causal and *process analysis* are two other forms of intellectual practice that can shape your critical approaches to topics. **Causal analysis,** sometimes called **cause-and-effect analysis,** answers the basic human question *Why?* It deals with a chain of happenings and the predictable consequences of these happenings. Like all the forms of thinking presented in this introductory section, causal analysis parallels our everyday thinking patterns. When we ask why terrorists bombed New York and Washington, why so many people in the **Third World** oppose globalization, or why the Internet can foster international cooperation, we are looking for causes or conditions and examining consequences and results (or effects). **Process analysis,** on the other hand, answers the question *How?* It takes things apart in order to understand how they operate or function. Many varieties of process analysis deal with "how-to" subjects involving steps in a correct sequence—for example, how to prepare fajitas. But process analysis is also central to the treatment of broad global trends. How did globalization come about? How do we combat terrorism? How do we prevent global warming? Process analysis can help explain the subtle and complex nature of relationships existing within a chain of events.

The last major form of exposition is **classification,** in which information is divided into categories or groups for the purpose of clarifying relationships among them. Some experts would term classification a "higher-order" reasoning skill. In actuality, classification again resembles a great deal of everyday thinking: we classify friends, teachers, types of music, types of cuisine, and so forth. (One writer in this textbook, Octavio Paz, who won the Nobel Prize for Literature, writes an essay classifying types of national foods.) Classification is a way of taking a large body of information and breaking it down (dividing it) into categories for better understanding. It relies on analytical ability—critical thinking that explores parts within a whole. For example, if you were to write an essay entitled "Approaches to Globalization," you could establish three categories—political, economic, and cultural—to divide your subject into coherent parts. The secret to using classification effectively is to avoid the temptation to have your categories overlap excessively. (Did you notice that classification was used to organize this section on exposition?)

Writers skilled in exposition are smart and credible. They write with authority because they can think clearly in a variety of modes. With exposition you make critical thinking choices, selecting those rhetorical strategies that provide the best degree of understanding for your readers, your audience.

Argument and Persuasion

Argument is a special type of reasoning. It appears in texts—written, spoken, or visual—that express a debatable point of view. Stated more rigorously, argument is a process of reasoning in which the truth of some main proposition (or claim) is shown to be true (that is, based on the truth of other minor propositions or premises). Closely allied to argument is **persuasion,** in which you invite an audience through rational, emotional, and ethical appeals to adopt your viewpoint or embark on a course of action. Aristotle in his *Rhetoric* spoke of the appeals as *logos, ethos,* and *pathos*—reason, beliefs, and emotion working together to guide an audience to a proper understanding or judgment of an issue. Argument—the rational component in persuasion—enables you to think responsibly about global issues and present your viewpoints about them in convincing fashion.

The dividing line between various forms of exposition and argumentation is a fine one. Where does a *thesis* leave off and a *claim* (the main argumentative point) begin? Some experts would say that "everything's an argument," and in the arena of global affairs this seems to be true. Issues of religion, race, class, gender, and culture are woven into the very fabric of both our local and global lives, and all of these issues trigger vigorous positions and responses. And the international environment is such that conflict and change seemingly provoke argumentative viewpoints and positions.

The distinctive feature of argumentative thinking is that you give reasons in support of a **claim** or **major proposition.** The **claim** is what you are trying to prove in an argument. The **reasons,** also called **minor propositions,** offer proof for the major claim. And you support each minor proposition with **evidence**—those various types of illustration mentioned in the previous section as well as logical explanations or abstract thinking used to buttress your basic reasons. If you don't "have the facts"—let's say about global inequality, the Kyoto Protocol on Climate Change, or the worldwide reach of McDonald's—you will not be able to stake a claim and defend it vigorously.

The British philosopher Steven Toulmin emphasizes that underpinning any argument or claim is a **warrant,** which he defines as an assumption, belief, or principle that is taken for granted. The warrant validates the link between the claim and the support. It might be stated or unstated. Many practices of nations, beliefs of citizens, and policies of political groups rest on such warrants. For example, if you assume that the United States is now the world's only **superpower**—a warrant—you can use this principle to claim that the United States should use its power to intervene in rogue states. Or if you believe that people have the right to free themselves from oppression—a warrant at the heart of the Declaration of Independence—you might use this warrant to claim that oppressed citizens have the right to start revolutions to break their chains.

Consider the warrants concerning the war on terrorism embedded in the following paragraph, written by Harold Hongju Koh, a former assistant secretary of state in the Clinton administration and a professor of international law at Yale University:

> Our enemies in this war are out to destroy our society precisely because it is open, tolerant, pluralistic and democratic. In its place, they seek to promote one that is closed, vengeful, repressive and absolutist. To secure gen-

uine victory, we must make sure that they fail, not just in their assault on our safety but also in their challenge to our most fundamental values.

—"Preserving American Values"

Here the writer predicates his claim about the need to achieve victory over our "enemies" on an entire catalog of "fundamental values" that in essence are warrants—that is, principles and beliefs. Also notice the way in which he employs the comparative method to structure his argument in this brief but revealing paragraph.

Before launching arguments over "homeland security," the pros and cons of globalization, the Arab-Israeli conflict, the rise of interracial and intercultural dating, or any other global or transnational subject, you once again have an obligation to think clearly and critically about these matters. Argumentation provides a logical way to present a viewpoint, deal fairly with opposing viewpoints, and hopefully arrive at a consensus. The psychologist Carl Rogers offers a new way of looking at argumentation when he suggests that both the communicator presenting an argument and the audience are participants in a dialogue—much like psychotherapy—in which they try to arrive at knowledge, understanding, and truth. At its best, argument results in intelligent discourse, a meeting of the minds, and even a strengthening of civic values.

Thinking About an Essay

"Love and Race"

NICHOLAS D. KRISTOF

Nicholas D. Kristof is a reporter and columnist for the *New York Times*. He was born in Chicago, Illinois, in 1959 and received a B.A. degree from Harvard University (1981) and a law degree from Oxford University (1983). He also has a diploma in Arabic language from the American University in Cairo. He writes: "Since my student days, when I began to travel with a backpack around Africa and Asia, I have had a fascination with foreign lands, cultures, and languages." Kristof and his wife, Sheryl WuDunn, who is also a *New York Times* reporter, won the Pulitzer Prize for their coverage of the Tiananmen Square massacre in 1989. Based in Asia for many years, Kristof and WuDunn have used their experiences there to write *China Awakes* (1994), *The Japanese Economy at the Millennium* (1999), and *Thunder from the East: Portrait of a Rising Asia* (2000). In the following **op-ed** essay that appeared in the *New York Times* on December 6, 2002, Kristof turns his attention from foreign lands to the changing cultural scene in the United States.

In a world brimming with bad news, here's one of the happiest trends. Instead of preying on people of different races, young Americans are falling in love with them.

Whites and blacks can be found strolling together as couples even at the University of Mississippi, once the symbol of racial confrontation.

"I will say that they are always given a second glance," acknowledges C. J. Rhodes, a black student at Ole Miss. He adds that there are still misgivings about interracial dating, particularly among black women and a formidable number of "white Southerners who view this race-mixing as abnormal, frozen by fear to see Sara Beth bring home a brotha."

Mixed-race marriages in the U.S. now number 1.5 million and are roughly doubling each decade. About 40 percent of Asian-Americans and 6 percent of blacks have married whites in recent years.

Still more striking, one survey found that 40 percent of Americans had dated someone of another race.

In a country where racial divisions remain deep, all this love is an enormously hopeful sign of progress in bridging barriers. Scientists who study the human genome say that race is mostly a bogus distinction reflecting very little genetic difference, perhaps one-hundredth of 1 percent of our DNA.

Skin color differences are recent arising over only the last 100,000 years or so, a twinkling of an evolutionary eye. That's too short a period for substantial genetic differences to emerge, and so there is perhaps 10 times more genetic difference within a race than there is between races. Thus we should welcome any trend that makes a superficial issue like color less central to how we categorize each other.

The rise in interracial marriage reflects a revolution in attitudes. As recently as 1958 a white mother in Monroe, N.C., called the police after her little girl kissed a black playmate on the cheek; the boy, Hanover Thompson, 9, was then sentenced to 14 years in prison for attempted rape. (His appeals failed, but he was released later after an outcry.)

In 1963, 59 percent of Americans believed that marriage between blacks and whites should be illegal. At one time or another 42 states banned intermarriage, although the Supreme Court finally invalidated these laws in 1967.

Typically, the miscegenation laws voided any interracial marriages, making the children illegitimate, and some states included penalties such as enslavement, life imprisonment and whippings. My wife is Chinese-American, and our relationship would once have been felonious.

At every juncture from the 19th century on, the segregationists warned that granting rights to blacks would mean the start of a slippery slope, ending up with black men marrying white women. The racists were prophetic.

"They were absolutely right," notes Randall Kennedy, the Harvard 12
Law School professor and author of a dazzling new book, "Interracial Intimacies," to be published next month. "I do think [interracial marriage] is a good thing. It's a welcome sign of thoroughgoing desegregation. We talk about desegregation in the public sphere; here's desegregation in the most intimate sphere."

These days, interracial romance can be seen on the big screen, on TV 13
shows and in the lives of some prominent Americans. Former Defense Secretary William Cohen has a black wife, as does Peter Norton, the software guru. The Supreme Court justice Clarence Thomas has a white wife.

I find the surge in intermarriage to be one of the most positive fronts in 14
American race relations today, building bridges and empathy. But it's still in its infancy.

I was excited to track down interracial couples at Ole Miss, thinking 15
they would be perfect to make my point about this hopeful trend: But none were willing to talk about the issue on the record.

"Even if people wanted to marry [interracially], I think they'd keep it 16
kind of quiet," explained a minister on campus.

For centuries, racists warned that racial equality would lead to the 17
"mongrelization" of America. Perhaps they were right in a sense, for we're increasingly going to see a blurring of racial distinctions. But these distinctions acquired enormous social resonance without ever having much basis in biology.

Questions for Critical Thinking

1. What is *your* opinion of interracial love? What assumptions and attitudes do you bring to the subject? How open are you to an essay entitled "Love and Race"? Why would such a topic invite—almost demand—careful critical thinking? What assumptions do you think Kristof makes about his readers?

2. Why does Kristof refer to the University of Mississippi (Ole Miss) at the beginning and end of his essay (paragraphs 3 and 15)? Answer this question in groups of three or four class members, pooling your knowledge of civil rights history (and perhaps conducting some fast research on someone's laptop) to broaden your understanding of Kristof's purpose.

3. Where does Kristof use narration and description to organize part of the essay? What is the effect?

4. Kristof employs numerous expository strategies in this essay. Locate and identify them, explaining what they contribute to the substance and the organization of the essay.

5. Does Kristof construct an argument in this essay or is he simply reporting a cultural development? How do you know?

Reading Critically

Most of the essays in this book were written within the last ten years, but the ideas in them run through the history of cultures and civilizations. Consequently we have to "read" the contemporary ideas contained in these selections through lenses that scan centuries and continents. We have to read critically—analyzing, interpreting, and reassessing new and old ideas in the light of our own experience. When, for example, George Orwell in the oldest essay in this book, his famous "Shooting an Elephant," tells us about a personal experience during his days as an official of the British Empire in Asia, it behooves us to know something about the legacy of the English **imperialism** before finding its relevance to us today. Is the United States the new imperial power? Are we facing the same conflicts and contradictions that imperial powers through the ages have confronted? To read critically is to be able to think critically about ideas in texts that have deep roots in world history.

As you read the selections in this book, you will discover that careful, critical reading about global issues can complement the talent you already have as a member of the generation that has grown up during the **information age.** Some say that college students have so much trouble with written texts because their culture privileges new forms of technology—call it visual or computer literacy—over older forms of print like the essays you find in this collection. But just as you probably think critically about information acquired through electronic and visual media, you can readily acquire an ability to read written texts critically and to respond to them in discussion and writing. One of the paradoxes of our era is that although we are spending more and more time in front of our computers, we also are buying more books and magazines.

Our most respected thinkers still use the written word to convey their ideas about the issues of our day. They might post these texts on the Web in various forms ranging from online magazines to blogs, but the reality is that these texts appear before us as products of the print universe. Only print can fully convey the intricacy of ideas writers have about our contemporary lives. Speech cannot rival the power of the printed word, as our propensity for tuning out the "talking heads" on television demonstrates. Moreover, with speech we rarely have the opportunity to go back and evaluate what has been said; with written texts, we can assess the presentation of ideas. As readers, therefore, you have an obligation to deal seriously with the ideas presented by the writers (many of them famous) in this book, and to respond critically and coherently to them. You need to acquire a *process* that will permit you to read texts in this manner.

There are many theories of reading, but the one that works best for the essays in this book is what has become known loosely as **reader response theory.** As the phrase suggests, there are various ways in which readers can respond to any given text. You, a reader, bring varieties of personal experience—and indeed your personality—to a written text. You also have been influenced in your responses to texts by your social and cultural background. Reader response theory acknowledges that there are many ways for you to approach a text. Among these approaches, which in essence are new strategies for thinking critically about the printed word, are *experiential, textual, psychological, social,* and *cultural* theories of response.

Experiential Theories of Reader Response

Experiential theories of reader response make the reader instead of the writer the primary focus of attention. In other words, you bring numerous personal experiences to the reading of any given text. You also have a personality shaped by numerous influences, as well as a mind and emotions uniquely attuned to your world. You have attitudes and opinions, likes and dislikes. You construct meaning through these personal experiences, your cultural background, and the community in which you live. Therefore, a text exists only in relationship to its reader.

Textual Theories of Reader Response

Textual theories of reader response focus exclusively on the written text. In other words, you center all meaning not on your personal experience but instead on the work itself. This approach had its roots in the 1920s, when literary critics began to advocate the New Criticism, which rejected the subjective, impressionistic, moralistic, and biographical background of a text. According to the New Critics, the meaning of any given text is within the text itself, and it is there for the reader to discover or decode. Thus the reader becomes a hunter for the "truth" of a text, which is contained in the very language, style, and structure of the work under scrutiny. We might very well ask, "Who is the keeper of these truths?" Often the answer has been the professor, who after all is trained in the analysis of literature. But before dismissing textual theory (and the professor), it is best to acknowledge that there are certain rules and **conventions** embedded in texts that we must decode to obtain meaning.

Psychological Theories of Reader Response

With the contemporary interest in psychology, it is not surprising that psychological theories of response should be popular among reader response theorists. The basic premise of psychological theories of reader response is that to understand or read a text properly, we must understand how we think. Cognitive processes develop at different stages of maturation: young children are unable to distinguish fantasy from reality (which is why they respond so powerfully to fairy tales and cartoons); young teenagers seek one true meaning in a text, whereas older teenagers are able to consider multiple meanings or interpretations. Psychological theorists also consider the moral as well as cognitive development of the reader's mind; a younger reader might respond to an essay about injustice with a desire for revenge, while a more mature reader would see a need to evaluate broader understanding of the situation. The mature mind, according to "cognitive processing" experts, is one that reveals powerful tools for reasoning, hypothesizing, classifying, defining, and predicting, thereby being able to engage with a text through a variety of response strategies.

Social Theories of Reader Response

Social theories of reader response move away from the isolated reader of any given text to a consideration of the reader as part of a larger group. In other words, you are part of a community of readers, with this society built around such features as class, education, religion, politics, region, and gender. In such an environment—let's say the classroom you now find yourself in—the reader is not a solitary soul but rather responding to texts as part of a group. As a member of this group, you want to share insights with others for the purpose of mutual understanding. You do not surrender your individual or personal impressions of a text as much as you become a member of what the critic Stanley Fish calls the "interpretive community." In this book, you will have many occasions to test your reading skills within these interpretive or collaborative communities.

Cultural Theories of Reader Response

Cultural theories of reader response do not reject the ideas of social theorists as much as they suggest that the latter do not read deeply enough into the very structures or foundations that govern or even dictate our ways of reading. Cultural theorists assert that we have to find the substratum or bedrock that gives rise to our reading experience—indeed, our experience of the world. They view social configurations as being formed by these deeply held worldviews and ideologies—for instance, **capitalism** and **socialism,** or Islam and Christianity. Various institutions, power structures, cultural conventions, gender roles, and "fields of discourse" like medicine and law dictate the ways we respond to a text. Thus, as you read the essays in the next chapter, "New American Mosaic," from the perspective of a cultural theory, you will have to contend with how your viewpoints on **immigration** have been formed by these deep wellsprings of culture. Through such analysis, you can avoid biased, nationalistic, and religiously chauvinistic ways of thinking about a text and engage instead in reflective thought.

Steps to Reading Critically

With a basic understanding of how ways of reading can influence your approach to a text, you can now develop concrete steps that will enable you to read critically. Any "system" for critical reading should be treated flexibly, but with the conviction that it is important to extract and evaluate the meanings that professional writers want to convey to their audience. Here are some guidelines for effective critical reading.

1. *Start with the conviction that critical reading, like critical thinking, requires active reading.* It is not like passively watching television. Instead, critical reading involves intellectual engagement with the text. Consequently, read with a pen or pencil in hand, underlining or circling key words, phrases, and sentences, asking questions in the margins, making observations—a process called **annotation**. These annotations will serve as guidelines for a second reading and additional responses in writing.

2. *Pause from time to time to reflect on what you are reading.* What is the writer's main idea? What are his or her basic methods (recall the rhetorical strategies) for developing ideas? What tone, or voice, does the writer convey, and why? What is the writer's **purpose**: is it to argue an issue, explain, analyze, or what? What varieties of illustration or evidence does the writer provide?

3. *Employ your critical thinking skills to interrogate the text.* Use some of the reader response theories to explore its deepest meanings. For example, test the text against your personal experience, or against certain cultural preconceptions. Think critically about the writer's argument, if there is one, and whether it withstands the test of logic and the conventions of argumentation.

4. *Consider the implied **audience** for the text.* How does the writer address you as part of this audience? Do you actually feel that you are part of this primary audience, a secondary reader, or largely forgotten or excluded? If you feel excluded, what features of the essay have caused you to be removed from this community of readers? How might you make yourself a part of this "universe of discourse" nevertheless?

5. *Write a **précis**, or **summary** of the essay.* These "shorthand" techniques will help you to focus your thoughts and prepare for class discussions and subsequent writing assignments.

These five steps for critical reading should suggest that critical reading, much like critical thinking and critical writing, involves re-reading. If you follow these guidelines, you will be able to enter the classroom community of readers with knowledge and authority and be prepared for productive class discussion.

Reading Visual Texts

You have to read **visual texts**—advertisements, tables and graphs, cartoons, artwork, photographs and illustrations—with the same care you bring to the critical reading of written texts. Indeed, "visuals" seem like the new mother of our information age, for we are bombarded with images that invite, sometimes demand, our response. Whether dealing with spam on our computers, contending with that ubiquitous beer commercial on television, responding to a photograph of the latest disaster in a newspaper account, or trying to decipher what a graph on the federal deficit *really* means, we know that visual texts are constructions designed to influence us in carefully contrived ways.

We must, therefore, contrive to be critical readers of visual texts so that the powerful images of our culture and civilization do not seduce or overwhelm us without proper evaluation. Visual texts, after all, tend to be instruments of persuasion. A symbol like the American eagle, the Islamic crescent, or the red star of China can trigger powerful personal and collective responses. Similarly, political advertisements and commercials often manipulate visual texts to persuade voters to act for a candidate or against (as with negative ads) an opposing candidate. To bring this discussion to the local level, log on to your campus website. What forms of visual text do you encounter that enhance the written text? Look especially for images that suggest that your campus is culturally and globally diverse.

To read visual texts with the same critical authority you bring to scrutinizing written texts, you should consider the following questions:

- What implicit messages are conveyed by the images and symbols?
- How is the visual designed or organized, and what is the effect of this arrangement?
- What is the purpose of the visual? What does the visual want the viewer to believe?
- What evidence is provided, and how can it be verified?
- What is the relationship of the visual to the printed text?

Visual images have an impact that complement and at times overwhelm print or even make printed texts unnecessary. Whether appearing on T-shirts, in ads in the glossiest fashion magazines, or marching across a computer screen, visual images usher us into a world of meaning. And we need to apply the same critical perspective to this visual universe that we do to its print counterpart.

Reading an Essay Critically

"The Ladybugs"

RAY GONZALEZ | Ray Gonzalez, an award-winning poet and author, was born in El Paso, Texas, in 1952 and raised in this city. He received a B.A. degree from the University of Texas at El Paso (1975) and has taught in high schools, prisons, and colleges in the Southwest. Among his five collections of poetry are *Twilights and Chants* (1977) and *The Heart of Arrivals* (1996). Gonzalez also has edited several collections of literature by contemporary Latinos, including *Touching the Fire: Fifteen Poets of Today's Latino Renaissance* (1998). In the following essay from the anthology *September 11, 2001: American Writers Respond* (2003), Gonzalez recounts his first day back in the college classroom following the events of 9/11.

I walk into my university office the day after the World Trade Center and Pentagon attacks. Classes were cancelled the previous afternoon and I have not had a chance to talk to any of my students since the terror. I set my book bag down, turn to my desk, and notice a ladybug crawling up my shirt, its tiny red body moving over the buttons on my chest. My first impulse is to flick it off, but I like ladybugs and consider them signs of good luck. I gently place my fingertip in its path and the insect climbs aboard. I sit down and watch it move across my finger, then onto the desktop. Distracted by having to get ready for class, I flip through my lecture notes and check my email. When I turn back to the desk, the ladybug has disappeared. I search under papers and files, but it is gone. I don't want it harmed or find it crushed by a book, but where did it go?

I try to imagine how far I carried it on my clothes, when the exact moment of it landing on me took place. These thoughts in search of precise time come from the hours I spent in front of the television the previous day. After a while, the unforgettable images of the collapsing towers melted into exact moments of horror, the news commentators repeating what happened at what moment and at what human cost. My ladybug has vanished, its invisible ride on me a microscopic act in a world where it seems like each tiny thing we do has now been amplified by fire and fear.

I bring up the subject of the terrorists' attacks in my undergraduate nature writing class, but no one wants to join in. I manage to connect the optimism nature writers present in their work with a sense of hope for the future, in light of the terrorism. I insist nature literature is the kind of writing we should read in a shocking time. Torn between discussing Henry Thoreau and talking about thousands of deaths, I look at the thirty students huddled in the small room. They stare at me in silence, events in the outer world pressing against the old, ugly walls of the building. Even the students who regularly contribute to discussions are quiet. As teachers, do we allow this sudden tragedy to come into our classes, or do we try and shut the door? It seems the attacks have entered during the first day of school after the tragedy, but we don't know how to proceed. How will a catastrophic event affect my lesson plans and the way young people, never having known an environment of war, respond to the assigned readings? It is too much to ponder as I stand in front of them and awkwardly get back to the sanctuary of Walden Pond.

Is the subject I'm teaching influencing their silence? Has Thoreau's pastoral idealism dictated a quiet atmosphere among these students? Perhaps history and political science classes are reacting in more vocal ways as I analyze Thoreau's reasons for wanting to touch a loon, even becoming the bird in one of the better-known chapters of *Walden*. Transcendentalism and Thoreau's warnings to his fellow New England citizens to not abandon an essential harmony with nature appeal to the students. We wind up having a lively discussion about the loon in the pond and why Thoreau insisted that hunting without a gun was one way to move beyond the boundaries of civilization—a belief that fell on deaf ears. There is enough time left in the period to discuss another famous passage in Walden—the battle between the red and black ants Thoreau gathered in a jar. I exhaust every metaphor about armies, good and evil, and human behavior in a time of war. The session ends as we isolate transcendence with the loon and nature's violent character as two key lessons for our time. The students pile out of the room and I feel a sense of triumph and relief. Several of them connected the previous day's events with the timeless lessons of environmental literature.

I stand alone in the empty classroom and can't forget the images on campus from the previous day. When classes were cancelled on the eleventh, and I walked across campus to my car, I saw dozens of students in tears. Many of them were huddled in small groups; cell phones in hand, a few hugging each other as they cried. The day after, I stroll the three blocks to my parking garage in silence, passing dozens of students and seeing that the fear and uncertainty is still on their faces. I reach my car on the fourth level of the massive garage after having momentarily forgotten where I parked that day. I unlock the door, throw my book bag on the seat, and climb in. As I reach for the magnetic card that will open the gate on the ground level, I spot a ladybug moving across my bag. Is it the same one that appeared in my office? My bag was on a chair near my office door and I never set it near the desk where the first ladybug appeared. Can this be a second ladybug and another sign of good luck? Why would I be getting these kinds of clues in the midst of a terrible and frightening time? Where are the ladybugs coming from, when I rarely see them at other times of the year? Instead of leaving the ladybug to disappear inside my car, I roll down the window, place my finger in the path of the insect on my bag, and it climbs on. I shake my finger outside and the ladybug flies away in a miniature dot of light.

I sit in my car for several minutes, not wanting to leave yet. The garage is located one block from the edge of campus, so the bustle and activity of thousands of students is muted. An eerie silence hangs among the rows of parked cars and concrete pillars. They remind me of the towers and how I had to finally turn off the television. The class discussion on Thoreau and his ideas on wilderness and the encroachment of civilization ring in my ears, yet they seem so far away. He was writing about America in the mid-nineteenth century and tried to encourage people to pause from their hard work on their farms and look around. The power of nature in its wild state on the continent had not been diminished by a great nation yet. One hundred and fifty years later, it seems the only wildness we know is one of crushed concrete, elusive enemies, and a state where the survival of our way of life has nothing to do with the natural power of the earth.

I pull out of the garage and turn onto the street leading to the freeway   7 I take to get home. As I emerge from the shelter of the ramp, sunlight flashes across the windows and lights up the car. At that moment, I spot a ladybug clinging to the windshield on the outside directly at eye level. It stays on the glass as I turn into traffic. My impulse is to slow down, but I have increased my speed to keep up with the cars. As I switch lanes, the ladybug springs off the windshield, its flared wings the purest fire I have imagined that day.

Questions for Response

1. After reading Gonzalez's essay once, reread and annotate it. Underline or circle key words, phrases, and sentences. Ask questions and make observations in the margins. Next to the title, write a phrase or sentence explaining what you think the title means.

2. In class groups of three or four, discuss your personal responses to this essay. Share with group members your experience of the text and why you respond to it the way you do. How does your remembrance of 9/11 influence this response? Do you feel close to the narrative, distanced from it, or what? Do you need to have read Thoreau to appreciate the essay? Consider as many aspects of your personal response as possible. For example, what is your attitude toward teachers, and what do you think of Gonzalez? Would you want to take a course with him? Why or why not? And are you as interested in nature as Gonzalez? Finally, come to a group understanding about why an experiential theory of reader response is useful in getting at the heart of a text.

3. Staying with your group, but now using the instructor as a resource if necessary, develop a textual theory of reader response to the essay. Concentrate on the language, style, and structure of the text. Discuss the allusion to Thoreau's *Walden*. Has anyone in your group read it? If not, ask the instructor for information or quickly download it. Explain how Gonzalez's essay succeeds as an example of narrative and descriptive art.

4. Imagine that you are a public school teacher. How would you teach Gonzalez's essay to a class of sixth graders? Ninth graders? Twelfth graders? How would your varying lesson plans reflect the psychological or cognitive theories of reader response?

5. Consider the ways in which you could utilize social and cultural theories of reader response to understand Gonzalez's essay. Share your thoughts in class discussion.

Writing in Response to Reading

The distinguished writers in this book, many of them recipients of major awards like the Nobel and Pulitzer prizes, are professionals. When dealing typically with local and world events—especially with the relationship of a liberal and open society like the United States to the world community—they employ a broad range of stylistic and rhetorical skills to construct meaning. They write for numerous reasons or purposes, although an argumentative edge appears in many of the essays. All engage in strategic thinking and rethinking as they tackle the promises and prospects of our new global era.

It is useful at the outset of a course in college writing to think like a professional writer or at least a professional writer in the making. With each essay you write, imagine that you are trying to produce "publishable prose." Indeed, you will have the opportunity to write letters to the editor, post papers on the Web, pool and present research findings with other classmates, and engage in many tasks that assume the character of the professional writer who composes for a specific audience and for a specific purpose. At the least, by treating yourself as a writer capable of producing publishable prose, you will impress your instructor with your seriousness and aspirations.

Many of the issues and momentous events treated by the writers in this book demand no less than a "professional" response based on your ability to deal critically in writing with the strategic questions the essays raise. Indeed, critical thinking and writing about our common global condition is one measure of a pluralistic and tolerant society. By thinking and rethinking, writing and rewriting about your world, you contribute to the creation of open democratic discourse.

How, then, do you write about the new global era and its many challenges, or about any other topic for that matter? Globalization has changed the way people think about themselves and their relation to the world. Even ideas have become global; communication of these ideas now can span the world in milliseconds. As a writer in this brave new world of globalization, you need to apply in writing that repertoire of critical thinking skills mentioned at the outset of this chapter to make sense of contemporary life on this planet.

To start, you must have a basic understanding of the world of global interrelationships that characterizes life in the twenty-first century. The noted historian Paul Kennedy, who has an essay in this book, defines globalization as "the ever-growing integration of economies and societies because of new communications, newer trade and investment patterns, the transmissions of cultural images and messages, and the erosion of local and traditional ways of life in the face of powerful economic forces from abroad." Kennedy, as we might expect from a historian, is quick to note that this new world of globalization did not spring immediately from the ashes of 9/11 but can be detected in different guises in the rise and fall of great civilizations. For example, what the British Empire once termed "progress," we now call globalization. Today, the United States is the Great Power, its financial, cultural, military, and hi-tech capacities unrivaled by other nations. Whether or not its Great Power status—its overarching control of the forces of globalization—will create new forms of "progress" for peoples and nations around the world is the central debate underlying the chapters in this book.

Writers like Paul Kennedy are "professional" in the sense that they know their subject. They are informed. But their informed essays do not result from some divinely inspired moment of creativity. When professional writers sit down to tackle an issue of importance, they know that beyond the knowledge they bring to the subject, they will have to consider various perspectives on the subject and even experiment with various methods of composition. Everyone composes differently, but it is fair to say that a good essay is the result of planning, writing, and revision, and such an essay reflects some of the key thinking strategies outlined in the first part of this chapter. There is a common consensus among professionals, including teachers of writing, that a **composing process**, consisting of *prewriting, drafting*, and *revision*, is the best way to approach the creation of a successful essay.

Prewriting

Prewriting is that preliminary stage in the composing process in which you map out mentally and in writing your overall approach to the subject. Prewriting in the context of this book begins when you read critically and respond to an essay. Perhaps you annotate the essay, summarize it mentally, or take notes on paper or the computer. Or maybe you take notes during class discussion. Next, you size up the nature of the writing project appearing in the exercises at the end of the essay or provided by the instructor. At this early stage, it is clear that already you are thinking, responding, and writing critically about the project at hand.

Composing processes are unique to each writer, but there are certain areas of the prewriting process that are necessary for you to consider:

- *Who is your audience?* A college writing assignment means that your primary audience will be your professor, who knows the "print code" and anticipates well-organized and grammatically correct prose. But there are secondary audiences to consider as well, and you might have to adjust your level of discourse to them. If you are working collaboratively, you have members of the group to satisfy. If you exchange papers with another class member for evaluation, this also creates a new audience. Or perhaps you will need to create an electronic portfolio of your best work as a graduation requirement; here the people who assess the quality of the portfolio become judges of your work.

- *What is your purpose?* Is your purpose to tell a story, describe, inform, argue, evaluate, or combine any number of these basic goals? Knowing your purpose in advance of actually drafting the essay will permit you to control the scope, method, and tone of the composition.
- *What is your thesis or claim?* Every paper requires a controlling idea or assertion. Think about and write down, either in shorthand or as a complete sentence, the main idea or claim that you plan to center your paper on.
- *How will you design your essay?* Planning or outlining your paper in advance of actually writing it can facilitate the writing process. Complete outlines, sketch outlines, sequenced notes, visual diagrams: all serve as aids once the actual drafting begins.
- *How can you generate preliminary content?* Notes can be valuable. **Brainstorming,** in which you write without stop for a certain amount of time, can also activate the creative process. Joining online discussion groups or working collaboratively in the classroom also can result in raw content and ideas for development.

Prewriting provides both content and a plan of operation before moving to the next stage in the composing process.

Drafting

Once you have attended to the preliminary, or prewriting, stage in the composing process, you can move to the second stage, which is the actual **drafting** of the paper. Applying an Aristotelian formula, be certain to have a beginning, middle, and end. Your introduction, ideally one opening paragraph, should center the topic, be sufficiently compelling to engage your reader, and contain a thesis or claim. The body of the essay should offer a series of paragraphs supporting your main idea or central assertion. The conclusion should wrap things up in an emphatic or convincing way.

Here is a checklist for drafting an essay:

- Does your title illuminate the topic and capture the reader's interest?
- Does your opening paragraph "hook" the reader? Does it establish and limit the topic? Does it contain a thesis or claim?
- Do all body paragraphs support the thesis? Is there a main idea (called a **topic sentence**) controlling each paragraph? Are all paragraphs well developed? Do they contain sufficient examples or evidence?
- Does the body hold together? Is there a logical sequence to the paragraphs? In other words, is the body of the essay **unified** and **coherent**, with **transitions** flowing from sentence to sentence and paragraph to paragraph?
- Have you selected the best critical thinking strategies to develop the paper and meet the expectations set out in your introduction?
- Is your conclusion strong and effective?

Think of drafting as the creation of a well-constructed plot. This plot does not begin, develop, and end haphazardly, but rather in a carefully considered sequence. Your draft should reveal those strategies and elements of the composing process that produce an interesting and logically constructed plot.

Revision

There are professional writers who rarely if ever revise their work, and there are others who spend forever getting every word and sentence just right. Yet most professional writers do some amount of **revision,** either on their own initiative or in response to other experts, normally editors and reviewers. As the American poet Archibald MacLeish observed, the composing process consists of the "endless discipline of writing and rewriting and rewriting."

Think of the essay that in all likelihood you have put up on your computer screen not as a polished or final product but as a rough draft. Use the grammar and spell checker features of your software program to clean up this draft, remembering that this software is not infallible and sometimes is even misleading. Then revise your essay, creating a second draft, with the following questions serving as guidelines:

- Is the essay long enough to satisfy the demands of the assignment?
- Is the topic suitable for the assignment?
- Is there a clear thesis or claim?
- Is the purpose or intention of the essay clear?
- Is the essay organized sensibly? Are the best rhetorical patterns used to facilitate reader interest and comprehension?
- Are all sentences grammatically correct and sufficiently varied in structure?
- Is there sufficient evidence, and is all information derived from other sources properly attributed?
- Does the manuscript conform to acceptable guidelines for submitting written work?

Successful writing blends form and content to communicate effectively with an audience. The guidelines offered in this section tap your ability to think and write critically about the global issues raised in this book. To be a global citizen, you must become aware of others, make sense of the world, and evaluate varieties of experience. To be a global writer, you have to translate your understanding of these global relationships into well-ordered and perceptive prose.

Writing in Response to an Essay

"At Muslim Prom, It's a Girls-Only Night"

PATRICIA LEIGH-BROWN

> Patricia Leigh-Brown is a correspondent for the *New York Times* who writes about multicultural issues. In the following essay, which Leigh-Brown wrote for the June 9, 2003, issue of the *New York Times*, she reports on a new phenomenon in the traditional ritual of American prom night.

The trappings of a typical high school prom were all there: the strobe 1
lights, the garlands, the crepe pineapple centerpieces and even a tiara
for the queen. In fact, Fatima Haque's prom tonight had practically everything one might expect on one of a teenage girl's most important nights.
Except boys.

Ms. Haque and her friends may have helped initiate a new American 2
ritual: the all-girl Muslim prom. It is a spirited response to religious and
cultural beliefs that forbid dating, dancing with or touching boys or appearing without a hijab, the Islamic head scarf. While Ms. Haque and her
Muslim friends do most things other teenagers do—shopping for shoes at
Macy's, watching *The Matrix* at the mall or ordering Jumbo Jack burgers
and curly fries at Jack in the Box—an essential ingredient of the American
prom, boys, is off limits. So they decided to do something about it.

"A lot of Muslim girls don't go to prom," said Ms. Haque, 18, who re- 3
moved her hijab and shawl at the prom to reveal an ethereal silvery gown.
"So while the other girls are getting ready for their prom, the Muslim girls
are getting ready for our prom, so we won't feel left out."

The rented room at a community center here was filled with the sounds 4
of the rapper 50 Cent, Arabic pop music, Britney Spears and about two
dozen girls, including some non-Muslim friends. But when the sun went
down, the music stopped temporarily, the silken gowns disappeared beneath full-length robes, and the Muslims in the room faced toward Mecca
to pray. Then it was time for spaghetti and lasagna.

It is perhaps a new version of having it all: embracing the American 5
prom culture of high heels, mascara and adrenaline while being true to a
Muslim identity.

"These young women are being very creative, finding a way to con- 6
tinue being Muslim in the American context," said Jane I. Smith, a professor of Islamic studies at the Hartford Seminary in Connecticut.

"Before, young Muslims may have stuck with the traditions of their parents or rejected them totally to become completely Americanized. Now, they're blending them."

Non-Muslim students at San Jose High Academy, where Ms. Haque is 7 president of the student body, went to the school's coed prom last month— renting cars or limousines, dining at the Sheraton, going to breakfast at Denny's and, for some, drinking. Ms. Haque, meanwhile, was on her turquoise cellphone with the smiley faces organizing the prom. She posted an announcement on Bay Area Muslim Youth, a Yahoo news group scanned by young people throughout the San Francisco Bay area, home to one of the country's largest and most active Muslim communities.

"We got so close, we wanted to hang," said Fatin Alhadi, 17, a friend, 8 explaining the farewell-to-high-school celebration, which involved cooking, shopping and decorating the room, rented with a loan from Ms. Haque's parents. "It's an excuse to dress and put makeup on. Everyone has so much fun at the prom."

The sense of anticipation was palpable at Ms. Haque's house this af- 9 ternoon, including an occasional "Relax, mom!" For Ms. Haque and her friends, the Muslim prom—like any prom—meant getting your eyebrows shaped at the last minute and ransacking mother's jewelry box. It was a time to forget about the clock, to look in the mirror and see a glamorous woman instead of a teenager. To be radiant.

Ms. Haque and her Muslim girlfriends dwell in a world of exquisite 10 subtlety in which modesty is the underlying principle. Though she wears a hijab, Ms. Alhadi recently dyed her black hair auburn. "Everyone asks me why, because nobody sees it," she said. "But I like to look at myself."

Ms. Haque, who will attend the University of California at Berkeley in 11 the fall, is one of a growing number of young Muslim women who have adopted the covering their mothers rejected. Islamic dress, worn after puberty, often accompanies a commitment not to date or to engage in activities where genders intermingle.

Her parents immigrated from Pakistan, and her mother, Shazia, who 12 has a master's degree in economics, does not wear the hijab.

Ms. Haque's decision to cover herself, which she made in her freshman 13 year, was nuanced and thoughtful.

"I noticed a big difference in the way guys talked," she said. "They were 14 afraid. I guess they had more respect. You walked down the street and you didn't feel guys staring at you. You felt a lot more confident." Her parents were surprised but said it was her decision.

Ms. Haque faced some taunting after the terror attacks on Sept. 11, 15 2001. "They call you terrorist, or raghead because high school students are immature," she said.

But she and her friends say Muslim boys, who are not distinguished by 16
their dress, may have a tougher time in American society.

"The scarf draws the line," said Ms. Alhadi, the daughter of a Singa- 17
porean mother and Indonesian father. "It's already a shield. Without it
everything comes to you and you have to fight it yourself."

Ms. Haque is enrolled in the academically elite International Baccalau- 18
reate program at San Jose High Academy, a public school where, as her
friend Morgan Parker, 17, put it, "the jocks are the nerds."

But the social pressures on Muslims, especially in less-cloistered set- 19
tings, can be intense.

"I felt left out, big time," said Saira Lara, 17, a senior at Gunn High 20
School in Palo Alto, of her school's prom. But she gets a vicarious taste of
dating by talking with her non-Muslim friends.

"The drama that goes on!" Ms. Lara said, looking dazzling at the Mus- 21
lim prom in a flowing maroon gown. "The Valentine's Day without a
phone call or a box of chocolates!"

Imran Khan, 17, a senior at Los Altos High School, admitted that his 22
school's prom was not easy.

"When I told my friends I wasn't going, they all said, 'Are you crazy?'" 23
he said in a telephone interview. "Prom is a you-have-to-go kind of thing.
Obviously if all your friends are going and you're not, you're going to feel
something. That day I was, 'Oh man, my friends are having fun and I'm
not.' But I don't regret not going."

Most of Mr. Khan's school friends are not Muslim, and his Muslim 24
friends are scattered across the Bay area.

"A lot of times it's difficult," he said. "We guys blend in so you can't tell 25
we're Muslim. We're not supposed to touch the opposite gender. My friends
who are girls understand, but when other girls want to hug you or shake
your hand, it's hard. I don't want them to think I'm a jerk or something."

Adeel Iqbal, 18, a senior at Bellarmine College Preparatory, a boys' 26
Catholic school in San Jose, went stag to his coed senior prom. Mr. Iqbal
decided to go in his official capacity as student body president as well as a
representative of his Muslim beliefs.

"Every day we're bombarded with images of sex and partying and get- 27
ting drunk, in music and on TV, so of course there's a curiosity," he said.
"When you see your own peers engaging in these activities, it's kind of weird.
It takes a lot of strength to not participate. But that's how I've been raised.
When your peers see you're different in a positive way, they respect it."

Nearly all parents of adolescents worry about the pressures of sex, 28
drugs and alcohol, but the anxiety is especially acute in Muslim families
who strictly adhere to traditional Islamic dress and gender separation.
Many Muslim parents disapprove of what they see as an excessively secu-

larized and liberalized American culture, and are deeply concerned that young Muslims, especially girls, not be put in compromising situations.

Ms. Haque's father, Faisal, a design engineer at Cisco Systems, said that 29 the pressure to conform was "very significant." It is the subject of frequent family discussions.

"It's difficult at best," Mr. Haque said. "It takes a lot of self-control. I 30 have a lot of respect for these kids."

The Haques supported their daughter's decision to organize the Mus- 31 lim prom. "You have to live in this country," Mr. Haque said. "In order to function, the children have to adapt. Prom is a rite of passage. You don't want them to feel like they don't belong."

Ms. Haque would like the Muslim prom to become an annual event. 32 "My goal is an elegant ballroom with a three-course dinner—no paper plates—women waiters and a hundred girls," she said.

Tonight, the prom room was filled with promise as the young women 33 whirled around the dance floor, strobe lights blinking. "Show off whatever you've got!" Ms. Lara exhorted the throng, sounding like a D.J. "Come on, guys. This is the most magical night of your life!"

Responding in Writing

1. As a prewriting strategy, brainstorm about this article for five minutes. Write or keyboard without stopping. Do not worry about grammatical correctness or the sequence of ideas. Just try to capture your impressions of this essay as you respond to the elements in it.

2. With two other class members, create a plan for a global or multiethnic prom. What types of music will there be? What forms of dress will be recommended? Will there be dancing or not? What will the menu be? Answer these questions and any others you generate, and then turn this into an outline that you will present to the class.

3. Write an analysis of this essay. What is Leigh-Brown's purpose? What expectations does she have of her audience? What is her thesis? How does she develop her introduction, body, and conclusion? How does she assemble and present her evidence? What ideas does she want the audience to gain from a critical reading of her article?

4. In an essay, argue for or against the proposition that separate proms for separate people actually produce a fragmentation of experience that is not healthy for an open, democratic society.

5. Go online and try to find out more about the ways in which Muslim youth— or any other group of young people—are responding to patterns of American culture. Write a report of your findings and summarize your findings in an oral presentation to the class.

New American Mosaic: Are We Becoming a Universal Nation?

Martin Luther King Jr. believed in the need for what he termed a "world house," a commitment to a society of inclusion. "We are all caught up in an inescapable web of mutuality, tied in a single garment of destiny," he declared. Indeed, long before the September 11, 2001, terrorist attacks reminded us of the interconnected forces of our world, we were discovering how the United States (and Canada as well) was starting to reflect the rest of the planet. Accelerating this transformation has been the arrival of tens of millions of immigrants to the United States in the last quarter of the twentieth century. Instead of repeating earlier immigration patterns in which peoples arrived from Europe, these new immigrants travel here from all parts of the globe: Asia, Africa, the Caribbean, Central and South America. Today, new immigrants are changing the traditional notion of what it means to be "American." Arguably, because of the strikingly diverse nature of its citizenry, America is in the process of becoming a universal nation.

The writers in this chapter reflect in their own ethnic and racial origins the broad mosaic—some prefer to call it a kaleidoscope—that characterizes life in the United States today. Consider the historical magnitude of this national transformation. True, North America once belonged to native tribes—as N. Scott Momaday reminds us in the opening selection of this chapter. And the legacy of slavery, which began in 1621 when a Dutch man-of-war ship brought the first Africans to the Jamestown colony, served to diversify the nation. But from colonial times to 1965, the United States drew its population largely from Europe. First came the English, Scots-Irish, Germans, and French. The second great wave that began in the 1870s and continued up to World

Thinking About the Image

1. Are the people portrayed in this cartoon stereotypes? How can you tell? Do you find the stereotypes offensive, or do they help the cartoon make sense? Can you think of any comedians or hip-hop artists who use stereotypes in a way that points out an uncomfortable truth?

2. This cartoon uses irony to make its point. What specifically is ironic about this cartoon?

3. Read the next essay in this collection, "The Way to Rainy Mountain" by N. Scott Momaday. What might Momaday think about this cartoon?

4. What political situation or issue is Steve Kelley, the cartoonist, responding to in this cartoon? What is his opinion? Does he make his point effectively?

War I brought tens of millions of immigrants from southern and eastern Europe. For centuries, immigrants from non-European parts of the world were systematically excluded, with restrictive quotas preserving certain assumptions about the racial and ethnic character of the nation. For example, in her haunting memoir, *China Men*, the acclaimed writer Maxine Hong Kingston devotes an entire chapter to listing the dozens of immigration statutes designed to exclude people from China from America's shores.

The Immigration Act of 1965 abolished all such quotas and opened the United States—for the first time in the nation's history—to the world's population. Now everyone presumably had a fair opportunity to achieve the American Dream, whatever this ambiguous term might mean. And arrive they did—from Vietnam, India, Nigeria, Cuba, the Philippines, Iran, China—all seeking a place in the new global nation. Of course, this contemporary collision and intersection of peoples, races, and cultures is not only an American phenomenon; many countries in Europe are dealing with similar patterns. But nowhere is this new global reality more apparent than in the United States. In certain states—California, for example—and in many major American cities, "minorities" are becoming majorities. According to the most recent census data, by 2056 the "average" American will be as likely to trace his or her origins to the Hispanic world, Asia, or the Pacific islands as to Europe. These demographic changes are often reflected on college campuses, with students from scores of national backgrounds speaking dozens of languages sharing classes together.

The story of American civilization is still unfinished, but the authors in this chapter suggest certain directions it will take. They write about conflicts and challenges posed by the new American dream, which is ostensibly open to, if not necessarily desired by, all the peoples of the world. They wrestle with America's complex fate. They ask collectively: How can America continue to be a beacon for peoples from around the planet seeking work, safety, security, freedom, the right to freely practice and preserve their own customs and beliefs? They ask: Can America be—should it be—the model for a universal nation?

The Way to Rainy Mountain

N. SCOTT MOMADAY

Navarre Scott Momaday, born in Oklahoma in 1934, is a Native American—a member of the Kiowa tribe; consequently, he says that he is "vitally interested in American Indian history, art, and culture." After receiving his doctorate from Stanford University, where he studied under the famous poet and critic Ivor Winters, Momaday embarked on his own distinguished career as poet, novelist, critic, autobiographer, and, for many years, professor of English at the University of Arizona. He won the Pulitzer Prize for his novel *House Made of Dawn* (1968). Additional works include *The Way to Rainy Mountain* (1969), *The Names* (1976), *The Ancient Child* (1989), and *In the Presence of the Sun* (1991). In an interview, Momaday stated, "When I was growing up on the reservations of the Southwest, I saw people who were deeply involved in their traditional

life, in the memories of their blood. They had, as far as
I can see, a certain strength and beauty that I find missing in the modern world at large. I like to celebrate that
involvement in my writing." The following essay from
The Way to Rainy Mountain captures the sacredness
that Momaday finds in his Native American heritage
and the land of his ancestors.

Before Reading

What do you know about Native American history and culture? Where does this
knowledge come from? In what ways are Native Americans in the news today?
What do you anticipate about the essay that follows from Momaday's title?

A single knoll rises out of the plain in Oklahoma, north and west of the   1
Wichita Range. For my people, the Kiowas, it is an old landmark, and
they gave it the name Rainy Mountain. The hardest weather in the world
is there. Winter brings blizzards, hot tornadic winds arise in the spring, and
in summer the prairie is an anvil's edge. The grass turns brittle and brown,
and it cracks beneath your feet. There are green belts along the rivers and
creeks, linear groves of hickory and pecan, willow and witch hazel. At a
distance in July or August the steaming foliage seems almost to writhe in
fire. Great green and yellow grasshoppers are everywhere in the tall grass,
popping up like corn to sting the flesh, and tortoises crawl about on the red
earth, going nowhere in the plenty of time. Loneliness is an aspect of the
land. All things in the plain are isolate; there is no confusion of objects in
the eye, but *one* hill or *one* tree or *one* man. To look upon that landscape
in the early morning, with the sun at your back, is to lose the sense of proportion. Your imagination comes to life, and this, you think, is where Creation was begun.

I returned to Rainy Mountain in July. My grandmother had died in the   2
spring, and I wanted to be at her grave. She had lived to be very old and at
last infirm. Her only living daughter was with her when she died, and I was
told that in death her face was that of a child.

I like to think of her as a child. When she was born, the Kiowas were   3
living the last great moment of their history. For more than a hundred years
they had controlled the open range from the Smoky Hill River to the Red,
from the headwaters of the Canadian to the fork of the Arkansas and
Cimarron. In alliance with the Comanches, they had ruled the whole of the
southern Plains. War was their sacred business, and they were among the
finest horsemen the world has ever known. But warfare for the Kiowas was
preeminently a matter of disposition rather than of survival, and they never
understood the grim, unrelenting advance of the U.S. Cavalry. When at

last, divided and ill-provisioned, they were driven onto the Staked Plains in the cold rains of autumn, they fell into panic. In Palo Duro Canyon they abandoned their crucial stores to pillage and had nothing then but their lives. In order to save themselves, they surrendered to the soldiers at Fort Sill and were imprisoned in the old stone corral that now stands as a military museum. My grandmother was spared the humiliation of those high gray walls by eight or ten years, but she must have known from birth the affliction of defeat, the dark brooding of old warriors.

Her name was Aho, and she belonged to the last culture to evolve in   4
North America. Her forebears came down from the high country in western Montana nearly three centuries ago. They were a mountain people, a mysterious tribe of hunters whose language has never been positively classified in any major group. In the late seventeenth century they began a long migration to the south and east. It was a journey toward the dawn, and it led to a golden age. Along the way the Kiowas were befriended by the Crows, who gave them the culture and religion of the Plains. They acquired horses, and their ancient nomadic spirit was suddenly free of the ground. They acquired Tai-me, the sacred Sun Dance doll, from that moment the object and symbol of their worship, and so shared in the divinity of the sun. Not least, they acquired the sense of destiny, therefore courage and pride. When they entered upon the southern Plains they had been transformed. No longer were they slaves to the simple necessity of survival; they were a lordly and dangerous society of fighters and thieves, hunters and priests of the sun. According to their origin myth, they entered the world through a hollow log. From one point of view, their migration was the fruit of an old prophecy, for indeed they emerged from a sunless world.

Although my grandmother lived out her long life in the shadow of   5
Rainy Mountain, the immense landscape of the continental interior lay like memory in her blood. She could tell of the Crows, whom she had never seen, and of the Black Hills, where she had never been. I wanted to see in reality what she had seen more perfectly in the mind's eye, and traveled fifteen hundred miles to begin my pilgrimage.

Yellowstone, it seemed to me, was the top of the world, a region of deep   6
lakes and dark timber, canyons and waterfalls. But, beautiful as it is, one might have the sense of confinement there. The skyline in all directions is close at hand, the high wall of the woods and deep cleavages of shade. There is a perfect freedom in the mountains, but it belongs to the eagle and the elk, the badger and the bear. The Kiowas reckoned their stature by the distance they could see, and they were bent and blind in the wilderness.

Descending eastward, the highland meadows are a stairway to the   7
plain. In July the inland slope of the Rockies is luxuriant with flax and buckwheat, stonecrop and larkspur. The earth unfolds and the limit of the

land recedes. Clusters of trees, and animals grazing far in the distance, cause the vision to reach away and wonder to build upon the mind. The sun follows a longer course in the day, and the sky is immense beyond all comparison. The great billowing clouds that sail upon it are shadows that move upon the grain like water, dividing light. Farther down, in the land of the Crows and Blackfeet, the plain is yellow. Sweet clover takes hold of the hills and bends upon itself to cover and seal the soil. There the Kiowas paused on their way; they had come to the place where they must change their lives. The sun is at home on the plains. Precisely there does it have the certain character of a god. When the Kiowas came to the land of the Crows, they could see the dark lees of the hills at dawn across the Bighorn River, the profusion of light on the grain shelves, the oldest deity ranging after the solstices. Not yet would they veer southward to the caldron of the land that lay below; they must wean their blood from the northern winter and hold the mountains a while longer in their view. They bore Tai-me in procession to the east.

A dark mist lay over the Black Hills, and the land was like iron. At the   8
top of a ridge I caught sight of Devil's Tower upthrust against the gray sky as if in the birth of time the core of the earth had broken through its crust and the motion of the world was begun. There are things in nature that engender an awful quiet in the heart of man; Devil's Tower is one of them. Two centuries ago, because they could not do otherwise, the Kiowas made a legend at the base of the rock. My grandmother said:

> Eight children were there at play, seven sisters and their brother. Suddenly the boy was struck dumb; he trembled and began to run upon his hands and feet. His fingers became claws, and his body was covered with fur. Directly there was a bear where the boy had been. The sisters were terrified; they ran, and the bear after them. They came to the stump of a great tree, and the tree spoke to them. It bade them climb upon it, and as they did so it began to rise into the air. The bear came to kill them, but they were just beyond its reach. It reared against the tree and scored the bark all around with its claws. The seven sisters were borne into the sky, and they became the stars of the Big Dipper.

From that moment, and so long as the legend lives, the Kiowas have kins-   9
men in the night sky. Whatever they were in the mountains, they could be no more. However tenuous their well-being, however much they had suffered and would suffer again, they had found a way out of the wilderness.

My grandmother had a reverence for the sun, a holy regard that now is   10
all but gone out of mankind. There was a wariness in her, and an ancient awe. She was a Christian in her later years, but she had come a long way about, and she never forgot her birthright. As a child she had been to the Sun Dances; she had taken part in those annual rites, and by them she had

learned the restoration of her people in the presence of Tai-me. She was about seven when the last Kiowa Sun Dance was held in 1887 on the Washita River above Rainy Mountain Creek. The buffalo were gone. In order to consummate the ancient sacrifice—to impale the head of a buffalo bull upon the medicine tree—a delegation of old men journeyed into Texas, there to beg and barter for an animal from the Goodnight herd. She was ten when the Kiowas came together for the last time as a living Sun Dance culture. They could find no buffalo; they had to hang an old hide from the sacred tree. Before the dance could begin, a company of soldiers rode out from Fort Sill under orders to disperse the tribe. Forbidden without cause the essential act of their faith, having seen the wild herds slaughtered and left to rot upon the ground, the Kiowas backed away forever from the medicine tree. That was July 20, 1890, at the great bend of the Washita. My grandmother was there. Without bitterness, and for as long as she lived, she bore a vision of deicide.

Now that I can have her only in memory, I see my grandmother in the several postures that were peculiar to her: standing at the wood stove on a winter morning and turning meat in a great iron skillet; sitting at the south window, bent above her beadwork, and afterwards, when her vision failed, looking down for a long time into the fold of her hands; going out upon a cane, very slowly as she did when the weight of age came upon her; praying. I remember her most often at prayer. She made long, rambling prayers out of suffering and hope, having seen many things. I was never sure that I had the right to hear, so exclusive were they of all mere custom and company. The last time I saw her she prayed standing by the side of her bed at night, naked to the waist, the light of a kerosene lamp moving upon her dark skin. Her long, black hair, always drawn and braided in the day, lay upon her shoulders and against her breasts like a shawl. I do not speak Kiowa, and I never understood her prayers, but there was something inherently sad in the sound, some merest hesitation upon the syllables of sorrow. She began in a high and descending pitch, exhausting her breath to silence; then again and again—and always the same intensity of effort, of something that is, and is not, like urgency in the human voice. Transported so in the dancing light among the shadows of her room, she seemed beyond the reach of time. But that was illusion; I think I knew then that I should not see her again. 11

Houses are like sentinels in the plain, old keepers of the weather watch. There, in a very little while, wood takes on the appearance of great age. All colors wear soon away in the wind and rain, and then the wood is burned gray and the grain appears and the nails turn red with rust. The windowpanes are black and opaque; you imagine there is nothing within, and indeed there are many ghosts, bones given up to the land. They stand here 12 and there against the sky, and you approach them for a longer time than you expect. They belong in the distance; it is their domain.

Once there was a lot of sound in my grandmother's house, a lot of com- 13 ing and going, feasting and talk. The summers there were full of excitement and reunion. The Kiowas are a summer people; they abide the cold and keep to themselves, but when the season turns and the land becomes warm and vital they cannot hold still; an old love of going returns upon them. The aged visitors who came to my grandmother's house when I was a child were made of lean and leather, and they bore themselves upright. They wore great black hats and bright ample shirts that shook in the wind. They rubbed fat upon their hair and wound their braids with strips of colored cloth. Some of them painted their faces and carried the scars of old and cherished enmities. They were an old council of warlords, come to remind and be reminded of who they were. Their wives and daughters served them well. The women might indulge themselves; gossip was at once the mark and compensation of their servitude. They made loud and elaborate talk among themselves, full of jest and gesture, fright and false alarm. They went abroad in fringed and flowered shawls, bright beadwork and German silver. They were at home in the kitchen, and they prepared meals that were banquets.

There were frequent prayer meetings, and great nocturnal feasts. When 14 I was a child I played with my cousins outside, where the lamplight fell upon the ground and the singing of the old people rose up around us and carried away into the darkness. There were a lot of good things to eat, a lot of laughter and surprise. And afterwards, when the quiet returned, I lay down with my grandmother and could hear the frogs away by the river and feel the motion of the air.

Now there is funeral silence in the rooms, the endless wake of some fi- 15 nal word. The walls have closed in upon my grandmother's house. When I returned to it in mourning, I saw for the first time in my life how small it was. It was late at night, and there was a white moon, nearly full. I sat for a long time on the stone steps by the kitchen door. From there I could see out across the land; I could see the long row of trees by the creek, the low light upon the rolling plains, and the stars of the Big Dipper. Once I looked at the moon and caught sight of a strange thing. A cricket had perched upon the handrail, only a few inches away from me. My line of vision was such that the creature filled the moon like a fossil. It had gone there, I thought, to live and die, for there, of all places, was its small definition made whole and eternal. A warm wind rose up and purled like the longing within me.

The next morning I awoke at dawn and went out on the dirt road to 16 Rainy Mountain. It was already hot, and the grasshoppers began to fill the air. Still, it was early in the morning, and the birds sang out of the shadows. The long yellow grass on the mountain shone in the bright light, and a scissortail hied above the land. There, where it ought to be, at the end of a long and legendary way, was my grandmother's grave. Here and there on the dark stones were ancestral names. Looking back once, I saw the mountain and came away.

Thinking About the Essay

1. What aspects of the Native American worldview does Momaday present in this essay? What are the myths and legends? How are they related? What is the relationship of the first paragraph to the central meanings of this essay?

2. In your own words, state the thesis that emerges from Momaday's narrative. Does the thesis emerge from the title? Why or why not? How does the title reflect the writer's purpose?

3. The language in this essay reflects Momaday's reputation as a major poet. Locate instances of "poetic" language in the selection—**imagery, metaphors, symbols,** and other types of **figurative language** and sensory detail. How does this poetic use of language serve to capture Momaday's subject and thesis?

4. Explain the narrative and descriptive patterns that serve to structure and unify the essay. What cinematic elements can you detect?

5. Momaday is quite successful at creating a specific mood or atmosphere in this essay. How would you describe it? How do the land, the Kiowas, and Momaday's grandmother serve as focal points in the creation of this atmosphere? Explain the mood we, as readers, are left with in the concluding paragraph.

Responding in Writing

6. Write a narrative and descriptive essay in which you capture a specific place that you associate with a particular person. Be certain to state your thesis or, if you wish, have it grow from the narrative. Also try to create a specific mood in your essay.

7. Write an analysis of Momaday's essay, focusing on how the writer presents the worldview of the Kiowas.

8. Where is the rest of the United States—other peoples (especially whites) and other communities—in this essay? Is Momaday making any implicit comments about these other peoples, whether it is their relationship to myths, to heritage, to family, or to the land? Answer these questions in a **reflective essay.**

Networking

9. In groups of three or four, discuss what you have learned about Native American culture from Momaday's essay. Identify and list at least three key discoveries. Share your list in discussion with the rest of the class.

10. Go online and find out more about Momaday and about Kiowa culture. Download the most compelling material and share it in class discussion.

America: The Multinational Society

ISHMAEL REED

Ishmael Reed was born in 1938 in Chattanooga, Tennessee, and is a well-known novelist, poet, and essayist who lives in Oakland and teaches at the University of California at Berkeley. An activist who advocates the rights of people of color, and notably African Americans, he has been at the forefront of major literary and political movements for decades. Reed's extensive literary production includes such works of fiction as *Mumbo Jumbo* (1972) and *Japanese by Spring* (1993), volumes of verse such as *Secretary to the Spirits* (1975), and several collections of essays, among them *Airing Dirty Laundry* (1993). Reed also has been an editor, playwright, songwriter, television producer, and publisher. In the following essay, which first appeared in *Writin' Is Fightin'* (1988) and has become a contemporary classic, Reed argues for a new definition of American culture.

Before Reading

Do you think that the United States is becoming a universal nation, composed of peoples and cultural styles from around the world? Why or why not?

> At the annual Lower East Side Jewish Festival yesterday, a Chinese woman ate a pizza slice in front of Ty Thuan Duc's Vietnamese grocery store. Beside her a Spanish-speaking family patronized a cart with two signs: "Italian Ices" and "Kosher by Rabbi Alper." And after the pastrami ran out, everybody ate knishes.
>
> —*The New York Times,* June 23, 1983

On the day before Memorial Day, 1983, a poet called me to describe a 1
city he had just visited. He said that one section included mosques, built by the Islamic people who dwelled there. Attending his reading, he

said, were large numbers of Hispanic people, forty thousand of whom lived in the same city. He was not talking about a fabled city located in some mysterious region of the world. The city he'd visited was Detroit.

A few months before, as I was leaving Houston, Texas, I heard it announced on the radio that Texas's largest minority was Mexican American, and though a foundation recently issued a report critical of bilingual education, the taped voice used to guide the passengers on the air trams connecting terminals in Dallas Airport is in both Spanish and English. If the trend continues, a day will come when it will be difficult to travel through some sections of the country without hearing commands in both English and Spanish; after all, for some western states, Spanish was the first written language and the Spanish style lives on in the western way of life.

Shortly after my Texas trip, I sat in an auditorium located on the campus of the University of Wisconsin at Milwaukee as a Yale professor—whose original work on the influence of African cultures upon those of the Americas has led to his ostracism from some monocultural intellectual circles—walked up and down the aisle, like an old-time southern evangelist, dancing and drumming the top of the lectern, illustrating his points before some serious Afro-American intellectuals and artists who cheered and applauded his performance and his mastery of information. The professor was "white." After his lecture, he joined a group of Milwaukeeans in a conversation. All of the participants spoke Yoruban, though only the professor had ever traveled to Africa.

One of the artists told me that his paintings, which included African and Afro-American mythological symbols and imagery, were hanging in the local McDonald's restaurant. The next day I went to McDonald's and snapped pictures of smiling youngsters eating hamburgers below paintings that could grace the walls of any of the country's leading museums. The manager of the local McDonald's said, "I don't know what you boys are doing, but I like it," as he commissioned the local painters to exhibit in his restaurant.

Such blurring of cultural styles occurs in everyday life in the United States to a greater extent than anyone can imagine and is probably more prevalent than the sensational conflict between people of different backgrounds that is played up and often encouraged by the media. The result is what the Yale professor, Robert Thompson, referred to as a cultural bouillabaisse, yet members of the nation's present educational and cultural Elect still cling to the notion that the United States belongs to some vaguely defined entity they refer to as "Western civilization," by which they mean, presumably, a civilization created by the people of Europe, as if Europe can be viewed in monolithic terms. Is Beethoven's Ninth Symphony, which includes

Turkish marches, a part of Western civilization, or the late nineteenth- and twentieth-century French paintings, whose creators were influenced by Japanese art? And what of the cubists, through whom the influence of African art changed modern painting, or the surrealists, who were so impressed with the art of the Pacific Northwest Indians that, in their map of North America, Alaska dwarfs the lower forty-eight in size?

Are the Russians, who are often criticized for their adoption of "West-   6 ern" ways by Tsarist dissidents in exile, members of Western civilization? And what of the millions of Europeans who have black African and Asian ancestry, black Africans having occupied several countries for hundreds of years? Are these "Europeans" members of Western civilization, or the Hungarians, who originated across the Urals in a place called Greater Hungary, or the Irish, who came from the Iberian Peninsula?

Even the notion that North America is part of Western civilization be-   7 cause our "system of government" is derived from Europe is being challenged by Native American historians who say that the founding fathers, Benjamin Franklin especially, were actually influenced by the system of government that had been adopted by the Iroquois hundreds of years prior to the arrival of large numbers of Europeans.   8

Western civilization, then, becomes another confusing category like Third World, or Judeo-Christian culture, as man attempts to impose his small-screen view of political and cultural reality upon a complex world. Our most publicized novelist recently said that Western civilization was the greatest achievement of mankind, an attitude that flourishes on the street level as scribbles in public restrooms: "White Power," "Niggers and Spics Suck," or "Hitler was a prophet," the latter being the most telling, for wasn't Adolph Hitler the archetypal monoculturalist who, in his pig-headed arrogance, believed that one way and one blood was so pure that it had to be protected from alien strains at all costs? Where did such an attitude, which has caused so much misery and depression in our national life, which has tainted even our noblest achievements, begin? An attitude that caused the incarceration of Japanese-American citizens during World War II, the persecution of Chicanos and Chinese Americans, the near-extermination of the Indians, and the murder and lynchings of thousands of Afro-Americans.

Virtuous, hardworking, pious, even though they occasionally would   9 wander off after some fancy clothes, or rendezvous in the woods with the town prostitute, the Puritans are idealized in our schoolbooks as "a hardy band" of no-nonsense patriarchs whose discipline razed the forest and brought order to the New World (a term that annoys Native American historians). Industrious, responsible, it was their "Yankee ingenuity" and practicality that created the work ethic. They were simple folk who produced a number of good poets, and they set the tone for the American writing style, of lean and spare lines, long before Hemingway. They worshiped in churches whose colors blended in with the New England snow, churches with simple structures and ornate lecterns.

The Puritans were a daring lot, but they had a mean streak. They hated 10 the theater and banned Christmas. They punished people in a cruel and inhuman manner. They killed children who disobeyed their parents. When they came in contact with those whom they considered heathens or aliens, they behaved in such a bizarre and irrational manner that this chapter in the American history comes down to us as a late-movie horror film. They exterminated the Indians, who taught them how to survive in a world unknown to them, and their encounter with the calypso culture of Barbados resulted in what the tourist guide in Salem's Witches' House refers to as the Witchcraft Hysteria.

The Puritan legacy of hard work and meticulous accounting led to the 11 establishment of a great industrial society; it is no wonder that the American industrial revolution began in Lowell, Massachusetts, but there was the other side, the strange and paranoid attitudes toward those different from the Elect.

The cultural attitudes of that early Elect continue to be voiced in every- 12 day life in the United States: the president of a distinguished university, writing a letter to the *Times,* belittling the study of African civilizations; the television network that promoted its show on the Vatican art with the boast that this art represented "the finest achievements of the human spirit." A modern up-tempo state of complex rhythms that depends upon contacts with an international community can no longer behave as if it dwelled in a "Zion Wilderness" surrounded by beasts and pagans.

When I heard a schoolteacher warn the other night about the invasion 13 of the American educational system by foreign curriculums, I wanted to yell at the television set, "Lady, they're already here." It has already begun because the world is here. The world has been arriving at these shores for at least ten thousand years from Europe, Africa, and Asia. In the late nineteenth and early twentieth centuries, large numbers of Europeans arrived, adding their cultures to those of the European, African, and Asian settlers who were already here, and recently millions have been entering the country from South America and the Caribbean, making Yale Professor Bob Thompson's bouillabaisse richer and thicker.

One of our most visionary politicians said that he envisioned a time 14 when the United States could become the brain of the world, by which he meant the repository of all of the latest advanced information systems. I thought of that remark when an enterprising poet friend of mine called to say that he had just sold a poem to a computer magazine and that the editors were delighted to get it because they didn't carry fiction or poetry. Is that the kind of world we desire? A humdrum homogeneous world of all brains but no heart, no fiction, no poetry; a world of robots with human attendants bereft of imagination, of culture? Or does North America deserve a more exciting destiny? To become a place where the cultures of the world crisscross. This is possible because the United States is unique in the world: The world is here.

Thinking About the Essay

1. How does the author's introductory paragraph set the stage for the development of his main claim or argument? Explain his argument in your own words. Does Reed develop his argument through **induction** or **deduction**? How do you know?

2. Reed begins in a personal mode of discourse, frequently using an "I" **point of view.** He then shifts to a more objective analytical and argumentative style before returning to the first-person point of view at the end of the essay. What is his purpose here? Do you find this strategy to be effective or confusing, and why?

3. What types of details and examples does the author employ? Why does Reed use so many examples in a relatively brief essay?

4. Identify and analyze the various rhetorical strategies—especially definition and comparison and contrast—that appear in this essay.

5. Why does Reed develop a series of questions in his closing paragraph?

Responding in Writing

6. Demonstrate in a personal essay the ways in which you come into contact with various races, ethnicities, and cultures on a daily basis. Be certain that you establish a clear thesis and develop several examples.

7. Write an argumentative essay in which you state your position on Reed's key assertion that the idea of Western or European civilization is wrongheaded.

8. In an analytical essay, explain some of the ways in which America's perception of itself as a **monoculturalist** or **Eurocentric** nation has caused problems in its relationship with the rest of the world.

Networking

9. In small groups, discuss your response to Reed's key assertion that "the United States is unique in the world: The world is here."

10. Select a partner and search the Internet together for information on American Puritanism. Present a brief oral report on your findings, explaining how the Puritan legacy continues to operate—as Reed suggests—in American society.

Our Rainbow Underclass

MORTIMER B. ZUCKERMAN

> Mortimer B. Zuckerman was born in Quebec, Canada, in 1937. He attended McGill University in Montreal, graduating with first-class honors in both economics and political theory. Coming to the United States, Zuckerman subsequently received a law degree from Harvard University in 1967. Becoming a millionaire from investments in real estate, he then acquired the *Atlantic Monthly* and *U.S. News and World Report.* As owner and editor in chief of the latter publication, he takes clear—generally conservative—stands on social and political issues in his weekly editorials. In this 2002 essay from *U.S. News & World Report,* Zuckerman asserts that a national dialogue on immigration is long overdue.

Before Reading

Do you think that immigration to the United States is out of control? Why or why not?

The roll of honor read at the 9/11 ceremonies was a tapestry of America, of native-born Americans of all ethnic origins and more recent immigrants. Of course, we know too well that some of the assassins and others plotting against America were immigrants who betrayed our ideals, so it is natural that many people feel we should now close the door altogether, beginning with immigrants from Muslim countries. Natural, and wrong. What is long overdue, however, is a sustained national dialogue on immigration.

Most politicians fear offending blocs of votes—a cowardice that does not serve the country well. Immigration has been out of control since 1965, when Sen. Edward Kennedy introduced a "reform" bill that ended the historic basis of the American melting pot. It was a bill remarkable for the fact that every single one of the assurances he and others gave proved wildly wrong—not because they wanted to mislead but because the bill unleashed forces they did not foresee. Indeed, the ensuing Immigration Reform Act triggered an immigration explosion, involving millions more than any other period, plus millions of illegals. There was a gross miscalculation of the effect of basing entry on "family reunification"; the criterion of "immediate relatives" was lost in the daisy-chain effect of brothers sponsoring brothers sponsoring cousins. It was said the goal was not to upset "the ethnic mix of this country," but the opposite occurred. Traditional immigrants from northern and western Europe were discriminated against in favor of Third World immigrants.

Schooling is the ticket. What is more disturbing is that the longer these   3
new immigrants stay in the country the worse they do, reversing the history of upward mobility in previous waves of immigration. Why? Traditionally, there were well-paid manufacturing jobs for immigrants, enabling them to join the ranks of blue-collar workers who secured a middle-class lifestyle without much formal education. Those days are gone. Schooling is today's ticket for a better future—with a high school diploma as the minimum. The original European newcomers could also send their children to high-quality urban schools. Assimilation was swift. The immigrants, however numerous, were from many different countries, so they took to English more rapidly: There was no linguistic minority to dominate any large city the way Spanish speakers now dominate Miami and Los Angeles. Today Latino immigrants live in a subnation with their own radio and TV stations, newspapers, films, and magazines, stunting assimilation and diminishing economic opportunity. Mexican-born males, handicapped by low or nonexistent English ability, earn half of what non-Latino whites earn. Although Mexican immigrants are often perceived as highly reliable, disciplined workers, Harvard Prof. Christopher Jencks makes the point that "having the right attitude is often enough to get an $8-an-hour job; it is seldom enough to get one for $16 an hour."

A critical question that is almost never asked: What is the impact on the   4
children, the second generation? Some thrive, but the majority do not. They form a rainbow underclass, caught in a cycle of downward assimilation, poverty combined with racial segregation. Often separated for long periods from their parents, especially their fathers, during the immigration process, they stop doing homework, reject their parents' values, and succumb to the dangers of an overcrowded inner-city culture. They face overwhelmed teachers, limited social service resources, and a decaying infrastructure, and they often adopt the negative behavior pattern of their peer groups, such as academic indifference and substance abuse, leading to dropout rates three times as high as for native-born Americans. Even the stellar performance of Asian children declines—studies show that by the third generation, Chinese students no longer exceed whites in educational success.

There is another disquieting connection, the trifecta effect of rising immigrant fertility rates. Our population is projected to rise to over 500 mil-   5 lion by 2050, roughly double what America is today—with post-1965 immigrants and their descendants making up about half. The effect of these numbers on myriad aspects of our environment, from rush-hour traffic to air and water pollution and social tensions, is incalculable.

How, then, should we proceed? No matter what, we must find more resources for the schools and other institutions that will support the development of second-generation children. Second, we must rebalance the number of visas provided for extended-family programs and add more to attract immigrants with skills transferable to the information economy. Third, we should slow down the process until we can thoroughly assess how the children of today's immigrants will fare as adults. Only through such measures can a national consensus on these issues begin to be forged.

6

Thinking About the Essay

1. What is the **tone** of this essay? Cite examples from the text to support your response.

2. How does the writer present his position on immigration? What topics does he raise? What types of evidence does he provide to support his main points?

3. What level of **diction** does the writer employ? Why does he use such words as *illegals* (paragraph 2), *subnation* (paragraph 3), and *rainbow underclass* (paragraph 4)?

4. The author employs cause-and-effect analysis to present his thesis in this essay. How effective is this strategy? Explain.

5. How does the writer develop his concluding paragraph? What is the effect?

Responding in Writing

6. Compose a letter to the editor of your college newspaper in which you state your position on immigration to the United States.

7. Write an analysis of Zuckerman's editorial and the strategies he employs to advance his argument.

8. Do you think that immigrants actually have access to quality education? If so, why? If not, why not? Write an argumentative essay responding to this question.

Networking

9. Help divide the class evenly for a debate on current immigration. One side should support unrestricted immigration, and the other side should support restriction. Write down the reasons supporting the position of your group and take time to locate evidence. Finally, designate one person to present findings to the entire class.

10. Conduct a web search, keying in "immigration" and "education." Summarize your findings in a brief report.

Asian Immigrants: Actors in History

RONALD TAKAKI | Ronald Takaki, whose grandparents were Japanese plantation workers in Hawaii, was born in Honolulu in 1939. He received his Ph.D. degree from the University of California at Berkeley in 1967 and is now professor of ethnic studies at that institution. A prolific writer in the field of ethnic studies, Takaki is the author of *Strangers from a Distant Shore: A History of Asian Americans* (1989), *Iron Cages: Race and Culture in 19th-Century America* (1999), and *Hiroshima* (2001), among other works. Takaki contributes frequently to both scholarly and popular magazines, lectures widely, and appears regularly on television news channels. In this selection from *Strangers from a Distant Shore*, Takaki combines personal narrative and cultural analysis as he reflects on the internment of Japanese Americans during World War II.

Before Reading

Why do you think Japanese Americans were interned during World War II? Can you think of any similar situations in the United States today? How can the past history of Japanese American internment help us to understand and manage present situations?

To confront the current problems of racism, Asian Americans know   1
they must remember the past and break its silence. This need was felt deeply by Japanese Americans during the hearings before the commission reviewing the issue of redress and reparations for Japanese Americans interned during World War II. Memories of the internment nightmare have haunted the older generation like ghosts. But the former prisoners have been unable to exorcise them by speaking out and ventilating their anger.

> When we were children,
> you spoke Japanese
> in lowered voices
> between yourselves.
> Once you uttered secrets
> which we should not know,
> were not to be heard by us.
> When you spoke

of some dark secret
you would admonish us,
"Don't tell it to anyone else."
It was a suffocated vow of silence.[1]

"Stigmatized," the ex-internees have been carrying the "burden of   2
shame" for over forty painful years. "They felt like a rape victim," explained Congressman Norman Mineta, a former internee of the Heart Mountain internment camp. "They were accused of being disloyal. They were the victims but they were on trial and they did not want to talk about it." But Sansei, or third-generation Japanese Americans, want their elders to tell their story. Warren Furutani, for example, told the commissioners that young people like himself had been asking their parents to tell them about the concentration camps and to join them in pilgrimages to the internment camp at Manzanar. "Why? Why!" their parents would reply defensively. "Why would you want to know about it? It's not important, we don't need to talk about it." But, Furutani continued, they need to tell the world what happened during those years of infamy.[2]

Suddenly, during the commission hearings, scores of Issei and Nisei   3
came forward and told their stories. "For over thirty-five years I have been the stereotype Japanese American," Alice Tanabe Nehira told the commission. "I've kept quiet, hoping in due time we will be justly compensated and recognized for our years of patient effort. By my passive attitude, I can reflect on my past years to conclude that it doesn't pay to remain silent." The act of speaking out has enabled the Japanese-American community to unburden itself of years of anger and anguish. Sometimes their testimonies before the commission were long and the chair urged them to conclude. But they insisted the time was theirs. "Mr. Commissioner," protested poet Janice Mirikitani,

So when you tell me my time is
up I tell you this.
Pride has kept my lips
pinned by nails,
my rage coffined.

1. Richard Oyama, poem published in *Transfer 38* (San Francisco, 1979), p. 43, reprinted in Elaine Kim, *Asian American Literature: An Introduction to the Writings and Their Social Context* (Philadelphia, 1982), pp. 308–309.
2. Congressman Robert Matsui, speech in the House of Representatives on bill 442 for redress and reparations, September 17, 1987, *Congressional Record* (Washington, 1987), p. 7584; Congressman Norman Mineta, interview with author, March 26, 1988; Warren Furutani, testimony, reprinted in *Amerasia*, vol. 8, no. 2 (1981), p. 104.

> But I exhume my past
> to claim this time.[3]

The former internees finally had spoken, and their voices compelled   4
the nation to redress the injustice of internment. In August 1988, Congress passed a bill giving an apology and a payment of $20,000 to each of the survivors of the internment camps. When President Ronald Reagan signed the bill into law, he admitted that the United States had committed "a grave wrong," for during World War II, Japanese Americans had remained "utterly loyal" to this country. "Indeed, scores of Japanese Americans volunteered for our Armed Forces—many stepping forward in the internment camps themselves. The 442nd Regimental Combat Team, made up entirely of Japanese Americans, served with immense distinction to defend this nation, their nation. Yet, back at home, the soldiers' families were being denied the very freedom for which so many of the soldiers themselves were laying down their lives." Then the president recalled an incident that happened forty-three years ago. At a ceremony to award the Distinguished Service Cross to Kazuo Masuda, who had been killed in action and whose family had been interned, a young actor paid tribute to the slain Nisei soldier. "The name of that young actor," remarked the president, who had been having trouble saying the Japanese names, "—I hope I pronounce this right—was Ronald Reagan." The time had come, the president acknowledged, to end "a sad chapter in American history."[4]

Asian Americans have begun to claim their time not only before the   5
commission on redress and reparations but elsewhere as well, in the novels of Maxine Hong Kingston and Milton Murayama, the plays of Frank Chin and Philip Gotanda, the scholarly writings of Sucheng Chan and Elaine Kim, the films of Steve Okazaki and Wa Wang, and the music of Hiroshima and Fred Houn. Others, too, have been breaking silences. Seventy-five-year-old Tomo Shoji, for example, had led a private life, but in 1981 she enrolled in an acting course because she wanted to try something frivolous and to take her mind off her husband's illness. In the beginning, Tomo was hesitant, awkward on the stage. "Be yourself," her teacher urged. Then suddenly she felt something surge through her, springing from deep within, and she began to tell funny and also sad stories about her life. Now Tomo tours the West Coast, a wonderful wordsmith giving one-woman shows to packed audiences of young Asian Americans.

3. Alice Tanabe Nehira, testimony, reprinted in *Amerasia,* vol. 8, no. 2 (1981), p. 93; Janice Mirikitani, "Breaking Silences," reprinted ibid., p. 109.
4. "Text of Reagan's Remarks:" reprinted in *Pacific Citizen,* August 19–26, 1988, p. 5; *San Francisco Chronicle,* August 5 and 11, 1988.

"Have we really told our children all we have gone through?" she asks. Telling one of her stories, Tomo recounts: "My parents came from Japan and I was born in a lumber camp. One day, at school, my class was going on a day trip to a show, and I was pulled aside and told I would have to stay behind. All the white kids went." Tomo shares stories about her husband: "When I first met him, I thought, 'wow.' Oh, he was so macho! And he wanted his wife to be a good, submissive wife. But then he married me." Theirs had been at times a stormy marriage. "Culturally we were different because he was Issei and I was American, and we used to argue a lot. Well, one day in 1942 right after World War II had started he came home and told me we had to go to an internment camp. 'I'm not going to one because I'm an American citizen,' I said to him. 'You have to go to camp, but not me.' Well, you know what, that was one time my husband was right!" Tomo remembers the camp: "We were housed in barracks, and we had no privacy. My husband and I had to share a room with another couple. So we hanged a blanket in the middle of the room as a partition. But you could hear everything from the other side. Well, one night, while we were in bed, my husband and I got into an argument, and I dumped him out of the bed. The other couple thought we were making violent love." As she stands on the stage and talks stories excitedly, Tomo cannot be contained: "We got such good, fantastic stories to tell. All our stories are different."[5]

Today, young Asian Americans want to listen to these stories—to shatter images of themselves and their ancestors as "strangers" and to understand who they are as Asian Americans. "What don't you know?" their elders ask. Their question seems to have a peculiar frame: it points to the blank areas of collective memory. And the young people reply that they want "to figure out how the invisible world the emigrants built around [their] childhoods fit in solid America." They want to know more about their "no name" Asian ancestors. They want to decipher the signs of the Asian presence here and there across the landscape of America—railroad tracks over high mountains, fields of cane virtually carpeting entire islands, and verdant agricultural lands.

> Deserts to farmlands
> Japanese-American
> Page in history.[6]

5. Tomo Shoji, "Born Too Soon . . . It's Never Too Late: Growing Up Nisei in Early Washington," presentations at the University of California at Berkeley, September 19, 1987, and the Ohana Cultural Center, Oakland, California, March 4, 1988.
6. Maxine Hong Kingston, *The Woman Warrior,* p. 6; poem in Kazuo Ito, *Issei: A History of Japanese Immigrants in North America* (Seattle, 1973), p. 493.

They want to know what is their history and "what is the movies." 7
They want to trace the origins of terms applied to them. "Why are we
called 'Oriental'?" they question, resenting the appellation that has identified Asians as exotic, mysterious, strange, and foreign. "The word 'orient'
simply means 'east.' So why are Europeans 'West' and why are Asians
'East'? Why did empire-minded Englishmen in the sixteenth century determine that Asia was 'east' of London? Who decided what names would be
given to the different regions and peoples of the world? Why does 'American' usually mean 'white'?" Weary of Eurocentric history, young Asian
Americans want their Asian ancestral lives in America chronicled, "given
the name of a place." They have earned the right to belong to specific
places like Washington, California, Hawaii, Puunene, Promontory Point,
North Adams, Manzanar, Doyers Street. "And today, after 125 years of
our life here," one of them insists, "I do not want just a home that time allowed me to have." Seeking to lay claim to America, they realize they can
no longer be indifferent to what happened in history, no longer embarrassed by the hardships and humiliations experienced by their grandparents and parents.

> My heart, once bent and cracked, once
> ashamed of your China ways.
> Ma, hear me now, tell me your story
> again and again.[7]

As they listen to the stories and become members of a "community of 8
memory," they are recovering roots deep within this country and the
homelands of their ancestors. Sometimes the journey leads them to discover rich and interesting things about themselves. Alfred Wong, for example, had been told repeatedly for years by his father, "Remember your
Chinese name. Remember your village in Toisha. Remember you are Chinese. Remember all this and you will have a home." One reason why it
was so important for the Chinese immigrants to remember was that they
never felt sure of their status in America. "Unlike German and Scottish immigrants, the Chinese immigrants never felt comfortable here," Wong explained. "So they had a special need to know there was a place, a home
for them somewhere."[8]

7. Kingston, *The Woman Warrior*, p. 6; Robert Kwan, "Asian v. Oriental: A difference that
Counts," *Pacific Citizen*, April 25, 1980; Sir James Augustus Henry Murry (ed.), *The Oxford
English Dictionary* (Oxford, 1933), vol. 7, p. 200; Aminur Rahim, "Is Oriental an Occident?"
in *The Asiandian*, vol. 5, no. 1, April 1983, p. 20; Shawn Wong, *Homebase* (New York,
1979), p. 111; Nellie Wong, "From a Heart of Rice Straw," in Nellie Wong, *Dreams in Harrison Railroad Park*. (Berkeley, 1977), p. 41.
8. Robert Bellah et al., *Habits of the Heart: Individualism and Commitment in American Life*
(Berkeley, 1985), p. 153; Alfred Wong, interviewed by Carol Takaki, April 6 and 13, 1988.

But Wong had a particular reason to remember. His father had married   9
by mutual agreement two women on the same day in China and had come
to America as a merchant in the 1920s. Later he brought over one of his
wives. But she had to enter as a "paper wife," for he had given the immigration authorities the name of the wife he had left behind. Born here in
1938, Wong grew up knowing about his father's other wife and the other
half of the family in China; his parents constantly talked about them and
regularly sent money home to Quangdong. For years the "family plan" had
been for him to see China someday. In 1984 he traveled to his father's
homeland, and there in the family home—the very house his father had left
decades earlier—Alfred Wong was welcomed by his *Chunk Gwok Ma*
("China Mama"). "You look just like I had imagined you would look," she
remarked. On the walls of the house, he saw hundreds of photographs—
of himself as well as sisters, nieces, nephews, and his own daughter—that
had been placed there over the years. He suddenly realized how much he
had always belonged there, and had a warm connectedness. "It's like you
were told there was this box and there was a beautiful diamond in it,"
Wong said. "But for years and years you couldn't open the box. Then finally you got a chance to open the box and it was as wonderful as you had
imagined it would be."[9]

Mine is a different yet similar story. My father, Toshio Takaki, died in   10
1945, when I was only five years old; my mother married Koon Keu Young
about a year later, and I grew up knowing very little about my father. Many
years later, in 1968, after my parents had moved to Los Angeles, my mother
passed away and I had to clear out her room after the funeral. In one of her
dresser drawers, I found an old photograph of my father as a teenager: it
was his immigration photograph. I noticed some Japanese writing on the
back. Later a friend translated: "This is Toshio Takaki, registered as an em-
igrant in Mifune, Kumamoto Prefecture, 1918." I wondered how young
Toshio managed to come to the United States. Why did he go to Hawaii?
Did he go alone? What dreams burned within the young boy? But a huge
silence stood before me, and I could only speculate that he must have come
alone and entered as a student, since the 1908 Gentlemen's Agreement had
prohibited the immigration of Japanese laborers. In Hawaii, he met and
married my mother, Catherine Okawa, a Nisei. I had no Takaki relatives
in Hawaii, I thought.

Ten years later, while on a sabbatical in Hawaii, I was "talking story"   11
with my uncle Richard Okawa. I was telling him about the book I was then
writing—*Iron Cages,* a study of race and culture in America. Suddenly his
eyes lit up as he exclaimed: "Hey, why you no go write a book about us,

9. Ibid.

huh? About the Japanese in Hawaii. After all, your grandparents came here as plantation workers and your mother and all your aunts and uncles were born on the plantation." Smiling, I replied: "Why not?" I went on to write a history of the plantation laborers. The book was published in 1983, and I was featured on television news and educational programs in Hawaii. One of the programs was aired in January 1985; a plantation laborer on the Puunene Plantation, Maui, was watching the discussion on television when he exclaimed to his wife: "Hey, that's my cousin, Ronald!" "No joke with me," she said, and he replied: "No, for real, for real."

A few months later, in July, I happened to visit Maui to give a lecture on the plantation experience. While standing in the auditorium shortly before my presentation, I noticed two Japanese men approaching me. One of them draped a red carnation lei around my shoulders and smiled: "You remember me, don't you?" I had never seen this man before and was confused. Then he said again. "You remember me?" After he asked for the third time, he pulled a family photograph from a plastic shopping bag. I saw among the people in the picture my father as a young man, and burst out excitedly: "Oh, you're a Takaki!" He replied: "I'm your cousin, Minoru. I saw you on television last January and when I found out you were going to come here I wanted to see you again. You were five years old when I last saw you. I was in the army on my way to Japan and I came by your house in Palolo Valley. But I guess you don't remember. I've been wondering what happened to you for forty years." Our families had lost contact with each other because of the war, the isolation of the plantation located on another island, my father's death, and my mother's remarriage. Minoru introduced me to his brother Susumu and his son, Leighton, who works on the Puunene Plantation and represents the fourth generation of Takaki plantation workers. Afterward they took me to the Puunene Plantation, showing me McGerrow Camp, where my branch of the Takaki family had lived, and filling me with stories about the old days. "You also have two cousins, Jeanette and Lillian in Honolulu," Minoru said, "and a big Takaki family in Japan." 12

A year later I visited my Takaki family in Japan. On the day I arrived, my cousin Nobuo showed me a box of old photographs that had been kept for decades in an upstairs closet. "We don't know who this baby is," he said, pointing to a picture of a baby boy. "That's me!" I exclaimed in disbelief. The box contained many photographs of my father, mother, sister, and me. My father had been sending pictures to the family in Kumamoto. I felt a part of me had been there all along and I had in a sense come home. Nobuo's wife Keiko told me that I was *Kumamoto kenjin*—"one of the people of Kumamoto." During my visit, I was taken to the farm where my 13 father was born. We drove up a narrow winding road past waterfalls and streams, tea farms, and rice paddies, to a village nestled high in the mountains. The scene reminded me of old Zen paintings of Japanese landscapes and evoked memories of my mother telling me the story of Momotaro. Toshino Watanabe, an old woman in her eighties, gave me a family portrait that her sister had sent in 1915; there they were in fading sepia—my uncle Teizo, grandfather Santaro, aunt Yukino, cousin Tsutako, uncle Nobuyoshi, and father Toshio, just fourteen years old—in McGerrow Camp on the Puunene Plantation.

The stories of Alfred Wong and myself branch from the late history of   14
Asian Americans and America itself—from William Hooper and Aaron Palmer, westward expansion, the economic development of California and Hawaii, the Chinese Exclusion Act, the Gentlemen's Agreement. The history of America is essentially the story of immigrants, and many of them, coming from a "different shore" than their European brethren, had sailed east to this new world. After she had traveled across the vast Pacific Ocean and settled here, a woman captured the vision of the immigrants from Asia in haiku's seventeen syllables:

> All the dreams of youth
> Shipped in emigration boats
> To reach this far shore.[10]

In America, Asian immigrants and their offspring have been actors in   15
history—the first Chinese working on the plantations of Hawaii and in the gold fields of California, the early Japanese immigrants transforming the brown San Joaquin Valley into verdant farmlands, the Korean immigrants struggling to free their homeland from Japanese colonialism, the Filipino farm workers and busboys seeking the America in their hearts, the Asian-Indian immigrants picking fruit and erecting Sikh temples in the West, the American-born Asians like Jean Park and Jade Snow Wong and Monica Sone trying to find an identity for themselves as Asian Americans, the second-wave Asian immigrants bringing their skills and creating new communities as well as revitalizing old communities with culture and enterprise, and the refugees from the war-torn countries of Southeast Asia trying to put their shattered lives together and becoming our newest Asian Americans. Their dreams and hopes unfurled here before the wind, all of them—from the first Chinese miners sailing through the Golden Gate to the last Vietnamese boat people flying into Los Angeles International Airport—have been making history in America. And they have been telling us about it all along.

10. Poem by Shigeko, in Kazuo Ito, *Issei,* p. 40.

Thinking About the Essay

1. What is Takaki's thesis? Where does it appear? What does the writer mean when he states, "Asian Americans have begun to claim their time" (paragraph 5)?

2. Why does Takaki present poetry in this essay? What is the relationship between the placement of each poem and the paragraphs surrounding it? How does the writer manage to maintain coherence?

3. Categorize the types of examples the writer uses to develop the essay and support the thesis.

4. Explain Takaki's argumentative stance. What is his claim, and where are his support and evidence?

5. Examine the writer's conclusion. Why is it so long? What is Takaki's purpose in providing so much information?

Responding in Writing

6. What stories have parents and relatives told you about your culture? What has been your response? Based on your response, write an essay in which you argue for or against the proposition that it is important for people to know about their culture.

7. Analyze the techniques used by Takaki to organize his essay. Provide examples and commentary. Explain why you think his method is successful—or not.

8. Based on the information Takaki provides, write an extended definition of "Asian American." Discuss the danger of stereotyping but the need also for understanding the specific cultures and heritages that make up the American mosaic or kaleidoscope.

Networking

9. In small groups, discuss this challenging essay in terms of Takaki's relationship to his material. What is the value of having an author inject himself personally into an analytical or argumentative essay? What are the dangers? Be prepared to present your conclusions to the class.

10. Download photographs of life in the Japanese American detention camps of World War II. For a group project, create a file of all these photographs—at least one photograph for each member of the class. Then have each class member write a brief caption for one or more photographs.

American Dreamer

Bharati Mukherjee

Bharati Mukherjee was born in Calcutta, India, in 1940. She attended the universities of Calcutta and Baroda, where she received a master's degree in English and ancient English culture. In 1961 she came to the United States to attend the Writer's Workshop at the University of Iowa, receiving a Ph.D. degree in English and comparative literature. Mukherjee became an American citizen in 1988; she is married to the writer Clark Blaise, with whom she has published two books, *Days and Nights in Calcutta* and *The Sorrow of the Terror*. Mukherjee's books of fiction include *The Middleman and Other Stories*, which won the 1988 National Book Critics Circle Award for fiction; *Jasmine* (1989); and *The Holder of the World* (1993). She is currently professor of English at the University of California at Berkeley. In the following essay, which was published in 1993 in *Mother Jones*, Mukherjee displays both narrative power and keen analytical strength in rejecting any hyphenated status as an American.

Before Reading

Mukherjee, writing in 1993, hyphenates such words as African-American and Asian-American. As a matter of style, why don't we use hyphenated race compounds today? Why do these terms even exist?

The United States exists as a sovereign nation. "America," in contrast, 1 exists as a myth of democracy and equal opportunity to live by, or as an ideal goal to reach.

I am a naturalized U.S. citizen, which means that, unlike native-born 2 citizens, I had to prove to the U.S. government that I merited citizenship. What I didn't have to disclose was that I desired "America," which to me is the stage for the drama of self-transformation.

I was born in Calcutta and first came to the United States—to Iowa 3 City, to be precise—on a summer evening in 1961. I flew into a small airport surrounded by cornfields and pastures, ready to carry out the two commands my father had written out for me the night before I left Calcutta: Spend two years studying creative writing at the Iowa Writers' Workshop, then come back home and marry the bridegroom he selected for me from our caste and class.

In traditional Hindu families like ours, men provided and women were   4
provided for. My father was a patriarch and I a pliant daughter. The neighborhood I'd grown up in was homogeneously Hindu, Bengali-speaking,
and middle-class. I didn't expect myself to ever disobey or disappoint my
father by setting my own goals and taking charge of my future.

When I landed in Iowa 35 years ago, I found myself in a society in   5
which almost everyone was Christian, white, and moderately well-off. In
the women's dormitory I lived in my first year, apart from six international
graduate students (all of us were from Asia and considered "exotic"), the
only non-Christian was Jewish, and the only nonwhite an African-
American from Georgia. I didn't anticipate then, that over the next 35
years, the Iowa population would become so diverse that it would have
6,931 children from non-English-speaking homes registered as students in
its schools, nor that Iowans would be in the grip of a cultural crisis in which
resentment against immigrants, particularly refugees from Vietnam, Sudan, and Bosnia, as well as unskilled Spanish-speaking workers, would become politicized enough to cause the Immigration and Naturalization
Service to open an "enforcement" office in Cedar Rapids in October for
the tracking and deporting of undocumented aliens.

In Calcutta in the '50s, I heard no talk of "identity crisis"—communal   6
or individual. The concept itself—of a person not knowing who he or she
is—was unimaginable in our hierarchical, classification-obsessed society.
One's identity was fixed, derived from religion, caste, patrimony, and
mother tongue. A Hindu Indian's last name announced his or her forefathers' caste and place of origin. A Mukherjee could *only* be a Brahmin from
Bengal. Hindu tradition forbade intercaste, interlanguage, interethnic marriages. Bengali tradition even discouraged emigration: To remove oneself
from Bengal was to dilute true culture.

Until the age of 8, I lived in a house crowded with 40 or 50 relatives. My   7
identity was viscerally connected with ancestral soil and genealogy. I was
who I was because I was Dr. Sudhir Lal Mukherjee's daughter, because I was
a Hindu Brahmin, because I was Bengali-speaking, and because my *desh*—
the Bengali word for homeland—was an East Bengal village called Faridpur.

The University of Iowa classroom was my first experience of coeducation.   8
And after not too long, I fell in love with a fellow student named Clark
Blaise, an American of Canadian origin, and impulsively married him dur-
ing a lunch break in a lawyer's office above a coffee shop.

That act cut me off forever from the rules and ways of upper-middle-   9
class life in Bengal, and hurled me into a New World life of scary im-
provisations and heady explorations. Until my lunch-break wedding, I

had seen myself as an Indian foreign student who intended to return to India to live. The five-minute ceremony in the lawyer's office suddenly changed me into a transient with conflicting loyalties to two very different cultures.

The first 10 years into marriage, years spent mostly in my husband's native Canada, I thought of myself as an expatriate Bengali permanently stranded in North America because of destiny or desire. My first novel, *The Tiger's Daughter*, embodies the loneliness I felt but could not acknowledge, even to myself, as I negotiated the no man's land between the country of my past and the continent of my present. Shaped by memory, textured with nostalgia for a class and culture I had abandoned, this novel quite naturally became an expression of the expatriate consciousness. 10

It took me a decade of painful introspection to put nostalgia in perspective and to make the transition from expatriate to immigrant. After a 14-year stay in Canada, I forced my husband and our two sons to relocate to the United States. But the transition from foreign student to U.S. citizen, from detached onlooker to committed immigrant, has not been easy. 11

The years in Canada were particularly harsh. Canada is a country that officially, and proudly, resists cultural fusion. For all its rhetoric about a cultural "mosaic," Canada refuses to renovate its national self-image to include its changing complexion. It is a New World country with Old World concepts of a fixed, exclusivist national identity. Canadian official rhetoric designated me as one of the "visible minority" who, even though I spoke the Canadian languages of English and French, was straining "the absorptive capacity" of Canada. Canadians of color were routinely treated as "not real" Canadians. One example: In 1985 a terrorist bomb, planted in an Air-India jet on Canadian soil, blew up after leaving Montreal, killing 329 passengers, most of whom were Canadians of Indian origin. The prime minister of Canada at the time, Brian Mulroney, phoned the prime minister of India to offer Canada's condolences for India's loss. 12

Those years of race-related harassments in Canada politicized me and deepened my love of the ideals embedded in the American Bill of Rights. I don't forget that the architects of the Constitution and the Bill of Rights were white males and slaveholders. But through their declaration, they provided us with the enthusiasm for human rights, and the initial framework from which other empowerments could be conceived and enfranchised communities expanded. 13

I am a naturalized U.S. citizen and I take my American citizenship very seriously. I am not an economic refugee, nor am I a seeker of political asylum. I am a voluntary immigrant. I became a citizen by choice, not by simple accident of birth. 14

Yet these days, questions such as who is an American and what is Amer- 15
ican culture are being posed with belligerence, and being answered with violence. Scapegoating of immigrants has once again become the politicians'
easy remedy for all that ails the nation. Hate speeches fill auditoriums for
demagogues willing to profit from stirring up racial animosity. An April
Gallup poll indicated that half of Americans would like to bar almost all
legal immigration for the next five years.

The United States, like every sovereign nation, has a right to formulate 16
its immigration policies. But in this decade of continual, large-scale diasporas, it is imperative that we come to some agreement about who "we"
are, and what our goals are for the nation, now that our community includes people of many races, ethnicities, languages, and religions.

The debate about American culture and American identity has to date 17
been monopolized largely by Eurocentrists and ethnocentrists whose rhetoric has been flamboyantly divisive, pitting a phantom "us" against a demonized "them."

All countries view themselves by their ideals. Indians idealize the cultural 18
continuum, the inherent value system of India, and are properly incensed
when foreigners see nothing but poverty, intolerance, strife, and injustice.
Americans see themselves as the embodiments of liberty, openness, and individualism, even as the world judges them for drugs, crime, violence, bigotry, militarism, and homelessness. I was in Singapore in 1994 when the
American teenager Michael Fay was sentenced to caning for having spray-
painted some cars. While I saw Fay's actions as those of an individual, and
his sentence as too harsh, the overwhelming local sentiment was that van-
dalism was an "American" crime, and that flogging Fay would deter Singapore youths from becoming "Americanized."

Conversely, in 1994, in Tavares, Florida, the Lake County School Board 19
announced its policy (since overturned) requiring middle school teachers to
instruct their students that American culture, by which the board meant
European-American culture, is inherently "superior to other foreign or historic cultures." The policy's misguided implication was that culture in the
United States has not been affected by the American Indian, African-
American, Latin-American, and Asian-American segments of the population. The sinister implication was that our national identity is so fragile
that it can absorb diverse and immigrant cultures only by recontextualiz-
ing them as deficient.

Our nation is unique in human history in that the founding idea of 20
"America" was in opposition to the tenet that a nation is a collection of
like-looking, like-speaking, like-worshipping people. The primary criterion

for nationhood in Europe is homogeneity of culture, race, and religion—which has contributed to blood-soaked balkanization in the former Yugoslavia and the former Soviet Union.

America's pioneering European ancestors gave up the easy homogeneity 21 of their native countries for a new version of Utopia. Now, in the 1990s, we have the exciting chance to follow that tradition and assist in the making of a new American culture that differs from both the enforced assimilation of a "melting pot" and the Canadian model of a multicultural "mosaic."

The multicultural mosaic implies a contiguity of fixed, self-sufficient, 22 utterly distinct cultures. Multiculturalism, as it has been practiced in the United States in the past 10 years, implies the existence of a central culture, ringed by peripheral cultures. The fallout of official multiculturalism is the establishment of one culture as the norm and the rest as aberrations. At the same time, the multiculturalist emphasis on race- and ethnicity-based group identity leads to a lack of respect for individual differences within each group, and to vilification of those individuals who place the good of the nation above the interests of their particular racial or ethnic communities.

We must be alert to the dangers of an "us" vs. "them" mentality. In Cal- 23 ifornia, this mentality is manifesting itself as increased violence between minority, ethnic communities. The attack on Korean-American merchants in South Central Los Angeles in the wake of the Rodney King beating trial is only one recent example of the tragic side effects of this mentality. On the national level, the politicization of ethnic identities has encouraged the scapegoating of legal immigrants, who are blamed for economic and social problems brought about by flawed domestic and foreign policies.

We need to discourage the retention of cultural memory if the aim of 24 that retention is cultural balkanization. We must think of American culture and nationhood as a constantly reforming, transmogrifying "we."

In this age of diasporas, one's biological identity may not be one's only 25 identity. Erosions and accretions come with the act of emigration. The experience of cutting myself off from a biological homeland and settling in an adopted homeland that is not always welcoming to its dark-complexioned citizens has tested me as a person, and made me the writer I am today.

I choose to Fdescribe myself on my own terms as an American, rather than 26 as an Asian-American. Why is it that hyphenation is imposed only on non-white Americans? Rejecting hyphenation is my refusal to categorize the cultural landscape into a center and its peripheries; it is to demand that the American nation deliver the promises of its dream and its Constitution to all its citizens equally.

My rejection of hyphenation has been misrepresented as race treachery 27
by some India-born academics on U.S. campuses who have appointed
themselves guardians of the "purity" of ethnic cultures. Many of them,
though they reside permanently in the United States and participate in its
economy, consistently denounce American ideals and institutions. They direct their rage at me because, by becoming a U.S. citizen and exercising my
voting rights, I have invested in the present and not the past; because I have
committed myself to help shape the future of my adopted homeland; and
because I celebrate racial and cultural mongrelization.

What excites me is that as a nation we have not only the chance to re- 28
tain those values we treasure from our original cultures but also the chance
to acknowledge that the outer forms of those values are likely to change.
Among Indian immigrants, I see a great deal of guilt about the inability to
hang on to what they commonly term "pure culture." Parents express rage
or despair at their U.S.-born children's forgetting of, or indifference to,
some aspects of Indian culture. Of those parents I would ask: What is it we
have lost if our children are acculturating into the culture in which we are
living? Is it so terrible that our children are discovering or are inventing
homelands for themselves?

Some first-generation Indo-Americans, embittered by racism and by un- 29
official "glass ceilings," construct a phantom identity, more-Indian-than-
Indians-in-India, as a defense against marginalization. I ask: Why don't you
get actively involved in fighting discrimination? Make your voice heard.
Choose the forum most appropriate for you. If you are a citizen, let your vote
count. Reinvest your energy and resources into revitalizing your city's disadvantaged residents and neighborhoods. Know your constitutional rights, and
when they are violated, use the agencies of redress the Constitution makes
available to you. Expect change, and when it comes, deal with it!

As a writer, my literary agenda begins by acknowledging that America 30
has transformed me. It does not end until I show that I (along with the hundreds of thousands of immigrants like me) am minute by minute transforming America. The transformation is a two-way process: It affects both
the individual and the national-cultural identity.

Others who write stories of migration often talk of arrival at a new 31
place as a loss, the loss of communal memory and the erosion of an original culture. I want to talk of arrival as a gain.

Thinking About the Essay

1. What is the significance of the title? How is Mukherjee a dreamer? Why
   does the idea of America inspire dreams? What impact does the American

Dream have on one's identity? For example, Mukherjee says in paragraph 6 that she had a clear sense of identity when she was in India. How has this sense of identity changed now that she is an American?

2. What is Mukherjee's purpose in writing this essay? Does she want to tell a story, analyze an issue, argue a position? Remember that this article appeared in *Mother Jones,* a progressive or left-of-center magazine. What does her primary audience tell you about her intentions?

3. Why does Mukherjee divide her essay into four parts? What are the relationships among these sections? Why has she used this pattern of organization? Where does she employ comparison and contrast and definition to achieve coherence among these parts?

4. Mukherjee refers to Eurocentrics and ethnocentrics. What do these terms mean to you? Discuss your understanding of these terms with other members of the class.

Responding in Writing

5. Write a summary of Mukherjee's essay, capturing as many of her major ideas as possible in no more than 300 words.

6. Write your own essay titled "American Dreamer," referring specifically to the dreams that immigrants—perhaps even you or members of your family—have had about coming to this country.

7. Mukherjee asserts, "We must be alert to the dangers of an 'us' vs. 'them' mentality (paragraph 23)." Write an argumentative essay responding to this statement, referring to other assertions by Mukherjee to amplify your own position.

Networking

8. In small groups, develop a summary of Mukherjee's essay. Next, compose a list of outstanding questions you still might have about her essay. For example, has she overlooked or diminished the importance of a specific topic, or has she personalized the subject too much? Finally, collaborate on a letter to the author in which you lay out your concerns.

9. Download from a search engine all the information that you can find about Bharati Mukherjee. Then compose a brief analytical profile of the author in which you highlight her career and the impact that living in several cultures has had on her work. Use "American Dreamer" as a foundation for this presentation, and be certain to provide citations for your web research. (For information on citing online sources, see Appendix A: Conducting Research in the New Global Era.)

The Cult of Ethnicity

ARTHUR M. SCHLESINGER JR.

> Arthur Meine Schlesinger Jr. was born in Columbus, Ohio, in 1917. Graduating from Harvard University in 1938, he embarked on a multifaceted career as historian, popular writer, university professor, political activist, and advisor to presidents. Among other positions he has held, he served as President Kennedy's special assistant for Latin American affairs. Schlesinger published dozens of books, most notably *The Age of Jackson*, which received the 1946 Pulitzer Prize for history, and *A Thousand Days*, which won the Pulitzer for biography in 1966. Although he never received an advanced degree, Schlesinger was awarded numerous honorary doctorates and for years was distinguished professor at the Graduate Center of the City University of New York. In the essay that follows, which was published in *Time* Magazine in 1991, Schlesinger offers a critique of multiculturalism and an endorsement of those values and attitudes that frame our commonality.

Before Reading

Do you support various ethnic studies programs and departments on your campus? Would you major in such a discipline? Why or why not?

The history of the world has been in great part the history of the mix-   1
ing of peoples. Modern communication and transport accelerate mass migrations from one continent to another. Ethnic and racial diversity is more than ever a salient fact of the age.

But what happens when people of different origins, speaking different   2
languages and professing different religions, inhabit the same locality and live under the same political sovereignty? Ethnic and racial conflict—far more than ideological conflict—is the explosive problem of our times.

On every side today ethnicity is breaking up nations. The Soviet Union,   3
India, Yugoslavia, Ethiopia, are all in crisis. Ethnic tensions disturb and divide Sri Lanka, Burma, Indonesia, Iraq, Cyprus, Nigeria, Angola, Lebanon, Guyana, Trinidad—you name it. Even nations as stable and civilized as Britain and France, Belgium and Spain, face growing ethnic troubles. Is there any large multiethnic state that can be made to work?

The answer to that question has been, until recently, the United States.   4
"No other nation," Margaret Thatcher has said, "has so successfully com-

bined people of different races and nations within a single culture." How have Americans succeeded in pulling off this almost unprecedented trick?

We have always been a multiethnic country. Hector St. John de Creve-   5
coeur, who came from France in the 18th century, marveled at the astonishing diversity of the settlers—"a mixture of English, Scotch, Irish,
French, Dutch, Germans and Swedes . . . this promiscuous breed." He pro-
pounded a famous question: "What then is the American, this new man?"
And he gave a famous answer: "Here individuals of all nations are melted
into a new race of men." *E pluribus unum.*

The U.S. escaped the divisiveness of a multiethnic society by a brilliant   6
solution: the creation of a brand-new national identity. The point of America was not to preserve old cultures but to forge a new, American culture.
"By an intermixture with our people," President George Washington told
Vice President John Adams, immigrants will "get assimilated to our customs, measures and laws: in a word, soon become one people." This was
the ideal that a century later Israel Zangwill crystallized in the title of his
popular 1908 play *The Melting Pot.* And no institution was more potent
in molding Crevecoeur's "promiscuous breed" into Washington's "one
people" than the American public school.

The new American nationality was inescapably English in language,   7
ideas and institutions. The pot did not melt everybody, not even all the
white immigrants; deeply bred racism put black Americans, yellow Americans, red Americans and brown Americans well outside the pale. Still, the
infusion of other stocks, even of nonwhite stocks, and the experience of the
New World reconfigured the British legacy and made the U.S., as we all
know, a very different country from Britain.

In the 20th century, new immigration laws altered the composition of   8
the American people, and a cult of ethnicity erupted both among non-
Anglo whites and among nonwhite minorities. This had many healthy consequences. The American culture at last began to give shamefully overdue
recognition to the achievements of groups subordinated and spurned during the high noon of Anglo dominance, and it began to acknowledge the
great swirling world beyond Europe. Americans acquired a more complex
and invigorating sense of their world—and of themselves.

But, pressed too far, the cult of ethnicity has unhealthy consequences.   9
It gives rise, for example, to the conception of the U.S. as a nation composed not of individuals making their own choices but of inviolable ethnic
and racial groups. It rejects the historic American goals of assimilation and
integration.

And, in an excess of zeal, well-intentioned people seek to transform our   10
system of education from a means of creating "one people" into a means

of promoting, celebrating and perpetuating separate ethnic origins and identities. The balance is shifting from *unum* to *pluribus*.

That is the issue that lies behind the hullabaloo over "multiculturalism" 11 and "political correctness," the attack on the "Eurocentric" curriculum and the rise of the notion that history and literature should be taught not as disciplines but as therapies whose function is to raise minority self-esteem. Group separatism crystallizes the differences, magnifies tensions, intensifies hostilities. Europe—the unique source of the liberating ideas of democracy, civil liberties and human rights—is portrayed as the root of all evil, and non-European cultures, their own many crimes deleted, are presented as the means of redemption.

I don't want to sound apocalyptic about these developments. Education 12 is always in ferment, and a good thing too. The situation in our universities, I am confident, will soon right itself. But the impact of separatist pressures on our public schools is more troubling. If a Kleagle of the Ku Klux Klan wanted to use the schools to disable and handicap black Americans, he could hardly come up with anything more effective than the "Afrocentric" curriculum. And if separatist tendencies go unchecked, the result can only be the fragmentation, resegregation and tribalization of American life.

I remain optimistic. My impression is that the historic forces driving to- 13 ward "one people" have not lost their power. The eruption of ethnicity is, I believe, a rather superficial enthusiasm stirred by romantic ideologues on the one hand and by unscrupulous con men on the other: self-appointed spokesmen whose claim to represent their minority groups is carelessly accepted by the media. Most American-born members of minority groups, white or nonwhite, see themselves primarily as Americans rather than primarily as members of one or another ethnic group. A notable indicator today is the rate of intermarriage across ethnic lines, across religious lines, even (increasingly) across racial lines. "We Americans," said Theodore Roosevelt, "are children of the crucible."

The growing diversity of the American population makes the quest for 14 unifying ideals and a common culture all the more urgent. In a world savagely rent by ethnic and racial antagonisms, the U.S. must continue as an example of how a highly differentiated society holds itself together.

Thinking About the Essay

1. Why does the writer employ the word *cult* in the title? What connotations does this word have? How does it affect the tone of the essay?

2. Consider the first two paragraphs of this essay, which constitute the writer's introduction. What thesis or claim does the writer advance? Why does he present his main idea in two brief paragraphs instead of one?

3. Summarize Schlesinger's argument. How does he state the problem and then proceed to offer a solution?

4. Note the many references to historical figures that the writer presents. Why has he employed this technique?

5. Examine paragraph 11, which consists of two very long sentences and one shorter one. How does the writer achieve coherence? Why does he place certain words within quotation marks? What assumptions does he make about his audience in presenting relatively complex sentence structures?

Responding in Writing

6. Schlesinger writes, "The balance is shifting from *unum* to *pluribus*" (paragraph 10). Write an essay in which you agree or disagree with this statement, offering your own reasons and support for the position you take.

7. Write an essay with the title "The Cult of——." You might want to select sports, celebrity, thinness, or any other subject that appeals to you.

8. Do you think that our commonality as Americans and citizens of the world outweighs our uniqueness? How can the two be reconciled? Write an essay that explores this issue.

Networking

9. In small groups talk about whether Schlesinger's portrait of America rings true, whether it describes you and your classmates as college students. What would you add to the writer's remarks? What, if anything, do you consider misleading or exaggerated? On the basis of your collective views, write notes for a letter to Schlesinger about his essay.

10. Using any search engine, download information on multiculturalism. Use the material you have assembled to write an essay in which you offer your own extended definition of this term. Be certain to cite at least three sources that you have discovered. (For information on citing online sources, see Appendix A.)

Go North, Young Man

RICHARD RODRIGUEZ

Richard Rodriguez, born in 1944 in San Francisco, has gained national fame for his articles, books, and broadcasts on issues of immigration, **multiculturalism,** and gender. After receiving degrees from both Stanford University and Columbia University, he also pursued graduate study at the University of California at Berkeley and the Warburg Institute, London. In his autobiography,

Hunger of Memory: The Education of Richard Rodriguez (1982), he offers a memorable portrait of a young man trying to reconcile his Hispanic heritage and the dominant American culture. Rodriguez's opposition to bilingualism and affirmative action has been controversial, but he brings sharp critical perceptions to every subject he treats. Rodriguez's most recent book is *Brown: The Last Discovery of America* (2002). In "Go North, Young Man," published in the July/August 1995 issue of *Mother Jones,* he shows how the new immigrants have altered the entire worldview of what it means to be American and a citizen of the Western world.

Before Reading

How do you define yourself as a person from a specific part of the country or the world? What assumptions do you bring about yourself from the place where you live? How do you think others perceive you?

Traditionally, America has been an east-west country. We have read 1 our history, right to left across the page. We were oblivious of Canada. We barely noticed Mexico, except when Mexico got in the way of our westward migration, which we interpreted as the will of God, "manifest destiny."

In a Protestant country that believed in rebirth (the Easter promise), 2 land became our metaphor for possibility. As long as there was land ahead of us—Ohio, Illinois, Nebraska—we could believe in change; we could abandon our in-laws, leave disappointments behind, to start anew further west. California symbolized ultimate possibility, future-time, the end of the line, where loonies and prophets lived, where America's fads necessarily began.

Nineteenth-century real estate developers and 20th-century Hollywood 3 moguls may have advertised the futuristic myth of California to the rest of America. But the myth was one Americans were predisposed to believe. The idea of California was invented by Americans many miles away. Only a few early voices from California ever warned against optimism. Two decades after California became American territory, the conservationist John Muir stood at the edge of California and realized that America is a finite idea: We need to preserve the land, if the dream of America is to survive. Word of Muir's discovery slowly traveled backward in time, from the barely populated West (the future) to the crowded brick cities of the East Coast (the past).

I grew up in California of the 1950s, when the state was filling with 4
people from New York and Oklahoma. Everyone was busy losing weight
and changing hair color and becoming someone new. There was, then, still
plenty of cheap land for tract houses, under the cloudless sky.

The 1950s, the 1960s—those years were our golden age. Edmund 5
G. "Pat" Brown was governor of optimism. He created the University of
California system, a decade before the children of the suburbs rebelled,
portraying themselves as the "counterculture." Brown constructed freeways that permitted Californians to move farther and farther away from
anything resembling an urban center. He even made the water run up the
side of a mountain.

By the 1970s, optimism was running out of space. Los Angeles needed 6
to reinvent itself as Orange County. Then Orange County got too crowded
and had to reinvent itself as North County San Diego. Then Californians
started moving into the foothills or out to the desert, complaining all the
while of the traffic and of the soiled air. And the immigrants!

Suddenly, foreign immigrants were everywhere—Iranians were buying 7
into Beverly Hills; the Vietnamese were moving into San Jose; the Chinese
were taking all the spaces in the biochemistry courses at UCLA. And Mexicans, poor Mexicans, were making hotel beds, picking peaches in the Central Valley, changing diapers, even impersonating Italian chefs at Santa
Monica restaurants.

The Mexicans and the Chinese had long inhabited California. But they 8
never resided within the golden myth of the state. Nineteenth-century California restricted the Chinese to Chinatowns or to a city's outskirts. Mexicans were neither here nor there. They were imported by California to
perform cheap labor, then deported in bad economic times.

The East Coast had incorporated Ellis Island in its myth. The West 9
Coast regarded the non-European immigrant as doubly foreign. Though
Spaniards may have colonized the place and though Mexico briefly
claimed it, California took its meaning from "internal immigrants"—
Americans from Minnesota or Brooklyn who came West to remake their
parents' version of America.

But sometime in the 1970s, it became clear to many Californians that the 10
famous blond myth of the state was in jeopardy. ("We are sorry to intrude,
señor, we are only looking for work.") Was L. A. "becoming" Mexican?

Latin Americans arrived, describing California as "el norte." The 11
"West Coast" was a finite idea; *el norte* in the Latin American lexicon
means wide-open. Whose compass was right?

Meanwhile, with the lifting of anti-Asian immigration restrictions, 12
jumbo jets were arriving at LAX from Bangkok and Seoul. People getting

off the planes said about California, "This is where the United States begins." Californians objected, "No, no. California is where the United States
comes to an end—we don't have enough room for you." Whose compass
was truer?

It has taken two more decades for the East Coast to get the point. Maga- 13
zines and television stories from New York today describe the golden state
as "tarnished." The more interesting possibility is that California has become the intersection between comedy and tragedy. Foreign immigrants
are replanting optimism on California soil; the native-born know the wisdom of finitude. Each side has a knowledge to give the other.

Already, everywhere in California, there is evidence of miscegenation— 14
Keanu Reeves, sushi tacos, blond Buddhists, Salvadoran Pentecostals.
But the forces that could lead to marriage also create gridlock on the
Santa Monica freeway. The native-born Californian sits disgruntled in
traffic going nowhere. The flatbed truck in front of him is filled with
Mexicans; in the Mercedes next to him is a Japanese businessman using
a car phone.

There are signs of backlash. Pete Wilson has become the last east-west 15
governor of California. In a state founded by people seeking a softer winter and famous internationally for being "laid back," Californians vote for
Proposition 187, hoping that illegal immigrants will stay away if there are
no welfare dollars.

But immigrants are most disconcerting to California because they are 16
everywhere working, transforming the ethos of the state from leisure to labor. Los Angeles is becoming a vast working city, on the order of Hong
Kong or Mexico City. Chinese kids are raising the admission standards to
the University of California. Mexican immigrant kids are undercutting
union wages, raising rents in once-black neighborhoods.

Californians used to resist any metaphor drawn from their state's 17
perennial earthquakes and floods and fires. Now Californians take their
meaning from natural calamity. People turn away from the sea, imagine the
future as existing backward in time.

> "I'm leaving California, I'm going to Colorado."
> "I'm headed for Arizona."

After hitting the coastline like flies against glass, we look in new direc- 18
tions. Did Southern California's urban sprawl invent NAFTA? For the first
time, Californians now talk of the North and the South—new points on
our national compass.

> "I've just bought a condo in Baja."
> "I'm leaving California for Seattle."

"I'm moving to Vancouver. I want someplace cleaner."

"Go North, young man."

Puerto Ricans, Mexicans: early in this century we were immigrants. Or not immigrants exactly. Puerto Ricans had awakened one day to discover that they suddenly lived on U.S. territory. Mexicans had seen Mexico's northern territory annexed and renamed the southwestern United States.

We were people from the South in an east-west country. We were people of mixed blood in a black and white nation. We were Catholics in a Protestant land. Many millions of us were Indians in an east-west country that imagined the Indian to be dead. 19

Today, Los Angeles is the largest Indian city in the United States, though Hollywood filmmakers persist in making movies about the dead Indian. (For seven bucks, you can see cowboys slaughter Indians in the Kevin Costner movie—and regret it from your comfortable chair.) On any day along Sunset Boulevard you can see Toltecs and Aztecs and Mayans. 20

Puerto Ricans, Mexicans—we are the earliest Latin American immigrants to the United States. We have turned into fools. We argue among ourselves, criticize one another for becoming too much the gringo or maybe not gringo enough. We criticize each other for speaking too much Spanish or not enough Spanish. We demand that politicians provide us with bilingual voting ballots, but we do not trouble to vote. 21

Octavio Paz, the Mexican writer, has observed that the Mexican-American is caught between cultures, thus a victim of history—unwilling to become a Mexican again, unable to belong to the United States. Michael Novak, the United States writer, has observed that what unites people throughout the Americas is that we all have said goodbye to our motherland. To Europe. To Africa. To Asia. Farewell! 22

The only trouble is: *Adios* was never part of the Mexican-American or Puerto Rican vocabulary. There was no need to turn one's back on the past. Many have traveled back and forth, between rivals, between past and future, commuters between the Third World and First. After a few months in New York or Los Angeles, it would be time to head "home." After a few months back in Mexico or Puerto Rico, it would be time to head "home" to the United States. 23

We were nothing like the famous Ellis Island immigrants who arrived in America with no expectation of return to the "old country." In a nation that believed in the future, we were a puzzle. 24

We were also a scandal to Puerto Rico and Mexico. Our Spanish turned bad. Our values were changing—though no one could say why or how exactly. *Abuelita* (grandmother) complained that we were growing more guarded. Alone. 25

There is a name that Mexico uses for children who have forgotten their   26
true address: *pocho*. The *pocho* is the child who wanders away, ends up in
the United States, among the gringos, where he forgets his true home.

The Americas began with a confusion about maps and a joke about our fa-   27
ther's mistake. Columbus imagined himself in a part of the world where
there were Indians.

We smile because our 15th-century *papi* thought he was in India. I'm   28
not certain, however, that even today we know where in the world we live.
We are only beginning to look at the map. We are only beginning to wonder what the map of the hemisphere might mean.

Latin Americans have long complained that the gringo, with character-   29
istic arrogance, hijacked the word *American* and gave it all to himself—
"the way he stole the land." I remember, years ago, my aunt in Mexico City
scolding me when I told her I came from "America." *Pocho!* Didn't I realize that the entire hemisphere is America? "Listen," my Mexican aunt told
me, "people who live in the United States are *norteamericanos*."

Well, I think to myself—my aunt is now dead, God rest her soul—I   30
wonder what she would have thought a couple of years ago when the great
leaders—the president of Mexico, the president of the United States, the
Canadian prime minister—gathered to sign the North American Free
Trade Agreement. Mexico signed a document acknowledging that she is a
North American.

I predict that Mexico will suffer a nervous breakdown in the next 10   31
years. She will have to check into the Betty Ford Clinic for a long rest. She
will need to determine just what exactly it means that she is, with the dread
gringo, a *norteamericana*.

Canada, meanwhile, worries about the impact of the Nashville music   32
channel on its cable TV; Pat Buchanan imagines a vast wall along our
southern flank; and Mexican nationalists fear a Clinton bailout of the
lowly peso.

We all speak of North America. But has anyone ever actually met a   33
North American? Oh, there are Mexicans. And there are Canadians. And
there are so-called Americans. But a North American?

I know one.   34

Let me tell you about him—this North American. He is a Mixteco In-   35
dian who comes from the Mexican state of Oaxaca. He is trilingual. His
primary language is the language of his tribe. His second language is Spanish, the language of Cortes. Also, he has a working knowledge of U.S. English, because, for several months of the year, he works near Stockton,
Calif.

He commutes over thousands of miles of dirt roads and freeways, 36
knows several centuries, two currencies, two sets of hypocrisy. He is a criminal in one country and an embarrassment to the other. He is pursued as an
"illegal" by the U.S. border patrol. He is preyed upon by Mexican officers
who want to shake him down because he has hidden U.S. dollars in his
shoes.

In Oaxaca, he lives in a 16th-century village, where his wife watches 37
blond Venezuelan soap operas. A picture of la Virgen de Guadalupe rests
over his bed. In Stockton, there is no Virgin Mary, only the other Madonna—
the material girl.

He is the first North American. 38

A journalist once asked Chou En-lai, the Chinese premier under Mao Ze- 39
dong, what he thought of the French Revolution. Chou En-lai gave a wonderful Chinese reply: "It's too early to tell."

I think it may even be too early to tell what the story of Columbus 40
means. The latest chapter of the Columbus saga may be taking place right
now, as Latin American teenagers with Indian faces violate the U.S. border.
The Mexican kids standing on the line tonight between Tijuana and San
Diego—if you ask them why they are coming to the United States of America, they will not say anything about Thomas Jefferson or The Federalist
Papers. They have only heard that there is a job in a Glendale dry cleaner's
or that some farmer is hiring near Fresno.

They insist: They will be returning to Mexico in a few months. They are 41
only going to the United States for the dollars. They certainly don't intend
to become gringos. They don't want anything to do with the United States,
except the dollars.

But the months will pass, and the teenagers will be changed in the 42
United States. When they go back to their Mexican village, they will no
longer be easy. They will expect an independence and an authority that the
village cannot give them. Much to their surprise, they will have been Americanized by the job in Glendale.

For work in the United States is our primary source of identity. There 43
is no more telling question we Americans ask one another than "What do
you do?" We do not ask about family or village or religion. We ask about
work.

The Mexican teenagers will return to Glendale. 44

Mexicans, Puerto Ricans—most of us end up in the United States, living in 45
the city. Peasants end up in the middle of a vast modern metropolis, having known only the village, with its three blocks of familiar facades.

The arriving generation is always the bravest. New immigrants often   46
change religion with their move to the city. They need to make their peace
with isolation, so far from relatives. They learn subway and bus routes that
take them far from [home] every day. Long before they can read English,
they learn how to recognize danger and opportunity. Their lives are defined
by change.

Their children or their grandchildren become, often, very different.   47
The best and the brightest, perhaps, will go off to college—become the
first in their family—but they talk about "keeping" their culture. They
start speaking Spanish, as a way of not changing: they eat in the cafeteria
only with others who look like themselves. They talk incessantly about
"culture" as though it were some little thing that can be preserved and kept
in a box.

The unluckiest children of immigrants drop out of high school. They   48
speak neither good English nor Spanish. Some end up in gangs—family,
man—"blood." They shoot other kids who look exactly like themselves.
If they try to leave their gang, the gang will come after them for their act
of betrayal. If they venture to some other part of the city, they might get
shot or they might merely be unable to decipher the freeway exits that
speed by.

They retreat to their "turf"—three blocks, just like in their grand-   49
mother's village, where the journey began.

One of the things that Mexico had never acknowledged about my father—   50
I insist that you at least entertain this idea—is the possibility that my father
and others like him were the great revolutionaries of Mexico. *Pocho* pio-
neers. They, not Pancho Villa, not Zapata, were heralds of the modern age
in Mexico. They left for the United States and then they came back to Mexico. And they changed Mexico forever.

A childhood friend of my father's—he worked in Chicago in the 1920s,   51
then returned one night to his village in Michoacan with appliances for *ma-
masita* and crisp dollars. The village gathered round him—this is a true
story—and asked, "What is it like up there in Chicago?"

The man said, "It's OK."   52

That rumor of "OK" spread across Michoacan, down to Jalisco, all the   53
way down to Oaxaca, from village to village to village.

Futurists and diplomats talk about a "new moment in the Ameri-   54
cas." The Latin American elite have condos in Miami and send their
children to Ivy League schools. U.S. and Canadian businessmen project
the future on a north-south graph. But for many decades before any of
this, Latin American peasants have been traveling back and forth, north
and south.

Today, there are remote villages in Latin America that are among the 55 most international places on earth. Tiny Peruvian villages know when farmers are picking pears in the Yakima valley in Washington state.

I am the son of a prophet. I am a fool. I am a victim of history. I am 56 confused. I do not know whether I am coming or going. I speak bad Spanish. And yet I tell Latin America this: Because I grew up Hispanic in California, I know more Guatemalans than I would if I had grown up in Mexico, more Brazilians than if I lived in Peru. Because I live in California, it is routine for me to know Nicaraguans and Salvadorans and Cubans. As routine as knowing Chinese or Vietnamese.

My fellow Californians complain loudly about the uncouth southern 57 invasion. I say this to California: Immigration is always illegal. It is a rude act, the leaving of home. Immigration begins as a violation of custom, a youthful act of defiance, an insult to the village. I know a man from El Salvador who has not spoken to his father since the day he left his father's village. Immigrants horrify the grandmothers they leave behind.

Illegal immigrants trouble U.S. environmentalists and Mexican nation- 58 alists. Illegal immigrants must trouble anyone, on either side of the line, who imagines that the poor are under control.

But they have also been our civilization's prophets. They, long before 59 the rest of us, saw the hemisphere whole.

Thinking About the Essay

1. What is the thesis of this essay? Where is the thesis most clearly stated?

2. Rodriguez divides his essay into seven parts. Summarize each section. Why does he employ this organizational strategy? What relationships do you see among the parts?

3. Analyze the tone of this essay. What is Rodriguez's attitude toward the "new" immigrants? How does his notion of "myth" influence the tone? Cite specific examples to support your response.

4. How does the writer's unique style make his argument all the more compelling? Identify sentences and paragraphs in which the language influences your response to the writer's claims.

5. Which paragraphs constitute the writer's conclusion? Are they effective? Why or why not?

Responding in Writing

6. Write a personal essay in which you explain why you consider yourself an American or, if you are from another country, what it would take for you to be an American in terms of your attitudes and values.

7. In an essay of 750–1,000 words, argue for or against the proposition that new patterns of immigration are dooming the "America for Americans" movement.

8. Write an essay explaining how the idea of what constitutes a North American must necessarily change.

Networking

9. Organize an online computer chat with three or four members of your class. Adopt a temporary screen name that identifies you as a person from a specific immigrant group, and role-play that person. Report on your experience with your classmates in a brief essay.

10. In another chat group, adopt a screen name, and anonymously explain your views on contemporary immigration. Report on your online chat in a brief essay.

Speaking in Tongues: Does Language Unify or Divide Us?

T he multicultural voices in the previous chapter reflect some of the numerous ethnic and racial diversities of the American mosaic. Along with this mosaic comes a variety of languages. Of course, you have been taught to speak and write the same language—that standard variety of English that places you in the college classroom today. Knowing the standard English "code" provides you with a powerful tool, offering pragmatic and liberating ways to gain control over your world. However, other languages might compete for your attention, especially if there are other languages that you speak at home or in your community. Powerful constituencies—politicians and advertisers among them—exploit this fact; for example, some decidedly Anglo politicians try to speak Spanish to Latino crowds (often to the amusement of native Spanish speakers). Other constituencies, threatened by our multilingual world, try to enact "English-only" laws in various states. Language can unify or divide a community or country, but basically it quite simply is a mark of your identity. To know a language or languages permits you to navigate your community, culture, and even global society.

Imagine, for example, what it would be like if you were illiterate. You wouldn't be here in college. You might not be able to read a menu or fill out a job application. You might not be interested in voting because you cannot read the names of the candidates. Illiteracy in reality is common around the world—and far more common in the United States than you might think.

We have vivid reminders of both the cost of illiteracy and also the power of literacy in film and literature. In the film *Driving Miss Daisy,*

The neighborhood of Elmhurst, Queens, in New York City, is one of the most ethnically and linguistically diverse places in the world. At Elmhurst's Newtown High School alone, students come from more than 100 countries and at least 39 languages are spoken. In this photograph, local schoolchildren take part in the neighborhood's annual International Day Festival on May 27, 1999.

Thinking About the Image

1. Recall a class photograph from your childhood. Was your school as diverse as this group of schoolchildren, or not? What are the advantages of being exposed to so many nationalities and languages at such a young age? What are the disadvantages?

2. News photographers often shoot many images of the same event, sometimes even multiple rolls of film, and then decide with their editors which unique image best captures the spirit of the event. Why do you think this photo was selected?

3. Are there parades for various ethnic or social groups in your community? How are those events covered in the local news media?

4. Would this parade have achieved its purpose, or appealed to its audience, as effectively if the marchers were adults instead of children? Why, or why not? Would the message (or purpose) have been different? In what way?

the character played by Morgan Freeman goes through most of his life pretending to read the daily newspaper. When Daisy (played by Jessica Tandy) teaches him to read, his world—and his comprehension of it—expands. Or consider one of the memorable sequences in *The Autobiography of Malcolm X*. Malcolm teaches himself to read and write when he is in prison. He starts at the beginning of the dictionary and works his way to the end. Going into prison as Richard Little, he comes out as Malcolm X, his identity reconstructed not only by the acquisition of a new system of belief—Islam—but also by a newly acquired literacy. In his writing and in his recovered life, Malcolm X harnessed the power of language to transform himself and his understanding of the world.

Think of language, then, as a radical weapon. Language permits you to share experiences and emotions, process information, analyze situations and events, defend a position, advocate a cause, make decisions. Language contributes to the growth of the self. Language is the bedrock of our academic, social, and professional lives. Language is a liberating force.

The idea that language is the key to our identity and our perception of the world is not new. Early Greek and Roman philosophers believed that you could not be a good thinker or writer unless you were a good person. Assuming that you are a good person, you possess a repertoire of mental skills that you can bring to bear on various situations and dimensions of your life. You can draw inferences, interpret conditions, understand causal relationships, develop arguments, make intelligent choices, and so forth. But have you ever found yourself in a situation where you know what you mean but not how to say it? Or think of how difficult it must be for people acquiring a second language; they know what they mean in their primary language but cannot express it in their new one. The essays in this chapter deal with precisely this situation.

The writers in this chapter illuminate the power and paradox of language. They link language, culture, and identity. They use language with skill and feeling. They work with the problems and contradictions of language, seeking answers to the question, Who am I, and where do my words—my languages—fit into the American mosaic?

Mother Tongue

AMY TAN

Amy Tan was born in San Francisco, California, in 1952, only two and a half years after her parents emigrated from China to the United States. She was educated at San Jose State University and the University of California at Berkeley and then worked as a reporter and technical writer. Tan is best known as a novelist whose fiction focuses on the conflict in culture between

Chinese parents and their Americanized children. Her first novel, *The Joy Luck Club* (1989), was highly popular and adapted by Hollywood as a feature film. Tan's other novels are *The Kitchen God's Wife* (1991), *The Hundred Secret Senses* (1995), and *The Bonesetter's Daughter* (2001). Tan's complicated relationship with her mother, Daisy, who died of Alzheimer's disease in 1999 at the age of eighty-three, is central to much of her fiction. In this essay, published in 1990 in *The Threepenny Reviews*, Tan, who has a master's degree in linguistics, invokes her mother in exploring the "Englishes" that immigrants employ as they navigate American culture.

Before Reading

How many "Englishes" do you speak, and what types of English do you speak in various situations? Is the English you speak in the classroom the same as you speak in your home or dormitory?

I am not a scholar of English or literature. I cannot give you much more   1
than personal opinions on the English language and its variations in this country or others.

I am a writer. And by that definition, I am someone who has always   2
loved language. I am fascinated by language in daily life. I spend a great deal of my time thinking about the power of language—the way it can evoke an emotion, a visual image, a complex idea, or a simple truth. Language is the tool of my trade. And I use them all—all the Englishes I grew up with.

Recently, I was made keenly aware of the different Englishes I do use. I   3
was giving a talk to a large group of people, the same talk I had already given to half a dozen other groups. The nature of the talk was about my writing, my life, and my book, *The Joy Luck Club*. The talk was going along well enough, until I remembered one major difference that made the whole talk sound wrong. My mother was in the room. And it was perhaps the first time she had heard me give a lengthy speech, using the kind of English I have never used with her. I was saying things like, "The intersection of memory upon imagination" and "There is an aspect of my fiction that relates to thus-and-thus"—a speech filled with carefully wrought grammatical phrases, burdened, it suddenly seemed to me, with nominalized forms, past perfect tenses, conditional phrases, all the forms of standard English that I had learned in school and through books, the forms of English I did not use at home with my mother.

Just last week, I was walking down the street with my mother, and I 4
again found myself conscious of the English I was using, the English I do
use with her. We were talking about the price of new and used furniture
and I heard myself saying this: "Not waste money that way." My husband
was with us as well, and he didn't notice any switch in my English. And
then I realized why. It's because over the twenty years we've been together
I've often used that same kind of English with him, and sometimes he even
uses it with me. It has become our language of intimacy, a different sort of
English that relates to family talk, the language I grew up with.

So you'll have some idea of what this family talk I heard sounds like, 5
I'll quote what my mother said during a recent conversation which I video-
taped and then transcribed. During this conversation, my mother was talking about a political gangster in Shanghai who had the same last name as
her family's, Du, and how the gangster in his early years wanted to be
adopted by her family, which was rich by comparison. Later, the gangster
became more powerful, far richer than my mother's family, and one day
showed up at my mother's wedding to pay his respects. Here's what she
said in part:

"Du Yusong having business like fruit stand. Like off the street kind. 6
He is Du like Du Zong—but not Tsung-ming Island people. The local people call putong, the river east side, he belong to that side local people. That
man want to ask Du Zong father take him in like become own family. Du
Zong father wasn't look down on him, but didn't take seriously, until that
man big like become a mafia. Now important person, very hard to inviting
him. Chinese way, came only to show respect, don't stay for dinner. Respect
for making big celebration, he shows up. Mean gives lots of respect. Chinese custom. Chinese social life that way. If too important won't have to
stay too long. He come to my wedding. I didn't see, I heard it. I gone to
boy's side, they have YMCA dinner. Chinese age I was nineteen."

You should know that my mother's expressive command of English be- 7
lies how much she actually understands. She reads the *Forbes* report, lis-
tens to *Wall Street Week*, converses daily with her stockbroker, reads all of
Shirley MacLaine's books with ease—all kinds of things I can't begin to understand. Yet some of my friends tell me they understand 50 percent of
what my mother says. Some say they understand 80 to 90 percent. Some
say they understand none of it, as if she were speaking pure Chinese. But
to me, my mother's English is perfectly clear, perfectly natural. It's my
mother tongue. Her language, as I hear it, is vivid, direct, full of observation and imagery. That was the language that helped shape the way I saw
things, expressed things, made sense of the world.

Lately, I've been giving more thought to the kind of English my mother   8
speaks. Like others, I have described it to people as "broken" or "fractured" English. But I wince when I say that. It has always bothered me that
I can think of no way to describe it other than "broken," as if it were damaged and needed to be fixed, as if it lacked a certain wholeness and soundness. I've heard other terms used, "limited English," for example. But they
seem just as bad, as if everything is limited, including people's perceptions
of the limited English speaker.

I know this for a fact, because when I was growing up, my mother's   9
"limited" English limited *my* perception of her. I was ashamed of her English. I believed that her English reflected the quality of what she had to say.
That is, because she expressed them imperfectly her thoughts were imperfect. And I had plenty of empirical evidence to support me: the fact that
people in department stores, at banks, and at restaurants did not take her
seriously, did not give her good service, pretended not to understand her,
or even acted as if they did not hear her.

My mother has long realized the limitations of her English as well.   10
When I was fifteen, she used to have me call people on the phone to pretend I was she. In this guise, I was forced to ask for information or even to
complain and yell at people who had been rude to her. One time it was a
call to her stockbroker in New York. She had cashed out her small portfolio and it just so happened we were going to go to New York the next week,
our very first trip outside California. I had to get on the phone and say in
an adolescent voice that was not very convincing, "This is Mrs. Tan."

And my mother was standing in the back whispering loudly, "Why he   11
don't send me check, already two weeks late. So mad he lie to me, losing
me money."

And then I said in perfect English, "Yes, I'm getting rather concerned.   12
You had agreed to send the check two weeks ago, but it hasn't arrived."

Then she began to talk more loudly. "What he want, I come to New   13
York tell him front of his boss, you cheating me?" And I was trying to calm
her down, make her be quiet, while telling the stockbroker, "I can't tolerate
any more excuses. If I don't receive the check immediately, I am going to
have to speak to your manager when I'm in New York next week." And sure
enough, the following week there we were in front of this astonished stockbroker, and I was sitting there red-faced and quiet, and my mother, the real
Mrs. Tan, was shouting at his boss in her impeccable broken English.

We used a similar routine just five days ago, for a situation that was   14
far less humorous. My mother had gone to the hospital for an appointment, to find out about a benign brain tumor a CAT scan had revealed a
month ago. She said she had spoken very good English, her best English,

no mistakes. Still, she said, the hospital did not apologize when they said they had lost the CAT scan and she had come for nothing. She said they did not seem to have any sympathy when she told them she was anxious to know the exact diagnosis, since her husband and son had both died of brain tumors. She said they would not give her any more information until the next time and she would have to make another appointment for that. So she said she would not leave until the doctor called her daughter. She wouldn't budge. And when the doctor finally called her daughter, me, who spoke in perfect English—lo and behold—we had assurances the CAT scan would be found, promises that a conference call on Monday would be held, and apologies for any suffering my mother had gone through for a most regrettable mistake.

I think my mother's English almost had an effect on limiting my possi- 15 bilities in life as well. Sociologists and linguists probably will tell you that a person's developing language skills are more influenced by peers. But I do think that the language spoken in the family, especially in immigrant families which are more insular, plays a large role in shaping the language of the child. And I believe that it affected my results on achievement tests, IQ tests, and the SAT. While my English skills were never judged as poor, compared to math, English could not be considered my strong suit. In grade school I did moderately well, getting perhaps B's, sometimes B-pluses, in English and scoring perhaps in the sixtieth or seventieth percentile on achievement tests. But those scores were not good enough to override the opinion that my true abilities lay in math and science, because in those areas I achieved A's and scored in the ninetieth percentile or higher.

This was understandable. Math is precise; there is only one correct an- 16 swer. Whereas, for me at least, the answers on English tests were always a judgment call, a matter of opinion and personal experience. Those tests were constructed around items like fill-in-the-blank sentence completion, such as, "Even though Tom was _____, Mary thought he was _____." And the correct answer always seemed to be the most bland combinations of thoughts, for example, "Even though Tom was shy, Mary thought he was charming," with the grammatical structure "even though" limiting the correct answer to some sort of semantic opposites, so you wouldn't get answers like, "Even though Tom was foolish, Mary thought he was ridiculous." Well, according to my mother, there were very few limitations as to what Tom could have been and what Mary might have thought of him. So I never did well on tests like that.

The same was true with word analogies, pairs of words in which you were 17 supposed to find some sort of logical, semantic relationship—for example, "*Sunset* is to *nightfall* as _____ is to _____." And here you would be presented with a list of four possible pairs, one of which showed the same kind of relationship: *red* is to *stoplight, bus* is to *arrival, chills* is to *fever, yawn* is to *boring.* Well, I could never think that way. I knew what the tests were asking, but I could not block out of my mind the images already created by the first pair, *"sunset* is to *nightfall"*—and I would see a burst of colors against a darkening sky, the moon rising, the lowering of a curtain of stars. And all the other pairs of words—red, bus, stoplight, boring—just threw up a mass of confusing images, making it impossible for me to sort out something as logical as saying: "A sunset precedes nightfall" is the same as "a chill precedes a fever." The only way I would have gotten that answer right would have been to imagine an associative situation, for example, my being disobedient and staying out past sunset, catching a chill at night, which turns into feverish pneumonia as punishment, which indeed did happen to me.

I have been thinking about all this lately, about my mother's English, 18 about achievement tests. Because lately I've been asked, as a writer, why there are not more Asian Americans represented in American literature. Why are there few Asian Americans enrolled in creative writing programs? Why do so many Chinese students go into engineering? Well, these are broad sociological questions I can't begin to answer. But I have noticed in surveys—in fact, just last week—that Asian students, as a whole, always do significantly better on math achievement tests than in English. And this makes me think that there are other Asian-American students whose English spoken in the home might also be described as "broken" or "limited." And perhaps they also have teachers who are steering them away from writing and into math and science, which is what happened to me.

Fortunately, I happen to be rebellious in nature and enjoy the challenge 19 of disproving assumptions made about me. I became an English major my first year in college, after being enrolled as pre-med. I started writing nonfiction as a freelancer the week after I was told by my former boss that writing was my worst skill and I should hone my talents toward account management.

But it wasn't until 1985 that I finally began to write fiction. And at first 20 I wrote using what I thought to be wittily crafted sentences, sentences that would finally prove I had mastery over the English language. Here's an example from the first draft of a story that later made its way into *The Joy Luck Club,* but without this line: "That was my mental quandary in its nascent state." A terrible line, which I can barely pronounce.

Fortunately, for reasons I won't get into today, I later decided I should 21 envision a reader for the stories I would write. And the reader I decided upon was my mother, because these were stories about mothers. So with this reader in mind—and in fact she did read my early drafts—I began to write stories using all the Englishes I grew up with: the English I spoke to my mother, which for lack of a better term might be described as "simple"; the English she used with me, which for lack of a better term might be described as "broken"; my translation of her Chinese, which could certainly be described as "watered down"; and what I imagined to be her translation of her Chinese if she could speak in perfect English, her internal language, and for that I sought to preserve the essence, but neither an English nor a Chinese structure. I wanted to capture what language ability tests can never reveal: her intent, her passion, her imagery, the rhythms of her speech and the nature of her thoughts.

Apart from what any critic had to say about my writing, I knew I had   22 succeeded where it counted when my mother finished reading my book and gave me her verdict: "So easy to read."

Thinking About the Essay

1. Explain the multiple meanings of Tan's title and how they illuminate the essay. What are the four ways Tan says language can work?

2. What is Tan's thesis, and where does it appear? How do we know her point of view about other "Englishes"? Does she state it directly or indirectly, and where?

3. How do narration and description interact in this essay? How does Tan describe her mother? What is the importance of dialogue?

4. What is Tan's viewpoint about language? Does she state that language should always be "simple"? Why or why not? To the extent that Tan's mother is an intended audience for her essay, is her language simple? Explain your answer by specific reference to her words and sentences. Finally, why does Tan's mother find her daughter's writing easy to understand?

5. How and where does Tan use humor in this essay? Where does Tan employ amusing anecdotes? What is her purpose in presenting these anecdotes, and how do they influence the essay's overall tone?

Responding in Writing

6. Tan suggests that the way we use language reflects the way we see the world. Write an essay based on this observation. Feel free to present an analytical paper or a narrative and descriptive essay, or to blend these patterns as does Tan.

7. Should all Americans speak and write the same language? Answer this question in an argumentative essay.

8. Tan writes about the "shame" she once experienced because of her mother's speech (paragraph 9). Write an essay about the dangers of linking personality or behavior to language. Can this linkage be used to promote racist, sexist, or other discriminatory ideas?

Networking

9. With two other class members, draw up a list of all the "Englishes" you have encountered. For example, how do your parents speak? What about relatives? Friends? Classmates? Personalities on television? Share your list with the class.

10. Conduct Internet or library research on the role of stereotyping by language in American radio and/or film. You might want to look into the popularity of the Charlie Chan series or Amos and Andy, or focus on a particular film that stereotypes a group. Present your information in an analytical and evaluative essay.

Mute in an English-Only World

CHANG-RAE LEE | Chang-rae Lee was born in 1965 in Seoul, South Korea. He and his family emigrated to the United States in 1968. Lee attended public schools in New Rochelle, New York; graduated from Yale University (B.A., 1987); and received an M.F.A. degree from the University of Oregon (1993). His first novel, *Native Speaker* (1995), won several prizes, including the Ernest Hemingway Foundation/PEN Award for First Fiction. He has also written *A Gesture Life* (1999) and *Aloft* (2004), and has published fiction and nonfiction in many magazines, including the *New Yorker* and *Time*. Lee has taught in the creative writing programs at the University of Oregon and Hunter College; today he is part of the Humanities Council and creative writing program at Princeton University. In the following essay, which appeared on the op-ed page of the *New York Times* in 1996, Lee remembers his mother's efforts to learn English, using literary memoir to comment on recent laws passed by certain towns in New Jersey requiring English on all commercial signs.

Before Reading

Should all commercial signs have English written on them, in addition to any other language? What about menus in ethnic restaurants?

When I read of the troubles in Palisades Park, N.J., over the prolifera- 1
tion of Korean-language signs along its main commercial strip, I unexpectedly sympathized with the frustrations, resentments and fears of the
longtime residents. They clearly felt alienated and even unwelcome in a vital part of their community. The town, like seven others in New Jersey, has
passed laws requiring that half of any commercial sign in a foreign language be in English.

Now I certainly would never tolerate any exclusionary ideas about who 2
could rightfully settle and belong in the town. But having been raised in a
Korean immigrant family, I saw every day the exacting price and power of
language, especially with my mother, who was an outsider in an English-
only world.

In the first years we lived in America, my mother could speak only the 3
most basic English, and she often encountered great difficulty whenever she
went out.

We lived in New Rochelle, N.Y., in the early 70's, and most of the local 4
businesses were run by the descendants of immigrants who, generations
ago, had come to the suburbs from New York City. Proudly dotting Main
Street and North Avenue were Italian pastry and cheese shops, Jewish tai-
lors and cleaners and Polish and German butchers and bakers. If my
mother's marketing couldn't wait until the weekend, when my father had
free time, she would often hold off until I came home from school to buy
the groceries.

Though I was only 6 or 7 years old, she insisted that I go out shopping 5
with her and my younger sister. I mostly loathed the task, partly because it
meant I couldn't spend the afternoon playing catch with my friends but
also because I knew our errands would inevitably lead to an awkward
scene, and that I would have to speak up to help my mother.

I was just learning the language myself, but I was a quick study, as chil- 6
dren are with new tongues. I had spent kindergarten in almost complete silence, hearing only the high nasality of my teacher and comprehending little
but the cranky wails and cries of my classmates. But soon, seemingly mere
months later, I had already become a terrible ham and mimic, and I would
crack up my father with impressions of teachers, his friends and even himself. My mother scolded me for aping his speech, and the one time I attempted to make light of hers I rated a roundhouse smack on my bottom.

For her, the English language was not very funny. It usually meant trou- 7
ble and a good dose of shame, and sometimes real hurt. Although she had
a good reading knowledge of the language from university classes in South
Korea, she had never practiced actual conversation. So in America, she
used English flashcards and phrase books and watched television with us

kids. And she faithfully carried a pocket workbook illustrated with stick-figure people and compound sentences to be filled in.

But none of it seemed to do her much good. Staying mostly at home to care for us, she didn't have many chances to try out sundry words and phrases. When she did, say, at the window of the post office, her readied speech would stall, freeze, sometimes altogether collapse. 8

One day was unusually harrowing. We ventured downtown in the new Ford Country Squire my father had bought her, an enormous station wagon that seemed as long—and deft—as an ocean liner. We were shopping for a special meal for guests visiting that weekend, and my mother had heard that a particular butcher carried fresh oxtails—which she needed for a traditional soup. 9

We'd never been inside the shop, but my mother would pause before its window, which was always lined with whole hams, crown roasts and ropes of plump handmade sausages. She greatly esteemed the bounty with her eyes, and my sister and I did also, but despite our desirous cries she'd turn us away and instead buy the packaged links at the Finast supermarket, where she felt comfortable looking them over and could easily spot the price. And, of course, not have to talk. 10

But that day she was resolved. The butcher store was crowded, and as we stepped inside the door jingled a welcome. No one seemed to notice. We waited for some time, and people who entered after us were now being served. Finally, an old woman nudged my mother and waved a little ticket, which we hadn't taken. We patiently waited again, until one of the beefy men behind the glass display hollered our number. 11

My mother pulled us forward and began searching the cases, but the oxtails were nowhere to be found. The man, his big arms crossed, sharply said, "Come on, lady, whaddya want?" This unnerved her, and she somehow blurted the Korean word for oxtail, soggori. 12

The butcher looked as if my mother had put something sour in his mouth, and he glanced back at the lighted board and called the next number. 13

Before I knew it, she had rushed us outside and back in the wagon, which she had double-parked because of the crowd. She was furious, almost vibrating with fear and grief, and I could see she was about to cry. 14

She wanted to go back inside, but now the driver of the car we were blocking wanted to pull out. She was shooing us away. My mother, who had just earned her driver's license, started furiously working the pedals. But in her haste she must have flooded the engine, for it wouldn't turn over. The driver started honking and then another car began honking as well, and soon it seemed the entire street was shrieking at us. 15

In the following years, my mother grew steadily more comfortable with 16 English. In Korean, she could be fiery, stern, deeply funny and ironic; in English, just slightly less so. If she was never quite fluent, she gained enough confidence to make herself clearly known to anyone, and particularly to me.

Five years ago, she died of cancer, and some months after we buried her 17 I found myself in the driveway of my father's house, washing her sedan. I liked taking care of her things; it made me feel close to her. While I was cleaning out the glove compartment, I found her pocket English workbook, the one with the silly illustrations. I hadn't seen it in nearly 20 years. The yellowed pages were brittle and dog-eared. She had fashioned a plain-paper wrapping for it, and I wondered whether she meant to protect the book or hide it.

I don't doubt that she would have appreciated doing the family shop- 18 ping on the new Broad Avenue of Palisades Park. But I like to think, too, that she would have understood those who now complain about the Korean-only signs.

I wonder what these same people would have done if they had seen my 19 mother studying her English workbook—or lost in a store. Would they have nodded gently at her? Would they have lent a kind word?

Thinking About the Essay

1. What is the author's purpose? Is he trying to paint a picture of his mother, describe an aspect of the immigrant experience, convey a thesis, argue a point, or what? Explain your response.

2. What is unusual about Lee's introduction? How does his position on the issue raised defy your expectations?

3. Lee offers stories within stories. How are they ordered? Which tale receives greatest development, and why?

4. Lee uses **colloquial language** in this essay. Identify some examples. What is the effect?

5. What is the dominant impression that you have of Lee's mother? How does he bring her to life?

Responding in Writing

6. Construct a profile of the writer. What do we learn about Lee? What are his values? What is his attitude toward English? How does this son of immigrant parents establish himself as an authority? How does he surprise us with his perspective on language?

7. In a personal essay, tell of a time when you were embarrassed either by the language of someone close to you or by your own use of language in a social or business situation.

8. Both Amy Tan and Chang-rae Lee focus on their mothers' handling of their second language—English. Write a comparative essay in which you explain the similarities and differences in the authors' approaches to their subject.

Networking

9. With two other class members, discuss the emotional appeal of Lee's essay. Look especially at his conclusion. Share your responses with the class.

10. Write an e-mail to your instructor, suggesting two additional questions you would ask about Lee's essay if *you* were teaching it.

Spanglish

Janice Castro, with Dan Cook and Cristina García

Janice Castro, born and raised in California, is a senior editor for *Time* magazine. She was the lead writer for *Time*'s 1991 Special Issue on Women and writes frequently on a range of cultural issues. Castro has written *The American Way of Health: How Medicine Is Changing, and What It Means to You* (1994). In the following essay, which she wrote for *Time* in 1988 with the assistance of *Time* staffers Dan Cook and Cristina García, she offers a crisp, concise definition of that hybrid and increasingly common form of language known as "Spanglish."

Before Reading

Why has Spanish been the most popular second language for students in high school and college for more than forty years? What Spanish "crossover" words do you know? Do you think that it is natural for languages—for example, Spanish and English—to borrow from each other, creating a new language in the process? Why or why not?

In Manhattan a first-grader greets her visiting grandparents, happily exclaiming, "Come here, *siéntate!*" Her bemused grandfather, who does not speak Spanish, nevertheless knows she is asking him to sit down. A Miami personnel officer understands what a job applicant means when he says, "*Quiero un* part time." Nor do drivers miss a beat reading a billboard alongside a Los Angeles street advertising CERVEZA—SIX-PACK!

This free-form blend of Spanish and English, known as Spanglish, is   2
common linguistic currency wherever concentrations of Hispanic Americans are found in the U.S. In Los Angeles, where 55% of the city's 3 million inhabitants speak Spanish, Spanglish is as much a part of daily life as
sunglasses. Unlike the broken-English efforts of earlier immigrants from
Europe, Asia and other regions, Spanglish has become a widely accepted
conversational mode used casually—even playfully—by Spanish-speaking
immigrants and native-born Americans alike.

Consisting of one part Hispanicized English, one part Americanized   3
Spanish and more than a little fractured syntax, Spanglish is a bit like a
Robin Williams comedy routine: a crackling line of cross-cultural patter
straight from the melting pot. Often it enters Anglo homes and families
through the children, who pick it up at school or at play with their young
Hispanic contemporaries. In other cases, it comes from watching TV; many
an Anglo child watching *Sesame Street* has learned *uno dos tres* almost as
quickly as one two three.

Spanglish takes a variety of forms, from the Southern California Anglos   4
who bid farewell with the utterly silly "*hasta la* bye-bye" to the Cuban-
American drivers in Miami who *parquean* their *carros.* Some Spanglish sentences are mostly Spanish, with a quick detour for an English word or two.
A Latino friend may cut short a conversation by glancing at his watch and
excusing himself with the explanation that he must "*ir al* supermarket."

Many of the English words transplanted in this way are simply handier   5
than their Spanish counterparts. No matter how distasteful the subject, for
example, it is still easier to say "income tax" than *impuesto sobre la renta.*
At the same time, many Spanish-speaking immigrants have adopted such
terms as VCR, microwave and dishwasher for what they view as largely
American phenomena. Still other English words convey a cultural context
that is not implicit in the Spanish. A friend who invites you to *lonche* most
likely has in mind the brisk American custom of "doing lunch" rather than
the languorous afternoon break traditionally implied by *almuerzo.*

Mainstream Americans exposed to similar hybrids of German, Chi-   6
nese or Hindi might be mystified. But even Anglos who speak little or no
Spanish are somewhat familiar with Spanglish. Living among them, for
one thing, are 19 million Hispanics. In addition, more American high
school and university students sign up for Spanish than for any other foreign language.

Only in the past ten years, though, has Spanglish begun to turn into a   7
national slang. Its popularity has grown with the explosive increases in U.S.
immigration from Latin American countries. English has increasingly col-
lided with Spanish in retail stores, offices and classrooms, in pop music and

on street corners. Anglos whose ancestors picked up such Spanish words as *rancho, bronco, tornado* and *incommunicado,* for instance, now freely use such Spanish words as *gracias, bueno, amigo* and *por favor.*

Among Latinos, Spanglish conversations often flow easily from Span-   8
ish into several sentences of English and back.

Spanglish is a sort of code for Latinos: the speakers know Spanish, but   9
their hybrid language reflects the American culture in which they live. Many lean to shorter, clipped phrases in place of the longer, more graceful expressions their parents used. Says Leonel de la Cuesta, an assistant professor of modern languages at Florida International University in Miami: "In the U.S., time is money, and that is showing up in Spanglish as an economy of language." Conversational examples: *taipiar* (type) and *winshi-wiper* (windshield wiper) replace *escribir a máquina* and *limpiaparabrisas.*

Major advertisers, eager to tap the estimated $134 billion in spending   10
power wielded by Spanish-speaking Americans, have ventured into Spanglish to promote their products. In some cases, attempts to sprinkle Spanish through commercials have produced embarrassing gaffes. A Braniff airlines ad that sought to tell Spanish-speaking audiences they could settle back *en* (in) luxuriant *cuero* (leather) seats, for example, inadvertently said they could fly without clothes *(encuero).* A fractured translation of the Miller Lite slogan told readers the beer was "Filling, and less delicious." Similar blunders are often made by Anglos trying to impress Spanish-speaking pals. But if Latinos are amused by mangled Spanglish, they also recognize these goofs as a sort of friendly acceptance. As they might put it, *no problema.*

Thinking About the Essay

1. What is the writers' purpose in developing this essay? What is the thesis? Is this thesis stated or implied? Explain.

2. Who is the audience for this essay? What assumptions do the writers make about this audience?

3. Where is the concise definition of "Spanglish" that the writers provide? How do they employ other rhetorical techniques—illustration, comparison and contrast, process analysis—to create an extended definition?

4. The writers use several types of illustration to develop their definition. Locate and identify these various forms. What is the overall effect?

5. Explain the tone of this essay. In other words, what is the writers' attitude toward their subject? Do they simply want to inform readers about Spanglish, want us to approve or disapprove of it, accept or reject it, or what? How do you know?

Responding in Writing

6. Do you think that "foreign" and hybrid languages are a threat to the purity of English in the United States? Answer this question in an argumentative essay.

7. Write an essay in which you discuss Spanglish, dialect, and slang as varieties of English. This will be a classification essay. Provide examples to support your thesis.

8. In an analytical essay, explore the relationship of language to cultural identity. Why is this issue especially significant in the United States today?

Networking

9. Exchange your essay with a class member, and evaluate it according to the following criteria: Is the thesis clearly stated? What patterns of development have been used, and how effective are they? Are there sufficient examples to support major points? Is there a consistent and effective style and tone throughout the essay? Revise your paper based on your classmate's remarks.

10. Consult several search engines to locate advertisements that reflect the hybrid use of language. Share your findings with the class. Appoint one class member to prepare a disk of the best advertisements for future use.

If Black English Isn't a Language, Then Tell Me, What Is?

JAMES BALDWIN | James Baldwin, born in 1924 in New York City, was a major novelist, short story writer, essayist, playwright, and public figure during much of his adult life. The son of a stern clergyman, Baldwin was a youth minister at Fireside Pentecostal Assembly in Harlem while still attending DeWitt Clinton High School, from which he graduated in 1942. After high school, Baldwin found work in the defense industry in New Jersey, where he encountered the racism, discrimination, and homophobia that would preoccupy him as a writer and spokesperson for oppressed peoples. Subsequently he moved to Greenwich Village, determined to be a writer. African American novelist Richard Wright helped him to obtain a prestigious Saxton Fellowship to advance his career. Frustrated by segregation in the United States, Baldwin moved to Paris in 1948, spending most of his remaining life overseas. "Once I found myself on the other side of the ocean," Baldwin told the *New York Times*, "I could see where I came from very clearly . . . I am the grandson of a slave, and I am a writer. I must deal with both." Baldwin's novels include *Go Tell It on the Mountain* (1953), *Giovanni's Room* (1977), *Another Country* (1962), and *If Beale Street Could Talk* (1974). Many critics think that Baldwin is an even better essayist than fiction writer; such collections as *Notes of a Native Son* (1955), *Nobody Knows My Name* (1961), and *The Price of the Ticket: Collected Nonfiction* (1985) establish him as a unique commentator on the African American condition. Baldwin died of stomach cancer in St-Paul de Vence, France, in 1987. In this essay first published in the *New York Times* in 1979, Baldwin takes an aggressive approach to the controversy over Black English, making clear his position on the political and sociological implications of the issue.

Before Reading

Do you think black English is a legitimate form of English? What about Ebonics or Spanglish? What about various regional dialects? Do any of these "Englishes," to use Amy Tan's phrase, have the same validity as Standard English? Why or why not?

The argument concerning the use, or the status, or the reality, of black 1 English is rooted in American history and has absolutely nothing to do with the question the argument supposes itself to be posing. The argument has nothing to do with language itself but with the role of language. Language, incontestably, reveals the speaker. Language, also, far more dubiously, is meant to define the other—and, in this case, the other is refusing to be defined by a language that has never been able to recognize him.

People evolve a language in order to describe and thus control their cir- 2 cumstances or in order not to be submerged by a situation that they cannot articulate. (And if they cannot articulate it, they are submerged.) A Frenchman living in Paris speaks a subtly and crucially different language from that of the man living in Marseilles; neither sounds very much like a man living in Quebec; and they would all have great difficulty in apprehending what the man from Guadeloupe, or Martinique, is saying, to say nothing of the man from Senegal—although the "common" language of all these areas is French. But each has paid, and is paying, a different price for this "common" language, in which, as it turns out, they are not saying, and cannot be saying, the same things: They each have very different realities to articulate, or control.

What joins all languages, and all men, is the necessity to confront life, in order, not inconceivably, to outwit death: The price for this is the acceptance, and achievement, of one's temporal identity. So that, for example, though it is not taught in the schools (and this has the potential of becoming a political issue) the south of France still clings to its ancient and musical Provençal, which resists being described as a "dialect." And much of the tension in the Basque countries, and in Wales, is due to the Basque and Welsh determination not to allow their languages to be destroyed. This determination also feeds the flames in Ireland for among the many indignities the Irish have been forced to undergo at English hands is the English contempt for their language.

It goes without saying, then, that language is also a political instrument, means, and proof of power. It is the most vivid and crucial key to identity. It reveals the private identity, and connects one with, or divorces one from, the larger, public, or communal identity. There have been, and are, times and places, when to speak a certain language could be dangerous, even fatal. Or, one may speak the same language, but in such a way that one's antecedents are revealed, or (one hopes) hidden. This is true in France, and is absolutely true in England: The range (and reign) of accents on that damp little island make England coherent for the English and totally incomprehensible for everyone else. To open your mouth in England is (if I may use black English) to "put your business in the street." You have confessed your parents, your youth, your school, your salary, your self-esteem, and, alas, your future.

Now, I do not know what white Americans would sound like if there had never been any black people in the United States, but they would not sound the way they sound. *Jazz,* for example, is a very specific sexual term, as in *jazz me, baby,* but white people purified it into the Jazz Age. *Sock it to me,* which means, roughly, the same thing, has been adopted by Nathaniel Hawthorne's descendants with no qualms or hesitations at all, along with *let it all hang out* and *right on! Beat to his socks,* which was once the black's most total and despairing image of poverty, was transformed into a thing called the Beat Generation, which phenomenon was, largely, composed of *uptight,* middle-class white people, imitating poverty, trying to *get down,* to get *with it,* doing their *thing,* doing their despairing best to be *funky,* which we, the blacks, never dreamed of doing—we were funky, baby, like *funk* was going out of style.

Now, no one can eat his cake, and have it, too, and it is late in the day   6
to attempt to penalize black people for having created a language that permits the nation its only glimpse of reality, a language without which the nation would be even more *whipped* than it is.

I say that the present skirmish is rooted in American history, and it is.   7
Black English is the creation of the black diaspora. Blacks came to the United States chained to each other, but from different tribes. Neither could speak the other's language. If two black people, at that bitter hour of the world's history, had been able to speak to each other, the institution of chattel slavery could never have lasted as long as it did. Subsequently, the slave was given, under the eye, and the gun, of his master, Congo Square, and the Bible—or, in other words, and under those conditions, the slave began the formation of the black church, and it is within this unprecedented tabernacle that black English began to be formed. This was not, merely, as in the European example, the adoption of a foreign tongue, but an alchemy that transformed ancient elements into a new language: *A language comes into existence by means of brutal necessity, and the rules of the language are dictated by what the language must convey.*

There was a moment, in time, and in this place, when my brother, or   8
my mother, or my father, or my sister, had to convey to me, for example, the danger in which I was standing from the white man standing just behind me, and to convey this with a speed and in a language, that the white man could not possibly understand, and that, indeed, he cannot understand, until today. He cannot afford to understand it. This understanding would reveal to him too much about himself and smash that mirror before which he has been frozen for so long.

Now, if this passion, this skill, this (to quote Toni Morrison) "sheer in-   9
telligence," this incredible music, the mighty achievement of having brought a people utterly unknown to, or despised by "history"—to have brought this people to their present, troubled, troubling, and unassailable and unanswerable place—if this absolutely unprecedented journey does not indicate that black English is a language, I am curious to know what definition of languages is to be trusted.

A people at the center of the western world, and in the midst of so hos-   10
tile a population, has not endured and transcended by means of what is patronizingly called a "dialect." We, the blacks, are in trouble, certainly, but we are not inarticulate because we are not compelled to defend a morality that we know to be a lie.

The brutal truth is that the bulk of the white people in America never   11
had any interest in educating black people, except as this could serve white purposes. It is not the black child's language that is despised. It is his ex-

perience. A child cannot be taught by anyone who despises him, and a child cannot afford to be fooled. A child cannot be taught by anyone whose demand, essentially, is that the child repudiate his experience, and all that gives him sustenance, and enter a limbo in which he will no longer be black, and in which he knows that he can never become white. Black people have lost too many black children that way.

And, after all, finally, in a country with standards so untrustworthy, 12 a country that makes heroes of so many criminal mediocrities, a country unable to face why so many of the nonwhite are in prison, or on the needle, or standing, futureless, in the streets—it may very well be that both the child, and his elder, have concluded that they have nothing whatever to learn from the people of a country that has managed to learn so little.

Thinking About the Essay

1. How does Baldwin present his argument in the opening paragraph? How does he use negation to clarify his position and limit his argument?

2. Is there a clearly stated claim or major proposition in this essay? If so, where is it?

3. What are the main reasons Baldwin offers in support of his argument?

4. An argument will often appeal to emotion, especially if the topic is personally important to the writer. Would you characterize Baldwin's essay as especially emotional? Why or why not?

5. What is the purpose of illustration in this essay? With so many examples, how does Baldwin maintain coherence?

6. How does Baldwin use causal analysis to advance his argument?

Responding in Writing

7. Baldwin writes, "There have been, and are, times, and places, where to speak a certain language could be dangerous, even fatal" (paragraph 4). In what cases might this be true? What is the double meaning of the phrase "a certain language"? Can you point to historical or current events that support Baldwin's statement? Write an essay dealing with his statement and these questions.

8. Write an argumentative essay in which you defend a position as to whether or not black English is a language in its own right.

9. Baldwin claims that "language is also a political instrument, means, and proof of power. It is the most vivid and crucial key to identity" (paragraph 4). Respond to his statement in an analytical essay.

Networking

10. Paragraph 5 illustrates how certain expressions from black English have become common in all Americans' daily speech. In a group of five, make a list of words or expressions from various cultural or ethnic groups that have also entered the common language. Read your list to the general class.

11. Recently, there have been legislative efforts to make English (presumably Standard English) the official language of certain states or the United States as a whole. Try to find an Internet forum or chat room dealing with this issue. Report your findings and your position on the issue in a brief essay.

Spanglish: The Making of a New American Language

ILAN STAVANS

Ilan Stavans was born in Mexico in 1961 to an Eastern European Jewish family and moved to New York City in the mid-1980s to attend Columbia University. Stavans is the editor of *The Oxford Book of Latin American Essays, The Oxford Book of Jewish Stories,* and the author of numerous works on Hispanic literature and culture. In genres ranging from literary criticism to the memoir, he has explored issues of language and identity in books including *Imagining Columbus: The Literary Voyage* (2001); *The Hispanic Condition: The Power of a People* (1995); and with Chicano artist Lalo Alcaraz, *LatinoUSA: A Cartoon History* (2000). A collection of his short stories, *The One-Handed Pianist and Other Stories,* appeared in 1996. Stavans, the recipient of a Guggenheim Fellowship and the Latino Literature Prize, is currently the Lewis-Sebring Professor in Latin-American and Latino Culture at Amherst College. In the following selection, which appears in *Spanglish: The Making of a New American Language* (2003), Stavans combines personal and analytical writing to explore a popular form of discourse.

Before Reading

What is your response to being required to speak or write a certain kind of English in the classroom and, perhaps, in the workplace? Why do these requirements, which may create tensions between people of different backgrounds, exist?

¿Cómo empezó everything? How did I stumble upon it? Walking the   1
streets of El Barrio in New York City, at least initially. Wandering around, as the Mexican expression puts it, con la oreja al vuelo, with ears

wide open. Later on, of course, my appreciation for Spanglish evolved dramatically as I traveled around los Unaited Esteits. But at the beginning was New York. It always is, isn't it?

I had arrived in Manhattan in the mid-eighties. My first one-room   2
apartment, which I shared with three roommates, was on Broadway and 122nd Street. The area was bustling with color: immigrants from the Americas, especially from the Dominican Republic, Mexico, El Salvador, and Colombia, intermingling with students from Columbia University, Barnard and Teacher's College, and with future ministers and rabbis from Union Theological Seminary and The Jewish Theological Seminary. The ethnic juxtaposition was exhilarating indeed. But sight wasn't everything. Sound was equally important. Color and noise went together, as I quickly learned.

I was enthralled by the clashing voices I encountered on a regular walk   3
in the Upper West Side: English, Spanish, Yiddish, Hebrew . . . Those voices often changed as one oscillated to different areas of the city: Arabic, French, Polish, Russian, Swahili and scores of other tongues were added to the mix. What kind of symphony was I immersed in? Was this the sound of the entire universe or only of my neighborhood?

There was a newspaper stand on the corner of 110th and Broadway, next   4
to a bagel bakery and a Korean grocery store. I regularly made my shopping in those blocks, so I regularly stopped to browse. Newspapers and magazines in English predominated in it, and Chinese and Israeli periodicals were also for sale. But the owner displayed the Spanish-language items with emphasis: *El Diario/La Prensa, Noticias del Mundo, Diario de las Américas, Cosmopolitan, Imagen* . . . As a Mexican native, I often bought one of them in the morning, "just to keep up with what's up," as I would tell my friends. But to keep up with these publications was also to invite your tongue for a bumpy ride. The grammar and syntax used in them was never fully "normal," e.g., it replicated, often unconsciously, English-language patterns. It was obvious that its authors and editors were americanos with a loose connection to la lengua de Borges. "Están contaminaos . . . ," a teacher of mine in the Department of Spanish at Columbia would tell me. "Pobrecitos . . . They've lost all sense of verbal propriety."

Or had they?   5

My favorite section to read in *El Diario/La Prensa*, already then the   6
fastest-growing daily in New York, where I eventually was hired to be a columnist, was the hilarious classified section. "Conviértase en inversor del Citibank," claimed an ad. Another one would state: " Para casos de divorcio y child support, llame a su advocate personal al (888) 745-1515." And: "¡¡¡ Alerta!!! Carpinteros y window professionals. Deben tener 10 años de experiencia y traer tools." Or, "Estación de TV local está

buscando un editor de lineal creativo. Debe tener conocimiento del 'Grass Valley Group VPE Series 151'. En The Bronx. Venga en persona: (718) 601-0962." One morning I came across one that announced pompously: "Hoy más que nunca, tiempo is money." And I stumbled upon another that read: "Apartments are selling like pan caliente and apartments de verdad."

Today I use the term *hilarious* in a reverent fashion. Over the years my admiration for Spanglish has grown exponentially, even though I'm perfectly conscious of its social and economic consequences. Only 14 percent of Latino students in the country graduate from college. The majority complain that the cultural obstacles along the way are innumerable: the closely knit family dynamic, the need to help support their family, the refusal to move out from home in order to go to school . . . And language, naturally: for many of them proficiency in the English language is too high a barrier to overcome. English is the door to the American Dream. Not until one masters el inglés are the fruits of that dream attainable.

Spanglish is often described as the trap, la trampa Hispanics fall into on the road to assimilation—el obstáculo en el cainino. Alas, the growing lower class uses it, thus procrastinating the possibility of un futuro mejor, a better future. Still, I've learned to admire Spanglish over time. Yes, it is the tongue of the uneducated. Yet, it's a hodgepodge . . . But its creativity astonished me. In many ways, I see in it the beauties and achievements of jazz, a musical style that sprung up among African-Americans as a result of improvisation and lack of education. Eventually, though, it became a major force in America, a state of mind breaching out of the ghetto into the middle class and beyond. Will Spanglish follow a similar route?

Back then, as my early immigrant days unfolded, it was easier to denigrate it. Asked by a reporter in 1985 for his opinion on el espanglés, one of the other ways used to refer to the linguistic juxtaposition of south and north—some other categories are casteyanqui, inglañol, argot sajón, español bastardo, papiamento gringo, and caló pachuco—Octavio Paz, the Mexican author of *The Labyrinth of Solitude* (1950) and a recipient of the Nobel Prize for Literature, is said to have responded with a paradox: "ni es bueno ni es malo, sino abominable"—it is neither good nor bad but abominable. This wasn't an exceptional view: Paz was one of scores of intellectuals with a distaste for the bastard jargon, which, in his eyes, didn't have gravitas. Una lengua bastarda: illegitimate, even wrongful.

The common perception was that Spanglish was sheer verbal chaos—el habla de los bárbaros. As I browsed through the pages of Spanish-language periodicals, as I watched TV and listened to radio stations en español, this approach increasingly made me uncomfortable. There was something, un yo no sé qué, that was simply exquisite . . . Of course, it took me no time to recognize that standard English was the lingua franca of the middle and upper classes, but its domain was in question in the lower strata of the population. In that segment, I wasn't able to recognize the English I expected to hear: monolithic, homogenous, single-minded. Instead, I constantly awakened to a polyphonic reality.

Depending on the individual age, ethnicity, and educational background,   11
a vast number of dispossessed nuyorquinos spoke a myriad of rongues, a sum of parts impossible to define. Indeed, the metropolis seemed to me a veritable Tower of Babel. And among Hispanics—the rubric *Latino* was only then emerging—this hullabaloo, this mishmash was all the more intense.

Mishmash is a Hebrew term that means fusion. In and of itself, the word   12
Spanglish is that mixture: a collage, part Spanish, part English. I'm an etymological freak, always on the lookout for a lexicographic definition. I've sought for the inclusion and explanation of the word *Spanglish* in dictionaries.

Doctor Samuel Johnson, an idol of mine, once said that "dictionaries   13
are like watches: the worst is better than none, and the best cannot be expected to go quite true." Perhaps that is the reason why so many ignore so common a verbal phenomenon: the best lexicon is never good enough, or the worst will build a fence around it not to let undignified terms irrupt on its pages. For shouldn't a lexicon, seeking to categorize the rowdy and infinite Spanglish exchanges, "to go as true as it might," in Johnson's mindset, begin by giving the meaning of the word?

Again, think of el jazz. In the seventies, Herbie Hancock offered a bril-   14
liant analogy: "It is something very hard to define," he said, "but very easy to recognize." Spanglish, I'm convinced, fits the same bill: it's not that it is impossible to define, but that people simply refuse to do it. And yet, nobody has the slightest doubt that it has arrived, que ya llegó . . . It is also a common vehicle of communication in places like Miami, Los Angeles, San Antonio, Houston, Albuquerque, Phoenix, Denver, and Tallahassee, as well as in countless rural areas, wherever the 35.3 million documented Latinos—this is the official number issued by the 2000 U.S. Census Bureau, which in 2003 jumped to 38.8 million, de facto making Hispanics the largest minority north of the Rio Grande—find themselves.

And, atención, Spanglish isn't only a phenomenon that takes place en   15
los Unaited Esteits: in some shape or form, with English as a merciless global force, it is spoken—and broken: no es solamente hablado sino quebrado—all across the Hispanic world, from Buenos Aires to Bogotá, from Barcelona to Santo Domingo.

Beware: Se habla el espanglés everywhere these days!   16

To contradict Paz—and perhaps to correct him—let me attempt my own def- 17
inition of Spanglish, once as succinct and encompassing as possible: "Spanglish, n. The verbal encounter between Anglo and Hispano civilizations."

As is always the case with these types of dictionary "explications," it 18
already makes me unhappy. For one thing, I was tempted to write *clash* instead of *encounter,* and *language* instead of *civilization*. But then again, by
doing so I would have reduced Spanglish to a purely linguistic phenomenon, which it isn't. Para nada . . .

At any rate, one thing is to get exposed to Spanish in the streets of New 19
York, another altogether different is to use it effortlessly. As an immigrant,
my road to full participation in American life was—as it has been and continues to be for any immigrant, regardless the origin—through English. I
had come with primitive skills in Shakespeare's tongue, so during almost
my entire first decade this side of the Rio Grande, my sole objective was to
master it de la mejor manera posible, to the best of my capacity. Spanish
was the language of the past for me, English the language of my future. It
was only when I was already comfortable in both Spanish and English (as
comfortable as one is ever likely to be) that I suddenly detected the possibilities of Spanglish.

This sequence of events, no doubt, has enlarged my overall apprecia- 20
tion of it. I date my full-grown descubrimiento in the early nineties. By then
I had already left Manhattan and was living in a small New England town,
where I taught at a small liberal arts college. My responsibilities included
courses on colonial and present-day Latin America, and, on occasion, also
on Hispanic culture in Anglolandia. The latter courses were invariably
more challenging for me to teach. Students didn't register for them with the
mere hope of learning about a specific period in history. Instead, their objective was psychological; they were eager to turn the classroom into a laboratory of identity.

They wanted to ask out loud: Quiénes somos? What makes us unique? 21
And why are we here? Are we members of a single minority—the Latinos—
or are we instead peoples of different ethnic, class, religious, and national
backgrounds? In the isolated milieu of Amherst, Massachusetts, the language my Latino students used was recognizable to me. But I didn't pay
much notice until Lisa Martinez showed up. (The name is fictitious and so
are some of her circumstances.) Or better, until she was a punto de
desvanecerse, about to disappear.

Originally from Istlos (e.g., East Los Angeles), Lisa, a junior, had taken a 22
number of classes with me: on popular culture—comic strips, TV soaps,
thrillers, music . . .—on autobiography, and on Argentine letters. We had established a solid relationship. Her odyssey was remarkable: Lisa had grown

up in the inner city; she had been an active gang member and had seen a number of relatives and friends shot or imprisoned—vapuleados por el sistema; and she was initiated into Catholic life by an activist priest. Her tenure in Amherst, Massachusetts, was, hence, a radical change of scene for Lisa.

During her freshman year, Lisa felt disoriented, nostalgic for la casa, anxious to finish and return home. She also expressed her ambivalence at being an affirmative action student, enticed to the place by a full fellowship, but often looked at suspiciously by her Anglo counterparts because of her skin color, su pigmentación mestiza and her ethnic idiosyncrasy. Still, in her third year of college she appeared to have found inner and outer balance. 23

However, in recent times, whenever we stumbled across one another in the hallway, Lisa looked at peace with herself. It was somewhat surprising, therefore, that one frigid February, Lisa came to my office to say adiós. 24

"Ya me voy, profe . . . ," she announced. 25

I wasn't completely sure I understood her statement, so I asked Lisa where she was going. She answered that she was going back to her hood, to Califas, where people "no son tan fregados. They are más calientes, with a little bit of dignidad." Lisa was tired of the WASPy culture of the small liberal arts college she was invited to attend with an ethnic scholarship. 26

"Aqui no soy más que un prieto, profe. They want me pa'las quotas, so the place might say 'Chicanos are also part of our diverse student population.' Pero pa'qué, profe? I don't feel bien. I'm just a strange animal brought in a cage to be displayed pa'que los gringos no sientan culpa." 27

I begged her to be patient. 28

She was almost finished with her education, I said. Estaba casi de salida . . . One and a half more years—is that too much? But she wouldn't listen. Our entire tête-à-tête took approximately five minutes. 29

I never succeeded in changing Lisa's mind, nunca la convencí, and to this day I regret it. Somehow, seeing her walk toward the podium during Commencement to get her Bachelor's diploma would have been a better conclusion to the New England chapter of her journey. 30

In retrospect, Lisa's goodbye, su partida, was quite painful. Me rompió el corazón. I felt genuine affection for her. But the scene that took place between us in my office was more than about dropping out from college—at least for me. For, as I recall the occasion, the moment I opened my mouth, I realized every one of the words I uttered felt artificial, anomalous. I had wanted to tell Lisa that the separation from home is painful for everyone, that for some, like her, the separation isn't only emotional but also geographical and cultural. I told her it was important to keep in mind that H*O*M*E—and I pronounced the word patiently, comfortably, sweetly—acquires a different value, it becomes symbolic, the moment one leaves it 31 behind. Or doesn't it? Even if she went back, her status as her mother's daughter would be different. And . . .

Pero no habia vuelta de hoja. 32

To my consternation, though, I couldn't express myself. The more I 33 tried to articulate my words, first in Spanish, then in English, the more dissatisfied I became. Any why? Because I was overwhelmed with envy. To announce her sudden farewell, Lisa wasn't using the traditional college language a pupil is expected to articulate in the professor's designated space. Instead, judging by her vocabulary and syntax, she had already departed New England for Los Angeles: she was inhabiting the language of her turf, su propia habla, not the language of the alien environment where she found herself at present.

And what was expected of me: to ask her, in that troublesome situation, 34 to switch to a more proper lengua?

That, no doubt, would have been counterproductive. What I desper- 35 ately needed was for her to feel cómoda.

But what actually happened to me is that, instead of wanting her to 36 "talk like me," my secret desire was the other way around: I wanted to use her own lingo.

Yes, en Spanglish—Lisa and I began to communicate in the jargon I had 37 frequently heard, and had been enthralled by, en las calles de Nuyol.

Was I happy with my switch? 38

To my chagrin, I was . . . And what did I do? Nothing, absolutamente 39 nada. I just let myself be taken by the verbal cadence of the conversation. Where is it written that faculty should elevate itself intellectually far beyond the reach of the students? Where does it say that professors cannot talk slang too? No sooner did I switch to Spanglish, though, that I realized that, as a teacher, I had crossed a dangerous line—una línea peligrosa.

My immediate, mechanical reaction was in tune with the milieu I 40 came from as a middle-class Jew from Mexico whose choice it was to emigrate to El Norte: What on earth es ésto? I asked myself. Why was I mimicking Lisa? Wasn't my role as an intellectual and teacher to protect the purity and sanctity of el español and el inglés, rather than endorse this verbal promiscuity?

If I, and others like me, endorse this chaos of words, where is this syn- 41 tactical amalgam leading us if not to hell? These were not easy questions. My tongue was moving in one direction and my heart in another. The more I rationalized what I was doing, the more guilt I felt. But I also realized that, through my standard English and Spanish, I lived in a verbal stratosphere remote from the universe I purported to invoke—and teach—in the classroom, for pupils just like my dear Lisa Martinez. Besides, in Spanglish I felt freer, más libre. I didn't sense it as an imported, unnatural self. On the contrary, using it made me blissful.

Me sentí feliz!   42

Over the years, I've returned to that fated encounter hundreds of times.   43
A door closed for Lisa Martinez that day but another one opened for me, a door se abrió and I walked through only to be radically transformed by the path I followed. That door has led me to more difficult questions.

Thinking About the Essay

1. What is Stavans's thesis? Is his thesis the same as Castro's essay on Spanglish (see page 88)? Justify your response.

2. What connections does Stavans draw between racism and language? How does he develop this connection? Point to specific passages to support your answer.

3. Stavans combines narrative and exposition in this essay. What stories does he tell? How does he order them within the essay? What comparative elements does he develop?

4. Part of our interest in this essay—and in Stavans—is his personal voice, the way in which he struggles to find a language to capture his identity. How does he go about doing this? What self-image does he create? Justify your answer by reference to the text.

5. Castro and Stavans develop extended definitions of Spanglish. In what ways are their approaches similar and different? How would you explain the differences in terms of the primary audience each writer addresses?

Responding in Writing

6. Stavans speaks of his discovery of Spanglish. Have you undergone a similar connection of your language to your identity? Write a personal essay on this topic.

7. In his conversations with his student Lisa, Stavans comes to realize that "it is important that H*O*M*E—and I pronounce the word patiently, comfortably, sweetly—acquires a different value, it becomes symbolic, the moment one leaves it behind" (paragraph 31). Write an essay responding to his observation, focusing on the role of language in creating a sense of "home."

8. Write an essay on Stavans's contention that "English is the door to the American Dream" (paragraph 7). Do you agree or disagree with his statement? Be sure to support your argument with examples and illustrations.

Networking

9. With another class member, look into popular web sites for Latino/Latina/ Hispanic culture in urban North America. To what extent do these websites use "Spanglish"?

10. Search the Internet for information on the Mexican Jewish community. Prepare notes for a five-minute lecture on the subject.

Multilingual America

WILLIAM H. FREY

> William H. Frey is a senior fellow of demographic studies at the Milken Institute in Santa Barbara, California. He is also on the faculty of the Population Studies Center at the University of Michigan. In the following essay, which appeared in the July/August 2002 issue of *American Demographics*, Frey analyzes the rise in American households where the inhabitants speak a language other than English. The writer offers data drawn from the 2000 United States Census to trace recent population shifts, the rise of ethnic communities in urban and nonurban areas, and the impact on the American "melting pot" of people who speak a language other than English at home.

Before Reading

How can English be taught to new immigrants who stay in their own ethnic communities and prefer to speak their own language at home? If you were involved in policymaking, what programs would you design for these individuals?

A merica's identity as a melting pot now extends beyond multiple races 1
and cultures to also include numerous languages. Ours is an increasingly multilingual nation, due to a new wave of immigration.

The number of individuals who speak a language other than English at 2
home is on the rise. This population is also on the move: No longer restricted to traditional port-of-entry cities, such as New York and Los Angeles, foreign-language speakers are now sprouting up in certain Southeastern and Western states.

For the first time, thanks to Census 2000 long-form data, we are able to 3
identify these new locations where residents who speak a foreign language are making their presence felt. Although relatively small, this population is beginning to constitute a critical mass in many communities—reason alone for businesses seeking new markets to take note.

Nationally, Americans age 5 and older who speak a language other 4
than English at home grew 47 percent in the past decade. According to
Census 2000, this group now accounts for slightly less than 1 in 5 Americans (17.9 percent). About three-fifths of this group speak Spanish at
home (59.9 percent), another fifth speaks another Indo-European language (21.3 percent) and almost 15 percent speak an Asian language.

Overall, foreign-language speakers grew by about 15 million during the 5
1990s, with new Spanish speakers contributing about 11 million people
and new Asian speakers almost 2.5 million. Continued immigration from
Latin America and Asia has increased the number of people who speak languages native to those regions.

Foreign-Language Havens

These foreign-language speakers are concentrated in 10 states, each where 6
20 percent or more of the residents speak a language other than English at
home. Led by California (40 percent), this group includes several other
Western states as well as New York, New Jersey, Florida and Rhode Island.
The concentration is even more evident when one looks at individual metropolitan areas. (See Table 3.1.)

In six metros, including Miami and Laredo, Texas, those who speak 7
only English at home are in the minority. In five Mexican border towns in
this category, Spanish accounts for more than 96 percent of non-English
languages spoken.

Other areas where more than one-third of the population speaks a language other than English at home include Los Angeles, San Antonio, San 8
Francisco, New York and San Diego.

By far, the two largest metros that house the most foreign-language- 9
speakers are Los Angeles and New York, with more than 7 million and
6 million foreign-language speakers, respectively. Together, these two gateways increased their foreign-language-speaking populations by 3.5 million
between 1990 and 2000, accounting for 24 percent of the country's total
gain. (See Figure 3.1.)

Eight metropolitan areas with the largest populations that speak a foreign 10
language accounted for almost half (46 percent) of the nation's total gain.
Others include Phoenix, Atlanta, Las Vegas, Seattle and Denver—cities that
became secondary magnets for new immigrant groups during the 1990s.

Multilingual Expansion

Although many immigrant gateway metros still hold the lion's share of in- 11
habitants who speak a foreign language, the 1990s was a decade of extensive
redistribution of foreign-born residents and hence, of foreign-language speakers. Areas that had little prior familiarity with Spanish-speaking residents or

TABLE 3.1   Spanish and Asian Language Magnets

There is some overlap between the lists of communities forming new, fast-growing enclaves [of] speakers of Spanish and Asian languages. The areas below all have at least 5,000 Spanish-speaking or Asian-speaking residents.

Persons speaking Spanish at home: Metro areas with greatest growth, 1990–2000	% Increase 1990–2000
Fayetteville-Springdale-Rogers, AR MSA*	609%
Elkhart-Goshen, IN MSA	403%
Raleigh-Durham–Chapel Hill, NC MSA	381%
Charlotte-Gastonia–Rock Hill, NC-SC MSA	376%
Greensboro-Winston-Salem–High Point, NC MSA	367%
Green Bay, WI MSA	354%
Hickory-Morganton-Lenoir, NC MSA	338%
Atlanta, GA MSA	314%
Fort Smith, AR-OK MSA	310%
Sioux City, IA-NE MSA	306%
Persons speaking Asian language at home: Metro areas with greatest growth, 1990–2000	
Hickory-Morganton-Lenoir, NC MSA	467%
Las Vegas, NV-AZ MSA	220%
Charlotte-Gastonia–Rock Hill, NC-SC MSA	182%
Lincoln, NE MSA	172%
Greenville-Spartanburg-Anderson, SC MSA	170%
Atlanta, GA MSA	157%
Greensboro-Winston-Salem–High Point, NC MSA	156%
Austin-San Marcos, TX MSA	156%
Raleigh-Durham–Chapel Hill, NC MSA	128%
Grand Rapids-Muskegon-Holland, MI MSA	127%

Source: William H. Frey analysis, 1990 and 2000 U.S. Census.
*MSA = Metropolitan Statistical Area as defined by the Office of Management and Budget.

those who speak an Asian language gained exposure to cultural as well as linguistic differences in their communities.

States that now have the fastest growing non-English-speaking populations are not typically those with the highest percentages of such people. (See Figure 3.2.) Most are Southeastern and Western states that began to attract new immigrants, often in response to an increased demand for services due to an influx of migrants from other states.

FIGURE 3.1 Native Tongues

Ten states have the largest shares of foreign-language speakers (more than one in five speaks a foreign language at home). These include several Western states, New York, New Jersey, Florida, and Rhode Island.

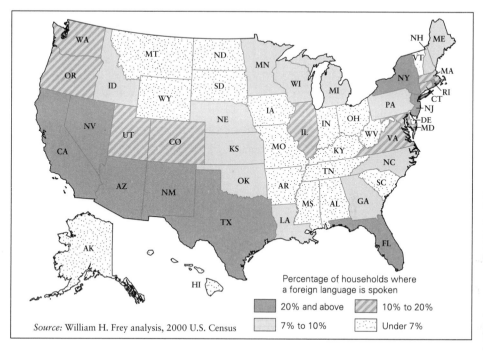

Source: William H. Frey analysis, 2000 U.S. Census

Percentage of households where a foreign language is spoken

- 20% and above
- 10% to 20%
- 7% to 10%
- Under 7%

In the Southeast, this includes Georgia, North Carolina, Arkansas, Tennessee and Virginia; in the West, Arizona, Nevada, Utah, Oregon, Washington, Idaho and Colorado. Several interior states with small foreign-born populations, such as Nebraska, are also attracting new non-English-speaking residents to take a variety of service jobs.   13

Similar geographic patterns are evident in metropolitan areas with the fastest growth of foreign-language speakers. For example, Fayetteville, Ark., increased its non-English-speaking population by a whopping 368 percent during the 1990s. Six of the seven fastest-growing areas (Las Vegas being the exception) are in the South, including the North Carolina metros of Hickory, Raleigh-Durham–Chapel Hill, Charlotte and Greensboro.   14

Although in many of these enclaves foreign-language speakers account for only a small percentage of the area's total population, this is not the case for all. Las Vegas, for example, increased its share of residents who speak a foreign language to 24 percent, from 13 percent, between 1990 and   15

FIGURE 3.2   Foreign-Language Growth, 1990–2000

The states with the fastest-growing non-English-speaking populations are not typically those with the highest percentages of foreign-language speakers. Such states include Georgia and North Carolina as well as Nebraska and Washington.

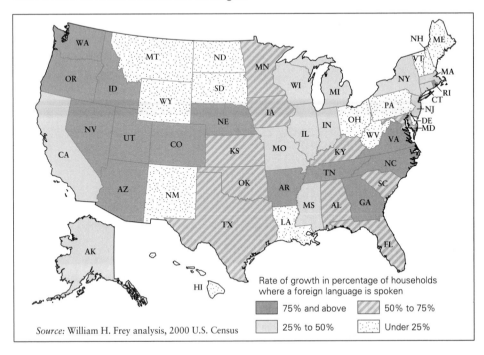

Rate of growth in percentage of households where a foreign language is spoken

■ 75% and above   ▨ 50% to 75%
□ 25% to 50%   ⬚ Under 25%

Source: William H. Frey analysis, 2000 U.S. Census

2000. Similar increases can be seen for Orlando and Naples, Fla.; Phoenix and Dallas. Significant gains also occurred in small Iowa cities, such as Sioux City, Waterloo and Des Moines.

Spanish and Asian Language Magnets

While Spanish dominates the foreign languages spoken at home on the na- 16
tional level, this is not true for all parts of the United States. For example, fewer than half the foreign-language speakers in San Francisco and New York City speak Spanish. In the former, nearly as many speak Asian languages; in the latter, a large number of residents continue to speak other European languages at home.

Spanish represents more than half the foreign languages spoken at 17
home in only nine states. These are located mostly on the Mexican border and in the West. Metro areas with the largest Spanish-speaking shares of their populations reflect the same geographic pattern.

TABLE 3.2 Metros with Highest Shares of Foreign-Language Speakers, 2000
Six metros, including Laredo and Miami, have populations where the minority speak only English at home. In five Mexican border towns in this category, Spanish is the non-English language spoken in more than 96 percent of homes.

Name	Percent speaking non-English language at home	Percent who speak these languages at home			
		Spanish	Asian language	European language	Other
Laredo, TX MSA	91.9%	99.4%	0.3%	0.3%	0.0%
McAllen-Edinburg-Mission, TX MSA	83.1%	99.0%	0.5%	0.4%	0.0%
Brownsville-Harlingen–San Benito, TX MSA	79.0%	99.1%	0.4%	0.4%	0.1%
El Paso, TX MSA	73.3%	97.1%	1.0%	1.6%	0.3%
Las Cruces, NM MSA	54.4%	96.7%	0.7%	1.9%	0.7%
Miami–Fort Lauderdale, FL CMSA	51.5%	80.0%	1.9%	16.7%	1.4%
Salinas, CA MSA	47.3%	83.5%	9.1%	6.5%	0.9%
Los Angeles–Riverside–Orange County, CA CMSA	46.8%	70.7%	18.2%	9.1%	1.9%
Yuma, AZ MSA	45.5%	95.6%	1.5%	1.9%	0.9%
Merced, CA MSA	45.2%	77.7%	11.6%	10.4%	0.4%

Source: William H. Frey analysis, 2000 U.S. Census.

In contrast, metropolitan areas that house large shares of Asian populations are fewer and farther between. Honolulu tops the group, with Asian languages spoken by almost 9 out of 10 people who speak a non-English language at home, followed by San Francisco, Los Angeles, San Diego and Stockton, Calif.

Considerable overlap exists between communities forming new, fast-growing enclaves for Spanish speakers and those who speak an Asian language. (See Tables 3.2 and 3.3.) Of the 15 metro areas with the fastest-growing Spanish-speaking populations, six are on the list of fast-growing, Asian-language-speaking areas. These include Atlanta and Las Vegas, as well as North Carolina metros Raleigh-Durham, Charlotte, Greensboro and Hickory.

TABLE 3.3   Metros with Largest Number of Foreign-Language Speakers, 2000

The two largest metros with foreign-language speakers are Los Angeles and New York. Together they increased their foreign-language-speaking population by 3.5 million during the 1990s— about 24 percent of the nation's total gain.

Largest number of foreign-language speakers, 2000	*Number of people*
Los Angeles–Riverside–Orange County, CA CMSA	7,080.474
New York–Northern New Jersey–Long Island, NY-NJ-CT-PA CMSA	6,614.354
San Francisco–Oakland–San Jose, CA CMSA	2,368.377
Chicago-Gary-Kenosha, IL-IN-WI CMSA	2,116.043
Miami–Fort Lauderdale, FL CMSA	1,869.966
Houston-Galveston-Brazoria, TX CMSA	1,372.010
Dallas–Fort Worth, TX CMSA	1,163.502
Washington-Baltimore, DC-MD-VA-WV CMSA	1,158.677
Boston-Worcester-Lawrence, MA-NH-ME-CT CMSA	1,042.727

Source: William H. Frey analysis, 1990 and 2000 U.S. Census.

These areas are attracting new residents as a result of local universities 20 or the labor market pulls associated with general population growth and the fast-growing economies of the "New Sun Belt."

English Proficiency

One issue raised when people who speak a foreign language become new 21 residents of a community is how well they can conduct their lives in English. While it's no surprise that immigrants who have lived in the U.S. for a long time become fluent in English, Census 2000 reveals that this may not be the case with new arrivals.

The Census Bureau asked people who speak a language other than English at home this question: How well does this person speak English? (The choices were: very well, well, not well or not at all). Between 1990 and 2000, there was a larger increase of Spanish speakers who could not speak English very well than of those who could. However, for Asian language speakers, there was a larger increase between 1990 and 2000 of those who could speak English very well.

To a great extent, Spanish speakers arriving in non-gateway areas are 23 less likely to speak English very well. Among the metros with the lowest percentages of Spanish speakers speaking English very well are Greens-

boro, Raleigh-Durham, Charlotte and Hickory in North Carolina; Atlanta   24
and other newer destinations for Spanish-speaking residents.

Among areas where Spanish speakers have high levels of English proficiency are university towns like Gainesville, Fla., and Lubbock, Texas, as well as locales with long-standing Spanish-speaking residents, such as Albuquerque, N.M.

The same pattern occurs among residents who speak an Asian language, with lower levels of proficiency where such settlers are relatively   25
new (e.g., Lincoln, Neb.; Grand Rapids, Mich.; Minneapolis–St. Paul, Minn.; Greensboro, N.C. and Atlanta). High levels of proficiency tend to be in university communities such as Gainesville, Fla.; Raleigh-Durham and Chapel Hill, N.C.; Champagne-Urbana, Ill. and Colorado Springs, Colo.

These patterns of English proficiency mirror the national picture. States   26
with the lowest levels of English proficiency tend to be those that had the fastest growth of foreign-language residents during the 1990s. Nebraska, Nevada, Oregon, North Carolina and Georgia are part of this group of states, which also includes some longer-term havens for foreign-born and foreign-language-speaking residents. For example, less than half (49 percent) of California's foreign-born residents speak English very well.

The new census data provides insights into this fast growing group of   27
Americans who speak a language other than English at home. It also highlights the fact that if the U.S. is to continue to live up to its reputation as a melting pot, this influx of foreign-language speakers will require special efforts on the parts of schools, local organizations and grassroots groups to enable these new residents to become fully integrated members of their communities.

Thinking About the Essay

1. How would you describe the writer's audience for this essay? What assumptions does he make about this audience? How does he mold his style to the expectations of the audience?

2. Explain the significance of the writer's title. What approach does he take to his subject? In other words, what is his purpose? How does his purpose govern his thesis?

3. Where is the thesis stated? How does the conclusion reinforce the thesis or color it with a mildly argumentative edge?

4. Frey employs a considerable amount of data in this essay. How relevant are these data? What aspects of the data do you find interesting? What aspects, if any, do you find weak or irrelevant?

5. The author divides his essay into sections. Summarize each section. How does each section flow from the previous unit? Is the author able to achieve unity and coherence? Justify your response.

6. There are several visual illustrations in this essay. What types are they? How do you "read" them in terms of their significance? What do they contribute to the article?

Responding in Writing

7. Use the data provided by Frey to write your own essay entitled "Our Shrinking Language Tapestry." Make your essay more argumentative than Frey's. Take a stand on the demographics Frey provides, and back up your claim with at least three good reasons or minor propositions.

8. If you belong to a family in which members normally speak a language other than English, tell about their attitude toward the use of English. Or imagine that you are part of such a household. What would your perception of your native language and this second language—English—be?

9. In the last paragraphs, Frey implies that it is important to learn English to become "fully integrated" into one's community. In an argumentative essay, agree or disagree with his statement.

Networking

10. In groups of four, obtain a copy of the 2000 United States Census, and focus on the data about immigration patterns and language use that this document provides. Then construct a group report of approximately 1,000 words highlighting and interpreting this data.

11. Go to one or more search engines and type in "English only" or "English Only Movement." Try other combinations if necessary. Download relevant information, and then participate in a class discussion of this controversy.

Reading the History of the World

ISABEL ALLENDE | Isabel Allende, the daughter of a Chilean diplomat, was born in 1942 in Lima, Peru. Isabel moved from Peru to Chile, where she was living and working at the time her uncle, Salvador Allende, the president of Chile, was assassinated during an army coup, assisted by the CIA, in 1973. "In that moment," she says, "I realized that everything was possible—that violence was a dimension that was always around you." The Allende family did not think that the new regime would last, and Isabel Allende continued to work as a noted journalist.

However, when it became too dangerous to remain in Chile, the family went into exile in Venezuela. Allende's first novel, *The House of the Spirits* (1985), established her as a significant writer in the tradition of "magic realism" associated with the Nobel Prize winner Gabriel García Márquez. Other novels include *Of Love and Shadows* (1987), *Eva Luna* (1988), and *Daughter of Fortune* (1999). Allende has also written an autobiography, *Paula* (1995), and stories for children. Allende has spoken of the "wind of exile" that makes it necessary to recover memories of one's native land. In this essay, which appears in a collection of essays on reading by well-known writers, *Speaking of Reading* (1995), she invokes the act of reading as one way to salvage these memories.

Before Reading

Allende declares that only through reading can we fully become aware of "injustice and misery and violence." Would you agree or disagree, and why?

Reading is like looking through several windows which open to an infinite landscape. I abandon myself to the pleasure of the journey. How could I know about other people, how could I know about the history of the world, how could my mind expand and grow if I could not read? I began to read when I was very small; I learned to read and write practically when I was a baby. For me, life without reading would be like being in prison, it would be as if my spirit were in a straitjacket; life would be a very dark and narrow place. 1

I was brought up in a house full of books. It was a big, strange, somber house, the house of my grandparents. My uncle, who lived in the house, had a lot of books—he collected them like holy relics. His room held a ton of books. Few newspapers were allowed in that house because my grandfather was a very patriarchal, conservative man who thought that newspapers, as well as the radio, were full of vulgar ideas (at that time we didn't have TV), so the only contact I had with the world, really, was through my uncle's books. No one censored or guided my reading; I read anything I wanted. 2

I began reading Shakespeare when I was nine, not because of the language or the beauty, but because of the plot and the great characters. I have always been interested in adventure, plot, strong characters, history, animals. As a child, I read children's books, most of the Russian literature, many French authors, and later, Latin American writers. I think I belong to 3 the first generation of writers in Latin America who were brought up reading Latin American literature; earlier generations read European and North American literature. Our books were very badly distributed.

Books allow me to see my feelings put into words. After I read the feminist authors from North America, I could finally find words for the anger that I had all my life. I was brought up in a male chauvinist society and I had accumulated much anger, yet I couldn't express it. I could only be angry and do crazy things, but I couldn't put my anger into words and use it in a rational, articulate way. After I read those books, things became clearer to me, I could talk about that anger and express it in a more positive way.   4

The same thing happened with politics. I was aware of injustice and misery and political violence, but I couldn't express my feelings until I read about those issues and realized that other people had been dealing with them for centuries, and had already invented the words to express what I was feeling.   5

I have often been separated from my mother, whom I love very much. She now lives in Chile and we write a letter to each other every day. We talk about what we've read or what we are writing. I do it the first thing every morning of my life, even when I'm traveling. It's as if I were writing a journal. It's like having a long conversation with her; we are connected with a strong bond. This same bond also connects me with my daughter, who is living in Spain, because when I write the letter to my mother, I make a copy that goes to my daughter, and they do the same. This is becoming a very strange network of letters.   6

My mother is a much better reader than I. My reading is very fast, hectic, disorganized, and impatient. If I'm not caught in the first pages I abandon the book. My mother, however, is very patient and goes very slowly. She is the only person who reads my manuscripts, helping me to edit, revise, and correct them. She has a strong sense of poetry and such good taste. She's very well informed, very cultivated, very sensitive, and loves reading.   7

I have tried to give my children the love of books. My daughter is a good reader. She's a psychologist and has to read a lot of professional books, but she loves novels, short stories, poetry. My son, however, doesn't read any fiction. He's a scientific person with a mathematical mentality. I've tried to imagine how his mind and heart work, without nourishment from books, but I can't. He's a great boy, but how can he do it? I don't know.   8

My uncle, Salvador Allende, who was President of Chile before he was assassinated during the military coup, hardly affected my life. I liked him and loved him, but only as I do other relatives. He was the best man at my   9 wedding. I was never involved in politics, and never participated in his government. (I became interested in politics only after the coup.) He was not a very strong reader of fiction, actually. He was always reading reports, essays, books about politics, sociology, economy, etc. He was a very well-informed person and he read very fast, his eyes practically skimming across the page to get the necessary information, but when he wanted to relax, he would rather watch a movie than read.

During the three years of Allende's government, any Chilean could buy   10
books of "Quimantu," the state publishing house, for very little money, the equivalent of two newspapers. In this way he hoped to promote culture. His goal was that every single Chilean could read and write and be able to buy as many books as he or she wanted by the end of his term.

My own experience of life, my biography, my feelings, my self as a per-   11
son, affect my reading. The writer puts out half of the book, but then I read the book in my own unique manner. This is why reading is so interesting; we as readers don't have passive roles, but very active ones. We must integrate into the text our own experiences of life and our own feelings. While reading a book, we are constantly applying our own knowledge.

Our backgrounds determine our strengths and interests as readers.   12
Many themes that are extremely popular in North America are impossible for me to read because they aren't part of my culture—I just don't care about them. For example, I can't relate to those books by daughters who write against their mothers. But if I read a book by Toni Morrison or Louise Erdrich that deals with being a woman and part of an ethnic minority, I can relate to its content. Also, I like Latin American authors very much, especially Jorge Amado, García Márquez, Mario Vargas Llosa, Juan Rulfo, Jorge Luis Borges, and many others. There are a few Latin American women writers that I enjoy as well, but they have been badly distributed and poorly reviewed. Latin American literature has been an exclusively male club, to say the least.

I have met many people, including well-informed, educated people,   13
who actually take pride in the fact that they haven't read anything by a woman. Recently, I received a clipping from a newspaper in Chile. It was a public letter to me from a Chilean entertainer apologizing that he had never before read any of my books because I am a woman. He wrote that he never read literature written by women. After he made a special effort to read my books, he felt he must apologize to me and say that I could actually write.

I will always be interested in programs of illiteracy because it is such a   14
common problem in my continent: 50 percent of the population of Latin America cannot read or write, and of those who can, only a few can afford

books or have the habit of reading. To me, not reading is like having the spirit imprisoned.

Thinking About the Essay

1. List the images, metaphors, and **similes** that Allende presents in her introductory paragraph. What is her purpose? What is the effect?

2. State Allende's thesis. Is it stated or implied? Explain.

3. What strategies does Allende employ to blend personal experience and analysis? What, specifically, is she analyzing, and how does she develop her topics?

4. Allende devotes two paragraphs to her uncle, Salvador Allende (paragraphs 9 and 10). Why? How do these paragraphs influence the tone of the entire essay?

5. What causal connections does Allende establish between the acts of reading and writing and the state of society in Latin America?

Responding in Writing

6. Write an essay in which you describe your reading habits as a child and as an adult. Did you live in a house filled with books? Did you enjoy reading? What were your favorite books? Who were the readers and nonreaders in your family? Answer these questions in a personal essay.

7. Allende refers to the fact that half of the population in Latin America is illiterate. Write an analytical essay that examines the impact of illiteracy on a society or nation.

8. Imagine a reading plan for your children, and write about it. Will you leave reading development exclusively to teachers? How will you regulate your child's reading and television viewing habits? Do you agree with Allende that reading can open children to "an infinite landscape" (paragraph 1)?

Networking

9. Discuss in small groups the nature of your reading habits during various stages in your life. Report to the class on your discoveries.

10. Find out more about Salvador Allende and the Allende family. Search the Internet or conduct an advanced search with the assistance of a college librarian. Try to find specific information on Allende's literacy crusade.

Global Relationships: Are Sex and Gender Roles Changing?

As we move into the twenty-first century, the roles of men and women in the United States and around the world are in flux. In the United States, there are increasing numbers of American women in many professional fields—medicine, law, education, politics, corporate life. And, with more men staying home and caring for their children, either by preference or necessity, there is greater equality in domestic responsibilities. At the same time, a woman's right to choose or even obtain social services is under attack. And it was only in the summer of 2003 that the United States Supreme Court struck down a Texas law that had made sex between consenting adult males in the privacy of their homes a crime. This national opposition in certain quarters to equality of rights in human relations is reflected in reactionary global attitudes and practices. Issues of race, sexual orientation, and ethnicity complicate the roles of women and men on a global scale.

American women do seem to have advantages over many of their global counterparts, for when we consider the situation of women globally, the issue of equal rights and human rights becomes acute. From increasing AIDS rates among global women, to their exploitation as cheap labor or sex workers, to female infanticide, to the continuing resistance of men in traditional societies to any thought of gender equality, the lives of women in many parts of the world are perilous. Gendered value systems in traditional societies change glacially, and often under only the most extreme conditions. For example, before the massacre of more than 800,000 Tutsi by their Hutu neighbors in Rwanda in 1993, women could not work or appear alone in the market; with the killing of so many of the men, Rwandan women

117

Hindu women take part in a speed-dating event at a London nightclub. Daters meet for a few minutes before moving on to the next date. Traditionally, relationships and marriages in this community were arranged by the families of the potential bride and groom.

Thinking About the Image

1. You probably know how awkward it can be to meet someone new. How do you think this photographer captured such an intimate, difficult moment between these two people?

2. What key characteristics do you see that distinguish groups of people or ethnicities in this photograph?

3. This photograph originally accompanied "Arranged Marriages Get a Little Reshuffling" by Lizette Alvarez (p. 119) How accurately does the photograph illustrate the article? Newspaper editors have a limited amount of space to fill each day – why do you think this newspaper's editors wanted to include a photograph with this story?

4. If you could take a snapshot of dating culture in your own social group, what would you need to include in order to best capture its essence? Describe the image using very specific language.

suddenly had to assume responsibility for tasks they formerly had been excluded from. Women are the ones who are displaced disproportionately by wars, ethnic conflicts, famine, and environmental crises.

In this new global era, the destinies of women and men around the world are intertwined. Global forces have brought them together. The role of democracy in promoting human rights, the challenge to spread wealth from North to South and West to East, the need to prevent wars, even the degradation of the environment—have notable implications for men and women. Some argue that global forces—which we will detect in some essays in this chapter and study in detail in the next chapter—are notably hostile to women. Others argue that to the extent that nations can promote peace and democracy, produce prosperity, improve health and the environment, and reduce racism and ethnocentrism, both women and men will be the beneficiaries.

The essays in this chapter present insights into the roles of men and women around the world. The writers inquire into the impact of economics, politics, race, gender and sexual orientation, and culture on the lives of women and men. They invite us to reconsider the meaning of human rights, self-determination, and equality from a gendered perspective. In the twenty-first century, new ideas have emerged about the roles and rights of women and men. The essays that follow reveal some of the challenges that must be overcome before the concept of equal rights and opportunities for women and men can be realized.

Arranged Marriages Get a Little Reshuffling

LIZETTE ALVAREZ

In the following article, which appeared in the *New York Times* in 2003, Lizette Alvarez, a journalist for the newspaper, examines the changing attitudes and rituals concerning the traditional practice of arranged marriages. Writing from London, she focuses on "young, hip, South Asians." These young people do not reject traditions governing relations between the sexes. Instead, they "reshuffle" these conventions so that they may work successfully for them in the twenty-first century.

Before Reading

What is your attitude toward arranged marriage? In many Western nations, divorce rates approach 50 percent. Why not try arranged marriage if choosing your own mate is so frustrating and perilous?

They are young, hip, South Asians in their 20's who glide seamlessly be-   1
tween two cultures, carefully cherry picking from the West to modernize the East.

They can just as easily listen to Justin Timberlake, the pop star, as Rishi   2
Rich, the Hindu musical dynamo. They eat halal meat but wear jeans and
T-shirts to cafes.

Now these young Indians and Pakistanis are pushing the cultural   3
boundaries created by their parents and grandparents one step further:
they are reshaping the tradition of arranged marriages in Britain.

While couples were once introduced exclusively by relatives and   4
friends, the Aunt Bijis, as Muslims call their matchmakers, are now being
slowly nudged out by a boom in Asian marriage Web sites, chat rooms and
personal advertisements. South Asian speed dating—Hindus one night,
Muslims the next—is the latest phenomenon to hit London, with men and
women meeting each other for just three minutes at restaurants and bars
before moving on to the next potential mate.

Arranged marriages are still the norm within these clannish, tight-knit   5
communities in Britain, but, with the urging of second- and third-generation
children, the nature of the arrangement has evolved, mostly by necessity.

What the young Indians and Pakistanis of Britain have done, in effect,   6
is to modernize practices that had evolved among the urban middle class
in India in recent decades, allowing the prospective bride and groom a little more than one fleeting meeting to make up their minds.

The relaxation that had crept in since the 1960's allowed the couple, af-   7
ter an initial meeting before their extended families, to meet alone several
times, either with family members in another room or at a restaurant, before delivering a verdict. Now, the meetings take place in public venues
without the family encounter first.

"The term we use now is 'assisted' arranged marriage," said Maha   8
Khan, a 23-year-old London Muslim woman. "The whole concept has
changed a lot. Parents have become more open and more liberal in their
concept of marriage and courtship."

Gitangeli Sapra, a trendy, willowy British Sindhu who at 25 jokes that   9
she is on her way to spinsterhood, is an avid speed dater with no qualms
about advertising her love of modern arranged marriages. She even wrote
a column about it for *The Sunday Times*.

"It's not based on love," she said, "which can fizzle out."   10

Ms. Sapra had attended 10 of the more formal arranged meetings—   11
awkward, drawn-out affairs in which the young man, his mother and several other relatives came over to meet the young woman and her family.
She wore her best Indian outfit, a sari or elegant Indian pants and top. She
sat quietly, which is almost impossible to fathom, considering her chatti-
ness. When called upon, she poured tea, and then talked briefly to her potential mate in a side room.

"The matriarchs do the talking," she said over a glass of wine at an Italian restaurant. "You sit there looking cute and like the ideal housewife." 12

"To be honest, it's an easy way to get a rich man, with my mother's blessing," she added, with a laugh. 13

None of them worked out, though, and Ms. Sapra has moved on to speed dating with the blessings of her mother. 14

The very concept raises the hackles of some more old-fashioned parents, but many are coming around, in part out of desperation. If Ms. Sapra finds someone on a speed date, she will quickly bring him home to her mother. 15

The abiding principles behind an arranged marriage still remain strong—lust does not a lasting marriage make and family knows best. But parents and elders, eager to avoid alienating their children, making them miserable or seeing them go unmarried, have shown considerable flexibility. This is especially pronounced among the middle class, whose members tend to have integrated more into British life. 16

"The notion of arrangement has become more fluid," said Yunas Samad, a sociology professor at Bradford University, who has studied marriage in the Muslim community. "What is happening is that the arranged marriage is becoming a bit more open and children are getting a bit more say in this so it becomes a nice compromise. There is the comfort of family support and a choice in what they are doing." 17

"It's a halfway house, not completely traditional and not completely the same as what is happening in British society," he added. 18

To the surprise of parents and elders, this new hybrid between East and West has actually stoked enthusiasm for an age-old tradition that many young people privately viewed as crusty and hopelessly unhip. 19

Now they see it as an important way to preserve religion and identity, not to mention a low-maintenance way of finding a mate. "It's like your parents giving you a black book of girls," said Ronak Mashru, 24, a London comedian whose parents are from India. 20

The young people also recognize that arranged marriages—in which similar education and income levels, religious beliefs and character outweigh the importance of physical attraction—can well outlast love marriages. 21

"The falling-in-love system has failed," said Rehna Azim, a Pakistani family lawyer who founded an Asian magazine, *Memsahib*. 22

South Asian unions are viewed as marriages between families, not individuals. Divorce is anathema, while respect and standing within a community are paramount. A lot of people have much invested in making a match work. 23

Similarly, several customs have survived dating: decisions have to be made 24
relatively quickly, often after the second or third meeting, and, Ms. Sapra said,
"once you've said yes, there is no turning back."

Dowries remain common and background still matters, too. 25

"Our mums look at the C.V.'s," said Vani Gupta, 30, a speed dater. 26
"They figure out whether we're compatible on paper—right job, right
background, right caste. It's nice to know your parents have done the work
for you. You feel more secure."

These middle-class women, most of them educated professionals or 27
university students, are looking for more modern men, who accept working wives and help around the house. But a "mechanic won't try for a
lawyer and a lawyer would not look for a mechanic," she said.

Ms. Sapra, for example, is looking for a fellow Sindhu, and a Gujarati 28
Indian typically seeks another Gujarati.

Muslims still keep it mostly within the family and the same region of 29
Pakistan. Cousins still frequently marry cousins, or at least second or
third cousins, and many British Pakistanis still find their brides back in
Pakistan. But now more men are marrying white British women who convert to Islam, and others insist on finding a Muslim bride there who
speaks English, eats fish and chips and watches "East Enders," a popular
soap opera.

Parents and elders have had to adapt, in large part because the number 30
of potential partners is much smaller here than in their home countries.
Rather than see an educated daughter go unwed, parents and elders have
accepted these more modern approaches, "Women are not going to be put
back in some kind of bottle," Professor Samad said.

Ms. Azim said, "Parents can say my child had an arranged marriage, 31
and he can say, 'Yeah, it's arranged. But I like her.' "

Thinking About the Essay

1. Writing for the *New York Times,* Alvarez knows her primary audience. What
   assumptions does she make about this audience? What secondary audiences would be interested in her topic, and why?

2. Does this article have a thesis? If so, where is it? If not, why not?

3. How does this essay reflect journalistic practice? Point to aspects of style,
   paragraph organization, article length, and other journalistic features. Is
   the tone of the article strictly neutral and objective (one aspect of journalistic method), or does it shade toward commentary or perhaps even contain
   an implicit argument? Explain.

4. How many people were interviewed for this article? Who are they, and what
   are their backgrounds? Taken together, how do they embody some of the

main points that Alvarez wants to make about courtship practices among some Asians today?

5. What rhetorical practices—for example, definition, comparison and contrast, process and causal analysis—can you locate in this essay? Toward what purpose does the writer use them?

Responding in Writing

6. What is the difference between people who use Internet dating sites to make their own contacts and establish their own relationships, and people from traditional societies who use the Internet to "cherry pick" prospective mates, whom they then present to their parents for appraisal. Which method strikes you as safer or potentially more successful, and why?

7. What is so great about "modern" dating and courtship practices if they often end in frustration and failure? Why not try something old, tried, and tested—like arranged marriage? Imagine that your parents insist on an arranged marriage for you. Write a personal response to this situation. Do not write that you would try to subvert the entire ritual. Instead, explain how you might "manage" this process to make the outcome acceptable.

8. Alvarez, presenting one principle behind the need for arranged marriages, writes that "lust does not a lasting marriage work" (paragraph 16). Do you agree or disagree with this claim? Provide at least three reasons to justify your response.

Networking

9. In class discussion, design a questionnaire about attitudes toward arranged marriage. Aim for at least five questions that can be answered briefly. Then have each class member obtain several responses to the questionnaire from other students. Compile the results, discuss them, and arrive at conclusions.

10. Investigate an Internet dating site. Sign up for it if you feel comfortable, or simply monitor the site for information. Report your findings to the class.

In Africa, AIDS Has a Woman's Face

KOFI A. ANNAN | Kofi A. Annan was born in the Gold Coast, as Ghana was known under British rule, in 1938. The son of a Fonte nobleman, he graduated in 1957 from Mfantsipim, a prestigious boarding school for boys that had been founded by the Methodist Church; Ghana won its independence from Great Britain that same year. After studies at the University of Science and Technology in Kumasi, Annan came to the United States on a Ford Foundation fellowship in 1959, completing his degree in economics at Macalester College in St. Paul, Minnesota. He also has a master's degree in management from the Massachusetts Institute of Technology (1972). Annan has worked for the United Nations in various capacities for four decades and has been secretary general of the United Nations since 1997. In the following essay, which appeared in the *New York Times* in 2003, he writes about one of the many "problems without borders" that he believes we must deal with from an international perspective.

Before Reading

Consider the impact that AIDS has on a developing nation or an entire region. What are the economic consequences of the AIDS epidemic in these countries? What happens to the condition of women in such societies?

A combination of famine and AIDS is threatening the backbone of Africa—the women who keep African societies going and whose work makes up the economic foundation of rural communities. For decades, we have known that the best way for Africa to thrive is to ensure that its women have the freedom, power and knowledge to make decisions affecting their own lives and those of their families and communities. At the United Nations, we have always understood that our work for development depends on building a successful partnership with the African farmer and her husband.

Study after study has shown that there is no effective development strategy in which women do not play a central role. When women are fully involved, the benefits can be seen immediately: families are healthier; they are better fed; their income, savings and reinvestment go up. And, what is true of families is true of communities and, eventually, of whole countries.

But today, millions of African women are threatened by two simultaneous catastrophes: famine and AIDS. More than 30 million people are now at risk of starvation in southern Africa and the Horn of Africa. All of these predominantly agricultural societies are also battling serious AIDS epidemics. This is no coincidence: AIDS and famine are directly linked.

Because of AIDS, farming skills are being lost, agricultural development efforts are declining, rural livelihoods are disintegrating, productive capacity to work the land is dropping and household earnings are shrinking—all while the cost of caring for the ill is rising exponentially. At the same time,

H.I.V. infection and AIDS are spreading dramatically and disproportion-ately among women. A United Nations report released last month shows that women now make up 50 percent of those infected with H.I.V. world-wide—and in Africa that figure is now 58 percent. Today, AIDS has a woman's face.

AIDS has already caused immense suffering by killing almost 2.5 mil-lion Africans this year alone. It has left 11 million African children orphaned since the epidemic began. Now it is attacking the capacity of these countries to resist famine by eroding those mechanisms that enable populations to fight back—the coping abilities provided by women.

In famines before the AIDS crisis, women proved more resilient than men. Their survival rate was higher, and their coping skills were stronger. Women were the ones who found alternative foods that could sustain their children in times of drought. Because droughts happened once a decade or so, women who had experienced previous droughts were able to pass on survival techniques to younger women. Women are the ones who nurture social networks that can help spread the burden in times of famine.

But today, as AIDS is eroding the health of Africa's women, it is erod-ing the skills, experience and networks that keep their families and com-munities going. Even before falling ill, a woman will often have to care for a sick husband, thereby reducing the time she can devote to planting, har-vesting and marketing crops. When her husband dies, she is often deprived of credit, distribution networks or land rights. When she dies, the house-hold will risk collapsing completely, leaving children to fend for them-selves. The older ones, especially girls, will be taken out of school to work in the home or the farm. These girls, deprived of education and opportu-nities, will be even less able to protect themselves against AIDS.

Because this crisis is different from past famines, we must look beyond relief measures of the past. Merely shipping in food is not enough. Our ef-fort will have to combine food assistance and new approaches to farming with treatment and prevention of H.I.V. and AIDS. It will require creating early-warning and analysis systems that monitor both H.I.V. infection rates and famine indicators. It will require new agricultural techniques, appro-priate to a depleted work force. It will require a renewed effort to wipe out H.I.V.-related stigma and silence.

It will require innovative, large-scale ways to care for orphans, with specific measures that enable children in AIDS-affected communities to stay in school. Education and prevention are still the most powerful weapons against the spread of H.I.V. Above all, this new international ef-fort must put women at the center of our strategy to fight AIDS.

Experience suggests that there is reason to hope. The recent United 10
Nations report shows that H.I.V. infection rates in Uganda continue to
decline. In South Africa, infection rates for women under 20 have started
to decrease. In Zambia, H.I.V. rates show signs of dropping among
women in urban areas and younger women in rural areas. In Ethiopia, infection levels have fallen among young women in the center of Addis
Ababa.

We can and must build on those successes and replicate them else- 11
where. For that, we need leadership, partnership and imagination from the
international community and African governments. If we want to save
Africa from two catastrophes, we would do well to focus on saving Africa's
women.

Thinking About the Image

1. Although the map on the facing page did not appear with Kofi Annan's editorial, it was produced by a United Nations group formed to educate people
   about, and actively combat, HIV/AIDS. In what ways does this map visually
   represent the trends Annan describes? How does the map make the urgency of his argument more immediate?

2. Is there any information on the map that surprises you?

3. If you were a delegate to the United Nations from an African or Asian nation, what questions or responses would you have for Secretary-General
   Kofi Annan?

4. Use the information in this map to support your answer to any of the "Responding in Writing" questions.

Thinking About the Essay

1. What is the tone of Annan's introductory paragraph and the entire essay?
   What is his purpose? Point to specific passages to support your answer.

2. Annan employs causal analysis to develop this essay. Trace the causes
   and effects that he presents. What are some of the primary causes and
   effects? What secondary causes and effects does he mention?

3. This essay is rich in the use of examples. What types of illustration does
   Annan present to support his thesis?

4. Locate other rhetorical strategies—for example, comparision and
   contrast—that appear as structuring devices in this essay.

5. This essay presents a problem and offers a solution. Explain this strategy,
   paying careful attention to how the pattern evolves.

MAP 4.1   Regional Estimates of HIV/AIDS Infection as of December 2002.

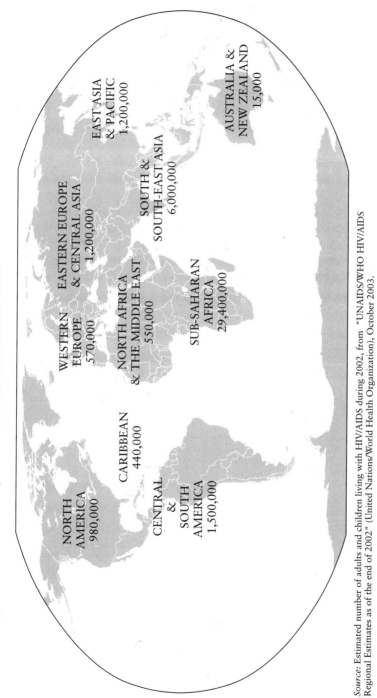

NORTH
AMERICA
980,000

CARIBBEAN
440,000

CENTRAL
&
SOUTH
AMERICA
1,500,000

WESTERN
EUROPE
570,000

EASTERN EUROPE
& CENTRAL ASIA
1,200,000

NORTH AFRICA
& THE MIDDLE EAST
550,000

SUB-SAHARAN
AFRICA
29,400,000

SOUTH &
SOUTH-EAST ASIA
6,000,000

EAST ASIA
& PACIFIC
1,200,000

AUSTRALIA &
NEW ZEALAND
15,000

Source: Estimated number of adults and children living with HIV/AIDS during 2002, from "UNAIDS/WHO HIV/AIDS Regional Estimates as of the end of 2002" (United Nations/World Health Organization), October 2003.

Responding in Writing

6. In a brief essay, explain what you have learned about AIDS in Africa from Annan's essay. Do you share his sense of optimism about the ability of the nations involved and the international community to solve the problem? Why or why not?

7. Explain your personal viewpoint on the increase of AIDS among the women of the world—not just in Africa but in Asia, Russia, Europe, and elsewhere.

8. Write an essay on another threat to women—either in a particular country or region, or around the world.

Networking

9. Form working groups of four or five class members, and draw up an action plan to solicit funds on your campus for United Nations AIDS relief efforts in sub-Saharan Africa. Then create a master plan based on the work of other class groups. Decide if you want to present this plan to the campus administration for approval.

10. Search the Internet for information on the United Nations programs to alleviate the AIDS epidemic around the world. Then write a letter to your congressional representative explaining why (or why not) Congress should support these efforts.

Polygamy

A. G. MOJTABAI | Ann Grace Mojtabai was born in Brooklyn, New York, in 1937 and was educated at Antioch College and Columbia University. She married a Muslim from Iran and lived for a number of years in Iran and Pakistan, where her husband was head of the Iranian cultural mission. Mojtabai writes both fiction and nonfiction. Her novels include *Mundome* (1974), *Autumn* (1982), *Ordinary Time* (1989), and *Called Out* (1994); her stories have been collected in *Soon: Tales from the Hospice* (1998). A reviewer of one of Mojtabai's works of nonfiction, *Blessed Assurance: At Home with the Bomb in Texas* (1986), observed that she listens carefully to people with whom she disagrees. In the following essay, first published in the *New York Times* in 1980, we see this ability on her part to listen and observe as she tries to understand a condition that most of us find alien to our beliefs and lives.

Before Reading

What do you know about polygamy? Where is it practiced in the United States and around the world? What are the grounds for polygamy? What is your attitude toward this phenomenon?

Teheran, 1960. A warm evening. The courtyard in which we were sitting was not very beautiful. There was a narrow strip of ground that ran along the edge of the wall, spotted with shrubbery and some insignificant roses; the rest was flagstone surrounding the customary small pool for ablutions, set like a turquoise in the center.

I had come to Iran expecting nightingales and roses, but had not yet heard a nightingale above the sounds of street hawkers and traffic, and the famed rose gardens of Persia were nowhere in evidence; they remained out of sight, if they ever existed, sealed off by high proprietary walls.

But my interest of the moment was not in the garden; my eyes were fixed on my father-in-law. He was a large, imposing man in his mid-90's, with high color, still-black eyebrows and the scrub of a heavy beard. He might have passed for a much younger man and, in fact, claimed to be in his young, vigorous 70's.

"What do you think of this?" he asked, pointing to his wives, one large, one small, on either side of him. His wives smiled in my direction, then at each other. My father-in-law continued to stare at me and to wait; he really wanted to know what I thought.

For the few separate moments it took to translate his question and my reply (with what distortion I shall never know), we gazed coolly at each other, each an anthropologist confronting opacity—the mind of a stranger. I thought I could hear him taking notes. I, for my part, was certainly jotting things down—but only impressions. I would see; I wasn't going to judge prematurely. My judgment, when it came, wouldn't be narrow, biased or culture-bound. "Customs differ," I said.

Long before meeting my father-in-law, I had been prepared for this— or, rather, I had been briefed, and imagined that I was prepared. It had been a briefing full of history (polygamy as a practical solution to the decimation of the male population in warfare and the resulting disproportionate preponderance of females over males); it had been a briefing on principle as well (the Koranic requirement that the husband distribute his affection equally among the co-wives).

But, of course, I was not ready to confront the live instance—three individuals who would bear an intimate family relation to me. Mother, father and what—aunt? mother-surrogate? I decided that the other party would simply be my Other Mother-in-Law. At that moment, the language barrier turned out to be an opportune cover for, really, I did not know what I thought.

The happy threesome sat cross-legged on a takhte, a low wooden plat-   8
form, covered with a rug. My particular mother-in-law, the tiny one, was the junior wife, chosen, I later learned, by the older woman as someone agreeable to herself, someone she thought the old man would like, too. The senior wife's passion was for talking, and her husband's silence had long been wearing her down. She wanted someone in the house willing to hear her out and, she hoped, to respond from time to time.

I was left to imagine the precise formalities, but it seemed to me to be   9
a marriage welcome to all the parties concerned. It was an arrangement not without its share of bickerings and quarrels, for however well-disposed the women were to each other, their respective children were rivals, and the wives were partisan for their children.

Still, as marriages go, theirs seemed to be a reasonably happy one.   10

When it grew chilly, we moved indoors. The sitting room was also my   11
father-in-law's bedroom. He sat on a fine, ancient rug, with bolsters at his back, a bay of windows on his left and, in front of him, an array of small vials: vitamins, elixirs, purges. He didn't believe in modern medicine, but was taking no chances.

Stiff, wooden chairs of mismatching shapes were lined against the walls   12
of the room. I eyed them, but, noticing that they were mantled in dust, furred with a thin, unbroken velvet, decided they were not really for use, and sat on the floor instead. In fact, the chairs were chiefly ceremonial, a reluctant concession to the times, to the imposition of Westernization around the world. Not like the television set, which was an ecstatic testimony to the march of *universal* human progress, and which held, along with the samovar, pride of place among the old man's possessions.

The wives stepped out to bring refreshments. With a sinking sense, I no-   13
ticed my husband getting up to speak to his mother in private. I was utterly adrift, alone with my father-in-law, a total stranger. The old man turned to me and said what I later learned was: "When hearts speak, no language is necessary." I recognized none of the words, but I guessed from his face and tone that whatever it was he had said was meant to be comforting and, trusting in a language of gesture and sign, I ventured a smile by way of reply.

Even today, I do not know what I think about polygamy. Or, perhaps,   14
I know what I think—it's only that my feelings are mixed. Abstractly, I oppose the custom. These bonds ought to be reciprocal, one-to-one. Sexual favors *may* be distributed equally as required (a night with A, a night with B), but I doubt whether affection can be distributed so neatly. And, of course, the custom speaks of the poverty of opportunities for women.

On the other hand, the custom of mut'a, or temporary marriage, prac- 15
ticed by Shiites, though not by Sunnites, seems to me to be possessed of
some merits and, on the whole, somewhat more enlightened than prostitution, or the vaguely polygamous custom of balancing wife (with legal
rights) with mistress (having no rights), which is so widely prevalent in the
West.

In the mut'a marriage, a term is stipulated—a night, a year, a decade, 16
an hour, whatever. A set term, a mehr—a wedding endowment for the
woman—mutual consent and a contract specifying all this are required.
The children of such unions are legitimate and entitled to a share of the father's inheritance, although the sigheh, the temporary wife, has no claim to
maintenance beyond the initial marriage endowment.

But polygamy is meant to be more than a mere alternative to such 17
clearly deficient institutions as prostitution. And my feelings for polygamy
as a true and viable form of marriage remain contrary, held in suspension.
My opposition in theory is muffled by my observation of one palpable contrary fact. I saw a polygamous marriage work, and work well. That my
mothers-in-law were deeply attached to each other, I have no doubt. I tend
to question rather more their devotion to the husband who brought them
together.

As for two mothers-in-law in one household, an old proverb would 18
seem to apply: "Better two tigers in one cage than two mistresses in one
household." But, in point of fact, the laws of addition don't always apply. After all, one shark and one codfish equal one shark; one raindrop
and one raindrop equal one raindrop. The two women worked off their
intensities on each other, with less energy left for me. So, actually, I had
one mother-in-law, which, as all the proverbs of all nations attest, was
quite sufficient.

Thinking About the Essay

1. How do paragraphs 1–5 establish the author's purpose? Why is this opening narrative effective?

2. What does Mojtabai mean when she describes her first meeting with her
   father-in-law as "each an anthropologist confronting opacity" (paragraph 5)?
   What level of language does that suggest that Mojtabai uses in this essay?
   How can these words be used by Westerners to describe aspects of various cultures?

3. The writer is both actor and observer. How does this affect the tone of the
   essay?

4. Why does Mojtabai devote considerable space to a description of *mut'a*? What elements of contrast does she utilize here? What is her purpose?

5. A subtle argument appears in this essay. Trace the course of this argument. What academic-sounding reasons for polygamy has Mojtabai been given? Do they help her confront the reality of it? Why, or why not? What is her final attitude toward polygamy? How do you know?

Responding in Writing

6. Polygamy is probably alien to your values. Write your own essay about this subject, comparing your response to Mojtabai's.

7. Does the United States have a more enlightened perspective on marriage than the one described by Mojtabai? Discuss this question in an argumentative essay.

8. Examine the effects of Westernization that appear in Mojtabai's essay. Of which ones do the Iranians approve? Of which ones do they disapprove? What does this situation tell you about the ways in which various cultures interact? Write an essay exploring this subject.

Networking

9. In small groups, discuss your personal response to Mojtabai's essay. Are you able to evaluate cultural situations that you might find alien as sympathetically as the writer? Summarize your discussion for the entire class.

10. Iran is very much in the news these days. Locate a website that can provide you with information on women's rights in the Islamic Republic, and write a report on your findings.

Justice for Women

ELLEN GOODMAN

Ellen Goodman was born in 1941 in Newton, Massachusetts, and received a B.A. degree from Harvard University in 1963. She is an award-winning journalist and columnist whose syndicated writing appears regularly in more than 250 newspapers. Goodman won the Pulitzer Prize for distinguished commentary in 1980. She also has been a commentator on radio and television. Among her books are *Close to Home* (1979), *At Large* (1981), *Value Judgments* (1993), and with Patricia O'Brien, *I Know Just What You Mean: The Power of Friendship in Women's Lives* (2000). Goodman is an adept practitioner of the personal essay, frequently bringing keen wit and humor to her subjects. However, Goodman employs invective and biting irony in the following essay from the *Boston Globe* (2002), in which she excoriates the Bush administration for its failure to promote women's rights.

Before Reading

Do you think that women have equal standing before courts of law in the United States? Around the world? Explain.

This time the dateline was Multan, Pakistan, although it could have 1 happened in any other place on the globe where women are the designated punching bags of injustice. An 18-year-old girl was "sentenced" to gang rape. Rape was the punishment allotted by a tribal council for her 11-year-old brother's "crime" of walking with an unchaperoned girl from a different tribe. For the sake of honor, four men took turns at sexual revenge, inflicting the "law" on the sister as she cried for help.

What shall we do with this unforgettable horror story? Shall we put it 2 in the folder next to stories of Nigerian women sentenced to be stoned to death for the crime of "adultery," whether sex was forced or consensual? Shall we add it to the studies coming out of the Barcelona AIDS conference reminding us that women's stunning vulnerability to this epidemic in sub-Saharan Africa is not just physiology but culture?

Ever since Afghanistan came upon our radar screen as the homeland of 3 woman-hating, we've paid more mind to the world's women. In one speech after another, President Bush has described the liberation of women as an American value worth fighting for. "A thriving nation," he told West Point graduates, "will respect the rights of women, because no society can prosper while denying opportunity to half its citizens."

In this atmosphere, how is it possible that our country cavalierly undermines its own stand on human rights? 4

Twenty-three years ago [1979] the United States helped write an international women's bill of rights. Since then, 170 countries have ratified the UN's Convention on the Elimination of All Forms of Discrimination Against Women. 5

Words like "discrimination" seem far too mild to describe female genital mutilation or sexual trafficking. But women from Colombia to Rwanda have used the treaty as a standard to rewrite laws on inheritance and domestic abuse, to change the patterns of education and employment. The treaty has been a tool in the long, slow evolution toward women's human rights. But who has not ratified the treaty? Countries like Somalia, Sudan, Iran. And the United States of America. 6

This year, I thought we would leave such embarrassing companions be-   7
hind. After all, the Bush administration offered a "general approval" for
the treaty early on. The Senate Foreign Relations Committee finally held
hearings in June [2000].

But on the way to ratification, women's rights took a right turn. First,   8
the conservative watchdog John Ashcroft declared that the treaty needed
more "study." Last Monday, Colin Powell made it clear to Joe Biden, the
chair of the Senate Foreign Relations Committee, that the State Department is not cramming to finish this "study." Powell's letter placed the
women's rights treaty behind 17 others waiting for Senate approval.

The administration is clearly trying to balance international women's   9
rights and the domestic political right. And politics may win.

The UN treaty brings out all the ancient enemies and hoary arguments   10
once launched against the Equal Rights Amendment. Conservative op-ed
mills and politicians proclaim that the treaty is simultaneously toothless
and radical. They offer a litany of alarms about the destruction of the family and even the bizarre idea that the treaty would eliminate, maybe even
criminalize, Mother's Day.

This international agreement can't trump national laws. Saudi Arabia,   11
no poster child for women's rights, has signed the treaty. So has Pakistan,
the scene of the rape sentence.

Slowly, though, more citizens hold countries up to their own signatures.   12
This new consciousness about human rights was surely one reason for the
Pakistani government's arrest of the rapist-jurists.

By not joining the international community, America damages its au-   13
thority to call others to account. As human rights advocate Steve Rickard
says, "We powerfully assist the Talibans of the world who want to argue
that the treaty isn't universal because we're not a party to it."

Biden, joining in, says, "The plain fact of the matter is that we should   14
provide a tool for women fighting for their lives in these countries." He
plans to bring up this plain fact next week in executive session of the Foreign Relations Committee and expects it to be voted onto the Senate floor.
"I want people to be counted," he says. But will that count add up to a two-
thirds majority?

Over the past two decades, nearly every president has signed an inter-   15
national human rights treaty. Ronald Reagan signed the genocide treaty.
The first George Bush signed the torture convention. Clinton signed the
race treaty. Will the man who takes pride in freeing Afghan women see
himself as a liberator or a rear guard?

Meanwhile, the stories accumulate. Every time we read about the   16
women of the world, there is an impulse to do something. This treaty is the
least we can do.

Thinking About the Essay

1. This is a topical essay, filled with references to figures in the Bush administration. Do these references limit the importance or lasting significance of the article? Why or why not?

2. How would you describe Goodman's tone in this essay? How does the tone affect her selection of information and her approach to the political environment she discusses?

3. Explain the effectiveness of Goodman's introduction. What is her purpose?

4. Trace the development of Goodman's argument. What is her claim? What reasons and evidence in support of her claim does she present?

5. Goodman's paragraphs are brief, reflecting the demands and expectations of opinion writing for the **op-ed** page of newspapers. What benefits do you see in her paragraphs, some of which are only one sentence? What is the downside to this strategy? How well, do you think, does she operate within the conventions of the op-ed piece?

Responding in Writing

6. Write an essay in which you agree or disagree with Goodman's charges against the Bush administration.

7. Write a letter to the editor of your college newspaper in which you explain how your campus can be more involved in the campaign for equal rights for women around the world.

8. Argue for or against the proposition that women need a human rights treaty to protect them and to achieve equality.

Networking

9. In groups of four or five class members, research the status of the UN's Convention on the Elimination of All Forms of Discrimination Against Women. Also determine the current administration's position on this document. Share your findings with the class.

10. Do a computer search for information on women's rights in India or Pakistan. Draft a report outlining your findings.

Family Values

RICHARD RODRIGUEZ

Richard Rodriguez, born in San Francisco in 1944, has gained national fame for his articles, books, and radio and television broadcasts on issues of race, immigration, multiculturalism, and gender. After receiving degrees from Stanford University and Columbia University, Rodriguez pursued graduate work at the University of California at Berkeley and the Warburg Institute, London. In his autobiography, *Hunger of Memory: The Education of Richard Rodriguez* (1982), he offers a memorable portrait of a young man trying to reconcile his Hispanic heritage and the dominant American culture. Rodriguez's opposition to bilingualism and affirmative action, as well as his advocacy of gay rights (which we see in the following essay), has been controversial, but he brings sharp critical insights to every subject he treats. Rodriguez's most recent book is *Brown: The Last Discovery of America* (2002). In "Family Values," published in the *Los Angeles Times* in 1992, Rodriguez argues that contrary to certain claims, homosexuality actually strengthens rather than weakens family structures.

Before Reading

Many college instructors see homophobia as the most intractable problem to deal with in the classroom—much more than sexism, racism, or any other type of discrimination. Why might this be the case? What is your own attitude toward homosexuality? What is your family's attitude? What is your culture or religion's attitude?

I am sitting alone in my car, in front of my parents' house—a middle-aged   1
man with a boy's secret to tell. What words will I use to tell them? I hate the word *gay*, find its little affirming sparkle more pathetic than assertive. I am happier with the less polite *queer*. But to my parents I would say *homosexual*, avoiding the Mexican slang *joto* (I had always heard it said in our house with hints of condescension), though *joto* is less mocking than the sissy-boy *maricon*.

The buzz on everyone's lips now: Family values. The other night on TV,   2
the vice president of the United States, his arm around his wife, smiled into the camera and described homosexuality as "mostly a choice." But how would he know? Homosexuality never felt like a choice to me.

A few minutes ago Rush Limbaugh, the radio guy with a voice that re-   3
minds me, for some reason, of a butcher's arms, was banging his console and booming a near-reasonable polemic about family values. Limbaugh was not very clear about which values exactly he considers to be family values. A divorced man who lives alone in New York?

My parents live on a gray, treeless street in San Francisco not far from   4
the ocean. Probably more than half of the neighborhood is immigrant. In-

dia lives next door to Greece, who lives next door to Russia. I wonder what the Chinese lady next door to my parents makes of the politicians' phrase *family values*.

What immigrants know, what my parents certainly know, is that when you come to this country, you risk losing your children. The assurance of family—continuity, inevitability—is precisely what America encourages its children to overturn. *Become your own man.* We who are native to this country know this too, of course, though we are likely to deny it. Only a society so guilty about its betrayal of family would tolerate the pieties of politicians regarding family values.

On the same summer day that Republicans were swarming in Houston (buzzing about family values), a friend of mine who escaped family values awhile back and who now wears earrings resembling intrauterine devices, was complaining to me over coffee about the Chinese. The Chinese will never take over San Francisco, my friend said, because the Chinese do not want to take over San Francisco. The Chinese do not even see San Francisco! All they care about is their damn families. All they care about is double-parking smack in front of the restaurant on Clement Street and pulling granny out of the car—and damn anyone who happens to be in the car behind them or the next or the next.

Politicians would be horrified by such an American opinion, of course. But then what do politicians, Republicans or Democrats, really know of our family life? Or what are they willing to admit? Even in that area where they could reasonably be expected to have something to say—regarding the relationship of family life to our economic system—the politicians say nothing. Republicans celebrate American economic freedom, but Republicans don't seem to connect that economic freedom to the social breakdown they find appalling. Democrats, on the other hand, if more tolerant of the drift from familial tradition, are suspicious of the very capitalism that creates social freedom.

How you become free in America: Consider the immigrant. He gets a job. Soon he is earning more money than his father ever made (his father's authority is thereby subtly undermined). The immigrant begins living a life his father never knew. The immigrant moves from one job to another, changes houses. His economic choices determine his home address—not the other way around. The immigrant is on his way to becoming his own man.

When I was broke a few years ago and trying to finish a book, I lived with my parents. What a thing to do! A major theme of America is leaving home. We trust the child who forsakes family connections to make it on his own. We call that the making of a man.

Let's talk about this man stuff for a minute. America's ethos is anti-domestic. We may be intrigued by blood that runs through wealth—the Kennedys or the Rockefellers—but they seem European to us. Which is to say, they are movies. They are Corleones. Our real pledge of allegiance: We say in America that nothing about your family—your class, your race, your pedigree—should be as important as what you yourself achieve. We end up in 1992 introducing ourselves by first names. 10

What authority can Papa have in a country that formed its identity in an act of Oedipal rebellion against a mad British king? Papa is a joke in America, a stock sitcom figure—Archie Bunker or Homer Simpson. But my Mexican father went to work every morning, and he stood in a white smock, making false teeth, oblivious of the shelves of grinning false teeth mocking his devotion. 11

The nuns in grammar school—my wonderful Irish nuns—used to push Mark Twain on me. I distrusted Huck Finn, he seemed like a gringo kid I would steer clear of in the schoolyard. (He was too confident.) I realize now, of course, that Huck is the closest we have to a national hero. We trust the story of a boy who has no home and is restless for the river. (Huck's Pap is drunk.) Americans are more forgiving of Huck's wildness than of the sweetness of the Chinese boy who walks to school with his mama or grandma. (There is no worse thing in America than to be a mama's boy, nothing better than to be a real boy—all boy—like Huck, who eludes Aunt Sally, and is eager for the world of men.) 12

There's a bent old woman coming up the street. She glances nervously as she passes my car. What would you tell us, old lady, of family values in America? 13

America is an immigrant country, we say. Motherhood—parenthood—is less our point than adoption. If I had to assign gender to America, I would note the consensus of the rest of the world. When America is burned in effigy, a male is burned. Americans themselves speak of Uncle Sam. 14

Like the Goddess of Liberty, Uncle Sam has no children of his own. He steals children to make men of them, mocks all reticence, all modesty, all memory. Uncle Sam is a hectoring Yankee, a skinflint uncle, gaunt, un-couth, unloved. He is the American Savonarola—hater of moonshine, de-stroyer of stills, burner of cocaine. Sam has no patience with mamas' boys. 15

You betray Uncle Sam by favoring private over public life, by seeking to exempt yourself, by cheating on your income taxes, by avoiding jury duty, by trying to keep your boy on the farm. 16

Mothers are traditionally the guardians of the family against America—though even Mom may side with America against queers and deserters, at least when the Old Man is around. Premature gray hair. Arthritis in her 17 shoulders. Bowlegged with time, red hands. In their fiercely flowered housedresses, mothers are always smarter than fathers in America. But in reality they are betrayed by their children who leave. In a thousand ways. They end up alone.

We kind of like the daughter who was a tomboy. Remember her? It was 18 always easier to be a tomboy in America than a sissy. Americans admired Annie Oakley more than they admired Liberace (who, nevertheless, always remembered his mother). But today we do not admire Annie Oakley when we see Mom becoming Annie Oakley.

The American household now needs two incomes, everyone says. 19 Meaning: Mom is *forced* to leave home out of economic necessity. But lots of us know lots of moms who are sick and tired of being mom, or only mom. It's like the nuns getting fed up, teaching kids for all those years and having those kids grow up telling stories of how awful Catholic school was! Not every woman in America wants her life's work to be forgiveness. Today there are moms who don't want their husbands' names. And the most disturbing possibility: What happens when Mom doesn't want to be Mom at all? Refuses pregnancy?

Mom is only becoming an American like the rest of us. Certainly, peo- 20 ple all over the world are going to describe the influence of feminism on women (all over the world) as their "Americanization." And rightly so.

Nothing of this, of course, will the politician's wife tell you. The politi- 21 cian's wife is careful to follow her husband's sentimental reassurances that nothing has changed about America except perhaps for the sinister influence of deviants. Like myself.

I contain within myself an anomaly at least as interesting as the Re- 22 publican Party's version of family values. I am a homosexual Catholic, a communicant in a tradition that rejects even as it upholds me.

I do not count myself among those Christians who proclaim themselves 23 protectors of family values. They regard me as no less an enemy of the family than the "radical feminists." But the joke about families that all homosexuals know is that we are the ones who stick around and make families possible. Call on us. I can think of 20 or 30 examples. A gay son or daughter is the only one who is "free" (married brothers and sisters are too busy). And, indeed, because we have admitted the inadmissible about ourselves (that we are queer)—we are adepts at imagination—we can even imagine those who refuse to imagine us. We can imagine Mom's loneliness, for example. If Mom needs to be taken to church or to the doctor or ferried between Christmas dinners, depend on the gay son or lesbian daughter.

I won't deny that the so-called gay liberation movement, along with fem- 24 inism, undermined the heterosexual household, if that's what politicians mean when they say family values. Against churchly reminders that sex was for procreation, the gay bar as much as the birth-control pill taught Americans not to fear sexual pleasure. In the past two decades—and, not coincidentally, parallel to the feminist movement—the gay liberation movement moved a generation of Americans toward the idea of a child-less adulthood. If the women's movement was ultimately more concerned about getting out of the house and into the workplace, the gay movement was in its way more subversive to puritan America because it stressed the importance of play.

Several months ago, the society editor of the morning paper in San   25 Francisco suggested (on a list of "must haves") that every society dame must have at least one gay male friend. A ballet companion. A lunch date. The remark was glib and incorrect enough to beg complaints from homo-sexual readers, but there was a truth about it as well. Homosexual men have provided women with an alternate model of masculinity. And the truth: The Old Man, God bless him, is a bore. Thus are we seen as pre-serving marriages? Even Republican marriages?

For myself, homosexuality is a deep brotherhood but does not involve   26 domestic life. Which is why, my married sisters will tell you, I can afford the time to be a writer. And why are so many homosexuals such wonder-ful teachers and priests and favorite aunts, if not because we are freed from the house? On the other hand, I know lots of homosexual couples (male and female) who model their lives on the traditional heterosexual version of domesticity and marriage. Republican politicians mock the notion of a homosexual marriage, but ironically such marriages honor the heterosex-ual marriage by imitating it.

"The only loving couples I know," a friend of mine recently remarked,   27 "are all gay couples."

This woman was not saying that she does not love her children or that   28 she is planning a divorce. But she was saying something about the sadness of American domestic life: the fact that there is so little joy in family inti-macy. Which is perhaps why gossip (public intrusion into the private) has become a national industry. All day long, in forlorn houses, the television lights up a freakish parade of husbands and mothers-in-law and children upon the stage of Sally or Oprah or Phil. They tell on each other. The au-dience ooohhhs. Then a psychiatrist-shaman appears at the end to dispense prescriptions—the importance of family members granting one another more "space."

The question I desperately need to ask you is whether we Americans   29 have ever truly valued the family. We are famous, or our immigrant ances-tors were famous, for the willingness to leave home. And it is ironic that a crusade under the banner of family values has been taken up by those who would otherwise pass themselves off as patriots. For they seem not to understand America, nor do I think they love the freedoms America grants. Do they understand why, in a country that prizes individuality and is suspicious of authority, children are disinclined to submit to their parents? You cannot celebrate American values in the public realm without expecting them to touch our private lives. As Barbara Bush remarked recently, family values are also neighborhood values. It may be harmless enough for Barbara Bush to recall a sweeter America—Midland, Texas, in the 1950s. But the question left begging is why we chose to leave Midland, Texas. Americans like to say that we can't go home again. The truth is that we don't want to go home again, don't want to be known, recognized. Don't want to respond in the same old ways. (And you know you will if you go back there.)

Little 10-year-old girls know that there are reasons for getting away   30 from the family. They learn to keep their secrets—under lock and key— addressed to Dear Diary. Growing up queer, you learn to keep secrets as well. In no place are those secrets more firmly held than within the family house. You learn to live in closets. I know a Chinese man who arrived in America about 10 years ago. He got a job and made some money. And during that time he came to confront his homosexuality. And then his family arrived. I do not yet know the end of this story.

The genius of America is that it permits children to leave home, it per-   31 mits us to become different from our parents. But the sadness, the loneliness of America, is clear too.

Listen to the way Americans talk about immigrants. If, on the one   32 hand, there is impatience when today's immigrants do not seem to give up their family, there is also a fascination with this reluctance. In Los Angeles, Hispanics are considered people of family. Hispanic women are hired to be at the center of the American family—to babysit and diaper, to cook and to clean and to ease the dying. Hispanic attachment to family is seen by many Americans, I think, as the reason why Hispanics don't get ahead. But if Asians privately annoy us for being so family oriented, they are also stereotypically celebrated as the new "whiz kids" in school. Don't Asians go to college, after all, to honor their parents?

More important still is the technological and economic ascendancy of   33 Asia, particularly Japan, on the American imagination. Americans are starting to wonder whether perhaps the family values of Asia put the United States at a disadvantage. The old platitude had it that ours is a vibrant, robust society for being a society of individuals. Now we look to Asia and see team effort paying off.

In this time of national homesickness, of nostalgia, for how we imagine 34 America used to be, there are obvious dangers. We are going to start blaming each other for the loss. Since we are inclined, as Americans, to think of ourselves individually, we are disinclined to think of ourselves as creating one another or influencing one another.

But it is not the politician or any political debate about family values 35 that has brought me here on a gray morning to my parents' house. It is some payment I owe to my youth and to my parents' youth. I imagine us sitting in the living room, amid my mother's sentimental doilies and the family photographs, trying to take the measure of the people we have turned out to be in America.

A San Francisco poet, when he was in the hospital and dying, called a 36 priest to his bedside. The old poet wanted to make his peace with Mother Church. He wanted baptism. The priest asked why. "Because the Catholic Church has to accept me," said the poet. "Because I am a sinner."

Isn't willy-nilly inclusiveness the point, the only possible point to be de- 37 rived from the concept of family? Curiously, both President Bush and Vice President Quayle got in trouble with their constituents recently for expressing a real family value. Both men said that they would try to dissuade a daughter or granddaughter from having an abortion. But, finally, they said they would support her decision, continue to love her, never abandon her.

There are families that do not accept. There are children who are forced 38 to leave home because of abortions or homosexuality. There are family secrets that Papa never hears. Which is to say there are families that never learn the point of families.

But there she is at the window. My mother has seen me and she waves 39 me in. Her face asks: Why am I sitting outside? (Have they, after all, known my secret for years and kept it, out of embarrassment, not knowing what to say?) Families accept, often by silence. My father opens the door to welcome me in.

Thinking About the Essay

1. Rodriguez's title is exceedingly compelling in light of his essay. Why is this title so powerful? What ironies do the title and the text reveal? Point to specific instances of irony in the essay.

2. Consider the introduction and conclusion of this essay. Why does Rodriguez begin and end on a personal note? What is his purpose? How does personal narrative enhance what is basically an expository essay?

3. How would you describe the writer's style in this essay? What types of sentences does he prefer? What are some of his more arresting phrases and

figures of speech? How does he generate an emotional mood and tone that pervades the entire essay? How would you describe this tone?

4. In many ways, this essay involves a definition—and a meditation—on the family and family values. What rhetorical strategies does Rodriguez use to develop his extended definitions? Would you say that his definitions are stipulative (that is, strictly personal and therefore limited in application) or universally true? Explain.

5. Analyze this essay as an argument. What is Rodriguez's claim? What are his key reasons supporting his claim? What types of evidence does he provide in support of these reasons? Finally, how convincing is his argument? Does he convince you? Has your thinking been changed in any way? Explain.

Responding in Writing

6. Rodriguez states that gay men and women frequently are the strongest defenders of traditional values within families (paragraph 23). Write an argumentative essay in which you agree or disagree with this proposition.

7. Write your own definition of "family values." Be certain to create a tone that captures your feelings about this term and about the people and groups who use it to advance a certain agenda.

8. Write a comparative paper treating the two essays by Rodriguez that appear in this text. State a clear thesis or claim, and back it up with at least three key points and supporting evidence drawn from the essays.

Networking

9. With two other class members, have a serious discussion of the issues raised by Rodriguez in his essay and your personal response to them. Share your opinions and feelings with the rest of the class.

10. Locate a "family values" website. What does this website say about homosexuality? Report your findings to the class.

Traveling Alone

MARY MORRIS | Mary Morris, who was born in 1947 in Chicago, Illinois, is a self-described "wanderer of the planet." After receiving her B.A. degree from Tufts College, followed by graduate degrees from Columbia University, Morris embarked on a career as a writer of fiction and travel narratives. Her first book was *Vanishing Animals and Other Stories* (1979). Morris then wrote several novels, including *Crossroads* (1983),

The Night Sky (1997), and *Acts of God* (2000). "As a writer," she says, "my life has always been connected with journeys; I have been a kind of compulsive traveler since I can remember. My stories have evolved out of those experiences." This essay, from Morris's *Nothing to Declare: Memoirs of a Woman Traveling Alone* (1988), offers insight into the possibilities and perils the author encounters as she travels through Mexico and Central America.

Before Reading

What unique problems do women encounter when they travel alone? Do these problems differ qualitatively from the problems that men might encounter? Defend your position.

Women who travel as I travel are dreamers. Our lives seem to be lives 1 of endless possibility. Like readers of romances we think that anything can happen to us at any time. We forget that this is not our real life— our life of domestic details, work pressures, attempts and failures at human relations. We keep moving. From anecdote to anecdote, from hope to hope. Around the next bend something new will befall us. Nostalgia has no place for the woman traveling alone. Our motion is forward, whether by train or daydream. Our sights are on the horizon, across strange terrain, vast desert, unfordable rivers, impenetrable ice peaks.

I wanted to keep going forever, to never stop, that morning when 2 the truck picked me up at five A.M. It was like a drug in me. As a traveler I can achieve a kind of high, a somewhat altered state of consciousness. I think it must be what athletes feel. I am transported out of myself, into another dimension in time and space. While the journey is on buses and across land, I begin another journey inside my head, a journey of memory and sensation, of past merging with present, of time growing insignificant.

My journey was now filled with dreams of other journeys to cool, 3 breezy places. The plateaus of Tibet, the altiplano of Bolivia, cold places, barren, without tropical splendor. I did not dream of Africa and its encompassing heat. I longed for white Siberia, for Tierra del Fuego, the Arctic tundra, vast desolate plains. I longed for what came next. Whatever the next stop, the next love, the next story might be.

Josh was sitting in the back of the truck when it pulled up to my pension. 4 "I thought you were going to Guatemala City," I said.

"Well," he said, smiling, "there are other ways to get to Panama." He 5 grabbed my duffel and pulled me on. Then we sat across from each other as we set out through a lush pass in the mountains, bouncing in the back through a very misty morning, past charging rivers, herds of cattle and goats, toward the border of Honduras.

At about five-thirty the driver stopped to pick up two women. They 6 were teachers who worked in one-room schoolhouses in the hills. One of them told us she walked an hour from where the truck would drop her to her school and she did this twice a day every day.

"You must be exhausted every day," I said. 7

She had a bright smile, sleek black hair, and dark eyes. "Oh, no." She 8 laughed. "The walk is beautiful and I always arrive feeling refreshed."

"You never get tired of it?" I asked, incredulous. 9

"There is always something to see," she said, smiling. At six-thirty, she 10 got off, heading toward the mountains, waving, then disappeared along a trail.

At seven we reached the frontier and found it closed. We took our bags, 11 waved good-bye to our pickup, and waited for the border to open and for some other vehicle, which we assumed would materialize, to appear. For an hour or so we clomped around, taking pictures of an enormous cow that was nearby. At last the border opened. "You want to go into Honduras?" the guard said with a bit of a sneer.

"Yes, we're going to the ruins." I have no idea why I felt the need to say 12 that, but I did.

"Well, if you want to go into Honduras, that's your problem." He 13 stamped our passports just as another minibus arrived, heading for Copán.

We spent the day at the ruins. We had no plan, really, no sense of whether 14 we would stay there or try to get out of the jungle and to some city by night. The ruins were fairly deserted and we spent the day climbing around. We had not gone far when we startled an enormous blue-black snake that had been asleep. The snake rose up on its side, then chased us along the path for several feet. I had never been chased by a snake before and was amazed at how fast it could move. Josh hurled a stone at it and the snake disappeared into the jungle.

We walked deeper into the jungle and a wasp stung me twice on the 15 knee. Josh scooped wet mud and packed it around the bites. My knee became very stiff and I thought I couldn't go on, but he coaxed me and I did.

We came to a pyramid. It was hardly excavated. The steps were bro- 16 ken, stones were covered with moss, but we climbed. My knee hurt, but I didn't care. We climbed and climbed. It was a very high pyramid and when we reached the top, we were silent. We sat still on the top of this unexcavated pyramid, looking at the tremendous jungle that stretched before us.

I liked Josh. What more can I say. I liked him. I wanted to go with him   17
to Panama. I had only just met him and I hadn't thought it through, but I wanted to go. Thinking about it now, I'm not sure what it was that I liked about him so much—he was, in fact, rather ordinary—but I think it had something to do with the fact that he was an American. He was an intelligent American male and he represented for me all those things that were now missing in my life. He could have dinner with my parents at my father's club. The men would wear suits and ties and discuss the market over Scotch and soda. My mother would wink at me across the table. Later she'd take me aside and say what a nice man he was and how they hoped they'd be seeing more of him.

I thought about Alejandro, sitting in that dark apartment, waiting for   18
my return, telegram in hand, but all I could think about was going on with Josh to Panama. That afternoon as we walked, we spoke of more personal things. I told him I had a boyfriend in Mexico City. He said he had just broken up with a woman in Berkeley.

We checked into the Mayan Copán and had dinner on the patio. Sitting   19
there with Josh in the steam of the jungle brought back to me what until now had seemed farthest away—the hot summer days and nights of Manhattan. Suddenly I found myself longing for a dripping ice cream cone while the plaintive song of a saxophonist echoed up the avenue. I longed for the heat of the pavement, cheap wine during a concert in the park, and black children jumping double-Dutch while illegal aliens sold assorted ices—pineapple, anise, coconut. I wanted to be transplanted, to feel the pace of the city in summer—an afternoon spent at the matinee, a weekend flight to Jones Beach. I even longed for what repulsed me—the garbage, the stench of urine, the homeless, the yellow smogged sky. All the things I swore I'd never miss.

After dinner we sat on the porch of the hotel, drinking rum and Cokes   20
and speaking of our travels. Josh told me about trekking through Afghanistan and hiking across the Khyber Pass, about wanting to walk to Turkistan and getting captured by rebels somewhere along the way. He said that he had talked his way into and out of every situation you could imagine. "But if I were a woman," he said, "I don't know if I'd do it alone."

"It has its ups and downs," I said.   21

"Have you ever had anything bad happen to you?"   22

I shrugged. "Some near-misses, that's all."   23

He sipped his rum contemplatively. "I've heard terrible stories." 24

"Like what?" 25

He leaned over and kissed me on the lips. "I don't want to ruin your 26 evening."

"You may as well tell me now." 27

He pulled his chair closer. "Well, this happened to a friend of a friend 28 of mine. Not someone I really know. I met him once, that's all. I'm not even sure it happened the way my friend said. This man went to Turkey with his wife. To Istanbul. He never talks about it, but they went to Istanbul. It was a kind of second honeymoon. They wanted to start a family, so anyway, they went on this second honeymoon—"

I reached across, touching his hand. "Just tell me the story." He held 29 onto my fingers and did not let go until he was done.

"All right. So they went. They were at the bazaar one day and his wife 30 wanted to buy a dress. She was a pretty woman, blond. So they went into a store and after a while he got bored and said he wanted to take a walk. He said he'd go have a cigarette and be back in half an hour. They had a little fight about this, but he went anyway. When he came back, the dress shop was closed and no one was there. So he thought they'd closed early and he went to the hotel and waited for his wife to meet him there. But she never went back to the hotel. He waited and waited, but she never came back. He talked to the police and the next day they went to the shop, but the people, people he recognized from the day before, said they had never seen the woman and she'd never been there. He stayed in Istanbul for weeks, but they never found his wife."

"And he thinks she was kidnapped by the people who owned the dress 31 shop?"

Josh nodded. "Kidnapped. And sold." 32

"Sold?" 33

"That's right. Sold." 34

We sat in silence for a long time, listening to the jungle noises. After 35 a while, Josh pulled me by my hand. "Come on," he said. "Let's go to sleep."

In the morning we boarded the minibus. The women who got on all had 36 holes cut in their dresses where their nipples hung out and small children suckled. The men carried machetes, which they checked with the bus driver by tucking them under his seat. Many of the men had slash marks on their arms or faces and many were missing fingers and limbs, so it appeared that this precaution was a necessary one. I was reminded of the movies about the Wild West, where the gunslingers check their guns at the saloon door.

Several hours later we reached La Entrada. Everyone there carried a 37
machete. We went to a bar to have a beer and a man walked in. Both his
hands had been chopped off above the wrist and his nose was missing. "A
machete did that," Josh said.

Suddenly I could not bear the thought of spending a moment alone. The 38
story he had told me of the woman in Istanbul stayed in my mind and I
knew that having heard it, I'd never be quite the same.

Josh was undecided about which direction he would take and I was un- 39
decided as to whether or not I would go with him. I wanted him to ask me.
I thought that if he asked me, I'd go. From La Entrada there were buses to
either coast and points east and west. The choices were infinite. But Josh
had taken a liking to inland Honduras and the guidebook said there were
some things to see in a neighboring town called Florida. "Look," Josh said.
"How often are you going to be in this part of Honduras?"

"Not often," I said. And we hitched a ride with a farmer in the back of 40
his pickup truck.

Josh had heard about a gas station attendant in Florida who knew 41
everything there was to know about the Mayan ruins in the vicinity.

"I thought you were tired of ruins." 42

"Well, we're here. We may as well make the most of it." 43

We found the gas station attendant and he sent us in the direction of 44
some ruins not far from the border. We crawled around in the heat of the
day while Josh tried to decide what kind of people lived in this place. A dog
that was skin and bones followed us. I threw him scraps of sandwich, but
Josh kept trying to chase the dog away.

Later that night while a tropical breeze blew in through the windows of 45
our small room, Josh told me he was going to go to Salvador. I thought to
myself how, having lost all sense of proportion, I'd follow this man anywhere, and after about thirty seconds I said, "Mind if I come with you?"

"Not at all," he said. "But what about your boyfriend in Mexico?" 46

"What about him?" 47

"Well, won't he be upset?" 48

"Do you want me to go with you or not?" I asked, pressing the point. 49

"I want you to do whatever makes you happy," he said. 50

"Well, then I'm going with you." 51

He drifted right to sleep, but I stayed awake. I could not stop thinking 52
about that woman he'd told me about the night before, a captive in some
harem, a woman used and tossed aside, trying endlessly to plan her escape.
A blond among dark people. A woman who could not speak their tongue.
Perhaps she had been ingenious, learning their ways, and had made a life
for herself wherever her prison was. Perhaps she had fallen into the hands

of a benevolent sheik who took pity on her, and though his pride would not permit him to release her, he would not abuse her, either.

But I think the scenario is much darker than this. That woman would 53 never be free. She would never return. If it were me, when I realized that rescue wouldn't come, that I would not be found, that I would never go home and would always be a prisoner of men, I would lose my mind. I would die of grief or by my own hand.

In the morning we stood at the crossroads at La Entrada, waiting for the 54 bus for Salvador. Until the bus arrived, I wasn't sure what I was going to do, but as soon as I saw it, kicking up dust, puffing in the distance, I knew what lay before me. When the driver stopped and opened the ancient door, I kissed Josh. "Have a safe journey," I said.

"What? Aren't you coming?" 55

"I'm going to Tegucigalpa." If he begs me, I told myself, I'll go. 56

"Well, whatever suits you." 57

He wasn't begging. He wasn't even asking. "Yes, I guess this suits me." 58 I waved good-bye. Sitting on my duffel in the sun—though dreaming of the way I could have gone with him—I felt sure I was on the right road. About an hour later the bus for Tegucigalpa approached. The bus driver asked me if I was a *gente de la sandía,* a watermelon person. A joke on the Sandinistas, and I said no, I was a tourist from the United States. He nodded and I took a seat in the rear.

It was a big bus this time, heading for the capital. Not long after I 59 boarded a young girl and her father got on, and they sat near the front. After about an hour the bus stopped and the father got off. He kissed his daughter good-bye and waved as the bus drove away. The girl was perhaps thirteen or fourteen and after a few moments she began to cry. She cried uncontrollably and the driver stopped. Women rushed to her, then came away shaking their heads. She was an idiot, one of the women told me. Her father had abandoned her here on this bus. "Too expensive to feed," the man behind me muttered. "Too expensive to keep."

Thinking About the Essay

1. How does the introductory paragraph set the stage and create the mood for this essay? What is the overall tone and effect of the first section (paragraphs 1–3)?

2. Morris presents herself in this essay as a traveler and dreamer. She also is quite candid in creating a **persona**, or self-image. What do we learn about this "I" narrator? How does she establish her reliability as a narrator? Point to specific passages to support your response.

3. Morris divides her narrative into several sections. What is her purpose? How does each section serve to advance the narrative? What contrasts does she draw between her own culture and the culture and civilizations she encounters?

4. In this narrative essay, Morris creates an atmosphere of potential danger and of possible conflict. How does she accomplish this? What is her point?

5. How does the concluding paragraph serve as a coda for the entire essay? What thesis does Morris reinforce in this last paragraph?

Responding in Writing

6. Are you a traveler and a dreamer, or just a dreamer who would like to travel but never manages to? Write a response to this question.

7. Part of Morris's purpose in this essay is to suggest that she needs to travel, even though she realizes that by "traveling alone" as a woman there could be problems. Reread her essay and then write a paper in which you outline her reasons for travel and the challenges she must confront. Do you sympathize with her, or is your final response different? Be certain to explain your response in your essay.

8. Write an essay explaining the ways in which gender could affect one's experience of a foreign country.

Networking

9. Discuss in groups of five or six class members the various experiences of travel that each person has had. What problems arose? Ultimately was the experience good or bad? What is the value of travel, either within your own country or abroad? Take notes on your discussion and share them when the entire class reassembles.

10. Go to an Internet travel site like Expedia or Travelocity and plan an itinerary for a trip to the one destination that you would like to visit. Why do you "dream" of this destination? Would you go on your own? Why or why not?

Life on the Global Assembly Line

BARBARA EHRENREICH AND ANNETTE FUENTES

Barbara Ehrenreich was born in 1941 in Butte, Montana. She attended Reed College (B.A., 1963) and Rockefeller University (Ph.D. in biology, 1968). A self-described socialist and **feminist**, Ehrenreich uses her scientific training to investigate a broad range of social issues: health care, the plight of the poor, the condition of women around the world. Her scathing critiques of American health care in such books as *The American Health Empire* (with John Ehrenreich, 1970), *Complaints and Disorders: The Sexual Politics of Sickness* (with Deirdre English, 1973), and *For Her Own Good* (with English, 1978) established her as an authority in the field. In her provocative *The Hearts of Men: American Dreams and the Flight from Commitment* (1983), Ehrenreich surveys the decline of male investment in the family from the 1950s to the 1980s. A prolific writer during the 1980s and 1990s, Ehrenreich most recently published the award-winning book *Nickel and Dimed: On (Not) Getting By in America* (2001). She is also a frequent contributor to magazines, including *Nation, Esquire, Radical America, New Republic,* and the *New York Times,* while serving as a contributing editor to *Ms.* and *Mother Jones.* The classic essay that appears here, written for *Ms.* in 1981 with Annette Fuentes, a New York–based journalist and adjunct professor at Columbia University, was among the first articles to expose the plight of working women around the world.

Before Reading

What experiences or expectations do you bring to a new job? What happens if you discover you are being exploited?

Ms.; 1981 January　　　　　　　　　　　　　　　　　　　　　　1

flash forward　　　　　　　　　　　　　　　　　　　　　　　　2

> Globalization has changed the rules of the game. The nation-state as　3
> we understand it is a state that is bargaining, struggling, being swallowed up by the forces of globalization. In 1985, on the eve of the Nairobi conference, our message about development was really new, that you can't just talk about gender equality without considering equality of what. Do you want equal shares of a poisoned pie? It was a message that had a galvanizing effect on people, because by Beijing, globalization issues had become part of everyone's vocabulary. No longer was it a situation where the North worries about gender equality and the South about development.
>
> —Economist Gita Sen, *Ford Foundation Report,* Winter 2000

Every morning, between four and seven, thousands of women head out　4
for the day shift. In Ciudad Juarez, they crowd into *ruteras* (run-down vans) for the trip from the slum neighborhoods to the industrial parks on

This three-year-old in India helps her mother and sisters make soccer balls—for 75 cents a day.

the outskirts of the city. In Penang they squeeze, 60 or more at a time, into buses for the trip to the low, modern factory buildings of the Bayan Lepas free trade zone. In Taiwan, they walk from the dormitories—where the night shift is already asleep in the still-warm beds—through the checkpoints in the high fence surrounding the factory zone.

This is the world's new industrial proletariat: young, female, Third   5
World. Viewed from the "first world," they are still faceless, genderless "cheap labor," signaling their existence only through a label or tiny imprint "made in Hong Kong," or Taiwan, Korea, the Dominican Republic, Mexico, the Philippines. But they may be one of the most strategic blocs of womanpower in the world. Conservatively, there are 2 million Third World female industrial workers employed now, millions more looking for work, and their numbers are rising every year.

It doesn't take more than second-grade arithmetic to understand what's   6
happening. In the U.S., an assembly-line worker is likely to earn, depend-

ing on her length of employment, between $3.10 and $5 an hour. In many Third World countries, a woman doing the same work will earn $3 to $5 a day.

And so, almost everything that can be packed up is being moved out to the Third World: garment manufacture, textiles, toys, footwear, pharmaceuticals, wigs, appliance parts, tape decks, computer components, plastic goods. In some industries, like garment and textile, American jobs are lost in the process, and the biggest losers are women, often black and Hispanic. But what's going on is much more than a matter of runaway shops. Economists are talking about a "new international division of labor," in which the process of production is broken down and the fragments are dispersed to different parts of the world, while control over the overall process and technology remains safely at company headquarters in "first world" countries. 7

The American electronics industry provides a classic example: circuits are printed on silicon wafers and tested in California; then the wafers are shipped to Asia for the labor-intensive process by which they are cut into tiny chips and bonded to circuit boards; final assembly into products such as calculators or military equipment usually takes place in the United States. Garment manufacture too is often broken into geographically separated steps, with the most repetitive, labor-intensive jobs going to the poor countries of the southern hemisphere. 8

So much any economist could tell you. What is less often noted is the gender breakdown of the emerging international division of labor. Eighty to 90 percent of the low-skilled assembly jobs that go to the Third World are performed by women in a remarkable switch from earlier patterns of foreign-dominated industrialization. Until now, "development" under the aegis of foreign corporations has usually meant more jobs for men and— compared to traditional agricultural society—a diminished economic status for women. But multinational corporations and Third World governments alike consider assembly-line work—whether the product is Barbie dolls or missile parts—to be "women's" work. 9

It's an article of faith with management that only women can do, or will do, the monotonous, painstaking work that American business is exporting to the Third World. The personnel manager of a light assembly plant in Taiwan told anthropologist Linda Gail Arrigo, "Young male workers are too restless and impatient to do monotonous work with no career value. If displeased, they sabotage the machines and even threaten the foreman. But girls? At most, they cry a little." 10

A top-level management consultant who specializes in advising American companies on where to relocate, gave us this global generalization: 11

"The [factory] girls genuinely enjoy themselves. They're away from their families. They have spending money. Of course it's a regulated experience too—with dormitories to live in—so it's a healthful experience."

What is the real experience of the women in the emerging Third World   12 industrial work force? Rachael Grossman, a researcher with the Southeast Asia Resource Center, found women employees of U.S. multinational firms in Malaysia and the Philippines living four to eight in a room in boarding-houses, or squeezing into tiny extensions built onto squatter huts near the factory. Where companies do provide dormitories, they are not of the "healthful," collegiate variety. The American Friends Service Committee reports that dormitory space is "likely to be crowded—while one shift works, another sleeps, as many as twenty to a room."

Living conditions are only part of the story. The work that multina-   13 tional corporations export to the Third World is not only the most tedious, but often the most hazardous part of the production process. The countries they go to are, for the most part, those that will guarantee no interference from health and safety inspectors, trade unions, or even free-lance reformers.

Consider the electronics industry, which is generally thought to be the   14 safest and cleanest of the exported industries. The factory buildings are low and modern, like those one might find in a suburban American industrial park. Inside, rows of young women, neatly dressed in the company uniform or Tshirt, work quietly at their stations. There is air conditioning (not for the women's comfort, but to protect the delicate semiconductor parts they work with), and high-volume piped-in Bee Gees hits (not so much for entertainment, as to prevent talking).

For many Third World women, electronics is a prestige occupation,   15 at least compared to other kinds of factory work. They are unlikely to know that in the United States the National Institute on Occupational Safety and Health (NIOSH) has placed electronics on its select list of "high health-risk industries using the greatest number of toxic substances." If electronics assembly work is risky here, it is doubly so in countries where there is no equivalent of NIOSH to even issue warnings. In many plants toxic chemicals and solvents sit in open containers, filling the work area with fumes that can literally knock you out. "We have been told of cases where ten to twelve women passed out at once," an AFSC field worker in northern Mexico told us, "and the newspapers report this as 'mass hysteria.' "

Some of the worst conditions have been documented in South Korea,   16 where the garment and textile industries have helped spark that country's "economic miracle." Workers are packed into poorly lit rooms, where summer temperatures rise above 100 degrees. Textile dust, which can cause permanent lung damage, fills the air. Management may require forced overtime of as much as 48 hours at a stretch, and if that seems to go beyond the limits of human endurance, pep pills and amphetamine injections are thoughtfully provided. In her diary (originally published in a magazine now banned by the South Korean government) Min Chong Suk, 30, a sewing-machine operator, wrote of working from 7 A.M. to 11:30 P.M. in a garment factory: "When [the apprentices] shake the waste threads from the clothes, the whole room fills with dust, and it is hard to breathe. Since we've been working in such dusty air, there have been increasing numbers of people getting tuberculosis, bronchitis, and eye diseases. Since we are women, it makes us so sad when we have pale, unhealthy, wrinkled faces like dried-up spinach. It seems to me that no one knows our blood dissolves into the threads and seams, with sighs and sorrow."

In all the exported industries, the most invidious, inescapable health 17 hazard is stress. Lunch breaks may be barely long enough for a woman to stand in line at the canteen or hawkers' stalls. Visits to the bathroom are treated as privileges. Rotating shifts—the day shift one week, the night shift the next—wreak havoc with sleep patterns. Because inaccuracies or failure to meet production quotas can mean substantial pay losses, the pressures are quickly internalized; stomach ailments and nervous problems are not unusual.

As if poor health and the stress of factory life weren't enough to drive 18 women into early retirement, management actually encourages a high turnover in many industries. "As you know, when seniority rises, wages rise," the management consultant to U.S. multinationals told us. He explained that it's cheaper to train a fresh supply of teenagers than to pay experienced women higher wages. "Older" women, aged 23 or 24, are likely to be laid off and not rehired.

The lucky ones find husbands. The unlucky ones find themselves at the 19 margins of society—as bar girls, "hostesses," or prostitutes.

There has been no international protest about the exploitation of Third 20 World women by multinational corporations—no thundering denunciations from the floor of the United Nations' General Assembly, no angry resolutions from the Conference of the Non-Aligned Countries. Sociologist Robert Snow, who has been tracing the multinationals on their way south and east-ward for years, explained why. "The Third World governments want the multinationals to move in. There's cutthroat competition to attract the corporations."

The governments themselves gain little revenue from this kind of 21 investment—especially since most offer tax holidays and freedom from export duties in order to attract the multinationals in the first place. Nor do the people as a whole benefit, according to a highly placed Third World woman within the U.N. "The multinationals like to say they're contributing to development," she told us, "but they come into our countries for one thing—cheap labor. If the labor stops being so cheap, they can move on. So how can you call that development? It depends on the people being poor and staying poor." But there are important groups that do stand to gain when the multinationals set up shop in their countries: local entrepreneurs who subcontract to the multinationals; "technocrats" who become local management; and government officials who specialize in cutting red tape for an "agent's fee" or an outright bribe.

In the competition for multinational investment, local governments 22 advertise their women shamelessly. An investment brochure issued by the Malaysian government informs multinational executives that: "the manual dexterity of the Oriental female is famous the world over. Her hands are small, and she works fast with extreme care. . . . Who, therefore, could be better qualified by nature and inheritance, to contribute to the efficiency of a bench-assembly production line than the Oriental girl?"

Many "host" governments are willing to back up their advertising with 23 whatever brutality it takes to keep "their girls" just as docile as they look in the brochures. Even the most polite and orderly attempts to organize are likely to bring down overkill doses of police repression:

In Guatemala in 1975 women workers in a North American-owned 24 garment factory drew up a list of complaints that included insults by management, piecework wages that turned out to be less than the legal minimum, no overtime pay, and "threats of death." In response, the American boss called the local authorities to report that he was being harassed by "Communists." When the women reported for work the next day they found the factory surrounded by two fully armed contingents of military police. The "Communist" ringleaders were picked out and fired.

In the Dominican Republic in 1978, workers who attempted to organ- 25 ize at La Romana industrial zone were first fired, then obligingly arrested by the local police. Officials from the AFLCIO have described the zone as a "modern slave-labor camp," where workers who do not meet their production quotas during their regular shift must stay and put in unpaid overtime until they do meet them, and many women workers are routinely strip-searched at the end of the day. During the 1978 organizing attempt, the government sent in national police in full combat gear armed with automatic weapons. Gulf & Western supplements the local law with its own company-sponsored motorcycle club, which specializes in terrorizing suspected union sympathizers.

In Inchon, South Korea, women at the Dong-II Textile Company 26 (which produces fabrics and yarn for export to the United States) had succeeded in gaining leadership in their union in 1972. But in 1978 the government-controlled, male-dominated Federation of Korean Trade Unions sent special "action squads" to destroy the women's union. Armed with steel bars and buckets of human excrement, the goons broke into the union office, smashed the office equipment, and smeared the excrement over the women's bodies and in their hair, ears, eyes, and mouths.

Crudely put (and incidents like this do not inspire verbal delicacy), the 27 relationship between many Third World governments and the multinational corporations is not very different from the relationship between a pimp and his customers. The governments advertise their women, sell them, and keep them in line for the multinational "johns." But there are other parties to the growing international traffic in women—such as the United Nations' Industrial Development Organization (UNIDO), the World Bank, and the United States government itself.

UNIDO has been a major promoter of "free trade zones." These are 28 enclaves within nations that offer multinationals a range of creature comforts, including: freedom from paying taxes and export duties; low-cost water, power, and buildings; exemption from whatever labor laws may apply in the country as a whole; and, in some cases, such security features as barbed-wire, guarded checkpoints, and government-paid police.

Then there is the World Bank, which over the past decade has lent sev- 29 eral billion dollars to finance the roads, airports, power plants, and even the first-class hotels that multinational corporations need in order to set up business in Third World countries.

But the most powerful promoter of exploitative conditions for Third 30 World women workers is the United States government itself. For example, the notoriously repressive Korean textile industry was developed with the help of $400 million in aid from the U.S. State Department. Malaysia became a low-wage haven for the electronics industry thanks to technical assistance financed by AID and to U.S. money (funneled through the Asian Development Bank) to set up free trade zones.

But the most obvious form of United States involvement, according 31 to Lenny Siegel, the director of the Pacific Studies Center, is through "our consistent record of military aid to Third World governments that are capitalist, politically repressive, and are not striving for economic independence."

What does our government have to say for itself? According to AID 32 staffer Emmy Simmons, "we can get hung up in the idea that it's exploitation without really looking at the alternatives for women. These people have to go somewhere."

Anna, for one, has nowhere to go but the maquiladora. Her family left 33 the farm when she was only six, and the land has long since been bought up by a large commercial agribusiness company. After her father left to find work north of the border, money was scarce for years. So when the factory where she now works opened, Anna felt it was "the best thing that had ever happened" to her. As a wage-earner, her status rose compared to her brothers with their on-again, off-again jobs. Partly out of her new sense of confidence she agreed to meet with a few other women one day after work to talk about wages and health conditions. That was the way she became what management called a "labor agitator" when, six months later, 90 percent of the day shift walked out in the company's first south-of-the-border strike.

Women like Anna need their jobs desperately. They know the risks of 34 organizing. Beyond that—if they do succeed in organizing—the company can always move on in search of a still-docile, job-hungry work force. Yet thousands of women in the Third World's industrial work force have chosen to fight for better wages and working conditions.

One particularly dramatic instance took place in South Korea in 1979. 35 Two hundred young women employees of the YH textile-and-wig factory staged a peaceful vigil and fast to protest the company's threatened closing of the plant. On the fifth day of the vigil, more than 1,000 riot police, armed with clubs and steel shields, broke into the building where the women were staying and forcibly dragged them out. Twenty-one-year-old Kim Kyong-suk was killed during the melee. It was her death that touched off widespread rioting throughout Korea that many thought led to the overthrow of President Park Chung Hee.

So far, feminism, first-world style, has barely begun to acknowledge 36 the Third World's new industrial womanpower. Jeb Mays and Kathleen Connell, cofounders of the San Francisco-based Women's Network on Global Corporations, are two women who would like to change that: "There's still this idea of the Third World woman as 'the other'—someone exotic and totally unlike us," Mays and Connell told us. "But now we're talking about women who wear the same styles in clothes, listen to the same music, and may even work for the same corporation. That's an irony the multinationals have created. In a way, they're drawing us together as women."

Saralee Hamilton, an AFSC staff organizer says: "The multinational 37 corporations have deliberately targeted women for exploitation. If feminism is going to mean anything to women all over the world, it's going to have to find new ways to resist corporate power internationally." She envisions a global network of grass-roots women capable of sharing experiences, transmitting information, and—eventually—providing direct support for each other's struggles. It's a long way off; few women anywhere have the money for intercontinental plane flights or even long-distance calls, but at least we are beginning to see the way. "We all have the same hard life," wrote Korean garment worker Min Chong Suk. "We are bound together with one string."

Thinking About the Essay

1. Describe the writers' argumentative purpose in this essay. Is it to convince or persuade—or both? Explain.

2. Who is the intended audience for this essay? What is the level of diction? How are the two connected?

3. Examine the writers' use of illustration in this essay. How do they use these illustrations to support a series of generalizations? Ehrenreich and Fuentes cite various studies and authorities. Identify these instances and explain the cumulative effect.

4. Ehrenreich and Fuentes draw on a number of rhetorical strategies to advance their argument. Explain their use of comparison and cause-and-effect analysis.

5. Evaluate the writers' conclusion. Does it effectively reinforce their argument? Why or why not?

Responding in Writing

6. Ehrenreich and Fuentes wrote this article originally for *Ms.* magazine. Why would the essay appeal to the *Ms.* audience? What elements would also appeal to a general audience? Write a brief essay that answers these questions, providing specific examples from the text.

7. Write a personal essay in which you describe a job that you had (or have) in which you were exploited. Provide sufficient illustrations to support your thesis.

8. The writers imply that workforce women around the world are exploited more than men. Write an essay in which you agree or disagree with their claim.

Networking

9. Form small groups, and read the drafts of each other's essays. After general comments about how to improve the first draft, concentrate on ways to provide even greater illustration to support each writer's thesis or claim.

10. With another class member, do a web search for new examples of the global exploitation of working women. Limit your focus to one of the countries mentioned by Ehrenreich and Fuentes. Think about whether the conditions that the two writers exposed more than twenty years ago are better or worse today. Share your conclusions with the rest of the class.

Culture or Conflict?
Images of Globalization

This portfolio of images from around the world presents a visual paradox: Is global culture a happy consumer wonderland where the fries are always crisp and the music always loud? Or has globalization simply packaged and marketed a bland, simplified version of the basics of culture, such as food and fashion, to an increasingly busy and distracted global population?

For millennia, trade between nation-states has introduced and shared aspects of culture, but the electronic telecommunication that is available now between countries has enabled instant blending of customs and has caused regional cultures and languages to fight to keep their own traditions vibrant. French-speaking Quebecois agitate for independence from the rest of English-speaking Canada. The ecotourism movement struggles to maintain the integrity of fragile cultures and environments even as it imports Western tourists with their cash, cameras, and expectations for plumbing. The slow-food movement, which originated in Italy, calls on communities to nurture biodiversity and sustainable agriculture through renewed appreciation of their culinary heritage.

As you examine the following images, be especially attentive to the irony that lies in the details. *Irony* is a quality of being unexpected, incongruous, or out of place; juxtapositions that make something as seemingly common as a bottle of soda seem suddenly, entirely strange. That strangeness leads to a realization that there's more to the image than meets the eye; the nomad's tent topped by a satellite dish or the camel carrying an expensive mountain bicycle can be perceived either as a widening of opportunities and experiences or a flattening out of cultural vitality.

Many readings in this book describe the clashing of cultures and civilizations. Can consumer culture, based on these images, foster cooperation rather than clashes? After all, in a 1996 *New York Times* op-ed piece, foreign correspondent Thomas Friedman argued that no two countries that both have a McDonald's have ever fought a war against each other. What do you think?

Coca-Cola in Egypt. An Egyptian girl drinks from a bottle of Coca-Cola in a shop in downtown Cairo, Egypt. After an Internet rumor that the Coca-Cola logo, if looked at upside-down or in a mirror, reads "No Mohammed, No Mecca" in Arabic, a top religious authority in Egypt studied the label and finally declared that "there is no defamation to the religion of Islam from near or far."

Considering the Image

1. Why would Coca-Cola be a target for such a rumor? Can you think of other examples in which consumer goods were boycotted as the symbols of a larger culture, value system, or belief?

2. What, to your eye, is particularly revealing or compelling about this image? What does the photographer want you to see? Does this image support or contradict images that you see in the media about women in the Middle East?

Big Bird in Shanghai. More than 90 percent of the households in the twelve major cities of the People's Republic of China have television sets. One of the favorite programs, reaching 120 million Chinese viewers, is *Sesame Street.* Here, Big Bird, known as *Zhima Jie,* appears on Shanghai television.

Considering the Image

1. How did the photographer capture a specific mood in this picture? What is the expression on the children's faces? Why does Big Bird loom over them? Do you think that there are universal values that make *Sesame Street* popular not just in China but throughout the world? Justify and explain your response.

2. Do you think the photographer wants to make a statement about "cultural imperialism" or the impact of globalization on national cultures, or simply capture a specific moment and scene? Explain your response. Why might globalization, which involves in part the transnational movement of media across cultures, be a force for democracy in China and elsewhere?

Ecotourists.   Tourists photograph a Huli Wigman, a representative of the Huli people of Papua New Guinea. The Huli are an indigenous people whose subsistence-based way of life has changed little for centuries. They have a particular reverence for birds; the Wigmen (certain men in this intricate clan-based society) wear elaborate headdresses woven of human hair and decorated with flowers and feathers to perform ritual dances that suggest the behavior of local birds.

Considering the Image

1. This photograph was used to illustrate a report on the rights and responsibilities of ecotourists and the groups that sponsor and profit from ecotourism. Why would that group, which advocates for the well-being of indigenous peoples and the preservation of endangered environments, consider this photograph a compelling example of the need for rights to be respected and responsibilities to be upheld?

2. Whose perspective do you assume as you look at this photograph: the native person's, the tourists', or the photographer's taking in the entire scene?

Sophisticated Ladies. Nakshatra Reddy is a biochemist who is married to a prosperous businessman in Mumbai (formerly Bombay). Her daughter, Meghana, dressed in a PVC suit of her own design, is a model and former host on a local music channel.

Considering the Image

1. How does the photographer stage or set up this scene? How does the photographer emphasize certain cultural contrasts between mother and daughter, and what is the purpose? Why is it important for viewers to know that mother and daughter represent a wealthy Indian family rather than a middle class or poor one?

2. The daughter in this family represents a familiar Western type. How would you describe her? What are her sources of imitation? Do you think that the daughter has succumbed to the lure of Western popular culture, or might she be making a statement about her global identity? Explain your response.

Inclusion Movement. In 2001, immigrants from several countries in Europe rallied in Valencia, Spain, to protest a new Spanish law that threatened to expel tens of thousands of undocumented aliens. The banner in the foreground reads, "We are human beings, we have rights."

Considering the Image

1. From what vantage point did the photographer shoot this image? What is the effect or dominant impression? If you know Spanish, what other inscriptions on placards can you translate? Does the photographer want to make a statement or simply capture a moment in time? How do you know?

2. The essays in Chapter 2 deal with the impact of immigration on the United States. Were you surprised to discover from this photograph that nations in Europe contend today with similar issues? Why would Spain want to expel undocumented aliens? Conduct research with two other class members to find out more about the impact of recent immigration on Spain, France, Italy, Germany, or Great Britain.

Separatist Movement.   Recent years have seen several referenda in Quebec Province on the issue of sovereignty or separation from the rest of Canada. Sentiment in Quebec has been divided on the issue, but all efforts to create a separate state have failed. In this photo, taken during the 1995 referendum, Quebec's separatist party rallies on election eve.

Considering the Image

1. How does this photo capture the emotions provoked in Canadians over the issue of separation for Quebec? How does the photographer capture these emotions? What details stand out?

2. As late as 1950, there were about 100 nations worldwide. Today, at the beginning of the twenty-first century, there are more than 200. What new countries can you name? Why have they come into existence? Do you think that their creation has been beneficial to world peace or harmful? Justify your response.

Modern Conveniences. The *ger* is the traditional, portable home of the nomadic people of Mongolia. A cone-shaped structure of felt stretched over a timber frame, with an opening in the top or a pipe to vent smoke from the stove, the *ger* is a symbol both of freedom and of hospitality. Many residents of Mongolia's capital, Ulaan Baatar, still live in traditional *gers,* and in keeping with their nomadic routes, any visitor is warmly greeted and offered shelter and food, as well as many modern conveniences. Here, a *ger* is outfitted with a satellite dish.

Considering the Image

1. This photo suggests not so much a clash of cultures as a fusion of ancient ways and modern technology. Why might a nomadic culture, like that of rural Mongolia, value the latest in communications technology?

2. Many writers in Chapter 9 define the so-called electronic gap or digital divide as one of the great challenges—and opportunities—for the new century. What does this image suggest to you about the digital divide? Granted, we don't know from this photograph if that satellite dish is being used to watch CNN or MTV; should that even matter? Why, or why not?

CHAPTER 5

The Challenge of Globalization: What Are the Consequences?

Q uick! Where was your cell phone manufactured? Where was the clothing you are wearing today made—and how much do you think the workers were paid to produce it? What type of food do you plan to eat for lunch or dinner: pizza, fried rice, tacos, a Big Mac? The ordinary features of our daily lives capture the forces of globalization that characterize our new century and our changed world. *New York Times* columnist Thomas Friedman, who writes persuasively on the subject—and who has an essay in this chapter as well as a later one—terms globalization the "super-story," the one all-embracing subject that dominates national and transnational developments today. As we see from the essays in this chapter, the concept of globalization already influences many major trends in economic, social, cultural, and political life in the twenty-first century.

It could be argued, of course, that globalization is nothing new: after all, Greece "globalized" much of the known world as far as India. Then Rome created its global dominion from England to Persia. More recently, for almost three centuries—from the seventeenth to the twentieth—England ruled the waves and a majority of the world's nations. And from the twentieth century to the present, the United States has assumed the mantle of the world's major globalizing power. (Some critics claim that globalization might simply be a mask for "Americanization.") With anti-globalization demonstrations and riots now commonplace in the United States, Europe, and the Third World, we have to acknowledge that there *is* something about contemporary globalization that prompts debate and demands critical analysis. Ralph Nader states the case against globalization boldly: "The essence of glob-alization is a subordination of human rights, of labor rights, consumer

161

A multiethnic group of protesters representing a wide range of causes marches in Richmond, California, to protest globalization.

Thinking About the Image

1. How many different ideas or causes do you see represented in this photograph? What does that suggest about this particular protest? About the anti-globalization movement in general?

2. What is the photographer's perspective on this event? Is anyone looking directly at the lens? Would your response to the photograph—or the story it tells—be different if there was a focus on just one or two people? If the photographer was further away and captured a larger crowd in the frame?

3. What other kinds of images do you associate with street protests? Based on the fact that this one photograph was chosen to represent an entire day of protest, what can you infer about the tone of the protest and the response of the community?

4. Street protest is a kind of rhetoric, in that the demonstrators have a purpose and an audience. How clear is the purpose of these protesters? Who is their audience? Do you think such protests will make any difference to people like the child on p. 152?

rights, environmental rights, democracy rights, to the imperatives of global trade and investment." But is Nader correct? Robert Rubin, the very able secretary of the treasury during the Clinton administration and highly respected throughout the world financial community, objects: "I think a healthy economy is the best environment in which to pursue human rights." The oppositional viewpoints of Nader and Rubin suggest that discussion of globalization often produces diverse opinions, and that consequently we must think carefully and openly about the globalizing trends molding our lives today.

One trend that is clear today, as the twenty-first century begins, is that capitalism has triumphed over all its main rivals: communism, fascism, and socialism. Thus capitalism is the dominant if not the sole model of development for the nations of the world. Where capitalism collides with alternative visions of development—for example, Islamic economics in Iran—the result proves disastrous. The question that many people—especially young people on college and university campuses around the world—ask is whether or not capitalism can meaningfully address the numerous questions of social justice raised by globalization. If, for example, the environmental policy of the United States aids the interests of its energy companies, can this policy benefit others in the developing world? Or does the policy exclude almost everyone in a developing nation? Such questions can be asked about virtually every key issue raised by Ralph Nader and others who are skeptical of globalization as an overpowering economic force around the world.

The writers in this chapter and the next offer a variety of perspectives and critical insights into the nature and effects of globalization trends. Because of developments in information technology, peoples in the most distant parts of the world now are as close to us as someone in the dorm room next door—and perhaps more compelling. We certainly see poverty, famine, the degradation of the environment, and civil wars close up. But is all this suffering the result of predatory multinational corporations and runaway capitalism? After all, both globalization *and* civil society are increasing worldwide, and the connections between the two require subtle critical analysis. The writers in this chapter bring such critical ability to their treatment of the social implications of current globalization trends.

Prologue: The Super-Story

THOMAS L. FRIEDMAN

A noted author, journalist, and television commentator, and currently an op-ed contributor to the *New York Times,* Thomas L. Friedman writes and speaks knowledgeably about contemporary trends in politics and global development. He was born in Minneapolis, Minnesota, in 1953, and was educated at Brandeis University

(B.A., 1975) and St. Anthony's College (M.A., 1978). Friedman covered the Middle East for the *New York Times* for ten years, and for five years he was bureau chief in Beirut, writing about both the Lebanese civil war and the Israel-Palestine conflict. He recorded these experiences in *From Beirut to Jerusalem* (1989), for which he won the National Book Award for nonfiction. A strong proponent of American intervention to solve seemingly intractable problems like the Arab-Israeli conflict, Friedman writes at the end of *From Beirut to Jerusalem,* "Only a real friend tells you the truth about yourself. An American friend has to help jar these people out of their fantasies by constantly holding up before their eyes the mirror of reality." In 2002, Friedman received the Pulitzer Prize for commentary for his reports on terrorism for the *New York Times.* His other books include *The Lexus and the Olive Tree: Understanding Globalization* (2000) and a collection of articles and essays, *Longitudes and Attitudes: Exploring the World After September 11* (2002), in which the following selection serves as the book's prologue.

Before Reading

How would you define the word *globalization*? Is it simply a trend in which nations interrelate economically, or are other forces involved? Do you think that globalization is good or bad? Justify your response.

I am a big believer in the idea of the super-story, the notion that we all   1
carry around with us a big lens, a big framework, through which we look at the world, order events, and decide what is important and what is not. The events of 9/11 did not happen in a vacuum. They happened in the context of a new international system—a system that cannot explain everything but *can* explain and connect more things in more places on more days than anything else. That new international system is called globalization. It came together in the late 1980s and replaced the previous international system, the cold war system, which had reigned since the end of World War II. This new system is the lens, the super-story, through which I viewed the events of 9/11.

I define globalization as the inexorable integration of markets, trans-   2
portation systems, and communication systems to a degree never witnessed before—in a way that is enabling corporations, countries, and individuals to reach around the world farther, faster, deeper, and cheaper than ever before, and in a way that is enabling the world to reach into cor-

porations, countries, and individuals farther, faster, deeper, and cheaper than ever before.

Several important features of this globalization system differ from those 3
of the cold war system in ways that are quite relevant for understanding the events of 9/11. I examined them in detail in my previous book, *The Lexus and the Olive Tree,* and want to simply highlight them here.

The cold war system was characterized by one overarching feature— 4
and that was *division.* That world was a divided-up, chopped-up place, and whether you were a country or a company, your threats and opportunities in the cold war system tended to grow out of who you were divided from. Appropriately, this cold war system was symbolized by a single word— *wall,* the Berlin Wall.

The globalization system is different. It also has one overarching 5
feature—and that is *integration.* The world has become an increasingly interwoven place, and today, whether you are a company or a country, your threats and opportunities increasingly derive from who you are connected to. This globalization system is also characterized by a single word—*web,* the World Wide Web. So in the broadest sense we have gone from an international system built around division and walls to a system increasingly built around integration and webs. In the cold war we reached for the hotline, which was a symbol that we were all divided but at least two people were in charge—the leaders of the United States and the Soviet Union. In the globalization system we reach for the Internet, which is a symbol that we are all connected and nobody is quite in charge.

Everyone in the world is directly or indirectly affected by this new sys- 6
tem, but not everyone benefits from it, not by a long shot, which is why the more it becomes diffused, the more it also produces a backlash by people who feel overwhelmed by it, homogenized by it, or unable to keep pace with its demands.

The other key difference between the cold war system and the global- 7
ization system is how power is structured within them. The cold war system was built primarily around nation-states. You acted on the world in that system through your state. The cold war was a drama of states confronting states, balancing states, and aligning with states. And, as a system, the cold war was balanced at the center by two superstates, two superpowers: the United States and the Soviet Union.

The globalization system, by contrast, is built around three balances, 8
which overlap and affect one another. The first is the traditional balance of power between nation-states. In the globalization system, the United States is now the sole and dominant superpower and all other nations are subordinate to it to one degree or another. The shifting balance of power between

the United States and other states, or simply between other states, still very much matters for the stability of this system. And it can still explain a lot of the news you read on the front page of the paper, whether it is the news of China balancing Russia, Iran balancing Iraq, or India confronting Pakistan.

The second important power balance in the globalization system is   9
between nation-states and global markets. These global markets are made up of millions of investors moving money around the world with the click of a mouse. I call them the Electronic Herd, and this herd gathers in key global financial centers—such as Wall Street, Hong Kong, London, and Frankfurt—which I call the Supermarkets. The attitudes and actions of the Electronic Herd and the Supermarkets can have a huge impact on nation-states today, even to the point of triggering the downfall of governments. Who ousted Suharto in Indonesia in 1998? It wasn't another state, it was the Supermarkets, by withdrawing their support for, and confidence in, the Indonesian economy. You also will not understand the front page of the newspaper today unless you bring the Supermarkets into your analysis. Because the United States can destroy you by dropping bombs, but the Supermarkets can destroy you by downgrading your bonds. In other words, the United States is the dominant player in maintaining the globalization game board, but it is hardly alone in influencing the moves on that game board.

The third balance that you have to pay attention to—the one that is really the newest of all and the most relevant to the events of 9/11—is the   10
balance between individuals and nation-states. Because globalization has brought down many of the walls that limited the movement and reach of people, and because it has simultaneously wired the world into networks, it gives more power to *individuals* to influence both markets and nation-states than at any other time in history. Whether by enabling people to use the Internet to communicate instantly at almost no cost over vast distances, or by enabling them to use the Web to transfer money or obtain weapons designs that normally would have been controlled by states, or by enabling them to go into a hardware store now and buy a five-hundred-dollar global positioning device, connected to a satellite, that can direct a hijacked airplane—globalization can be an incredible force-multiplier for individuals. Individuals can increasingly act on the world stage directly, unmediated by a state.

So you have today not only a superpower, not only Supermarkets, but   11
also what I call "super-empowered individuals." Some of these super-empowered individuals are quite angry, some of them quite wonderful—but all of them are now able to act much more directly and much more powerfully on the world stage.

Osama bin Laden declared war on the United States in the late 1990s. 12
After he organized the bombing of two American embassies in Africa, the
U.S. Air Force retaliated with a cruise missile attack on his bases in
Afghanistan as though he were another nation-state. Think about that: on
one day in 1998, the United States fired 75 cruise missiles at bin Laden. The
United States fired 75 cruise missiles, at $1 million apiece, at a person! That
was the first battle in history between a superpower and a super-
empowered angry man. September 11 was just the second such battle.

Jody Williams won the Nobel Peace Prize in 1997 for helping to build 13
an international coalition to bring about a treaty outlawing land mines. Although nearly 120 governments endorsed the treaty, it was opposed by
Russia, China, and the United States. When Jody Williams was asked,
"How did you do that? How did you organize one thousand different citizens' groups and nongovernmental organizations on five continents to
forge a treaty that was opposed by the major powers?" she had a very brief
answer: "E-mail." Jody Williams used e-mail and the networked world to
super-empower herself.

Nation-states, and the American superpower in particular, are still 14
hugely important today, but so too now are Supermarkets and super-
empowered individuals. You will never understand the globalization system, or the front page of the morning paper—or 9/11—unless you see each
as a complex interaction between all three of these actors: states bumping
up against states, states bumping up against Supermarkets, and Supermarkets and states bumping up against super-empowered individuals—many
of whom, unfortunately, are super-empowered angry men.

Thinking About the Essay

1. Friedman constructs this essay and entitles it a "prologue." What is the
   purpose of a prologue? What subject matter does the writer provide in his
   prologue?

2. The writer is not afraid to inject the personal "I" into his analysis—a strategy that many composition teachers will warn you against. Why does Friedman start with his personal voice? Why can he get away with it? What does
   the personal voice contribute to the effect of the essay?

3. In addition to his personal voice, what other stylistic features make Friedman's essay, despite its complicated subject matter, accessible to ordinary
   readers? How does he establish a colloquial style?

4. This essay offers a series of definitions, comparisons, and classifications
   as structuring devices. Locate instances of these three rhetorical strategies and explain how they complement each other.

5. Friedman uses September 11 as a touchstone for his essay. Why does he do this? What is the effect?

Responding in Writing

6. Write a 250-word summary of Friedman's essay, capturing all the important topics that he presents.

7. Take one major point that Friedman makes in this essay and write a paper on it. For example, you might want to discuss why September 11 represents a key transition point in our understanding of globalization. Or you might focus on the concept of the Supermarket or the Electronic Herd.

8. Think about the world today, and write your own "super-story" in which you define and classify its primary features.

Networking

9. Divide into two roughly equal groups, and conduct a debate on whether or not globalization is a good or bad phenomenon. Use Friedman's essay as a reference point. Your instructor should serve as the moderator for this debate.

10. Join the Electronic Herd and develop a list of links to sites that deal with globalization. Contribute your list to the others generated by class members in order to create a superlist for possible future use.

The Global Village Finally Arrives

PICO IYER

Pico Iyer was born in 1957, in Oxford, England, to Indian parents, both of them university professors. Educated at Oxford University and Harvard University, Iyer has been a writer for *Time* magazine since 1982 and a prolific author of travel books, essays, and fiction. His first full-length travel book is the acclaimed *Video Night in Kathmandu: And Other Reports from the Not-so-Far East* (1988). He followed the success of this book with *The Lady and the Monk: Four Seasons in Kyoto* (1991), *Tropical Classical: Essays from Several Directions* (1997), and *The Global Soul: Jet Lag, Shopping Malls, and the Search for Home* (2000), among others. Iyer also has published a novel, *Cuba and the Night* (1995). Iyer calls writing "an intimate letter to a stranger." In this essay, published in *Time* Magazine on December 2, 1993, he invites us to view his world in southern California—and the world in general—in polyglot terms.

Before Reading

Look around you or think about your college—its students, courses, clubs, cultural programs, and so forth. Would you say that your campus reflects what Iyer terms a "diversified world"? Why or why not?

This is the typical day of a relatively typical soul in today's diversified 1 world. I wake up to the sound of my Japanese clock radio, put on a T shirt sent me by an uncle in Nigeria and walk out into the street, past German cars, to my office. Around me are English-language students from Korea, Switzerland and Argentina—all on this Spanish-named road in this Mediterranean-style town. On TV, I find, the news is in Mandarin; today's baseball game is being broadcast in Korean. For lunch I can walk to a sushi bar, a tandoori palace, a Thai cafe or the newest burrito joint (run by an old Japanese lady). Who am I, I sometimes wonder, the son of Indian parents and a British citizen who spends much of his time in Japan (and is therefore—what else?—an American permanent resident)? And where am I?

I am, as it happens, in Southern California, in a quiet, relatively unin- 2 ternational town, but I could as easily be in Vancouver or Sydney or London or Hong Kong. All the world's a rainbow coalition, more and more; the whole planet, you might say, is going global. When I fly to Toronto, or Paris, or Singapore, I disembark in a world as hyphenated as the one I left. More and more of the globe looks like America, but an America that is itself looking more and more like the rest of the globe. Los Angeles famously teaches 82 different languages in its schools. In this respect, the city seems only to bear out the old adage that what is in California today is in America tomorrow, and next week around the globe.

In ways that were hardly conceivable even a generation ago, the new 3 world order is a version of the New World writ large: a wide-open frontier of polyglot terms and postnational trends. A common multiculturalism links us all—call it Planet Hollywood, Planet Reebok or the United Colors of Benetton. Taxi and hotel and disco are universal terms now, but so too are karaoke and yoga and pizza. For the gourmet alone, there is tiramisu at the Burger King in Kyoto, echt angel-hair pasta in Saigon and enchiladas on every menu in Nepal.

But deeper than mere goods, it is souls that are mingling. In Brussels, a 4 center of the new "unified Europe," 1 new baby in every 4 is Arab. Whole parts of the Paraguayan capital of Asunción are largely Korean. And when the prostitutes of Melbourne distributed some pro-condom pamphlets, one of the languages they used was Macedonian. Even Japan, which prides itself on its centuries-old socially engineered uniculture, swarms with Iranian illegals, Western executives, Pakistani laborers and Filipina hostesses.

The global village is defined, as we know, by an international youth cul- 5
ture that takes its cues from American pop culture. Kids in Perth and
Prague and New Delhi are all tuning in to *Santa Barbara* on TV, and wrig-
gling into 501 jeans, while singing along to Madonna's latest in English.
CNN (which has grown 70-fold in 13 years) now reaches more than 140
countries; an American football championship pits London against
Barcelona. As fast as the world comes to America, America goes round the
world—but it is an America that is itself multi-tongued and many hued, an
America of Amy Tan and Janet Jackson and movies with dialogue in
Lakota.

For far more than goods and artifacts, the one great influence being 6
broadcast around the world in greater numbers and at greater speed than
ever before is people. What were once clear divisions are now tangles of
crossed lines: there are 40,000 "Canadians" resident in Hong Kong, many
of whose first language is Cantonese. And with people come customs:
while new immigrants from Taiwan and Vietnam and India—some of the
so-called Asian Calvinists—import all-American values of hard work and
family closeness and entrepreneurial energy to America, America is sending its values of upward mobility and individualism and melting-pot hope-
fulness to Taipei and Saigon and Bombay.

Values, in fact, travel at the speed of fax; by now, almost half the 7
world's Mormons live outside the U.S. A diversity of one culture quickly
becomes a diversity of many: the "typical American" who goes to Japan
today may be a third-generation Japanese American, or the son of a
Japanese woman married to a California serviceman, or the offspring of
a Salvadoran father and an Italian mother from San Francisco. When he
goes out with a Japanese woman, more than two cultures are brought
into play.

None of this, of course, is new: Chinese silks were all the rage in Rome 8
centuries ago, and Alexandria before the time of Christ was a paradigm of
the modern universal city. Not even American eclecticism is new: many a
small town has long known Chinese restaurants, Indian doctors and
Lebanese grocers. But now all these cultures are crossing at the speed of
light. And the rising diversity of the planet is something more than mere
cosmopolitanism: it is a fundamental recoloring of the very complexion of
societies. Cities like Paris, or Hong Kong, have always had a soigné, international air and served as magnets for exiles and émigrés, but now smaller
places are multinational too. Marseilles speaks French with a distinctly
North African twang. Islamic fundamentalism has one of its strongholds in
Bradford, England. It is the sleepy coastal towns of Queensland, Australia,
that print their menus in Japanese.

The dangers this internationalism presents are evident: not for nothing 9 did the Tower of Babel collapse. As national borders fall, tribal alliances, and new manmade divisions, rise up, and the world learns every day terrible new meanings of the word Balkanization. And while some places are wired for international transmission, others (think of Iran or North Korea or Burma) remain as isolated as ever, widening the gap between the haves and the have-nots, or what Alvin Toffler has called the "fast" and the "slow" worlds. Tokyo has more telephones than the whole continent of Africa.

Nonetheless, whether we like it or not, the "transnational" future is 10 upon us: as Kenichi Ohmae, the international economist, suggests with his talk of a "borderless economy," capitalism's allegiances are to products, not places. "Capital is now global," Robert Reich, the Secretary of Labor, has said, pointing out that when an Iowan buys a Pontiac from General Motors, 60% of his money goes to South Korea, Japan, West Germany, Taiwan, Singapore, Britain and Barbados. Culturally we are being reformed daily by the cadences of world music and world fiction: where the great Canadian writers of an older generation had names like Frye and Davies and Laurence, now they are called Ondaatje and Mistry and Skvorecky.

As space shrinks, moreover, time accelerates. This hip-hop mishmash is 11 spreading overnight. When my parents were in college, there were all of seven foreigners living in Tibet, a country the size of Western Europe, and in its entire history the country had seen fewer than 2,000 Westerners. Now a Danish student in Lhasa is scarcely more surprising than a Tibetan in Copenhagen. Already a city like Miami is beyond the wildest dreams of 1968; how much more so will its face in 2018 defy our predictions of today?

It would be easy, seeing all this, to say that the world is moving toward 12 the Raza Cosmica (Cosmic Race), predicted by the Mexican thinker José Vasconcelos in the '20s—a glorious blend of mongrels and mestizos. It may be more relevant to suppose that more and more of the world may come to resemble Hong Kong, a stateless special economic zone full of expats and exiles linked by the lingua franca of English and the global marketplace. Some urbanists already see the world as a grid of 30 or so highly advanced city-regions, or technopoles, all plugged into the same international circuit.

The world will not become America. Anyone who has been to a base- 13 ball game in Osaka, or a Pizza Hut in Moscow, knows instantly that she is not in Kansas. But America may still, if only symbolically, be a model for the world. E Pluribus Unum, after all, is on the dollar bill. As Federico Mayor Zaragoza, the director-general of UNESCO, has said, "America's main role in the new world order is not as a military superpower, but as a multicultural superpower."

The traditional metaphor for this is that of a mosaic. But Richard Rod-   14
riguez, the Mexican-American essayist who is a psalmist for our new hybrid forms, points out that the interaction is more fluid than that, more human, subject to daily revision. "I am Chinese," he says, "because I live in San Francisco, a Chinese city. I became Irish in America. I became Portuguese in America." And even as he announces this new truth, Portuguese women are becoming American, and Irishmen are becoming Portuguese, and Sydney (or is it Toronto?) is thinking to compare itself with the "Chinese city" we know as San Francisco.

Thinking About the Essay

1. How does Iyer's introductory paragraph set the stage for the rest of the essay? What is the setting? Why does he use a personal voice? What is his reason for writing? Is his thesis stated or implied? Explain.

2. Iyer presents us with an interesting example of an illustrative essay. Draw up a list of all the examples, references, authorities, and allusions that he presents. Why—from start to finish and in every paragraph—does he offer so many illustrations? What is the overall effect?

3. Does the writer have an argument or claim that he develops in this essay, or does he merely want to make a major point? Explain your response.

4. What is the tone of this essay? Put differently, do you think that Iyer embraces his new "transnational" world, likes it, dislikes it, is worried about it, or what? Locate passages that confirm your response.

5. How does Iyer use definitions in constructing his analysis of the global village? Cite examples of his approach.

Responding in Writing

6. Narrate—as Iyer does at the start of his essay—a typical day in your life. Turn this day into an exploration of how you fit into the "Global Village." Provide examples throughout the essay to support your thesis.

7. "The world," writes Iyer, "will not become America" (paragraph 13). Write an essay arguing for or against his view.

8. Write an extended definition of *globalization*. Refer to Iyer's essay for ideas as you develop this paper.

Networking

9. Iyer's professional address is Time Magazine, 1271 Avenue of the Americas, Rockefeller Center, New York, NY 10021. Discuss his essay with class

members, and then write a collective letter telling him of the group's discussion. Ask about his interest in travel and globalization, and pose one or two questions for his response.

10. As a travel writer, Iyer has visited some of the more remote and exotic parts of the planet. What exotic or romantic part of the world interests you? Go online and find information about this place. Plan travel arrangements and a budget. Prepare an outline or itinerary for a two-week trip to your dream destination.

The Noble Feat of Nike

JOHAN NORBERG

> Johan Norberg contributed this article to London's *The Spectator* in June 2003. In the essay, he takes issue with those who think that globalization is the invention of "ruthless international capitalists." In arguing his case, Norberg centers his discussion on one symbol of globalization—Nike—suggesting that we simply have to look at our "feet" to understand Nike's "feat" in advancing a benign form of globalization. Norberg is the author of *In Defense of Global Capitalism*, and writer and presenter of the recent documentary *Globalization Is Good*.

Before Reading

Check your sneakers. Where were they made? What do you think the workers earned to manufacture them? Do you think they were exploited? Explain your response.

Nike. It means victory. It also means a type of expensive gym shoe. In   1
the minds of the anti-globalisation movement, it stands for both at once. Nike stands for the victory of a Western footwear company over the poor and dispossessed. Spongy, smelly, hungered after by kids across the world, Nike is the symbol of the unacceptable triumph of global capital.

A Nike is a shoe that simultaneously kicks people out of jobs in the   2
West, and tramples on the poor in the Third World. Sold for 100 times more than the wages of the peons who make them, Nike shoes are hate-objects more potent, in the eyes of the protesters at this week's G8 riots, than McDonald's hamburgers. If you want to be trendy these days, you don't wear Nikes; you boycott them.

So I was interested to hear someone not only praising Nike sweatshops,   3
but also claiming that Nike is an example of a good and responsible business. That someone was the ruling Communist party of Vietnam.

Today Nike has almost four times more workers in Vietnam than in the   4
United States. I travelled to Ho Chi Minh to examine the effects of multinational corporations on poor countries. Nike being the most notorious
multinational villain, and Vietnam being a dictatorship with a documented
lack of free speech, the operation is supposed to be a classic of conscience-
free capitalist oppression.

In truth the work does look tough, and the conditions grim, if we com-   5
pare Vietnamese factories with what we have back home. But that's not the
comparison these workers make. They compare the work at Nike with the
way they lived before, or the way their parents or neighbours still work.
And the facts are revealing. The average pay at a Nike factory close to Ho
Chi Minh is $54 a month, almost three times the minimum wage for a
state-owned enterprise.

Ten years ago, when Nike was established in Vietnam, the workers had   6
to walk to the factories, often for many miles. After three years on Nike
wages, they could afford bicycles. Another three years later, they could afford scooters, so they all take the scooters to work (and if you go there, beware; they haven't really decided on which side of the road to drive). Today,
the first workers can afford to buy a car.

But when I talk to a young Vietnamese woman, Tsi-Chi, at the factory,   7
it is not the wages she is most happy about. Sure, she makes five times more
than she did, she earns more than her husband, and she can now afford to
build an extension to her house. But the most important thing, she says, is
that she doesn't have to work outdoors on a farm any more. For me, a
Swede with only three months of summer, this sounds bizarre. Surely working conditions under the blue sky must be superior to those in a sweatshop?
But then I am naively Eurocentric. Farming means 10 to 14 hours a day in
the burning sun or the intensive rain, in rice fields with water up to your
ankles and insects in your face. Even a Swede would prefer working nine
to five in a clean, air-conditioned factory.

Furthermore, the Nike job comes with a regular wage, with free or sub-   8
sidised meals, free medical services and training and education. The most
persistent demand Nike hears from the workers is for an expansion of the
factories so that their relatives can be offered a job as well.

These facts make Nike sound more like Santa Claus than Scrooge. But   9
corporations such as Nike don't bring these benefits and wages because
they are generous. It is not altruism that is at work here; it is globalisation.
With their investments in poor countries, multinationals bring new machinery, better technology, new management skills and production ideas, a
larger market and the education of their workers. That is exactly what

raises productivity. And if you increase productivity—the amount a worker can produce—you can also increase his wage.

Nike is not the accidental good guy. On average, multinationals in the least developed countries pay twice as much as domestic companies in the same line of business. If you get to work for an American multinational in a low-income country, you get eight times the average income. If this is exploitation, then the problem in our world is that the poor countries aren't sufficiently exploited.

The effect on local business is profound: "Before I visit some foreign factory, especially like Nike, we have a question. Why do the foreign factories here work well and produce much more?" That was what Mr. Kiet, the owner of a local shoe factory who visited Nike to learn how he could be just as successful at attracting workers, told me: "And I recognise that productivity does not only come from machinery but also from satisfaction of the worker. So for the future factory we should concentrate on our working conditions."

If I was an antiglobalist, I would stop complaining about Nike's bad wages. If there is a problem, it is that the wages are too high, so that they are almost luring doctors and teachers away from their important jobs.

But—happily—I don't think even that is a realistic threat. With growing productivity it will also be possible to invest in education and healthcare for Vietnam. Since 1990, when the Vietnamese communists began to liberalise the economy, exports of coffee, rice, clothes and footwear have surged, the economy has doubled, and poverty has been halved. Nike and Coca-Cola triumphed where American bombs failed. They have made Vietnam capitalist.

I asked the young Nike worker Tsi-Chi what her hopes were for her son's future. A generation ago, she would have had to put him to work on the farm from an early age. But Tsi-Chi told me she wants to give him a good education, so that he can become a doctor. That's one of the most impressive developments since Vietnam's economy was opened up. In ten years 2.2 million children have gone from child labour to education. It would be extremely interesting to hear an antiglobalist explain to Tsi-Chi why it is important for Westerners to boycott Nike, so that she loses her job, and has to go back into farming, and has to send her son to work.

The European Left used to listen to the Vietnamese communists when they brought only misery and starvation to their population. Shouldn't they listen to the Vietnamese now, when they have found a way to improve people's lives? The party officials have been convinced by Nike that ruthless multinational capitalists are better than the state at providing workers with high wages and a good and healthy workplace. How long will it take for our own anticapitalists to learn that lesson?

Thinking About the Essay

1. Examine the writer's introduction. Why is it distinctive? How does Norberg "hook" us and also set the terms of his argument? Why is Nike an especially potent symbol around which to organize an essay on globalization?

2. Explain the writer's claim and how he defends it. Identify those instances in which he deals with the opposition. How effective do you think his argument is? Justify your answer.

3. What is the writer's tone in this essay? Why is the tone especially effective in conveying the substance of Norberg's argument?

4. Analyze the writer's style and how it contributes to his argument. Identify specific stylistic elements that you consider especially effective.

5. To a large extent, the writer bases his argument on direct observation. How can you tell that he is open-minded and truthful in the presentation of facts? What is the role of a newspaper or journal in claiming responsibility for the accuracy of this information?

Responding in Writing

6. Select a symbol of globalization and write an essay about it. You may use Nike if you wish, or Coca-Cola, McDonald's, or any other company that has a global reach.

7. Write a rebuttal to Norberg's essay. Try to answer him point by point.

8. Why have clothing manufacturing and other forms of manufacturing fled from the United States and other industrialized nations to less developed parts of the world? Write a causal analysis of this trend, being certain to state a thesis or present a claim that illustrates your viewpoint on the issue.

Networking

9. In groups of four, examine your clothes. List the countries where they were manufactured. Share the list with the class, drawing a global map of the countries where the various items were produced.

10. Check various Internet sites for information on Nike and its role in globalization. On the basis of your findings, determine whether or not this company is sensitive to globalization issues. Participate in a class discussion of this topic.

Fear Not Globalization

JOSEPH S. NYE JR.

> Joseph Samuel Nye Jr. was born in South Orange, New Jersey, in 1937; his father was a stockbroker and his mother an art gallery owner. He received undergraduate degrees from Princeton University (1958) and Oxford University (1960), and a Ph.D. degree from Harvard University (1964) in political science. Currently he is dean of Harvard's Kennedy School of Government. A prolific writer and well-known authority in international relations, Nye has served in the U.S. Department of State and on the committees of such prominent organizations as the Ford Foundation and the Carnegie Endowment for International Peace. A frequent guest on television programs, including *Nightline* and the *McNeil-Lehrer Report,* Nye also writes frequently for the *New York Times, Christian Science Monitor, Atlantic Monthly,* and *New Republic.* His most recent book is *Understanding International Conflicts: An Introduction to Theory and History* (2000). The title of the following essay, which appeared in *Newsday* on October 8, 2002, captures Nye's essential thesis about the forces of globalization in today's world.

Before Reading

Is globalization a force for good or bad? Will it turn all nations, cultures, and peoples into reflections of each other?

When anti-globalization protesters took to the streets of Washington 1
recently, they blamed globalization for everything from hunger to the destruction of indigenous cultures. And globalization meant the United States.

The critics call it Coca-Colonization, and French sheep farmer Jose 2
Bove has become a cult figure since destroying a McDonald's restaurant in 1999.

Contrary to conventional wisdom, however, globalization is neither ho- 3
mogenizing nor Americanizing the cultures of the world.

To understand why not, we have to step back and put the current pe- 4
riod in a larger historical perspective. Although they are related, the long-term historical trends of globalization and modernization are not the same. While modernization has produced some common traits, such as large

cities, factories and mass communications, local cultures have by no means been erased. The appearance of similar institutions in response to similar problems is not surprising, but it does not lead to homogeneity.

In the first half of the 20th century, for example, there were some sim-   5
ilarities among the industrial societies of Britain, Germany, America and Japan, but there were even more important differences. When China, India and Brazil complete their current processes of industrialization and modernization, we should not expect them to be replicas of Japan, Germany or the United States.

Take the current information revolution. The United States is at the   6
forefront of this great movement of change, so the uniform social and cultural habits produced by television viewing or Internet use, for instance, are often attributed to Americanization. But correlation is not causation. Imagine if another country had introduced computers and communications at a rapid rate in a world in which the United States did not exist. Major social and cultural changes still would have followed. Of course, since the United States does exist and is at the leading edge of the information revolution, there is a degree of Americanization at present, but it is likely to diminish over the course of the 21st century as technology spreads and local cultures modernize in their own ways.

The lesson that Japan has to teach the rest of the world is that even a   7
century and a half of openness to global trends does not necessarily assure destruction of a country's separate cultural identity. Of course, there are American influences in contemporary Japan (and Japanese influences such as Sony and Pokemon in the United States). Thousands of Japanese youths are co-opting the music, dress and style of urban black America. But some of the groups they listen to dress up like samurai warriors on stage. One can applaud or deplore such cultural transfers, but one should not doubt the persistence of Japan's cultural uniqueness.

The protesters' image of America homogenizing the world also reflects   8
a mistakenly static view of culture. Efforts to portray cultures as unchanging more often reflect reactionary political strategies than descriptions of reality. The Peruvian writer Mario Vargas Llosa put it well when he said that arguments in favor of cultural identity and against globalization "betray a stagnant attitude toward culture that is not borne out by historical fact. Do we know of any cultures that have remained unchanged through time? To find any of them one has to travel to the small, primitive, magico-religious communities made up of people . . . who, due to their primitive condition, become progressively more vulnerable to exploitation and extermination."

Vibrant cultures are constantly changing and borrowing from other   9
cultures. And the borrowing is not always from the United States. For ex-

ample many more countries turned to Canada than to the United States as a model for constitution-building in the aftermath of the Cold War. Canadian views of how to deal with hate crimes were more congenial to countries such as South Africa and the post-Communist states of Eastern Europe than America's First Amendment practices.

Globalization is also a two-edged sword. In some areas, there has been   10 not only a backlash against American cultural imports, but also an effort to change American culture itself. American policies on capital punishment may have majority support inside the United States, but they are regarded as egregious violations of human rights in much of Europe and have been the focus of transnational human rights campaigns. American attitudes toward climate change or genetic modification of food draw similar criticism. More subtly, the openness of the United States to the world's diasporas both enriches and changes American culture.

Transnational corporations are changing poor countries but not ho-   11 mogenizing them. In the early stages of investment, a multinational company with access to the global resources of finance, technology and markets holds the high cards and often gets the best of the bargain with the poor country. But over time, as the poor country develops a skilled workforce, learns new technologies, and opens its own channels to global finance and markets, it is often able to renegotiate the bargain and capture more of the benefits.

As technical capabilities spread and more and more people hook up to   12 global communications systems, the U.S.' economic and cultural preponderance may diminish. This in turn has mixed implications for American "soft" power, our ability to get others to do what we want by attraction rather than coercion. Less dominance may mean less anxiety about Americanization, fewer complaints about American arrogance and a little less intensity in the anti-American backlash. We may have less control in the future, but we may find ourselves living in a world somewhat more congenial to our basic values of democracy, free markets and human rights.

Thinking About the Essay

1. What is Nye's purpose in writing this article? How can you tell? What type of audience does Nye have in mind for his essay? Why does he produce such an affirmative tone in dealing with his subject?

2. Which paragraphs constitute Nye's introduction? Where does he place his thesis, and how does he state it?

3. Break down the essay into its main topics. How does Nye develop these topics? What strategies does he employ—for example, causal analysis, comparison and contrast, illustration—and where?

4. Analyze Nye's topic sentences for his paragraphs. How do they serve as clear guides for the development of his paragraphs? How do they serve to unify the essay?

5. How does Nye's concluding paragraph serve as an answer both to the issue raised in his introduction and to other concerns expressed in the body of the essay?

Responding in Writing

6. From your own personal experience of globalization, write an essay in which you agree or disagree with Nye's assertion that there is little to fear from globilization.

7. Try writing a rebuttal to Nye's argument, explaining why there is much to fear about globalization. Deal point by point with Nye's main assertions. Be certain to provide your own evidence in support of your key reasons.

8. Write an essay that responds to the following topic sentence in Nye's essay: "Vibrant cultures are constantly changing and borrowing from other cultures" (paragraph 9). Base your paper on personal experience, your reading, and your knowledge of current events.

Networking

9. With four other classmates, imagine that you have to teach Nye's essay to a class of high school seniors. How would you proceed? Develop a lesson plan that you think would appeal to your audience.

10. With the entire class, arrange a time when you can have an online chat about Nye's essay. As a focal point for your discussion, argue for or against the idea that he does not take the dangers of globalization seriously enough.

Globalisation

ANTHONY GIDDENS

Anthony Giddens, born in 1938, is arguably England's most prominent sociologist and cultural critic. He received his B.A. degree from the University of Hull (1959), an M.A. degree (with distinction) from the London School of Economics (1961), and a Ph.D. degree from the University of Cambridge (1976). Director of the London School of Economics and chairman of Polity Press, Giddens enjoys an international reputation; he has been a distinguished lecturer and professor at universities around the world, including Harvard University, Stanford University, the University of Rome, and the University of Paris. He has published dozens of books on modern social theory, including *The Consequences of Modernity* (1990), *The Third Way: The Renewal of Social Democracy* (1999), and *Runaway World: How Globalization Is Reshaping Our Lives* (2000). With "Globalisation," part of a series he presented for the BBC Reith Lectures in 1999, Giddens offers a succinct definition of globalization as "a complex set of processes."

Before Reading

In this essay, Giddens asks, "Is globalisation a force promoting the general good?" Based on your reading and writing so far, what is *your* answer?

A friend of mine studies village life in central Africa. A few years ago, she paid her first visit to a remote area where she was to carry out her fieldwork. The evening she got there, she was invited to a local home for an evening's entertainment. She expected to find out about the traditional pastimes of this isolated community. Instead, the evening turned out to be a viewing of *Basic Instinct* on video. The film at that point hadn't even reached the cinemas in London.

Such vignettes reveal something about our world. And what they reveal isn't trivial. It isn't just a matter of people adding modern paraphernalia—videos, TVs, personal computers and so forth—to their traditional ways of life. We live in a world of transformations, affecting almost every aspect of what we do. For better or worse, we are being propelled into a global order that no one fully understands, but which is making its effects felt upon all of us.

Globalisation is the main theme of my lecture tonight, and of the lectures as a whole. The term may not be—it isn't—a particularly attractive or elegant one. But absolutely no-one who wants to understand our prospects and possibilities at century's end can ignore it. I travel a lot to speak abroad. I haven't been to a single country recently where globalisation isn't being intensively discussed. In France, the word is *mondialisation*. In Spain and Latin America, it is *globalización*. The Germans say *Globalisierung*.

The global spread of the term is evidence of the very developments to which it refers. Every business guru talks about it. No political speech is complete without reference to it. Yet as little as 10 years ago the term was hardly used, either in the academic literature or in everyday language. It has come from nowhere to be almost everywhere. Given its sudden popularity, we shouldn't be surprised that the meaning of the notion isn't always clear, or that an intellectual reaction has set in against it. Globalisation has something to do with the thesis that we now all live in one world—but in what ways exactly, and is the idea really valid?

Different thinkers have taken almost completely opposite views about globalisation in debates that have sprung up over the past few years. Some dispute the whole thing. I'll call them the sceptics. According to the sceptics, all the talk about globalisation is only that—just talk. Whatever its benefits, its trials and tribulations, the global economy isn't especially different from that which existed at previous periods. The world carries on much the same as it has done for many years.

Most countries, the sceptics argue, only gain a small amount of their income from external trade. Moreover, a good deal of economic exchange is between regions, rather than being truly world-wide. The countries of the European Union, for example, mostly trade among themselves. The same is true of the other main trading blocs, such as those of the Asia Pacific or North America.

Others, however, take a very different position. I'll label them the radicals. The radicals argue that not only is globalisation very real, but that its consequences can be felt everywhere. The global marketplace, they say, is much more developed than even two or three decades ago, and is indifferent to national borders. Nations have lost most of the sovereignty they once had, and politicians have lost most of their capability to influence events. It isn't surprising that no one respects political leaders any more, or has much interest in what they have to say. The era of the nation state is over. Nations, as the Japanese business writer Keniche Ohmae puts it, have become mere "fictions." Authors like Ohmae see the economic difficulties of last year and this as demonstrating the reality of globalisation, albeit seen from its disruptive side.

The sceptics tend to be on the political left, especially the old left. For if all of this is essentially a myth, governments can still intervene in economic life and the welfare state remain intact. The notion of globalisation, according to the sceptics, is an ideology put about by free-marketeers who wish to dismantle welfare systems and cut back on state expenditures. What has happened is at most a reversion to how the world was a century ago. In the late 19th Century there was already an open global economy, with a great deal of trade, including trade in currencies.

Well, who is right in this debate? I think it is the radicals. The level of world trade today is much higher than it ever was before, and involves a much wider range of goods and services. But the biggest difference is in the level of finance and capital flows. Geared as it is to electronic money—

money that exists only as digits in computers—the current world economy has no parallels in earlier times. In the new global electronic economy, fund managers, banks, corporations, as well as millions of individual investors, can transfer vast amounts of capital from one side of the world to another at the click of a mouse. As they do so, they can destabilise what might have seemed rock-solid economies—as happened in East Asia.

The volume of world financial transactions is usually measured in US dollars. A million dollars is a lot of money for most people. Measured as a stack of thousand dollar notes, it would be eight inches high. A billion dollars—in other words, a million million—would be over 120 miles high, 20 times higher than Mount Everest.   10

Yet far more than a trillion dollars is now turned over each day on global currency markets, a massive increase from only 10 years ago, let alone the more distant past. The value of whatever money we may have in our pockets, or our bank accounts, shifts from moment to moment according to fluctuations in such markets. I would have no hesitation, therefore, in saying that globalisation, as we are experiencing it, is in many respects not only new, but revolutionary.   11

However, I don't believe either the sceptics or the radicals have properly understood either what it is or its implications for us. Both groups see the phenomenon almost solely in economic terms. This is a mistake. Globalisation is political, technological and cultural, as well as economic. It has been influenced above all by developments in systems of communication, dating back only to the late 1960's.   12

In the mid-19th Century, a Massachusetts portrait painter, Samuel Morse, transmitted the first message, "What hath god wrought?", by electric telegraph. In so doing, he initiated a new phase in world history. Never before could a message be sent without someone going somewhere to carry it. Yet the advent of satellite communications marks every bit as dramatic a break with the past. The first communications satellite was launched only just over 30 years ago. Now there are more than 200 such satellites above the earth, each carrying a vast range of information. For the first time ever, instantaneous communication is possible from one side of the world to the other. Other types of electronic communication, more and more integrated with satellite transmission, have also accelerated over the past few years. No dedicated transatlantic or transpacific cables existed at all until the late 1950's. The first held less than 100 voice paths. Those of today carry more than a million.   13

On the first of February 1999, about 150 years after Morse invented his system of dots and dashes, Morse code finally disappeared from the world stage, discontinued as a means of communication for the sea. In its   14 place has come a system using satellite technology, whereby any ship in distress can be pinpointed immediately. Most countries prepared for the transition some while before. The French, for example, stopped using Morse as a distress code in their local waters two years ago, signing off with a Gallic flourish: "Calling all. This is our last cry before our eternal silence."

Instantaneous electronic communication isn't just a way in which news   15
or information is conveyed more quickly. Its existence alters the very texture of our lives, rich and poor alike. When the image of Nelson Mandela maybe is more familiar to us than the face of our next door neighbour, something has changed in the nature of our everyday experience.

Nelson Mandela is a global celebrity, and celebrity itself is largely a   16
product of new communications technology. The reach of media technologies is growing with each wave of innovation. It took 40 years for radio in the United States to gain an audience of 50 million. The same number were using personal computers only 15 years after the PC was introduced. It needed a mere four years, after it was made available for 50 million Americans to be regularly using the Internet.

It is wrong to think of globalisation as just concerning the big systems,   17
like the world financial order. Globalisation isn't only about what is "out there" remote and far away from the individual. It is an "in here" phenomenon too, influencing intimate and personal aspects of our lives. The debate about family values, for example, that is going on in many countries, might seem far removed from globalising influences. It isn't. Traditional family systems are becoming transformed, or are under strain, in many parts of the world, particularly as women stake claim to greater equality. There has never before been a society, so far as we know from the historical record, in which women have been even approximately equal to men. This is a truly global revolution in everyday life, whose consequences are being felt around the world in spheres from work to politics.

Globalisation thus is a complex set of processes, not a single one. And   18
these operate in a contradictory or oppositional fashion. Most people think of it as simply "pulling away" power or influence from local communities and nations into the global arena. And indeed this is one of its consequences. Nations do lose some of the economic power they once had. However, it also has an opposite effect. Globalisation not only pulls upwards, it pushes downwards, creating new pressures for local autonomy. The American sociologist Daniel Bell expresses this very well when he says that the nation becomes too small to solve the big problems, but also too large to solve the small ones.

Globalisation is the reason for the revival of local cultural identities in   19
different parts of the world. If one asks, for example, why the Scots want more independence in the UK, or why there is a strong separatist move-

ment in Quebec, the answer is not to be found only in their cultural history. Local nationalisms spring up as a response to globalising tendencies, as the hold of older nation-states weakens.

Globalisation also squeezes sideways. It creates new economic and cultural zones within and across nations. Examples are the Hong Kong region, northern Italy, or Silicon Valley in California. The area around Barcelona in northern Spain extends over into France. Catalonia, where Barcelona is located, is closely integrated into the European Union. It is part of Spain, yet also looks outwards. 20

The changes are being propelled by a range of factors, some structural, others more specific and historical. Economic influences are certainly among the driving forces, especially the global financial system. Yet they aren't like forces of nature. They have been shaped by technology, and cultural diffusion, as well as by the decisions of governments to liberalise and deregulate their national economies. 21

The collapse of Soviet communism has added further weight to such developments, since no significant group of countries any longer stands outside. That collapse wasn't just something that happened to occur. Globalisation explains both why and how Soviet communism met its end. The Soviet Union and the East European countries were comparable to the West in terms of growth rates until somewhere around the early 1970s. After that point, they fell rapidly behind. Soviet communism, with its emphasis upon state-run enterprise and heavy industry, could not compete in the global electronic economy. The ideological and cultural control upon which communist political authority was based similarly could not survive in an era of global media. 22

The Soviet and the East European regimes were unable to prevent the reception of western radio and TV broadcasts. Television played a direct role in the 1989 revolutions, which have rightly been called the first "television revolutions." Street protests taking place in one country were watched by the audiences in others, large numbers of whom then took to the streets themselves. 23

Globalisation, of course, isn't developing in an even-handed way, and is by no means wholly benign in its consequences. To many living outside Europe and North America, it looks uncomfortably like Westernisation—or, perhaps, Americanisation, since the US is now the sole superpower, with a dominant economic, cultural and military position in the global order. Many of the most visible cultural expressions of globalisation are American—Coca-Cola, McDonald's. 24

Most of giant multinational companies are based in the US too. Those that aren't all come from the rich countries, not the poorer areas of the world. A pessimistic view of globalisation would consider it largely an affair of the 25 industrial North, in which the developing societies of the South play little or no active part. It would see it as destroying local cultures, widening world inequalities and worsening the lot of the impoverished. Globalisation, some argue, creates a world of winners and losers, a few on the fast track to prosperity, the majority condemned to a life of misery and despair.

And indeed the statistics are daunting. The share of the poorest fifth of   26 the world's population in global income has dropped from 2.3% to 1.4% over the past 10 years. The proportion taken by the richest fifth, on the other hand, has risen from 70% to 85%. In Sub-Saharan Africa, 20 countries have lower incomes per head in real terms than they did two decades ago. In many less developed countries, safety and environmental regulations are low or virtually non-existent. Some trans-national companies sell goods there that are controlled or banned in the industrial countries—poor quality medical drugs, destructive pesticides or high tar and nicotine content cigarettes. As one writer put it recently, rather than a global village, this is more like global pillage.

Along with ecological risk, to which it is related, expanding inequality   27 is the most serious problem facing world society. It will not do, however, merely to blame it on the wealthy. It is fundamental to my argument that globalisation today is only partly Westernisation. Of course the western nations, and more generally the industrial countries, still have far more influence over world affairs than do the poorer states. But globalisation is becoming increasingly de-centred—not under the control of any group of nations, and still less of the large corporations. Its effects are felt just as much in the western countries as elsewhere.

This is true of the global financial system, communications and media,   28 and of changes affecting the nature of government itself. Examples of "reverse colonisation" are becoming more and more common. Reverse colonisation means that non-western countries influence developments in the west. Examples abound—such as the Latinising of Los Angeles, the emergence of a globally-oriented high-tech sector in India, or the selling of Brazilian TV programmes to Portugal.

Is globalisation a force promoting the general good? The question can't   29 be answered in a simple way, given the complexity of the phenomenon. People who ask it, and who blame globalisation for deepening world inequalities, usually have in mind economic globalisation, and within that, free trade. Now it is surely obvious that free trade is not an unalloyed benefit. This is especially so as concerns the less developed countries. Opening up a country, or regions within it, to free trade can undermine a local subsistence economy. An area that becomes dependent upon a few products sold on world markets is very vulnerable to shifts in prices as well as to technological change.

Trade always needs a framework of institutions, as do other forms of 30
economic development. Markets cannot be created by purely economic
means, and how far a given economy should be exposed to the world marketplace must depend upon a range of criteria. Yet to oppose economic
globalisation, and to opt for economic protectionism, would be a misplaced tactic for rich and poor nations alike. Protectionism may be a necessary strategy at some times and in some countries. In my view, for
example, Malaysia was correct to introduce controls in 1998, to stem the
flood of capital from the country. But more permanent forms of protectionism will not help the development of the poor countries, and among
the rich would lead to warring trade blocs.

The debates about globalisation I mentioned at the beginning have con- 31
centrated mainly upon its implications for the nation-state. Are nation-
states, and hence national political leaders, still powerful, or are they
becoming largely irrelevant to the forces shaping the world? Nation-states
are indeed still powerful and political leaders have a large role to play in
the world. Yet at the same time the nation-state is being reshaped before
our eyes. National economic policy can't be as effective as it once was.
More importantly, nations have to rethink their identities now the older
forms of geopolitics are becoming obsolete. Although this is a contentious
point, I would say that, following the dissolving of the cold war, nations no
longer have enemies. Who are the enemies of Britain, or France, or Japan?
Nations today face risks and dangers rather than enemies, a massive shift
in their very nature.

It isn't only of the nation that such comments could be made. Every- 32
where we look, we see institutions that appear the same as they used to be
from the outside, and carry the same names, but inside have become quite
different. We continue to talk of the nation, the family, work, tradition, nature, as if they were all the same as in the past. They are not. The outer shell
remains, but inside all is different—and this is happening not only in the
US, Britain, or France, but almost everywhere. They are what I call shell institutions, and I shall talk about them quite a bit in the lectures to come.
They are institutions that have become inadequate to the tasks they are
called upon to perform.

As the changes I have described in this lecture gather weight, they are 33
creating something that has never existed before, a global cosmopolitan society. We are the first generation to live in this society, whose contours we
can as yet only dimly see. It is shaking up our existing ways of life, no matter where we happen to be. This is not—at least at the moment—a global
order driven by collective human will. Instead, it is emerging in an anar-
chic, haphazard, fashion, carried along by a mixture of economic, technological and cultural imperatives.

It is not settled or secure, but fraught with anxieties, as well as scarred 34
by deep divisions. Many of us feel in the grip of forces over which we have
no control. Can we re-impose our will upon them? I believe we can. The
powerlessness we experience is not a sign of personal failings, but reflects
the incapacities of our institutions. We need to reconstruct those we have,
or create new ones, in ways appropriate to the global age.

We should and we can look to achieve greater control over our runaway 35
world. We shan't be able to do so if we shirk the challenges, or pretend that
all can go on as before. For globalisation is not incidental to our lives today.
It is a shift in our very life circumstances. It is the way we now live.

Thinking About the Essay

1. Did you notice how Giddens spells *globalisation*? Why does the English
   spelling differ from the American? Where does Giddens allude to the word
   in other languages? What can you infer from these variant spellings and
   translations?

2. Giddens begins his essay with the personal example of an unnamed friend.
   Why? What other types of illustration does he use in this essay?

3. The writer presents an *extended definition* of globalization. What aspects of
   globalization does he define and in what sequence? What thesis emerges
   from this definition? In what place (or places) does his thesis appear?

4. According to Giddens, how did globalization come about? What historical
   processes, causes and effects does he trace in his presentation?

5. How does Giddens use the comparative method and classification to frame
   his analysis of globalization? Identify specific paragraphs and passages
   where these strategies serve his purpose.

Responding in Writing

6. Giddens suggests—most clearly in his conclusion—that today we live in a
   "runaway world." Do you have the same thoughts or feelings? Is your response a result of the forces of globalization? Write an essay that answers
   these questions.

7. Giddens wrote this piece as a lecture. Write your own lecture, about ten
   minutes long, on globalization. Assume that you must define and discuss
   the word for an educated radio or television audience. Adjust your style to
   the expectations of this audience.

8. Giddens speaks of "sceptics," "radicals," and a third group he doesn't
   name but whom we might call "comparative analysts" who are capable of
   understanding the complexities of globalization. Write a classification essay
   in which you present at least three types or ways of looking at globalization.
   Feel free to use one or more of Giddens's categories in your paper.

Thinking About the Image

1. What is ironic about the narrative in this cartoon?

2. What do the visual images contribute to this man's story?

3. Giddens divides people who think about globalization into "sceptics," "radicals," and what might be called "comparative analysts." How would each group respond to this cartoon?

4. Cartoons are also a kind of rhetoric, in that they have a purpose and an audience. A cartoonist uses visuals as well as language to move or persuade that audience. How effective is Horsey's rhetoric in serving his purpose? Who is his audience, and how effectively does he address them?

Networking

9. In small groups, construct an extended definition of globalization. Feel free to use information in Giddens's essay as well as other selections in this chapter. Then distill this definition to a 300-word summary that one member of your group presents to the class.

10. Go online and locate transcripts of the entire series of lectures on globalization given by Giddens on the British Broadcasting System. Review the content and write a brief report on your findings.

On Seeing England for the First Time

JAMAICA KINCAID

> Jamaica Kincaid was born Elaine Potter Richardson in 1949 in St. John's, Antigua, in the West Indies. After emigrating to the United States, she became a staff writer for the *New Yorker,* with her short stories also appearing in *Rolling Stone,* the *Paris Review,* and elsewhere. She has taught at Harvard University and other colleges while compiling a distinguished body of fiction and nonfiction, notably *Annie John* (1958), *A Small Place* (1988), *Lucy* (1991), and *The Autobiography of My Mother* (1996). The stories collected in *At the Bottom of the River* won the Morton Dauwen Zabel Award from the American Academy and Institute of Arts and Letters. Although Kincaid has turned recently in her writing to the relatively peaceful world of gardening, the typical tone of her fiction and essays is severely critical of the social, cultural, and political consequences of colonialism and immigration. In "On Seeing England for the First Time," published in *Transition* in 1991, Kincaid thinks about the time when Great Britain was associated with the forces of globalization throughout the world.

Before Reading

It was once said that the sun never sets on the British Empire. What does this statement mean? Could the same be said for the United States today?

When I saw England for the first time, I was a child in school sitting at   1
a desk. The England I was looking at was laid out on a map gently, beautifully, delicately, a very special jewel; it lay on a bed of sky blue—the

background of the map—its yellow form mysterious, because though it looked like a leg of mutton, it could not really look like anything so familiar as a leg of mutton because it was England—with shadings of pink and green, unlike any shadings of pink and green I had seen before, squiggly veins of red running in every direction. England was a special jewel all right, and only special people got to wear it. The people who got to wear England were English people. They wore it well and they wore it everywhere: in jungles, in deserts, on plains, on top of the highest mountains, on all the oceans, on all the seas, in places where they were not welcome, in places they should not have been. When my teacher had pinned this map up on the blackboard, she said, "This is England"—and she said it with authority, seriousness, and adoration, and we all sat up. It was as if she had said, "This is Jerusalem, the place you will go to when you die but only if you have been good." We understood then—we were meant to understand then—that England was to be our source of myth and the source from which we got our sense of reality, our sense of what was meaningful, our sense of what was meaningless—and much about our own lives and much about the very idea of us headed that last list.

At the time I was a child sitting at my desk seeing England for the first time, I was already very familiar with the greatness of it. Each morning before I left for school, I ate a breakfast of half a grapefruit, an egg, bread and butter and a slice of cheese, and a cup of cocoa; or half a grapefruit, a bowl of oat porridge, bread and butter and a slice of cheese, and a cup of cocoa. The can of cocoa was often left on the table in front of me. It had written on it the name of the company, the year the company was established, and the words "Made in England." Those words, "Made in England," were written on the box the oats came in too. They would also have been written on the box the shoes I was wearing came in; a bolt of gray linen cloth lying on the shelf of a store from which my mother had bought three yards to make the uniform that I was wearing had written along its edge those three words. The shoes I wore were made in England; so were my socks and cotton undergarments and the satin ribbons I wore tied at the end of two plaits of my hair. My father, who might have sat next to me at breakfast, was a carpenter and cabinet maker. The shoes he wore to work would have been made in England, as were his khaki shirt and trousers, his underpants and undershirt, his socks and brown felt hat. Felt was not the proper material from which a hat that was expected to provide shade from the hot sun should be made, but my father must have seen and admired a picture of an Englishman wearing such a hat in England, and this picture that he saw must have been so compelling that it caused him to wear the wrong hat for a hot climate most of his long life. And this hat—a brown felt hat—became so central to his character that it was the first thing he put on in the morning as he stepped out of bed and the last thing he took off before he stepped back into bed at night. As we sat at breakfast a car might go by. The car, a Hillman or a Zephyr, was made in England. The very idea of the meal itself, breakfast, and its substantial quality and quantity was an idea from England; we somehow knew that in England they began the day with this meal called breakfast and a proper breakfast was a big breakfast. No one I knew liked eating so much food so early in the day; it made us feel sleepy, tired. But this breakfast business was Made in England like almost everything else that surrounded us, the exceptions being the sea, the sky, and the air we breathed.

At the time I saw this map—seeing England for the first time—I did not 3 say to myself, "Ah, so that's what it looks like," because there was no longing in me to put a shape to those three words that ran through every part of my life, no matter how small; for me to have had such a longing would have meant that I lived in a certain atmosphere, an atmosphere in which those three words were felt as a burden. But I did not live in such an atmosphere. My father's brown felt hat would develop a hole in its crown, the lining would separate from the hat itself, and six weeks before he thought that he could not be seen wearing it—he was a very vain man—he would order another hat from England. And my mother taught me to eat my food in the English way: the knife in the right hand, the fork in the left, my elbows held still close to my side, the food carefully balanced on my fork and then brought up to my mouth. When I had finally mastered it, I overheard her saying to a friend, "Did you see how nicely she can eat?" But I knew then that I enjoyed my food more when I ate it with my bare hands, and I continued to do so when she wasn't looking. And when my teacher showed us the map, she asked us to study it carefully, because no test we would ever take would be complete without this statement: "Draw a map of England."

I did not know then that the statement "Draw a map of England" was 4 something far worse than a declaration of war, for in fact a flat-out declaration of war would have put me on alert, and again in fact, there was no need for war—I had long ago been conquered. I did not know then that this statement was part of a process that would result in my erasure, not my physical erasure, but my erasure all the same. I did not know then that this statement was meant to make me feel in awe and small whenever I heard the word "England": awe at its existence, small because I was not from it. I did not know very much of anything then—certainly not what a blessing it was that I was unable to draw a map of England correctly.

After that there were many times of seeing England for the first time. I 5
saw England in history. I knew the names of all the kings of England. I
knew the names of their children, their wives, their disappointments, their
triumphs, the names of people who betrayed them; I knew the dates on
which they were born and the dates they died. I knew their conquests and
was made to feel glad if I figured in them; I knew their defeats. I knew the
details of the year 1066 (the Battle of Hastings, the end of the reign of the
Anglo-Saxon kings) before I knew the details of the year 1832 (the year
slavery was abolished). It wasn't as bad as I make it sound now; it was
worse. I did like so much hearing again and again how Alfred the Great,
traveling in disguise, had been left to watch cakes, and because he wasn't
used to this the cakes got burned, and Alfred burned his hands pulling them
out of the fire, and the woman who had left him to watch the cakes
screamed at him. I loved King Alfred. My grandfather was named after
him; his son, my uncle, was named after King Alfred; my brother is named
after King Alfred. And so there are three people in my family named after
a man they have never met, a man who died over ten centuries ago. The
first view I got of England then was not unlike the first view received by
the person who named my grandfather.

This view, though—the naming of the kings, their deeds, their disap- 6
pointments—was the vivid view, the forceful view. There were other views,
subtler ones, softer, almost not there—but these were the ones that made
the most lasting impression on me, these were the ones that made me really feel like nothing. "When morning touched the sky" was one phrase,
for no morning touched the sky where I lived. The mornings where I lived
came on abruptly, with a shock of heat and loud noises. "Evening approaches" was another, but the evenings where I lived did not approach; in
fact, I had no evening—I had night and I had day and they came and went
in a mechanical way: on, off; on, off. And then there were gentle mountains
and low blue skies and moors over which people took walks for nothing
but pleasure, when where I lived a walk was an act of labor, a burden,
something only death or the automobile could relieve. And there were
things that a small turn of a head could convey—entire worlds, whole lives
would depend on this thing, a certain turn of a head. Everyday life could
be quite tiring, more tiring than anything I was told not to do. I was told
not to gossip, but they did that all the time. And they ate so much food, violating another of those rules they taught me: do not indulge in gluttony.
And the foods they ate actually: if only sometime I could eat cold cuts after theater, cold cuts of lamb and mint sauce, and Yorkshire pudding and
scones, and clotted cream, and sausages that came from up-country (imagine, "up-country"). And having troubling thoughts at twilight, a good time

to have troubling thoughts, apparently; and servants who stole and left in the middle of a crisis, who were born with a limp or some other kind of deformity, not nourished properly in their mother's womb (that last part I figured out for myself; the point was, oh to have an untrustworthy servant); and wonderful cobbled streets onto which solid front doors opened; and people whose eyes were blue and who had fair skins and who smelled only of lavender, or sometimes sweet pea or primrose. And those flowers with those names: delphiniums, foxgloves, tulips, daffodils, floribunda, peonies; in bloom, a striking display, being cut and placed in large glass bowls, crystal, decorating rooms so large twenty families the size of mine could fit in comfortably but used only for passing through. And the weather was so remarkable because the rain fell gently always, only occasionally in deep gusts, and it colored the air various shades of gray, each an appealing shade for a dress to be worn when a portrait was being painted; and when it rained at twilight, wonderful things happened: people bumped into each other unexpectedly and that would lead to all sorts of turns of events—a plot, the mere weather caused plots. I saw that people rushed: they rushed to catch trains, they rushed toward each other and away from each other; they rushed and rushed and rushed. That word: rushed! I did not know what it was to do that. It was too hot to do that, and so I came to envy people who would rush, even though it had no meaning to me to do such a thing. But there they are again. They loved their children; their children were sent to their own rooms as a punishment, rooms larger than my entire house. They were special, everything about them said so, even their clothes; their clothes rustled, swished, soothed. The world was theirs, not mine; everything told me so.

If now as I speak of all this I give the impression of someone on the outside looking in, nose pressed up against a glass window, that is wrong. My nose was pressed up against a glass window all right, but there was an iron vise at the back of my neck forcing my head to stay in place. To avert my gaze was to fall back into something from which I had been rescued, a hole filled with nothing, and that was the word for everything about me, nothing. The reality of my life was conquests, subjugation, humiliation, enforced amnesia. I was forced to forget. Just for instance, this: I lived in a part of St. John's, Antigua, called Ovals. Ovals was made up of five streets, each of them named after a famous English seaman—to be quite frank, an officially sanctioned criminal: Rodney Street (after George Rodney), Nelson Street (after Horatio Nelson), Drake Street (after Francis Drake), Hood Street, and Hawkins Street (after John Hawkins). But John Hawkins was knighted after a trip he made to Africa, opening up a new trade, the slave trade. He was then entitled to wear as his crest a Negro bound with a cord.

Every single person living on Hawkins Street was descended from a slave. John Hawkins's ship, the one in which he transported the people he had bought and kidnapped, was called *The Jesus*. He later became the treasurer of the Royal Navy and rear admiral.

Again, the reality of my life, the life I led at the time I was being shown   8
these views of England for the first time, for the second time, for the one-hundred-millionth time, was this: the sun shone with what sometimes seemed to be a deliberate cruelty; we must have done something to deserve that. My dresses did not rustle in the evening air as I strolled to the theater (I had no evening, I had no theater; my dresses were made of a cheap cotton, the weave of which would give way after not too many washings). I got up in the morning, I did my chores (fetched water from the public pipe for my mother, swept the yard), I washed myself, I went to a woman to have my hair combed freshly every day (because before we were allowed into our classroom our teachers would inspect us, and children who had not bathed that day, or had dirt under their fingernails, or whose hair had not been combed anew that day, might not be allowed to attend class). I ate that breakfast. I walked to school. At school we gathered in an auditorium and sang a hymn, "All Things Bright and Beautiful," and looking down on us as we sang were portraits of the Queen of England and her husband; they wore jewels and medals and they smiled. I was a Brownie. At each meeting we would form a little group around a flagpole, and after raising the Union Jack, we would say, "I promise to do my best, to do my duty to God and the Queen, to help other people every day and obey the scouts' law."

Who were these people and why had I never seen them, I mean really   9
seen them, in the place where they lived? I had never been to England. No one I knew had ever been to England, or I should say, no one I knew had ever been and returned to tell me about it. All the people I knew who had gone to England had stayed there. Sometimes they left behind them their small children, never to see them again. England! I had seen England's representatives. I had seen the governor general at the public grounds at a ceremony celebrating the Queen's birthday. I had seen an old princess and I had seen a young princess. They had both been extremely not beautiful, but who of us would have told them that? I had never seen England, really seen it, I had only met a representative, seen a picture, read books, memorized its history. I had never set foot, my own foot, in it.

The space between the idea of something and its reality is always wide   10
and deep and dark. The longer they are kept apart—idea of thing, reality of thing—the wider the width, the deeper the depth, the thicker and darker

the darkness. This space starts out empty, there is nothing in it, but it rapidly becomes filled up with obsession or desire or hatred or love—sometimes all of these things, sometimes some of these things, sometimes only one of these things. The existence of the world as I came to know it was a result of this: idea of thing over here, reality of thing way, way over there. There was Christopher Columbus, an unlikable man, an unpleasant man, a liar (and so, of course, a thief) surrounded by maps and schemes and plans, and there was the reality on the other side of that width, that depth, that darkness. He became obsessed, he became filled with desire, the hatred came later, love was never a part of it. Eventually, his idea met the longed-for reality. That the idea of something and its reality are often two completely different things is something no one ever remembers; and so when they meet and find that they are not compatible, the weaker of the two, idea or reality, dies. That idea Christopher Columbus had was more powerful than the reality he met, and so the reality he met died.

And so finally, when I was a grown-up woman, the mother of two children, the wife of someone, a person who resides in a powerful country that takes up more than its fair share of a continent, the owner of a house with many rooms in it and of two automobiles, with the desire and will (which I very much act upon) to take from the world more than I give back to it, more than I deserve, more than I need, finally then, I saw England, the real England, not a picture, not a painting, not through a story in a book, but England, for the first time. In me, the space between the idea of it and its reality had become filled with hatred, and so when at last I saw it I wanted to take it into my hands and tear it into little pieces and then crumble it up as if it were clay, child's clay. That was impossible, and so I could only indulge in not-favorable opinions. [11]

There were monuments everywhere; they commemorated victories, battles fought between them and the people who lived across the sea from them, all vile people, fought over which of them would have dominion over the people who looked like me. The monuments were useless to them now, people sat on them and ate their lunch. They were like markers on an old useless trail, like a piece of old string tied to a finger to jog the memory, like old decoration in an old house, dirty, useless, in the way. Their skins were so pale, it made them look so fragile, so weak, so ugly. What if I had the power to simply banish them from their land, send boat after boatload of them on a voyage that in fact had no destination, force them to live in a place where the sun's presence was a constant? This would rid them of their pale complexion and make them look more like me, make them look more like the people I love and treasure and hold dear, and more like the people who occupy the near and far reaches of my imagination, my history, my ge- [12]

ography, and reduce them and everything they have ever known to fig-
urines as evidence that I was in divine favor, what if all this was in my
power? Could I resist it? No one ever has.

And they were rude, they were rude to each other. They didn't like each   13
other very much. They didn't like each other in the way they didn't like me,
and it occurred to me that their dislike for me was one of the few things
they agreed on.

I was on a train in England with a friend, an English woman. Before   14
we were in England she liked me very much. In England she didn't like
me at all. She didn't like the claim I said I had on England, she didn't like
the views I had of England. I didn't like England, she didn't like England,
but she didn't like me not liking it too. She said, "I want to show you my
England, I want to show you the England that I know and love." I had
told her many times before that I knew England and I didn't want to love
it anyway. She no longer lived in England; it was her own country, but
it had not been kind to her, so she left. On the train, the conductor was
rude to her; she asked something, and he responded in a rude way. She
became ashamed. She was ashamed at the way he treated her; she was
ashamed at the way he behaved. "This is the new England," she said. But
I liked the conductor being rude; his behavior seemed quite appropriate.
Earlier this had happened: we had gone to a store to buy a shirt for my
husband; it was meant to be a special present, a special shirt to wear on
special occasions. This was a store where the Prince of Wales has his
shirts made, but the shirts sold in this store are beautiful all the same. I
found a shirt I thought my husband would like and I wanted to buy him
a tie to go with it. When I couldn't decide which one to choose, the
salesman showed me a new set. He was very pleased with these, he said,
because they bore the crest of the Prince of Wales, and the Prince of
Wales had never allowed his crest to decorate an article of clothing before. There was something in the way he said it; his tone was slavish, rev-
erential, awed. It made me feel angry; I wanted to hit him. I didn't do
that. I said, my husband and I hate princes, my husband would never
wear anything that had a prince's anything on it. My friend stiffened.
The salesman stiffened. They both drew themselves in, away from me.
My friend told me that the prince was a symbol of her Englishness, and
I could see that I had caused offense. I looked at her. She was an English
person, the sort of English person I used to know at home, the sort who
was nobody in England but somebody when they came to live among the
people like me. There were many people I could have seen England with;
that I was seeing it with this particular person, a person who reminded
me of the people who showed me England long ago as I sat in church or

at my desk, made me feel silent and afraid, for I wondered if, all these years of our friendship, I had had a friend or had been in the thrall of a racial memory.

I went to Bath—we, my friend and I, did this, but though we were to- 15 gether, I was no longer with her. The landscape was almost as familiar as my own hand, but I had never been in this place before, so how could that be again? And the streets of Bath were familiar, too, but I had never walked on them before. It was all those years of reading, starting with Roman Britain. Why did I have to know about Roman Britain? It was of no real use to me, a person living on a hot, drought-ridden island, and it is of no use to me now, and yet my head is filled with this nonsense, Roman Britain. In Bath, I drank tea in a room I had read about in a novel written in the eighteenth century. In this very same room, young women wearing those dresses that rustled and so on danced and flirted and sometimes disgraced themselves with young men, soldiers, sailors, who were on their way to Bristol or someplace like that, so many places like that where so many adventures, the outcome of which was not good for me, began. Bristol, England. A sentence that began "That night the ship sailed from Bristol, England" would end not so good for me. And then I was driving through the countryside in an English motorcar, on narrow winding roads, and they were so familiar, though I had never been on them before; and through little villages the names of which I somehow knew so well though I had never been there before. And the countryside did have all those hedges and hedges, fields hedged in. I was marveling at all the toil of it, the planting of the hedges to begin with and then the care of it, all that clipping, year after year of clipping, and I wondered at the lives of the people who would have to do this, because wherever I see and feel the hands that hold up the world, I see and feel myself and all the people who look like me. And I said, "Those hedges" and my friend said that someone, a woman named Mrs. Rothchild, worried that the hedges weren't being taken care of properly; the farmers couldn't afford or find the help to keep up the hedges, and often they replaced them with wire fencing. I might have said to that, well if Mrs. Rothchild doesn't like the wire fencing, why doesn't she take care of the hedges herself, but I didn't. And then in those fields that were now hemmed in by wire fencing that a privileged woman didn't like was planted a vile yellow flowering bush that produced an oil, and my friend said that Mrs. Rothchild didn't like this either; it ruined the English countryside, it ruined the traditional look of the English countryside.

It was not at that moment that I wished every sentence, everything I 16 knew, that began with England would end with "and then it all died; we don't know how, it just all died." At that moment, I was thinking, who are these people who forced me to think of them all the time, who forced me to think that the world I knew was incomplete, or without substance, or did not measure up because it was not England; that I was incomplete, or without substance, and did not measure up because I was not English. Who were these people? The person sitting next to me couldn't give me a clue; no one person could. In any case, if I had said to her, I find England ugly, I hate England; the weather is like a jail sentence, the English are a very ugly people, the food in England is like a jail sentence, the hair of English people is so straight, so dead looking, the English have an unbearable smell so different from the smell of people I know, real people of course, she would have said that I was a person full of prejudice. Apart from the fact that it is I—that is, the people who look like me—who made her aware of the unpleasantness of such a thing, the idea of such a thing, prejudice, she would have been only partly right, sort of right: I may be capable of prejudice, but my prejudices have no weight to them, my prejudices have no force behind them, my prejudices remain opinions, my prejudices remain my personal opinion. And a great feeling of rage and disappointment came over me as I looked at England, my head full of personal opinions that could not have public, my public, approval. The people I come from are powerless to do evil on grand scale.

The moment I wished every sentence, everything I knew, that began 17 with England would end with "and then it all died, we don't know how, it just all died" was when I saw the white cliffs of Dover. I had sung hymns and recited poems that were about a longing to see the white cliffs of Dover again. At the time I sang the hymns and recited the poems, I could really long to see them again because I had never seen them at all, nor had anyone around me at the time. But there we were, groups of people longing for something we had never seen. And so there they were, the white cliffs, but they were not that pearly majestic thing I used to sing about, that thing that created such a feeling in these people that when they died in the place where I lived they had themselves buried facing a direction that would allow them to see the white cliffs of Dover when they were resurrected, as surely they would be. The white cliffs of Dover, when finally I saw them, were cliffs, but they were not white; you would only call them that if the word "white" meant something special to you; they were dirty and they were steep; they were so steep, the correct height from which all my views of England, starting with the map before me in my classroom and ending with the trip I had just taken, should jump and die and disappear forever.

Thinking About the Essay

1. Based on your careful reading of this essay, summarize Kincaid's understanding of globalization. Does the fact that she writes about England and not the United States diminish the importance of her argument? Explain.

2. Kincaid divides her essay into two major parts. What is her intention? What is the effect?

3. Kincaid establishes several contrasts between England and Antigua. What are they? How does this comparative method serve to organize the essay?

4. The writer's paragraphs tend to be quite long. Analyze the way she develops her introductory and concluding paragraphs. Also examine the longest paragraph in the essay (paragraph 6) and explain how she achieves coherence in the presentation of her ideas.

5. How does Kincaid's use of the personal voice—the "I" point of view—affect the tone and purpose of her essay? By adopting this personal perspective, what does Kincaid want the audience to infer about her and her experience of globalization?

Responding in Writing

6. Write an account of your early education. What did you learn about the country where you were born and its relationship to the rest of the world? How did your early education influence or mold your global understanding today?

7. Write an essay analyzing Kincaid's various views on England, and what they ultimately mean to her. Has she convinced you about her perspective on the subject? Why or why not? Be certain to deal with her concluding paragraph and her reference to the "white cliffs of Dover."

8. Imagine that you live in a country that has a history of colonization. (Perhaps you or your family has actually experienced this condition.) What would your attitude toward the colonizing or globalizing power be? Write a paper exploring this real or imaginary situation.

Networking

9. With three other class members, draw up a complete list of the contrasts that Kincaid establishes between Antigua and England. Arrive at a consensus about why she is so preoccupied with England—not just as a child but also as an adult writing about the experience. Select one member of your group as a representative in a class panel discussion that talks about these contrasts.

10. Go online and find information about Antigua. Evaluate Kincaid's impressions of her native island with what you have learned about it.

The Educated Student: Global Citizen or Global Consumer?

BENJAMIN BARBER

> Born in New York City in 1939, Benjamin Barber attended school in Switzerland and London before receiving a B.A. degree from Grinnell College in 1960 and a Ph.D. degree from Harvard University in 1966. For years he was Walt Whitman Professor of Political Science and director of the Walt Whitman Center for the Culture and Politics of Democracy at Rutgers University. Currently he holds an endowed professorship at the University of Maryland and is principal of the Democracy Collaborative. A charismatic speaker in great demand at major conferences and a frequent guest on television news programs, Barber is also a prolific writer on a wide range of issues, many of them centering on the need for participatory democracy around the world. His numerous books include *Jihad Versus McWorld* (1995), *A Passion for Democracy* (1998), and *A Place for Us: Civilizing Society and Domesticating the Marketplace* (1998). He is also a playwright and author, with Patrick Watson, of *The Struggle for Democracy* television series. In the essay that appears next, which appeared in the magazine *Liberal Education* (a publication of the Association of Colleges and Universities) in 2002, Barber raises important questions about the status of civic education in the contemporary global era.

Before Reading

Should today's college students be educated in global affairs? If so, how should such programs be handled by schools and colleges? If not, why not? What connections do you see between education and citizenship?

I want to trace a quick trajectory from July 4, 1776 to Sept. 11, 2001. It takes us from the Declaration of Independence to the declaration of interdependence—not one that is actually yet proclaimed but one that we educators need to begin to proclaim from the pulpits of our classrooms and administrative suites across America.

In 1776 it was all pretty simple for people who cared about both education and democracy. There was nobody among the extraordinary group of men who founded this nation who did not know that democracy—then an inventive, challenging, experimental new system of government—was dependent for its success not just on constitutions, laws, and institutions, but dependent for its success on the quality of citizens who would constitute the new republic. Because democracy depends on citizenship, the emphasis then was to think about what and how to constitute a competent and virtuous citizen body. That led directly, in almost every one of the founders' minds, to the connection between citizenship and education.

Whether you look at Thomas Jefferson in Virginia or John Adams in   3
Massachusetts, there was widespread agreement that the new republic, for all of the cunning of its inventive and experimental new Constitution, could not succeed unless the citizenry was well educated. That meant that in the period after the Revolution but before the ratification of the Constitution, John Adams argued hard for schools for every young man in Massachusetts (it being the case, of course, that only men could be citizens). And in Virginia, Thomas Jefferson made the same argument for public schooling for every potential citizen in America, founding the first great public university there. Those were arguments that were uncontested.

By the beginning of the nineteenth century this logic was clear in the   4
common school movement and later, in the land grant colleges. It was clear in the founding documents of every religious, private, and public higher education institution in this country. Colleges and universities had to be committed above all to the constituting of citizens. That's what education was about. The other aspects of it—literacy, knowledge, and research—were in themselves important. Equally important as dimensions of education and citizenship was education that would make the Bill of Rights real, education that would make democracy succeed.

It was no accident that in subsequent years, African Americans and   5
then women struggled for a place and a voice in this system, and the key was always seen as education. If women were to be citizens, then women's education would have to become central to suffragism. After the Civil War, African Americans were given technical liberty but remained in many ways in economic servitude. Education again was seen as the key. The struggle over education went on, through *Plessy vs. Ferguson* in 1896—separate, but equal—right down to the 1954 *Brown vs. Board of Education*, which declared separate but equal unconstitutional.

In a way our first 200 years were a clear lesson in the relationship be-   6
tween democracy, citizenship, and education, the triangle on which the freedom of America depended. But sometime after the Civil War with the emergence of great corporations and of an economic system organized around private capital, private labor, and private markets, and with the import from Europe of models of higher education devoted to scientific research, we began to see a gradual change in the character of American

education generally and particularly the character of higher education in America's colleges and universities. From the founding of Johns Hopkins at the end of the nineteenth century through today we have witnessed the professionalization, the bureaucratization, the privatization, the commercialization, and the individualization of education. Civics stopped being the envelope in which education was put and became instead a footnote on the letter that went inside and nothing more than that.

With the rise of industry, capitalism, and a market society, it came to pass that young people were exposed more and more to tutors other than teachers in their classrooms or even those who were in their churches, their synagogues—and today, their mosques as well. They were increasingly exposed to the informal education of popular opinion, of advertising, of merchandising, of the entertainment industry. Today it is a world whose messages come at our young people from those ubiquitous screens that define modern society and have little to do with anything that you teach. The large screens of the multiplex promote content determined not just by Hollywood but by multinational corporations that control information, technology, communication, sports, and entertainment. About ten of those corporations control over 60 to 70 percent of what appears on those screens.

Then, too, there are those medium-sized screens, the television sets that peek from every room of our homes. That's where our children receive not the twenty-eight to thirty hours a week of instruction they might receive in primary and secondary school, or the six or nine hours a week of classroom instruction they might get in college, but where they get anywhere from forty to seventy hours a week of ongoing "information," "knowledge," and above all, entertainment. The barriers between these very categories of information and entertainment are themselves largely vanished.

Then, there are those little screens, our computer screens, hooked up to the Internet. Just fifteen years ago they were thought to be a potential new electronic frontier for democracy. But today very clearly they are one more mirror of a commercialized, privatized society where everything is for sale. The Internet which our children use is now a steady stream of advertising, mass marketing, a virtual mall, a place where the violence, the values—for better or worse—of these same universal corporations reappear in video games and sales messages. Ninety-five to 97 percent of the hits on the Internet are commercial. Of those, 25 to 30 percent are hits on pornographic sites. Most of our political leaders are deeply proud that they have hooked up American schools to the Internet, and that we are a "wired nation." We have, however, in effect hooked up our schools to what in many ways is a national sewer.

In the nineteenth century, Alexis de Tocqueville talked about the "im-   10
mense tutelary power" of that other source of learning, not education, but
public opinion. Now public opinion has come under the control of corporate conglomerates whose primary interest is profit. They are willing to put
anything out there that will sell and make a profit.

We have watched this commercialization and privatization, a distortion   11
of the education mission and its content, going to the heart of our schools
themselves. Most American colleges and universities now are participants—
and in some ways beneficiaries—but ultimately victims of the cola wars. Is
your college a Pepsi college or a Coke college? Which do you have a contract
with? And which monopoly do your kids have to drink the goods of? While
you are busy teaching them the importance of critical choices, they can only
drink one cola beverage on this campus. Choice ends at the cafeteria door.

Go to what used to be the food services cafeteria of your local college   12
or university and in many cases you will now find a food court indistin-
guishable from the local mall featuring Taco Bell, Starbucks, McDonald's,
and Burger King. Yes, they are feeding students, but more importantly, they
are creating a venue in the middle of campus for what is not education, but
an acquisition-of-brands learning. Brand learning means getting young
people on board: any merchandiser will tell you, "If we can get the kids
when they are in high school and college to buy into our brand, we've got
them for life."

Consequences of De-funding

Part of privatization means the de-funding of public institutions, of culture   13
and education, and the de-funding of universities, and so these institutions
make a pact with the devil. A real mischief of the modern world (one that
colleges haven't yet encountered) is Channel One, which goes into our nation's junior high schools and high schools—particularly the poor ones,
those in the inner-city that can't afford their own technology or their own
equipment. It makes this promise: "We're not going to give it to you, but
we'll lease you some equipment: television sets, maybe a satellite dish, some
modems, maybe even a few computers, if you do one thing. Once a day
make sure that every student in this school sits in the classroom and
watches a very nice little twelve-minute program. Only three minutes of it
will be advertising. Let us feed advertising to your kids during a history or
a social studies class, and we will lend you some technology."

Most states—New York state is the only one that has held out—in   14
America have accepted Channel One, which is now in over twelve or thirteen thousand high schools around the nation. Our students sit during class
time, possibly a social studies or history class, and watch advertising. I dare

say, if somebody said they were going to give you some equipment as long as you watch the message of Christ or the church of Christ for three minutes a day, or said they were going to give you some equipment as long as you listen to the message of the Communist Party or the Democratic party during class for three out of twelve minutes, there would be an outcry and an uproar. Totalitarianism! State propaganda! Theocracy! But because they have been so degradingly de-funded, we have allowed our schools to be left without the resources to resist this deal with the devil.

Tell me why it is in the modern world that when a political party or a   15 state takes over the schools and spews its propaganda into them and takes over every sector of society, we call that political totalitarianism and oppose it as the denial of liberty. And when a church or a religion takes over every sector of society and spews its propaganda forth in its schools, we call it theocratic and totalitarian and go to war against it. But when the market comes in with its brands and advertising and takes over every sector of society and spews its propaganda in our schools, we call it an excellent bargain on the road to liberty. I don't understand that, and I don't think we should put up with it, and I don't think America should put up with it. I know the people who sell it would not sit still for a minute if their own children, sitting in private schools somewhere, were exposed to that commercial advertising. They're not paying $25,000 a year to have their kids watch advertising in the classroom. But, of course, it's not their children's schools that are at risk; it's mostly the schools of children of families who don't have much of a say about these things.

Imagine how far Channel One has come from Jefferson's dream, from   16 John Adams's dream, the dream of the common school. And how low we have sunk as a society where we turn our heads and say, "Well, it's not so bad, it's not really, it's just advertising." Advertisers know how valuable the legitimizing venue of the classroom is and pay double the rates of prime time to advertise on Channel One, not because the audience is so broad but because it is the perfect target audience and because it gets that extraordinary legitimization of the American classroom where what kids believe you "learn" in your classroom has to be true.

Commercialization and privatization go right across the board. You   17 see them in every part of our society. You see cultural institutions increasingly dependent on corporate handouts. Because we will not fund the arts, the arts, too, like education have to make a profit. In our universities and colleges, scientists are now selling patents and making deals that the research they do will benefit not humanity and their students, but the shareholders of corporations, and so their research will otherwise be kept private. Again, most administrators welcome that because they don't have to raise faculty research budgets. The corporate world will take care of that.

These practices change the nature of knowledge and information. They 18 privatize, making research a part of commercial enterprise. That's the kind of bargain we have made with our colleges and universities. We hope that somehow the faculty will remain insulated from it. We hope the students won't notice, but then when they're cynical about politics and about the administration, and cynical about their own education, and when they look to their own education as a passport to a hot job and big money—and nothing else—we wonder what's going on with them.

But of course students see everything; they have noses for hypocrisy. 19 Students see the hypocrisy of a society that talks about the importance of education and knowledge and information while its very educational institutions are selling their own souls for a buck, and they're doing it because the society otherwise won't support them adequately, is unwilling to tax itself, is unwilling to ask itself for sufficient funds to support quality education. That's where we are. That's where we were on September 10.

What We've Learned

On September 11 a dreadful, pathological act occurred, which nonetheless 20 may act in a brutal way as a kind of tutorial for America and for its educators. On that day, it suddenly became apparent to many people who'd forgotten it that America was no longer a land of independence or sovereignty, a land that could "go it alone." America was no longer capable of surviving as a free democracy unless it began to deal in different terms with a world that for 200 years it had largely ignored and in the last fifty or seventy-five years had treated in terms of that sad phrase "collateral damage." Foreign policy was about dealing with the collateral damage of America being America, America being commercialized, America being prosperous, America "doing well" in the economic sense—if necessary, at everybody else's expense.

September 11 was a brutal and perverse lesson in the inevitability of in- 21 terdependence in the modern world—and of the end of independence, where America could simply go it alone. It was the end of the time in which making a buck for individuals would, for those that were doing all right, be enough; somehow the fact that the rest of the world was in trouble and that much of America was in trouble—particularly its children (one out of five in poverty)—was incidental. After thirty years of privatization and commercialization, the growing strength of the ideology that said the era not just of government, but of big government was over; that said, this was to be the era of markets, and markets will solve every problem: education, culture, you name it, the markets can do it.

On September 11 it became clear that there were areas in which the 22 market could do nothing: terrorism, poverty, injustice, war. The tragedy pointed to issues of democracy and equality and culture, and revealed a foreign policy that had been paying no attention. In the early morning of September 12, nobody called Bill Gates at Microsoft or Michael Eisner at Disney and said "Help us, would you? You market guys have good solutions. Help us get the terrorists." Indeed, the heroes of September 11 were public officials, public safety officers: policemen, firemen, administrators, even a mayor who found his soul during that period. Those were the ones we turned to and suddenly understood that they played a public role representing all of us.

Suddenly, Americans recognized that its citizens were the heroes. Not 23 the pop singers, fastball pitchers, and the guys who make all the money in the NBA; not those who've figured out how to make a fast buck by the time they're thirty, the Internet entrepreneurs. In the aftermath of 9/11, it was particularly those public-official-citizens. All citizens because in what they do, they are committed to the welfare of their neighbors, their children, to future generations. That's what citizens are supposed to do: think about the communities to which they belong and pledge themselves to the public good of those communities.

Hence the importance of the civic professions like teaching. In most 24 countries, in fact, teachers and professors are public officials. They are seen, like firemen and policemen, as guardians of the public good, of the res publica, those things of the public that we all care about. On September 11 and the days afterwards, it became clear how important those folks were. As a consequence, a kind of closing of a door occasioned by the fall of the towers became an opening of a window of new opportunities, new possibilities, new citizenship: an opportunity to explore interdependence. Interdependence is another word for citizenship.

Citizenship in the World

The citizen is the person who acknowledges and recognizes his or her inter- 25 dependence in a neighborhood, a town, a state, in a nation—and today, in the world. Anyone with eyes wide open during the last thirty to forty years has known that the world has become interdependent in ineluctable and significant ways. AIDS and the West Nile Virus don't carry passports. They go where they will. The Internet doesn't stop at national boundaries; it's a worldwide phenomenon. Today's telecommunications technologies define communications and entertainment all over the world without regard to borders. Global warming recognizes no sovereignty, and nobody can say he or she won't have to suffer the consequences of polluted air. Ecology, technology, and of course economics and markets are global in character, and no nation can pretend that its own destiny is any longer in its own hands in the manner of eighteenth and nineteenth century nations.

In particular, this nation was the special land where independence had 26 been declared, and our two oceans would protect us from the world. We went for several hundred years thinking America was immune to the problems and tumult and prejudices of the wars of the world beyond the oceans. And then 9/11—and suddenly it became clear that no American could ever rest comfortably in bed at night if somewhere, someone else in the world was starving or someone's children were at risk. With 9/11 it became apparent that whatever boundaries once protected us and whatever new borders we were trying to build including the missile shield (a new technological "virtual ocean" that would protect us from the world) were irrelevant.

Multilateralism becomes a new mandate of national security, a neces- 27 sity. There are no oceans wide enough, there are no walls high enough to protect America from the rest of our world. What does that say about education? It means that for the first time a lot of people who didn't care about civic education—the education of citizens, the soundness of our own democracy, the ability of our children to understand the world—now suddenly recognize this is key, that education counts. Multicultural education counts because we have to understand the cultures of other worlds. Language education counts because language is a window on other cultures and histories.

Citizenship is now the crucial identity. We need to think about what an 28 adequate civic education means today, and what it means to be a citizen. We need education-based community service programs. We need experiential learning, not just talking about citizenship but exercises in doing it. We need to strongly support the programs around the country that over the '80s and '90s sprang up but have recently been in decline.

But we also need new programs in media literacy. I talked about the 29 way in which a handful of global corporations control the information channels of television, the Internet, and Hollywood. We need young people who are sophisticated in media, who understand how media work, how media affect them, how to resist, how to control, how to become immune to media. Media literacy and media studies from my point of view become a key part of how we create a new civic education. Of course history, the arts, sociology, and anthropology, and all of those fields that make young people aware of the rest of the world in a comparative fashion are more important than ever before.

We are a strange place because we are one of the most multicultural na- 30
tions on Earth with people in our schools from all over the world, and yet
we know less than most nations about the world from which those people
come. At one and the same time, we are truly multicultural, we represent
the globe, and yet we know little about it.

Coming Full Circle

In coming full circle, the trajectory from the Declaration of Independence 31
200 years ago to the declaration of interdependence that was sounded on
September 11 opens an opportunity for us as educators to seize the initiative to make civic education central again. The opportunity to free education from the commercializers and privatizers, to take it back for civic
education and for our children, and to make the schools of America and
the world the engines of democracy and liberty and freedom that they were
supposed to be. And that's not just an abstraction. That starts with ad-
dressing commercialization directly: confronting Channel One and the
food court at your local college, the malling of your cafeterias, and the sell-
out of corporate research.

There are things that every one of us can do inside our own colleges 32
and universities. If we do, our students will notice. And if we really make
our colleges and universities democratic, civic, independent, au-
tonomous, international, and multilateral again, we will no longer even
need civics classes. Our students will take one look at what we've done
in the university and understand the relationship between education and
democracy. That must be our mission. I hope that as individual citizens,
teachers, administrators, you will take this mission seriously. I certainly
do, and I know that as before, the future of liberty, the future of democracy in both America and around the world, depends most of all on its
educational institutions and on the teachers and administrators who control them. Which means we really are in a position to determine what our
future will be.

Thinking About the Essay

1. This essay reflects Barber's deep historical and political knowledge and his
passionate concern for the role of education in civic and global life. What
assumptions does he make about his primary audience—who, we can infer
from the place of publication—are educators? What "message" does he
want to convey to his primary audience? What secondary audiences might
he have in mind, and how does he manage to appeal to them?

2. State Barber's thesis in your own words. Does he ever present a thesis
statement or does he imply it? Explain.

3. In part, this essay reflects a rhetorical strategy known as process analysis. How does Barber take us through a step-by-step historical process? Point to specific stages in this process. How does the process come full circle? In other words, how does he tie September 11, 2001, to July 4, 1776?

4. Barber divides his essay into five parts. Summarize each part. What logical relationships do you see between and among them? How do these sections progress logically from one stage of Barber's argument to the next?

5. What definitions does Barber offer for such key terms as *democracy, education, civic responsibility, globalization,* and *multilateralism*? What is his purpose? Why does he introduce such abstract terms? What other broad abstractions does he discuss, and where?

Responding in Writing

6. In a personal essay, discuss the quality of your own education. To what extent do you feel your education has provided you with a sense of what it takes to create or sustain a democracy or a sense of civic responsibility? To what extent have you been encouraged to think of yourself as a citizen of the world? To what extent have you been affected by the forces of consumerism? Explore these issues—and any others raised by Barber—in your paper.

7. Barber writes that "students see everything; they have noses for hypocrisy" (paragraph 19). Clearly you agree with this notion. But what precisely are *you* hypocritical about when you think about education, democracy, terrorism, consumerism, and some of the other "big" words that Barber discusses? In fact, do you have a nose for hypocrisy or might you actually be hypocritical? (For example, if you believe in democracy as a necessary civic institution, do you vote in elections?) Write an essay exploring the subject of hypocrisy.

8. Are you a global citizen or a global consumer? Must you be one or the other, or can you be both and still be a good citizen—of your country and of the world? Examine this subject in a reflective essay.

Networking

9. In small groups, look over the syllabi for the various courses that you are taking this term. Which ones explicitly address some of the main issues raised by Barber? Does the English course in which you're presently enrolled reflect these issues? Present your findings to the class.

10. Locate websites for the Walt Whitman Center for the Culture and Politics of Democracy or the Democracy Collaborative. Take notes on these organizations, and then prepare a paper on their missions and programs.

Culture Wars: Whose Culture Is It, Anyway?

A s we have seen in earlier chapters, the power and influence of the United States radiate outward to the rest of the world in many ways. Nowhere is this more visible than in the impact of various American cultural manifestations—ranging from food, to clothing, to music, to television and film—on other countries. When a French farmer burns down a McDonald's or terrorists destroy a disco in Bali, killing more than two hundred people, we sense the opposition to American cultural hegemony. Conversely, when young Iranians turn on their banned satellite systems to catch the latest *Simpsons* episode, or when street merchants in Kenya sell University of Michigan T-shirts, we detect the flip side of the culture wars— the mesmerizing power of American culture throughout the world. Sometimes it seems that American culture, wittingly or unwittingly, is in a battle for the world's soul.

We also have to acknowledge that the culture wars color American life as well. At home, current debates over immigration, affirmative action, bilingual education, and much more impinge on our daily lives and dominate media presentations. It might be fashionable to say that we all trace our DNA to Africa and that ideally we are all citizens of the world, but the issue of what sort of culture we represent individually or collectively is much more complicated. Tiger Woods might be the icon for the New American, or for the new Universal Person, but his slightest actions and words prompt cultural controversy. American culture cuts many ways; it is powerful, but also strange and contradictory.

The culture wars take us to the borders of contradiction both at home and abroad. It is too facile to say that we are moving "beyond" monoculturalism at home or that the rest of the world doesn't have to

French farmer José Bové, who leads a radical farmer's union in France protesting the encroachments of American fast-food culture, is shown here after having been released from prison for vandalizing a McDonald's restaurant in France. To celebrate, he dines on local French bread, Roquefort cheese, and wine.

Thinking About the Image

1. If McDonald's is stereotypically American, what is stereotypically French about this image? Why do you think José Bové is emphasizing those stereotypes?

2. Think about other images of protest you have seen in this book (see p. 162). Clearly, José Bové's delicious meal was intended for an audience, and had a clear purpose. How effective is the "rhetoric" of his protest here?

3. In 2003, some Americans boycotted French products (such as wine and cheese) in protest over France's refusal to support the United States in its war against Iraq. Why is something so seemingly basic as food such a potent symbol of cultural meaning and pride?

4. Read Carol Norris's essay "Eat All of Your McAfrika, Honey, Because I Have a Funny Feeling There Might Be Starving People Out There Somewhere." In what ways are her argument and Bové's agenda similar? Could this photograph be used accurately to illustrate her essay? Why, or why not?

embrace American culture if it doesn't want to. What is clear is that the very *idea* of American culture, in all its diversity, is so pervasive that it spawns numerous viewpoints and possibilities for resolution. After all, culture is a big subject: it embraces one's ethnic, racial, class, religious, sexual, and national identity. We can't be uncritical about culture. We have to understand how culture both molds and reflects our lives.

The writers in this chapter offer perspectives—all of them provocative and engaging—on national and transnational culture. They deal with the ironies of culture at home and the paradoxes of American cultural influence abroad. Some of the writers engage in self-reflection, others in rigorous analysis. All refuse to view culture in simplistic terms. In reading them, you might discover that whether you grew up in the United States or another country, culture is at the heart of who you are.

Cultural Baggage

BARBARA EHRENREICH

Barbara Ehrenreich was born in 1941 in Butte, Montana. She attended Reed College (B.A., 1963) and Rockefeller University (Ph.D. in biology, 1968). A self-described socialist and feminist, Ehrenreich uses her scientific training to investigate a broad range of social issues: health care, the plight of the poor, the condition of women around the world. Her scathing critiques of American health care in such books as *The American Health Empire* (with John Ehrenreich, 1970), *Complaints and Disorders: The Sexual Politics of Sickness* (with Deirdre English, 1973), and *For Her Own Good* (with English, 1978) established her as an authority in the field. In her provocative *The Hearts of Men: American Dreams and the Flight from Commitment* (1983), Ehrenreich surveys the decline of male investment in the family from the 1950s to the 1980s. A prolific writer during the 1980s and 1990s, Ehrenreich most recently published the award-winning book, *Nickel and Dimed: On (Not) Getting By in America* (2001). She is also a frequent contributor to magazines, including *Nation, Esquire, Radical America, New Republic,* and the *New York Times,* while serving as a contributing editor to *Ms.* and *Mother Jones.* Her fresh insights into the complex contours of American society can be seen in "Cultural Baggage," published in the *New York Times* Magazine in 1992, where Ehrenreich offers a new slant on the idea of "heritage."

Before Reading

What is your ethnic or religious heritage? Do you feel comfortable explaining or defending it? Why or why not?

An acquaintance was telling me about the joys of rediscovering her eth- 1
nic and religious heritage. "I know exactly what my ancestors were doing 2,000 years ago," she said, eyes gleaming with enthusiasm, "and I can do the same things now." Then she leaned forward and inquired politely, "And what is your ethnic background, if I may ask?"

"None," I said, that being the first word in line to get out of my mouth. 2
Well, not "none," I backtracked. Scottish, English, Irish—that was something, I supposed. Too much Irish to qualify as a WASP; too much of the hated English to warrant a "Kiss Me, I'm Irish" button; plus there are a number of dead ends in the family tree due to adoptions, missing records, failing memories and the like. I was blushing by this time. Did "none" mean I was rejecting my heritage out of Anglo-Celtic self-hate? Or was I revealing a hidden ethnic chauvinism in which the Britannically derived serve as a kind of neutral standard compared with the ethnic "others"?

Throughout the 1960s and '70s I watched one group after another— 3
African Americans, Latinos, Native Americans—stand up and proudly reclaim their roots while I just sank back ever deeper into my seat. All this excitement over ethnicity stemmed, I uneasily sensed, from a past in which their ancestors had been trampled upon by my ancestors, or at least by people who looked very much like them. In addition, it had begun to seem almost un-American not to have some sort of hyphen at hand, linking one to more venerable times and locales.

But the truth is, I was raised with none. We'd eaten ethnic foods in my 4
childhood home, but these were all borrowed, like the pasties, or Cornish meat pies, my father had picked up from his fellow miners in Butte, Montana. If my mother had one rule, it was militant ecumenism in all matters of food and experience. "Try new things," she would say, meaning anything from sweet-breads to clams, with an emphasis on the "new."

As a child, I briefly nourished a craving for tradition and roots. I im- 5
mersed myself in the works of Sir Walter Scott. I pretended to believe that the bagpipe was a musical instrument. I was fascinated to learn from a grandmother that we were descended from certain Highland clans and longed for a pleated skirt in one of their distinctive tartans.

But in *Ivanhoe*, it was the dark-eyed "Jewess" Rebecca I identified 6
with, not the flaxen-haired bimbo Rowena. As for clans: Why not call them tribes—those bands of half-clad peasants and warriors whose idea of cuisine was stuffed sheep gut washed down with whisky? And then there was

the sting of Disraeli's remark—which I came across in my early teens—to the effect that his ancestors had been leading orderly, literate lives when my ancestors were still rampaging through the Highlands daubing themselves with blue paint.

Motherhood put the screws on me, ethnicity-wise. I had hoped that by marrying a man of Eastern European Jewish ancestry I would acquire for my descendants the ethnic genes that my own forebears so sadly lacked. At one point I even subjected the children to a seder of my own design, including a little talk about the flight from Egypt and its relevance to modern social issues. But the kids insisted on buttering their matzos and snickering through my talk. "Give me a break, Mom," the older one said. "You don't even believe in God." 7

After the tiny pagans had been put to bed, I sat down to brood over Elijah's wine. What had I been thinking? The kids knew that their Jewish grandparents were secular folks who didn't hold seders themselves. And if ethnicity eluded me, how could I expect it to take root in my children, who are not only Scottish English Irish, but Hungarian Polish Russian to boot? 8

But, then, on the fumes of Manischewitz, a great insight took form in my mind. It was true, as the kids said, that I didn't "believe in God." But this could be taken as something very different from an accusation—a reminder of a genuine heritage. My parents had not believed in God either, nor had my grandparents or any other progenitors going back to the great-great level. They had become disillusioned with Christianity generations ago—just as, on the in-law side, my children's other ancestors had shaken off their Orthodox Judaism. This insight did not exactly furnish me with an "identity," but it was at least something to work with: We are the kind of people, I realized—whatever our distant ancestors' religions—who do not believe, who do not carry on traditions, who do not do things just because someone has done them before. 9

The epiphany went on: I recalled that my mother never introduced a procedure for cooking or cleaning by telling me, "Grandma did it this way." What did Grandma know, living in the days before vacuum cleaners and disposable toilet mops? In my parents' general view, new things were better than old and the very fact that some ritual had been performed in the past was a good reason for abandoning it now. Because what was the past, as our forebears knew it? Nothing but poverty, superstition and grief. "Think for yourself," Dad used to say. "Always ask why." 10

In fact, this may have been the ideal cultural heritage for my particular ethnic strain—bounced as it was from the Highlands of Scotland across the sea, out to the Rockies, down into the mines and finally spewed out into high-tech, suburban America. What better philosophy, for a race of 11 migrants, than "think for yourself"? What better maxim, for a people whose whole world was rudely inverted every 30 years or so, than "try new things"?

The more tradition-minded, the newly enthusiastic celebrants of Purim   12
and Kwanzaa and Solstice, may see little point to survival if the survivors carry no cultural freight—religion, for example, or ethnic tradition. To which I would say that skepticism, curiosity and wide-eyed ecumenical tolerance are also worthy elements of the human tradition and are at least as old as such notions as "Serbian" or "Croatian," "Scottish" or "Jewish." I make no claims for my personal line of progenitors except that they remained loyal to the values that may have induced all of our ancestors, long, long ago, to climb down from the trees and make their way into the open plains.

A few weeks ago I cleared my throat and asked the children, now   13
mostly grown and fearsomely smart, whether they felt any stirrings of ethnic or religious identity, which might have been, ahem, insufficiently nourished at home. "None," they said, adding firmly, "and the world would be a better place if nobody else did, either." My chest swelled with pride, as would my mother's, to know that the race of "none" marches on.

Thinking About the Essay

1. Why is Ehrenreich's title perfect for the essay that she writes?

2. What is Ehrenreich's purpose in asking so many questions in this essay? Is the strategy effective? Why or why not?

3. How would you describe the tone of this essay—the writer's attitude or approach to her subject? Locate phrases, sentences, and passages that support your response.

4. Ehrenreich traces a pattern of causality in this essay as she describes not only her own experience of ethnic and religious heritage but that of others as well. Trace this pattern of cause and effect throughout the article. Where do other rhetorical strategies—for example, illustration, comparison, or definition—come into play?

5. Examine paragraphs 10–13. How do they serve as an extended conclusion to the argument Ehrenreich presents?

Responding in Writing

6. Write your own personal essay with the title "Cultural Baggage." Like Ehrenreich, use the personal, or "I," point of view and focus on your own experience of your ethnic and religious heritage. Be certain to have a clear thesis that helps to guide your approach to the subject.

7. As an exercise, argue against Ehrenreich's claim that it is best to have "no cultural freight—religion, for example, or ethnic tradition" (paragraph 12).

8. Write a comparative paper in which you analyze the concepts of *cultural pride* and *cultural baggage*. Establish a controlling thesis, and develop at least three major comparative topics for this essay.

Networking

9. Form two equal groups of class members. One group should develop an argument in favor of cultural heritage, the other opposing it. Select one spokesperson from each group and have them debate the issue in front of the class.

10. Ehrenreich says she is a socialist. Go online and locate information on this term, as well as additional information on Ehrenreich herself. Then use this information to write a paper describing how "Cultural Baggage" reflects Ehrenreich's socialist views.

Eat All of Your McAfrika, Honey, Because I Have a Funny Feeling There Might Be Starving People Out There Somewhere

CAROL NORRIS | Carol Norris, a freelance writer and psychotherapist, writes for several liberal and online magazines, including *Common Dreams*, where the following essay first appeared in August 2002. In this article, Norris takes aim at one of America's most venerated symbols—the twin golden arches of McDonald's—as she proposes several new types of Big Macs that might appeal to residents in various nations.

Before Reading

Why do you like or dislike McDonald's? Is there a McDonald's on or near your campus? Have you ever eaten at a McDonald's in another country? How do you account for the presence of so many McDonald's restaurants in the United States and around the world?

McDonald's recently launched a new burger-in-a-pita product in Norway: The "McAfrika." 1

And with this they have inadvertently created a brilliantly succinct 2 metaphor for the increasingly blatant corporate takeover of the Earth—

country by Mccountry, continent by Mccontinent. I wonder if McDonald's, its arches a great, snapping, golden maw, gobbling up one country's burger market share while digesting a bit of another continent's culture, created this product to honor the 12 million Africans doing their best to stave off unspeakable famine, or to pay tribute to the millions dying of AIDS, or perhaps to give a nod to the ever-growing numbers left without clean, public drinking water. It's tough to say.

And I thought Disney putting on an Electricland Parade in California during last year's blackouts so that all of us Blackouters, intermittently bereft of electricity, could get a little glimpse of 20 foot tall, light-bulb covered bumblebees was a gauche juxtaposition. At least McDonald's had the decency to do it in Norway, away from all that unappetizing African suffering. Disney did it right here in California. But, nobody said a word about it as far as I can tell; unlike in Norway where some people like the Norwegian Red Cross and Norwegian Church Aid have seen the incongruity. These groups have confronted McDonald's and met with its representatives to discuss the issue and the possibility of sharing proceeds of its sales with the aid agencies helping Africans. Nothing yet. Maybe you should go to McDonald's website and email this suggestion to them.

Yes, yes, I know. See the cup half full. The McAfrika could be hailed as a celebration of Africa and the wonderful new possibilities its rich culture can offer the ingredient-locked hamburger. Africans should be happy and proud as they wait in line for their daily emergency protein biscuit. Maybe they will all be so full from the heaping dose of irony, they won't even need it.

This is not an invective against McDonald's. It just happens to be McDonald's. It could just as easily be any other multinational corporation doing something similar. The only thing I can figure is that maybe the people at McDonald's don't know what is going on in Africa, just like the guy down the street from me who herds those three pesky cigarette butts off the sidewalk into the gutter for twenty-five minutes every day with increasingly precious water spewed from his garden hose doesn't know there is a huge drought going on in the Southwest, not to mention the clean water crisis in developing countries and soon, perhaps, the world. Or just like my neighbor who uses a disposable bib on her kid and then cleans him up with disposable baby wipes and then changes his disposable diapers while using disposable mop covers to clean the mess on the floor and then afterward washes her face and hands with disposable "cleansing cloths" says to me "it's not like I'm throwing away plutonium, for chrissakes."

So, I was thinking: as long as we are appropriating a little culture from 6
large land masses, creating yummy burgers for corporate gain, I'd like to
offer a few burger suggestions of my own:

McMexico Burger: Made in an American-owned factory relocated to 7
Mexico. Includes a yummy GMO corn tortilla hand wrapped by Mexicans. Don't worry, no unions allowed! And, you know what that means:
lower labor standards and sub-living wages. And that equals dirt-cheap
prices for you! Get yours while the burgers and the workers last! [Also af-
fectionately known by some as the McNAFTA Burger.]

McVenezuela Burger: Delicious. But, you can only get it if you secretly 8
abet the Venezuelan Rightist in line with you and he is able to successfully
oust the democratically elected Shift Manager. [Limited to American government officials only.]

McDeveloping Country Burger: Basic burger. Comes with a $19, 6 oz. 9
cup of newly privatized water. [Cup and debt relief sold separately and only
for those who have proof of a World Bank/IMF-endorsed contract with a
big water company. No exceptions.] Some of the only uncontaminated water left in the country!! Time limited offer. Offer while water supplies last.
Bribes welcome.

McEvil Axis Burger: [Also called the McBrave New World Burger.] In- 10
cludes an absolutely FREE Bonus Ingredient: Valium. Yep, just another
idea American military chiefs here in the ole' US are reportedly thinking
about to mellow out the evil out there. Offer limited to large, hostile populations and certified evildoers only. Yes, the McJust as Evil Country, But
Strategically Important and Therefore Our Friend Burger has the exact
same ingredients as the McEvil Axis Burger. Sorry, but we've completely
sold out.

McIraq Burger: Basically, just some flat bread dripping in lots and lots 11
and lots of oil. All the other ingredients have been sanctioned. We know
Westerners are just dying to sink their teeth into this one. Remember, Iraq
reserves the right to refuse service to anyone.

McEngland Burger: Kinda bland. Special orders? We'll take 'em, what- 12
ever you want. Just tell us what you want! Your loyalty is important to us!
[This offer is limited to American power holders only.]

McUSA Burger: Offered only in the USofA. We use pasteurized beef! 13
[Okay, alright, irradiated beef. Po-TAY-to, Po-TAH-to. Whatever.] If
your budget is tight and you only make $5.15 an hour, the federal mini-
mum wage that congress has frozen for a while now, phone your con-
gressperson and ask him/her to take you out to lunch. Because, unlike
what they've done for you, they just voted themselves their yearly pay
raise. They should all be pretty flush with cash. Soon to be made with

100% unadvertised, genetically modified ingredients. Yum! Comes with a side of beef-broth flavored vegetarian fries. Wrapped in a disposable, non-biodegradable American flag. But, really, order whatever you want, it's a free country; nobody's stopping you. Only be very, very careful to order things that are with us, not against us. Come to think of it, it doesn't really matter what you order because with that new technology out of MIT that can falsify images, we can film you on our cameras and with a little digital alteration we can make it look exactly like you ordered an Extra-Large Weapon of Mass Destruction and a side of Anthrax.

Bon appetit. . . . 14

Thinking About the Essay

1. Norris begins her essay with a one-sentence paragraph. What is the effect? How does the sentence relate to the next fully developed paragraph? Where else does she employ this single-sentence approach to paragraph design, and why?

2. The writer adopts an informal, colloquial style in this essay. Why? Point to aspects of this style in the essay.

3. Explain Norris's classification scheme. What is the tone in these paragraphs?

4. Does Norris have an argument in this essay? Why or why not? Where might it be stated most clearly? Why does she use satire to advance her claim?

5. What, ultimately, does Norris say about globalization? How does she define it, and where?

Responding in Writing

6. Write a personal essay about your experience with fast food. Have you worked in a fast-food restaurant? Are you a fast-food junkie, an occasional consumer, a die-hard resister? Do you think about the global reach of various fast-food franchises as you bite into your Big Mac, Whopper, or KFC? Try to adopt a comic tone in developing this essay.

7. Compare and contrast the essays by Goodman (see Chapter 4) and Norris. Focus on subject, thesis, tone, and any other aspects of the two essays that you consider important.

8. Develop a classification essay in which you analyze the following forms or types of American cultural influence that you detect in the world today: food, television, music, and film. Explain why these types of cultural influence (some would call it cultural imperialism) are so powerful throughout the contemporary world.

Networking

9. Norris suggests in her essay that you go to the McDonald's website and e-mail them about the McAfrika controversy. In a group of three or four class members, compose a joint e-mail and then transmit it to McDonald's. Ask specifically about the controversy—and also about McDonald's efforts to share its resources with other nations around the world.

10. For a brief research paper, go online and find information about McDonald's worldwide operations. Write a paper in which you take a position on the corporation's global research. Incorporate documentation into your paper.

Whose Culture Is It, Anyway?

HENRY LOUIS GATES JR.

Henry Louis Gates Jr. is one of the most respected figures in the field of African American studies. Born in 1950 in Keyser, West Virginia, he received a B.A. degree (summa cum laude) from Harvard University (1973) and M.A. (1974) and Ph.D. degrees (1979) from Clare College, Cambridge University. A recipient of numerous major grants, including the prestigious MacArthur Prize Fellowship, and a professor at Harvard University, Gates in numerous essays and books argues for a greater diversity in arts, literature, and life. In one of his best-known works, *Loose Canons: Notes on the Culture Wars* (1992), Gates states, "The society we have made simply won't survive without the values of tolerance. And cultural tolerance comes to nothing without cultural understanding." Among his many publications are *The Signifying Monkey: Toward a Theory of Afro-American Literary Criticism* (1988), which won both a National Book Award and an American Book Award; *Colored People, A Memoir* (1994); *The Future of the Race* (with Cornel West, 1996); and *Wonders of the African World* (1999). In the following essay, which appeared originally in the *New York Times* on May 4, 1991, Gates analyzes the cultural diversity movement in American colleges and universities.

Before Reading

Gates argues elsewhere that we must reject "ethnic absolutism" of all kinds. What do you think he means by this phrase? Exactly how does a college or university—perhaps your institution—transcend this problem?

I recently asked the dean of a prestigious liberal arts college if his school   1
would ever have, as Berkeley has, a 70 percent non-white enrollment.
"Never," he replied. "That would completely alter our identity as a center
of the liberal arts."

The assumption that there is a deep connection between the shape of a   2
college's curriculum and the ethnic composition of its students reflects a
disquieting trend in education. Political representation has been confused
with the "representation" of various ethnic identities in the curriculum.

The cultural right wing, threatened by demographic changes and the   3
ensuing demands for curricular change, has retreated to intellectual protectionism, arguing for a great and inviolable "Western tradition," which
contains the seeds, fruit and flowers of the very best thought or uttered in
history. (Typically, Mortimer Adler has ventured that blacks "wrote no
good books.") Meanwhile, the cultural left demands changes to accord
with population shifts in gender and ethnicity. Both are wrongheaded.

I am just as concerned that so many of my colleagues feel that the ra-   4
tionale for a diverse curriculum depends on the latest Census Bureau report
as I am that those opposed see pluralism as forestalling the possibility of a
communal "American" identity. To them, the study of our diverse cultures
must lead to "tribalism" and "fragmentation."

The cultural diversity movement arose partly because of the fragmen-   5
tation of society by ethnicity, class and gender. To make it the culprit for
this fragmentation is to mistake effect for cause. A curriculum that reflects
the achievement of the world's great cultures, not merely the West's, is not
"politicized"; rather it situates the West as one of a community of civilizations. After all, culture is always a conversation among different voices.

To insist that we "master our own culture" before learning others—as   6
Arthur Schlesinger Jr. has proposed—only defers the vexed question: What
gets to count as "our" culture? What has passed as "common culture" has
been an Anglo-American regional culture, masking itself as universal. Significantly different cultures sought refuge underground.

Writing in 1903, W. E. B. Du Bois expressed his dream of a high culture   7
that would transcend the color line: "I sit with Shakespeare and he winces
not." But the dream was not open to all. "Is this the life you grudge us,"
he concluded, "O knightly America?" For him, the humanities were a conduit into a republic of letters enabling escape from racism and ethnic chauvinism. Yet no one played a more crucial role than he in excavating the long
buried heritage of Africans and African-Americans.

The fact of one's ethnicity, for any American of color, is never neutral: 8
One's public treatment, and public behavior, are shaped in large part by
one's perceived ethnic identity, just as by one's gender. To demand that

Americans shuck their cultural heritages and homogenize themselves into a "universal" WASP culture is to dream of an America in cultural white face, and that just won't do.

So it's only when we're free to explore the complexities of our hyphen- 9 ated culture that we can discover what a genuinely common American culture might actually look like.

Is multiculturalism un-American? Herman Melville didn't think so. As 10 he wrote: "We are not a narrow tribe, no. . . . We are not a nation, so much as a world." We're all ethnics; the challenge of transcending ethnic chauvinism is one we all face.

We've entrusted our schools with the fashioning and refashioning of a 11 democratic polity. That's why schooling has always been a matter of political judgment. But in a nation that has theorized itself as plural from its inception, schools have a very special task.

Our society won't survive without the values of tolerance, and cultural 12 tolerance comes to nothing without cultural understanding. The challenge facing America will be the shaping of a truly common public culture, one responsive to the long-silenced cultures of color. If we relinquish the ideal of America as a plural nation, we've abandoned the very experiment America represents. And that is too great a price to pay.

Thinking About the Essay

1. Gates poses a question in his title. How does he answer it? Where does he state his thesis?

2. The essay begins with an anecdote. How does it illuminate a key aspect of the problem Gates analyzes?

3. Gates makes several references to other writers—Mortimer Adler, Arthur Schlesinger Jr. (who appears in an earlier chapter), W. E. B. Du Bois, and Herman Melville. Who are these figures, and how do they provide a frame or context for Gates's argument?

4. How does the writer use comparison and contrast and causal analysis to advance his argument?

5. How does the concluding paragraph serve as a fitting end to the writer's argument?

Responding in Writing

6. Write a comparative essay in which you analyze the respective approaches to multiculturalism by Arthur Schlesinger Jr. (see Chapter 2) and Gates.

7. Gates speaks of "our hyphenated culture" (paragraph 9). Write a paper examining this phrase and applying it to your own campus.

8. Are you on "the cultural left" or "the cultural right" (to use Gates's words in paragraph 3), or somewhere in the middle? Write a personal essay responding to this question.

Networking

9. Form four working groups of classmates. Each group should investigate the ethnic composition of your campus, courses and programs designed to foster pluralism and multiculturalism, and the institution's policy on affirmative action. Draft a document in which you present your findings and conclusions concerning the state of the cultural diversity movement on your campus.

10. Search the World Wide Web for sites that promote what Gates terms "universal WASP culture" (paragraph 8). What sort of ideology do they promote? Where do they stand in terms of the culture wars? What impact do you think they have on the course of contemporary life in the United States?

Hygiene and Repression

OCTAVIO PAZ

Octavio Paz was born in 1914 near Mexico City, into a family that was influential in the political and cultural life of the nation. Paz published poetry and short stories as a teenager and came to the attention of the famous Chilean poet Pablo Neruda, who encouraged him to attend a congress of leftist writers in Spain. Subsequently, Paz was drawn into the Spanish Civil War, fighting against the Fascist forces of Francisco Franco. Paz moved continuously for decades—Los Angeles, New York, Mexico City, and France—and served in his country's diplomatic corps for twenty years. During this time he published one of his most famous works, *The Labyrinth of Solitude* (1950), a study of Mexican culture and identity. A prolific writer of both poetry and prose, the author of more than four dozen books, Paz was awarded the Nobel Prize for Literature in 1990. He died in April 1998. Paz was a professor of comparative literature at Harvard University from 1973 to 1980, and during this period he wrote the following essay, which appears in *Convergences Essays on Art and Literature* (1997). In this essay, Paz offers a fine comparative investigation of rival cultural cuisines.

Before Reading

How would you describe "American" food? How does it reflect American culture? And how would you describe Spanish or French or Indian cuisine and the ways it captures its respective culture?

Traditional American cooking is a cuisine without mystery: simple, nourishing, scantily seasoned foods. No tricks: a carrot is a homely, honest carrot, a potato is not ashamed of its humble condition, and a steak is a big, bloody hunk of meat. This is a transubstantiation of the democratic virtues of the Founding Fathers: a plain meal, one dish following another like the sensible, unaffected sentences of a virtuous discourse. Like the conversation among those at table, the relation between substances and flavors is direct: sauces that mask tastes, garnishes that entice the eye, condiments that confuse the taste buds are taboo. The separation of one food from another is analogous to the reserve that characterizes the relations between sexes, races, and classes. In our countries food is communion, not only between those together at table but between ingredients; Yankee food, impregnated with Puritanism, is based on exclusions. The maniacal preoccupation with the purity and origin of food products has its counterpart in racism and exclusivism. The American contradiction—a democratic universalism based on ethnic, cultural, religious, and sexual exclusions—is reflected in its cuisine. In this culinary tradition our fondness for dark, passionate stews such as moles, for thick and sumptuous red, green, and yellow sauces, would be scandalous, as would be the choice place at our table of *huitlacoche,* which not only is made from diseased young maize but is black in color. Likewise our love for hot peppers, ranging from parakeet green to ecclesiastical purple, and for ears of Indian corn, their grains varying from golden yellow to midnight blue. Colors as violent as their tastes. Americans adore fresh, delicate colors and flavors. Their cuisine is like watercolor painting or pastels.

American cooking shuns spices as it shuns the devil, but it wallows in slews of cream and butter. Orgies of sugar. Complementary opposites: the almost apostolic simplicity and soberness of lunch, in stark contrast to the suspiciously innocent, pregenital pleasures of ice cream and milkshakes. Two poles: the glass of milk and the glass of whiskey. The first affirms the primacy of home and mother. The virtues of the glass of milk are twofold: it is a wholesome food and it takes us back to childhood. Fourier detested the family repast, the image of the family in civilized society, a tedious daily ceremony presided over by a tyrannical father and a phallic mother. What would he have said of the cult of the glass of milk? As for whiskey and gin, they are drinks for loners and introverts. For Fourier, Gastrosophy was the science of combining not only foods but guests at table: matching the variety of dishes is the variety of persons sharing the meal. Wines, spirits, and liqueurs are the complement of a meal, hence their object is to stimulate the relations and unions consolidated round a table. Unlike wine, pulque, champagne, beer, and vodka, neither whiskey nor gin accompanies meals. Nor are they apéritifs or digestifs. They are drinks that accentuate uncommunicativeness and unsociability. In a gastrosophic age they would not enjoy much of a reputation. The universal favor accorded them reveals the situation of our societies, ever wavering between promiscuous association and solitude.

Ambiguity and ambivalence are resources unknown to American cooking. Here, as in so many other things, it is the diametrical opposite of the extremely delicate French cuisine, based on nuances, variations, and modulations—transitions from one substance to another, from one flavor to another. In a sort of profane Eucharist, even a glass of water is transfigured into an erotic chalice: 3

> *Ta lèvre contre le cristal*
> *Gorgée à gorgée y compose*
> *Le souvenir pourpre et vital*
> *De la moins éphémère rose.**

It is the contrary as well of Mexican and Hindu cuisine, whose secret is the shock of tastes: cool and piquant, salt and sweet, hot and tart, pungent and delicate. Desire is the active agent, the secret producer of changes, whether it be the transition from one flavor to another or the contrast between several. In gastronomy as in the erotic, it's desire that sets substances, bodies, and sensations in motion; this is the power that rules their conjunction, commingling, and transmutation. A reasonable cuisine, in which each substance is what it is and in which both variations and contrasts are avoided, is a cuisine that has excluded desire.

Pleasure is a notion (a sensation) absent from traditional Yankee cuisine. Not pleasure but health, not correspondence between savors but the satisfaction of a need—these are its two values. One is physical and the other moral; both are associated with the idea of the body as work. Work in turn is a concept at once economic and spiritual: production and redemption. We are condemned to labor, and food restores the body after the pain and punishment of work. It is a real *reparation*, in both the physical and the moral sense. Through work the body pays its debt; by earning its 4

---

*Your lip against the crystal / Sip by sip forms therein / The vital deep crimson memory / Of the least ephemeral rose.—Stéphane Mallarmé, "Verre d'eau."

physical sustenance, it also earns its spiritual recompense. Work redeems us and the sign of this redemption is food. An active sign in the spiritual economy of humanity, food restores the health of body and soul. If what we eat gives us physical and spiritual health, the exclusion of spices for moral and hygienic reasons is justified: they are the signs of desire, and they are difficult to digest.

Health is the condition of two activities of the body, work and sports. 5 In the first, the body is an agent that produces and at the same time redeems; in the second, the sign changes: sports are a wasteful expenditure of energy. This is a contradiction in appearance only, since what we have here in reality is a system of communicating vessels. Sports are a physical expenditure that is precisely the contrary of what happens in sexual pleasure, since sports in the end become productive—an expenditure that produces health. Work in turn is an expenditure of energy that produces goods and thereby transforms biological life into social, economic, and moral life. There is, moreover, another connection between work and sports: both take place within a context of rivalry; both are competition and emulation. The two of them are forms of Fourier's "Cabalist" passion. In this sense, sports possess the rigor and gravity of work, and work possesses the gratuity and levity of sports. The play element of work is one of the few features of American society that might have earned Fourier's praise, though doubtless he would have been horrified at the commercialization of sports. The preeminence of work and sports, activities necessarily excluding sexual pleasure, has the same significance as the exclusion of spices in cuisine. If gastronomy and eroticism are unions and conjunctions of substances and tastes or of bodies and sensations, it is evident that neither has been a central preoccupation of American society—as ideas and social values, I repeat, not as more or less secret realities. In the American tradition the body is not a source of pleasure but of health and work, in the material and the moral sense.

The cult of health manifests itself as an "ethic of hygiene." I use the 6 word ethic because its prescriptions are at once physiological and moral. A despotic ethic: sexuality, work, sports, and even cuisine are its domains. Again, there is a dual concept: hygiene governs both the corporeal and the moral life. Following the precepts of hygiene means obeying not only rules concerning physiology but also ethical principles: temperance, moderation, reserve. The morality of separation gives rise to the rules of hygiene, just as the aesthetics of fusion inspires the combinations of gastronomy and erotics. In India I frequently witnessed the obsession of Americans with hygiene. Their dread of contagion seemed to know no bounds; anything and everything might be laden with germs: food, drink, objects, people, the very air. These preoccupations are the precise counterpart of the ritual preoccupations of Brahmans fearing contact with certain foods and impure things, not to mention people belonging to a caste different from their own. Many will say that the concerns of the American are justified, whereas those of the Brahman are superstitions. Everything depends on the point of view: for the Brahman the bacteria that the American fears are illusory, while the moral stains produced by contact with alien people are real. These stains are stigmas that isolate him: no member of his caste would dare touch him until he had performed long and complicated rites of purification. The fear of social isolation is no less intense than that of illness. The hygienic taboo of the American and the ritual taboo of the Brahman have a common basis: the concern for purity. This basis is religious even though, in the case of hygiene, it is masked by the authority of science.

In the last analysis, the cult of hygiene is merely another expression of   7 the principle underlying attitudes toward sports, work, cuisine, sex, and races. The other name of purity is separation. Although hygiene is a social morality based explicitly on science, its unconscious root is religious. Nonetheless, the form in which it expresses itself, and the justifications for it, are rational. In American society, unlike in ours, science from the very beginning has occupied a privileged place in the system of beliefs and values. The quarrel between faith and reason never took on the intensity that it assumed among Hispanic peoples. Ever since their birth as a nation, Americans have been modern; for them it is natural to believe in science, whereas for us this belief implies a negation of our past. The prestige of science in American public opinion is such that even political disputes frequently take on the form of scientific polemics, just as in the Soviet Union they assume the guise of quarrels about Marxist orthodoxy. Two recent examples are the racial question and the feminist movement: are intellectual differences between races and sexes genetic in origin or a historico-cultural phenomenon?

The universality of science (or what passes for science) justifies the   8 development and imposition of collective patterns of normality. Obviating the necessity for direct coercion, the overlapping of science and Puritan morality permits the imposition of rules that condemn peculiarities, exceptions, and deviations in a manner no less categorical and implacable than religious anathemas. Against the excommunications of science, the individual has neither the religious recourse of abjuration nor the legal one of *habeas corpus*. Although they masquerade as hygiene and science, these patterns of normality have the same function in the realm of eroticism as "healthful" cuisine in the sphere of gastronomy: the extirpation or the separation of what is alien, different, ambiguous, impure. One and the same condemnation applies to blacks, Chicanos, sodomites, and spices.

Thinking About the Essay

1. Paz's title is intriguing—as challenging perhaps as the essay. How does the title capture the substance of the essay?

2. Explain Paz's argument. What is his claim? What are his warrants? What support does he present, and how is it organized?

3. The writer composes dense, relatively long paragraphs, filled with figurative language, various allusions (notably to Fourier), difficult words, and complex sentences. Take one paragraph and analyze it as completely as possible. Would you say that Paz is writing for a Harvard audience? What exactly *is* a Harvard audience?

4. Sexuality is a theme, or motif, that runs through this essay. Trace its development in the essay and explain its contribution to the selection.

5. Paz uses a variety of rhetorical strategies—notably comparison and contrast—to organize his essay. Identify these strategies and explain how they function.

Responding in Writing

6. Select your favorite cuisine, and in an analytical essay explain why you prefer it to all other cuisines.

7. Write an essay comparing any two cuisines. Be certain to link these two cuisines to the nations or cultures they illuminate.

8. Paz makes an implicit criticism of American food in his essay. Write an argumentative essay in which you agree or disagree with his thoughts on the subject.

Networking

9. In small groups, select just one dish—for example, pizza or tacos or hamburger—and discuss ways in which this food reflects its culture. Draw up a list of these cultural attributes, and present it to the class.

10. Go to Google or another search engine and find out more about Octavio Paz. Focus on his thoughts about politics and then, in class discussion, show how his political views are reflected in the tone of "Hygiene and Repression."

That's Entertainment? Hollywood's Contribution to Anti-Americanism Abroad

MICHAEL MEDVED

Michael Medved, born in 1948 in Philadelphia, Pennsylvania, received his B.A. degree from Yale University (1969) and attended Yale Law School for one year before leaving to serve as a speechwriter for congressional and presidential campaigns from 1970 to 1972. After receiving an M.F.A. degree from San Francisco State University in 1974, Medved became a film reviewer for cable television station WTBS and Cable News Network, Los Angeles. Today he is a movie critic and co-host of *Sneak Previews*, PBS-TV; chief film critic for the *New York Post*; and Hollywood correspondent for the London *Sunday Times*. Medved's interests as a writer are quite broad: in addition to his film and cultural criticism, which appears notably in *Hollywood vs. America: Popular Culture and the War on Traditional Values* (1992), he has also written *What Really Happened to the Class of 65?* (1976), *The Shadow Presidents: The Secret History of the Chief Executives and Their Top Aides* (1979), and *Saving Childhood: Protecting Our Children from the National Assault on Innocence* (1998). In "That's Entertainment?"—published in the *National Interest* in the summer of 2002—Medved explains how Hollywood's depiction of the seedier aspects of American culture contributes to the unfavorable impression viewers abroad have of the United States.

Before Reading

Do you think that various American cultural manifestations—notably Hollywood films, television programs, and music—contribute to anti-Americanism around the world? Why or why not?

"THINK AMERICA: WHY THE HOLE WORLD HATES YOU?"   1

This message, proudly proclaimed in a hand-lettered sign held aloft by   2
a scowling, bearded Pakistani protestor during one of the angry demonstrations that followed September 11, continues to challenge the

world's dominant power. In responding to such disturbing questions about the origins of anti-Americanism, glib commentators may cite the imperial reach of U.S. corporations, or Washington's support for Israel, or sheer envy for the freedom and prosperity of American life. But they must also contend with the profound impact of the lurid Hollywood visions that penetrate every society on earth. The vast majority of people in Pakistan or Peru, Poland or Papua New Guinea, may never visit the United States or ever meet an American face to face, but they inevitably encounter images of L.A. and New York in the movies, television programs and popular songs exported everywhere by the American entertainment industry.

Those images inevitably exert a more powerful influence on overseas 3 consumers than they do on the American domestic audience. If you live in Seattle or Cincinnati, you understand that the feverish media fantasies provided by a DMX music video or a Dark Angel TV episode do not represent everyday reality for you or your neighbors. If you live in Indonesia or Nigeria, however, you will have little or no first-hand experience to balance the negative impressions provided by American pop culture, with its intense emphasis on violence, sexual adventurism, and every inventive variety of anti-social behavior that the most overheated imagination could concoct. No wonder so many Islamic extremists (and so many others) look upon America as a cruel, Godless, vulgar society—a "Great Satan," indeed.

During violent anti-American riots in October 2001, mobs in Quetta, 4 Pakistan specifically targeted five movie theaters showing U.S. imports and offered their negative review of this cinematic fare by burning each of those theaters to the ground. "Look what they did!" wailed Chaudary Umedali amid the smoking ruins of his cinema. He said that a thousand rioters smashed the doors of his theater and threw firebombs inside because "they didn't like our showing American films." Ironically, the last movie he had offered his Quetta customers was *Desperado*—a hyper-violent, R-rated 1995 shoot-em-up with Antonio Banderas and Salma Hayek, specifically designed by its Texas-born director Robert Rodriguez for export outside the United States (in this case, to worldwide Hispanic audiences).

Even the President of the United States worries publicly about the dis- 5 torted view of this embattled nation that Hollywood conveys to the rest of the world. In his eloquent but uncelebrated address to students at Beijing's Tsinghua University on February 22, George W. Bush declared: "As America learns more about China, I am concerned that the Chinese people do not always see a clear picture of my country. This happens for many reasons, and some of them of our own making. Our movies and television shows often do not portray the values of the real America I know."

Ironically, the President assumed in his remarks that the Beijing students he addressed felt repulsed by the messages they received from American entertainment—despite abundant evidence that hundreds of millions of Chinese, and in particular the nation's most ambitious young people, enthusiastically embrace our pop culture. During the tragic Tiananmen Square rebellion more than a decade ago, pro-democracy reformers not only seized on the Statue of Liberty as a symbol of their movement, but indulged their taste for the music and fashions identified everywhere as part of American youth culture. American conservatives may abhor the redoubtable Madonna and all her works, but the youthful activists who brought about the Velvet Revolution in Prague reveled in her cultural contributions.

This contradiction highlights the major dispute over the worldwide influence of Hollywood entertainment. Do the spectacularly successful exports from the big show business conglomerates inspire hatred and resentment of the United States, or do they advance the inevitable, End-of-History triumph of American values? Does the near-universal popularity of national icons from Mickey Mouse to Michael Jackson represent the power of our ideals of free expression and free markets, or do the dark and decadent images we broadcast to the rest of the world hand a potent weapon to America-haters everywhere?

Telling It Like It Isn't

OF COURSE, apologists for the entertainment industry decry all attempts to blame Hollywood for anti-Americanism, insisting that American pop culture merely reports reality, accurately reflecting the promise and problems of the United States, and allowing the worldwide audience to respond as they may to the best and worst aspects of our society. During a forum on movie violence sponsored by a group of leading liberal activists, movie director Paul Verhoeven (author of such worthy ornaments to our civilization as *Robocop* and *Basic Instinct*) insisted: "Art is a reflection of the world. If the world is horrible, the reflection in the mirror is horrible." In other words, if people in developing countries feel disgusted by the Hollywood imagery so aggressively marketed in their homelands, then the problem cannot be pinned on the shapers of show business but rather arises from the authentic excesses of American life.

This argument runs counter to every statistical analysis of the past twenty years on the distorted imagery of American society purveyed by the entertainment industry. All serious evaluations of movie and television versions of American life suggest that the pop culture portrays a world that is far more violent, dangerous, sexually indulgent (and, of course, dramatic) than everyday American reality. George Gerbner, a leading analyst of media violence at the Annenberg School of Communications at the University of Pennsylvania, concluded after thirty years of research that characters on network television fall victim to acts of violence at least fifty times more frequently than citizens of the real America.

If anything, the disproportionate emphasis on violent behavior only intensifies with the export of American entertainment. For many years, so-called action movies have traveled more effectively than other genres, since explosions and car crashes do not require translation. This leads to the widespread assumption abroad that the United States, despite the dramatically declining crime rate of the last decade, remains a dangerous and insecure society. On a recent trip to England, I encountered sophisticated and thoughtful Londoners who refused to travel across the Atlantic because of their wildly exaggerated fear of American street crime—ignoring recent statistics showing unequivocally that muggings and assaults are now more common in London than in New York. On a similar note, a recent traveler in rural Indonesia met a ten-year old boy who, discovering the American origins of the visitor, asked to see her gun. When she insisted that she didn't carry any firearms, the child refused to believe her: he knew that all Americans carried guns because he had seen them perpetually armed on TV and at the movies.

The misleading media treatment of sexuality has proven similarly unreliable in its oddly altered version of American life. Analysis by Robert and Linda Lichter at the Center for Media and Public Affairs in Washington, DC reveals that on television, depictions of sex outside of marriage are nine to fourteen times more common than dramatizations of marital sex. This odd emphasis on non-marital intercourse leads to the conclusion that the only sort of sexual expression frowned upon by Hollywood involves physical affection between husband and wife. In reality, all surveys of intimate behavior (including the famous, sweeping 1994 national study by the University of Chicago) suggest that among the more than two-thirds of American adults who are currently married, sex is not only more satisfying, but significantly more frequent, than it is among their single counterparts. One of pop culture's most celebrated representatives of the "swinging singles" lifestyle today, Kim Cattrall of *Sex and the City*, recently published a best-selling book full of revealing confessions. In *Satisfaction: The Art of the Female Orgasm*, Cattrall describes a life dramatically different from the voracious and promiscuous escapades of the character she portrays on television. In the intimate arena, she felt frustrated and unfulfilled as do nearly half of American females, she maintains—until the loving ministrations of her husband, Mark Levinson, finally enabled her to experience gratification and joy.

Even without Cattrall's revelations, anyone acquainted with actual un- 12
attached individuals could confirm that *Friends* and *Ally McBeal* hardly
represent the common lot of American singles. On television and at the
movies, the major challenge confronted by most unmarried characters is
trying to decide among a superficially dazzling array of sexual alternatives.
The entertainments in question may suggest that these explorations will
prove less than wholly satisfying, but to most American viewers, single or
married, they still look mightily intriguing. To most viewers in more traditional societies, by contrast, they look mightily decadent and disrespectful.

Consider, too, the emphasis on homosexuality in contemporary televi- 13
sion and movies. In less than a year between 2001 and 2002, three major
networks (NBC, HBO, MTV) offered different, competing dramatizations
of the murder of Matthew Shepherd—the gay Wyoming college student
beaten to death by two thugs. No other crime in memory—not even the
murder of Nicole Brown Simpson—has received comparable attention by
major entertainment companies. The message to the world at large not
only calls attention to homosexual alternatives in American life, but focuses on our brutal and criminal underclass.

The Gay and Lesbian Alliance Against Defamation (GLAAD) publishes 14
an annual scorecard in which it celebrates the number of openly gay characters who appear regularly on national television series, and recently
counted more than thirty. This trendy fascination with homosexuality (as
illustrated by the worshipful attention given to Rosie O'Donnell's hugely
publicized "coming out") obviously overstates the incidence of out-of-the-
closet gay identity; all scientific studies suggest that less than 3 percent of
adults unequivocally see themselves as gay.

For purposes of perspective, it is useful to contrast the pop culture fo- 15
cus on gay orientation with media indifference to religious commitment.
A handful of successful television shows such as *Touched By An Angel*
and *Seventh Heaven* may invoke elements of conventional faith, if often
in simplistic, childlike form, but ardent and mature believers remain rare
on television and at the movies. The Gallup Poll and other surveys suggest that some 40 percent of Americans attend religious services on a
weekly basis—more than four times the percentage who go to the movies
on any given week. Church or synagogue attendance, however, hardly
ever appears in Hollywood or television portrayals of contemporary
American society, while mass media feature gay references far more frequently than religious ones. This is hardly an accurate representation of
mainstream America, and the distortion plays directly into the hands of
some of our most deadly enemies. In October 2001, an "official" press
spokesman for Osama bin Laden's Al-Qaeda terror network summarized

the struggle between Islamic fanatics and the United States as part of the eternal battle "between faith and atheism." Since the United States represents by far the most religiously committed, church-going nation in the Western world, this reference to the nation's godlessness gains credibility abroad only because of Hollywood's habitual denial or downplaying of the faith-based nature of our civilization.

The ugly media emphasis on the dysfunctional nature of our national   16
life transcends examples of widely decried, tacky and exploitative entertainment, and pointedly includes the most prodigiously praised products of the popular culture. In recent years, some 1.5 billion people around the world watch at least part of Hollywood's annual Oscar extravaganza, and in April 2000 they saw the Motion Picture Academy confer all of its most prestigious awards (Best Picture, Best Actor, Best Director, Best Screenplay) on a puerile pastiche called *American Beauty.* This embittered assault on suburban family life shows a frustrated father (Kevin Spacey) who achieves redemption only through quitting his job, lusting after a teenaged cheerleader, insulting his harridan wife, compulsively exercising and smoking marijuana. The only visibly loving and wholesome relationship in this surreal middle class nightmare flourishes between two clean-cut gay male neighbors. The very title, *American Beauty,* ironically invokes the name of an especially cherished flower to suggest that all is not, well, rosy with the American dream. If the entertainment establishment chooses to honor this cinematic effort above all others, then viewers in Kenya or Kuala Lumpur might understandably assume that it offers a mordantly accurate assessment of the emptiness and corruption of American society.

Explaining Media Masochism

This prominent example of overpraised artistic ambition suggests that the   17
persistent problems in Hollywood's view of America go far beyond the normal pursuit of profit. While *American Beauty* director Sam Mendes and screenwriter Alan Ball might well aspire to critical acclaim, the movie's producers always understood that this tale of suburban dysfunction probably would not be a slam-dunk box office blockbuster (though the Oscars ensured that it did quite well commercially). The most common excuse for the ferocious focus on violence and bizarre behavior—the argument that the "market made me do it" and that public demands leave entertainment executives with no choice—falls apart in the face of the most rudimentary analysis.

Every year, the American movie industry releases more than 300 films,   18
with a recent average of 65 percent of those titles rated "R"—or adults only—by the Motion Picture Association of America. Conventional wisdom

holds that the big studios emphasize such disturbing, edgy R-rated releases precisely because they perform best at the box office, but an abundance of recent studies proves that the public prefers feel-good, family fare. A recent comprehensive analysis confirms the conclusions on this point in my 1992 book, *Hollywood Vs. America.* Two economists, Arthur DeVany of the University of California at Irvine and W. David Walls of the University of Hong Kong, summarized their research: "This paper shows that Medved is right: there are too many R-rated movies in Hollywood's portfolio. . . . We show that, as Medved claimed, R-rated movies are dominated by G, PG and PG-13 movies in all three dimensions of revenues, costs, return on production cost, and profits."

The other argument in defense of the entertainment emphasis on trou- 19 bled aspects of American life involves the inherently dramatic nature of social dysfunction. According to the celebrated Tolstoyan aphorism, "All happy families are the same; every unhappy family is unhappy in its own way." This logic suggests an inevitable tendency to highlight the same sort of unpleasant but gripping situations so memorably brought to life by eminent pre-cinematic screenwriters like Sophocles and Shakespeare. Divorce and adultery offer more obvious entertainment value than marital bliss; criminality proves more instantly compelling than good citizenship. In an intensely competitive international marketplace, the dark—even deviant— obsessions of the present potentates of pop culture may seem to make a crude sort of sense.

This approach, however, ignores the striking lessons of Hollywood's 20 own heritage and the wholesome basis on which our star-spangled entertainment industry came to conquer the world. In the 1920s and 1930s, the American movie business faced formidable competition from well-developed production centers in Italy, France, Germany, England and even Russia. Obvious political disruptions (including the brutal intrusion of fascist and communist tyranny) helped U.S. corporations triumph over their European rivals, and drove many of the most talented individuals to seek refuge across the Atlantic. But even more than the historic circumstances that undermined America's competitors, Hollywood managed to dominate international markets because of a worldwide infatuation with the America it both exploited and promoted. Without question, iconic homegrown figures such as Jimmy Stewart, Mae West, Henry Fonda, Shirley Temple, Clark Gable, Jimmy Cagney and John Wayne, in addition to charismatic imports like Charlie Chaplin, Cary Grant and Greta Garbo, projected qualities on screen that came to seem quintessentially, irresistibly American. As film critic Richard Grenier aptly commented during a March 1992 symposium:

Aside from the country's prominence, there seems to have been an irresistible magnetism about a whole assemblage of American attitudes—optimism, hope, belief in progress, profound assumptions of human equality, informality—often more apparent to foreigners than to Americans themselves, that the outside world has found compelling. Over many decades these attitudes became so entrenched in world opinion as "American" that in recent times, when certain Hollywood films have taken on a distinctly negative tone, America has still retained its dramatic power, Hollywood, as it were, living on its spiritual capital.

In other words, in its so-called Golden Age, the entertainment industry 21 found a way to make heroism look riveting, even fashionable, and to make decency dramatic. In contrast to the present day, when most of the world watches American pop culture with the sort of guilty fascination we might lavish on a particularly bloody car crash, people in every corner of the globe once looked to our entertainment exports as a source of inspiration, even enlightenment. As the English producer David Puttnam revealed in an eloquent 1989 interview with Bill Moyers, he cherished the days of his childhood when

> the image that was being projected overseas was of a society of which I wanted to be a member. Now cut to twenty years later—the image that America began projecting in the 1970s, of a self-loathing, very violent society, antagonistic within itself—that patently isn't a society that any thinking person in the Third World or Western Europe or Eastern Europe would wish to have anything to do with. America has for some years been exporting an extremely negative notion of itself.

The change came about in part because of a change in the people run- 22 ning the major studios and television networks. As movie historian Neal Gabler perceptively observed in his influential book, *An Empire of Their Own,* Hollywood's founding generation consisted almost entirely of East European immigrant Jews who craved American acceptance so powerfully that they used celluloid fantasies to express their ongoing adoration for their adopted country. Their successors, on the other hand, came from far more "respectable" backgrounds—in some cases as the privileged children and grandchildren of the founders themselves. In the 1960s and 1970s, they sought to establish their independence and artistic integrity by burnishing their countercultural credentials. To illustrate the magnitude and speed of the change, the 1965 Academy Award for Best Picture went to the delightful and traditionally romantic musical, *The Sound of Music.* A mere four years later, that same coveted Oscar went to *Midnight Cowboy*—the gritty story of a down-and-out male hustler in New York City, and the only X-rated feature ever to win Best Picture.

From the beginning and through to the present day, the leaders of the 23
entertainment community have felt a powerful need to be taken seriously.
The creators of the industry were born outsiders who earned that respect
by expressing affection for America; the moguls of the later generations
have been for the most part born insiders who earned their respect by expressing their alienation. This negativity naturally found an eager international audience during the Vietnam War era and in the waning years of the
Cold War with the widespread dismissal of the "cowboy culture" of Rea-
ganism. Even after the collapse of the Soviet Empire, anti-Americanism remained fashionable among taste-setting elites in much of the world,
appealing with equal fervor to critics from the Right and the Left. In
Afghanistan in the 1980s, for example, the beleaguered Russian Communists and the indefatigable mujaheddin might agree on very little—but they
both felt powerful contempt for the free-wheeling and self-destructive
mores of American culture as promoted everywhere by the Hollywood entertainment machine.

Even as post–Cold War globalization enhanced the economic power 24
and political influence of the United States, it helped the entertainment
industry sustain its anti-American attitudes. With the removal of the
Iron Curtain, vast new markets opened up for Hollywood entertainment, with developing economies in Asia and Latin America, too, providing hundreds of millions of additional customers. Between 1985 and
1990, inflation-adjusted revenues from overseas markets for U.S. feature films rose 124 percent at a time when domestic proceeds remained
relatively flat. As a result, the portion of all movie income derived from
foreign distribution rose from 30 percent in 1980 to more than 50 percent in 2000. James G. Robinson, influential chairman of Morgan
Creek Productions, was right to have predicted to the *Los Angeles
Times* in March 1992: "All of the real growth in the coming years will
be overseas."

The fulfillment of his forecast has served to further detach today's pro- 25
ducers from any sense of patriotic or parochial identification, encouraging
their pose as Americans who have nobly transcended their own Americanism. A current captain of the entertainment industry need not ask whether
a putative project will "play in Peoria"—so long as it plays in Paris, St. Pe-
tersburg and Panama City. As I argued in the pages of *Hollywood Vs.
America in* 1992: "While the populist products of Hollywood's Golden
Age most certainly encouraged the world's love affair with America, today's nihilistic and degrading attempts at entertainment may, in the long
run, produce the opposite effect, helping to isolate this country as a symbol of diseased decadence."

Why Do They Watch It?

With that isolation increasingly apparent after the unprecedented assault 26 of 9/11, the question remains: Why does so much of the world still seem so single-mindedly obsessed with American entertainment, for all its chaotic and unrepresentative elements?

The most likely answer involves what might be described as the "*Na-* 27 *tional Enquirer* appeal" of Hollywood's vision of life in the United States. While waiting in the supermarket checkout lines, we turn to the scandal-ridden tabloids not because of our admiration for the celebrities they expose, but because of our uncomfortable combination of envy and resentment toward them. The tabloids compel our attention because they allow us to feel superior to the rich and famous. For all their wealth and glamor and power, they cannot stay faithful to their spouses, avoid drug addiction, or cover up some other guilty secret. We may privately yearn to change places with some star of the moment, but the weekly revelations of the *National Enquirer* actually work best to reassure us that we are better off as we are.

In much the same way, Hollywood's unpleasant images of America en- 28 able the rest of the world to temper inevitable envy with a sense of their own superiority. The United States may be rich in material terms (and movies and television systematically overstate that wealth), but the violence, cruelty, injustice, corruption, arrogance and degeneracy so regularly included in depictions of American life allow viewers abroad to feel fortunate by comparison. Like the *Enquirer* approach to the private peccadilloes of world-striding celebrities, you are supposed to feel fascinated by their profligate squandering of opportunity and power.

In this sense, American pop culture is not so much liberating as it is an- 29 archic and even nihilistic. Our entertainment offerings do not honor our freedom and liberty as political or cultural values so much as they undermine all restraints and guidelines, both the tyrannical and the traditional. As Dwight Macdonald wrote in his celebrated 1953 essay, "A Theory of Mass Culture": "Like 19th-century capitalism, Mass Culture is a dynamic, revolutionary force, breaking down the old barriers of class, tradition, taste, and dissolving all cultural distinctions." Amplifying Macdonald's work, Edward Rothstein of the *New York Times* wrote in March 2002: "There is something inherently disruptive about popular culture. It undermines the elite values of aristocratic art, displaces the customs of folk culture and opposes any limitation on art's audiences or subjects. It asserts egalitarian tastes, encourages dissent and does not shun desire." It should come as no surprise, then, that even those who embrace the symbols and themes of American entertainment may feel little gratitude toward a force that casts them loose from all traditional moorings, but offers no organized system of ideas or values by way of replacement.

Patriotism and Profit

In 1994, I participated in an international conference on the family in War- 30 saw and listened to the plaintive recollections of a troubled Polish priest. He recalled the days of the Cold War, "when we listened in basements to illegal radios to Radio Free Europe so we could get a little bit of hope, a little bit of truth, from the magical land of America." After the collapse of Communism, however, America's message seemed dangerous and decadent rather than hopeful. "All of a sudden, we're struggling against drugs and free sex and AIDS and crime and all of that seems to be an import from America. It's like the message of freedom that we heard before was only the freedom to destroy ourselves."

On a similar note, an American businessman of my acquaintance trav- 31 eling in Beirut struck up a conversation with the proprietor of a falafel stand who announced himself an enthusiastic supporter of the radical, pro-Iranian terrorist group, Hizballah. Ironically, his small business featured a faded poster showing a barechested, machine-gun toting Sylvester Stallone as Rambo. My friend asked about the place of honor provided to an American movie hero. "We all like Rambo," the Hizballah supporter unblushingly declared. "He is a fighter's fighter." But wouldn't that make the Lebanese dissident more favorably inclined toward the United States, the visitor inquired. "Not at all," was the response. "We will use Rambo's methods to destroy the evil America."

This love-hate relationship with Hollywood's twisted imagery also 32 characterized the 19 conspirators who made such a notable attempt to "destroy evil America" with their September 11 atrocities. During their months and years in the United States, Mohammed Atta and his colleagues savored the popular culture-renting action videos and visiting bars, peep shows, lap dancing parlors and Las Vegas—immersing themselves in Western degradation to stiffen their own hatred (and self-hatred?) of it.

In response to the terrorist attacks and to the onset of the war that fol- 33 lowed, leaders of the Hollywood community expressed some dawning awareness that they may have indeed contributed to some of the hatred of America expressed around the world. Beyond a brief flurry of flag-waving, and the generous contributions to the 9/11 fund by leading celebrities from Julia Roberts to Jim Carrey, members of the entertainment elite showed a new willingness to cooperate with the defense establishment. Working through the Institute for Creative Technologies at USC (originally created to enlist Hollywood talent for shaping virtual reality simulators for military training), creators of movies like *Die Hard, Fight Club* and even *Being John Malkovich* brainstormed with Pentagon brass. Their purpose, according to several press reports, involved an attempt to concoct the next possible plot that might be launched against the United States, and then to devise strategies to counteract it.

In a sense, this unconventional program acknowledged the fact that vi-   34
olent, demented, anti-social and conspiratorial thinking has come to characterize a major segment of the entertainment establishment. How else could an objective observer interpret the idea that the military turned first to millionaire screenwriters in order to understand the thought processes of mass-murdering terrorists?

Beyond this strange collaboration, top show business executives met   35
with Karl Rove, political representative of President Bush, in an attempt to mobilize Hollywood creativity to serve America in the war against terror. The well-publicized "summit" discussed public service ads to discourage bigotry against Muslims in America and additional productions to give the United States a more benign image in the Islamic world. A handful of top directors, including William Friedkin (*The French Connection, The Exorcist* and the excellent *Rules of Engagement*) expressed their willingness to drop all their pressing projects and enlist full-time to help the American war effort. In this determination, these pop culture patriots hoped to follow the example of the great Golden Age director Frank Capra, who served his country during World War II through the creation of the epic *Why We Fight* series.

Alas, the White House and the Pentagon failed to take advantage of the   36
self-sacrificing spirit of the moment, or to pursue the entertainment industry opportunities that presented themselves after September 11. As the trauma of terrorist attacks gradually recedes into memory and the nation loses focus on its sense of patriotic purpose, the popular culture is displaying few long-term changes. Perhaps a more positive attitude toward the military may be the chief legacy of the deadly attacks—an attitude publicly celebrated so far in a handful of movies (*Behind Enemy Lines, Black Hawk Down, We Were Soldiers*), incidentally, all produced before the September 11 catastrophe. More significant changes, involving a new sense of responsibility for the images of America that pop culture transmits around the world, never even merited serious discussion in Hollywood. For the top entertainment conglomerates, this may count as an unseized opportunity for public service, but also a missed chance for corporate profit.

In his February speech in Beijing, President Bush held the Chinese stu-   37
dents transfixed with a picture of America that departed dramatically from the visions they had received from made-in-USA music, movies and

television. "America is a nation guided by faith," the President declared. "Someone once called us 'a nation with the soul of a church.' This may interest you—95 percent of Americans say they believe in God, and I'm one of them." Bush went on to appeal to the family priorities that have characterized Chinese culture for more than 3,000 years: "Many of the values that guide our life in America are first shaped in our families, just as they are in your country. American moms and dads love their children and work hard and sacrifice for them because we believe life can always be better for the next generation. In our families, we find love and learn responsibility and character."

If Hollywood's leaders placed themselves within the context of the wider 38 American family, they might also learn responsibility and character—and discover that a more wholesome, loving and balanced portrayal of the nation they serve could enhance rather than undermine their worldwide popularity.

Thinking About the Essay

1. Medved's essay is relatively long. What does he assume about his audience's willingness to follow his well-developed argument? What strategies does he use to sustain the reader's interest?

2. Trace the development of Medved's argument from section to section. What is the writer's thesis or claim? Where does he state it most clearly?

3. What types of illustration does Medved employ to support his argument? Cite passages where these various forms of exemplification appear. Why does the writer provide so much illustration in this article? What is the overall effect?

4. One attribute of an effective argument is the writer's willingness to acknowledge the opposition, present its views fairly, and then refute these views. Where does Medved engage in refutation? Is it effective? Why or why not?

5. How does comparison and contrast serve to bolster Medved's argument? Point to instances where this comparative method appears.

Responding in Writing

6. Medved is known as a relatively conservative commentator on American culture. Reread his essay and then write a paper in which you analyze the nature of his conservatism and how and where he expresses it.

7. Write a paper in which you agree or disagree with the idea that American popular culture contributes to anti-Americanism abroad. Be certain to provide examples to support your main points.

8. Medved refers to numerous television programs and films in his essay. Select one film or television series, and imagine how viewers overseas would respond to it. Does the film or television series fairly depict the nature of American life? Why or why not?

Networking

9. In groups of four or five, agree on the one movie, television program, or music video that presents the *worst* image of American culture. Explain to the class why this negative example could damage America's reputation abroad.

10. Go online and locate information on the impact of the American media overseas. Narrow the search to one area that interests you. Then prepare a brief research paper on your findings.

The Culture of Liberty

Mario Vargas Llosa

Mario Vargas Llosa, born in Arequipa, Peru, in 1936, is a major figure in contemporary Latin American and world literature. An acclaimed novelist, playwright, critic, and essayist, Vargas Llosa was a self-imposed exile from his native land for three decades, living in Paris, London, and Barcelona. He received a Ph.D. degree from the University of Madrid in 1959. Returning to Peru, he ran for president in 1990; he had a big lead initially but lost in the end to Alberto Fujimori. In his writing, broadcasting, and frequent lecturing, Vargas Llosa has been a persistent critic of violence, tyranny, and all forms of political oppression. A Marxist in his youth, Vargas Llosa in recent years has been a strong supporter of democracy. "If you are a writer in a country like Peru," he told an interviewer, "you're a privileged person because you know how to read and write, you have an audience, and you are respected. It is a moral obligation of a writer in Latin America to be involved in civic activities." Today Vargas Llosa is a citizen of Spain. Among his many notable novels are *Aunt Julia and the Scriptwriter* (1982), *In Praise of the Stepmother* (1990), and *The Feast of the Goat* (2001). In the essay that follows, which appeared in the journal *Foreign Policy* in 2001, Vargas Llosa examines the relationship between local culture and globalization.

Before Reading

Do you think that it is too simplistic to say that local cultures around the world cannot survive the impact of globalization? Why or why not?

The most effective attacks against globalization are usually not those related to economics. Instead, they are social, ethical, and, above all, cultural. These arguments surfaced amid the tumult of Seattle in 1999 and have resonated more recently in Davos, Bangkok, and Prague. They say this:

The disappearance of national borders and the establishment of a world interconnected by markets will deal a deathblow to regional and national cultures and to the traditions, customs, myths, and mores that determine each country or region's cultural identity. Since most of the world is incapable of resisting the invasion of cultural products from developed countries—or, more to the point, from the superpower, the United States—that inevitably trails the great transnational corporations, North American culture will ultimately impose itself, standardizing the world and annihilating its rich flora of diverse cultures. In this manner, all other peoples, and not just the small and weak ones, will lose their identity, their soul, and will become no more than 21st-century colonies—zombies or caricatures modeled after the cultural norms of a new imperialism that, in addition to ruling over the planet with its capital, military might, and scientific knowledge, will impose on others its language and its ways of thinking, believing, enjoying, and dreaming.

This nightmare or negative utopia of a world that, thanks to globalization, is losing its linguistic and cultural diversity and is being culturally appropriated by the United States, is not the exclusive domain of left-wing politicians nostalgic for Marx, Mao, or Che Guevara. This delirium of persecution—spurred by hatred and rancor toward the North American giant—is also apparent in developed countries and nations of high culture and is shared among political sectors of the left, center, and right.

The most notorious case is that of France, where we see frequent government campaigns in defense of a French "cultural identity" supposedly threatened by globalization. A vast array of intellectuals and politicians is alarmed by the possibility that the soil that produced Montaigne, Descartes, Racine, and Baudelaire—and a country that was long the arbiter of fashion in clothing, thought, art, dining, and in all domains of the spirit—can be invaded by McDonald's, Pizza Hut, Kentucky Fried Chicken, rock, rap, Hollywood movies, bluejeans, sneakers, and T-shirts. This fear has resulted, for instance, in massive French subsidies for the local film industry and demands for quotas requiring theaters to show a certain number of national films and limit the importation of movies from the United States. This fear is also the reason why municipalities issued severe directives penalizing with high fines any publicity announcements that littered with Anglicisms the language of Molière. (Although, judging by the view of a pedestrian on the streets of Paris, the directives were not quite respected.) This is the reason why José Bové, the farmer-cum-crusader against *la malbouffe* (lousy food), has become no less than a popular hero in France. And with his recent sentencing to three months in prison, his popularity has likely increased.

Even though I believe this cultural argument against globalization is 5 unacceptable, we should recognize that deep within it lies an unquestionable truth. This century, the world in which we will live will be less picturesque and imbued with less local color than the one we left behind. The festivals, attire, customs, ceremonies, rites, and beliefs that in the past gave humanity its folkloric and ethnological variety are progressively disappearing or confining themselves to minority sectors, while the bulk of society abandons them and adopts others more suited to the reality of our time. All countries of the earth experience this process, some more quickly than others, but it is not due to globalization. Rather, it is due to modernization, of which the former is effect, not cause. It is possible to lament, certainly, that this process occurs, and to feel nostalgia for the eclipse of the past ways of life that, particularly from our comfortable vantage point of the present, seem full of amusement, originality, and color. But this process is unavoidable. Totalitarian regimes in countries like Cuba or North Korea, fearful that any opening will destroy them, close themselves off and issue all types of prohibitions and censures against modernity. But even they are unable to impede modernity's slow infiltration and its gradual undermining of their so-called cultural identity. In theory, perhaps, a country could keep this identity, but only if—like certain remote tribes in Africa or the Amazon—it decides to live in total isolation, cutting off all exchange with other nations and practicing self-sufficiency. A cultural identity preserved in this form would take that society back to prehistoric standards of living.

It is true that modernization makes many forms of traditional life disappear. But at the same time, it opens opportunities and constitutes an important step forward for a society as a whole. That is why, when given the option to choose freely, peoples, sometimes counter to what their leaders 6 or intellectual traditionalists would like, opt for modernization without the slightest ambiguity.

The allegations against globalization and in favor of cultural identity 7 reveal a static conception of culture that has no historical basis. Which cultures have ever remained identical and unchanged over time? To find them we must search among the small and primitive magical-religious communities that live in caves, worship thunder and beasts, and, due to their primitivism, are increasingly vulnerable to exploitation and extermination. All other cultures, in particular those that have the right to be called modern and alive, have evolved to the point that they are but a remote reflection of what they were just two or three generations before. This evolution is easily apparent in countries like France, Spain, and England, where the changes over the last half century have been so spectacular and profound that a Marcel Proust, a Federico García Lorca, or a Virginia Woolf would hardly recognize today the societies in which they were born—the societies their works helped so much to renew.

The notion of "cultural identity" is dangerous. Form a social point of 8 view, it represents merely a doubtful, artificial concept, but from a political perspective it threatens humanity's most precious achievement: freedom. I do not deny that people who speak the same language, were born and live in the same territory, face the same problems, and practice the same religions and customs have common characteristics. But that collective denominator can never fully define each one of them, and it only abolishes or relegates to a disdainful secondary plane the sum of unique attributes and traits that differentiates one member of the group from the others. The concept of identity, when not employed on an exclusively individual scale, is inherently reductionist and dehumanizing, a collectivist and ideological abstraction of all that is original and creative in the human being, of all that has not been imposed by inheritance, geography, or social pressure. Rather, true identity springs from the capacity of human beings to resist these influences and counter them with free acts of their own invention.

The notion of "collective identity" is an ideological fiction and the 9 foundation of nationalism. For many ethnologists and anthropologists, collective identity does not represent the truth even among the most archaic communities. Common practices and customs may be crucial to the defense of a group, but the margin of initiative and creativity among its members to emancipate themselves from the group is invariably large, and individual differences prevail over collective traits when individuals are examined on their own terms, and not as mere peripheral elements of collectivity. Globalization extends radically to all citizens of this planet the possibility to construct their individual cultural identities through voluntary action, according to their preferences and intimate motivations. Now, citizens are not always obligated, as in the past and in many places in the present, to respect an identity that traps them in a concentration camp from which there is no escape—the identity that is imposed on them through the language, nation, church, and customs of the place where they were born. In this sense, globalization must be welcomed because it notably expands the horizons of individual liberty.

One Continent's Two Histories

Perhaps Latin America is the best example of the artifice and absurdity of trying to establish collective identities. What might be Latin America's cultural identity? What would be included in a coherent collection of beliefs, customs, traditions, practices, and mythologies that endows this region with a singular personality, unique and nontransferable? Our history has been forged in intellectual polemics—some ferocious—seeking to answer this question. The most celebrated was the one that, beginning in the early 20th century, pitted Hispanists against indigenists and reverberated across the continent.

For Hispanists like José de la Riva-Agüero, Victor Andrés Belaúnde, and Francisco Garcia Calderón, Latin America was born when, thanks to the Discovery and the Conquest, it joined with the Spanish and Portuguese languages and, adopting Christianity, came to form part of Western civilization. Hispanists did not belittle pre-Hispanic cultures, but considered that these constituted but a layer—and not the primary one—of the social and historical reality that only completed its nature and personality thanks to the vivifying influence of the West.

Indigenists, on the other hand, rejected with moral indignation the alleged benefits that Europeans brought to Latin America. For them, our identity finds its roots and its soul in pre-Hispanic cultures and civilizations, whose development and modernization were brutally stunted by violence and subjected to censure, repression, and marginalization not only during the three colonial centuries but also later, after the advent of republicanism. According to indigenist thinkers, the authentic "American expression" (to use the title of a book by José Lezama Lima) resides in all the cultural manifestations—from the native languages to the beliefs, rites, arts, and popular mores—that resisted Western cultural oppression and endured to our days. A distinguished historian of this vein, the Peruvian Luis E. Valcárcel, even affirmed that the churches, convents, and other monuments of colonial architecture should be burned since they represented the "Anti-Peru." They were impostors, a negation of the pristine American identity that could only be of exclusively indigenous roots. And one of Latin America's most original novelists, José María Arguedas, narrated, in stories of great delicacy and vibrant moral protest, the epic of the survival of the Quechua culture in the Andean world, despite the suffocating and distortionary presence of the West.

Hispanicism and indigenism produced excellent historical essays and 13 highly creative works of fiction, but, judged from our current perspective, both doctrines seem equally sectarian, reductionist, and false. Neither is capable of fitting the expansive diversity of Latin America into its ideological straitjacket, and both smack of racism. Who would dare claim in our day that only what is "Hispanic" or "Indian" legitimately represents Latin America?

Nevertheless, efforts to forge and isolate our distinct "cultural identity" 14 continue today with a political and intellectual zeal deserving of worthier causes. Seeking to impose a cultural identity on a people is equivalent to locking them in a prison and denying them the most precious of liberties— that of choosing what, how, and who they want to be. Latin America has not one but many cultural identities; no one of them can claim more legitimacy or purity than the others. Of course, Latin America embodies the pre-Hispanic world and its cultures, which, in Mexico, Guatemala, and the Andean countries, still exert so much social force. But Latin America is also a vast swarm of Spanish and Portuguese speakers with a tradition of five centuries behind them whose presence and actions have been decisive in giving the continent its current features. And is not Latin America also something of Africa, which arrived on our shores together with Europe? Has not the African presence indelibly marked our skin, our music, our idiosyncrasies, our society? The cultural, ethnic, and social ingredients that make up Latin America link us to almost all the regions and cultures of the world. We have so many cultural identities that it is like not having one at all. This reality is, contrary to what nationalists believe, our greatest treasure. It is also an excellent credential that enables us to feel like full-fledged citizens in our globalized world.

Local Voices, Global Reach

The fear of Americanization of the planet is more ideological paranoia than 15 reality. There is no doubt, of course, that with globalization, English has become the general language of our time, as was Latin in the Middle Ages. And it will continue its ascent, since it is an indispensable instrument for international transactions and communication. But does this mean that English necessarily develops at the expense of the other great languages? Absolutely not. In fact, the opposite is true. The vanishing of borders and an increasingly interdependent world have created incentives for new generations to learn and assimilate to other cultures, not merely as a hobby but also out of necessity, since the ability to speak several languages and navigate comfortably in different cultures has become crucial for professional success. Consider the case of Spanish. Half a century ago, Spanish speakers were an inward-looking community; we projected ourselves in only very limited ways beyond our traditional linguistic confines. Today, Spanish is dynamic and thriving, gaining beachheads or even vast landholdings on all five continents. The fact that there are some 25 to 30 million Spanish speakers in the United States today explains why the two recent U.S. presidential candidates, Texas Governor George W. Bush and Vice President Al Gore, campaigned not only in English but also in Spanish.

How many millions of young men and women around the globe have 16 responded to the challenges of globalization by learning Japanese, German, Mandarin, Cantonese, Russian, or French? Fortunately, this tendency will only increase in the coming years. That is why the best defense of our own cultures and languages is to promote them vigorously throughout this new world, not to persist in the naive pretense of vaccinating them against the menace of English. Those who propose such remedies speak much about culture, but they tend to be ignorant people who mask their true vocation: nationalism. And if there is anything at odds with the universalist propensities of culture, it is the parochial, exclusionary, and confused vision that nationalist perspectives try to impose on cultural life. The most admirable lesson that cultures teach us is that they need not be protected by bureaucrats or commissars, or confined behind iron bars, or isolated by customs services in order to remain alive and exuberant; to the contrary, such efforts would only wither or even trivialize *culture*. Cultures must live freely, constantly jousting with different cultures. This renovates and renews them, allowing them to evolve and adapt to the continuous flow of life. In antiquity, Latin did not kill Greek; to the contrary, the artistic originality and intellectual depth of Hellenic culture permeated Roman civilization and, through it, the poems of Homer and the philosophies of Plato and Aristotle reached the entire world. Globalization will not make local cultures disappear; in a framework of worldwide openness, all that is valuable and worthy of survival in local cultures will find fertile ground in which to bloom.

This is happening in Europe, everywhere. Especially noteworthy is 17 Spain, where regional cultures are reemerging with special vigor. During the dictatorship of General Francisco Franco, regional cultures were repressed and condemned to a clandestine existence. But with the return of democracy, Spain's rich cultural diversity was unleashed and allowed to develop freely. In the country's regime of autonomies, local cultures have had an extraordinary boom, particularly in Catalonia, Galicia, and the Basque country, but also in the rest of Spain. Of course, we must not confuse this regional cultural rebirth, which is positive and enriching, with the phenomenon of nationalism, which poses serious threats to the culture of liberty.

In his celebrated 1948 essay "Notes Towards the Definition of Culture," T. S. Eliot predicted that in the future, humanity would experience a renaissance of local and regional cultures. At the time, his prophecy seemed quite daring. However, globalization will likely make it a reality in the 21st century, and we must be happy about this. A rebirth of small, local cultures will give back to humanity that rich multiplicity of behavior and expressions that the nation-state annihilated in order to create so-called national cultural identities toward the end of the 18th, and particularly in the 19th, century. (This fact is easily forgotten, or we attempt to forget it because of its grave moral connotations.) National cultures were often forged in blood and fire, prohibiting the teaching or publication of vernacular languages or the practice of religions and customs that dissented from those the nation-state considered ideal. In this way, in many countries of the world, the nation-state forcibly imposed a dominant culture upon local ones that were repressed and abolished from official life. But, contrary to the warnings of those who fear globalization, it is not easy to completely erase cultures—however small they may be—if behind them is a rich tradition and people who practice them, even if in secret. And today, thanks to the weakening of the nation-state, we are seeing forgotten, marginalized, and silenced local cultures reemerging and displaying dynamic signs of life in the great concept of this globalized planet.

Thinking About the Essay

1. Is this essay about *culture* or *globalization*—or both? How do you know? Does the title provide a hint or is it incomplete or misleading? What is Vargas Llosa's thesis, and how does this thesis provide an answer to the first question?

2. Vargas Llosa divides his essay into three sections. What is the focus of each section? How do the parts interrelate?

3. What types of illustration does he use to structure his definition and analysis of culture? Identify some of these.

4. This essay involves considerable causal analysis and comparison and contrast. What causal and comparative patterns of development can you detect? What assumptions does the writer make about the reader's ability to follow these patterns of thought and organization? In terms of audience analysis, how does his overall style of writing presuppose a highly literate readership?

5. Select three paragraphs that capture Vargas Llosa's optimistic tone. Does he deal adequately with the pessimistic side of his subject? Why or why not?

Responding in Writing

6. Vargas Llosa writes: "Cultures must live freely, constantly jousting with different cultures" (paragraph 16). Write a paper responding to Vargas Llosa's statement. Provide sufficient reasons and illustrations to support your position.

7. Define what you mean by *culture,* and how this relates to your own family's cultural origins and attitudes.

8. Write an essay in which you tackle the problem of the relationship between culture and globalization. Feel free to consult the essays in the previous chapter for ideas.

Networking

9. In small groups, develop a formal outline of Vargas Llosa's relatively complex essay. Put your collective product on the chalkboard or on a transparency so that you can evaluate your outline against the results of the other class groups.

10. Search the Internet for reviews of Vargas Llosa's recent novel, *The Feast of the Goat.* After reading these reviews, decide whether you would like to read the novel, and explain your response to other members of the class.

Simpson Agonistes

PAUL A. CANTOR

Paul Arthur Cantor was born in Brooklyn, New York, in 1945. He received his B.A. (1966) and Ph.D. (1971) degrees from Harvard University, where he taught as an assistant professor from 1971 to 1977. He is currently a professor of English at the University of Virginia. From 1992 to 1999, he served on the National Council on the Humanities. He is the author of *Shakespeare's Rome: Republic and Empire* (1976), *Creature and Creator: Mythmaking and English Romanticism* (1984), and *Gilligan Unbound: Popular Culture in the Age of Globalization* (2001). Cantor's essays on popular culture have appeared in *The Weekly Standard, Reason, The American Enterprise,* and elsewhere. In the following selection, a section of *Gilligan Unbound,* Cantor analyzes one of television's longest running shows, *The Simpsons,* finding numerous transcultural connections in Springfield's inhabitants and the rest of the world.

Before Reading

Which televsion programs do you think convey an accurate vision of life in the United States? Which programs project distortions? Can any one television series provide a complete picture of American culture? Why or why not?

Given the negative portrait of national politics in *The Simpsons,* it is 1 thus not surprising that the Springfielders are attached to their local community and not to larger political units. But the devaluation of politics on the national level in the show has other consequences. The Springfielders' disillusionment with and lack of concern for national politics lead them to think globally even as they act locally. *The Simpsons* can thus serve as a representative of the new developments in television in what I am calling the global era. Working to reduce the power of the national networks, cable TV and other technological breakthroughs have allowed television to become at once more local and more global as a medium. To be sure, *The Simpsons* is not itself a cable TV program; shown by the Fox Network, the series is in fact an example of broadcast television. But the rise of Fox in the 1980s and 1990s was one of the central events in the great change in the television landscape that is often called the cable revolution but should perhaps more properly be called the globalization of television. As a fourth network challenging the supremacy of the seemingly entrenched and untouchable Big Three—CBS, NBC, and ABC—Fox was instrumental in undermining the centrality of the traditional national networks in American culture, and it did so precisely by promoting untraditional TV programming such as *The Simpsons.* Many analysts have attributed the success of Fox largely to *The Simpsons.* William Shawcross, for example, writes: " 'The Simpsons' was the show that fanned Fox's flame and gained it the respect of the television industry. . . . [P]rograms like 'The Simpsons' made Fox the darling of media buyers. . . . Bart Simpson had done the impossible. He had created a fourth national network."[1]

The Simpsons illustrates the economic logic of globalization that has 2 transformed television. The show is largely created in the United States, but

1. William Shawcross, *Murdoch: The Making of a Media Empire* (New York: Simon & Schuster, 1997), 281. In his January 11, 2000, AP story, Sutel reports that Sandy Grushow, chairman of the Fox TV Entertainment Group, said: "The bottom line is that 'The Simpsons' is this network's flagship show. It's largely responsible for putting this network on the map." Sutel adds that "he said 'The Simpsons' and 'The X-Files' are the two most profitable series Fox ever made."

to save money, the episodes are in fact animated in Korea. This outsourcing of the production of the show is typical of the modern globalized economy. For all the obvious logistical problems, it is still cheaper to have the cartoons drawn halfway around the world. Moreover, as a Fox program, *The Simpsons* is ultimately financed by an Australian, media mogul Rupert Murdoch. Murdoch actually appears in one episode ("Sunday, Cruddy Sunday," #AABF08, 1/31/99), describing himself as a "billionaire tyrant." Thus *The Simpsons* itself is a perfect example of globalization: an American show financed by an Australian and animated by Koreans, now shown all around the earth. No wonder globalization emerges as one of the recurrent themes in the show.

For small-town people, the Springfielders are in their own way remarkably cosmopolitan, especially when compared to their antecedents in the sitcoms of the 1950s. The Springfield of *Father Knows Best* did not have a convenience store, but if it did, it would not have been operated by a practicing Hindu like Apu. Unlike Bart and Lisa Simpson, Bud and Kathy Anderson of *Father Knows Best* never met a Hindu, practicing or otherwise, in their lives. One can say that this merely mirrors the realities of life in the United States at the end of the twentieth century, but that is just the point. Without trumpeting the fact, *The Simpsons* effectively portrays the globalization of America in the 1990s. Simply by virtue of living when they do, the Simpson family has opportunities that were denied to their counterparts in sitcoms in the heyday of the national networks. *Leave It to Beaver* devoted a whole episode to the chaos that results when Wally and the Beav simply take a bus beyond the borders of Mayfield. *My Three Sons* thought it was being quite daring when it took the Douglas family to Hawaii for a two-part episode. By contrast, the Simpsons have taken trips to Australia and Japan and taken them in stride. It is of course much easier to transport characters halfway around the globe in a cartoon. But the jet-setting of the Simpsons still points to a fundamental transformation in their lives that the show consistently documents. For all their small-town mentality, they have become citizens of the world.

A fundamental reason for the demotion of the nation as a concern in the minds of the Springfielders is the fact that *The Simpsons* portrays a world fundamentally at peace and this in turn leads to a broadening of the cultural horizons of the characters in the series. It is appropriate that the show made its debut as a full-length program at the end of 1989 (in a Christmas special on December 17), that is, shortly after the fall of the Berlin Wall and hence the "official" end of the Cold War. Real war is no longer a threat in the world of *The Simpsons*. Bart is sent in one episode to a military academy, but it is to punish him, not to train him for a life of combat in the army.[2] In the many visions the show offers of Bart's future, it never imagines him having to go to war for his country. In fact, in "Homer's Phobia," when Homer is worried that the influence of a friendly gay man (voiced by John Waters) may be affecting Bart's sexual orientation, he and Moe momentarily think of turning to the military to make a man out of the boy, but the bartender quickly points out that this option has been foreclosed by the success of 1990s diplomacy: "There's not even any war anymore, thank you, Warren Christopher."

For real wars, *The Simpsons* must look back to the past. One episode 5 deals with Grandpa Simpson's service in World War II,[3] and Principal Skinner is constantly referring to his experiences in Vietnam (in one episode the truth about his past in the Vietnam War comes back to haunt him).[4] The elimination of war as a palpable threat significantly reduces the importance of the nation-state in the minds of the Springfielders. They no longer feel that the government is necessary to protect them from aggressive foreigners, and they no longer think in terms of giving up their lives in battle for the sake of the United States. Hence their nation cannot possibly mean as much to them as it did to Abraham Simpson in his youth, when Americans were marching off to fight the Germans and the Japanese in a kind of national crusade. In the world of *The Simpsons,* the Germans now can try to purchase Mr. Burns's nuclear power plant and the Japanese open up a sushi restaurant in Springfield (The Happy Sumo), admittedly nearly killing Homer in the process, but not as a hostile act of war.[5]

The Simpsons rests so firmly on the premise of peace in the post–Cold 6 War era that the show can even play with the idea of nuclear annihilation. In one of the Halloween episodes, one segment deals with the hellish aftermath when Springfield is hit by a neutron bomb from France, delivered in retaliation for a rude remark about the French made by Mayor Quimby.[6] The absurdity of this segment underscores the point—if the French are all that Americans need worry about anymore, then they need not really

---

2. "The Secret War of Lisa Simpson," #4F21, 5/18/97. The February 25, 2001, episode of *The Simpsons* portrays the U.S. military so desperate to recapture the interest of America's youth that the navy implants subliminal recruiting messages in the music of a new boy band featuring Bart.

3. "Raging Abe Simpson and His Grumbling Grandson in 'The Curse of the Flying Hellfish,' " #3F19, 4/28/96.

4. "The Principal and the Pauper," #4F23, 9/28/97. Skinner's most pointed reflection on his experience in Vietnam occurs during the episode about his school being closed down by a blizzard, broadcast on December 17, 2000. In a flashback to his internment in a Vietnamese prison camp, Skinner recalls one of his comrades saying: "Let's make a break for it while the guards are partying with Jane Fonda."

5. "One Fish, Two Fish, Blowfish, Blue Fish," #7F11, 1/24/91.

6. "The Homega Man" in "Treehouse of Horror VIII," #5F02, 10/26/97.

worry at all. *The Simpsons* even toys with the idea that the end of the Cold War may have been a Russian trick. In the episode called "Simpson Tide" (#4G04, 3/29/98), Homer joins the naval reserve, not because he has a sudden surge of partiotism but because he has been fired from his job at the nuclear power plant. In one imaginative sequence, the Russians reveal that the end of their hostilities with the West was just a ruse, as a seemingly peaceful parade in Red Square mutates into an old Soviet-style display of aggressive military might. Lenin's corpse springs back to life, solemnly intoning: "Must crush capitalism," and in the most emblematic moment, the Berlin Wall suddenly pops back up. Just by raising the possibility of this reversal, *The Simpsons* reveals how crucial it is in fact to the series that the Cold War really is over. In the absence of a credible threat to the United States, and hence in the absence of the need for the national government to defend the citizens of Springfield, they are free to pay less attention to national concerns, to neglect many of the demands the nation-state has traditionally made, and to devote themselves to local matters. But the end of the Cold War also frees the Springfielders to take a more global view of their lives. No longer feeling threatened by foreign enemies, they are more open to influences from abroad and are willing to enter into dealings with people from other nations.

This is the subject of one of the earliest episodes of *The Simpsons*, and still my personal favorite, "The Crepes of Wrath," a marvelously absurd episode, but one that also shows the remarkable range of cultural reference in the series. Bart pushes his luck with Principal Skinner too far and ends up in an exchange-student scheme, largely designed just to get him out of the country. Bart is sent to France, and in his place an exchange student from Albania, named Adil Hoxha, comes to Springfield Elementary School. To my knowledge, *The Simpsons* is the only American TV program that has ever played with the name of an Albanian dictator (Enver Hoxha). "The Crepes of Wrath" is the show's backhanded tribute to the end of the Cold War. By 1990 one had to go to the depths of darkest Albania to find anyone still committed to Communist ideology and hence implacably opposed to the United States. Indeed, in trying to explain Albania to Homer, Lisa tells her father that its "main export is furious political thought." This episode can be viewed in two ways, as reflecting either the parochialism of Americans or their cosmopolitanism, their orientation toward the local or toward the global. On the one hand, "The Crepes of Wrath" offers a compendium of American prejudices against foreigners. The French live up to their stereotype of being hostile to Americans when Bart is treated miserably in France. The men in whose care he is placed, Ugolin and Cesar, force him to work like a slave in their vineyard and even use him to test the wine they have laced with antifreeze. As for the innocent-looking Adil, he turns out to be an American's worst nightmare—a sinister secret agent working for a foreign enemy. He exploits Homer's American hospitality to obtain secret information about the Springfield nuclear power plant, which he dutifully broadcasts back to his Communist masters in Albania. In short, the episode seems to confirm the nasty suspicions Americans tend to harbor about foreigners—they are all evil and anti-American at heart.

On the other hand, the episode does show Springfield welcoming Adil 8 with open arms, and even as the evidence against him mounts, Homer is so receptive to his foreign guest that he refuses to believe that the young boy has done anything wrong. Bart grudgingly sums up his trip abroad: "So basically, I met one nice French person," but the fact is that a gendarme did save him from his plight. More to the point, the only reason the policeman rescued him is that Bart suddenly found himself explaining his predicament in fluent French. After failing to learn the language by study, Bart picked it up by osmosis, just as Principal Skinner predicted: "When he's totally immersed in a foreign language, the average child can become fluent in weeks." Once he actually goes abroad, even the unstudious Bart Simpson is open to the influence of a foreign culture and he ends up quite a devotee of all things French by the close of the episode. He returns from France wearing a beret and bearing all sorts of French gifts for his family, including a toy guillotine for Lisa. Homer ends the episode saying proudly: "You hear that, Marge, my boy speaks French"—not realizing that Bart has just used his newly acquired mastery of the language to call his father a "buffoon." For an American cartoon, "The Crepes of Wrath" has a remarkably polyglot texture, with whole scenes not just in French but even in Albanian.

Principal Skinner sums up the ambivalent response of Springfield to 9 foreigners when he originally introduces Adil at school:

> You may find his accent peculiar. Certain aspects of his culture may seem absurd, perhaps even offensive. But I urge you all to give little Adil the benefit of the doubt. In this way, and only in this way, can we hope to better understand our backward neighbors throughout the world.

Here is the strange combination of being both open and closed to the rest of the globe that characterizes Springfield. Skinner may regard all foreigners as backward, but he would still like to understand them better. And, when one adds up what happens in "The Crepes of Wrath," one finds a Springfield strangely integrated into the world community, with its children being educated in France and foreigners coming to learn about the workings of its advanced technology. Though a small town, Springfield has an international airport, with direct flights from Paris according to the PA announcements we hear, and, even more remarkably, from Tirana, the capital of Albania. It is a small world after all.

Thus, for all its parochial qualities, Springfield emerges as a globalized 10 community in *The Simpsons*. Even after Adil is returned under a cloud to his native Albania, the town continues to have a foreign exchange student in the person of Uter, complete with his German accent and *Lederhosen*. One of Springfield's most distinguished residents also has a heavy German accent, Rainier Wolfcastle, the actor who plays the action hero McBain (obviously modeled on the Austrian-born movie star Arnold Schwarzenegger). Perhaps the presence of so many German speakers in Springfield explains the interest of German businessmen in buying the nuclear power plant from Burns. The prospect of this foreign takeover reflects the increasingly multinational nature of business at the end of the twentieth century. We see Burns's flunky, Waylon Smithers, using audiotapes labeled "Sycophantic German" to get ready for his new bosses, learning such useful phrases as: "You looken sharpen todayen, mein herr" ("Burns Verkaufen der Kraftwerk"). As for the polyglot character of Springfield, this small town even has a Spanish-language sitcom on its Channel Ocho, featuring the famous Bumblebee Man. When Lisa takes the wrong bus and gets lost in Springfield, she discovers to her surprise whole ethnic neighborhoods in the town, including one in which everybody speaks Russian.[7] As we see in the episode called "Mom and Pop Art" (#AABF15, 4/11/99), Springfield is sufficiently Europeanized to support a trendy art community. Filled with homages to masterpieces of European art, from Rousseau's *Sleeping Gypsy* to Dali's *The Persistence of Memory*, this episode deals with Homer's brief triumph as an "outsider artist," due to the support of a group of foreign admirers, semi-affectionately referred to as "Eurotrash." But perhaps the most telling detail of the episode is the fact that Homer obtains his art supplies from "Mom & Pop Hardware," which turns out upon closer inspection to be "A Subsidiary of Global Dynamics, Inc." In late 1990s Springfield, a seemingly local business operation is really part of a multinational corporation. *The Simpsons* truly grasps the dynamics of the contemporary world, as everywhere one turns the local is globalized and the global is localized.

In one particularly bizarre subplot (in "In Marge We Trust"), Homer 11 finds to his dismay that halfway around the earth his face has mysteriously become the logo for a Japanese soap product called "Mr. Sparkle." The episode features a brilliant parody of a Japanese TV commercial that reveals how aware the creators of the show are of what is happening on

7. "Lost Our Lisa," #5F17, 5/10/98.

television around the globe. Indeed, as part of portraying the globalization of the world, *The Simpsons* repeatedly portrays the globalization of television. And in an odd case of life imitating art imitating life, *The Simpsons* has itself emerged as a perfect example of globalized television. The program is now shown all around the world and has been dubbed into over twenty languages, often illustrating the complexities and paradoxes of contemporary globalized culture. As an example of local variations on a global theme, *The Simpsons* is dubbed into French in both France and Quebec and thus ends up existing in "two parallel francophone universes" according to an article in the Canadian magazine *Saturday Night*. The dubbers in France and Quebec often come up with different solutions to the problem of translating American idiom. "Where American Homer describes his shrewish sisters-in-law as the 'gruesome twosome,' French Homère labels them *les sorcières Siamoises* (the Siamese witches), in Quebec, they're called *deux airs de boeuf* (the two grouches)."[8] Sometimes the seemingly simple act of translation can take on a political dimension. "The French are confident enough to let an anglicism or two slip into the dub. In Quebec, apparently, the fear is that if you give the English an inch, they'll swamp your whole language. So Homer's doughnuts remain *les donuts* in France, but in Quebec become *les beignes*." Who would have thought that Homer's donuts could spark such cultural controversy? But evidently translating *The Simpsons* into French raises all sorts of issues of race and class, as the dubbers in both France and Quebec scramble to find local equivalents of the various social and ethnic types in the original American program. For example, in France Apu is "given a quasi-Arabic accent," whereas in Quebec, "Apu's accent sounds more like Haitian Creole spoken *à la* Québecoise."

It is appropriate that Apu should provide a measure of the complexity 12 of the spread of *The Simpsons* around the globe, because within the series, he is the central symbol of the globalization of Springfield. Nothing is more integrated into the daily lives of the Springfielders than their local convenience store, and yet it turns out to be run by a foreigner, and one whose customs are distinctly foreign to the town's inhabitants. Apu is, for example, a strict vegetarian, even though—or perhaps precisely because—he is given to selling spoiled meat. Though Apu generally tries to keep a low profile in Springfield and assimilates to its ways as much as possible, his mere presence in the town and the example he sets with his exotic customs work to broaden the Springfielders' horizons. Just when Lisa is about to abandon her dogmatic vegetarianism, Apu reinforces her beliefs by revealing to her that he shares her philosophy and by introducing her to two other foreign-

8. Jonathan Kay, "Caste of Characters," *Saturday Night*, 9 September 2000, 16.

ers in Springfield who are also vegetarians—Paul and Linda McCartney
("Lisa the Vegetarian"). Only the presence of these impressive resident
aliens in Springfield allows Lisa to resist the relentless American propaganda in favor of eating meat to which she is subjected, which even makes
it seem a patriotic duty in the educational short Lisa is forced to watch,
"The Meat Council Presents Meat and You: Partners in Freedom."

Thus, although *The Simpsons* portrays Apu struggling to assimilate to
America, it also shows members of the Springfield community assimilating
to his ways. That is the meaning of globalization in the contemporary
world, which *The Simpsons,* unlike *Gilligan's Island,* portrays as a two-
way street. Apu is the embodiment of the American dream—a small businessman, determined to make his fortune solely on the basis of his hard
work and entrepreneurial skills. And as a convenience store, the Kwik-E-
Mart seems to be the quintessential American institution. And yet like
"Mom & Pop Hardware," the very local Kwik-E-Mart turns out to be integrated into the global economy. In "Homer and Apu" (#1F10, 2/10/94),
we learn that the Kwik-E-Mart is in fact part of a chain headquartered in
India. When Apu is fired, Homer, to help him get his job back, accompanies him to the corporate headquarters in the Himalayas, where they meet
the Maharishi-like CEO of Kwik-E-Mart. They even have the epiphanic experience of viewing the world's first convenience store high in the mountains ("This isn't very convenient," observes Homer). Its sign combines the
timeless wisdom of the East with the time-tested business acumen of the
West: "The Master Knows Everything Except Combination to Safe." *The
Simpsons* could offer no better image of the bizarre logic of contemporary
globalization than a worldwide convenience store empire run by an enlightened guru from the sacred mountains of India.

The Simpsons has devoted several episodes to Apu, who clearly has
emerged as one of the most popular characters in the series. Apu at first
threatened to become the one negative ethnic stereotype in the show,[9] but
the more we have gotten to know him, the more admirable he has appeared, and as is typical in the series, he has evolved from a mere cartoon
caricature to a complex and sympathetically portrayed human being. Apu
has become so admirable that at the Charity Bachelors Auction in Springfield, when all the other candidates are rejected, he is the one man the
women eagerly bid for.[10] Just at the moment when Apu becomes the most
popular date in Springfield and starts to live the life of a playboy, he

13

14

---

9. In an article in *TV Guide* (21 October 2000), Matt Groening admitted about Apu: "We
were worried he might be considered an offensive stereotype," but as the magazine points out:
"The writers made Apu a Pakistani [sic] of great dignity and industry" (20).
10. "The Two Mrs. Nahasapeemapetilons," #5F04, 11/16/97.

receives word from his mother back in India that he must now go through with his prearranged marriage to a young Hindu woman. In the face of a scheme Homer concocts to claim that Apu is already married, first Mrs. Nahasapeemapetilon and then his betrothed, Manjula, arrive in Springfield. To chart the progress of globalization in Springfield since the first-season "The Crepes of Wrath," there now are no less than three flights daily arriving direct from India at the town's international airport. Once Apu sees how beautiful Manjula is, he is eager to marry her, and in another emblematic moment of globalization, the terminally Protestant Reverend Lovejoy performs the Hindu ceremony. Mistakenly thinking that Apu is still reluctant to get married, Homer tries to stop the ceremony the only way he can—he puts on an elephant head, pretends that he is the Hindu god Ganesh, and forbids the marriage. When a dolt like Homer Simpson shows that he is familiar with the gods of the Hindu pantheon, it is fair to say that the globalization of Springfield is proceeding apace. Indeed the episode ends with Springfield joyously embracing the Nahasapeemapetilon family with all its foreign customs into the community.

But things do not always go smoothly for Apu in Springfield, and in one   15
episode *The Simpsons* tackles the dark side of globalization—the controversial issue of immigration. Apu's status as a resident alien in the United States had been left unclear and in "Much Apu About Nothing" (#3F20, 5/5/96), it comes back to haunt him. Forced to raise taxes in Springfield (the tax issue again!), Mayor Quimby puts the blame on illegal aliens and sponsors a ballot proposition to deport all immigrants. (The episode is clearly a satire on California's famous Proposition 187.) The campaign for Proposition 24 stirs up the lingering nationalism in the Springfielders, who are soon sporting signs proclaiming: "United States for United Statesians." More ominously, the proposition brings out the latent xenophobia in the town and especially the suspicion of foreign business interests.[11] People picket Apu's store with signs saying: "Buy American," "The Only Good Foreigner is Rod Stewart," and "Get Eurass Back to Eurasia." Faced with this mounting wave of nationalist hysteria, Apu buys a fake American identity from the local mobster, Fat Tony, who goes on to reassure him and yet caution him: "You're an American now. Remember you were born in Green Bay,

---

11. *The Simpsons* occasionally seems to reflect anxieties about the impact of foreign competition on American economic interests, though it usually satirizes those anxieties and shows its global perspective by portraying the foreign interests positively. In a flashback in "Last Exit to Springfield" (#9F15, 3/11/93), a disgruntled worker at a plant owned by Burns's grandfather makes the ominous (and accurate) prediction: "One day we'll form a union and get the fair and equitable treatment we deserve! Then we'll go too far, and get corrupt and shiftless, and the Japanese will eat us alive!" In "Burns Verkaufen der Kraftwerk," Lisa's characterization of the Germans taking over the plant sounds a warning to America: "They're efficient and punctual with a strong work ethic."

Wisconsin. Your parents were Herb and Judy Nahasapeemapetilon. And if you do not wish to arouse suspicion, I strongly urge you to act American." But despite his willingness to put on a cowboy hat, Apu is finally too proud of his Indian heritage to pander to stereotypes of American identity: "I cannot deny my roots and I cannot keep up this charade. I only did it because I love this land, where I have the freedom to say, and to think, and to charge whatever I want."

In his devotion to the cause of freedom and free enterprise, Apu comes across in this episode as more American than the native-born Americans trying to deport him. On the political issue of immigration, the sympathies of *The Simpsons* seem clear—the show sides with the immigrants and against the likes of Proposition 24 or 187. The way the show has Chief Wiggum issue the orders for deportation reveals that it regards the anti-immigration position as a betrayal of the basic American heritage of open borders. In his characteristic Edward G. Robinson voice, the chief stands the Statue of Liberty on its head: "All right men, here's the order of deportation. First we'll be rounding up your tired, then your poor, then your huddled masses yearning to breathe free." "Much Apu About Nothing" highlights everything that is nasty about Springfield as a small town—above all its small-mindedness—and reminds us that, although powerful forces may be driving the globalization of America, other powerful forces are resisting the process. The episode shows Springfield torn between its traditional attachment to the local and its newfound attraction to the global. The Springfielders may hate immigrants in the abstract, but they have grown to like concrete examples of immigration such as Apu. Homer represents the divided response of Springfield to Apu: "I got so swept up in the scapegoating and fun of Proposition 24, I never stopped to think it might affect someone I cared about. You know what, Apu? I am really, really gonna miss you." Though in his oafish way Homer at first sides against Apu, he soon reverses himself and rallies to his support. In the end, although Proposition 24 wins, Apu is able to avoid deportation by passing a test in American history and becoming a U.S. citizen. One might say that the show thereby cops out and ducks the very tough issue of immigration it raised in the first place, but a more charitable interpretation would be that *The Simpsons* does a good job of portraying how difficult it is for ordinary Americans to come to terms with immigration in an age of globalization.

16

Thinking About the Essay

1. What assumptions does Cantor make about his audience? For instance, can you identify the significance of the title? How does he address the needs of those readers who might not be *Simpsons* fans or viewers?

2. What is Cantor's purpose in writing about *The Simpsons*? Does he want to inform, entertain, argue, or what? What is his tone? Point to passages of the essay to support your responses.

3. Trace the causal connections between globalization and culture that Cantor analyzes in this essay. What thesis emerges from this analysis? Where is this thesis stated, or does Cantor rely on an implied thesis? Explain.

4. Cantor devotes a considerable amount of space in this essay to one *Simpsons* character, Apu. How can you justify his decision? Does the extended analysis of Apu detract from the balance of the essay? Explain.

5. Examine Cantor's footnotes. What do they tell you about his methodology, about the need for footnotes or citations, about the ways in which footnotes can enhance an essay?

Responding in Writing

6. View three or four *Simpsons* episodes, and then write an essay on the way in which the program reflects the impact of transnational culture on Springfield.

7. Children around the world watch American cartoons. What impact do you think these cartoons have on these children? What images of America are transmitted? Try to refer to specific cartoon series to bolster your analysis.

8. Write a careful analysis of the ways in which Cantor builds his case about globalization and culture in "Simpson Agonistes." Evaluate the relative success Cantor achieves in explaining his fascination with *The Simpsons* to an audience of educated readers.

Networking

9. Arrange with another class member to view one *Simpsons* episode or an episode of another television program that the two of you prefer. Then write a collaborative essay on cultural and transcultural messages the show conveys.

10. Join a *Simpsons* chat group on the Web. Why is the show so popular, especially with college students? What aspects of American and transnational culture do the participants focus on? Summarize your findings in a brief paper.

The Clash of Civilizations: Is Conflict Avoidable?

7

The spread of Coca-Cola, McDonald's, and Levi's jeans around the world—all the trappings of American popular culture—combined with the broader economic and political forces generated by America's superpower status, has resulted in what some call a "clash of civilizations." The phrase, coined by the American political scientist Samuel Huntington, who has an essay in this chapter, suggests that we are in a new era in which the forces of globalization have brought entire civilizations, rather than mere nations, into conflict with each other. The nature of this conflict goes to the heart of what we mean by cultural identity—who am I, and where do I belong?—and how we see ourselves in relation to our civilization and others we come into contact with.

According to Huntington, whose long article appeared in the summer 1993 issue of *Foreign Affairs* and subsequently in an expanded book, *The Clash of Civilizations and the Remaking of World Order* (1996), the world can be divided into seven or perhaps eight contemporary civilizations: Western, Latin American, Islamic, Sinic or Chinese (which includes China, Taiwan, Korea, and Vietnam), Japanese, Hindu, Orthodox (Russia, Serbia, Greece), and African. "Human history," writes Huntington, "is the history of civilizations. It is impossible to think of the development of humanity in any other terms." Historically there have been numerous conflicts between and among these civilizations. However, Huntington's thesis is that with the rise of the West since 1500, other civilizations—notably the Islamic and Chinese—have resented this "rise" and reacted against it. Furthermore, in the inevitable cycles of history, other civilizations will rise in reaction to the dominance of the Western world and become dominant themselves, thus leading to a new clash with global consequences.

In Santiago, Chile, demonstrators hold a vigil in response to the terrorist attacks of September 11, 2001, as well as the impending United States retaliatory strikes on Afghanistan. The sign held by the protesters is addressed to President George W. Bush of the United States and Osama Bin-Laden, leader of the terrorist group Al-Qaeda.

Thinking About the Image

1. Why is the banner in English instead of Spanish (the language spoken in Chile)? (Again, think of the rhetoric of public protest: who is the audience, and what is the purpose?)

2. What would have been your response to this photo on the day it was taken? Has your response changed based on events since September 11?

3. Why did these demonstrators choose to hold their protest outside of a cathedral?

4. Why do some protesters, such as these Chileans and those on p. 162, take to the streets, rather than writing or phoning their government representatives directly?

Huntington's broad thesis has come under scrutiny and attack on all sides, and some of his critics appear in this chapter. Yet it could be argued that what we see most clearly in the world today—the conflict between the Western and Islamic worlds, or the gradual ascendancy of China as the next major world power—confirms Huntington's basic claim. Conversely, if you think that reality actually contradicts Huntington's thesis, then you could argue that Western forms of culture, democracy, and modernization actually are cutting across all civilizations and triumphing over them. Benjamin Barber (whose essay appears in Chapter 5) maintains that there will be raging conflicts among civilizations in the future, but that "McWorld," as he terms the West, will triumph over "Jihad." Thus Western civilization will not decline but will defeat the forces of fundamentalism and totalitarianism.

The essays in this chapter deal with the clash of civilizations from a variety of perspectives. We can't deny that conflicts among civilizations exist; some are religious, others ethnic, still others cultural. Beginning with a classic essay by George Orwell, the writers invite us to consider our own loyalties, and whether we associate with one culture, nation, or civilization or with many. Are there commonalities among civilizations, or must we be forever in conflict? Must we always deal with threats to our gods, our ancestors, our civilization? Or, in a world of 6 billion people, are there tangible signs that we needn't think of "inferior" and "superior" civilizations but rather of a world showing signs of heightened tolerance, integration, and harmony? The way we answer these questions will determine the fabric of future civilizations.

Shooting an Elephant

GEORGE ORWELL

George Orwell (1903–1950) was the pseudonym of Eric Blair, an English novelist, essayist, and political commentator. He was born in Bengal, India, to parents who were members of the British Civil Service; as a young man, he joined the Imperial Police in Burma from 1922 to 1927. Ironically he turned against colonialism, became a socialist, and fought against the Fascists under Franco (and was wounded) in the Spanish Civil War. His disenchantment with communism appears in two classic novels, the allegorical fable *Animal Farm* (1945), which is a satire against Stalinism; and the bleak "dystopian" novel *1984* (1949), depicting a futuristic world in which human beings are controlled by "Big Brother." (The phrase "Big Brother is watching you" comes from this novel.) Orwell wrote a number of highly influential essays that serve to rank him among

> the greatest prose writers of the twentieth century. In this essay, first published in 1936, Orwell relates a personal narrative in order to expose the contradictions of British imperialism.

Before Reading

What do we mean by *imperialism*? What, as Orwell indicates, is "the real nature of imperialism"?

In Moulmein, in Lower Burma, I was hated by large numbers of people—   1 the only time in my life that I have been important enough for this to happen to me. I was sub-divisional police officer of the town, and in an aimless, petty kind of way anti-European feeling was very bitter. No one had the guts to raise a riot, but if a European woman went through the bazaars alone somebody would probably spit betel juice over her dress. As a police officer I was an obvious target and was baited whenever it seemed safe to do so. When a nimble Burman tripped me up on the football field and the referee (another Burman) looked the other way, the crowd yelled with hideous laughter. This happened more than once. In the end the sneering yellow faces of young men that met me everywhere, the insults hooted after me when I was at a safe distance, got badly on my nerves. The young Buddhist priests were the worst of all. There were several thousands of them in the town and none of them seemed to have anything to do except stand on street corners and jeer at Europeans.

All this was perplexing and upsetting. For at that time I had already   2 made up my mind that imperialism was an evil thing and the sooner I chucked up my job and got out of it the better. Theoretically—and secretly, of course—I was all for the Burmese and all against their oppressors, the British. As for the job I was doing, I hated it more bitterly than I can perhaps make clear. In a job like that you see the dirty work of Empire at close quarters. The wretched prisoners huddling in the stinking cages of the lockups, the grey, cowed faces of the long-term convicts, the scarred buttocks of the men who had been flogged with bamboos—all these oppressed me with an intolerable sense of guilt. But I could get nothing into perspective. I was young and ill-educated and I had had to think out my problems in the utter silence that is imposed on every Englishman in the East. I did not even know that the British Empire is dying, still less did I know that it is a great deal better than the younger empires that are going to supplant it. All I knew was that I was stuck between my hatred of the empire I served and my rage against the evil-spirited little beasts who tried to make my job impossible. With one part of my mind I thought of the British Raj as an unbreakable tyranny, as something clamped down, *in saecula saeculorum,* upon the will of prostrate peoples; with another part I thought that the greatest joy in the world would be to drive a bayonet into a Buddhist priest's guts. Feelings like these are the normal by-products of imperialism; ask any Anglo-Indian official, if you can catch him off duty.

One day something happened which in a roundabout way was enlight-   3
ening. It was a tiny incident in itself, but it gave me a better glimpse than I had had before of the real nature of imperialism—the real motives for which despotic governments act. Early one morning the sub-inspector at a police station at the other end of the town rang me up on the phone and said that an elephant was ravaging the bazaar. Would I please come and do something about it? I did not know what I could do, but I wanted to see what was happening and I got on to a pony and started out. I took my ri-fle, an old .44 Winchester and much too small to kill an elephant, but I thought the noise might be useful *in terrorem.* Various Burmans stopped me on the way and told me about the elephant's doings. It was not, of course, a wild elephant, but a tame one which had gone "must." It had been chained up as tame elephants always are when their attack of "must" is due, but on the previous night it had broken its chain and escaped. Its mahout, the only person who could manage it when it was in that state, had set out in pursuit, but he had taken the wrong direction and was now twelve hours' journey away, and in the morning the elephant had suddenly reappeared in the town. The Burmese population had no weapons and were quite helpless against it. It had already destroyed somebody's bamboo hut, killed a cow and raided some fruit-stalls and devoured the stock; also it had met the municipal rubbish van, and, when the driver jumped out and took to his heels, had turned the van over and inflicted violence upon it.

The Burmese sub-inspector and some Indian constables were waiting   4
for me in the quarter where the elephant had been seen. It was a very poor quarter, a labyrinth of squalid bamboo huts, thatched with palm-leaf, winding all over a steep hillside. I remember that it was a cloudy stuffy morning at the beginning of the rains. We began questioning the people as to where the elephant had gone, and, as usual, failed to get any definite information. That is invariably the case in the East; a story always sounds clear enough at a distance, but the nearer you get to the scene of events the vaguer it becomes. Some of the people said that the elephant had gone in one direction, some said that he had gone in another, some professed not even to have heard of any elephant. I had almost made up my mind that the whole story was a pack of lies, when we heard yells a little distance away. There was a loud, scandalised cry of "Go away, child! Go away this instant!" and an old woman with a switch in her hand came round the

corner of a hut, violently shooing away a crowd of naked children. Some more women followed, clicking their tongues and exclaiming; evidently there was something there that the children ought not to have seen. I rounded the hut and saw a man's dead body sprawling in the mud. He was an Indian, a black Dravidian coolie, almost naked, and he could not have been dead many minutes. The people said that the elephant had come suddenly upon him round the corner of the hut, caught him with its trunk, put its foot on his back and ground him into the earth. This was the rainy season and the ground was soft, and his face had scored a trench a foot deep and a couple of yards long. He was lying on his belly with arms crucified and head sharply twisted to one side. His face was coated with mud, the eyes wide open, the teeth bared and grinning with an expression of unendurable agony. (Never tell me, by the way, that the dead look peaceful. Most of the corpses I have seen looked devilish.) The friction of the great beast's foot had stripped the skin from his back as neatly as one skins a rabbit. As soon as I saw the dead man I sent an orderly to a friend's house nearby to borrow an elephant rifle. I had already sent back the pony, not wanting it to go mad with fright and throw me if it smelled the elephant.

The orderly came back in a few minutes with a rifle and five cartridges,   5 and meanwhile some Burmans had arrived and told us that the elephant was in the paddy fields below, only a few hundred yards away. As I started forward practically the whole population of the quarter flocked out of their houses and followed me. They had seen the rifle and were all shouting excitedly that I was going to shoot the elephant. They had not shown much interest in the elephant when he was merely ravaging their homes, but it was different now that he was going to be shot. It was a bit of fun to them, as it would be to an English crowd; besides, they wanted the meat. It made me vaguely uneasy. I had no intention of shooting the elephant—I had merely sent for the rifle to defend myself if necessary—and it is always unnerving to have a crowd following you. I marched down the hill, looking and feeling a fool, with the rifle over my shoulder and an evergrowing army of people jostling at my heels. At the bottom, when you got away from the huts, there was a metalled road and beyond that a miry waste of paddy fields a thousand yards across, not yet ploughed but soggy from the first rains and dotted with coarse grass. The elephant was standing eighty yards from the road, his left side towards us. He took not the slightest notice of the crowd's approach. He was tearing up bunches of grass, beating them against his knees to clean them and stuffing them into his mouth.

I had halted on the road. As soon as I saw the elephant I knew with per-   6 fect certainty that I ought not to shoot him. It is a serious matter to shoot a working elephant—it is comparable to destroying a huge and costly piece of machinery—and obviously one ought not to do it if it can possibly be avoided. And at that distance, peacefully eating, the elephant looked no more dangerous than a cow. I thought then and I think now that his attack of "must" was already passing off; in which case he would merely wander harmlessly about until the mahout came back and caught him. Moreover, I did not in the least want to shoot him. I decided that I would watch him for a little while to make sure that he did not turn savage again, and then go home.

But at that moment I glanced round at the crowd that had followed me. 7 It was an immense crowd, two thousand at the least and growing every minute. It blocked the road for a long distance on either side. I looked at the sea of yellow faces above the garish clothes—faces all happy and excited over this bit of fun, all certain that the elephant was going to be shot. They were watching me as they would watch a conjuror about to perform a trick. They did not like me, but with the magical rifle in my hands I was momentarily worth watching. And suddenly I realised that I should have to shoot the elephant after all. The people expected it of me and I had got to do it; I could feel their two thousand wills pressing me forward, irresistibly. And it was at this moment, as I stood there with the rifle in my hands, that I first grasped the hollowness, the futility of the white man's dominion in the East. Here was I, the white man with his gun, standing in front of the unarmed native crowd—seemingly the leading actor of the piece; but in reality I was only an absurd puppet pushed to and fro by the will of those yellow faces behind. I perceived in this moment that when the white man turns tyrant it is his own freedom that he destroys. He becomes a sort of hollow, posing dummy, the conventionalised figure of a sahib. For it is the condition of his rule that he shall spend his life in trying to impress the "natives" and so in every crisis he has got to do what the "natives" expect of him. He wears a mask, and his face grows to fit it. I had got to shoot the elephant. I had committed myself to doing it when I sent for the rifle. A sahib has got to act like a sahib; he has got to appear resolute, to know his own mind and do definite things. To come all that way, rifle in hand, with two thousand people marching at my heels, and then to trail feebly away, having done nothing—no that was impossible. The crowd would laugh at me. And my whole life, every white man's life in the East, was one long struggle not to be laughed at.

But I did not want to shoot the elephant. I watched him beating his 8 bunch of grass against his knees, with that preoccupied grandmotherly air that elephants have. It seemed to me that it would be murder to shoot him. At that age I was not squeamish about killing animals, but I had never shot an elephant and never wanted to. (Somehow it always seems worse to kill a *large* animal.) Besides, there was the beast's owner to be considered. Alive, the elephant was worth at least a hundred pounds; dead, he would only be worth the value of his tusks—five pounds, possibly. But I had got to act quickly. I turned to some experienced-looking Burmans who had been there when we arrived, and asked them how the elephant had been behaving. They all said the same thing: he took no notice of you if you left him alone, but he might charge if you went too close to him.

It was perfectly clear to me what I ought to do. I ought to walk up to 9 within, say, twenty-five yards of the elephant and test his behaviour. If he charged I could shoot, if he took no notice of me it would be safe to leave him until the mahout came back. But also I knew that I was going to do no such thing. I was a poor shot with a rifle and the ground was soft mud into which one would sink at every step. If the elephant charged and I missed him, I should have about as much chance as a toad under a steam-roller. But even then I was not thinking particularly of my own skin, only the watchful yellow faces behind. For at that moment, with the crowd watching me, I was not afraid in the ordinary sense, as I would have been if I had been alone. A white man mustn't be frightened in front of "natives"; and so, in general, he isn't frightened. The sole thought in my mind was that if anything went wrong those two thousand Burmans would see me pursued, caught, trampled on and reduced to a grinning corpse like that Indian up the hill. And if that happened it was quite probable that some of them would laugh. That would never do. There was only one alternative. I shoved the cartridges into the magazine and lay down on the road to get a better aim.

The crowd grew very still, and a deep, low, happy sigh, of people who 10 see the theatre curtain go up at last, breathed from innumerable throats. They were going to have their bit of fun after all. The rifle was a beautiful German thing with cross-hair sights. I did not then know that in shooting an elephant one should shoot to cut an imaginary bar running from ear-hole to ear-hole. I ought therefore, as the elephant was sideways on, to have aimed straight at his ear-hole; actually I aimed several inches in front of this, thinking the brain would be further forward.

When I pulled the trigger I did not hear the bang or feel the kick—one 11 never does when a shot goes home—but I heard the devilish roar of glee that went up from the crowd. In that instant, in too short a time, one would have thought, even for the bullet to get there, a mysterious, terrible change had come over the elephant. He neither stirred nor fell, but every line of his body had altered. He looked suddenly stricken, shrunken, immensely old, as though the frightful impact of the bullet had paralysed him without knocking him down. At last, after what seemed a long time—it might have been five seconds, I dare say—he sagged flabbily to his knees. His mouth slobbered. An enormous senility seemed to have settled upon him. One could have imagined him thousands of years old. I fired again into the same spot. At the second shot he did not collapse but climbed with desperate slowness to his feet and stood weakly upright, with legs sagging and head drooping. I fired a third time. That was the shot that did for him. You could see the agony of it jolt his whole body and knock the last remnant of strength from his legs. But in falling he seemed for a moment to rise, for as his hindlegs collapsed beneath him he seemed to tower upwards like a huge rock toppling, his trunk reaching skyward like a tree. He trumpeted, for the first and only time. And then down he came, his belly towards me, with a crash that seemed to shake the ground even where I lay.

I got up. The Burmans were already racing past me across the mud. It 12 was obvious that the elephant would never rise again, but he was not dead. He was breathing very rhythmically with long rattling gasps, his great mound of a side painfully rising and falling. His mouth was wide open—I could see far down into caverns of pale pink throat. I waited a long time for him to die, but his breathing did not weaken. Finally I fired my two remaining shots into the spot where I thought his heart must be. The thick blood welled out of him like red velvet, but still he did not die. His body did not even jerk when the shots hit him, the tortured breathing continued without a pause. He was dying, very slowly and in great agony, but in some world remote from me where not even a bullet could damage him further. I felt that I had got to put an end to that dreadful noise. It seemed dreadful to see the great beast lying there, powerless to move and yet powerless to die, and not even to be able to finish him. I sent back for my small rifle and poured shot after shot into his heart and down his throat. They seemed to make no impression. The tortured gasps continued as steadily as the ticking of a clock.

In the end I could not stand it any longer and went away. I heard later 13 that it took him half an hour to die. Burmans were arriving with dahs and baskets even before I left, and I was told they had stripped his body almost to the bones by the afternoon.

Afterwards, of course, there were endless discussions about the shoot- 14 ing of the elephant. The owner was furious, but he was only an Indian and could do nothing. Besides, legally I had done the right thing, for a mad elephant has to be killed, like a mad dog, if its owner fails to control it. Among the Europeans opinion was divided. The older men said I was right, the younger men said it was a damn shame to shoot an elephant for killing a coolie, because an elephant was worth more than any damn Coringhee coolie. And afterwards I was very glad that the coolie had been killed; it put me legally in the right and it gave me a sufficient pretext for shooting the elephant. I often wondered whether any of the others grasped that I had done it solely to avoid looking a fool.

Thinking About the Essay

1. Examine the first two paragraphs. What purpose do they serve? Does Orwell state his thesis anywhere in these paragraphs? Why or why not?

2. The events in this essay occur in Burma (also called Myanmar since 1989). What techniques does Orwell use to develop the action? How does he dramatize events, and from what perspectives? Why, ultimately, does he kill the elephant? Why is the elephant's death so prolonged?

3. Point to specific details that capture the reader's interest. Why does Orwell rely on the heavy accumulation of detail in this essay?

4. How does Orwell use irony and paradox to highlight the ethical issues he raises? Point to specific passages to support your response.

5. This is a personal essay, told by Orwell from the first-person point of view. How is he both a participant and an observer in the action? Do you find him to be reliable or unreliable as a narrator? Explain. What profile of the author emerges from this narrative?

Responding in Writing

6. Analyze Orwell's essay as an example of the "clash of civilizations." Explain the writer's attitude toward the Burmese people, his understanding of imperialism, and the "real nature of imperialism" as he sees it.

7. Orwell, who wrote this essay in 1936, states that "I did not even know that the British Empire is dying, still less did I know that it is a great deal better than the younger empires that are going to supplant it" (paragraph 2). Write an essay in response to his observation. What "younger empires" have emerged since then?

8. Write a personal essay of your own in which you describe an event that brought you into contact or conflict with people representing a "civilization" different from yours.

Networking

9. In small groups, read drafts of each other's papers for the "Responding in Writing" activities. Look especially at the clarity of each member's thesis and the insights brought to the subject.

10. For a research project, consult library sources *and* Internet sites, and then write a report, including documentation from books and online sources, on the importance of Orwell as an essayist.

When Afghanistan Was at Peace

MARGARET ATWOOD

> Margaret Atwood, born in 1939, is a Canadian novelist, poet, short story writer, and literary critic whose work explores the troubled contours of the modern world. Atwood's second collection of poetry, *The Circle Game* (1966), was published to critical acclaim. Equally impressive is a distinguished series of novels, including *Life Before Man* (1979), *The Handmaid's Tale* (1986), *Cat's Eye* (1988), and *The Blind Assassin* (2000). Atwood's writing often blends the intensely personal experience with global realties. In "When Afghanistan Was at Peace," published in October 2001 in the *New York Times Magazine,* Atwood describes a world ruined by clashing civilizations.

Before Reading

Reflect on what you know about Afghanistan. How many "civilizations" have attempted to conquer and control it? What problems do you foresee for Afghanistan's future?

In February 1978, almost 23 years ago, I visited Afghanistan with my spouse, Graeme Gibson, and our 18-month-old daughter. We went there almost by chance: we were on our way to the Adelaide literary festival in Australia. Pausing at intervals, we felt, would surely be easier on a child's time clock. (Wrong, as it turned out.) We thought Afghanistan would make a fascinating two-week stopover. Its military history impressed us—neither Alexander the Great nor the British in the 19th century had stayed in the country long because of the ferocity of its warriors.

"Don't go to Afghanistan," my father said when told of our plans. "There's going to be a war there." He was fond of reading history books. "As Alexander the Great said, Afghanistan is easy to march into but hard to march out of." But we hadn't heard any other rumors of war, so off we went.

We were among the last to see Afghanistan in its days of relative peace—relative, because even then there were tribal disputes and superpowers in play. The three biggest buildings in Kabul were the Chinese Embassy, the Soviet Embassy and the American Embassy, and the head of the country was reportedly playing the three against one another.

The houses of Kabul were carved wood, and the streets were like a living "Book of Hours": people in flowing robes, camels, donkeys, carts with huge wooden wheels being pushed and pulled by men at either end. There were few motorized vehicles. Among them were buses covered with ornate Arabic script, with eyes painted on the front so the buses could see where they were going.

We managed to hire a car in order to see the terrain of the famous and disastrous British retreat from Kabul to Jalalabad. The scenery was breathtaking: jagged mountains and the "Arabian Nights" dwellings in the valleys—part houses, part fortresses—reflected in the enchanted blue-green of the rivers. Our driver took the switchback road at breakneck speed since we had to be back before sundown because of bandits.

The men we encountered were friendly and fond of children: our curly-headed, fair-haired child got a lot of attention. The winter coat I wore had a large hood so that I was sufficiently covered and did not attract undue notice. Many wanted to talk; some knew English, while others spoke through our driver. But they all addressed Graeme exclusively. To have spoken to me would have been impolite. And yet when out interpreter negotiated our entry into an all-male teahouse, I received nothing worse than uneasy glances. The law of hospitality toward visitors ranked higher than the no-women-in-the-teahouse custom. In the hotel, those who served meals and cleaned rooms were men, tall men with scars either from dueling or from the national sport, played on horseback, in which gaining possession of a headless calf is the aim.

Girls and women we glimpsed on the street wore the chador, the long, pleated garment with a crocheted grill for the eyes that is more comprehensive than any other Muslim coverup. At that time, you often saw chic boots and shoes peeking out from the hem. The chador wasn't obligatory back then; Hindu women didn't wear it. It was a cultural custom, and since I had grown up hearing that you weren't decently dressed without a girdle and white gloves, I thought I could understand such a thing. I also knew that clothing is a symbol, that all symbols are ambiguous and that this one might signify a fear of women or a desire to protect them from the gaze of strangers. But it could also mean more negative things, just as the color red can mean love, blood, life, royalty, good luck—or sin.

I bought a chador in the market. A jovial crowd of men gathered around, amused by the spectacle of a Western woman picking out such a non-Western item. They offered advice about color and quality. Purple was better than light green or the blue, they said. (I bought the purple.) Every writer wants the Cloak of Invisibility—the power to see without being seen—or so I was thinking as I donned the chador. But once I had put it on, I had an odd sense of having been turned into negative space, a blank in the visual field, a sort of antimatter—both there and not there. Such a space has power of a sort, but it is a passive power, the power of taboo.

Several weeks after we left Afghanistan, the war broke out. My father 9
was right, after all. Over the next years, we often remembered the people
we met and their courtesy and curiosity. How many of them are now dead,
through no fault of their own?

Six years after our trip, I wrote "The Handmaid's Tale," a speculative 10
fiction about an American theocracy. The women in that book wear out-
fits derived in part from nuns' costumes, partly from girls' schools' hem-
lines and partly—I must admit—from the faceless woman on the Old
Dutch Cleanser box, but also partly from the chador I acquired in
Afghanistan and its conflicting associations. As one character says, there is
freedom to and freedom from. But how much of the first should you have
to give up in order to assure the second? All cultures have had to grapple
with that, and our own—as we are now seeing—is no exception. Would I
have written the book if I never had visited Afghanistan? Possibly. Would
it have been the same? Unlikely.

Thinking About the Essay

1. Does Atwood provide a thesis sentence in this essay? Why or why not?
   How does her title imply a thesis? If you were writing a thesis sentence of
   your own for this essay, what would it be?

2. What is Atwood's purpose in writing this narrative essay? Consider that this
   essay was published shortly after the events of 9/11. Is narration an appropriate strategy for her purpose? Why or why not?

3. Narrative essays typically use description to flesh out the story. Find descriptive details that Atwood provides, and explain what these details contribute to the overall effect.

4. Analyze the point of view in this essay. Is Atwood an observer, a participant, or both? Is she neutral or involved? Support your opinion.

5. Consider the relationship of the introductory paragraphs to the conclusion.
   Why does Atwood use the introduction and conclusion to expand the time
   frame of her main narrative?

Responding in Writing

6. Write an editorial for your college newspaper supporting or attacking the
   role of Western powers in Afghanistan today.

7. Imagine that you are traveling to Afghanistan on assignment for a newspaper. Report back, telling readers about what you see and where you go.
   Feel free to research the subject prior to writing the essay.

8. What does Atwood say about the clash of civilizations in this essay? Answer
   this question by analyzing the strategies she uses to convey her thesis.

Networking

9. In groups of two or three, pool your knowledge of Afghanistan. Prepare a brief report to be presented to the class.

10. In her essay, Atwood alludes to some of the nations and civilizations that have tried to conquer Afghanistan over the centuries. For research, conduct a library or Internet search on the history of Afghanistan, and how it has been a crossroads in the clash of civilizations. Prepare a brief report on your findings.

The World in 1500—or the West as Backwater

DINESH D'SOUZA

Dinesh D'Souza was born in 1961 in Bombay, India, and came to the United States in 1978 as an exchange student. After completing high school, he attended Dartmouth College, where he served as editor of the conservative magazine *Dartmouth Review* before graduation in 1983. Subsequently D'Souza contributed articles to several magazines, notably the *National Review,* before becoming a policy analyst for the Reagan administration. His longer work appears in *Illiberal Education: The Politics of Race and Sex on Campus* (1991), *The End of Racism: Principles for a Multi-Cultural Society* (1995), and *The Virtue of Prosperity: Finding Values in an Age of Techno-Affluence* (2001). D'Souza is a visiting scholar at the Hoover Institution. The following selection appears in his most recent book *What's So Great About America* (2002); here D'Souza offers an interesting perspective on the history of civilizations.

Before Reading

Think about all the great civilizations of the past and present. What causes them to rise and fall? Is it possible that Western civilization will suffer the same fate as other civilizations have? Why or why not?

For most of human history, other civilizations have proven far more   1
advanced than the West. They were more advanced in learning, in wealth, in exploration, in inventions—and in cultural sophistication and works of the mind. We can see this clearly by taking an imaginative leap

back in time to the year 1500, when "the West" as we know it now was just starting to emerge.

In 1500, there were several civilizations dotting the globe. However, two of them stood out in resplendence: the civilization of China—and the civilization of the Arab-Islamic world. During the Ming dynasty, the wealth, knowledge and power of China astonished all those who came into contact with it. Chinese astronomers knew more about eclipses and heavenly orbits than anyone else at the time. The Chinese were responsible for inventions of surpassing importance—printing, gunpowder and the compass. In the 15th century, the Chinese sent a fleet of ships—the largest and most sophisticated of their kind—to explore the shores of Africa, India and other countries. At home, the Chinese ruling class presided over an empire distinguished by its size and cohesion. Confucian philosophy gave a kind of moral and intellectual unity to Chinese civilization. The Chinese had a merit system of government appointments. This was all the more impressive as most of the world operated on traditional systems of nepotism and patronage. Chinese society showed a refinement in porcelain work, in silk embroidery—and in social refinement—that no other society could match. No wonder the Chinese emperors regarded themselves as the "sons of Heaven"—and their part of the world as the center of the universe.

Equally impressive in the year 1500 were the achievements of Islamic civilization. Starting in the 7th century, the Islamic empire spread rapidly until it sprawled across three continents: Europe, Asia—and Africa. The Muslims unified their enormous empire around a single faith, Islam—and a single language, Arabic. The Islamic world enjoyed a flourishing economy, enriched by trade with India and the Far East, and a largely uniform system of laws. The Muslims built spectacular cities—Baghdad, Damascus, Cairo, Istanbul, Seville, Granada—distinguished by architectural and literary splendor. Islamic literature and thought exhibited a richness, variety—and complexity—that far surpassed that of Europe at the time. Islam produced great men of learning, such as Ibn Sinha (Avicenna), Ihn Rushd (Averroes), Ibn Khaldun, al-Ghazali, al-Farabi and al-Kindi. Indeed, much of Greco-Roman knowledge—including the works of Aristotle—that had been lost in Europe during the Dark Ages was preserved in the Islamic world. It is no exaggeration to write, in the words of historian David Landes, that during this period "Islam was Europe's teacher."

Nothing could compare to China and the Islamic empire, but there were other civilizations in the world in the year 1500. There was the civilization of India, renowned for its spiritual depth as the original home of two of the world's great religions: Hinduism and Buddhism. India was also famous for its wealth and mathematical learning. In Africa, there were the kingdoms of Ghana, Mali and Songhay—which were large, orderly and rich in gold. Finally, in the Americas, there were the Aztec and Inca civilizations. Despite their reputation for brutality and human sacrifice, these were impressive for their architecture, social organization—and city planning.

Meanwhile, Western civilization—then called Christendom—was a relative backwater. Mired in the Dark Ages, Christendom was characterized by widespread ignorance, poverty and incessant clashes between warring tribes— and between kings and the Church. Indeed, Islamic writers who encountered the West in the late Middle Ages described it as remote, uninteresting—and primitive. A Muslim traveler described Europeans as "more like beasts than like men. They lack keenness of understanding and clarity of intelligence—and are overcome by ignorance and apathy, lack of discernment and stupidity." Another Muslim writer gives an account of the state of European medicine. He tells of a knight who came to a European physician complaining of an abscess on his leg. The physician seized an ax and chopped off the leg with one blow—"and the man died at once." Bernard Lewis, the Princeton historian, finds in such Muslim writings "the same note of amused disdain as we sometimes find among European travelers in Africa and Asia many centuries later."   5

How then did this relatively impoverished, backward civilization accumulate so much economic, political and military power that it was able to conquer and subdue all the other cultures of the world put together? The truth is that, throughout history, Western civilization has gained immensely from its absorption of the ideas and inventions of other cultures. From the Muslims, the West recovered parts of its own Greco-Roman heritage. From Hindus, the West learned its numeral system.   6

Civilizational development does not always go to the group that invents things. It frequently goes to the people who are able to take the inventions— and run with them.   7

Thinking About the Essay

1. What do you expect from D'Souza's title? Does he satisfy your expectations? Why or why not?

2. D'Souza is known as a conservative. Does he offer a conservative's view of the history of civilizations or not? Is his tone, for example, biased or objective? Explain your answer by referring to specific aspects of the essay.

3. Explain D'Souza's typical approach to paragraph development. What types of examples does he provide in these paragraphs? How does he achieve *coherence*?

4. How does D'Souza use classification as a main technique of organization in this essay?

5. Examine D'Souza's conclusion. What is significant about it?

Responding in Writing

6. Write an essay in which you maintain that the West *today* is or is not a "backwater."

7. In an argumentative paper, argue for or against the idea that the civilizations that D'Souza mentions in his essay are still vibrant and capable of coexisting.

8. Imagine that you represent a civilization *other* than the one you actually belong to. In an explanatory essay, tell why this civilization is noteworthy. You may want to conduct research for this paper.

Networking

9. In groups of four or five, review the drafts you have written. Focus on how well each writer has constructed a compelling presentation of the idea of civilization that has to be central to the essay assignment selected.

10. Search the Internet for information on D'Souza. Then join a class discussion in which you share your information and explore the reasons he is such a controversial figure.

American Dream Boat

K. OANH HA

K. Oanh Ha was born in Vietnam in 1973. As she relates in the following essay, she left Vietnam with her family in July 1979, journeying with other "boat people" to the United States. Raised in California, she is a staff writer for the *San Jose Mercury News*. She is working on a novel that is based loosely on her family's escape from Vietnam. In this personal narrative that she published in *Modern Maturity* in 2002, Ha provides a gentle affirmation of how—when it comes to love—civilizations need not clash.

Before Reading

Have you dated someone whose background represents a civilization entirely different from yours? If not, do you know of a couple who signify this coming together of civilizations? How do you—or they—work out any "clashes"?

The wedding day was only two weeks away when my parents called   1
with yet another request. In accordance with Vietnamese custom, they
fully expected Scott Harris, my fiancé, and his family to visit our family on
the morning of the wedding, bearing dowry gifts of fruit, candies, jewelry,
and a pig, in an elaborate procession.

"But it's not going to mean anything to Scott or his family. They're not   2
Vietnamese!" I protested. My parents were adamant: "Scott is marrying a
Vietnamese. If he wants to marry you, he'll honor our traditions."

Maybe there's no such thing as a stress-free wedding. Small or large,   3
there's bound to be pressure. But our February 12 wedding was a large
do-it-yourselfer that required a fusion of Vietnamese and American
traditions—a wedding that forced me and my parents to wrestle with
questions about our identities, culture, and place in America. After
nearly 20 years here, my family, and my parents in particular, were determined to have a traditional Vietnamese wedding of sorts, even if their
son-in-law and Vietnam-born, California-raised daughter are as American as they can be.

And so I grudgingly called Scott that night to describe the wedding pro-   4
cession and explain the significance of the ritual. It's a good thing that he
is a patient, easygoing man. "I'll bring the pig," he said, "but I'm worried
it'll make a mess in the car."

"Oh! It's a *roasted* pig," I told him, laughing.   5

I was six years old when my family fled Vietnam in July 1979, just one   6
family among the thousands who collectively became known as the "boat
people," families who decided it was better to risk the very real possibility
of death at sea than to live under Communist rule. But, of course, I never
understood the politics then. I was just a child following my parents.

My memories are sketchy. There was the time that Thai pirates wield-   7
ing saber-like machetes raided our boat. Two years ago, I told my mother,
Kim Hanh Nguyen, how I remembered a woman dropping a handful of
jewelry into my rice porridge during the raid with the instructions to keep
eating. "That was no woman," my mother said. "That was me!" When we
reached the refugee camp in Kuala Lumpur, my mother used the wedding
ring and necklace to buy our shelter.

In September 1980, we arrived in Santa Ana, California, in Orange   8
County, now home to the largest Vietnamese community outside of Vietnam. Those who had left in 1975, right after the end of the war and the
American withdrawal, had been well-educated, wealthy, and connected
with the military. My family was part of the wave of boat people—
mostly middle-class and with little education—who sought refuge in
America.

For nearly a year after we arrived, we crowded into the same three- 9
bedroom apartment, all 13 of us: brothers, sisters, cousins, uncles, aunts,
sisters-in-law, and my father's mother. There were only four of us children
in my immediate family then, three born in Vietnam and one born shortly
after our resettlement in the U.S.

We started school and watched Mr. Rogers on PBS in the afternoons, 10
grew to love hamburgers and ketchup and longed to lose our accents. We
older kids did lose our accents—and those who came later never had accents to begin with because they were born here. When we first came, I was
the oldest of three children, all born in Vietnam. Now I have seven siblings,
22 years separating me from my youngest brother, who will start kindergarten in the fall.

In some ways, I was the stereotypical Asian nerd. I took honors 11
classes, received good grades, played the violin and cello. But there was
a part of me that also yearned to be as American as my blond-haired
neighbors across the street. I joined the school's swim and tennis teams,
participated in speech competitions (which were attended by mostly
white students) and worshipped Esprit and Guess. My first serious
boyfriend was white but most of my friends were Asians who were either born in the U.S. or immigrated when they were very young. None
of us had accents and we rarely spoke our native languages around one
another. The last thing we wanted to be mistaken for was FOBs—fresh
off the boat. I even changed my name to Kyrstin, unaware of its Nordic
roots.

I wanted so badly to be a full-fledged American, whatever that meant. 12
At home though, my parents pushed traditional Vietnamese values. I spent
most of my teenage years baby-sitting and had to plead with my then overly
strict parents to let me out of the house. "Please, please. I just want to be
like any other American kid."

My parents didn't understand. "You'll always be Vietnamese. No one's 13
going to look at you and say you're an American," was my mother's often-
heard refrain.

I saw college as my escape, the beginning of the trip I would undertake 14
on my own. We had come to America as a family but it was time I navi-
gated alone. College was my flight from the house that always smelled of
fish sauce and jasmine tea.

At UCLA, I dated the man who would become my husband. Though 15
he's 17 years older than I am, my parents seemed to be more concerned
with the cultural barriers than our age difference. "White Americans are
fickle. They don't understand commitment and family responsibility like
we Asians do," I was told.

Soon after I announced my engagement, my father, Minh Phu Ha, and 16
I had a rare and intimate conversation. "I'm just worried for you," he said.
"All the Vietnamese women I know who have married whites are divorced
from them. Our cultures are too far apart."

My father, I think, is worried that none of his kids will marry Viet- 17
namese. My sisters are dating non-Vietnamese Asians while my brother is
dating a white American. "It's just that with a Vietnamese son-in-law, I can
talk to him," my father explained to me one day. "A Vietnamese son-in-
law would call me 'Ba' and not by my first name."

Although my parents have come to terms with having Scott as their son- 18
in-law and to the prospect of grandchildren who will be racially mixed,
there are still times when Scott comes to visit that there are awkward silences. There are still many cultural barriers.

I still think of what it all means to marry a white American. I worry that 19
my children won't be able to speak Vietnamese and won't appreciate that
part of their heritage. I also wonder if somehow this is the ultimate fulfillment of a latent desire to be "American."

Vietnamese-Americans, like Chinese-Americans, Indian-Americans, 20
and other assimilated immigrants, often speak of leading hyphenated lives,
of feet that straddle both cultures. I've always been proud of being Vietnamese. As my family and I discussed and heatedly debated what the wedding event was going to look like, I began to realize just how "American"
I had become.

And yet there was no denying the pull of my Vietnamese roots. Four 21
months before the wedding, I traveled back to Vietnam for the second time
since our family's escape. It was a trip I had planned for more than a year.
I was in Saigon, the city of my birth, to research and write a novel that
loosely mirrors the story of my own family and our journey from Vietnam.
The novel is my tribute to my family and our past. I'm writing it for myself as much as for my younger siblings, so they'll know what our family's
been through.

I returned to Vietnam to connect with something I can't really name but 22
know I lost when we left 20 years ago. I was about to start a new journey
with the marriage ahead, but I needed to come back to the place where my
family's journey began.

Scott came along for the first two weeks and met my extended family. 23
They all seemed to approve, especially when he showed he could eat pungent fish and shrimp sauce like any other Vietnamese.

During my time there I visited often with family members and talked 24
about the past. I saw the hospital where I was born, took a walk through
our old house, chatted with my father's old friends. The gaps in the circle

of my hyphenated life came closer together with every new Vietnamese word that I learned, with every Vietnamese friend that I made.

I also chose the fabric for the tailoring of the *ao dai,* the traditional Viet- 25 namese dress of a long tunic over flowing pants, which I would change into at the reception. I had my sisters' bridesmaid gowns made. And I had a velvet ao dai made for my 88-year-old maternal grandmother, *Bā Ngoai,* to wear to the wedding of her oldest grandchild. "My dream is to see you on your wedding day and eat at your wedding feast," she had told me several times.

Bā Ngoai came to the U.S. in 1983, three years after my family landed 26 in Orange County as war refugees. As soon as we got to the United States, my mother filed immigration papers for her. Bā Ngoai made that journey at age 73, leaving the only home she had known to be with my mother, her only child. Bā Ngoai nurtured and helped raise us grandchildren.

I had extended my stay in Vietnam. Several days after my original de- 27 parture date, I received a phone call. Bā Ngoai had died. I flew home carrying her ao dai. We buried her in it.

In Vietnamese tradition, one is in mourning for three years after the loss 28 of a parent or grandparent. Out of respect and love for the deceased, or *hieu,* decorum dictates that close family members can't get married until after the mourning period is over. But my wedding was only a month and a half away.

On the day we buried my grandmother, my family advised me to burn 29 the white cloth headband that symbolized my grief. By burning it, I ended my official mourning.

Through my tears I watched the white cloth become wispy ashes. My 30 family was supportive. "It's your duty to remember and honor her," my father told me. "But you also need to move forward with your life."

On the morning of our wedding, Scott's family stood outside our house 31 in a line bearing dowry gifts. Inside the house, Scott and I lighted incense in front of the family altar. Holding the incense between our palms, we bowed to my ancestors and asked for their blessings. I looked at the photo of Bā Ngoai and knew she had to be smiling.

Thinking About the Essay

1. How do you interpret the title? What aspects of the essay does it capture?

2. There are several characters in this essay. Who are they? How are they described? What sort of persona does Ha create for herself as the "I" narrator?

3. Why does Ha begin the essay in the present and then shift to the past? Trace the narrative pattern throughout her essay.

4. Often when you write a personal essay, it is valuable to create a central conflict. What is the conflict (or conflicts) in this selection? How does Ha develop and resolve it? Does this conflict lead to a thesis? Why or why not?

5. Explain the various moods and tones that Ha imbues her narrative with. Do they "clash" or not? Are they finally reconciled? Justify your response.

Responding in Writing

6. In a 500–750-word paper, explain why Ha's essay tells us about the clash of civilizations and how we might resolve it.

7. Write a narrative essay in which you tell of a relationship in which the people come from different civilizations. You can base this essay on personal experience, the experience of family or friends, or a situation drawn from television or film.

8. Do you think that the narrator and her husband will have a happy marriage? Why or why not? Cite what you have learned about them in the essay as support for your response.

Networking

9. In a group of four, discuss the relationship between Scott and "Kyrstin" Oanh. Do you think it is healthy and viable, or do you sense potential problems? Summarize your decision for the rest of the class.

10. Search the Internet for more information on the Vietnamese boat people. Where have they settled in the United States? How do they preserve their culture and civilization? How often do they intermarry with Americans outside their background? Discuss your findings with the class.

The West and the Rest: Intercivilizational Issues

SAMUEL P. HUNTINGTON

Samuel Phillips Huntington was born in New York City in 1927. He received his education at Yale University (B.A., 1946), the University of Chicago (M.A., 1948), and Harvard University (Ph.D., 1951). A leading authority on international affairs, Huntington has worked and consulted for numerous government and private organizations, including the National Security Council, the National War College, and the Office of the Secretary of Defense. He is professor of government at Harvard University and director of its Center for Strategic Studies. Among his many books are *The Soldier and the*

State (1957), *Political Order in Changing Societies* (1968), *American Military Strategy* (1986), and *The Clash of Civilizations and the Remaking of World Order* (1996), from which this essay is taken.

Before Reading

Do you think that Western civilization is under assault from Islamic, Chinese, or other civilizations? Why or why not?

Western Universalism

In the emerging world, the relations between states and groups from different civilizations will not be close and will often be antagonistic. Yet some intercivilization relations are more conflict-prone than others. At the micro level, the most violent fault lines are between Islam and its Orthodox, Hindu, African, and Western Christian neighbors. At the macro level, the dominant division is between "the West and the rest," with the most intense conflicts occurring between Muslim and Asian societies on the one hand, and the West on the other. The dangerous clashes of the future are likely to arise from the interaction of Western arrogance, Islamic intolerance, and Sinic assertiveness.

Alone among civilizations the West has had a major and at times devastating impact on every other civilization. The relation between the power and culture of the West and the power and cultures of other civilizations is, as a result, the most pervasive characteristic of the world of civilizations. As the relative power of other civilizations increases, the appeal of Western culture fades and non-Western peoples have increasing confidence in and commitment to their indigenous cultures. The central problem in the relations between the West and the rest is, consequently, the discordance between the West's—particularly America's—efforts to promote a universal Western culture and its declining ability to do so.

The collapse of communism exacerbated this discordance by reinforcing in the West the view that its ideology of democratic liberalism had triumphed globally and hence was universally valid. The West, and especially the United States, which has always been a missionary nation, believe that the non-Western peoples should commit themselves to the Western values of democracy, free markets, limited government, human rights, individualism, the rule of law, and should embody these values in their institutions. Minorities in other civilizations embrace and promote these values, but the dominant attitudes toward them in non-Western cultures range from widespread skepticism to intense opposition. What is universalism to the West is imperialism to the rest.

The West is attempting and will continue to attempt to sustain its pre-   4
eminent position and defend its interests by defining those interests as the
interests of the "world community." That phrase has become the eu-
phemistic collective noun (replacing "the Free World") to give global legitimacy to actions reflecting the interests of the United States and other
Western powers. The West is, for instance, attempting to integrate the
economies of non-Western societies into a global economic system which
it dominates. Through the IMF and other international economic institutions, the West promotes its economic interests and imposes on other nations the economic policies it thinks appropriate. In any poll of
non-Western peoples, however, the IMF undoubtedly would win the support of finance ministers and a few others but get an overwhelmingly unfavorable rating from almost everyone else, who would agree with Georgi
Arbatov's description of IMF officials as "neo-Bolsheviks who love expro-
priating other people's money, imposing undemocratic and alien rules of
economic and political conduct and stifling economic freedom."[1]

Non-Westerners also do not hesitate to point to the gaps between   5
Western principle and Western action. Hypocrisy, double standards, and
"but nots" are the price of universalist pretensions. Democracy is promoted but not if it brings Islamic fundamentalists to power; nonproliferation is preached for Iran and Iraq but not for Israel; free trade is the elixir
of economic growth but not for agriculture; human rights are an issue
with China but not with Saudi Arabia; aggression against oil-owning
Kuwaitis is massively repulsed but not against non-oil-owning Bosnians.
Double standards in practice are the unavoidable price of universal standards of principle.

Having achieved political independence, non-Western societies wish to   6
free themselves from Western economic, military, and cultural domination.
East Asian societies are well on their way to equalling the West economically. Asian and Islamic countries are looking for shortcuts to balance the
West militarily. The universal aspirations of Western civilization, the declining relative power of the West, and the increasing cultural assertiveness
of other civilizations ensure generally difficult relations between the West
and the rest. The nature of those relations and the extent to which they are
antagonistic, however, vary considerably and fall into three categories.
With the challenger civilizations, Islam and China, the West is likely to
have consistently strained and often highly antagonistic relations. Its relations with Latin America and Africa, weaker civilizations which have in
some measure been dependent on the West, will involve much lower levels

---

1. Georgi Arbatov, "Neo-Bolsheviks of the I.M.F.," *New York Times*, 7 May 1992, p. A27.

of conflict, particularly with Latin America. The relations of Russia, Japan, and India to the West are likely to fall between those of the other two groups, involving elements of cooperation and conflict, as these three core states at times line up with the challenger civilizations and at times side with the West. They are the "swing" civilizations between the West, on the one hand, and Islamic and Sinic civilizations, on the other.

Islam and China embody great cultural traditions very different from 7 and in their eyes infinitely superior to that of the West. The power and assertiveness of both in relation to the West are increasing, and the conflicts between their values and interests and those of the West are multiplying and becoming more intense. Because Islam lacks a core state, its relations with the West vary greatly from country to country. Since the 1970s, however, a fairly consistent anti-Western trend has existed, marked by the rise of fundamentalism, shifts in power within Muslim countries from more pro-Western to more anti-Western governments, the emergence of a quasi war between some Islamic groups and the West, and the weakening of the Cold War security ties that existed between some Muslim states and the United States. Underlying the differences on specific issues is the fundamental question of the role these civilizations will play relative to the West in shaping the future of the world. Will the global institutions, the distribution of power, and the politics and economies of nations in the twenty-first century primarily reflect Western values and interests or will they be shaped primarily by those of Islam and China? . . .

The issues that divide the West and these other societies are increasingly 8 important on the international agenda. Three such issues involve the efforts of the West: (1) to maintain its military superiority through policies of nonproliferation and counterproliferation with respect to nuclear, biological, and chemical weapons and the means to deliver them; (2) to promote Western political values and institutions by pressing other societies to respect human rights as conceived in the West and to adopt democracy on Western lines; and (3) to protect the cultural, social, and ethnic integrity of Western societies by restricting the number of non-Westerners admitted as immigrants or refugees. In all three areas the West has had and is likely to continue to have difficulties defending its interests against those of non-Western societies. . . .

The changing balance of power among civilizations makes it more and 9 more difficult for the West to achieve its goals with respect to weapons proliferation, human rights, immigration, and other issues. To minimize its losses in this situation requires the West to wield skillfully its economic resources as carrots and sticks in dealing with other societies, to bolster its unity and coordinate its policies so as to make it more difficult for other societies to play one Western country off against another, and to promote and exploit differences among non-Western nations. The West's ability to pursue these strategies will be shaped by the nature and intensity of its conflicts with the challenger civilizations, on the one hand, and the extent to which it can identify and develop common interests with the swing civilizations, on the other.

Thinking About the Essay

1. How would you characterize the tone of this essay? Does Huntington present himself as argumentative, opinioned, objective, fair-minded, liberal, conservative, or what? Identify words, sentences, and passages that support your assessment of the writer's voice.

2. Summarize Huntington's argument. What is his thesis or claim? What types of support does he provide?

3. What aspects of Huntington's language tell you that he writes for an audience that can follow his rapid sweep of the civilizations and institutions of the world? To what extent does he employ "loaded" language to advance his argument? Explain.

4. Huntington employs numerous rhetorical strategies to develop his argument, among them comparison and contrast, classification, and illustration. Locate examples of these strategies in the essay.

5. What, in Huntington's view, is the answer to the clash of civilizations? How does he prepare the reader for his answer? Trace the "logic" of his answer through the essay.

Responding in Writing

6. Compare and contrast the essays by Orwell and Huntington. Establish a clear thesis concerning their views about the conflict of civilizations, and the different ways they approach the subject. Develop at least three key topics.

7. Do you agree or disagree with Huntington's analysis and argument? Explain your response in an argumentative paper of your own.

8. Respond in an analytical essay to Huntington's statement, "Alone among civilizations the West has had a major and at times devastating impact on every other civilization."

Networking

9. Discuss Huntington's essay in groups of three or four. Draw up a list of all the key elements in his argument. Then join a general class discussion on why his argument has caused so much controversy.

10. Go online and conduct a Boolean search on "Samuel Huntington" and "Clash of Civilizations." How has the debate developed since the time Huntington first published his ideas? Summarize the controversy in a brief paper.

A World Not Neatly Divided

AMARTYA SEN | Amartya K. Sen, the 1998 Nobel Prize winner in economics, was born in 1933 in Santiniketan, India. After studying at Presidency College in Calcutta, Sen emigrated to England, where he received B.A. (1955), M.A., and Ph.D. (1959) degrees from Trinity College, Cambridge. Master of Trinity College since 1998, Sen also has taught at Oxford University, the London School of Economics, Harvard University, and Cornell University. Sen is credited with bringing ethical considerations into the study of economics. He has done groundbreaking work in establishing techniques for assessing world poverty and the relative wealth of nations, the causes of famine, and the economic impact of health and education on developing societies. His study, *Collective Choice and Social Welfare* (1970), in which he uses the tools of economics to study such concepts as fairness, liberty, and justice, brings to economic theory a dimension of moral philosophy that has made Sen an influential figure in contemporary thought. Other notable works include *Poverty and Famines: An Essay on Entitlement and Deprivation* (1981), *On Ethics and Economics* (1987), and *Development as Freedom* (1999). As this essay from the *New York Times*, November 23, 2001, demonstrates, Sen commands a lucid prose style that enables him to make complex issues accessible to general readers. Here, he argues for a more nuanced approach to the idea of civilization than the one posed by Samuel Huntington.

Before Reading

Is it necessary to divide the world into various types of civilizations? What is the purpose of such classification, and what are the possible results?

When people talk about clashing civilizations, as so many politicians   1
and academics do now, they can sometimes miss the central issue.
The inadequacy of this thesis begins well before we get to the question of

whether civilizations must clash. The basic weakness of the theory lies in its program of categorizing people of the world according to a unique, allegedly commanding system of classification. This is problematic because civilizational categories are crude and inconsistent and also because there are other ways of seeing people (linked to politics, language, literature, class, occupation or other affiliations).

The befuddling influence of a singular classification also traps those   2
who dispute the thesis of a clash: To talk about "the Islamic world" or "the Western world" is already to adopt an impoverished vision of humanity as unalterably divided. In fact, civilizations are hard to partition in this way, given the diversities within each society as well as the linkages among different countries and cultures. For example, describing India as a "Hindu civilization" misses the fact that India has more Muslims than any other country except Indonesia and possibly Pakistan. It is futile to try to understand Indian art, literature, music, food or politics without seeing the extensive interactions across barriers of religious communities. These include Hindus and Muslims, Buddhists, Jains, Sikhs, Parsees, Christians (who have been in India since at least the fourth century, well before England's conversion to Christianity), Jews (present since the fall of Jerusalem), and even atheists and agnostics. Sanskrit has a larger atheistic literature than exists in any other classical language. Speaking of India as a Hindu civilization may be comforting to the Hindu fundamentalist, but it is an odd reading of India.

A similar coarseness can be seen in the other categories invoked, like   3
"the Islamic world." Consider Akbar and Aurangzeb, two Muslim emperors of the Mogul dynasty in India. Aurangzeb tried hard to convert Hindus into Muslims and instituted various policies in that direction, of which taxing the non-Muslims was only one example. In contrast, Akbar reveled in his multiethnic court and pluralist laws, and issued official proclamations insisting that no one "should be interfered with on account of religion" and that "anyone is to be allowed to go over to a religion that pleases him."

If a homogeneous view of Islam were to be taken, then only one of these   4
emperors could count as a true Muslim. The Islamic fundamentalist would have no time for Akbar; Prime Minister Tony Blair, given his insistence that tolerance is a defining characteristic of Islam, would have to consider excommunicating Aurangzeb. I expect both Akbar and Aurangzeb would protest, and so would I. A similar crudity is present in the characterization of what is called "Western civilization." Tolerance and individual freedom have certainly been present in European history. But there is no dearth of diversity here, either. When Akbar was making his pronouncements on re-

ligious tolerance in Agra, in the 1590's, the Inquisitions were still going on; in 1600, Giordano Bruno was burned at the stake, for heresy, in Campo dei Fiori in Rome.

Dividing the world into discrete civilizations is not just crude. It propels 5 us into the absurd belief that this partitioning is natural and necessary and must overwhelm all other ways of identifying people. That imperious view goes not only against the sentiment that "we human beings are all much the same," but also against the more plausible understanding that we are diversely different. For example, Bangladesh's split from Pakistan was not connected with religion, but with language and politics.

Each of us has many features in our self-conception. Our religion, im- 6 portant as it may be, cannot be an all-engulfing identity. Even a shared poverty can be a source of solidarity across the borders. The kind of division highlighted by, say, the so-called "anti-globalization" protesters— whose movement is, incidentally, one of the most globalized in the world—tries to unite the underdogs of the world economy and goes firmly against religious, national or "civilizational" lines of division.

The main hope of harmony lies not in any imagined uniformity, but in 7 the plurality of our identities, which cut across each other and work against sharp divisions into impenetrable civilizational camps. Political leaders who think and act in terms of sectioning off humanity into various "worlds" stand to make the world more flammable—even when their intentions are very different. They also end up, in the case of civilizations defined by religion, lending authority to religious leaders seen as spokesmen for their "worlds." In the process, other voices are muffled and other concerns silenced. The robbing of our plural identities not only reduces us; it impoverishes the world.

Thinking About the Essay

1. How does Sen begin his essay? What is his argument and how does he present it in the opening paragraph?

2. Sen uses several illustrations to support his argument about "singular classification." Locate three of these examples and explain how they advance his claim.

3. Any discussion of types—whether types of civilizations or types of teachers—lends itself to classification. How does Sen use classification and division to organize his argument and his essay?

4. What transitional devices serve to unify this essay?

5. Does Sen's concluding paragraph serve to confirm his thesis or claim? Explain your answer.

Responding in Writing

6. What is so wrong about "singular classification," especially when considering nations, cultures, and civilizations? Write a response to this question, referring to Sen's essay in the process.

7. Write a complete analysis of the ways in which Sen composes his argument in "A World Not Neatly Divided."

8. Write a comparative paper analyzing the essays by Sen and Samuel Huntington.

Networking

9. In small groups, select a city, region, country, or civilization, and then draw up a list of traits or attributes—a singular classification—illuminating your subject. Present the list to class members, and as a group discuss the advantages and disadvantages of singular classification.

10. Conduct online research on an international city. Then write a travel blurb stressing both the singular nature of this city and also its diversity.

Andalusia's Journey

EDWARD SAID

Edward W. Said was born in 1935 in Jerusalem, Palestine, and grew up in Egypt. His family moved to the United States in 1951. Educated at Princeton University (B.A., 1957) and Harvard University (Ph.D., 1964), Said was an influential literary and cultural critic and a noted supporter of the Palestinian cause. University Professor of English and comparative literature at Columbia, he was best known to the general public as a commentator on radio and television on Middle Eastern affairs. Perceived as a public intellectual, Said for decades advocated Palestinian rights even as he criticized Palestinian policies and leadership. His books *The Question of Palestine* (1979), *Covering Islam* (1981), and *The Politics of Dispossession: The Struggle for Palestinian Self-Determination* (1994) offer penetrating analyses of this troubled region. Said was also a distinguished literary critic, the author of the groundbreaking study *Orientalism* (1978), *Culture and Imperialism* (1993), and other books and collections of essays. In the early 1990s Said was diagnosed with leukemia; his illness prompted him to write an autobiography, *Out of Place:*

A *Memoir* (1999), tracing his life and journeys as an exile. Said died in 2003. In the following essay, published in *Travel and Leisure* in 2002, Said offers a personal impression of one region in Spain that has been a crossroads in the convergence of civilizations.

Before Reading

Said speaks of Andalusia—the region in southern Spain where Arab, Latin, and Jewish civilizations came together for seven hundred years—as representing a dialogue rather than clash of civilizations. What is necessary for such a dialogue to occur in the world today?

> Poverty turns our country into a foreign land, and riches our place of exile into our home. For the whole world, in all its diversity, is one. And all its inhabitants our brothers and neighbors.
>
> —Abu Muhammad al-Zubaydi, Seville, A.D. 926–989

For an Arab, such as myself, to enter Granada's 13th-century Alhambra palace is to leave behind a modern world of disillusionment, strife, and uncertainty. In this, the calmest, most harmonious structure ever built by Arab Muslims, the walls are covered with dizzying arabesques and geometric patterns, interspersed with Arabic script extolling God and his regents on earth. The repetition of a basically abstract series of motifs suggests infinity, and serves to pull one through the palace's many rooms. The palace's Generalife gardens, punctuated by cooling streams, are a miracle of balance and repose. The Alhambra, like the great ninth-century mosque-cum-cathedral of Cordova, La Mezquita, invites believer and nonbeliever alike with opulence and rigorous discipline of ornament, and almost imperceptible changes in perspective from one space to the next. The whole composition is always in evidence—always changing yet always somehow the same—a unity in multiplicity.

I have been traveling for four decades to southern Spain, Andalucía as it is called by Spaniards, al-Andalus by Arabs, drawn there by its magnificent architecture, and the amazingly mixed Arab, Jewish, and Latin cultural centers of Cordova, Granada, and Seville. The turmoil of Andalusia's extraordinary past seems to hover just beneath the surface of its pleasant landscapes and generally small-scaled urban life. In its medieval heyday, Andalusia, established by the Arab general Tariq bin Ziyad and continuously fought over by numerous Muslim sects (among them Almoravids, Nasrids, and Almohads) and by Catholics as far north as Galicia, was a particularly lively instance of the dialogue, much more than the clash, of

A 16th-century plate from Valencia (once part of the Caliphate of Cordova), on which Arabic and Spanish designs merge.

cultures. Muslims, Jews, and Christians co-existed with astonishing harmony. Today its periods of fruitful cultural diversity may provide a model for the co-existence of peoples, a model quite different from the ideological battles, local chauvinism, and ethnic conflict that finally brought it down—and which ironically enough threaten to engulf our own 21st-century world.

When I first visited, in the summer of 1966, Franco-era Andalusia 3 seemed like a forgotten, if wonderfully picturesque, province of Catholic Spain. Its fierce sun accentuated the area's rigors: the scarcity of good accommodations, the difficulty of travel, the heaviness of the cuisine, the unyielding spirit of a people living in relative poverty and obdurate pride, the political and religious repression under which the country suffocated. The splendor of its great buildings was evident but seemed part of a distant backdrop to more urgent and more recent times: the Civil War of 1936–39 and Hemingway's sentimentalized view of it; the burgeoning and quite sleazy mass tourist trade that had put down roots in Málaga (not to mention the ghastly neighboring village of Torremolinos) and that was creeping slowly westward toward Portugal's Algarve (from the Arabic *al-gharb min al-Andalus,* "west of Andalusia").

Even in the summer of 1979, when I spent a few weeks in the area with 4 my wife and two young children, the Alhambra was all but deserted. You could stroll into it as you would into a public park. (Today, visiting the place is more like going to Disneyland. There are five gigantic parking lots and you must reserve well in advance.) For its part, Seville was a pleasant, somewhat subdued city of modest restaurants and family-style hotels. Franco had disappeared in 1975, of course, but the prosperous Spain of

The Alhambra's repeating arches.

solidly based, open democracy had not yet arrived. You could still feel the Church's cold impress and the vestiges of the fascist dictatorship. Europe was a long distance away, beyond the Pyrenees, to the north.

In the 1980's and 90's Spain awakened into modernity and globalization. NATO's Spain, the EU's Spain, took over the peninsula's identity. There is now no shortage of excellent hotels or good restaurants, although it must again be admitted, as the Michelin Guide put it in the 1960's, that for the most part "Spanish cuisine is more complicated than it is refined." But for me, and indeed for many Arabs, Andalusia still represents the finest flowering of our culture. That is particularly true now, when the Arab Middle East seems mired in defeat and violence, its societies unable to arrest their declining fortunes, its secular culture so full of almost surreal crisis, shock, and nihilism.

A spate of recent Arabic and Muslim writing has redirected attention to Andalusia as a mournful, tantalizing emblem of what a glorious civilization was lost when Islamic rule ended. This literature serves only to accentuate the conditions of decline and loss that have so diminished modern Arab life—and the conquests that have dominated it. Thus, for instance, the 1992 appearance of Palestinian poet Mahmud Darwish's great *qasida*, or ode, *Ahd Ashr Kawkaban Ala Akhir Almashad Al-Andalusi* (Eleven Stars over the Last Moments of Andalusia). The poem was written about— and served to clarify—what the Palestinians felt they had lost not just once but time after time. The Palestinian national poet seems to be asking, What do we do after the last time, after the new conquerors have entered our palaces and consumed our still hot tea and heard our mellifluous music?

The palace's Generalife gardens.

Swearing allegiance at the Alhambra, as imagined by Filippo Baratti, one of many 19th-century European artists captivated by Andalusia's history.

Does it mean that as Arabs we exist only as a footnote to someone else's history?

> Our tea is green and hot: drink it. Our pistachios are fresh; eat them.
> The beds are of green cedar, fall on them,
> following this long siege, lie down on the feathers of our dream.
> The sheets are crisp, perfumes are ready by the door, and there are plenty of mirrors:
> Enter them so we may exist completely. Soon we will search

MAP 7.1   The Iberian Peninsula and North Africa

The map shows the extent of the Moorish conquest from the 9th through the 12th centuries c.e.

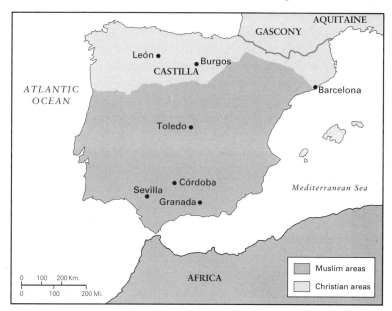

> In the margins of your history, in distant countries,
> For what was once our history. And in the end we will ask ourselves:
> Was Andalusia here or there? On the land . . . or in the poem?

It is difficult to overestimate the searing poignancy of these lines. They recall not only the self-destructive demise of the Andalusian kings and their *tawai'f* but also present-day Arab disunity and consequent weakness. (*Tawai'f* is the plural of the Arabic *ta'ifa*, used to refer both to the independent Muslim kingdoms that began in 1023, and also to modern-day confessional sects, of the sort common in Lebanon during its recent civil war. The references are lost on no one whose language is Arabic.) For a visitor from either North Africa or the Arab countries east of Suez, including Egypt, Andalusia is idealized as a kind of lost paradise, which fell from the brilliance of its medieval apex into terrible squabbles and petty jealousies. This perhaps makes a rather too facile moral lesson of the place.

Andalusia's unthreatening landscape—tranquil hills, agreeable towns, and rich green fields—survived a turbulent and deeply unsavory history. Running through its convoluted past was a steady current of unrest, of trust betrayed. It seems to have been made up of composite or converted souls, Mozarabs (Arabized Christians) and *muwallads* (Christian converts to

Islam). Nothing and no one is simple. Several of its city-states (there were no fewer than 12 at the height of the internecine conflict) were occasionally ruled by poets and patrons of the arts, such as Seville's 11th-century al-Mutamid, but they were often jealous and even small-minded schemers. Andalusia multiplies in the mind with its contradictions and puzzles; its history is a history of the masks and assumed identities it has worn.

Was Andalusia largely Arab and Muslim, as it certainly seems to have been, and if so why was it so very different from, say, Syria, Egypt, and Iraq, themselves great centers of civilization and power? And how did the Jews, the Visigoth Catholics, and the Romans who colonized it before the Arabs play their role in Andalusia's makeup and identity? However all these components are sorted out, a composite Andalusian identity anchored in Arab culture can be discerned in its striking buildings, its tiles and wooden ceilings, its ornate pottery and neatly constructed houses. And what could be more Andalusian than the fiery flamenco dancer, accompanied by hoarse *cantaores,* martial hand-clapping, and hypnotically strummed guitars, all of which have precedents in Arabic music? 9

On this trip I wanted to discover what Andalusia was from my perspective as a Palestinian Arab, as someone whose diverse background might offer a way of seeing and understanding the place beyond illusion and romance. I was born in Jerusalem, Andalusia's great Eastern antipode, and raised as a Christian. Though the environment I grew up in was both colonial and Muslim, my university education and years of residence in the United States and Europe allow me to see my past as a Westerner might. Standing before the monumental portal of Seville's Alcázar (the Hispanicized word for *al-qasr,* "castle"), every inch of which is covered in raised florid swirls and interlocking squares. I was reminded of similar surfaces from my earlier years in Cairo, Damascus, and Jerusalem, strangely present before me now in southern Europe, where Arab Muslims once hoped to set up an Umayyad empire in the West to rival the one in Syria. The Arabs journeyed along the shores of the Mediterranean through Spain, France, and Italy, all of which now bear their traces, even if those traces are not always acknowledged. 10

Perhaps the most striking feature of Andalusia historically was the care lavished on such aspects of urban life as running water, leafy gardens, viewing places (*miradores*), and graceful wall and ceiling designs. Medieval Europe, all rough skins, drafty rooms, and meaty cuisine, was barbaric by comparison. This is worth noting, since the interiors of Andalusia's palaces today are presented as out of time, stripped of their luxurious silks and divans, their heady perfumes and spices, their counterpoint of din and lyrical poetry. 11

Except for Cordova's immense Mezquita, the choice spaces of what has been known historically as Muslim Spain are generally not very large. Even Seville's Alcázar, big enough as a castle or palace, doesn't dominate 12

Seville's Alcázar palace, one of the best surviving examples of Mudejar architecture, a late Andalusian style.

at all. The Arabs who gave Andalusia its characteristic features generally used architecture to refashion and enhance nature, to create symmetrical patterns that echo Arabic calligraphy. Streets are pleasant to saunter in, rather than utilitarian thoroughfares. Curved ornaments—such as highly patterned vases and metal utensils—abound, all part of a wonderfully relaxed worldliness.

That worldliness, which reached its apex between the 9th and 12th cen-   13
turies, testifies to the extraordinary diversity of Islam itself, so often
thought of today as a monolithic block of wild-eyed terrorists, bent on destruction and driven by fanaticism. Yes, there were feuding factions, but
rarely before or after did the Islamic kings and princes produce a civilization of such refinement with so many potentially warring components.
Consider that in Cordova's heyday the Jewish sage Maimonides and Islam's greatest thinker, Ibn Rushd (Averroës), lived in Cordova at the same
time, each with his own disciples and doctrines, both writing and speaking
in Arabic. Part of the Damascus-based Umayyad empire that had fallen to
the Baghdad-based Abbasids in 750, the Spanish territories always retained
an eagerness to be recognized by, and an ambition to surpass the achievements of, their Eastern cousin.

Quite soon, Andalusia became a magnet for talent in many arenas: mu-   14
sic, philosophy, mysticism, literature, architecture, virtually all of the sciences, jurisprudence, religion. The monarchs Abd ar-Rahman I (731–788)
and Abd ar-Rahman III (891–961) gave Cordova its almost mythic status.
Three times the size of Paris (Europe's second-largest city in the 10th century), with 70 libraries, Cordova also had, according to the historian Salma
Kahdra Jayyusi, "1,600 mosques, 900 baths, 213,077 homes for ordinary
people, 60,300 mansions for notables, officials, and military commanders,
and 80,455 shops." The mystics and poets Ibn Hazm and Ibn Arabi, Jewish writers Judah ha-Levi and Ibn Gabirol, the colloquial but lyrical *zajals*
and wonderful strophic songs, or *muwashshah,* that seemed to emerge as
if from nowhere and later influenced the troubadors, provided al-Andalus
with verse, music, and atmosphere such as Europe had never had before.

The Arab general Tariq bin Ziyad and his desert army streamed across   15
the Gibraltar straits in 711; on later forays he brought with him many
North African Berbers, Yemenis, Egyptians, and Syrians. In Spain they encountered Visigoths and Jews, plus the remnants of a once thriving Roman
community, all of whom at times co-existed, and at times fought with one
another. No harmony was stable for very long—too many conflicting elements were always in play. Andalusia's reign of relative tolerance (three
monotheistic faiths in complex accord with one another) abruptly ended
when King Ferdinand and Queen Isabella seized the region and imposed a
reign of terror on non-Christians. Significantly, one of the towering figures
of the Andalusian cultural synthesis, Ibn Khaldun, a founder of sociology
and historiography, came from a prominent Seville family, and was perhaps
the greatest analyst of how nations rise and fall.

The last king of Granada, the luckless Boabdil (Abu Abd Allah Muham-   16
mad), was expelled along with the Jews in 1492, weeping or sighing—choose

your version. The unhappy Moor quickly became the emblem of what the Arabs had lost. Yet most people who are gripped by the pathos of the king's departure may not know that Boabdil negotiated very profitable surrender terms—some money, and land outside Granada—before he left the city to the Castilian monarchs.

Despite the richness of Andalusia's Islamic past and its indelible presence   17 in Spain's subsequent history after the Reconquista, for years the Church and royalist ideologues stressed the purgation of Spain's Islamic and Jewish heritage, insisting that Christian Spain was restored in 1492 as if little had happened to disturb its ascendancy in the seven preceding centuries. Not for nothing has the cult of Santiago (Saint James) been highlighted in Catholic Spain: St. James was, among other things, the patron saint of the Spanish in their battles against the Moors, hence his nickname Matamoros, "Killer of Moors." Yet, classical Mudejar art, with its typically florid arabesques and geometrical architecture, was produced after the Muslims were defeated. As far away as Catalonia, Gaudí's obsession with botanical motifs shows the Arab influence at its most profound. Why did it linger so if Arabs had represented only a negligible phase in Spanish history?

The Jews and Muslims who weren't thrown out or destroyed by the   18 Inquisition remained as conversos and Moriscos, men and women who had converted to Catholicism to preserve their lives. No one will ever know whether the identity they abandoned was really given up or whether it continued underground. Miguel de Cervantes's magnificent novel *Don Quixote* draws attention to its supposed author, the fictional Arab Sidi Hamete Benengeli, which—it is plausibly alleged—was a way of masking Cervantes's own secret identity as an unrepentant converso. The wars between Muslims and Catholics turn up again and again in literature, including of course the *Chanson de Roland* (in which Charlemagne's Frankish army is defeated in 778 by Abd ar-Rahman's men) and Spain's national epic, *El Poema del Cid*. About 60 percent of the Spanish language is made up of Arabic words and phrases: *alcalde* (mayor), *barrios* (quarters of a city), *aceite* (oil), *aceitunas* (olives). Their persistence indicates that Spain's identity is truly, if perhaps also uneasily, bicultural.

It took the great Spanish historian and philologist Américo Castro,   19 who taught for many years at Princeton, to establish the enduring pervasiveness of the country's repressed past in his monumental work *The Structure of Spanish History* (1954). One of Spain's finest contemporary novelists, Juan Goytisolo, has also inspired interest in Andalusia's Arab and Muslim origins, and done much to reassert Spain's non-European past. His *Count Julian,* which centers on the treacherous Catholic whom Spaniards hold responsible for bringing in the Moors, challenges the myth that Visigoth Spain's rapid fall in 711 can be explained by nothing other than the nobleman's betrayal.

Andalusia's identity was always in the process of being dissolved and lost, 20 even when its cultural life was at its pinnacle. Every one of its several strands—Arabic, Muslim, Berber, Catholic, Jewish, Visigothic, Roman— calls up another. Cordova was a particularly wonderful case in point. A much smaller city today than under Abd ar-Rahman I, it is still dominated by the mosque that he began in 785. Erected on the site of a Christian church, it was an attempt to assert his identity as a Umayyad prince flee- ing Damascus, to make a cultural statement as a Muslim exiled to a place literally across the world from where he had come.

The result is, in my experience, the greatest and most impressive religious 21 structure on earth. The mosque-cathedral, La Mezquita, stretches effortlessly for acres in a series of unending double arches, whose climax is an incredi- bly ornate mihrab, the place where the muezzin or prayer leader stands. Its contours echo those of the great mosque in Damascus (from which Abd ar- Rahman I barely managed to escape when his Umayyad dynasty fell), while its arches are conscious quotations of Roman aqueducts. So assiduous was its architect in copying Damascus that the Cordovan mihrab actually faces south, rather than east—toward Mecca—as it should.

The great mosque was later barbarically seized by a Christian monarch 22 who turned it into a church. He did this by inserting an entire cathedral into the Muslim structure's center, in an aggressive erasure of history and statement of faith. He may also have had in mind the legend that Muslims had stolen the bells of the Cathedral of Santiago de Compostela, melted them down, and used them in the mosque, which also housed the Prophet Muhammad's hand. Today, though the Muslim idea of prayer remains dominant, the building exudes a spirit of inclusive sanctity and magna- nimity of purpose.

Beyond the mosque's imposing walls, Cordova retains its memorial splen- 23 dor and inviting shelter. To this day, the houses communicate a sense of wel- come: inner courtyards are often furnished with a fountain, and the rooms are dispersed around it, very much as they are in houses in Aleppo thousands of miles to the east. Streets are narrow and winding because, as in medieval Cairo, the idea is to cajole the pedestrian with promises of arrival. Thus one walks along without having to face the psychologically intimidating distance of the long, straight avenue. Moreover, Cordova is one of the few cities in the

Mediterranean where the intermingling of Arab and Jewish quarters doesn't immediately suggest conflict. Just seeing streets and squares named after Averroës and Maimonides in 21st-century Cordova, one gets an immediate idea of what a universal culture was like a thousand years ago.

Only five miles outside Cordova stand the partially restored ruins of 24 what must have been the most lavish, and certainly the most impressive, royal city in Europe, Madinat al-Zahra (City of the Flower). Begun by Abd ar-Rahman III in 936, it, too, was a vast echo of palace-cities in the Arab East, which it almost certainly overshadowed for a time. It is as if Andalusia's rulers and great figures were unable ever to rid their minds of the East. They relived its prior greatness on their terms, nowhere with more striving for effect than in Madinat al-Zahra.

Now an enormous excavation, Madinat al-Zahra is slowly being re- 25 stored. You can stand looking down on the symmetrical array of stables, military barracks, reception rooms, courtyards—all pointing at the great central hall in which the king received his guests and subjects. According to some scholars. Abd ar-Rahman wanted not only to assume the mantle of the caliphate, thereby wresting it from the Abbasid king in Baghdad (who couldn't have paid much attention to Abd ar-Rahman's posturings), but also to establish political authority as something that belonged in the West but had meaning only if snatched from the East. For an Arab visitor, it is hard not to be struck by the rather competitive Andalusian reference to the better-known Eastern Muslim empires, mainly those of the Abbasids and Fatimids, who to this day form the core of what is taught and propagated as Arab culture.

A special poignancy hangs over Andalusia's impressively animated spaces. 26 It derives not only from a pervasive sense of former grandeur but also from what, because so many people hoped to possess it, Andalusia tried to be— and what it might have been. Certainly Granada's Alhambra is a monument to regret and the passage of time. Next to the wonderful 13th- to 14th-century Nasrid palace and superb Generalife gardens looms the ponderous 16th-century castle of the Spanish king and Holy Roman Emperor Charles V, who obviously wanted his rather ostentatious abode to acquire some of the luster of the Arab complex. Yet, despite the Alhambra's opulence and its apparently hedonistic celebration of the good life (for rulers, mainly), its arabesque patterns can seem like a defense against mortality or the ravages of human life. One can easily imagine the beleaguered and insecure Boabdil using it as a place of perfumed forgetfulness—perhaps even at times reexperiencing the studied oblivion cultivated by Sufi masters such as Ibn Arab.

The schizophrenia inherent in Spain's identity is more apparent in 27 Granada than anywhere else in Andalusia. Because the Alhambra sits on one of several hills high above the city, Granada proper has paid the price in clogged streets and overbuilt residential and commercial quarters through which the Arab palace must be approached. Granada as a whole embodies this tension between high and low. A mazelike system of one-way streets connects the Alhambra to Albaicín, the old Muslim quarter. Despite the wonders of the Alhambra, being in Albaicín is like feeling the fantasy of summer and the realities of a grim winter very close to each other. The resemblances between Albaicín and Cordova's barrios are striking, except that, as the name suggests, Albaicín—Arabic for "the downtrodden and hopeless"—was indeed an area for the poor and, one can't help feeling, where the last Arabs and Jews huddled together before their eviction in 1492. Nothing evokes Granada's riven history more superbly than the "Albaicín" movement in Isaac Albéniz's greatest musical work, the redoubtably difficult-to-perform piano collection *Iberia*.

By contrast, Seville's spirit is very much of this world—part feline, 28 part macho, part dashing sparkle, part somber colonialism. Seville contains Spain's finest *plaza de toros* and also its largest cathedral. And it is here that all the archives of Spain's imperial conquests are housed. But before 1492, Seville was the administrative capital of the Arab monarchy that held sway over Andalusia. Where the Catholic empire-builders set their sights on the New World, the Arabs were taken up with the Old: Morocco, which before the final Reconquista was considered to be part of Andalusia. Similarities in metal, leather, and glazed pottery design between Spain and North Africa reinforce a prevailing unity of vision and religious discourse.

If Seville is a city where Catholic and Muslim cultures interact, it is to 29 the decided advantage of the former—though given Seville's special status in the Western romantic imagination as an extension of the Orient, it's probably truer to say that Seville is the triumph of Andalusian style. This, after all, is the city of Mérimée's and Bizet's *Carmen*, the heart of Hemingway's bullfighting obsession, and a favorite port of call for northern European poets and writers for whom citrus blossoms represent the salutary opposite of their dreary climates. Stendhal's *espagnolisme* derives from Sevillian themes, and the city's Holy Week parades and observances have gripped many peregrinating artists.

Not that the Arabs haven't made their own indelible mark on the city. 30 Standing watch over the landscape is the four-sided Giralda, a minaret built by an Almohad (basically an austere fundamentalist sort of Islam) king in the late 12th century. Its upper third was added to, for purposes of "improvement," by zealous Christians 400 years later. Despite some unnecessary flourishes, the tower was so magnetic that a contemporary chronicler observed, "From a distance it would appear that all the stars of the Zodiac had stopped in the heart of Seville." Incorporated into the cathedral, whose awesome bulk testifies to Catholic ambition and consolidation of power (Christopher Columbus's tomb is inside), the Giralda leads an independent existence as an ornate symbol of how even the harshest of ideologies can be filled with grace.

In the long run, and almost in spite of its kings and magistrates, the Andalusian style seems to have fostered movement and discovery rather than monumentality and stability. It enacted an earlier version of our own hybrid world, one whose borders were also thresholds, and whose multiple identities formed an enriched diversity.   31

Thinking About the Essay

1. Said wrote this article for *Travel and Leisure.* What does he assume about the readership of this specific magazine? How does he make the essay both an introduction to a tourist destination and a serious explanation of the importance of the region? Do you think he succeeds in his dual purpose? Why or why not?

2. Where does Said state his thesis? Why is his thesis personally important?

3. Trace the historical process that Said presents in this essay, moving section by section through the article. What are some of the main topics and points he draws from his historical analysis?

4. What mood or sense of place does Said create in this essay? Identify aspects of style and language that convey mood and atmosphere.

5. What *definition* of culture and civilization does Said present in this essay? Locate examples of various strategies he employs to create this definition.

Responding in Writing

6. Explain why, after reading Said's essay, you might want to visit Andalusia on your own or on a group tour. Where would you visit? What would you look for? What would you hope to learn from this trip?

7. Said raises the prospect that civilizations don't necessarily have to clash. Reread his essay, and then write a paper in which you outline the necessary conditions required for a dialogue of civilizations.

8. How can travel alert us to the history and contours of civilizations? Answer this question in a reflective essay. If you have traveled to the various centers of civilization or have read about them, incorporate this knowledge into the paper.

Networking

9. In small groups, work through Said's essay section by section. Then devise a sketch outline of the entire essay. Put your outline on the chalkboard or blackboard for the class to view.

10. Go to the library or online to find additional information on Andalusia. Then prepare a report in which you determine whether Said's presentation of the region is accurate or biased.

The Age of Terror: What Is the Just Response?

Just as changes in United States demographics, patterns of cultural change, the forces of globalization, and the "clash" of civilizations have brought us into expanding contact with the peoples of the world, recent events remind us of how dangerous this new world can be. Indeed, in the years since the September 11, 2001, attack, we have had to reorient our thinking about numerous critical issues: the war on terrorism; the erosion of our sense of individual and collective security; the need to achieve a balance between individual rights and common security. Above all, Americans now face the ethical, political, and historical challenge of being the world's single superpower. There are people and nations who hate America's standing in the world. And hatred and cruelty, as Isaac Bashevis Singer, a winner of the Nobel Prize for Literature, once observed, only produce more of the same.

The 9/11 terrorist attack was so profoundly unnerving that virtually all of us can remember where we were when the planes hijacked by terrorists crashed into New York's World Trade Center and the Pentagon in Washington, D.C. This was a primal national event, similar in impact to the raid on Pearl Harbor in 1941 or the assassinations of President John Kennedy and Martin Luther King Jr. in the 1960s. These prior events, whether taking the lives of thousands or just one, serve to define entire American generations. Today, America faces a new defining event—the war on terrorism. We seemingly live in an age of terror, and we have to find ways in which national and global communities can deal with this unnerving reality.

In a sense, the September 11 attack and subsequent assaults—from Bali to Africa to the Persian Gulf—have forced America to look inward and outward for intelligent responses. Looking inward, we

Members of the Sikh community in Bhopal, central India, share grief with the relatives of the people killed in Tuesday's terrorist attacks in the United States, Sunday, Sept. 16, 2001. They later held a prayer meeting for the victims of the attacks. (AP Photo/Prakash Hatvalne)

Thinking About the Image

1. Is it at all ironic that this particular Indian community, given its recent tragic history, should express its "solidarity " with America after September 11? Why, or why not?

2. Why are these demonstrators holding signs in English? Who is their intended audience? What is the effect of this photograph?

3. Why do you think it might have been important for the Sikh community to demonstrate its support for America immediately after the terrorist attacks? Using a newspaper or magazine database, research acts of discrimination, racial profiling, or hate crimes committed against Sikhs, Indians, and others, in the mistaken belief that they were Muslim, immediately after September 11.

4. Is there anything similar in this image, or the message of these demonstrators, and the Chilean demonstrators depicted on p. 264?

Two women hold each other as they watch the World Trade Center burn following a terrorist attack on the twin skyscrapers in New York on Tuesday, Sept. 11, 2001. Terrorists crashed two planes into the World Trade Center and the twin 110-story towers collapsed Tuesday morning. (AP Photo/Ernesto Mora)

Thinking About the Image

1. On September 11, 2001, New York City was the center of the world's media attention. Cameras seemed to document every single moment of the disaster, from the first plane's impact through the seemingly endless search for remains. Why do you think the author of this textbook chose this particular image—rather than, say, an image of one of the buildings in flames—to illustrate this chapter?

2. Compare this photograph with others throughout this text. What is most strikingly different about this image?

3. Is the photographer violating the privacy of these women in a moment of obviously tremendous grief and distress? How do you think news photographers might cope with the responsibility of documenting such tragic or frightening events?

4. Which of the essays in this chapter do you think this photograph best illustrates? Why?

often have to deal with our own anger, insecurity, and hatred of other peoples who commit these crimes against unsuspecting humanity. These are primal emotions that affect our sense of personal identity. At the same time, we must understand how others around the world view our country and must gain knowledge of peoples and cultures we once knew little or nothing about. For example, are the terrorists who planned and launched the 9/11 attack a mere aberration—some delusional distortion of the great culture and civilization of Islam? Or do they reflect the consensus of the Arab street? Where do college students—who should be committed to liberal learning—go to find answers to such large and complex questions? What courses exist on your campus? What organizations foster transnational or global understanding?

Ultimately—as writers in this chapter and throughout the text suggest—we have to read across cultures and nations to understand the consequences of 9/11. We have to reflect on our own backgrounds. We have to be candid about how our individual experience molds our attitudes toward "others"—most of whom are like us but some of whom want to do us harm. Liberal education, as the American philosopher William James stated at the beginning of the last century, makes us less fanatical. Against the backdrop of contemporary terrorism, we have to search for wisdom and for sustaining values.

To Any Would-Be Terrorists

NAOMI SHIHAB NYE

Naomi Shihab Nye was born in 1952 in St. Louis, Missouri. Her family background is Palestinian American. She graduated from Trinity University (B.A., 1974) and subsequently started a career as a freelance writer and editor. Today Nye is known for her award-winning poetry, fiction for children, novels, and essays. She has been a visiting writer at the University of Texas, the University of Hawaii, the University of California at Berkeley, and elsewhere. Among Nye's books are the prize-winning poetry collection *Different Ways to Pray* (1980); several other poetry volumes, including *Yellow Glove* (1986), incorporating poems dealing with Palestinian life; a book of essays, *Never in a Hurry* (1996); and a young adult novel, *Habibi* (1997), which draws on Nye's own childhood experience of living in Jerusalem in the 1970s, which at that time was part of Jordan. Among her many awards are the Peter I. B. Lavin Younger Poets Award from the Academy of American Poets and a Guggenheim Fellowship. Starting with the provocative title of the following essay, Nye speaks as a Palestinian American to an extremist audience that needs "to find another way to live."

Before Reading

If you had an opportunity to address a terrorist, what would you say and how would you say it?

I am sorry I have to call you that, but I don't know how else to get your attention. I hate that word. Do you know how hard some of us have worked to get rid of that word, to deny its instant connection to the Middle East? And now look. Look what extra work we have.

Not only did your colleagues kill thousands of innocent, international people in those buildings and scar their families forever; they wounded a huge community of people in the Middle East, in the United States and all over the world. If that's what they wanted to do, please know the mission was a terrible success, and you can stop now.

Because I feel a little closer to you than many Americans could possibly feel, or ever want to feel, I insist that you listen to me. Sit down and listen. I know what kinds of foods you like. I would feed them to you if you were right here, because it is very important that you listen.

I am humble in my country's pain and I am furious.

My Palestinian father became a refugee in 1948. He came to the United States as a college student. He is 74 years old now and still homesick. He has planted fig trees. He has invited all the Ethiopians in his neighborhood to fill their little paper sacks with his figs. He has written columns and stories saying the Arabs are not terrorists; he has worked all his life to defy that word. Arabs are businessmen and students and kind neighbors. There is no one like him and there are thousands like him—gentle Arab daddies who make everyone laugh around the dinner table, who have a hard time with headlines, who stand outside in the evenings with their hands in their pockets staring toward the far horizon.

I am sorry if you did not have a father like that.

I wish everyone could have a father like that.

My hard-working American mother has spent 50 years trying to convince her fellow teachers and choirmates not to believe stereotypes about the Middle East. She always told them, there is a much larger story. If you knew the story, you would not jump to conclusions from what you see in the news. But now look at the news. What a mess has been made.

Sometimes I wish everyone could have parents from different countries or ethnic groups so they would be forced to cross boundaries, to believe in mixtures, every day of their lives. Because this is what the world calls us to do. WAKE UP!

The Palestinian grocer in my Mexican-American neighborhood paints pictures of the Palestinian flag on his empty cartons. He paints trees and rivers. He gives his paintings away. He says, "Don't insult me" when I try to pay him for a lemonade. Arabs have always been famous for their generosity. Remember?

My half-Arab brother with an Arabic name looks more like an Arab   10
than many full-blooded Arabs do and he has to fly every week.

My Palestinian cousins in Texas have beautiful brown little boys. Many   11
of them haven't gone to school yet. And now they have this heavy word to
carry in their backpacks along with the weight of their papers and books.
I repeat, the mission was a terrible success. But it was also a complete, total tragedy, and I want you to think about a few things.

1.

Many people, thousands of people, perhaps even millions of people, in the   12
United States are very aware of the long unfairness of our country's policies
regarding Israel and Palestine. We talk about this all the time. It exhausts
us and we keep talking. We write letters to newspapers, to politicians, to
each other. We speak out in public even when it is uncomfortable to do so,
because that is our responsibility. Many of these people aren't even Arabs.
Many happen to be Jews who are equally troubled by the inequity. I promise you this is true. Because I am Arab-American, people always express
these views to me, and I am amazed how many understand the intricate situation and have strong, caring feelings for Arabs and Palestinians even
when they don't have to. Think of them, please: All those people who have
been standing up for Arabs when they didn't have to.

But as ordinary citizens we don't run the government and don't get to   13
make all our government's policies, which makes us sad sometimes. We believe in the power of the word and we keep using it, even when it seems no
one large enough is listening. That is one of the best things about this country: the free power of free words. Maybe we take it for granted too much.
Many of the people killed in the World Trade Center probably believed in
a free Palestine and were probably talking about it all the time.

But this tragedy could never help the Palestinians. Somehow, miracu-   14
lously, if other people won't help them more, they are going to have to help
themselves. And it will be peace, not violence, that fixes things. You could
ask any one of the kids in the Seeds of Peace organization and they would
tell you that. Do you ever talk to kids? Please, please, talk to more kids.

2.

Have you noticed how many roads there are? Sure you have. You must check   15
out maps and highways and small alternate routes just like anyone else. There
is no way everyone on earth could travel on the same road, or believe in exactly the same religion. It would be too crowded: it would be dumb. I don't
believe you want us all to be Muslims. My Palestinian grandmother lived to

be 106 years old and did not read or write, but even she was much smarter than that. The only place she ever went beyond Palestine and Jordan was to Mecca, by bus, and she was very proud to be called a Hajji and to wear white clothes afterwards. She worked very hard to get stains out of everyone's dresses—scrubbing them with a stone. I think she would consider the recent tragedies a terrible stain on her religion and her whole part of the world. She would weep. She was scared of airplanes anyway. She wanted people to worship God in whatever ways they felt comfortable. Just worship. Just remember God in every single day and doing. It didn't matter what they called it. When people asked her how she felt about the peace talks that were happening right before she died, she puffed up like a proud little bird and said, in Arabic, "I never lost my peace inside." To her, Islam was a welcoming religion. After her home in Jerusalem was stolen from her, she lived in a small village that contained a Christian shrine. She felt very tender toward the people who would visit it. A Jewish professor tracked me down a few years ago in Jerusalem to tell me she changed his life after he went to her village to do an oral history project on Arabs. "Don't think she only mattered to you!" he said. "She gave me a whole different reality to imagine—yet it was amazing how close we became. Arabs could never be just a 'project' after that."

Did you have a grandmother? Mine never wanted people to be pushed 16 around. What did yours want?

Reading about Islam since my grandmother died, I note the "tolerance" 17 that was "typical of Islam" even in the old days. The Muslim leader Khalid ibn al-Walid signed a Jerusalem treaty which declared, "in the name of God . . . you have complete security for your churches which shall not be occupied by the Muslims or destroyed."

It is the new millennium in which we should be even smarter than we 18 used to be, right? But I think we have fallen behind.

3.

Many Americans do not want to kill any more innocent people anywhere in 19 the world. We are extremely worried about military actions killing innocent people. We didn't like this in Iraq, we never liked it anywhere. We would like no more violence, from us as well as from you. We would like to stop the terrifying wheel of violence, just stop it, right on the road, and find something more creative to do to fix these huge problems we have. Violence is not creative, it is stupid and scary, and many of us hate all those terrible movies and TV shows made in our own country that try to pretend otherwise. Don't watch them. Everyone should stop watching them. An appetite for explosive sounds and toppling buildings is not a healthy thing for anyone in any country. The USA should apologize to the whole world for sending this trash out into the air and for paying people to make it.

But here's something good you may not know—one of the best-selling books of poetry in the United States in recent years is the Coleman Barks translation of Rumi, a mystical Sufi poet of the 13th century, and Sufism is 20 Islam and doesn't that make you glad?

Everyone is talking about the suffering that ethnic Americans are going through. Many will no doubt go through more of it, but I would like to thank everyone who has sent me a condolence card. Americans are usually 21 very kind people. Didn't your colleagues find that out during their time living here? It is hard to imagine they missed it. How could they do what they did, knowing that?

4.

We will all die soon enough. Why not take the short time we have on this delicate planet and figure out some really interesting things we might do together? I promise you, God would be happier. So many people are always 22 trying to speak for God—I know it is a very dangerous thing to do. I tried my whole life not to do it. But this one time is an exception. Because there are so many people crying and scared and confused and complicated and exhausted right now—it is as if we have all had a giant simultaneous break-down.

I beg you, as your distant Arab cousin, as your American neighbor, listen to me.

Our hearts are broken: as yours may also feel broken in some ways, we can't understand, unless you tell us in words. Killing people won't tell us. 23 We can't read that message.

Find another way to live. Don't expect others to be like you. Read 24 Rumi. Read Arabic poetry. Poetry humanizes us in a way that news, or even religion, has a harder time doing. A great Arab scholar, Dr. Salma Jayyusi, said, "If we read one another, we won't kill one another." Read 25 American poetry. Plant mint. Find a friend who is so different from you, you can't believe how much you have in common. Love them. Let them love you. Surprise people in gentle ways, as friends do. The rest of us will try harder too. Make our family proud.

Thinking About the Essay

1. How does Nye address her primary audience—"would-be terrorists"? What tone or voice does she employ? What are some of the words and phrases she uses to get their attention? Of course, Nye also writes for a broader audience of readers—us. How does she make her message appealing to this larger audience?

2. Nye presents an elaborate argument in this essay. What is her central claim? What reasons or minor propositions does she give in support of her claim? How do the events of September 11 condition the nature of her ar-

gument? What types of appeal does she make to convince her audience to think, feel, and act differently?

3. Examine the introductory paragraphs—paragraphs 1–11. Why does Nye use a first-person ("I") point of view? What is her purpose? What is the effect?

4. Analyze sections 1–4 of Nye's essay (paragraphs 12–25). What is the subject matter of each? How does the sequence of sections serve to advance the writer's argument? What transitional techniques permit essay coherence and unity?

5. Why is Nye's last paragraph a fitting conclusion to the essay? What elements from the body of the essay does this concluding paragraph reinforce and illuminate?

Responding in Writing

6. Write your own letter to any would-be terrorists. Address this audience in a personal voice. Use a variety of appeals to make your case.

7. In an analytical essay, examine the ways in which Nye tries to make her case in "To Any Would-be Terrorists."

8. Write a letter to Naomi Shihab Nye in which you agree or disagree with the content of her essay.

Networking

9. Exchange your paper with another class member and evaluate it for content, grammar and syntax, organization, and tone. Make revisions based on your discussion.

10. Either on the computer or in person, consult your college library's holdings for books by Rumi and works about this poet. Prepare a bibliography and also a brief biography of the poet, explaining why Naomi Shihab Nye would invite us to read Rumi.

One Day, Now Broken in Two

ANNA QUINDLEN

Anna Quindlen was born in 1953 in Philadelphia and graduated from Barnard College. She began her writing career as a reporter for the *New York Post.* Quindlen then served as a columnist and deputy metropolitan editor for the *New York Times* before retiring from that post in order to devote full time to writing. Today she is known as a provocative columnist for *Newsweek* magazine as well as an acclaimed novelist. In 1991 she published a novel entitled *Object Lessons,* and in 1992 she received the Pulitzer Prize for commentary. One of her novels, *One True Thing* (1994), was made into a film starring Meryl Streep and

William Hurt. In an interview in *Commonweal,* Quindlen states, "I tend to write about what we have come, unfortunately, to call women's issues." In the following essay, which appeared in *Newsweek* on September 9, 2002, she offers an intensely personal response to 9/11.

Before Reading

Imagine that your birthday is 9/11. What feelings would you anticipate? How would you celebrate this birthday? How would family and friends be likely to deal with it?

September 11 is my eldest child's birthday. When he drove cross-country 1 this spring and got pulled over for pushing the pedal on a couple of stretches of monotonous highway, two cops in two different states said more or less the same thing as they looked down at his license: aw, man, you were really born on 9-11? Maybe it was coincidence, but in both cases he got a warning instead of a ticket.

Who are we now? A people who manage to get by with the help of the 2 everyday, the ordinary, the mundane, the old familiar life muting the terror of the new reality. The day approaching will always be bifurcated for me: part September 11, the anniversary of one of the happiest days of my life, and part 9-11, the day America's mind reeled, its spine stiffened and its heart broke.

That is how the country is now, split in two. The American people used 3 their own simple routines to muffle the horror they felt looking at that indelible loop of tape—the plane, the flames, the plane, the fire, the falling bodies, the falling buildings. Amid the fear and the shock there were babies to be fed, dogs to be walked, jobs to be done. After the first months almost no one bought gas masks anymore; fewer people than expected in New York City asked for the counseling that had been provided as part of the official response. Slowly the planes filled up again. A kind of self-hypnosis prevailed, and these were the words used to induce the happy trance: life goes on.

Who are we now? We are better people than we were before. That's 4 what the optimists say, soothed by the vision of those standing in line to give blood and money and time at the outset, vowing to stop and smell the flowers as the weeks ticked by. We are people living in a world of unimaginable cruelty and savagery. So say the pessimists. The realists insist that both are right, and, as always, they are correct.

We are people whose powers of imagination have been challenged by the 5 revelations of the careful planning, the hidden leaders, the machinations from within a country of rubble and caves and desperate want, the willingness to slam headlong into one great technological achievement while piloting another as a way of despising modernity. Why do they hate us, some asked afterward, and many Americans were outraged at the question, confusing the search for motivation with mitigation. But quietly, as routine returned, a new routine based on a new bedrock of loss of innocence and loss of life, a new question crept almost undetected into the national psyche: did we like ourselves? Had we become a people who confused prosperity with probity, whose culture had become personified by oversize sneakers and KFC? Our own individual transformations made each of us wonder what our legacy would be if we left the world on a sunny September day with a "to do" list floating down 80 stories to the street below.

So we looked at our lives a little harder, called our friends a little more of- 6
ten, hugged our kids a little tighter. And then we complained about the long lines at the airport and obsessed about the stock market in lieu of soul-searching. Time passed. The blade dulled. The edges softened. Except, of course, for those who lived through birthdays, anniversaries, holidays, without someone lost in the cloud of silvery dust, those families the living embodiment of what the whole nation had first felt and then learned not to feel.

We are people of two minds now, the one that looks forward and the one 7
that unwillingly and unexpectedly flashes back. Flying over lower Manhattan, the passengers reflexively lean toward the skyline below, looking for ghost buildings. "Is everything back to normal?" someone asked me in another country not long ago, and I said yes. And no. The closest I could come to describing what I felt was to describe a bowl I had broken in two and beautifully mended. It holds everything it once did; the crack is scarcely visible. But I always know it's there. My eye worries it without even meaning to.

On Sept. 10 of last year my daughter and I went to the funeral of a 8
neighbor we both loved greatly. We rushed home so I could go to the hospital, where my closest friend had just had serious surgery. Someone else took the cat to the vet after we discovered that he was poisoned and was near death. That night, as my daughter got ready for bed I said to her, without the slightest hint of hyperbole, "Don't worry, honey. We'll never again have a day as bad as this one."

Who are we now? We are people who know that we never understood 9
what "bad day" meant until that morning that cracked our world cleanly in two, that day that made two days, September 11 and 9-11. The mundane and the monstrous. "Tell me how do you live brokenhearted?" Bruce Springsteen sings on his new album about the aftermath. September 11 is my boy's birthday; 9-11 is something else. That is the way we have to live, or we cannot really go on living at all.

Thinking About the Essay

1. Why does the writer personalize the events of 9/11 in her introductory paragraph? In what other paragraphs do you detect this personal frame of reference? What is the overall effect?

2. What comparative perspectives does Quindlen bring to this essay? How does comparison and contrast as a rhetorical strategy serve as the essay's organizing principle?

3. Note that the writer begins paragraphs 2, 4, and 9 with the same question. What is this question, and what does its repetition serve to emphasize? How does this question point to the thesis of the essay? State the thesis in your own words. Locate other examples of this questioning strategy.

4. Identity certain aspects of Quindlen's style—for example, her use of figurative language—that make the essay so compelling.

5. Analyze the final paragraph. How does it serve as a fitting conclusion for the essay? What ideas does it recapitulate? Why is the allusion to Bruce Springsteen so appropriate? How does the conclusion serve to confirm the meaning of the title?

Responding in Writing

6. Assume that you were born on September 11, and write a personal essay on how this fact will always cause you to be "split in two."

7. Write an analysis and evaluation of Quindlen's essay, stating why or why not you were affected by it.

8. Answer Quindlen's main question, "Who are we now?" in an essay of 750–1,000 words. Frame your answer in terms of 9/11 and its aftermath.

Networking

9. In groups of three or four class members, discuss where you were on 9/11 and how you felt as you watched television replays of the attacks on the Twin Towers and the Pentagon. Have one member take notes and another member report on the group's responses.

10. Search the World Wide Web for images of the September 11, 2001, attacks. Then write an essay on how the event affected you then and now.

And Our Flag Was Still There

BARBARA KINGSOLVER

Barbara Kingsolver, best-selling novelist and essayist, was born in 1955 in Annapolis, Maryland. Educated at De-Pauw University (B.A.) and the University of Arizona (M.S.), Kingsolver as a writer focuses on the lives of middle-class Americans, infusing her characters with strength in their struggle to survive. Her first novel, *The Bean Trees* (1988), received wide critical praise for its depiction of the lives of a group of women—all seeking, as the author observes, "a new comprehension of responsibility." With the publication of *The Poisonwood Bible* (1998), she produces an epic story of a family serving in the Congo as missionaries and the tragedies they both uncover and precipitate. Kingsolver also writes nonfiction and poetry and is a human rights activist. "I'm extremely interested in cultural difference," she writes, "in social and political history, and the sparks that fly when people with different ways of looking at the world come together and need to reconcile or move through or celebrate those differences." In the following essay, written shortly after the 9/11 attacks, and published in the *San Francisco Chronicle* on September 25, 2001, Kingsolver offers a stipulative definition of patriotism.

Before Reading

What are some of the virtues and dangers in being patriotic? How has our patriotism been tested by the events of 9/11 and the aftermath?

My daughter came home from kindergarten and announced, "Tomorrow we all have to wear red, white and blue."   1

"Why?" I asked, trying not to sound wary.   2

"For all the people that died when the airplanes hit the buildings."   3

I fear the sound of saber-rattling, dread that not just my taxes but even   4 my children are being dragged to the cause of death in the wake of death. I asked quietly, "Why not wear black, then? Why the colors of the flag, what does that mean?"

"It means we're a country. Just all people together."   5

So we sent her to school in red, white and blue, because it felt to her   6 like something she could do to help people who are hurting. And because my wise husband put a hand on my arm and said, "You can't let hateful people steal the flag from us."

He didn't mean terrorists, he meant Americans. Like the man in a city   7 near us who went on a rampage crying "I'm an American" as he shot at foreign-born neighbors, killing a gentle Sikh man in a turban and terrifying every brown-skinned person I know. Or the talk-radio hosts, who are viciously bullying a handful of members of Congress for airing sensible skepticism at a time when the White House was announcing preposterous things in apparent self-interest, such as the "revelation" that terrorists had aimed to hunt down Air Force One with a hijacked commercial plane. Rep. Barbara Lee cast the House's only vote against handing over virtually unlimited war powers to one man that a whole lot of us didn't vote for. As a consequence, so many red-blooded Americans have now threatened to kill her, she has to have additional bodyguards.

Patriotism seems to be falling to whoever claims it loudest, and we're 8
left struggling to find a definition in a clamor of reaction. This is what I'm
hearing: Patriotism opposes the lone representative of democracy who was
brave enough to vote her conscience instead of following an angry mob.
(Several others have confessed they wanted to vote the same way, but
chickened out.) Patriotism threatens free speech with death. It is infuriated
by thoughtful hesitation, constructive criticism of our leaders and pleas for
peace. It despises people of foreign birth who've spent years learning our
culture and contributing their talents to our economy. It has specifically
blamed homosexuals, feminists and the American Civil Liberties Union. In
other words, the American flag stands for intimidation, censorship, violence, bigotry, sexism, homophobia, and shoving the Constitution through
a paper shredder? Who are we calling terrorists here? Outsiders can destroy airplanes and buildings, but it is only we, the people, who have the
power to demolish our own ideals.

It's a fact of our culture that the loudest mouths get the most airplay, 9
and the loudmouths are saying now that in times of crisis it is treasonous
to question our leaders. Nonsense. That kind of thinking let fascism grow
out of the international depression of the 1930s. In critical times, our leaders need most to be influenced by the moderating force of dissent. That is
the basis of democracy, in sickness and in health, and especially when national choices are difficult, and bear grave consequences.

It occurs to me that my patriotic duty is to recapture my flag from the 10
men now waving it in the name of jingoism and censorship. This isn't easy
for me.

The last time I looked at a flag with unambiguous pride, I was 13. Right 11
after that, Vietnam began teaching me lessons in ambiguity, and the lessons
have kept coming. I've learned of things my government has done to the
world that made me direly ashamed. I've been further alienated from my
flag by people who waved it at me declaring I should love it or leave it. I
search my soul and find I cannot love killing for any reason. When I look
at the flag, I see it illuminated by the rocket's red glare.

This is why the warmongers so easily gain the upper hand in the patriot 12
game: Our nation was established with a fight for independence, so our
iconography grew out of war. Our national anthem celebrates it; our language
of patriotism is inseparable from a battle cry. Our every military campaign is
still launched with phrases about men dying for the freedoms we hold dear,
even when this is impossible to square with reality. In the Persian Gulf War
we rushed to the aid of Kuwait, a monarchy in which women enjoyed approximately the same rights as a 19th century American slave. The values we
fought for and won there are best understood, I think, by oil companies.
Meanwhile, a country of civilians was devastated, and remains destroyed.

Stating these realities does not violate the principles of liberty, equality, 13
and freedom of speech; it exercises them, and by exercise we grow stronger.
I would like to stand up for my flag and wave it over a few things I believe
in, including but not limited to the protection of dissenting points of view.
After 225 years, I vote to retire the rocket's red glare and the bullet wound
as obsolete symbols of Old Glory. We desperately need a new iconography
of patriotism. I propose we rip stripes of cloth from the uniforms of public
servants who rescued the injured and panic-stricken, remaining at their post
until it fell down on them. The red glare of candles held in vigils everywhere
as peace-loving people pray for the bereaved, and plead for compassion and
restraint. The blood donated to the Red Cross. The stars of film and theater
and music who are using their influence to raise money for recovery. The
small hands of schoolchildren collecting pennies, toothpaste, teddy bears,
anything they think might help the kids who've lost their moms and dads.

My town, Tucson, Ariz., has become famous for a simple gesture in 14
which some 8,000 people wearing red, white or blue T-shirts assembled
themselves in the shape of a flag on a baseball field and had their photograph taken from above. That picture has begun to turn up everywhere,
but we saw it first on our newspaper's front page. Our family stood in silence for a minute looking at that photo of a human flag, trying to know
what to make of it. Then my teenage daughter, who has a quick mind for
numbers and a sensitive heart, did an interesting thing. She laid her hand
over a quarter of the picture, leaving visible more or less 6,000 people, and
said, "That many are dead." We stared at what that looked like—all those
innocent souls, multicolored and packed into a conjoined destiny—and
shuddered at the one simple truth behind all the noise, which is that so
many beloved people have suddenly gone from us. That is my flag, and
that's what it means: We're all just people together.

Thinking About the Essay

1. Kingsolver begins her essay with a brief anecdote involving her daughter. Why
   does she start in this personal way? How effective is this strategy? Explain.

2. What is Kingsolver's thesis in this essay? Where does she state it? What
   is her tone as she develops her thesis?

3. How does Kingsolver build an extended definition of patriotism in this essay? Would you say that she constructs a "negative" definition? Why or why
   not? Find examples of other common techniques of definition, such as illustration, comparison and contrast, reference to authority, and identification of causes and effects.

4. Kingsolver's essay contains several arguments. Identify these arguments
   or claims. Are they credible? Why or why not?

5. How does Kingsolver's concluding paragraph reflect the technique of the opening of this essay? Why does the writer employ this strategy?

Responding in Writing

6. Write your own definition of *patriotism,* using Kingsolver's essay and her ideas as a foundation for your approach. Use one or more of the techniques that Kingsolver employs—for example, personal experience, observation, or negation—to develop this extended definition. You might want to conduct research, which can be as simple as consulting an online dictionary or as challenging as a complete Google search, to provide a full definition of the word.

7. In light of the events since 9/11, do you think that Kingsolver's definition of *patriotism* is correct and appropriate? Why or why not? Write an argumentative essay responding to this question.

8. Write a letter to the editor of your campus newspaper in which you take a position on the prevalence (or lack of it) of patriotism at your college. Explain to your readers why discussion or recognition of patriotism should be an issue worthy of campus attention.

Networking

9. In class, divide into two roughly equal groups of classmates. Next, prepare to debate the following proposition: *Patriotism is a sign of a nation's strength, especially in times of conflict or war.* One side should defend this proposition and the other oppose it. (Do not worry if you find yourself on the side that expresses views antithetical to your own. Be a good sport!) Each group should take time to identify key reasons in support of its position and to generate useful evidence. Finally, designate one member of the group to argue your position before the class.

10. Compose an e-mail to the editor of the *San Francisco Chronicle,* where this article first appeared, explaining your response to Kingsolver's definition of *patriotism.* What would you add, if anything? What would you suggest is exaggerated or misleading? Be certain to explain what *patriotism* means to you.

Letter from New York

PETER CAREY | Born in Victoria, Australia, in 1943, Peter Carey attended Monash University briefly before working part-time in advertising and starting a literary career, first as a short story writer and then as a novelist. His second collection of short fiction, *War Crimes* (1979), received numerous prizes, including Australia's National Book Council Award. In 1988, he won England's most

prestigious literary award, the Booker Prize, for his
novel *Oscar and Lucinda;* the novel was adapted as a
film starring Cate Blanchett and Ralph Fiennes. Carey
has written a number of other award-winning novels,
including the acclaimed historical novel *True History of
the Kelly Gang* (2000). In his fiction, Carey is a
dazzling stylist and inventive formalist, often producing
quirky and bizarre narratives in which eccentric
characters cope with the mysteries of existence. Carey
now lives in New York City with his wife, Alison
Summers, who is mentioned in the following article. He
wrote this piece in the form of an open letter to his
friend Robert McCrum, the literary editor of the British
Observer, only days after the 9-11 disaster.

Before Reading

Where were you on the day of the 9/11 attack on the World Trade Center?
What do you remember? What were your immediate feelings and thoughts
about the attack?

[September 23, 2001]
Dear Robert

The last week is a great blur with no divisions between night and day. 1
Time is broken. The events of the first day bleed into the next and all
the powerful emotions and disturbing sights are now so hard to put in
proper sequence.

I was sitting here in this office which you know so well, looking out 2
over that little garden. I heard a passenger jet fly over, very large, very low.
I did feel momentarily alarmed. Air disaster crossed my mind, but only for
a moment. It was probably 10 minutes before I went out to the street, and
then only to buy a can of food for the starving cat. I wandered up to the
corner deli. As I entered, a young Asian American woman smiled at me, as
New Yorkers will when something weird is happening. I was puzzled. I
wondered if she was a student I'd forgotten.

I got the cat food, and suddenly realised that the deli radio was playing 3
very loud. What is it? I asked the girl. She said: a plane has crashed into the
World Trade Centre. Of course it was a terrorist attack. I never doubted it.
Crowds were now gathering around the loudspeaker in the little doorway.
They spilled into the street and looked down to the WTC. Smoke was al-
ready pouring from the upper floors.

In retrospect it seems an innocent and optimistic moment. We had no 4
idea how huge this disaster was. I knew my wife was in that building, not

because she had told me, or told the kids where she was going, but because all three of us males knew that this was her favourite time to pick up discount clothes at Century 21, just across the street from the north tower. You go through the 1 & 9 subway in the Trade Centre concourse to get there. Of course you now know Century 21 from TV—that blackened broken jigsaw of disaster that has not yet fallen down.

I wanted to wait by the phone for Alison. But I wanted to be in the street. I wanted to see my wife coming down from 6th Avenue, carrying those big plastic shopping bags filled with children's clothes. On the landing of our building I found my neighbour, Stu, crying. He had seen the plane crash into the building. So many friends were looking at the World Trade Centre at this moment. They now have this nightmare branded into the tissue of their cerebral cortex.

My friend Caz was jogging down the west side highway and witnessed it. Pure evil. Rocky was working on a roof on 11th street. He ducked as the 757 flew over his head, then stood to see hell arrive just down the road. Now he cannot sleep. Now none of us can sleep. Rocky thrashes and moans all night long. Charley our 11-year-old cannot sleep. He didn't see the plane but he was at school at Brooklyn Heights and his friends looked out the window and saw what they should never have seen and then the Manhattan kids all went through the difficulty, the uncertainty, of evacuation. Manhattan was burning. The bridges were closed. They did not know where their parents were. Now Charley faces the mornings exhausted, tearful, leaving a soggy bowl of half-eaten cereal on the table.

Our street drew us all outside. Our community was far more important than the television. We huddled together, on our landings, in the laundromat, at the corner deli.

From my doorway I saw MaryAnn from across the street. She was walking up and down with her baby in her arms. You could see, from the way she kissed her baby's head, that she feared her husband dead. Feeling her agony, we looked up towards 6th Avenue where the fire engines were already appearing in huge numbers. They drove the wrong way down the avenue, soon followed by black 4WDs with lights clamped on their roofs.

MaryAnn's husband entered the street. We were so happy to see him alive. "Lloyd, Lloyd." We called to him but he did not even hear us. He was a man who had seen something very bad. Now we started to hear about the attack on the second building, then the Pentagon. I ran back and forth between the silent phone and the street, like a madman on a leash. I could not be anywhere. I could not miss the phone. Could not be away from my neighbours.

Finally: a call. It was our friend Bea phoning from her apartment on 10 lower Broadway, just near City Hall. She had heard from my wife. Alison had buzzed from the street just as the second plane hit the South Tower, almost next door. Bea was distraught. She had seen bodies falling past her window. She was going to try to find my wife, but the street below was chaos, billowing malignant smoke, stretching to engulf whoever fell or stumbled. Bea said she would try to make her way to our house, a 15-minute walk, just north of Houston.

So I now knew that Alison had escaped the first building, but was she 11 safe? How could I know? I paced like MaryAnn had paced but outside the street was crowded. Pedestrians were fleeing from downtown. You could recognise these people straight away, the stark, seared horror in their eyes, the blankness, but also sometimes the frank appeals for human contact. They now begin to stream along Bedford Street in ever increasing numbers. These people have felt horror, they are like no other crowd I have ever seen.

Among them, finally, comes my wife, remarkable for the lack of trauma 12 her face reveals. It takes a little while for me to understand she was in the building when it hit. Only when I read her own account do I appreciate the extraordinary escape she has made, how lucky we are to have her alive.

We have two sons at different schools in Brooklyn and today we are 13 both very happy they are there. We discover our response is quite different to many other Manhattan parents who immediately set out through the ruined city, fighting the problems of closed bridges and roads and subways, to collect their children.

Bea's husband John is one of these. Why would you do that? I yell at 14 him. You're fucking nuts. Leave her there. She's safe. But his daughter wants to come home and he is her father and he sets off into the chaos of midtown traffic.

Although we believe that our kids are safe in Brooklyn, they are, just 15 the same, suffering their own traumas in their separate schools, knowing their mother is probably in the building, seeing weeping friends whose parents had offices in the WTC. Some of these stories will have happy resolutions, but not all.

Our neighbourhood is now cordoned off from the city. You needed ID 16 to get beneath Houston, to get back from above 14th Street. John succeeded in his insane trip across the 59th Bridge and up the Brooklyn Queens Expressway to Brooklyn Heights. He got his daughter, Leah, back home on a train that the news said was not running. Bea and John and Leah would not be able to return to her apartment for days. We cooked them pasta and made them beds and in the evenings that would follow listened to Bea as she arrived home after a traumatic day of grief counselling at

Bellevue—it was she who talked to all those people looking for husbands, wives, children, lovers.

Late that night we discovered the F train was running. Charley came 17 back to Manhattan with his best friend Matthew. I walked him home. He said the empty streets "creeped him out."

Our Brooklyn friend Betsy was caught in Manhattan with her beat-up 18 car and her cat and she too headed out on the 59th Street Bridge just as John had, but now the expressway was closed down and so she started a low meandering journey through the side streets of Queens and Brooklyn until she found herself—ah, Bonfire of the Vanities—a white Jew alone in the tough black area of East New York. "They were so sweet to me," she said. "These young men guided me to safety, getting this little white girl back to her own people."

Now our neighbourhood has become a command centre. That evening 19 we are standing on the corner of Houston and 6th Avenue watching the huge earth-moving equipment and heavy trucks rolling, bumper to bumper, in a never-ending parade towards the devastation. Here is the endless might and wealth of America. Here are the drivers, like soldiers, heroes. These are not military vehicles but huge trucks from small companies in Connecticut and New Jersey, from Bergen and Hackensack. Seeing all these individuals rise to the crisis, with their American flags stuck out of windows and taped to radio aerials, I am reminded of Dunkirk. I am moved. We are all moved. The crowds come out to cheer them. I do too, without reserve.

This is the same corner where we will soon be lighting candles for the 20 dead and missing, where 11-year-old Charley and I will stand for 20 silent minutes watching those photographs, of lost firefighters, wives, mothers, fathers, sons. It's hard not to cry. We watch the tender way our neighbours lay flowers and arrange the candles. We do not know all these people in the pictures, but we do know our firefighters. We shop with them. We wait in line at the supermarket while they buy Italian sausage and pasta for their dinner.

Pleasant, hoarse-voiced Jerry from the laundromat is there on the cor- 21 ner. He is always on the street, but tonight he wears a stars and stripes bandanna and he cannot be still. He has three grown-up sons downtown right now, working in that perilous pile of deadly pick-up sticks. Jerry and I embrace, because what else is there to do? When one of his sons almost loses his hand, it is miraculously sewn on by microsurgery. I am praying, says Jerry, there is just a lot of praying to do.

Everywhere people are touched by death. Our friend David across the 22 road has lost his best friend, the father of a new baby. Silvano the restaurateur has lost a fireman friend, and Charley and I are dismayed to see the huge piles of flowers outside that tiny station on West 3rd Street. The station was always so small, it looked like a museum. But now we stand, Charley and I, and we close our eyes and say a prayer, although I don't know who I'm praying to. There is no God for me.

Alison needs to stay home. She nests, tidies, spends several hours on small 23 domestic tasks. Then, finally, she begins to write a powerful piece about her escape. She works all day, all night, she cannot stop. As for me, I have to be outside, among the people. It is all that gives me any peace. I want to stand in the deli by the radio. There I can be with my neighbours. We touch, embrace, cry, are half wild with anger. Emotions are close to the surface.

One night 15-year-old Sam says he wants to walk around the city. He 24 wants to see Union Square where there is the biggest massing of candles and memorials. We walk along Houston Street which is now a war zone. Huge trucks from the New York Housing Authority stand in readiness to remove the rubble. We head east and then north. He is taller than me now, and likes to put his arm paternally around my shoulder. As we walk he says to me, apropos of nothing: "I love this city."

We walk to Union Square and I am proud of the complex, multifaceted 25 way Sam is talking about these events. He is concerned that local Muslims may be victimised because of our anger, cautious about retaliatory bombing, but mad too, like I am. We stand among the extraordinary shrine at Union Square where nuke-crazed groups stand next to pacifists, all united by their grief. The searing, murderous heat of that explosion has brought us all together.

We see so many people whom we know. The sweet-faced man from our 26 post office, whose continually lowered eyes have always given him a rather bemused and almost beatific expression, comes out of the dark to embrace me.

I am more vindictive than my son. I want to strike back, pulverise, kill, 27 obliterate anyone who has caused this harm to my city. I have become like the dangerous American the world has most reason to fear. This phase passes quickly enough. It has passed now. But on those first days and nights, I was overcome with murderous rage.

We are all changed by what has happened. Some of the changes have 28 been totally unexpected. Once, a year or so ago, I heard my son saying: "When we bombed Iraq."

"No," I said, "when they bombed Iraq." 29

"No," he said, "we." 30

It put a chill in me. I was very happy for him to be a New Yorker, but 31 I wasn't sure I wished him to be American.

But on the second day after the attack on the WTC, the day Sam turned   32
15, I bought him a large white T-shirt with an American flag printed on its
front. Sam is a very hard guy to buy a T-shirt for, but he put this one on immediately, and then we went out together again, out among the people, giving ourselves some strange and rather beautiful comfort in the middle of all
the horror that had fallen on our lives.

"I love this city, Dad. I love it more than ever." I did not disagree with   33
him.

Thinking About the Essay

1. Carey wrote this essay in the form of an open letter, probably with the expectation that it would be published. What aspects of the epistolary or letter style do you find in this piece? Cite specific examples. What are the
   benefits accruing to the epistolary style?

2. Who are Carey's primary and secondary audiences for this letter? Consider
   that Carey is an Australian, living in the United States, and writing to an
   English friend.

3. The writer is an acclaimed novelist. Point to examples of narrative and descriptive techniques that seem especially accomplished in this essay.

4. Does this essay contain a thesis, or is it simply a diffuse "letter from New
   York"? Justify your response by careful citation from the text.

5. What episode constitutes the writer's conclusion? Why is it so effective?
   What does Carey want to tell the reader at the end of his letter?

Responding in Writing

6. Write a letter to a close friend, reconstructing your response to the 9/11
   disaster. Try to employ narration and description to re-create the experience in as vivid a manner as possible.

7. In an analytical and evaluative essay, explain why you think Carey's essay
   does or does not capture a sense of life in New York immediately after the
   World Trade Center bombings.

8. Carey writes that at first he wanted to kill all terrorists but that his ideas
   and emotions quickly changed. Are you able to trace a similar pattern to
   your own behavior? Why or why not? Answer these questions in a personal
   essay.

Networking

9. In small groups, explain to class members exactly where you were on 9/11
   and how you responded to events during that first week. Then participate in
   a class discussion to create an inventory of responses.

10. Go to the Web and retrieve visual images of the World Trade Center disaster. Many are now famous. Which impress you, several years after they were taken? From a distance in time, how do you react to these images? Share one photograph with class members.

Bad Luck: Why Americans Exaggerate the Terrorist Threat

JEFFREY ROSEN | Jeffrey Rosen was born in 1964 in New York City and educated at Harvard University and Balliol College, Oxford University. He also has a J.D. degree from Yale Law School. Rosen currently teaches at George Washington Law School in Washington, D.C.; serves as legal affairs editor at the *New Republic*, where the following essay was published in November 2001; and also is a staff writer for the *New Yorker* magazine. In his recent book *The Unwanted Gaze: The Destruction of Privacy in America* (2000), Rosen explores the issue of privacy from the Middle Ages—when the Jewish ban on the "unwanted gaze" protected citizens from scrutiny—to such contemporary intrusions into the right of privacy as the Monica Lewinsky case. In this essay, Rosen (as we can infer from the title) offers a critical appraisal of our response to the terrorist threat.

Before Reading

What types of threats or fears have you experienced recently? Is the terrorist threat one of them? Why or why not?

The terrorist threat is all too real, but newspapers and TV stations 1 around the globe are still managing to exaggerate it. As new cases of anthrax infection continue to emerge, the World Health Organization is begging people not to panic. But tabloid headlines like this one from *The Mirror* in London send a different message: "panic." A Time/ CNN poll found that nearly half of all Americans say they are "very" or "somewhat" concerned that they or their families will be exposed to anthrax, even though only a handful of politicians and journalists have been targeted so far.

This isn't surprising. Terrorism is unfamiliar, it strikes largely at ran- 2 dom, and it can't be easily avoided by individual precautions. Criminologists tell us that crimes with these features are the most likely to create hysteria. If America's ability to win the psychological war against terrorism depends upon our ability to remain calm in the face of random violence, our reaction to similar threats in the past is not entirely reassuring.

In the academic literature about crime, scholars have identified a paradox: "Most surveys discover that people apparently fear most being a victim of precisely those crimes they are least likely to be victims of," writes Jason Ditton of the University of Sheffield. "Little old ladies apparently worry excessively about being mugged, but they are the least likely to be mugging victims." Women worry most about violent crime, though they have the lowest risk of being victims, while young men worry the least, though they have the highest risk. And because of their physical vulnerability, women tend to worry more about violence in general, even when the risk of experiencing a particular attack is evenly distributed. In a Gallup poll at the end of September, 62 percent of women said they were "very worried" that their families might be victimized by terrorist attacks. Only 35 percent of the men were similarly concerned.   3

Why are people most afraid of the crimes they are least likely to experience? According to Wesley Skogan of Northwestern University, "it may be the things we feel we can't control or influence, those uncontrollable risks, are the ones that make people most fearful." It's why people fear flying more than they fear being hit by a car. We think we can protect ourselves against cars by looking before crossing the street—and therefore underestimate the risk, even though it is actually higher than being killed in a plane crash.   4

People also overestimate the risk of crimes they have never experienced. The elderly are no more fearful than anyone else when asked how safe they feel when they go out at night. That's because many senior citizens don't go out at night, or they take precautions when they do. But when surveys ask how safe they would feel if they did go out at night more often, old people say they would be very afraid, since they have less experience to give them context. Instead they tend to assess risk based on media hype and rumors. "To be able to estimate the probability of an event occurring, you first have to know the underlying distribution of those events, and second the trend of those events—but when it comes to crime, people usually get both hugely wrong," writes Ditton.   5

The media is partly to blame. A survey by George Gerbner, former dean of the Annenberg School at the University of Pennsylvania, found that people who watch a lot of television are more likely than occasional viewers to overestimate their chances of being a victim of violence, to believe their neighborhood is unsafe, to say fear of crime is a very serious problem, to assume that crime is rising, and to buy locks, watchdogs, and guns. And   6 this distortion isn't limited to television. Jason Ditton notes that 45 percent of crimes reported in the newspaper involve sex or violence, even though they only represent 3 percent of crimes overall. When interviewed about how many crimes involve sex or violence, people tend to overestimate it by a factor of three or four. People believe they are more likely to be assaulted or raped than robbed, even though the robbery rate is much higher.

Will sensationalistic reports of worst-case terrorist scenarios exaggerate people's fear of being caught in an attack? There's every reason to believe that they will because of the media's tendency to exaggerate the scope and probability of remote risks. In a book called *Random Violence,* Joel Best, then of Southern Illinois University, examined the "moral panics" about a series of new crimes that seized public attention in the 1980s and '90s: freeway violence in 1987, wilding in 1989, stalking around 1990, kids and guns in 1991, and so forth. In each case, Best writes, television seized on two or three incidents of a dramatic crime, such as freeway shooting, and then claimed it was part of a broader trend. By taking the worst and most infrequent examples of criminal violence and melodramatically claiming they were typical, television created the false impression that everyone was equally at risk, thereby increasing its audience.

The risk of terrorism is more randomly distributed than the crimes the media has hyped in the past. This makes it even more frightening because it is hard to avoid through precautions. (The anthrax envelopes were more narrowly targeted than the World Trade Center attack, of course, but they still infected postal workers.) Contemporary Americans, in particular, are not well equipped to deal with arbitrary threats because, in so many realms of life, we refuse to accept the role of chance. In his nineteenth-century novel *The Gilded Age,* Mark Twain described a steamship accident that killed 22 people. The investigator's verdict: "nobody to blame." This attitude was reflected in nineteenth-century legal doctrines such as assumption of risk, which refused to compensate victims who behaved carelessly. In the twentieth century, by contrast, the United States developed what the legal historian Lawrence Friedman has called an expectation of "total justice"— namely, "the general expectation that somebody will pay for any and all calamities that happen to a person, provided only that it is not the victim's 'fault,' or at least not solely his fault."

This effort to guarantee total justice is reflected throughout American society—from the regulation of product safety to the elimination of legal doctrines like assumption of risk. Since September 11 the most egregious display of this total justice mentality has been the threat by various personal injury lawyers to sue the airlines, security officials, and the architects of the World Trade Center on behalf of the victims' families. One of their claims: Flaws in the design of the twin towers may have impeded escape.

Given America's difficulty in calculating and accepting unfamiliar risk, 10 what can be done, after September 11, to minimize panic? Rather than self-censoring only when it comes to the ravings of Osama bin Laden, the broadcast media might try to curb its usual focus on worst-case scenarios. Wesley Skogan found that when people were accurately informed about the real risk, they adjusted their fears accordingly. Politicians also need to be careful about passing on unspecified but terrifying threats of future attacks. In the middle of October the Justice Department warned that a terrorist attack might be imminent, but didn't say what the attack might be, or where it might strike. The vagueness of the warning only increased public fear and caused people to cancel travel plans. But it didn't make anyone more secure.

While Americans learn to take sensible precautions, we need to also 11 learn that there is no insurance against every calamity or compensation for every misfortune. There is something inegalitarian about risk: It singles out some people from the crowd for no good reason and treats them worse than everybody else. But even in the United States, there is no such thing as perfect equality or total justice. If the first foreign attack on U.S. soil helps teach Americans how to live with risk, then perhaps we can emerge from this ordeal a stronger society as well as a stronger nation.

Thinking About the Essay

1. In Rosen's opinion, who or what is to blame for Americans' preoccupation with threats of various kinds? How does a cause-and-effect pattern of development permit the writer to present a panorama of threats in this essay?

2. Rosen is trained in the law. How does his professional expertise influence the way he builds his "case" in this essay? What legal or "courtroom" techniques can you detect?

3. The writer constructs his argument through the use of numerous examples and forms of evidence. What types of evidence can you identify and where? What is the overall effect? Is his evidence convincing or not?

4. How does Rosen's level of language imply that he is writing for an audience that can follow logically the "rules of evidence" that he presents? Cite specific words and sentences to support your response.

5. To what extent, in your opinion, is Rosen's concluding paragraph an effective summation of his case? Is the tone of this last paragraph in keeping with the tone of the whole essay? Why or why not?

Responding in Writing

6. "The terrorist threat," says Rosen in the first sentence of paragraph 1, "is all too real, but newspapers and TV stations around the globe are still managing to exaggerate it." From your perspective, do you agree or disagree with his assertion? Write an essay in which you provide sufficient evidence to support your response.

7. In a personal essay, explain how the terrorist threat has affected any other fears or apprehensions that you have had to deal with.

8. In an illustrative essay, address a question posed by Rosen in paragraph 10: "Given America's difficulty in calculating and accepting unfamiliar risk, what can be done, after September 11, to minimize panic?" Develop at least three ways to reduce our sense of panic.

Networking

9. In groups of four or five, discuss the ways in which each member has developed ways to cope with a range of fears and phobias—not just the terrorist threat. Then list all the strategies for coping and share them in class discussion.

10. Go online and locate at least four reviews of Rosen's book *The Unwanted Gaze: The Destruction of Privacy in America* (2000). Download and take notes on the reviewers' comments. (You will discover that some reviewers think that the book is brilliant, whereas others have negative opinions.) Write a comparative essay in which you explain these diverging appraisals of Rosen's book.

Blaming America First

TODD GITLIN

Todd Gitlin, who was born in 1943, is noted for his perceptive explorations of contemporary cultural life, especially the complex ways in which the media affect society. Among his notable books on the mass media are *The Whole World Is Watching: Mass Media in the Making and Unmaking of the New Left* (1980) and *Inside Prime Time* (1983). Since the 1960s, when he was president of Students for a Democratic Society (SDS), Gitlin also has written about those power structures that influence and often control our lives in the United States and increasingly around the world. For several decades Gitlin has been a spokesperson for the New Left and, more recently, a chronicler of the decline in American liberalism. His books *The Sixties: Years of Hope, Days of Rage* (1987) and *The Twilight* of *Common Dreams: Why America Is Wracked by Culture Wars* (1995) trace the decline of New Left optimism. Gitlin has a Ph.D. degree in sociology from the University of California at Berkeley and is a professor of journalism, culture, and sociology at New York University. In the essay that follows, published in 2002 in the magazine *Mother Jones,* Gitlin examines why some liberals who profess sympathy for victims around the world find it difficult to express similar emotions for Americans who suffer because of the events surrounding 9/11.

Before Reading

What does it mean to be aligned politically with the "left"? Conversely, how would you define someone of the "right"? Where do you stand within this political spectrum?

As shock and solidarity overflowed on September 11, it seemed for a 1 moment that political differences had melted in the inferno of Lower Manhattan. Plain human sympathy abounded amid a common sense of grief and emergency. Soon enough, however, old reflexes and tones cropped up here and there on the left both abroad and at home—smugness, acrimony, even schadenfreude, accompanied by the notion that the attacks were, well, not a just dessert, exactly, but . . . damnable yet understandable payback . . . rooted in America's own crimes of commission and omission . . . reaping what empire had sown. After all, was not America essentially the oil-greedy, Islam-disrespecting oppressor of Iraq, Sudan, Palestine? Were not the ghosts of the Shah's Iran, of Vietnam, and of the Cold War Afghan jihad rattling their bones? Intermittently grandiose talk from Washington about a righteous "crusade" against "evil" helped inflame the rhetoric of critics who feared—legitimately—that a deepening war in Afghanistan would pile human catastrophe upon human catastrophe. And soon, without pausing to consider why the vast majority of Americans might feel bellicose as well as sorrowful, some on the left were dismissing the idea that the United States had any legitimate recourse to the use of force in self-defense—or indeed any legitimate claim to the status of victim.

I am not speaking of the ardent, and often expressed, hope that Sep- 2 tember 11's crimes against humanity might eventually elicit from America a greater respect for the whole of assaulted humanity. A reasoned, vigorous examination of U.S. policies, including collusion in the Israeli occupation, sanctions against Iraq, and support of corrupt regimes in Saudi Arabia and Egypt, is badly needed. So is critical scrutiny of the administration's actions in Afghanistan and American unilateralism on many fronts. But in the wake of September 11 there erupted something more primal and reflexive than criticism: a kind of left-wing fundamentalism, a negative faith in America the ugly.

In this cartoon view of the world, there is nothing worse than American power—not the woman-enslaving Taliban, not an unrepentant Al Qaeda committed to killing civilians as they please—and America is nothing but a self-seeking bully. It does not face genuine dilemmas. It never has legitimate reason to do what it does. When its rulers' views command popularity, this can only be because the entire population has been brainwashed, or rendered moronic, or shares in its leaders' monstrous values.

Of the perils of American ignorance, of our fantasy life of pure and unappreciated goodness, much can be said. The failures of intelligence that made September 11 possible include not only security oversights but a vast combination of stupefaction and arrogance—not least the all-or-nothing thinking that armed the Islamic jihad in Afghanistan in order to fight our own jihad against Soviet Communism—and a willful ignorance that not so long ago permitted half the citizens of a flabby, self-satisfied democracy to vote for a man unembarrassed by his lack of acquaintanceship with the world.

But myopia in the name of the weak is no more defensible than myopia in the name of the strong. Like jingoists who consider any effort to understand terrorists immoral, on the grounds that to understand is to endorse, these hard-liners disdain complexity. They see no American motives except oil-soaked power lust, but look on the bright side of societies that cultivate fundamentalist ignorance. They point out that the actions of various mass murderers (the Khmer Rouge, bin Laden) must be "contextualized," yet refuse to consider any context or reason for the actions of Americans.

If we are to understand Islamic fundamentalism, must we not also trouble ourselves to understand America, this freedom-loving, brutal, tolerant, shortsighted, selfish, generous, trigger-happy, dumb, glorious, fatheaded powerhouse?

Not a bad place to start might be the patriotic fervor that arose after the attacks. What's offensive about affirming that you belong to a people, that your fate is bound up with theirs? Should it be surprising that suffering close-up is felt more urgently, more deeply, than suffering at a distance? After disaster comes a desire to reassemble the shards of a broken community, withstand the loss, strike back at the enemy. The attack stirs, in other words, patriotism—love of one's people, pride in their endurance, and a desire to keep them from being hurt anymore. And then, too, the wound is inverted, transformed into a badge of honor. It is translated into protest ("We didn't deserve this") and indignation ("They can't do this to us"). Pride can fuel the quest for justice, the rage for punishment, or the pleasures of smugness. The dangers are obvious. But it should not be hard to understand that the American flag sprouted in the days after September 11, for many of us, as a badge of belonging, not a call to shed innocent blood.

This sequence is not a peculiarity of American arrogance, ignorance, and power. It is simply and ordinarily human. It operates as clearly, as humanly, among nonviolent Palestinians attacked by West Bank and Gaza settlers and their Israeli soldier-protectors as among Israelis suicide-bombed at a nightclub or a pizza joint. No government anywhere has the right to neglect the safety of its own citizens—not least against an enemy that swears it will strike again. Yet some who instantly, and rightly, understand that Palestinians may burn to avenge their compatriots killed by American weapons assume that Americans have only interests (at least the elites do) and gullibilities (which are the best the masses are capable of). 8

In this purist insistence on reducing America and Americans to a wicked stereotype, we encounter a soft anti-Americanism that, whatever takes place in the world, wheels automatically to blame America first. This is not the hard anti-Americanism of bin Laden, the terrorist logic under which, because the United States maintains military bases in the land of the prophet, innocents must be slaughtered and their own temples crushed. Totalitarians like bin Laden treat issues as fodder for the apocalyptic imagination. They want power and call it God. Were Saddam Hussein or the Palestinians to win all their demands, bin Laden would move on, in his next video, to his next issue. 9

Soft anti-Americans, by contrast, sincerely want U.S. policies to change— though by their lights, such turnabouts are well-nigh unimaginable—but they commit the grave moral error of viewing the mass murderer (if not the mass murder) as nothing more than an outgrowth of U.S. policy. They not only note but gloat that the United States built up Islamic fundamentalism in Afghanistan as a counterfoil to the Russians. In this thinking, Al Qaeda is an effect, not a cause; a symptom, not a disease. The initiative, the power to cause, is always American. 10

But here moral reasoning runs off the rails. Who can hold a symptom accountable? To the left-wing fundamentalist, the only interesting or important brutality is at least indirectly the United States' doing. Thus, sanctions against Iraq are denounced, but the cynical mass murderer Saddam Hussein, who permits his people to die, remains an afterthought. Were America to vanish, so, presumably, would the miseries of Iraq and Egypt. 11

In the United States, adherents of this kind of reflexive anti- 12
Americanism are a minority (isolated, usually, on campuses and in coastal
cities, in circles where reality checks are scarce), but they are vocal and
quick to action. Observing flags flying everywhere, they feel embattled and
draw on their embattlement for moral credit, thus roping themselves into
tight little circles of the pure and the saved.

The United States represents a frozen imperialism that values only un- 13
bridled power in the service of untrammeled capital. It is congenitally, geno-
cidally, irremediably racist. Why complicate matters by facing up to
America's self-contradictions, its on-again, off-again interest in extending
rights, its clumsy egalitarianism coupled with ignorant arrogance? America
is seen as all of a piece, and it is hated because it is hateful—period. One may
quarrel with the means used to bring it low, but low is only what it deserves.

So even as the smoke was still rising from the ground of Lower Man- 14
hattan, condemnations of mass murder made way in some quarters for a
retreat to the old formula and the declaration that the "real question" was
America's victims—as if there were not room in the heart for more than one
set of victims. And the seductions of closure were irresistible even to those
dedicated, in other circumstances, to intellectual glasnost. Noam Chomsky
bent facts to claim that Bill Clinton's misguided attack on a Sudanese pharmaceutical plant in 1998 was worse by far than the massacres of September 11. Edward Said, the exiled Palestinian author and critic, wrote of "a
superpower almost constantly at war, or in some sort of conflict, all over
the Islamic domains." As if the United States always picked the fight; as if
U.S. support of the Oslo peace process, whatever its limitations, could be
simply brushed aside; as if defending Muslims in Bosnia and Kosovo—
however dreadful some of the consequences—were the equivalent of practicing gunboat diplomacy in Latin America or dropping megatons of
bombs on Vietnam and Cambodia.

From the Indian novelist Arundhati Roy, who has admirably criticized 15
her country's policies on nuclear weapons and development, came the
queenly declaration that "American people ought to know that it is not
them but their government's policies that are so hated." (One reason why
Americans were not exactly clear about the difference is that the murderers of September 11 did not trouble themselves with such nice distinctions.)
When Roy described bin Laden as "the American president's dark doppelgänger" and claimed that "the twins are blurring into one another and
gradually becoming interchangeable," she was in the grip of a prejudice in-
vulnerable to moral distinctions.

Insofar as we who criticize U.S. policy seriously want Americans to 16
wake up to the world—to overcome what essayist Anne Taylor Fleming

has called our serial innocence, ever renewed, ever absurd—we must speak to, not at, Americans, in recognition of our common perplexity and vulnerability. We must abstain from the fairy-tale pleasures of oversimplification. We must propose what is practical—the stakes are too great for the luxury of any fundamentalism. We must not content ourselves with seeing what Washington says and rejecting that. We must forgo the luxury of assuming that we are not obligated to imagine ourselves in the seats of power.

Generals, it's said, are always planning to fight the last war. But they're 17 not alone in suffering from sentimentality, blindness, and mental laziness disguised as resolve. The one-eyed left helps no one when it mires itself in its own mirror-image myths. Breaking habits is desperately hard, but those who evade the difficulties in their purist positions and refuse to face *all* the mess and danger of reality only guarantee their bitter inconsequence.

Thinking About the Essay

1. Gitlin's introductory paragraph is quite long for a relatively short essay. Why does he start this way? Does he state a thesis? If so, where is it? If not, why not? Do you find the introduction effective? Explain.

2. Why does Gitlin's criticism of certain individuals on the left who cannot bring themselves to sympathize with the victims of terrorist attacks against Americans possess special weight or authority? (Review his biography for clues.) How does he use his special authority to control the tone and organization of the essay?

3. Analyze paragraph 6, which consists of one long sentence. How does the design of this sentence capture the logic and structure of Gitlin's approach to his subject?

4. What can you infer about Noam Chomsky, Edward Said, and Arundhati Roy (whose essay appears next), who are mentioned in paragraphs 14–15, from the context of this essay?

5. Explain the level of diction, style, and logic that Gitlin brings to this essay. How easy or difficult was it for you to follow his argument, and how do you account for this response?

Responding in Writing

6. Borrowing Gitlin's title, write your own essay, "Blaming America First." Deal with some of Gitlin's main points or claims as you develop this paper. To focus your essay, try to answer the question, Why do some Americans and others around the world refuse to acknowledge the benefits and altruism of United States foreign policy?

7. What do you think of Americans and others who criticize the nation's foreign policy? Do you sympathize with them, support them, loathe them, or

what? Under what conditions and circumstances do you support dissent, or do you think that dissent is an absolute right? Prepare a paper that ties these questions together.

8. Gitlin writes in paragraph 16, "We must forgo the luxury of assuming that we are not obligated to imagine ourselves in the seats of power." Write an essay in which you explore the implications of his statement, offering examples to support your primary points.

Networking

9. In groups of four or five class members, break down Gitlin's argument paragraph by paragraph. Paraphrase each paragraph and then reduce each paragraph to a single-sentence précis. Select one member to join a panel presentation of your findings.

10. Go online and locate information on three writers mentioned by the author: Noam Chomsky, Edward Said, and Arundhati Roy. Present your findings in a paper that focuses on their shared political orientation.

The Algebra of Infinite Justice

ARUNDHATI ROY

Arundhati Roy, born in Shillong, India, in 1961 and raised in Kerala, is the child of Syrian Christian and Hindu parents. Her first novel, *The God of Small Things* (1997), turned this former architecture student, actor, and screenwriter into an international celebrity. Steeped in the complex history of India, Roy's novel, which won the prestigious Booker Prize, is a dazzling portrayal of the lives of twin children as they move through the barriers of race, gender, and class on national and international levels of experience. To date, *The God of Small Things* has been published in twenty-seven languages. With her fame and royalties, Roy today is an activist, denouncing in extended essays the Indian government's destruction of the environment, criticizing nuclear proliferation, and subjecting other global issues to critical scrutiny. Her social and political criticism appears in *The Cost of Living* (1999) and *Power Politics* (2001). Roy received the $350,000 Lannam Foundation Prize for Cultural Freedom in 2002, announcing that she would donate the money to fifty educational institutions, publishing houses, and people's movements in India. In the following essay, published in *The Progressive* in December, 2001, Roy tries to explain why American foreign policy is so hated around the world.

Before Reading

Do you think that the United States government engages in policies around the world in order to promote "the American way of life"? Why or why not? What do you understand this term to mean? Why would peoples of other nations be skeptical of this effort?

It must be hard for ordinary Americans, so recently bereaved, to look up at the world with their eyes full of tears and encounter what might appear to them to be indifference. It isn't indifference. It's just augury. An absence of surprise. The tired wisdom of knowing that what goes around eventually comes around. The American people ought to know that it is not them, but their government's policies, that are so hated.

Bush's almost god-like mission—called Operation Infinite Justice until it was pointed out that this could be seen as an insult to Muslims, who believe that only Allah can mete out infinite justice, and was renamed Operation Enduring Freedom—requires some small clarifications. For example, Infinite Justice/Enduring Freedom for whom?

In 1996, Madeleine Albright, then the U.S. Ambassador to the United Nations, was asked on national television what she felt about the fact that 500,000 Iraqi children had died as a result of economic sanctions the U.S. insisted upon. She replied that it was "a very hard choice," but that all things considered, "we think the price is worth it." Albright never lost her job for saying this. She continued to travel the world representing the views and aspirations of the U.S. government. More pertinently, the sanctions against Iraq remain in place. Children continue to die.

So here we have it. The equivocating distinction between civilization and savagery, between the "massacre of innocent people" or, if you like, the "clash of civilizations" and "collateral damage." The sophistry and fastidious algebra of Infinite Justice. How many dead Iraqis will it take to make the world a better place? How many dead Afghans for every dead American? How many dead children for every dead man? How many dead mujahedeen for each dead investment banker?

The American people may be a little fuzzy about where exactly Afghanistan is (we hear reports that there's a run on maps of the country), but the U.S. government and Afghanistan are old friends. In 1979, after the Soviet invasion of Afghanistan, the CIA and Pakistan's ISI (Inter-Services Intelligence) launched the CIA's largest covert operation since the Vietnam War. Their purpose was to harness the energy of Afghan resistance and expand it into a holy war, an Islamic jihad, which would turn Muslim countries within the Soviet Union against the communist regime and eventually destabilize it. When it began, it was meant to be the Soviet Union's Vietnam. It turned out to be much more than that. Over the years, through the ISI, the CIA funded and recruited tens of thousands of radical mujahedeen from forty Islamic countries as soldiers for America's proxy war. The rank and file of the mujahedeen were unaware that their jihad was actually being fought on behalf of Uncle Sam.

In 1989, after being bloodied by ten years of relentless conflict, the Russians withdrew, leaving behind a civilization reduced to rubble. Civil war in Afghanistan raged on. The jihad spread to Chechnya, Kosovo, and eventually to Kashmir. The CIA continued to pour in money and military equipment, but the overhead had become immense, and more money was needed. 6

The mujahedeen ordered farmers to plant opium as a "revolutionary tax." Under the protection of the ISI, hundreds of heroin processing laboratories were set up across Afghanistan. Within two years of the CIA's arrival, the Pakistan/Afghanistan borderland had become the biggest producer of heroin in the world, and the single biggest source on American streets. The annual profits, said to be between $100 and $200 billion, were ploughed back into training and arming militants. 7

In 1996, the Taliban—then a marginal sect of dangerous, hard-line fundamentalists—fought its way to power in Afghanistan. It was funded by the ISI, that old cohort of the CIA, and supported by many political parties in Pakistan. The Taliban unleashed a regime of terror. Its first victims were its own people, particularly women. It closed down girls' schools, dismissed women from government jobs, enforced Sharia law—under which women deemed to be "immoral" are stoned to death and widows guilty of being adulterous are buried alive. 8

After all that has happened, can there be anything more ironic than Russia and America joining hands to redestroy Afghanistan? The question is, can you destroy destruction? Dropping more bombs on Afghanistan will only shuffle the rubble, scramble some old graves, and disturb the dead. The desolate landscape of Afghanistan was the burial ground of Soviet communism and the springboard of a unipolar world dominated by America. It made the space for neocapitalism and corporate globalization, again dominated by America: And now Afghanistan is poised to become the graveyard for the unlikely soldiers who fought and won this war for America. 9

India, thanks in part to its geography and in part to the vision of its former leaders, has so far been fortunate enough to be left out of this Great Game. Had it been drawn in, it's more than likely that our democracy, such as it is, would not have survived. After September 11, as some of us watched in horror, the Indian government furiously gyrated its hips, begging the U.S. to set up its base in India rather than Pakistan. Having had this ringside view of Pakistan's sordid fate, it isn't just odd, it's unthinkable, that India should want to do this. Any Third World country with a fragile economy and a complex social base should know by now that to invite a superpower such as America in (whether it says it's staying or just passing through) would be like inviting a brick to drop through your windscreen. 10

Operation Enduring Freedom is being fought ostensibly to uphold the 11
American Way of Life. It'll probably end up undermining it completely. It
will spawn more anger and more terror across the world. For ordinary people in America, it will mean lives lived in a climate of sickening uncertainty:
Will my child be safe in school? Will there be nerve gas in the subway? A
bomb in the cinema hall? Will my love come home tonight? Being picked
off a few at a time—now with anthrax, later perhaps with smallpox or
bubonic plague—may end up being worse than being annihilated all at
once by a nuclear bomb.

The U.S. government and governments all over the world are using the 12
climate of war as an excuse to curtail civil liberties, deny free speech, lay
off workers, harass ethnic and religious minorities, cut back on public
spending, and divert huge amounts of money to the defense industry. To
what purpose? President Bush can no more "rid the world of evildoers"
than he can stock it with saints.

It's absurd for the U.S. government to even toy with the notion that it 13
can stamp out terrorism with more violence and oppression. Terrorism is
the symptom, not the disease.

Terrorism has no country. It's transnational, as global an enterprise as 14
Coke or Pepsi or Nike. At the first sign of trouble, terrorists can pull up
stakes and move their "factories" from country to country in search of a
better deal. Just like the multinationals.

Terrorism as a phenomenon may never go away. But if it is to be con- 15
tained, the first step is for America to at least acknowledge that it shares
the planet with other nations, with other human beings, who, even if they
are not on TV, have loves and griefs and stories and songs and sorrows and,
for heaven's sake, rights.

The September 11 attacks were a monstrous calling card from a world 16
gone horribly wrong. The message may have been written by Osama bin
Laden (who knows?) and delivered by his couriers, but it could well have
been signed by the ghosts of the victims of America's old wars: the millions
killed in Korea, Vietnam, and Cambodia, the 17,500 killed when Israel—
backed by the U.S.—invaded Lebanon in 1982, the tens of thousands of
Iraqis killed in Operation Desert Storm, the thousands of Palestinians who
have died fighting Israel's occupation of the West Bank.

And the millions who died, in Yugoslavia, Somalia, Haiti, Chile, 17
Nicaragua, El Salvador, the Dominican Republic, Panama, at the hands of
all the terrorists, dictators, and genocidists whom the American government supported, trained, bankrolled, and supplied with arms. And this is
far from being a comprehensive list.

For a country involved in so much warfare and conflict, the American 18
people have been extremely fortunate. The strikes on September 11 were only

the second on American soil in over a century. The first was Pearl Harbor. The reprisal for this took a long route, but ended with Hiroshima and Nagasaki.

This time the world waits with bated breath for the horrors to come.   19

Someone recently said that if Osama bin Laden didn't exist, America   20 would have had to invent him. But in a way, America did invent him. He was among the jihadis who moved to Afghanistan in 1979 when the CIA commenced its operations there. Bin Laden has the distinction of being created by the CIA and wanted by the FBI. In the course of a fortnight, he was promoted from Suspect to Prime Suspect, and then, despite the lack of any real evidence, straight up the charts to "Wanted: Dead or Alive."

From what is known about bin Laden, it's entirely possible that he did   21 not personally plan and carry out the attacks—that he is the inspirational figure, "the CEO of the Holding Company." The Taliban's response to U.S. demands for the extradition of bin Laden was uncharacteristically reasonable: Produce the evidence, then we'll hand him over. President Bush's response was that the demand was "non-negotiable."

(While talks are on for the extradition of CEOs, can India put in a side-   22 request for the extradition of Warren Anderson of the USA? He was the chairman of Union Carbide, responsible for the 1984 Bhopal gas leak that killed 16,000 people. We have collated the necessary evidence. It's all in the files. Could we have him, please?)

But who is Osama bin Laden really? Let me rephrase that. What is   23 Osama bin Laden? He's America's family secret. He is the American President's dark doppelgänger. The savage twin of all that purports to be beautiful and civilized. He has been sculpted from the spare rib of a world laid to waste by America's foreign policy: its gunboat diplomacy, its nuclear arsenal, its vulgarly stated policy of "full spectrum dominance," its chilling disregard for non-American lives, its barbarous military interventions, its support for despotic and dictatorial regimes, its merciless economic agenda that has munched through the economies of poor countries like a cloud of locusts, its marauding multinationals that are taking over the air we breathe, the ground we stand on, the water we drink, the thoughts we think.

Now that the family secret has been spilled, the twins are blurring into   24 one another and gradually becoming interchangeable. Their guns, bombs, money, and drugs have been going around in the loop for a while. Now they've even begun to borrow each other's rhetoric. Each refers to the other as "the head of the snake." Both invoke God and use the loose millenarian currency of Good and Evil as their terms of reference. Both are engaged in unequivocal political crimes. Both are dangerously armed—one with the nuclear arsenal of the obscenely powerful, the other with the incandescent, destructive power of the utterly hopeless. The fireball and the ice pick. The bludgeon and the axe.

The important thing to keep in mind is that neither is an acceptable al- 25
ternative to the other.

President Bush's ultimatum to the people of the world—"Either you are 26
with us or you are with the terrorists"—is a piece of presumptuous arrogance.

It's not a choice that people want to, need to, or should have to make. 27

Thinking About the Essay

1. In the previous essay in this chapter, Todd Gitlin criticizes Arundhati Roy for her political views about the United States. What aspects of Roy's essay would prompt such criticism? Do you agree or disagree with Gitlin's assessment, or do you think that Roy actually has an important argument that we should treat seriously? Explain.

2. What does the title of the essay mean? Where does Roy expand on it? Why does she equate "justice" with "algebra"?

3. Point to paragraphs and sections of this essay where the writer uses process analysis, causal analysis, and comparison and contrast to advance her argument.

4. This essay seems to hop almost cinematically from point to point. Does Roy's technique damage the organization and coherence of her essay? Why or why not?

5. In the final analysis, does Roy make a compelling or logical argument in this essay? Explain your response.

Responding in Writing

6. Do you think that people around the world hate America's policies but not Americans—as Roy asserts? Write a paper responding to this question. Provide examples to support your position.

7. Write an argumentative essay in which you either support or rebut Roy's argument. Try to proceed point by point, moving completely through Roy's main reasons in defense of her claim.

8. What does the word *justice* mean to you? Did the American nation receive its due "justice" on September 11, 2001? Write an extended-definition essay responding to this notion.

Networking

9. In small groups, discuss each member's personal impression of Roy's essay. Try to explain the thoughts and emotions it prompts. Make a list of these responses, and share them with the rest of the class.

10. Enter an Internet forum dealing with American foreign policy and monitor what participants write about it. Prepare a summary of these responses, and post them—either on your own web page or as an e-mail attachment to friends.

The Digital Revolution: Will It Bring Us Together?

Today you arrive in class with cell phones, pagers, wireless laptops, and other forms of digital paraphernalia—some so miniaturized as to be unseen by the myopic instructor. You send e-mails to friends around the world while the professor spins a fantastic lecture; you enter a MUD while the teacher offers advice on comma splices. You probably know more about electronic technology and educational software than digitally challenged professors, for studies indicate that only 20 percent of them feel comfortable using computer technology. That is why you should plan to come to the aid of your instructor when computer equipment breaks down or Blackboard poses problems.

As a contemporary college student, you are a comfortable member of the digital revolution. In all likelihood you entered the digital world at an early age, typically by gaming. In fact, computer games are the digital drugs of choice; they serve as a gateway to the mystical electronic universe and might very well be a form of visual literacy that experts are only starting to examine. Along the way, you acquired keyboarding skills, troubleshooting talents, wisdom about sites for free software and music, and the value of communication with real and virtual friends around the world. You customized your website, and while your parents struggled with the problem of limiting your access to exotic Internet sources, found ways to block *them* from your digital universe. Now, in college, you are wired from your wrist to the dorm to the classroom. You *know* the extraordinary power and promise of the electronic universe because you are a privileged participant in it.

But have you considered the worldwide implications of the digital revolution? According to *Facts and Figures*, 94 percent of all Internet users live in the forty richest countries. It would take an average worker

An Azad University student uses an internet café in Tehran, Iran. Access to the internet is still highly restricted in some countries and by some cultures.

Thinking About the Image

1. Closely examine all of the details of this photograph (for example, what is on the table next to this woman's elbow?) In what ways does this photograph reinforce standard images in the American media of Muslim women? In what ways is the photograph surprising?

2. This photograph originally accompanied "The Digital Revolution and the New Reformation" by Ali Mazrui and Alamin Mazrui (p. 381). The authors write that "literacy as a source of empowerment has shifted from the print to the computer medium." Do you agree that access to the internet provides a kind of "empowerment"? Why, or why not?

3. In her essay "When Afghanistan Was at Peace," Margaret Atwood notes of her book *The Handmaid's Tale* (partly inspired by her travels in Afghanistan) that "there is freedom to and freedom from. But how much of the first should you have to give up in order to assure the second?" How would the Mazruis respond to that question? How might the woman in this photograph respond?

4. The English-language version of the web site for Azad University, where this woman is a student, is *http://www.azad.ac.ir/main/INDEX_Eng.htm*. Visit this website and compare it to that of your own college. What are the similarities between your schools and how they present themselves? How are they different? Are you surprised?

in Bangladesh roughly eight years of wages to purchase a basic computer. A child in Nigeria does not typically come into contact with computers in elementary school like his or her American counterparts. And with half the population in Latin America poor and illiterate, it seems cynical to speak about the digital revolution as a transformative force in their lives. In the world today, the age-old contest between the "haves" and "have-nots" has assumed digital proportions. There is a worldwide interconnectedness of effects—a global ecology involving class, income, literacy, geography, infrastructure, and now digital development—that has produced yet another challenge for our new century. Even in war, as recent events have demonstrated, the victory goes to the nations that are most electronically advanced.

What's the lesson here? Not, certainly, that the digital revolution is the devil in disguise. As the writers in this chapter attest, the electronic age is transforming our lives, and, as it spreads, it will change incrementally the lives of peoples in the least developed parts of the world. Perhaps the lesson we must learn is that there is a digital divide in the world today, but that there are ways to bridge it. Generations from now, a fair-minded narrative of the history of the early stages of the digital age will have to deal with just how well we managed to harness the power of the electronic revolution to benefit the world's peoples.

The Electronic Gap

PAUL KENNEDY | Born in Wallsend, England, in 1945, Paul Kennedy is a noted historian with a talent for making broad historical movements comprehensible to the lay reader. He received his doctorate degree from St. Anthony's College, Oxford, in 1970, and has taught at Yale University, where he holds an endowed professorship, since 1982. Kennedy has lectured throughout the United States and has appeared on the *Today Show* and *MacNeil-Lehrer Report.* His widely acclaimed book *The Rise and Fall of the Great Powers: Economic Change and Military Conflict from 1500 to 2000* (1988) offers a penetrating analysis of how certain empires or "power centers" lose strategic importance. His most controversial thesis in this study is that the United States has experienced historical decline since the peak of its power after World War II. He states, "If I'm going to preach about the lessons of history at all, it is that societies which did not invest in the future but invested too much either in defense or consumption were destined to be overtaken by those with a different set of priorities." Kennedy has written and edited almost two dozen books, including *Pacific Victory*

(1973), *Strategy and Diplomacy, 1870–1945* (1983), *Preparing for the Twenty-First Century* (1993), and *Global Sociology* (2000). This brief essay by Kennedy, which appeared in the UNESCO Courier in December 2001, offers a challenge to those who "want to work toward a knowledge-based society."

Before Reading

How does an "electronic gap" develop? What are the causes and implications? Could there be an electronic gap at your college? Why or why not? What electronic gaps do you think might exist in the United States?

In the United States, business journals, market gurus, economics professors and highly paid consultants talk incessantly about the coming global boom, the transformation of the workplace, the technology revolution and the knowledge explosion. It is implied that the world is slowly becoming a reproduction of Silicon Valley. It is asserted that this is the future. But instead of swallowing this hype, perhaps we should pull back and look at the globe as a whole.   1

The pessimistic view would be to point out what is currently occurring in Kosovo, West Africa, Rwanda, Chechnya, Kashmir and elsewhere. We might also follow Robert Kaplan in the trips he describes in *To the Ends of the Earth*,[1] only to discover that much of humanity is headed for disaster and self-destruction. I do not wish to be as negative as that. However, I would like to offer a caution to those who portray globalization in an uncritical and overly enthusiastic manner.   2

Each day I send and receive up to 40 messages on the Internet. From my home I can search the web sites of the World Bank and the United Nations to find new data, read the *New York Times* and check the 9 million book titles in the Yale University Library. The Internet gives me, my students and my children immediate access to knowledge, and the knowledge explosion is at the heart of the modernization and globalization of world society.   3

One in three Americans are regular, daily Internet users. Even within American society, the computer and e-mail have widened the gap between educated people (chiefly whites and Asians) and the less educated (chiefly black Americans). This gap will be felt in every aspect of life, whether it is in opportunities, potential, education or job-hunting. The United States will be divided into two groups, one which is computer-literate and the other which is not.   4

---

1. Robert Kaplan's book suggests that in most of the Third World conditions will get worse, largely because of the effects of overpopulation, environmental deterioration and social breakdown.

This phenomenon has been replicated at the international level. The most important fact is that we are in the midst of a technology revolution that seems less likely to close the gap between rich and poor countries than to widen the gap even further.

The technology revolution and the communications revolution still bypass billions of human beings. From UNESCO's standpoint, the Internet may have more influence than any single medium upon global educational and cultural developments in the coming century. Yet only 2.4 percent of the world's population is on the Internet, or one person out of 40. In Southeast Asia, only one person in 200 is linked to the Internet. In the Arab states, only one person in 500 has Internet access, while in Africa only one person in a 1,000 is an Internet user. This situation will not change as long as those lands lack electricity, telephone wires and infrastructure. They cannot afford either computers or the expensive software they require. If knowledge indeed equals power, the developing world may have less real power nowadays than it did 30 years ago, before the Internet was developed.

If we want to work toward a knowledge-based society in the coming century, over at least the next 10 years we need to make a concerted effort to bring poorer societies into the system of electronic communications. This effort will need to be coordinated by the World Bank, the UN Development Programme, UNESCO, the NGO community and the global business community.

The alternative is to perpetuate a world which is fundamentally undemocratic and structurally unsound. If we do nothing, if we let the knowledge explosion intensify in technology-rich societies while poorer societies fall further and further behind, the growing gap between haves and have-nots will lead to widespread discontent and threaten any prospect of global harmony and international understanding. This is the most significant challenge we face. We have no time to waste in responding.

Thinking About the Essay

1. Kennedy wrote this piece for the *UNESCO Courier,* an official publication of the United Nations. What internal evidence suggests his specialized audience? How does he manage to appeal to a broader secondary audience of readers? What thesis or argument does he want to convey to both audiences?

2. This essay is brief—similar in certain ways to the 500–750-word essays that you often are asked to write. What characteristics of Kennedy's piece could serve as a model for the brief essay?

3. How does Kennedy construct his argument? Where does he acknowledge opposing viewpoints, and how does he deal with them? Do you find the logic easy to follow and convincing? Why or why not?

4. Why does Kennedy introduce his personal voice into this essay?

5. What is the purpose of Kennedy's conclusion? Is it simply to convince, or are there other intentions at work?

Responding in Writing

6. Write a 500–750-word essay of your own entitled "The Electronic Gap." Make it an argumentative essay.

7. Kennedy writes about searching the Web for global information and contacts. In a personal essay, describe what you have learned about the world from your experience of the Internet, and what sort of global contacts you have established.

8. Do you think, as Kennedy warns, that the electronic gap could actually produce in the future a less democratic world? Consider this question in an analytical essay.

Networking

9. Go to the UNESCO website with another class member and scan current issues of the *UNESCO Courier*. What types of articles appear in this publication? What are its main concerns? Afterward, contribute to a class analysis of this publication.

10. Connect to a website such as eLibrary or InfoTrac, and download a list of articles that might contain information on the *electronic gap*. You might want to use terms other than *electronic gap* to complete this search. Tell the class about the nature of your search, the key words you employed, and the results.

A Map of the Network Society

ESTHER DYSON

Esther Dyson, who was born in Zurich, Switzerland, in 1941, is a deep thinker about the information age and the editor of one of the most influential newsletters in the computer industry, *Release 1.0*. Raised in Princeton, New Jersey, and educated at Harvard University, where she received a B.A. degree in economics in 1972, she is a frequent commentator on National Public Radio and a board member on numerous foundations, including the Institute for East/West Studies, Global Business Network, and the Eurasia Foundation. She also is president of Edventure Holdings and a managing partner of Edventure Ventures, a fund devoted to investments in information-oriented start-ups in Central and Eastern Europe. A self-described nomad, Dyson travels the world, looking for emerging trends in information technology and economics, new products, and new markets. With the publication of her book *Release 2.0: A Design for Living in the Digital Age* (1997), Dyson presented her ideas on the Internet and the culture it produces. In *Release 2.0,* she attempts to demystify the Internet and demonstrate how it can benefit education, commerce, the environment, and social relations. Dyson sees the Internet "as an environment for human beings, not as an alien or separate place." Hungary awarded Dyson the prestigious Von Neumann Medal in 1997 for her contributions to Eastern Europe's emerging computer market. This essay, which appeared in *New Perspectives Quarterly* in 1997, deals generally with the positive and negative power of the Internet and its relevance to developments in Eastern Europe.

Before Reading

Dyson claims that the Internet is "a powerful tool." What sort of "tool" do you think the Internet is? Could it be a tool for the good as well as the bad? Defend your response.

CYBERSPACE—Because I speculate about the Internet and am assumed 1 to have a social conscience, if only because I am female, people sometimes ask me whether the world is being divided into the wired haves and have-nots. I do not like to answer this question because it seems to imply that the Internet will make existing divisions worse: How can I babble on about the benefits it will bring if they come only to a limited elite?

The first point to understand is that few influential people involved 2 with the Internet claim it is a good in and of itself. It is a powerful tool for solving social problems, just as it is a tool for making money, finding lost relatives, receiving medical advice or, come to that, trading instructions for making bombs.

Precisely because it is such a powerful tool, it is incumbent on people 3 who want to change the world for the better to learn how to use it. As its use becomes more widespread, those without it will be at a disadvantage. So the question should not be "How can we encourage widespread adoption of this powerful tool by people whom it could benefit?" We should be asking how to help those still left behind.

But first, some background on the Internet and what it can and cannot 4 do. It is often likened to television or other mass media because it reaches a mass audience, at least in the United States. But it is more like a telephone system because it does not send information to everyone at random, but records conversations between individuals. Those conversations can then be read by thousands of other people.

Overall, the Internet is not so much a highway as an environment in 5
which an increasing amount of commerce and communication will take
place. It is not a monolithic environment either: It will have commercial
and non-profit sectors; those open to children and those limited to a few
members and sectors devoted to people with special interests.

At its worst the Internet is like a repository of the most inaccurate, ba- 6
nal and slanderous cocktail-party conversation. But at its best it allows intelligent people to discuss weighty issues among a large group without
regard to timing or geographical boundaries. It ties people together across
continents, gives programmers in India access to customers in the US and
helps victims of repression find a hearing outside their home countries.

What are we to do with this thing? Use it wisely, of course, and teach chil- 7
dren worldwide to do so. But access to the Internet is not a human right as,
say, access to education is or should be. Moreover, making it freely available
without providing the education to use it is pointless. Governments should
understand that the best way to foster the Internet is to allow it to grow commercially, encouraging cost-effective investment and competition.

If a government subsequently decides that a particular group in society 8
such as schools or hospitals needs Internet access, it should subsidize those
groups directly rather than providing access itself. When a government
"owns" the physical manifestation of the Internet within its borders, the
temptation to control it is hard to overcome.

Once you could achieve a semblance of equality by distributing land to 9
the peasants, or later by raising workers' salaries or even giving them profit-
sharing or a stock-ownership plan. But while such tactics may work in the
agricultural or industrial economy, they no longer work in the information
economy. People prosper less according to what they have in their hands or
bank accounts, and more according to what they can do with their minds.

This means that the task of fostering equality is more complex than a 10
simple redistribution of assets. Simply providing information does not do
the trick: people have to acquire the capacity to use it. The only feasible
way is education, a two-way process that requires participation from the
learner. Aside from law enforcement, it is about the most important job a
community can do. A free, privately owned press and information on the
Internet itself can continue the job for adults.

Education works best in the decentralized way fostered by the Internet, 11
yet the costs of access need to be spread broadly so that equal opportunities
are available to all, although people will make individual choices as to what
kind and level of education they want for their children and for themselves.

Although computers and the Net are important tools for education, 12
however, they cannot replace teachers as role models, mentors and moti-

vators. Children should learn to use the Internet as a tool for getting information and communicating with each other, just as adults do. But they need to get the basics of their moral and social education from their own families.

MORALS.COM: What will children find as they join the world of 13 work? First, it will not seem as foreign to them as it did to children in the industrial age, when adults worked in offices and factories. Many children are already writing programs or designing Web pages. The optimistic view is that more people will work from home, becoming closer to their families, and that the work itself will be more fulfilling, ecologically benign and productive. Such a trend could also foster home schooling, supplemented by Net educational resources. But the worker of the future may well hold several jobs at once, change jobs frequently and operate more as a freelance than as a loyal team member. This seems to be the norm in Silicon Valley, although companies such as Netscape and Hewlett Packard work hard to foster loyalty. In an increasingly competitive market where anyone can match salaries, the best long-term incentive for retaining employees is the presence of other people they respect and enjoy.

In fact, there will simply be a greater variety of arrangements. Some 14 people will enjoy the freedom to control their own careers and manage their own time. Others will find this mode of contract work scary, uncertain and alienating. And of course others, without the necessary skills, will be left out altogether.

Education will bear the burden of training people to operate in this new 15 world. And people will bear the burden of continuing their education throughout their lifetimes, ideally with some form of tax-advantaged education investment account. For those with the skills there should be ample work, whether it is managing online customer feedback services, designing new software, providing medical care or teaching children in a world that finally recognizes the importance of education.

People not properly prepared for this kind of world will become an in- 16 creasing problem for themselves and for the rest of society. Digital media are no panacea but they can contribute to solutions in a number of ways. These include supplementing teachers' efforts, letting children learn from other people and providing better sources of information about jobs, training and transport in disadvantaged communities. Because the physical channels themselves are relatively cheap, the capital costs of establishing community networks will be minimal for civic organizations, a situation that I hope will lead to a proliferation of such efforts.

The advent of the Internet will change the impact of geography. 17 One's future used to depend a great deal on the country of one's birth.

The Internet will create one large "country," a global marketplace not just for commerce but for ideas. Within each country, however, there will be a second marketplace cut off from the rest of the world. Those without connections to the world will be no more cut off than before, but their relative disadvantage will increase. Most members of the world community will be bilingual, speaking their mother tongue but using other international languages, of which the major one is English.

The challenge to each nation will be to help its citizens join the world community without leaving their home communities. For these lucky people the advantages will be great: higher salaries, more challenging and productive work and access to the rest of the world. Countries that try to cut their people off for whatever reason, such as political control, xenophobia or lack of investment, will doom themselves to second-rate status. Short-term inequality within each country should ultimately give way to greater benefits for the country as a whole as its citizens become more productive and able to market their labor and products worldwide. This benign view will never be fully realized, of course, but it is the goal for which we should strive. 18

The Internet's impact in Central and Eastern Europe will be very different than in the Third World. The countries of Central and Eastern Europe have highly literate populations able to make use of this technology to join the developed world. My own experience has been that in relative terms, the region is adopting this technology faster than Western Europe. 19

In Western Europe people generally take the attitude that if they already have faxes and portable phones for communication, why do they need the Internet? They have magazines, newspapers, libraries and assistants for information; advertising, representatives and distributors for markets. 20

In Central and Eastern Europe the Internet is seen not only as a source of information but as a way to appear closer to others than you really are. Let me illustrate. Some time ago, as part of the 24 Hours in Cyberspace project being presented at the 1997 World Economic Forum summit, I took a digital camera to the team at Poland Online. When I arrived in Warsaw and presented it with a flourish, people were crestfallen: This was a Macintosh camera and the equipment was Windows-based. 21

Marek Goschorski, Poland Online's chairman, sat in front of a workstation and called up the Kodak Web site. He quickly found instructions to download software that could reconfigure the camera to work with Windows. Had we been in the US he could have called Kodak's free 1–800 number probably 24 hours a day, seven days a week. In Germany, between the hours of nine and six on a weekday, he could have visited Kodak service center. But in Poland, before the Web, we would have been totally help- 22 less. What is a convenience in the US and a godsend in Germany is a true miracle in Poland.

And that is what the Web continues to be for many people, much of the 23 time. The good news is that it lets the elite, such as our team at Poland On-line, join in the world economy. The locals still do not have the commercial experience, business practices and infrastructure they need to compete on an equal basis, but at least they can be part of things. Companies online in Poland have access to the same information as companies online in Silicon Valley.

The challenge, of course, is how to encourage this good fortune to 24 trickle down to a broader sector of society. In Central and Eastern Europe, at least, it should be relatively easy. Start with computers in the schools and most children will take it from there. With the knowledge work they can perform on them, they will be able to take their place in the world economy relatively quickly—more quickly, indeed, than the illiterate dropout in Paris or the sweatshop child of the Third World.

Thinking About the Essay

1. How does Dyson define the Internet? What strategies for definition do you find in her essay?

2. Why does Dyson refer to her gender in the opening paragraph? What assumptions does she make about her audience and about her readers' understanding of the Internet? How does she adjust her style to meet the expectations of this audience?

3. How does Dyson organize her essay? What topics does she introduce, and in what sequence? How does she achieve geographic sweep to her coverage, and why does she do this?

4. Explain Dyson's use of comparison and contrast to frame some of her thoughts about the Internet. What parts of the essay benefit from this comparative strategy?

5. Why does Dyson focus on Eastern Europe in the closing section of the essay? Is this extended focus warranted? Why or why not?

Responding in Writing

6. Applying one of Dyson's rhetorical strategies, write a comparative essay in which you discuss the benefits and drawbacks of the Internet. Be certain to offer a definition of the Internet before proceeding to your comparative assessment.

7. Dyson states that "computers and the Net are important tools for education" (paragraph 12). Write an essay that expands upon her observation.

You may want to include information on the way in which computer technology affects your own education.

8. Write a narrative of your own experience with computers and the Internet. When did this experience begin? How advanced are you? Are you a novice, a geek, or somewhere in between?

Networking

9. Form the class into groups of four or five, and then select one part of the world in order to research the status of computers and the Internet in that region. You might want to focus, as Dyson does, on Eastern Europe, going to a site she mentions, Poland Online. Or you might want to research our own Silicon Valley in California or Silicon Alley in New York City. Report on your findings to the class.

10. Conduct an Internet search for biographical information on Esther Dyson. Be certain to consult the files in *Edventure Holdings, Release 1.0,* and *Wired,* along with any other sites you discover. Share your findings in class discussion.

Big Brother Is Us

JAMES GLEICK

James Gleick was born in New York City in 1954. He graduated from Harvard College in 1976 and worked for ten years as a reporter and editor for the *New York Times.* He was the founder and CEO of the Pipeline, one of the first Internet services. Gleick, whose writing has been published in more than two dozen languages, is a perceptive critic of the role of science and technology in contemporary society. He is the author of the bestselling *Chaos: Making a New Science* (1987), which explores the work of numerous scientists who are changing our understanding of the natural world. Gleick's next book, *Genius: The Life and Science of Richard Feynman* (1992), won a Pulitzer Prize. He has also written *Faster: The Acceleration of Just About Everything* (1999), an inquiry into our attempt to "save" time. Gleick says, "I really don't think of myself as a science writer. . . . I really see myself as a general non-fiction writer." In this essay, which appears in his collection *What Just Happened: A Chronicle of the Information Frontier* (2002), Gleick offers a sober, somewhat Orwellian set of prophecies about privacy in the new world of the Internet.

Before Reading

The Internet is a powerful tool for information gathering. What do you think those Big Brothers hiding behind the Net know about you?

For much of the twentieth century, 1984 was a year that belonged to the future—a strange, gray future at that. Then it slid painlessly into the past, like any other year. Big Brother arrived and settled in, though not at all in the way George Orwell had imagined. 1

Underpinning Orwell's 1948 anti-utopia—with its corruption of language and history, its never-ending nuclear arms race and its totalitarianism of torture and brainwashing—was the utter annihilation of privacy. Its single technological innovation, in a world of pig iron and pneumatic tubes and broken elevators, was the telescreen, transmitting the intimate sights and sounds of every home to the Thought Police. BIG BROTHER IS WATCHING YOU. "You had to live—did live, from habit that became instinct—" Orwell wrote, "in the assumption that every sound you made was overheard, and, except in darkness, every movement scrutinized." 2

It has turned out differently. We have had to wait a bit longer for interactive appliances to arrive in our bedrooms. Our telescreens come with hundreds of channels but no hidden cameras. If you want a device with a microphone to record and transmit your voice, you are better off with a multimedia PC or, for that matter, a dedicated Internet connection: hook up your camera and turn on the switch that Winston Smith could never turn off. People in large numbers are doing just this: acting out their private lives before online cameras, accessible to the world. Grim though Orwell's vision was, it never encompassed the Dan-O-Cam (H. Dan Smith at work in his office in Fresno, California), the LivingRoomCam (watch children and pets at play: "personal publishing of personal spaces"), and scores of similar Internet "cams"—evidence that some citizens of the twenty-first century, anyway, will not be grieving over their loss of privacy. 3

And yet . . . 4

Information-gathering about individuals has reached an astounding level of completeness, if not actual malevolence. So has fear of information-gathering, if not among the broad public, at least among those who pay attention to privacy as an issue of law and technology. Hundreds of privacy organizations, newsletters, annual conferences, information clearing-houses, mailing lists, and Web sites have sprung into existence—a societal immune-system response. 5

The rapid rise of the Internet surpasses the grimmest forecasts of interconnectedness among all these computer dossiers. Yet it defies those forecasts as well. Strangely enough, the linking of computers has taken place 6 democratically, even anarchically. Its rules and habits are emerging in the open light, rather than behind the closed doors of security agencies or corporate operations centers. It is clear that technology has the power not just to invade privacy but to protect it, through encryption, for example, which will be available to everyone, as soon as the government steps out of the way. The balance of power has already shifted from those who break codes—eavesdroppers and intelligence agencies—to those who wish to use them. In these closing years of the century, we are setting the laws and customs of a future built on networked communication, giant interlinked databases, electronic commerce, and digital cash. Historians will see our time as a time of transition. But transition to what?

"There's a very important and long-term debate taking place right now   7
about technologies of privacy in the next century," says Marc Rotenberg, director of the Electronic Privacy Information Center in Washington. "Privacy will be to the information economy of the next century what consumer protection and environmental concerns have been to the industrial society of the twentieth century."

Privacy is a construct of our age. As a tradition in law, it is young. When   8
Louis Brandeis issued his famous opinion in 1928 that privacy is "the right to be let alone—the most comprehensive of rights, and the right most valued by civilized men," he was looking to the future, because he was dissenting; the Supreme Court's majority was upholding the right of the police to tap telephone lines without warrants.

"In the beginning, there was no such thing as private life, no refuge   9
from the public gaze and its ceaseless criticism," writes Theodore Zeldin, a social historian, in *An Intimate History of Humanity.* Then, he says, "the middle classes began cultivating secrets." In villages and small towns, the secret life was rare. The neighbors knew far more about one's intimacies, from breakfast habits to clandestine affairs, than in any city of the twentieth century. One's shield, if a shield was needed, was a formal civility: rules of discourse that discouraged questions about money or sex. The pathological case of the private person was the hermit—hermits, by and large, have disappeared. The word is quaint. In a crowd, we can all be hermits now.

"Privacy means seeing only people whom one chooses to see," adds   10
Zeldin.

"The rest do not exist, except as ghosts or gods on television, the great   11
protector of privacy."

In public opinion surveys, Americans always favor privacy. Then they   12
turn around and sell it cheaply. Most vehemently oppose any suggestion of

a national identification system yet volunteer their telephone numbers and mothers' maiden names and even—grudgingly or not—Social Security numbers to merchants bearing discounts or Web services offering "membership" privileges. For most, the abstract notion of privacy suggests a mystical, romantic, cowboy-era set of freedoms. Yet in the real world it boils down to matters of small convenience. Is privacy about government security agents decrypting your e-mail and then kicking down the front door with their jackboots? Or is it about telemarketers interrupting your supper with cold calls?

It depends. Mainly, of course, it depends on whether you live in a to- 13 talitarian or a free society. If the government is nefarious or unaccountable to individuals—or if you believe it is—the efficient ideal of easy-to-use, perfectly linked and comprehensive national databases must be frightening indeed. But if, deep down, you feel secure in your relations with the state, then perhaps you are willing to let your guard down: put off till tomorrow your acquisition of that encryption software, send your e-mail in the clear, perhaps even set up an Internet camera at the kitchen table or discuss your sexual history with Oprah.

Certainly where other people's privacy is concerned, we seem willing to 14 lower our standards. We have become a society with a cavernous appetite for news and gossip. Our era has replaced the tacit, eyes-averted civility of an earlier time with exhibitionism and prying. Even borderline public figures must get used to the nation's eyes in their bedrooms and pocketbooks. That's not Big Brother watching. It's us.

Like any gossip, we trade information to get information. Over in the ad- 15 vanced research laboratories of the consumer electronics companies, futurists are readying little boxes that they believe you would like to carry around—not just telephones but perfect two-way Internet-connected pocket pals. They could use Global Positioning System satellites so that you always know where you are. They could let the Network know too: then the Network could combine its knowledge of your block-by-block location and your customary 2 A.M. hankering for sushi to beam live restaurant guidance to your pocket pal. Surely you don't mind if the Network knows all this.

It knows much more, of course. Here is what exists about you in gov- 16 ernment and corporate computers, even if you are not a particularly active (or unlucky) participant in the wired and unwired economy:

- Your health history; your credit history; your marital history; your educational history; your employment history.
- The times and telephone numbers of every call you make and receive.

- The magazines you subscribe to and the books you borrow from the library.
- Your travel history: you can no longer travel by air without presenting photographic identification; in a world of electronic fare cards tracking frequent-traveler data, computers could list even your bus and subway rides.
- The trail of your cash withdrawals.
- All your purchases by credit card or check. In a not-so-distant future, when electronic cash becomes the rule, even the purchases you still make by bills and coins could be logged.
- What you eat. No sooner had supermarket scanners gone online—to speed checkout efficiency—than data began to be tracked for marketing purposes. Large chains now invite customers to link personal identifying information with the records of what they buy, in exchange for discount cards or other promotions.
- Your electronic mail and your telephone messages. If you use a computer at work, your employer has the legal right to look over your shoulder while you type. More and more companies are quietly spot-checking workers' e-mail and even voice mail. In theory—though rarely in practice—even an online service or private Internet service provider could monitor you. "Anyway," advises a Web site at, naturally, paranoia.com, "you should assume that everything you do online is monitored by your service provider."
- Where you go, what you see on the World Wide Web. Ordinarily Net exploring is an anonymous activity, but many information services ask users to identify themselves and even to provide telephone numbers and other personal information. Once a user does that, his or her activity can be traced in surprising detail. Do you like country music? Were you thinking about taking a vacation in New Zealand? Were you perusing the erotic-books section of the online bookstore? Someone—some computer, anyway—probably already knows.

Many of these personal facts are innocuous in themselves. Some are 17 essentially matters of public record. What matters is mere efficiency—linkage. Your birth certificate was never private; it was always available to someone willing to stand in line and pay a few dollars to a clerk at town hall. Computers and telephone lines make that a bit more convenient, that's all—but it turns out that proficiency in compilation, sorting, and distribution can give sinister overtones to even simple collections of names and addresses. A Los Angeles television reporter, to make a point, recently bought a list of 5,000 children, with ages, addresses and phone numbers, in the name of Richard Allen Davis, the convicted murderer of a twelve-year-old girl. The company that sold the list, Metromail, boasts of compiling consumer information on 90 percent of United States households.

To David Burnham, the former *New York Times* reporter who wrote 18 the admonitory *Rise of the Computer State* more than a decade ago, this inexorably more detailed compiling of information about individuals amounted to one thing: surveillance. "The question looms before us," he wrote. "Can the United States continue to flourish and grow in an age when the physical movements, individual purchases, conversations and meetings of every citizen are constantly under surveillance by private companies and government agencies?" And he added, "Does not surveillance, even the innocent sort, gradually poison the soul of a nation?" Does it? If so, we're like sheep to the slaughter.

The right to be left alone—privacy on Brandeis's terms—is not exactly the 19 same as the right to vanish, the right to act in society without leaving traces, and the right to assume a false identity. Most privacy experts who have studied the possible futures of electronic money favor versions that allow for the anonymity of cash rather than the traceability of checks and credit cards. That is appealing; we ought to be able to make a contribution to a dissident political organization without fear of exposure.

Still, the people with the greatest daily, practical need for untraceable 20 cash are criminals: tax cheats, drug dealers, bribers, and extortionists.

Most drivers prove willing to use an electronic card to pass through 21 tollbooths without worrying about whether a database is logging their movements. Yet if cards like these replaced cash altogether, the net around us would unquestionably be drawn a notch tighter—especially if we are lying to our employers or spouses about our whereabouts, or if we are simply planning to take it on the lam, Bonnie and Clyde–style.

In a past world of intimate small towns, people could disappear. The 22 mere possibility was an essential aspect of privacy, in Rotenberg's view: "People left those small towns and re-emerged in other towns and created new identities." Could you disappear today: abandon all the computerized trappings of your identity, gather enough cash, vanish without leaving a trail and start life again? Probably not. Certainly, there have never been so many invisible chains to the life you now lead.

On the Internet, we are re-creating a small-town world, where people 23 mingle and share news easily and informally. But this time it is just one town.

Some of its residents advocate rights not just to passive privacy, the 24 right to be left alone, but to what might be called aggressive privacy: the right to retain anonymity even while acting with force and consequence on a broad public stage.

Passive privacy is the kind elegantly described by the Fourth Amend- 25 ment: "the right of the people to be secure in their persons, houses, papers, and effects, against unreasonable searches and seizures." We do have a lot of papers and effects these days.

Aggressive privacy implies much more. Telephone regulatory commis- 26 sions have listened to arguments that people have a right to remain anonymous, hiding their own numbers when placing telephone calls. On the Internet, surprising numbers of users insist on a right to hide behind false names while engaging in verbal harassment or slander.

The use of false online identities has emerged as a cultural phenome- 27 non. Those who cannot reinvent a new self in real life can easily do so online. Sometimes they are experimenting with role playing. Most often, though, as a practical reality, the use of false identity on the Internet has an unsavory flavor: marketers sending junk mail from untraceable sources; speculators or corporate insiders trying to influence stock prices; people violating copyrights or engaging in character assassination.

Changing personae like clothing—is that what the demand for pri- 28 vacy will come to mean? It's a game for people who choose a form of existence impossible in the old world, maybe hermits at that, hiding in digitally equipped homes, visiting by telecam. Something has been lost after all, in the rush to modernity: the chance to mingle freely and thoughtlessly in our communities, exposing our faces and brushing hands with neighbors who know what we had for breakfast and will remember if we lie about it.

In compensation, our reach is thousands of times longer. We meet 29 people, form communities, make our voices heard with a freedom unimaginable to a small-towner of the last century. But we no longer board airplanes or enter schools and courthouses secure in our persons and effects; we submit, generally by choice, to the most intrusive of electronic searches. In banks, at toll-booths, in elevators, in doorways, alongside highways, near public telephones, we submit to what used to be called surveillance. In Orwell's country, thousands of closed-circuit cameras are trained on public streets—pan, zoom, and infrared. Every suitcase bomb in a public park brings more cameras and, perhaps, more digital hermits.

We turn those cameras on ourselves. Then we beg for more gossip. We 30 invent diamond-hard technologies of encryption, but we rarely bother to use them.

If we want to live freely and privately in the interconnected world of the 31
twenty-first century—and surely we do—perhaps above all we need a revival of the small-town civility of the nineteenth century. Manners, not devices: sometimes it's just better not to ask, and better not to look.

Thinking About the Essay

1. This essay presupposes a basic knowledge about George Orwell. What information does Gleick provide for readers who know nothing about Orwell?
   How does he use references to Orwell to structure his essay?

2. What is Gleick's thesis? In what place (or places) does he state it?

3. Gleick divides his essay into four parts. What subject or topic dominates
   each part? How are these sections interconnected?

4. Identify the types of illustration that Gleick employs in this essay. What is
   the cumulative effect?

5. In the final analysis, what is the overall tone of Gleick's essay? Is he pessimistic, hopeful, cautiously optimistic, fatalistic, or what? Does the tone
   vary from section to section? Explain your response.

Responding in Writing

6. Write an essay entitled "BIG BROTHER IS WATCHING YOU." Connect the title to your understanding of the Internet and how it can be used to violate
   your privacy.

7. How can the Internet—as Gleick suggests—assist in the formation of
   "communities"? What are the implications of this electronic force for the
   preservation or creation of democracies around the world? Write an essay
   exploring this issue.

8. Gleick wrote this essay in 1996. Would you say that he was as prophetic
   as George Orwell? Why or why not? Answer this question in a brief essay.
   Conduct research on Orwell if necessary.

Networking

9. Discuss in groups of four or five class members some of the main issues
   concerning privacy and the Internet raised by Gleick. Have each member relate any instances in which his or her privacy has been violated by Internet
   intrusions. Consider strategies to protect your privacy in the Internet era.

10. Use the Internet to locate information on George Orwell's *1984*. Read
    or reread the book (or watch a film version). Then discuss in class the
    ways in which Orwell's vision of the future might relate to "information-
    gathering" today.

Webbed, Wired, and Worried

THOMAS L. FRIEDMAN

A noted author, journalist, and television commentator, and currently a columnist for the *New York Times,* Thomas L. Friedman writes and speaks knowledgeably about contemporary trends in politics and global development. He was born in Minneapolis, Minnesota, in 1953, and educated at Brandeis University (B.A., 1975) and St. Anthony's College, Oxford (M.A., 1978). Friedman covered the Middle East for the *New York Times* for ten years, and for five years he was bureau chief in Beirut, writing about both the Lebanese civil war and the Israel-Palestine conflict. He recorded these experiences in *From Beirut to Jerusalem* (1989), for which he won the National Book Award. A strong proponent of American intervention to solve seemingly intractable problems in the Arab-Israeli conflict, Friedman writes at the end of *From Beirut to Jerusalem,* "Only a real friend tells you the truth about yourself. An American friend has to help jar these people out of their fantasies by constantly holding up before their eyes the mirror of reality." In 2002, Friedman received the Pulitzer Prize for commentary for his reporting on terrorism for the *New York Times*. His other books include *The Lexus and the Olive Tree* (2000) and a collection of articles and essays, *Longitudes and Attitudes: America in the Age of Terrorism** (2002), which includes the following essay.

Before Reading

After the events of 9/11, do you think that access to the Internet should be limited, monitored, or controlled? If so, how? If not, why not?

Ever since I learned that Mohamed Atta made his reservation for September 11 using his laptop and the American Airlines Web site, and that several of his colleagues used Travelocity.com, I've been wondering how the entrepreneurs of Silicon Valley were looking at the 9/11 tragedy— whether it was giving them any pause about the wired world they've been building and the assumptions they are building it upon.   1

In a recent visit to Stanford University and Silicon Valley, I had a chance to pose these questions to techies. I found that at least some of their   2 libertarian technology-will-solve-everything cockiness was gone. I found a much keener awareness that the unique web of technologies Silicon Valley was building before 9/11—from the Internet to powerful encryption software—can be incredible force multipliers for individuals and small groups to do both good and evil. And I found an acknowledgment that all those technologies had been built with a high degree of trust as to how they would be used, and that that trust had been shaken. In its place is a greater appreciation that high-tech companies aren't just threatened by their competitors—but also by some of their users.

"The question 'How can this technology be used against me?' is now a   3
real R-and-D issue for companies, where in the past it wasn't really even being asked," said Jim Hornthal, a former vice chairman of Travelocity.com. "People here always thought the enemy was Microsoft, not Mohamed Atta."

It was part of Silicon Valley lore that successful innovations would fol-   4
low a well-trodden path beginning with early adopters, then early mass-appeal users, and finally the mass market. But it's clear now that there is also a parallel criminal path—starting with the early perverters of a new technology up to the really twisted perverters. For instance, the 9/11 hijackers may have communicated globally through steganography software, which lets users e-mail, say, a baby picture that secretly contains a 300-page compressed document or even a voice message.

"We have engineered large parts of our system on an assumption of   5
trust that may no longer be accurate," said Stanford law professor Joseph A. Grundfest. "Trust is hard-wired into everything from computers to the Internet to building codes. What kind of building codes you need depends on what kind of risks you thought were out there. The odds of someone flying a passenger jet into a tall building were zero before. They're not anymore. The whole objective of the terrorists is to reduce our trust in all the normal instruments and technologies we use in daily life. You wake up in the morning and trust that you can get to work across the Brooklyn Bridge—don't. This is particularly dangerous because societies which have a low degree of trust are backward societies."

Silicon Valley staunchly opposed the Clipper Chip, which would have   6
given the government a back-door key to all U.S. encrypted data. Now some wonder whether they shouldn't have opposed it. John Doerr, the venture capitalist, said, "Culturally, the Valley was already maturing before 9/11, but since then it's definitely developed a deeper respect for leaders and government institutions."

At Travelocity, Mr. Hornthal noted, whether the customer was Mo-   7
hamed Atta or Bill Gates, "our only responsibility was to authenticate your financial ability to pay. Did your name and credit card match your billing address? It was not our responsibility, nor did we have the ability, to au-

thenticate your intent with that ticket, which requires a much deeper sense
of identification. It may be, though, that this is where technology will have
to go—to allow a deeper sense of identification."

Speaking of identity, Bethany Hornthal, a marketing consultant, noted 8
that Silicon Valley had always been a multicultural place where young people felt they could go anywhere in the world and fit in. They were global
kids. "Suddenly after 9/11, that changed," she said. "Suddenly they were
Americans, and there was a certain danger in that identity. [As a result] the
world has become more defined and restricted for them. Now you ask,
Where is it safe to go as an American?" So there is this sense, she concluded, that thanks to technology and globalization, "the world may have
gotten smaller—but I can't go there anymore."

Or as my friend Jack Murphy, a venture capitalist, mused to me as we 9
discussed the low state of many high-tech investments, "Maybe I should
have gone into the fence business instead."

May 26, 2002

Thinking About the Essay

1. Friedman wrote this essay as an op-ed piece for the *New York Times;* thus
   we know something about his audience. But what is his purpose? What thesis does he present?

2. How do we know that Friedman uses a reporter's skills to develop this article? What evidence can you identify to support your response?

3. What is unusual about the introductory paragraph? How effective is it as an
   introduction? Explain your response.

4. Why does Friedman journey to Silicon Valley to conduct his research? What
   assumptions do we bring to our reading when the writer alludes to Silicon
   Valley? How does Friedman present the "myths" about this location?

5. How does Friedman establish a global context for his inquiry into the attitudes of the Silicon Valley spokespersons he quotes in the essay? How
   does he emphasize this context throughout the article?

Responding in Writing

6. Censorship of the Internet is a large and complex issue. Write an essay in
   which you focus on one aspect of Net censorship—for example, child
   pornography—and argue for or against restrictions.

7. Friedman quotes a Stanford law professor as saying that "societies which
   have a low degree of trust are backward societies." Does this mean that
   we should "trust" the digital revolution uncritically? Answer this question in
   an argumentative essay.

8. Analyze Friedman's article as a model of journalistic commentary. Focus on audience, style, methodology, and content.

Networking

9. In a group of three, write a collaborative op-ed article for your college newspaper on terrorist use of the Internet. Agree on a thesis or claim, and then work together to produce the piece. As with all newspaper writing, give yourselves a strict time frame to complete the article—twenty-four hours.

10. Friedman writes compellingly about the forces of tradition and globalization in *The Lexus and the Olive Tree.* Go online and find information and reviews of this book. Take notes for a possible discussion of the issues that Friedman raises in this text.

Fear, the New Virus of a Connected Era

MICHIKO KAKUTANI

Michiko Kakutani is widely recognized as an influential book critic and cultural commentator. For more than a decade she has been a reviewer for the *New York Times,* producing artful and provocative assessments of today's writers. Kakutani has a wide-ranging grasp of trends in literature, art, the media, and culture. Displaying sharp intellect and precise style, her reviews and essays seek the essence of a subject or reveal unique perspectives on pivotal events. Here, in an article from the *New York Times* in 2001, she offers insights into our digital world from the other side of the September 11 divide.

Before Reading

Kakutani introduces us to a word—*meme* (pronounced "meem")—and applies it to our digital world. A meme is a powerful idea or image that spreads through instant messaging. The Twin Towers is a tragic example of this concept. What *memes* have you encountered recently on the Internet? How do you respond to them, participate in them, or spread them?

In that distant world far, far away that was America before Sept. 11, much 1 was written about how the Internet and cable television were creating a newly fragmented, decentralized world—a culturally splintered world of niche marketing, special-interest publications and identity politics. As one

1990's survey of Internet politics concluded, virtual communities "resemble the semiprivate spaces of modern health clubs more than the public spaces of agoras": "instead of meeting to discuss and debate issues of common concern to the society, members of these virtual communities meet largely to promote their own interests and to reinforce their own like-mindedness."

As a result, the cultural critic David Shenk wrote in his book *Data Smog,* "It appears that rather than our world becoming a cozy village, we are instead retreating into an electronic Tower of Babel, a global skyscraper. Instead of gathering us into the town square, the new information technology clusters us into social cubicles. There are fewer central spaces, and not even a common channel." 2

All this changed in the wake of Sept. 11. The terrorist attacks not only unified the nation in obvious ways—provoking a shared sense of anger and grief, a rallying around the president and the flag, an initial urge to put partisan politics aside—but also created a ripple effect that moved across the land like a tsunami, revealing just how interconnected the country really is. 3

In the weeks after the World Trade Center disaster, Alaskan fishermen reported a 15 percent drop in the sales of halibut, as high-end restaurant orders contracted and shipments were disrupted by the temporary closing of the Fulton Fish Market in Manhattan. Meatpackers and bakeries in Minnesota and dairy cooperatives in Wisconsin were affected by the decision of Northwest Airlines in the days following the terrorist attacks to cancel most inflight meals. As for shoe manufacturers, one report indicated a 30 percent dip in the sales of high heels and a 40 percent dip in platform-shoe sales, as women—presumably worried about having to run for their lives—began turning to more sensible footwear. 4

Because all of America was affected by the events of Sept. 11, the Internet and 24-cable news shows quickly assumed the role of electronic town halls. But if those forms of communication initially brought the country together in displays of public grieving—through broadcasts of memorial services and Web site tributes to the victims—they have more lately become national forums for the expression of anxiety. 5

In the past, television brought the Vietnam conflict home to our living rooms, thereby accelerating, by many accounts, opposition to the war. With the Persian Gulf war, it enhanced an illusion of control and low-risk assault by showing us video-game images of smart bombs precisely destroying their targets. In contrast, the current war in Afghanistan has yielded fewer visuals, and talk on television and the Internet has focused more and more on fears of another terrorist attack at home—fears 6 that have been magnified by the electronic media's dynamic of feedback and iteration.

In the first weeks after Sept. 11, images of the second plane hitting the 7
World Trade Center, along with images of the towers collapsing, were played over and over again on television, goading people to relive those horrors. In the last two weeks (during which the F.B.I. responded to more than 2,300 reports of suspected anthrax or other dangerous substances) a new set of recycled images is being broadcast: shots of anthrax bacteria multiplying in petri dishes, and haz-mat inspectors in gas masks and protective suits examining suspected sites.

With 52 percent of Americans, according to one poll, saying they could 8
imagine themselves or a loved one being victims of a terrorist attack, talk online and onscreen has increasingly revolved around worries of bioterrorism. On MSNBC.com, for instance, people voiced an imaginative array of fears that could easily prove contagious. Someone from Mesa, Ariz., wondered if "terrorists working as production workers" could "contaminate consumer goods"—like cosmetics, vitamins, baby powder—"during manufacture." Someone from Coral Springs, Fla., worried that smallpox could be spread by "suicide disease carriers" walking around and infecting thousands. And someone from Massillon, Ohio, raised the possibility of the white powder used inside latex gloves being contaminated with anthrax.

False e-mail rumors—ranging from the loony ("Images of the World 9
Trade Center fire reveal the face of Satan!") to the portentous ("blue envelopes from the Klingerman Foundation containing sponges saturated with a deadly virus are being anonymously mailed to random Americans")—began to circulate with such virulence that several Web sites (including snopes2.com and truthorfiction.com) set up special pages to assess the veracity of such terrorist-related "urban legends." And with his "Nightline Fact Check," Ted Koppel has repeatedly tried to debunk widespread e-mails, including one about a woman whose Afghan former boyfriend warned her not to fly on Sept. 11 and not to visit any malls on Oct. 31; and another reporting that more than 30 Ryder, U-Haul and Verizon trucks had been stolen, many by individuals of Arab descent.

"It's like emptying the ocean with a spoon," Mr. Koppel observed. 10
"These are boom times for idiots with a misplaced sense of humor or malice."

They are boom times, of course, because in a day when the F.B.I. itself 11
is issuing ominously vague warnings about imminent terrorist attacks, it's harder to tell legitimate worries from out-and-out paranoia. Given the discovery of anthrax in Florida, New York City, New Jersey and Washington, given the decision of the House of Representatives to adjourn for five days

because of an anthrax scare, there is fear now in a handful of dust, in a handful of baby powder or pudding mix or artificial sweetener.

Before Sept. 11, it was easy enough for anyone with a little common sense to shrug off the nuttier rumors and conspiracy theories that flourish on the Net—the Area 51 UFO warnings, the Jimmy Hoffa sightings, the Hale-Bopp comet fantasies of the Heaven's Gate cult—but these days, when things once thought unimaginable (the twin towers' being brought down by hijacked airplanes, anthrax turning up in the mail) have come to pass, it's harder to separate the hysterical from the plausible. Indeed, recent television broadcasts by two usually sober news shows had a sensationalistic, what-if quality to them: "Nightline" staged a fictional scenario about an anthrax attack on a city's subway system, while "60 Minutes" did a segment on the dangers of a terrorist attack on the nation's nuclear power plants.   12

Uncertainty provides just the sort of environment in which rumors thrive, of course, and the Internet by its very nature tends to incubate ideas that might otherwise fade away. In Marshall McLuhan's terms, the Internet is a "cool" medium—leaving "much to be filled in or completed by the audience"—and by democratizing information, it gives equal weight to the opinions of specialists, ignoramuses and zealots, allowing users to pull in whatever data they want through their computers. Among the things that can be viewed on the Web today are recruitment videos from Al Qaeda and terrorist tradecraft tips from Osama bin Laden's followers, who have proven themselves remarkably adept at using the Internet to spread their message around the world.   13

What people tend to pull in from the Internet and television are those ideas and images they find most compelling; these "memes"—to use a term coined by the evolutionary biologist Richard Dawkins back in 1976—then spread from person to person through conversations, e-mails, bulletin boards, chat rooms and instant messages. What makes a meme spread quickly enough to cause a cultural epidemic? In the book *Thought Contagion,* Aaron Lynch suggested that anxiety-inducing memes tend to spread more quickly than others, because their carriers are driven by an urgent need to proselytize. And in *The Tipping Point,* Malcolm Gladwell argued that the "stickiness" of an idea—its irresistibility—is a crucial factor.   14

The fear of a Y2K meltdown was a meme that flourished right before the millennium. The vogue for low-riding jeans was a meme that seized hold of teenagers. The fascination with Monica Lewinsky was a meme embraced by the chattering classes in a more innocent time.   15

The fear of anthrax infection is a very real and legitimate worry in an America still recovering from Sept. 11 and reeling from new reports of ex-   16 posure. At the same time, however, it is also a remarkably hardy and widespread meme that has taken hold of the nation's collective unconscious—a mind virus spread by word of mouth and amplified by our electronic media, an epidemic that has united the country, but united it in anxiety and dread.

Thinking About the Essay

1. Why does Kakutani begin the essay with the phrase "In that distant world far, far away that was America before Sept. 11"? What does this phrase remind you of? How does she use the opening sentence to frame her first two paragraphs?

2. What simile does Kakutani create in the third paragraph? What point does she want to make from this comparison? What other forms of figurative language can you locate in the essay? What other aspects of her style do you find interesting?

3. Kakutani wrote this essay shortly after the events of September 11. What details and events tend to "date" this piece? Do you think this topicality reduces the quality of the essay? Why or why not? She also refers to writers, thinkers, and books. What does she presuppose about her readers? Are you put off by these references or interested in them? Explain your response.

4. How does the writer establish a connection between television and the Internet, and how does she use this comparative element to structure the body of her essay?

5. Is there one place where Kakutani establishes her thesis, or do we have to infer it from various signals throughout the essay? Justify your response.

Responding in Writing

6. Write an essay on a *meme* that has preoccupied you recently. Make special reference to its appearance on the Internet or in the media.

7. Kakutani writes about the power of the Internet to either bring us together as a community or separate us from each other. Present both sides of the argument in a comparative essay, but be certain to finally state your own position, paying special attention to reinforcing this position, as Kakutani does, in your concluding paragraph.

8. How do "talk" online and talk on television reinforce each other? Investigate this question in an essay that offers specific examples from the Internet and from talk programs on Fox, CNN, CNBC, or other channels.

Networking

9. With three other class members, discuss the implications of Kakutani's assertion—suggested throughout the essay and explicitly in the last

paragraph—that the nation after September 11 is susceptible to a "mind virus." Would you agree or disagree? Has this virus infected any member of your group? Appoint one member to represent your group in a class panel discussion.

10. Locate a site on the Net that projects a specific *meme* or, alternately, a "mind virus." Report on your findings in class discussion.

Silicon Snake Oil

CLIFFORD STOLL

Clifford Stoll is an astronomer who in recent years has become better known as a pioneering investigator of the computer world. Born in 1950 in Buffalo, New York, he received his B.A. degree from the University of Buffalo (1973) and a Ph.D. degree from the University of Arizona (1980). He has been affiliated with the Space Telescope Institute in Baltimore, the Lawrence Berkeley Laboratory's Keck Observatory, and the Harvard Smithsonian Institute for Astrophysics. Stoll has been involved with computer networking systems since their inception and has consistently stated that he is "deeply ambivalent" about the information highway. His first book, *The Cuckoo's Egg: Tracking a Spy Through the Maze of Computer Espionage* (1989), the story of how he discovered and tracked a German spy operating over the Internet, made him a bestselling author. His next book, *Silicon Snake Oil: Second Thoughts on the Information Highway* (1995), offers an amusing but ultimately serious critique of the dangers of computer technology, especially in education, a topic he pursues in another book, *High-Tech Heretic: Why Computers Don't Belong in the Classroom and Other Reflections by a Computer Contrarian* (1999). Stoll's feisty, conversational style makes him, as one critic observes, "a prophet crying out in the high-tech universe." The following selection is the first chapter *of Silicon Snake Oil*, which Stoll, in his typically wry fashion, entitles "A Speleological Introduction to the Author's Ambivalence."

Before Reading

What do you know about Multi-User Dungeons (MUDs)? Are you—or someone you know—frequent participants in them? Why are they so fascinating? What are their inherent dangers?

It's some caving trip: Far below you is an active volcano from which great gouts of molten lava come surging out, cascading back down into the depths. The glowing rock fills the farthest reaches of the cavern with a blood-red glare, giving everything an eerie, macabre appearance. The air is filled with flickering sparks of ash and a heavy smell of brimstone. Embedded in the jagged roof far overhead are myriad twisted formations composed of pure white alabaster, which scatter the murky light into sinister apparitions on the walls. To one side is a deep gorge filled with a bizarre chaos of tortured rock that seems to have been crafted by the devil himself. An immense river of fire crashes out from the depths of the volcano, burns its way through the gorge, and plummets into a bottom pit far off to your left. The far right wall is aflame with an incandescence of its own, which lends an additional infernal splendor to the already hellish scene.

Yow—this is heady stuff. The year: 1976. I'd just started graduate school at the University of Arizona in Tucson. Next to me is a homebrew computer with a row of toggle switches on the front panel. I've fired up a computer game called Adventure, written by Will Crowther and Don Wood. The object is to explore a cave and find hidden treasures. 1

I watch this purple passage scroll across my beat-up TV monitor. It's an early virtual-reality game, though that term, along with *Internet* and *cyberpunk,* has not yet been invented. I'm wasting time, the main occupation of grad students. 2

Nearly twenty years have passed. Today, nobody plays Adventure. It's been supplanted by MUDs—Multi-User Dungeons—where you not only explore programmed worlds, but interact with other users as well. These games are virtual realities over the Internet. Like their predecessor, these fantasy role-playing games are creatively programmed with tantalizing clues to solve dangerous quests. 3

Still, when it comes to caves, I've been swallowed up by the real thing, and it's far scarier and much muddier than anything you'll find on a computer screen. 4

But go back to 1976. Something didn't quite feel authentic about the words that flickered across my primitive screen. Alabaster in a lava cave? It didn't jibe with what I'd heard in my geology class. Basalt maybe. But not a carbonate rock. 5

So I ask the guy in the next cubicle. He's wearing a Hawaiian floral shirt, cutoff jeans, and no shoes. On his desk, a stack of physics texts, a slide rule, and a couple of stale burritos. His name is written on the side of a *Boy Scout Handbook:* Jon Gradie. 6

Jon looks up from a photomap of Mars. "Funny you should ask about cave formations," he replies. "I know a great cave fifty miles south of here. 7

It makes the lunar highlands look like a parking lot. C'mon along and see for yourself."

I've hardly met this guy—do I trust him enough to lead an expedition 8 through a maze of stalagmites, rubble, and guano? As an astronomer, he might know his way around the asteroid belt, but that doesn't mean much a hundred feet under a slab of Arizona limestone.

On the other hand, four other grad students were already planning to 9 go, and Jon promised a side trip to the core-mantle boundary. He also mentioned bringing along several members of the opposite sex. This was during Tucson's great woman shortage, so the question was settled.

Now, real cavers bring helmets, rope, three sources of light, and an experienced leader. We had baseball caps, a ball of string, a couple of feeble flashlights, and Jon Gradie. 10

Cave of the Bells is two miles up a dry gulch, down the slope from the 11 multimirror observatory. (Around Tucson, every hiking trail is downslope from some observatory.) There's barrel cactus along the way; nearby, a bird is singing.

"Just follow me," Jon tells us. "I came here with my fraternity three 12 years ago." This explains the beer bottles near the entrance, but doesn't exactly inspire confidence. Neither does the rattlesnake, hissing by the hole in the limestone wall. Jon waves a long stick, and it slithers away.

I'm wearing a grubby T-shirt, faded jeans, and cheap sneakers—same 13 as in class. We climb down a knotted rope into a pitch-black cavern that smells dank. The flashlights don't help much, and neither does one of the women, who's already babbling about claustrophobia. Still, we start in, trailing a string through the muddy tunnel—everything's covered with gunk, as are the six of us crawling behind Jon. Not your ordinary slimy, brown, backyard mud, either. This is the goop of inner-earth that works its way into your hair, socks, and underwear.

"This cave is easy," Jon explains as he crawls ahead of us. "It goes all 14 the way until it quits." Through twenty feet of tunnel, all I see of him is the bottoms of his shoes.

The ball of string is patently stupid: five hundred feet into the cave, the 15 twine runs out. Jon doesn't care—he's way ahead, yelling for us to hurry up. Slathered with mud, we follow, occasionally glancing back, wondering if we'll ever see daylight again. Time and distance have no meaning. How many turns have we made, how many rooms have we crawled through?

Ahead in the distance, echoes of Jon's voice, calling to hurry up. One of 16 the women sits down, swearing that she won't take another step without knowing where we're going. The rest of us plead with her to continue, seeing how Jon's still way beyond us, down some tunnel in the blackness.

Two of us are limping when we finally catch up with Jon, seven million 17
kilometers down. He's treading water in a cobalt-blue pool, flashlight
beam reflecting off delicate limestone stalagmites.

"The blue's from copper salts leached out of the Bisbee vein," Jon's ex- 18
plaining. "The same acids that eat through this limestone are chewing at
the metal ores up above."

There's Jon Gradie swimming in the nude, lecturing us on groundwater 19
percolation. "Those marks on the wall show how the water table has
dropped over the past century; probably as good of a record as exists." I
peel off mud-caked jeans, wondering how this guy, who's written a dozen
papers on infrared properties of asteroids, knows so much about hydrol-
ogy and karst geomorphology. And so little about leading a cave trip.

Three others have a water fight while I float on my back, looking up at 20
the shadowy ceiling. Way above, the desert might be shimmering in heat
for all I know. Down here in the dark and quiet, it's a constant seventy degrees, and I'm swimming in the biggest lake south of Tucson. Probably the
only lake south of Tucson.

Getting out is as bad as getting in. We're down to one flashlight, and 21
most of us have dinged our heads on stalactites. Jon's way ahead, calling
to hurry up; I'm trying to stay in sight. The knotted rope leads the way to
the surface. We crawl out of the pit to find Jon toasting some burritos over
a campfire. They taste muddy.

Report from the earth's core-mantle boundary: it's dark, humid, and 22
muddy. And the only women we found were covered with mud.

You're right: this has little to do with the Internet. But every time some- 23
one mentions MUDs and virtual reality, I think of a genuine reality with
muddier mud than anything a computer can deliver.

In 1986, the budding Internet linked perhaps sixty thousand people. To- 24
day, there's well beyond two million online. And a hundred thousand more
join every month. What once felt like a small town is now a congested, im-
personal New York City of the mind, where you no longer recognize the
person who's talking to you.

I sense an insatiable demand for connectivity. Maybe all these people 25
have discovered important uses for the Internet. Perhaps some of them feel
hungry for a community that our real neighborhoods don't deliver. At least
a few must wonder what the big deal is.

Being online conveys a strange type of prestige. Those with modems 26
display their network addresses on business cards and letterheads. What
was once as geeky as a pocket protector has become a status symbol. It's
the ultimate revenge of the nerds.

Used to be that only scientists, engineers, and academics used e-mail . . . 27
myself included. Networks were a part of the R and D culture—a useful tool
to communicate with colleagues and exchange data. While mainly technical and academic, the traffic on the networks slowly became less formal. By
the early nineties, the Internet had evolved into a self-contained, anarchis-
tic community, with nobody in charge. At the same time, it's promoted as a
legitimate conduit for governmental and public communication.

Public officials now speak of the Internet as a major resource in our na- 28
tion's commercial and academic infrastructure. No longer an experiment,
it's to become a part of our schools, our businesses, our homes, our lives.

Yet who knows what the proposed National Information Infrastructure 29
will be?

Will it be a scheme for hundreds of video channels over cable? Will it 30
become a way to bring the Internet out of the universities and into our
homes and public schools? Will it be primarily a commercial endeavor or
a public service? Will the government regulate its growth and content? Will
it be a part of the telephone or cable-television system? Should I worry that
local bulletin boards won't have access? Will the government further subsidize an industry that's making lots of money already?

The answer is yes to all of the above, and more. Authors of the National 31
Information Infrastructure Progress Report of September 1994 expect to
"reduce health care costs by some $36 billion per year, prepare our chil-
dren for the knowledge-based economy of the 21st century, add more than
$100 billion to our Gross Domestic Product over the next decade, and add
500,000 new jobs by 1996, while enhancing the quality of work life and
forming a labor-management partnership."

Such glowing pronouncements make me wonder if some lemminglike 32
madness has cursed our technologists. In turn, I ask myself why the networked world attracts such attention.

As I contemplate this silicon navel, I see a wide gulf between the real 33
networks that I use daily and the promised land of the information infrastructure.

Some without a modem worry that they're missing an important part 34
of modern living. Yet few aspects of daily life require computers, digital
networks, or massive connectivity. They're irrelevant to cooking, driving,
visiting, negotiating, eating, hiking, dancing, and gossiping. You don't need
a keyboard to bake bread, play touch football, piece a quilt, build a stone
wall, recite a poem, or say a prayer.

At the other end of the spectrum, I have friends who are online ten or 35
twelve hours a day. They spend a substantial part of their lives answering
e-mail, transferring files, playing games, reading net news, and exploring

the Internet. They'd take umbrage at the suggestion that they're missing out on something important—having a rich life.

Instead, these online addicts point out the importance of networks, 36 communications, and home computers. They see the Internet as both tool and community, essential to work and home.

I flat-out don't believe them. 37

Technology has become hip. I read about computer networks on the front 38 pages of newspapers and magazines; talk-show hosts give their e-mail addresses; commercials promise a wonderful future where anything's available via computer. Lots of excitement and plenty of glitz, but little substance and even less reflection.

I'm saddened that so many accept the false promises of a hyper-hyped 39 idea. Overpromoted, the small, intimate benefits of the Internet are being destroyed by their own success.

The glamour of the Internet attracts journalists who write laudatory ar- 40 ticles, technoburbling how this must be the wave of the future. The computer press reinforces the feeling that you must own the latest doodads—their reporters, smiling from behind laptop computers, sincerely believe that everyone needs the latest digital wonders.

It's just a short extrapolation to a society where we download the lat- 41 est news and movies, where talking yellow pages show up on computer screens, and where interactive compact discs replace books.

Well, I don't believe that phone books, newspapers, magazines, or cor- 42 ner video stores will disappear as computer networks spread. Nor do I think that my telephone will merge with my computer, to become some sort of information appliance.

Yet the effects of this online obsession are already being felt. Elemen- 43 tary and high schools are being sold down the networked river. To keep up with this educational fad, school boards spend way too much on technical gimmicks that teachers don't want and students don't need. And look at the appalling state of our libraries' book-acquisition programs!

Computers and their accoutrements cost money. Big heaps of moola— 44 whole swimming pools overflowing with bills and coins bilked from people who've paid zillions for equipment, software, and network connections, from which they may never get their money's worth.

OK, so I don't care how you spend your money. But I do care how schools, 45 libraries, and governments spend *my* money. And much of the software and services being sold aren't worth the floppy disks they're recorded on.

I see businesses squeeze their products into computers, even when 46 they don't fit. Books on paper work damned well, as do post offices, newspapers, and the telephone. Yet I find offerings from publishers and phone companies that leave me scratching my head. I've rarely met anyone who prefers to read digital books. I don't want my morning paper delivered over computer, or a CD-ROM stuffed with *National Geographic* photographs. Call me a troglodyte; I'd rather peruse those photos alongside my sweetheart, catch the newspaper on the way to work, and page through a real book.

47   I can't help but apologize for the obviousness of my comments.* Computers and online services frustrate virtually everyone. Read the computing literature to feel the aridity of the culture of computing. Or follow Usenet net news to see dolts posting utter drivel or flame wars reminiscent of the Ostrogoths and Visigoths. Watch any kid play Nintendo to sense the shallowness of computer games.

48   Despite the peasant mentality that's online, we're told that anyone without a modem is an inept bumpkin, hopelessly behind the times or afraid of the march of technology. Don't buy it, or the cyberbullies will bury us all.

49   In 1977, Ken Olson, president of Digital Equipment Corporation, proclaimed, "There is no reason for any individual to have a computer in their home."

50   A year earlier, I had built a dearly beloved home computer, a nifty stone-age box with 4K of memory that displayed text on a TV. Within five years, I'd connected to the predecessor to the Internet, the Arpanet. As the network grew, I wrote software and used the network for science and recreation.

51   But over the past few years, I've experienced something of a change of heart. What started out so various, so beautiful, so new, now appears to be less than meets the eye.

52   Occasionally, I yearn for the good ol' days, back when computers squatted in glass rooms and mechanical teletypes clattered. You could see the bits in a punch card, you could smell the ozone when the printer jammed.

53   But don't write me off as some digital Luddite, plotting to break silicon knitting frames. Like my friends on the network, I'm confident that the Internet will thrive.

54   I feel a bit like an axolotl who, having grown lungs and walked ashore, now wonders what happened to his gills. Yet that doesn't explain my nerd-

---

*Nor do I claim to have originated these ideas. Perceptive people galore have already discussed 'em. Thoughtful scholars have profoundly plumbed the depths of philosophical matters on which I can only back-float: semiotics, rationalism, theory of knowledge, epistemology, ethics, Neoplatonism, 'pataphysics, and radiative transfer in nongray atmospheres.

like glee for the next generation of microprocessors or why my Macintosh ever itches for faster modems. Using a Unix workstation, I daily log into six networks and as many bulletin boards; every week I hear someone forecast the imminent demise of the Usenet. Death of the network predicted, film at eleven.

Still, I can't help worrying about the gross disparity between the bally- 55 hooed electronic utopia and the mundane reality of today's networked community. It's a theme you'll hear me repeat many times. Listening to digital prophets pointing to the promised land makes me crotchety and prone to mutter.

So discount some of my comments as the grinching of an old grackle, 56 directed to a nebulous online community. Write off others as challenges to the technicians building the next incarnation of the Internet. And dismiss the rest as misguided rant from a scoffer.

For I'm mainly speaking to people who feel mystically lured to the In- 57 ternet: locus-eaters, beware. Life in the real world is far more interesting, far more important, far richer, than anything you'll ever find on a computer screen.

"Are you some kind of sentimental reactionary?" asked a librarian friend 58 after I'd aired my doubts. "Do you want to return to the days of postcards and card catalogs?" About the same time, several Berkeley computer jocks gave me the hairy eyeball, wondering if I was frightened of the digital frontier. On the Internet, I've read that I'm "the willing tool or unwitting dupe of the enemies of human survival."

No. I still love my networked community; the sense of belonging to a 59 neighborhood where I recognize my friends. Daily, I'm delighted to read e-mail from strangers and acquaintances, to chat online, and to explore the growing Internet. So why do I get this vague phobic feeling as I plop down at my workstation?

Am I purposely viewing only the worrisome and distasteful parts of this 60 pervasive medium?

Well, yes, to an extent. Technology needs no further hype these days. 61 Open any magazine and get your fill of dithering praise and glossy full-color wonderment. Chat with a devout computer jock and you'll hear how the electronic revolution is linking all of us together through the universal Internet and how online experiences can change your life for the better.

Or simply log in—spend a week connected to the electronic world. 62 You'll find a more complex environment than I'm letting on to here.

But remember, you're viewing a world that doesn't exist. During 63 that week you spend online, you could have planted a tomato garden, volunteered at a hospital, spoken with your child's teacher, and taught the kid down the block how to shag fly balls.

Claim that you can do all of those things while having a rich online 64 life? Nope. Every hour that you're behind the keyboard is sixty minutes that you're not doing something else. Throwing a vase on a potter's wheel takes the same concentration and dedication as exploring a Multi-User Dungeon. And only a little less than getting lost in a cave with Jon Gradie.

Thinking About the Essay

1. What is the purpose and effect of the prefatory extract preceding paragraph 1? How does Stoll connect this preface to paragraphs 1 and 2, while preparing the reader for the rest of the essay?

2. What elements of Stoll's style make this essay potentially appealing even for readers who are not especially interested in the Internet?

3. Explain the tone of Stoll's essay—his attitude toward his subject. Locate specific sentences and passages that best reveal his viewpoints.

4. Carefully examine each of the five sections in this essay. Establish the topic for each part, the ways Stoll develops it, and the linkages between and among these units. Would you say that the overall effect is unified and coherent? Why or why not?

5. Stoll tells a good story—or stories. What aspects of narrative technique do you find in this essay? Why does Stoll find narrative especially useful in presenting his thesis? Why, in fact, does he tell the story of his spelunking expedition?

Responding in Writing

6. Stoll says that reality is far more important to him than anything on the Internet. Would you agree or disagree? Tell a story that supports your viewpoint.

7. Do you think that Stoll is a "sentimental reactionary," as a friend calls him (paragraph 58)? In a critical essay, evaluate Stoll's argument and your response to it.

8. "Every hour that you're behind the keyboard is sixty minutes that you're not doing something else" (paragraph 64). Write a meditative essay based on this statement by Stoll in the last paragraph of his essay.

Networking

9. Participate in a poll of class members, finding out who supports Stoll's critique of the Internet and who opposes his viewpoints. Then decide on two

volunteers from each side to defend their positions. Be prepared to challenge, rebut, or cross-examine their statements.

10. Stoll is a popular writer on the information highway whose essays have
appeared in specialized journals like *Technical Communication* and *PC
World,* newspapers like the *New York Times* and the *Christian Science
Monitor,* business magazines like *Forbes* and *Barron's,* and publications
on the right and left of the political spectrum. Search the Net for representative selections. Report on some of the topics that Stoll develops for
his various audiences.

The Digital Revolution and the New Reformation

ALI MAZRUI AND ALAMIN MAZRUI

Ali Mazrui was born in Mombasa, Kenya, in 1933; his
father was a judge of Islamic law. Following his education at the University of Manchester (B.A., 1960), Columbia University (M.A., 1961), and Oxford University
(D.Phil., 1966), Mazrui taught political science and
served as dean of the Faculty of Social Sciences at Mak-
erere University in Kampala, Uganda. In 1967, he came
to the University of Michigan, where as professor of political science and director of the Center for Afroameri-
can and African Studies, he established himself as a
recognized expert on modern Africa. Among his numerous works are *The African Condition* (1980), *The
Africans: A Triple Heritage* (1986), *Cultural Forces in
World Politics* (1990), and *The Power of Babel* (1998).
Mazrui also is a poet, novelist, and literary critic. Active
in numerous international organizations and advisory
committees, Mazrui is a public intellectual known for
his quick wit and impenetrable logic He currently is director of the Institute for Global Cultural Studies at
SUNY Binghamton. His son, Alamin Mazrui, is professor of African American Studies at Ohio State University. In this essay, published in the *Harvard International
Review* in 2001, they analyze both sides of the digital divide from the perspective of culture and religion.

Before Reading

Is it possible—even thinkable— for peoples from diverse cultures and backgrounds around the world to embrace the digital revolution? What are the dangers if they don't? What are the dangers if they do?

Any major university in the United States may have more computer-literate individuals than several states of the Nigerian Federation. This disparity between computer-skilled and computer-challenged highlights the depth of the digital divide. Literacy as a source of empowerment has shifted from the print to the computer medium. There is the lingering danger that cyberspace will solidify the gap between the haves and the have-nots.

However, this gap cannot merely be reduced to economic difference and financial access to Internet technology. Certainly, what appear to be cultural reasons for the digital divide are often due to differences in economic opportunity. But while it is difficult to distinguish whether economic or cultural factors are more salient in explaining the digital divide, the different levels of interaction between religious traditions and technological changes raise several crucial questions: how will a computer revolution shape the changes within religious doctrine, and how do religious traditions affect people's ability to adapt to such a revolution?

Examining how technology has affected doctrine and gender in Islam will illuminate a key example of the interplay between technology and religion. By exploring the effect of the Internet on the internal logic of Islam, as well as the enlarged global influence Islam must play when digital barriers are broken, we hope to highlight the possibilities for a dual reformation.

Information to Reformation

The impact of the first industrial revolution on western Christianity undoubtedly led to the momentous movement of the Christian Reformation. Will the impact of the new revolution of information lead to a comparable Islamic Reformation? In the 20th century Westerners have debated whether the Protestant Reformation was the mother of capitalism in Europe or whether the Christian Reformation was itself a child of earlier phases of the capitalist revolution. Max Weber's book *The Protestant Ethic and the Spirit of Capitalism* advances the view that the Protestant Reformation was the mother of capitalism rather than a child of economic change. Other thinkers, however, have identified pre-Reformation technological inventions as part of the preparation for both the birth of Protestantism and modern-day capitalism.

Francis Robinson, professor of history at the University of London, has placed the printing press at the center of the Protestant movement and within the Catholic counter-offensive. He writes, "Print lay at the heart of that great challenge to religious authority, the Protestant Reformation; Lutheranism was the child of the printed book. Print lay at the heart of the

Catholic counter-offensive, whether it meant harnessing the press for the work of Jesuits and the office of Propaganda, or controlling the press through the machinery of the Papal Index and the Papal Imprimatur." The question here is whether the Internet and cyberspace and the third industrial revolution will do to Islam what the first industrial revolution did for Christianity.

In some respects the Christian Reformation was a return to the biblical 6 roots of Christianity. Likewise, the information revolution may help Islam realize some of its earliest aims more effectively. The first casualty of the information revolution, however, may be national sovereignty, which will shrink in the wake of the Internet and cyberspace. The printed word played a major role in the construction of nationhood and in reinforcing national consciousness. Computer communication, on the other hand, is contributing to the breakdown of nationhood and may play a role in the construction of trans-ethnic communities.

While the first industrial revolution of capitalist production and the 7 Christian Reformation became allied to the new forces of nationalism in the Western world, the third industrial revolution and any Islamic reformation will be increasingly hostile to the insularity of the state. Islam and the information revolution will be allies in breaking down the barriers of competing national sovereignties. The new technology will give Islam a chance to realize its original aim of transnational universalism. The Internet could become the Islamic super-highway.

Many Muslims have already risen to this challenge of the new infor- 8 mation age with Islamic resource guides on the Internet, Cyber Muslim Guides, the Islamic Information and News Network and web servers with Islamic material. As Childers writes, contrary to some assumptions that "modern communications would engender a new and generally Western-oriented cosmopolitanism, they are predominantly spreading the idea of a freedom that is translated by the receivers as endogenous freedom including freedom to rejoin one's real kinship (whether larger or smaller) and to re-examine the validity of one's own ancient social values." Thus, the Internet may have the effect of rekindling community.

The Ballot Enters the Harem

But there is one fundamental area where Islam and the new information 9 revolution have yet to converge: the relationship between men and women. Will the new information technology fundamentally alter gender relations?

The Muslim world has traditionally vacillated between two doctrines 10 on this issue. One doctrine has been to treat genders as separate but equal. Genders co-exist in homes; separation of genders is inevitably moderated by family ties. This is qualitatively different from the separation of races and ethnicities. The gender doctrine of "separate but equal" could survive the new information revolution.

Under the new technology the computerized hijab is at hand: women 11 can more easily stay at home while continuing to participate in a computerized workplace. This possibility is amply demonstrated by a woman from the British Asian community in her response to a BBC radio presenter who expressed concern that the computer can, in fact, enhance the isolation of women. The woman commented, "Well, if they're just stuck at home then why not use the Internet to get connectivity with people across the world . . . the Internet can also provide an access for women to possibly start providing their own services—maybe hobbies that they're interested in or business that they have a keen eye on." By gradually abolishing the distinction between home and the workplace, Internet technology may give women the opportunity to integrate themselves into the economic and political global community.

But many Muslim societies treat women as "separate and unequal." As- 12 pects of that perspective are rooted in a view of the Shari'a that dictates that women inherit half of what men inherit and that, in certain circumstances, holds the testimony of women in court to be worth less than that of men. Such Muslim societies have assumed that there were two different doors of knowledge, one for each gender. Many Muslim societies had assumed that there were branches of knowledge that were not fit for women and children under 16. The Taliban regime in Afghanistan has carried this theory of two tiers of gender knowledge to its extreme.

New information technology is going to destroy the social justification 13 for gender discrimination. Increased information may be insusceptible to gender differentiation. The digital divide may give way to digital democracy. While it is true that what men know about sex, pornography, politics, and corruption may also be accessible to women through the Internet, the new technology will pass a death sentence on the old tradition of female seclusion that has existed since the Abbasid dynasty in many Muslim societies. The traditional forms of seclusion of women will no longer survive a technology in which women can declare their presence and, in time, assert their rights.

Toward Islamizing the Internet

In spite of these new freedoms and new possibilities afforded by the Inter- 14 net, the technology is not necessarily free of influence from existing systems of economic, political, and social inequality. New computer technology and the Internet may be inaugurating new kinds of stratification and reform, and Muslim countries are bound to be affected. Distribution of real power in the world is not based on "who owns what" but on "who knows what." It has not been the power of property but the power of skill that has been the ultimate international arbiter. For example, oilrich Muslim countries like Saudi Arabia or Kuwait have not been able to exploit their own petroleum resources without the skills of Western companies and their engineers.

How is the Muslim *ummah* to relate to these "negative" consequences 15 of the Internet and computer communication? There is now a growing movement among Muslims that seeks to Islamize scientific (and other forms of) knowledge for the greater project of Islamizing modernity itself. The Islamization of computer communication is seen as a core component of this quest. As Nasim Butt explains, "As information technologies are becoming the basic tools of manipulation and control, access to them will become the decisive factor between control and power or manipulation and subservience. In this powerful dilemma, the way forward, surely, is to modify the technology at the point of use to meet the needs and requirements of Muslim society." Butt suggests an alternative scientific paradigm that supposedly maintains the values of Islam and provides some broad guidelines for the Islamization of science and technology.

Science in the more isolationist Muslim discourse has often been 16 viewed as distinct from religion. More recent Islamic revival initiatives, however, insist on a greater convergence between the two. There is a new nostalgia for ancient scientific practices. Advocates seek to enforce Islamic ethical parameters on both scientific research and, more importantly, on applied science. Some Islamicist interpretations would now regard any scientific venture that carries the potential for harmful or unnatural consequences as un-Islamic. Under this paradigm, research into germ warfare would probably be disallowed outright. But how about areas of mixed blessings, like genetic engineering, which may have beneficial or unnatural and harmful uses? The verdict here may depend on the particular application. For example, nuclear weapons have been seen as defensive against Zionist, Hindu, or Western enemies. Pakistan's development of a nuclear weapons program may be a rationalization of this interpretation.

The Islamization of science may also refer to attempts to accord science 17 greater Islamic identity and Muslim representation. At some point this quest may entail both indigenization and domestication. Indigenization involves increasing the use of indigenous resources, ranging from native personnel to aspects of traditional local knowledge, in the process making them more relevant to the modern age. Domestication, on the other hand, involves making imported versions of science and technology more relevant to local needs.

In the realm of computer technology, domestication would begin with   18
a substantial employment of indigenous personnel. This would require,
first, greater commitment by Muslim governments and institutions to promote relevant training at different levels for Muslims, both men and
women; second, readiness on the part of both governments and employers
to create a structure of incentives that would attract Muslim men and
women to those fields; third, greater political pressure on computer suppliers to facilitate training and cooperate in related tasks; and fourth,
stricter control by Muslim governments of the importation of computers.

The indigenization of high-level personnel in the local computer indus-   19
try should in time help indigenize the functions of computer technology.
When the most skilled roles in the computer industry in a Muslim country
are in the hands of Muslims themselves, new types of technological tasks
will emerge. This Islamization of computer personnel should also facilitate
further Islamization of users of computer services. But efficient indigenization and domestication of the computer still require a gradualist and
planned approach.

The difficulty of this task is compounded by the technological depend-   20
ence engendered by multinational corporations and their respective governments. As technology levels increase in Muslim countries, so too may
these countries' dependence on external corporations in order to maintain
the technology. Additional strategies for decolonization of computer technology are thus required. These may include diversification of the sources
on which a country is dependent, horizontal interpenetration to promote
greater exchange between Muslim countries themselves, and vertical counterpenetration to enable Muslim countries to work in the citadels of power
in the West.

Launching Islam

The possibility that the Internet may stimulate an "Islamic Reformation"   21
is based on the assumption that individual Muslim men and women are
real actors in the information revolution and not merely objects, and that
they are producers of knowledge and not merely consumers of knowledge.
Are Muslims of both genders making progress in narrowing the technological gap between Islam and the West?

But what would be the larger global implications of an Islamic Refor-   22
mation? Will not a reinvigorated Muslim *ummah* lead to the clash of civilizations, as predicted by Harvard professor Samuel Huntington? It can be
argued that Islamic renewal will not only galvanize the Muslim *ummah*

from within but also, by rekindling the spirit of *itihad*, it will reopen the doors of constructive engagement with other civilizations.

At the height of its glory Islam attempted to protect religious minori- 23 ties, even if Muslims did not always respect women's rights. Jews and Christians had special status as People of the Book, a fraternity of monotheists. Other religious minorities were later to be accorded the status of *dhimmis* (protected minorities). Under the system Jewish scholars rose to high positions in Muslim Spain. During the Ottoman Empire, Christians also sometimes attained high political office: Sulaiman 1 (1520–1566) had Christian ministers in his government, as did Salim III (1789–1807). The Mughal Empire integrated Hindus and Muslims into a consolidated Indian state; Emperor Akbar (1556–1605) carried furthest the Mughal policy of bringing Hindus into the government. All this may be an indication that Islam is inclusive and open to dialogue precisely when it is politically most influential. It is this historical precedent that is likely to undergo a resurgence under an Islamic Reformation. A self-confident and self-assured Islam is a better partner for peace than a threatened Islam.

The toughest synthesis of all is yet to come—synthesizing the rights of 24 women with the rights of men to create a more balanced moral equilibrium. It would be particularly fitting if the Martin Luther of the Islamic Reformation turned out to be a woman, posting her 95 theses of reform not on the door of a Wittenberg mosque but universally on the Internet.

Thinking About the Essay

1. This essay was published in the *Harvard International Review,* a scholarly journal read primarily by diplomats and policymakers. What distinguishing features does the article have from the other essays in this chapter? What similarities does it share with these essays?

2. Both authors clearly are specialists who are interested in Islam. How do they establish their authority? How do they make their views accessible and acceptable to an audience that perhaps has limited knowledge of Islam? What exactly is their purpose, and how do they achieve it?

3. Trace the argument of this essay. How successful are the authors in advancing it? Justify your response.

4. The authors employ many rhetorical techniques to organize materials in this essay. Explain especially how classification operates as a structuring principle. What other rhetorical elements do you encounter?

5. How does each subtitle prepare the reader for the information that follows? What interrelationships do you detect among the subtitles in this essay?

Responding in Writing

6. Write a précis of this rather complicated essay. Aim for 300 words, capturing all the most important points that the authors present.

7. Write a personal essay in which you explain what you have learned about Islam from this essay, and how the Islamic world might respond to the electronic revolution.

8. Argue for or against the following proposition, as it is stated by the authors: "The Internet could become the Islamic superhighway" (Paragraph 7).

Networking

9. Divide into groups of three and four, and consider the title of the essay. Have each member explain his or her interpretation of it. If possible, come up with a shared explanation. Present the group's response to the rest of the class.

10. Research the Islamic response to information technology on the Web. Based on this research, form your own opinion on the compatibility of Islam—or any other religion—and the information superhighway.

The Fate of the Earth: Can We Preserve the Global Environment?

10

CHAPTER

I t is tempting to think that at one time—was it before 9/11, or before the explosion of the first atomic bomb, or before the Black Death?— the problems of the world were simpler and more manageable. But were they? After all, the Black Death of the thirteenth century liquidated more than a third of Europe's population. There have always been world conflicts, and challenges that Earth's inhabitants have had to confront. So far, we have survived; we have not destroyed the planet. However, as the writers in this chapter attest, the fate of the Earth is uncertain, for humanity continues to be a flawed enterprise.

What is certain is that for the last several decades we have been moving into a new era in global history. This new era, as the writers in earlier chapters have revealed, is both like and unlike previous historical epochs. We do not have to accept the thesis of Francis Fukuyama, whose writing appears in this chapter, that we have reached the "end" of history. At the same time, we do have to acknowledge that new challenges—scientific, ecological, economic, political, and cultural— await us in the new millennium. Numerous local and global problems need our sustained attention. Over the past decade, in particular, we have come to recognize that we have relationships and obligations to the planet and its inhabitants. A dust storm originating in Africa can sweep across the Atlantic, affecting ecologies in other continents. A nuclear accident in Russia can affect the milk of cows in Nebraska. Even the cars that we purchase and drive—as one author in this chapter asserts—can have an impact on the world's climate.

Clearly, then, in this new millennial era, we are part of a global environment. We have mutual obligations not to waste natural resources, to respect the environment, to harness science and technology to human and

389

Tourists on a camel safari in Egypt clearly affect the local ecosystem and indigenous community.

Thinking About the Image

1. This photograph originally accompanied an article about "ecotourism." What do you know about ecotourism? Why do you think people would plan an "ecotourism" vacation?

2. What kind of story does this photograph tell about the relationship between the tourists and the "natives?"

3. Are you amused or surprised by what the camels are carrying?

4. What do you think is the point of view, or opinion, of the photographer who took this picture toward the people on the camels? How can you tell? Is there anything else that is amusing, sarcastic, or ironic about this photograph?

nonhuman benefit, and so much more. This new era is not necessarily more corrosive than previous epochs, but the stakes do seem to be higher. We now have to comprehend our reciprocal relationships at the numerous crossroads of nature and civilization. The *process* of civilization wherein we harness our physical, creative, scientific, political, intellectual, and spiritual resources is well advanced. However, the current condition of the global environment, as the writers in this last chapter testify, demands our attention.

By and large, the writers in this chapter, all of whom deal with subjects of consequence—global warming, biotechnology, environmental degradation, population growth, weapons of mass destruction—are not doomsday prophets. In fact, while offering cautionary statements about our shortsight-edness and wastefulness, they tend to find hope for the world's environment. Whether finding once again a small spot in Eden in a remote Amazon jungle or contemplating the consequences of driving an SUV, these writers try to establish a moral basis for the continuation of the species—not just our human species but all varieties of life on Earth. We are not caught in an endless spiral that will end in mass extinction. But we do have to harness what Albert Schweitzer called "the devils of our own creation." Ultimately, we must find ways to coexist on Earth with nature and all living things.

The Obligation to Endure

RACHEL CARSON

> Born in Pennsylvania in 1907, Rachel Carson became a leading figure in the world's emerging environmental movement. Abandoning an early interest in English literature, she concentrated instead on zoology, ultimately obtaining an advanced degree from the Graduate School of Johns Hopkins University. She was a marine biologist on the staff of the United States Fish and Wildlife Service for fifteen years, serving as editor in chief. Her first book was *Under the Sea Wind* (1941). With *The Sea Around Us* (1951), which sold millions of copies, was translated into dozens of languages, and won the National Book Award, Carson emerged as the best-known spokesperson for the preservation of the world's resources. In 1952, Carson resigned her government position to devote her time to writing. Her last book, *Silent Spring* (1964), from which the following essay is taken, aroused immediate controversy for its indictment of the use of pesticides. Carson died in 1964.

Before Reading

In the decades since *Silent Spring* was published, numerous pesticides have been banned—especially in the United States. Do you think that the problem no longer exists? Why or why not?

The history of life on earth has been a history of interaction between liv-   1
ing things and their surroundings. To a large extent, the physical form and the habits of the earth's vegetation and its animal life have been molded by the environment. Considering the whole span of earthly time, the opposite effect, in which life actually modifies its surroundings, has been relatively slight. Only within the moment of time represented by the present century has one species—man—acquired significant power to alter the nature of his world.

During the past quarter century this power has not only increased to one 2
of disturbing magnitude but it has changed in character. The most alarming
of all man's assaults upon the environment is the contamination of air, earth,
rivers, and sea with dangerous and even lethal materials. This pollution is for
the most part irrecoverable; the chain of evil it initiates not only in the world
that must support life but in living tissues is for the most part irreversible. In
this now universal contamination of the environment, chemicals are the sinister and little-recognized partners of radiation in changing the very nature
of the world—the very nature of its life. Strontium 90, released through nuclear explosions into the air, comes to earth in rain or drifts down as fallout,
lodges in soil, enters into the grass or corn or wheat grown there, and in time
takes up its abode in the bones of a human being, there to remain until his
death. Similarly, chemicals sprayed on croplands or forests or gardens lie
long in soil, entering into living organisms, passing from one to another in a
chain of poisoning and death. Or they pass mysteriously by underground
streams until they emerge and, through the alchemy of air and sunlight, combine into new forms that kill vegetation, sicken cattle, and work unknown
harm on those who drink from once pure wells. As Albert Schweitzer has
said, "Man can hardly even recognize the devils of his own creation."

It took hundreds of millions of years to produce the life that now in- 3
habits the earth—eons of time in which that developing and evolving and
diversifying life reached a state of adjustment and balance with its surroundings. The environment, rigorously shaping and directing the life it
supported, contained elements that were hostile as well as supporting. Certain rocks gave out dangerous radiation; even within the light of the sun,
from which all life draws its energy, there were shortwave radiations with
power to injure. Given time—time not in years but in millennia—life ad-
justs, and a balance has been reached. For time is the essential ingredient;
but in the modern world there is no time.

The rapidity of change and the speed with which new situations are cre- 4
ated follow the impetuous and heedless pace of man rather than the deliberate pace of nature. Radiation is no longer merely the background radiation of
rocks, the bombardment of cosmic rays, the ultraviolet of the sun that have
existed before there was any life on earth; radiation is now the unnatural creation of man's tampering with the atom. The chemicals to which life is asked
to make its adjustment are no longer merely the calcium and silica and copper and all the rest of the minerals washed out of the rocks and carried in
rivers to the sea; they are the synthetic creations of man's inventive mind,
brewed in his laboratories, and having no counterparts in nature.

To adjust to these chemicals would require time on the scale that is na- 5
ture's; it would require not merely the years of a man's life but the life of generations. And even this, were it by some miracle possible, would be futile, for

the new chemicals come from our laboratories in an endless stream; almost five hundred annually find their way into actual use in the United States alone. The figure is staggering and its implications are not easily grasped—500 new chemicals to which the bodies of men and animals are required somehow to adapt each year, chemicals totally outside the limits of biologic experience.

Among them are many that are used in man's war against nature. Since 6 the mid-1940's over 200 basic chemicals have been created for use in killing insects, weeds, rodents, and other organisms described in the modern vernacular as "pests"; and they are sold under several thousand different brand names.

These sprays, dusts, and aerosols are now applied almost universally to 7 farms, gardens, forests, and homes—nonselective chemicals that have the power to kill every insect, the "good" and the "bad," to still the song of birds and the leaping of fish in the streams, to coat the leaves with a deadly film, and to linger on in soil—all this though the intended target may be only a few weeds or insects. Can anyone believe it is possible to lay down such a barrage of poisons on the surface of the earth without making it unfit for all life? They should not be called "insecticides," but "biocides."

The whole process of spraying seems caught up in an endless spiral. 8 Since DDT was released for civilian use, a process of escalation has been going on in which ever more toxic materials must be found. This has happened because insects, in a triumphant vindication of Darwin's principle of the survival of the fittest, have evolved super races immune to the particular insecticide used, hence a deadlier one has always to be developed—and then a deadlier one than that. It has happened also because, for reasons to be described later, destructive insects often undergo a "flareback," or resurgence, after spraying in numbers greater than before. Thus the chemical war is never won, and all life is caught in its violent crossfire.

Along with the possibility of the extinction of mankind by nuclear war, 9 the central problem of our age has therefore become the contamination of man's total environment with such substances of incredible potential for harm—substances that accumulate in the tissues of plants and animals and even penetrate the germ cells to shatter or alter the very material of heredity upon which the shape of the future depends.

Some would-be architects of our future look toward a time when it will 10 be possible to alter the human germ plasm by design. But we may easily be doing so now by inadvertence, for many chemicals, like radiation, bring about gene mutations. It is ironic to think that man might determine his own future by something so seemingly trivial as the choice of an insect spray.

All this has been risked—for what? Future historians may well be 11 amazed by our distorted sense of proportion. How could intelligent beings seek to control a few unwanted species by a method that contaminated the entire environment and brought the threat of disease and death even to their own kind? Yet this is precisely what we have done. We have done it, moreover, for reasons that collapse the moment we examine them. We are told that the enormous and expanding use of pesticides is necessary to maintain farm production. Yet is our real problem not one of *overproduction*? Our farms, despite measures to remove acreages from production and to pay farmers *not* to produce, have yielded such a staggering excess of crops that the American taxpayer in 1962 is paying out more than one billion dollars a year as the total carrying cost of the surplus-food storage program. And is the situation helped when one branch of the Agriculture Department tries to reduce production while another states, as it did in 1958, "It is believed generally that reduction of crop acreages under provisions of the Soil Bank will stimulate interest in use of chemicals to obtain maximum production on the land retained in crops."

All this is not to say there is no insect problem and no need of control. 12 I am saying, rather, that control must be geared to realities, not to mythical situations, and that the methods employed must be such that they do not destroy us along with the insects.

The problem whose attempted solution has brought such a train of disaster in its wake is an accompaniment of our modern way of life. Long before the age of man, insects inhabited the earth—a group of extraordinarily varied and adaptable beings. Over the course of time since man's advent, a small percentage of the more than half a million species of insects have come into conflict with human welfare in two principal ways: as competitors for the food supply and as carriers of human disease.

Disease-carrying insects become important where human beings are 14 crowded together, especially under conditions where sanitation is poor, as in times of natural disaster or war or in situations of extreme poverty and deprivation. Then control of some sort becomes necessary. It is a sobering fact, however, as we shall presently see, that the method of massive chemical control has had only limited success, and also threatens to worsen the very conditions it is intended to curb.

Under primitive agricultural conditions the farmer had few insect problems. 15 These arose with the intensification of agriculture—the devotion of immense acreages to a single crop. Such a system set the stage for explosive increases in specific insect populations. Single-crop farming does not take advantage of the principles by which nature works; it is agriculture as an engineer might conceive it to be. Nature has introduced great variety into the landscape, but man has displayed a passion for simplifying it. Thus he undoes the built-in checks and balances by which nature holds the species within bounds. One important natural check is a limit on the amount of suitable habitat for each species. Obviously then, an insect that lives on wheat can build up its population to much higher levels on a farm devoted to wheat than on one in which wheat is intermingled with other crops to which the insect is not adapted.

The same thing happens in other situations. A generation or more ago, 16 the towns of large areas of the United States lined their streets with the noble elm tree. Now the beauty they hopefully created is threatened with complete destruction as disease sweeps through the elms, carried by a beetle that would have only limited chance to build up large populations and to spread from tree to tree if the elms were only occasional trees in a richly diversified planting.

Another factor in the modern insect problem is one that must be viewed 17 against a background of geologic and human history: the spreading of thousands of different kinds of organisms from their native homes to invade new territories. This worldwide migration has been studied and graphically described by the British ecologist Charles Elton in his recent book *The Ecology of Invasions*. During the Cretaceous Period, some hundred million years ago, flooding seas cut many land bridges between continents and living things found themselves confined in what Elton calls "colossal separate nature reserves." There, isolated from others of their kind, they developed many new species. When some of the land masses were joined again, about 15 million years ago, these species began to move out into new territories—a movement that is not only still in progress but is now receiving considerable assistance from man.

The importation of plants is the primary agent in the modern spread of 18 species, for animals have almost invariably gone along with the plants, quarantine being a comparatively recent and not completely effective innovation. The United States Office of Plant Introduction alone has introduced almost 200,000 species and varieties of plants from all over the world. Nearly half of the 180 or so major insect enemies of plants in the United States are accidental imports from abroad, and most of them have come as hitchhikers on plants.

In new territory, out of reach of the restraining hand of the natural enemies that kept down its numbers in its native land, an invading plant or 19 animal is able to become enormously abundant. Thus it is no accident that our most troublesome insects are introduced species.

These invasions, both the naturally occurring and those dependent on 20 human assistance, are likely to continue indefinitely. Quarantine and massive chemical campaigns are only extremely expensive ways of buying time. We are faced, according to Dr. Elton, "with a life-and-death need not just to find new technological means of suppressing this plant or that animal"; instead we need the basic knowledge of animal populations and their relations to their surroundings that will "promote an even balance and damp down the explosive power of outbreaks and new invasions."

Much of the necessary knowledge is now available but we do not use 21 it. We train ecologists in our universities and even employ them in our governmental agencies but we seldom take their advice. We allow the chemical death rain to fall as though there were no alternative, whereas in fact there are many, and our ingenuity could soon discover many more if given opportunity.

Have we fallen into a mesmerized state that makes us accept as in- 22 evitable that which is inferior or detrimental, as though having lost the will or the vision to demand that which is good? Such thinking, in the words of the ecologist Paul Shepard, "idealizes life with only its head out of water, inches above the limits of toleration of the corruption of its own environment. . . . Why should we tolerate a diet of weak poisons, a home in insipid surroundings, a circle of acquaintances who are not quite our enemies, the noise of motors with just enough relief to prevent insanity? Who would want to live in a world which is just not quite fatal?"

Yet such a world is pressed upon us. The crusade to create a chemically 23 sterile, insect-free world seems to have engendered a fanatic zeal on the part of many specialists and most of the so-called control agencies. On every hand there is evidence that those engaged in spraying operations exercise a ruthless power. "The regulatory entomologists . . . function as prosecutor, judge and jury, tax assessor and collector and sheriff to enforce their own orders," said Connecticut entomologist Neely Turner. The most flagrant abuses go unchecked in both state and federal agencies.

It is not my contention that chemical insecticides must never be used. I 24 do contend that we have put poisonous and biologically potent chemicals indiscriminately into the hands of persons largely or wholly ignorant of their potentials for harm. We have subjected enormous numbers of people to contact with these poisons, without their consent and often without their knowledge. If the Bill of Rights contains no guarantee that a citizen shall be secure against lethal poisons distributed either by private individuals or by public officials, it is surely only because our forefathers, despite their considerable wisdom and foresight, could conceive of no such problem.

I contend, furthermore, that we have allowed these chemicals to be used 25 with little or no advance investigation of their effect on soil, water, wildlife, and man himself. Future generations are unlikely to condone our lack of prudent concern for the integrity of the natural world that supports all life.

There is still very limited awareness of the nature of the threat. This is 26 an era of specialists, each of whom sees his own problem and is unaware of or intolerant of the larger frame into which it fits. It is also an era dominated by industry, in which the right to make a dollar at whatever cost is seldom challenged. When the public protests, confronted with some obvious evidence of damaging results of pesticide applications, it is fed little tranquilizing pills of half truth. We urgently need an end to these false assurances, to the sugar coating of unpalatable facts. It is the public that is being asked to assume the risks that the insect controllers calculate. The public must decide whether it wishes to continue on the present road, and it can do so only when in full possession of the facts. In the words of Jean Rostand, "The obligation to endure gives us the right to know."

Thinking About the Essay

1. What is Carson's thesis or claim? Where does it appear, or is it implied? Justify your response.

2. Explain the tone of Carson's essay. How do such words as *dangerous, evil,* and *sinister* reinforce this tone?

3. Evaluate Carson's essay as a model of argumentation. What reasons does she provide to demonstrate the overpopulation of insects? How does she convince us of "the obligation to endure"? What remedies does she propose? What appeals does she make?

4. Identify all instances where Carson uses expert testimony. How effective is this testimony in reinforcing the writer's argument?

5. What is Carson's purpose in her final paragraph? How effective is it? Explain.

Responding in Writing

6. Write your own essay entitled "The Obligation to Endure." You may focus on pesticides or any other topic—for example, genetically altered foods or global warming—to organize your paper.

7. In an essay, argue for or against the proposition that we spend too much time and money worrying about the state of the world environment.

8. Write a paper in which you present solutions to some of the problems that Carson raises in her essay.

Networking

9. Working in small groups, find out more about Rachel Carson and her involvement with environmental issues. In class discussion, evaluate her relevance to the environmental situation today.

10. Go online and find out more about pesticides commonly used today. Share your findings with the class. How safe are they? Would you use them as a homeowner, landscaper, farmer, or forestry official?

Talking Trash

ANDY ROONEY

Andrew A. Rooney, better known as "Andy" from his regular appearances on *60 Minutes* and his syndicated columns in more than two hundred newspapers, is one of the nation's best-know curmudgeons, a writer and commentator who is frequently at odds with conventional wisdom on various issues. Born in Albany, New York, in 1919, he attended Colgate University before serving in the U.S. Army from 1942 to 1945 as a reporter for *Stars and Stripes*. Rooney has written, produced, and narrated programs for some of the major shows in television history: he wrote material for Arthur Godfrey from 1949 to 1955, and for Sam Levenson, Herb Shriner, Victor Borge, Gary Moore, and other celebrities who define many of the high points of early television comedy. Over the decades, Rooney has also produced television essays, documentaries, and specials for ABC, CBS, and public television. A prolific writer, he is the author of more than a dozen books—most recently *My War* (1995), *Sincerely, Andy Rooney* (1999), *Common Nonsense* (2002), and *Years of Minutes* (2003). Known for his dry, unassuming, but acerbic wit (which from time to time has gotten him in trouble with viewers and television studios), Rooney is at his best when convincing readers about simple truths. In this essay, which appeared in 2002 in *Diversion*, he tells us the simple truth about our inability to moderate our wasteful ways.

Before Reading

Americans are perceived as being terribly wasteful. They discard food, appliances, clothing, and so much more that other peoples and societies would find useful. Do you agree or disagree with this profile of the wasteful American? And how do you fit into this picture?

L ast Saturday I filled the trunk of my car and the passenger seats be-   1
hind me with junk and headed for the dump. There were newspapers, empty cardboard boxes, bags of junk mail, advertising flyers, empty bottles, cans, and garbage. I enjoy the trip. Next to buying something new, throwing away something that is old is the most satisfying experience I know.

The garbage men come to my house twice a week, but they're very 2 fussy. If the garbage is not packaged the way they like it, they won't take it. That's why I make a trip to the dump every Saturday. It's two miles from our house, and I often think big thoughts about throwing things away while I'm driving there.

How much, I got to wondering last week, does the whole Earth weigh? 3 New York City alone throws away 24 million pounds of garbage a day. A day! How long will it take us to turn the whole planet Earth into garbage, throw it away, and leave us standing on nothing?

Oil, coal, and metal ore are the most obvious extractions, but any place 4 there's a valuable mineral, we dig beneath the surface, take it out, and make it into something else. We never put anything back. We disfigure one part of our land by digging something out and then move on to another spot after we've used up all its resources.

After my visit to the dump, I headed for the supermarket, where I 5 bought $34 worth of groceries. Everything was packed in something–a can, a box, a bottle, a carton, or a bag. When I got to the checkout counter, the cashier separated my cans, boxes, cartons, bottles, and bags and put three or four at a time into other bags, boxes, or cartons. Sometimes she put my paper bags into plastic bags. One bag never seemed to do. If something was in plastic, she put that into paper.

On the way home, I stopped at the dry cleaner. Five of my shirts, which 6 had been laundered, were in a cardboard box. There was a piece of cardboard in the front of each shirt and another cardboard cutout to fit the collar to keep it from getting wrinkled. The suit I had cleaned was on a throwaway hanger, in a plastic bag with a form-fitting piece of paper inside over the shoulders of my suit.

When I got home, I put the groceries where they belonged in various 7 places in the kitchen. With the wastebasket at hand, I threw out all the outer bags and wrappers. By the time I'd unwrapped and stored everything, I'd filled the kitchen wastebasket a second time.

It would be interesting to conduct a serious test to determine what per- 8 centage of everything we discard. It must be more than 25%. I drank the contents of a bottle of Coke and threw the bottle away. The Coca-Cola Company must pay more for the bottle than for what they put in it. Dozens of things we eat come in containers that weigh more and cost the manufacturer more than what they put in them.

We've gone overboard on packaging, and part of the reason is that a 9 bag, a can, or a carton provides a place for the producer to display advertising. The average cereal box looks like a roadside billboard.

The Earth could end up as one huge, uninhabitable dump. 10

Thinking About the Essay

1. What is Rooney's thesis? Where does he state it? What evidence does he provide to support his thesis?

2. Does Rooney, writing about a serious problem, maintain a serious tone in this essay? What evidence in the essay leads you to your view?

3. How does Rooney structure his argument? Does he provide enough supporting points to back up his major claim or proposition? Why or why not?

4. Is Rooney merely making value judgments about himself, or does he have a broader purpose? How do you know?

5. Explain the style of this essay. Are Rooney's language and sentence structure accessible or difficult? How does his style facilitate your reading and appreciation of the essay?

Responding in Writing

6. Argue for or against the proposition that we are a wasteful society. As Rooney does, organize your essay around your own personal experience or your knowledge of family and friends.

7. Write an imaginative essay about the year 2050. Center the essay on Rooney's last sentence: "The Earth could end up as one huge, uninhabitable dump."

8. Write a letter to your local congressman or congresswoman outlining the need for your community to do more about controlling its waste flow. Offer specific remedies for improvement.

Networking

9. Divide into groups of three or four, and jot down some of the instances of waste you have encountered on your campus. Compare your list with other group members' lists. Which problems seem to be most common? Which are singular? Share and discuss your results with the rest of the class.

10. Utilizing one or more web search engines, download information on waste management. What is the current status of this movement in the United States? Which cities or regions are doing the best job of managing their waste problems? Present your findings in class discussion.

Driving Global Warming

BILL MCKIBBEN | Bill McKibben was born in Palo Alto, California, in 1960 and studied at Harvard University (B.A., 1982). His writing focuses on the global ecosystem and the human impact on it. Frequently he brings moral and religious ideas to bear on the ways in which our behavior—from consumerism to industrial shortsightedness—degrades the natural world. McKibben says that with respect to nature and Earth's ecosystem, he tries "to counter despair." In books like *The End of Nature* (1989), *Hope, Human and Wild: True Stories of Living Lightly on the Earth* (1995), *Long Distance: A Year of Living Strenuously* (2000), and *Enough: Staying Human in an Engineered Age* (2003), McKibben balances a sense of alarm about our profligate waste of natural resources with a tempered optimism that we can revere and preserve our fragile planet. "What I have learned so far," McKibben observes, "is that what is sound and elegant and civilized and respectful of community is also environmentally benign." This essay by McKibben, which appeared in *The Christian Century* in 2001, poses a challenge: Why do we drive SUVs when clearly they degrade the environment?

Before Reading

What car or cars does your family own? Do you or other family members consider the impact on environment when purchasing vehicles? Why or why not? Is too much being made of the American propensity to drive large, gas-consuming cars? Justify your response.

Up until some point in the 1960s, people of a certain class routinely be- 1 longed to segregated country clubs without giving it much thought— it was "normal." And then, in the space of a few years, those memberships became immoral. As a society, we'd crossed some threshold where the benefits—a good place to play golf, a nice pool for the kids, business contacts, a sense of status and belonging—had to be weighed against the recognition that racial discrimination was evil. Belonging to Farflung Acres CC wasn't the same as bombing black churches (perfectly sweet and decent people did it) and quitting wasn't going to change the economic or social patterns of the whole society, but it had become an inescapable symbol.

Either you cared enough about the issue of race to make a stand and or you didn't. If you thought we were all made in God's image, and that Jesus had died to save us all, it was the least you could do.

For the past decade, buying a sport utility vehicle—an Explorer, a Navigator, a CRV, a Suburban, a Rover, and so on down the list—has seemed perfectly normal. Most people of a certain station did it. If you went to a grocery store in suburban Boston, you would think that reaching it required crossing flooded rivers and climbing untracked canyons. In any given parking lot, every other vehicle has four-wheel drive, 18 inches of clearance, step-up bumpers. They come with a lot of other features: leather seats, surround sound, comfort, status. Maybe even some sense of connection with nature, for they've been advertised as a way to commune with creation.

But now we've come to another of those threshold moments. In January, after five years of exhaustive scientific study, the International Panel on Climate Change announced the consensus of the world's leading experts: if we keep burning fossil fuels at anything like our present rate, the planet will warm four or five degrees, and perhaps as much as 11 degrees, before the century is out. Those temperatures would top anything we've seen for hundreds of millions of years. Already we can guess the effects. The decade we've just come through was the warmest on record in human history: it saw record incidence of floods and drought (both of which you'd expect with higher temperatures). Arctic ice, we now know, has thinned 40 percent in the last 40 years. Sea level is rising steadily.

And what has the SUV to do with all of this? Well, it is mostly a machine for burning gasoline. Say you switched from a normal car to a big sport "ute" and drove it for one year. The extra energy you use would be the equivalent of leaving the door to the fridge open for six years, or your bathroom light on for three decades. Twenty percent of America's carbon dioxide emissions come from automobiles. Even as we've begun to improve efficiency in factories and power plants, our cars and trucks have grown bigger and more wasteful: average fuel efficiency actually declined in the 1990s, even as engineers came up with one technology after another that could have saved gas. That's a big reason why Americans now produce 12 percent more CO_2, the main global warming gas, than they did when Bill Clinton took office.

If you drive an SUV, then you're "driving" global warming, even more than the rest of us.

In Bangladesh people spent three months of 1998 living in the thigh-deep water that covered two-thirds of the nation. The inundation came because the Bay of Bengal was some inches higher than normal (as climate changes, sea level rises because warm water takes up more space). That high water blocked the drainage of the normal summer floods, turning the nation into a vast lake. No one can say exactly how much higher that water was because of our recent fondness for semi-military transport in the suburbs. Maybe an inch, who knows?

But the connection is clear. If you care about the people in this world living closest to the margins, then you need to do everything in your power to slow the rate at which the planet warms, for they are the most vulnerable. I was naked and you did not clothe me. I was hungry and you drowned me with your Ford Explorer.

Here's more: Coral reefs the world over are dying as warmer sea water bleaches them to death—by some estimates, this whole amazing ecosystem, this whole lovely corner of God's brain, may be extinct by mid-century. In the far north, scientists recently found that polar bears were 20 percent scrawnier than they'd been just a few years before. As pack ice disappears, they can't hunt the seals that form the basis of their diet. And on and on— according to many experts, the extinction spasm caused by climate change and other environmental degradation in this century will equal or surpass those caused by crashing asteroids in geological times. But this time it's us doing the crashing.

If we care about creation, if we understand the blooming earth as an exhibit of what pleases God, then we've got to do what we can to slow these massive changes. "Where were you when I set the boundaries of the oceans, and told the proud waves here you shall come and no further?" God asks Job. We can either spit in the old geezer's face and tell him we're in charge of sea level from here on out, or we can throttle back, learn to live a little differently.

Not so differently. Giving up SUVs is not exactly a return to the Stone Age. After all, we didn't have them a decade ago, when people with large families transported themselves in considerably more fuel-efficient minivans or station wagons. The only reason we have them now is that the car companies make immense profits from them. Ford's lucky to clear a grand selling you an Escort, but there's $10,000 clear profit in an Explorer. Save for a very few special circumstances, we don't need them—nine in ten SUVs never even leave the pavement. Where I live, in the Adirondack mountains of New York, we have snow and ice six months of the year, bad roads and steep mountains. But we don't have many SUVs because no one has the money to buy one. Somehow we still get around.

Sometimes people cite safety as their cause for buying a behemoth. They reason that they need them because everyone else has them or because in an accident the other car will suffer more (a position that would probably not pass the test with many Christian ethicists). But even that's a flawed argument. It's true, says the *New York Times,* that in a collision an SUV is twice as likely as a car to kill the other driver. But because the things roll over so easily, overall "their occupants have roughly the same chance as car occupants of dying in a crash."

The big car companies are starting to sense that their franchise for may- 12 hem is running out. Last fall, after fuel prices soared and exploding tires killed dozens, the big car companies said that half a decade from now they would try to increase their fuel efficiency by 25 percent. Which is actually a nice start, but also sort of like the country club board of directors saying, "Wait five years and we'll find a few token blacks." Twenty-five percent better than 13 miles per hour is still a sick joke. Already Toyota and Honda have hybrid vehicles on the lot that can get 50, 60, 70 miles to the gallon. And we don't have five or ten or 15 years to wait.

No, the time has come to make the case in the strongest terms. Not to ha- 13 rass those who already own SUVs—in a way, they're the biggest victims, since they get to live in the same warmer world as the rest of us, but have each sent 40 grand to Detroit to boot. But it's time to urge everyone we know to stop buying them. Time to join the SUV protest in Boston on June 2. Time to pass petitions around church pews collecting pledges not to buy the things in the future. Time to organize your friends and neighbors to picket outside the auto dealerships, reminding buyers to ask about gas mileage, steering them away from the monster trucks.

Time, in short, to say that this is a moral issue every bit as compelling 14 as the civil rights movement of a generation ago, and every bit as demand- ing of our commitment and our sacrifice. It's not a technical question—it's about desire, status, power, willingness to change, openness to the rest of creation. It can't be left to the experts—the experts have had it for a decade now, and we're pouring ever more carbon into the atmosphere. It's time for all of us to take it on, as uncomfortable as that may be.

Calling it a moral issue does not mean we need to moralize. Every 15 American is implicated in the environmental crisis—there are plenty of other indulgences we could point at in our own lives, from living in over- sized houses to boarding jets on a whim. But there's no symbol much clearer in our time than SUVs. Stop driving global warming. If we can't do even that, we're unlikely ever to do much.

Thinking About the Essay

1. McKibben published this essay in *The Christian Century.* What evidence do you find in the essay that suggests he writes for an audience interested in religious matters? What assumptions does he make about his intended au-

dience? To what extent do you feel you are a member of that readership? Explain.

2. What exactly does the SUV symbolize? How does McKibben develop this symbol?

3. Why does McKibben create an introduction that seemingly is not directly relevant to the subject he develops? How *is* the content of this first paragraph relevant?

4. What is the author's argument? Where does he state his claim, and how effective is its placement? How does he employ personal experience, observation, and data to support his claim? Cite specific examples.

5. Explain the author's tone and how he achieves it. Is he optimistic or pessimistic about his subject? How do you know?

Responding in Writing

6. Write an essay explaining why you would or would not purchase an SUV. Be certain to provide reasons and evidence supporting your decision.

7. Argue for or against the proposition that moral and religious considerations should override personal preferences when we make decisions that might affect our environment adversely.

8. Write an essay that tries to present fairly both sides of the argument concerning SUVs. Create a thesis that reflects this attempt at objectivity.

Networking

9. Divide into groups of three or four and discuss your views on global warming. Do you think it is a serious problem or one that has been exaggerated? Share your answers with the rest of the class. Also, mention whether your views were modified or changed during group discussion.

10. Go online and read messages of some of the professional newsgroups whose members are in the environmental movement. Select several messages regarding global warming, and write a report on your findings.

In the Jungle

ANNIE DILLARD | Essayist, poet, autobiographer, novelist, and literary critic, Annie Dillard is best known for her keen descriptions and musings on nature. She was born in Pittsburgh, Pennsylvania, in 1945 and attended Hollins College in Virginia, where she received her B.A. (1967) and M.A. (1968) degrees. Her book *Pilgrim at Tinker Creek* (1974), a series of lyrical essays capturing the seasonal rhythms of her quiet life in Virginia's Roanoke Valley, received the Pulitzer Prize for general nonfiction. Among her other books are *Teaching a Stone to Talk* (1982), a collection of essays on nature and religion; *An American Childhood* (1987), an autobiography; *The Writing Life* (1989), a personal exploration of the creative process; and *Mornings Like This: Found Poems* (1995). She has been writer-in-residence at Wesleyan University in Connecticut since 1987. This essay, from *Teaching a Stone to Talk,* precise and poetic in style and meditative in its depiction of nature, reveals Dillard's unique ability to capture essential truths about our presence on Earth.

Before Reading

What do you expect to find in an essay with the title "In the Jungle"? What preconceptions do you have about jungles? What might you be able to learn about yourself and the human condition in a jungle?

Like any out-of-the-way place, the Napo River in the Ecuadorian jungle 1
seems real enough when you are there, even central. Out of the way of *what*? I was sitting on a stump at the edge of a bankside palm-thatch village, in the middle of the night, on the headwaters of the Amazon. Out of the way of human life, tenderness, or the glance of heaven?

A nightjar in a deep-leaved shadow called three long notes, and hushed. 2
The men with me talked softly in clumps: three North Americans, four Ecuadorians who were showing us the jungle. We were holding cool drinks and idly watching a hand-sized tarantula seize moths that came to the lone bulb on the generator shed beside us.

It was February, the middle of summer. Green fireflies spattered lights 3
across the air and illumined for seconds, now here, now there, the pale trunks of enormous, solitary trees. Beneath us the brown Napo River was rising, in all silence; it coiled up the sandy bank and tangled its foam in vines that trailed from the forest and roots that looped the shore.

Each breath of night smelled sweet, more moistened and sweet than any 4
kitchen, or garden, or cradle. Each star in Orion seemed to tremble and stir with my breath. All at once, in the thatch house across the clearing behind us, one of the village's Jesuit priests began playing an alto recorder, playing a wordless song, lyric, in a minor key, that twined over the village clearing, that caught in the big trees' canopies, muted our talk on the bankside, and wandered over the river, dissolving downstream.

This will do, I thought. This will do, for a weekend, or a season, or a 5
home.

Later that night I loosed my hair from its braids and combed it smooth— 6
not for myself, but so the village girls could play with it in the morning.

We had disembarked at the village that afternoon, and I had slumped 7
on some shaded steps, wishing I knew some Spanish or some Quechua so
I could speak with the ring of little girls who were alternately staring at me
and smiling at their toes. I spoke anyway, and fooled with my hair, which
they were obviously dying to get their hands on, and laughed, and soon
they were all braiding my hair, all five of them, all fifty fingers, all my hair,
even my bangs. And then they took it apart and did it again, laughing, and
teaching me Spanish nouns, and meeting my eyes and each other's with
open delight, while their small brothers in blue jeans climbed down from
the trees and began kicking a volleyball around with one of the North
American men.

Now, as I combed my hair in the little tent, another of the men, a free- 8
lance writer from Manhattan, was talking quietly. He was telling us the tale
of his life, describing his work in Hollywood, his apartment in Manhattan,
his house in Paris. . . . "It makes me wonder," he said, "what I'm doing in
a tent under a tree in the village of Pompeya, on the Napo River, in the jungle of Ecuador." After a pause he added, "It makes me wonder why I'm going *back*."

The point of going somewhere like the Napo River in Ecuador is not to 9
see the most spectacular anything. It is simply to see what is there. We are
here on the planet only once, and might as well get a feel for the place. We
might as well get a feel for the fringes and hollows in which life is lived, for
the Amazon basin, which covers half a continent, and for the life that—
there, like anywhere else—is always and necessarily lived in detail: on the
tributaries, in the riverside villages, sucking this particular white-fleshed
guava in this particular pattern of shade.

What is there is interesting. The Napo River itself is wide (I mean wider 10
than the Mississippi at Davenport) and brown, opaque, and smeared with
floating foam and logs and branches from the jungle. White egrets hunch
on shoreline deadfalls and parrots in flocks dart in and out of the light. Under the water in the river, unseen, are anacondas—which are reputed to
take a few village toddlers every year—and water boas, stingrays, croco-
diles, manatees, and sweet-meated fish.

Low water bares gray strips of sandbar on which the natives build tiny 11
palm-thatch shelters, arched, the size of pup tents, for overnight fishing
trips. You see these extraordinarily clean people (who bathe twice a day in

the river, and whose straight black hair is always freshly washed) paddling down the river in dugout canoes, hugging the banks.

Some of the Indians of this region, earlier in the century, used to sleep 12 naked in hammocks. The nights are cold. Gordon MacCreach, an American explorer in these Amazon tributaries, reported that he was startled to hear the Indians get up at three in the morning. He was even more startled, night after night, to hear them walk down to the river slowly, half asleep, and bathe in the water. Only later did he learn what they were doing: they were getting warm. The cold woke them; they warmed their skins in the river, which was always ninety degrees; then they returned to their hammocks and slept through the rest of the night.

The riverbanks are low, and from the river you see an unbroken wall of 13 dark forest in every direction, from the Andes to the Atlantic. You get a taste for looking at trees: trees hung with the swinging nests of yellow troupials, trees from which ant nests the size of grain sacks hang like black goiters, trees from which seven-colored tanagers flutter, coral trees, teak, balsa and breadfruit, enormous emergent silk-cotton trees, and the pale-barked *samona* palms.

When you are inside the jungle, away from the river, the trees vault out 14 of sight. It is hard to remember to look up the long trunks and see the fans, strips, fronds, and sprays of glossy leaves. Inside the jungle you are more likely to notice the snarl of climbers and creepers round the trees' boles, the flowering bromeliads and epiphytes in every bough's crook, and the fantastic silk-cotton tree trunks thirty or forty feet across, trunks buttressed in flanges of wood whose curves can make three high walls of a room—a shady, loamy-aired room where you would gladly live, or die. Butterflies, iridescent blue, striped, or clear-winged, thread the jungle paths at eye level. And at your feet is a swath of ants bearing triangular bits of green leaf. The ants with their leaves look like a wide fleet of sailing dinghies— but they don't quit. In either direction they wobble over the jungle floor as far as the eye can see. I followed them off the path as far as I dared, and never saw an end to ants or to those luffing chips of green they bore.

Unseen in the jungle, but present, are tapirs, jaguars, many species of 15 snake and lizard, ocelots, armadillos, marmosets, howler monkeys, toucans and macaws and a hundred other birds, deer, bats, peccaries, capybaras, agoutis, and sloths. Also present in this jungle, but variously distant, are Texaco derricks and pipelines, and some of the wildest Indians in the world, blowgun-using Indians, who killed missionaries in 1956 and ate them.

Long lakes shine in the jungle. We traveled one of these in dugout ca- 16 noes, canoes with two inches of freeboard, canoes paddled with machete-hewn oars chopped from buttresses of silk-cotton trees, or poled in the shallows with peeled cane or bamboo. Our part-Indian guide had cleared the path to the lake the day before; when we walked the path we saw where he had impaled the lopped head of a boa, open-mouthed, on a pointed stick by the canoes, for decoration.

The lake was wonderful. Herons, egrets, and ibises plodded the saw- 17 grass shores, kingfishers and cuckoos clattered from sunlight to shade, great turkeylike birds fussed in dead branches, and hawks lolled overhead. There was all the time in the world. A turtle slid into the water. The boy in the bow of my canoe slapped stones at birds with a simple sling, a rubber throng and leather pad. He aimed brilliantly at moving targets, always, and always missed; the birds were out of range. He stuffed his sling back in his shirt. I looked around.

The lake and river waters are as opaque as rain-forest leaves; they are 18 veils, blinds, painted screens. You see things only by their effects. I saw the shoreline water roil and the sawgrass heave above a thrashing *paichi,* an enormous black fish of these waters; one had been caught the previous week weighing 430 pounds. Piranha fish live in the lakes, and electric eels. I dangled my fingers in the water, figuring it would be worth it.

We would eat chicken that night in the village, and rice, yucca, onions, 19 beets, and heaps of fruit. The sun would ring down, pulling darkness after it like a curtain. Twilight is short, and the unseen birds of twilight wistful, uncanny, catching the heart. The two nuns in their dazzling white habits— the beautiful-boned young nun and the warm-faced old—would glide to the open cane-and-thatch schoolroom in darkness, and start the children singing. The children would sing in piping Spanish, high-pitched and pure; they would sing "Nearer My God to Thee" in Quechua, very fast. (To reciprocate, we sang for them "Old MacDonald Had a Farm"; I thought they might recognize the animal sounds. Of course they thought we were out of our minds.) As the children became excited by their own singing, they left their log benches and swarmed around the nuns, hopping, smiling at us, everyone smiling, the nuns' faces bursting in their cowls, and the clear-voiced children still singing, and the palm-leafed roofing stirred.

The Napo River: it is not out of the way. It is *in* the way, catching sun- 20 light the way a cup catches poured water; it is a bowl of sweet air, a basin of greenness, and of grace, and, it would seem, of peace.

Thinking About the Essay

1. What is Dillard's purpose in writing this essay? Does she simply want to provide vivid description of a place that we might find romantic or exotic, or does she want to argue a point or persuade us to see something? Explain.

How might description be used in the service of a larger purpose? Justify your answer with specific reference to the text.

2. Examine the first five paragraphs of this essay, which constitute the introduction. What is the effect of the first paragraph? How do paragraphs 1 to 5 set the stage for the ideas Dillard wants to develop in the rest of the essay?

3. Explain in your own words Dilllard's thesis. How does she use comparison and contrast to advance this thesis?

4. What is Dillard's attitude toward the natives she encounters? How does her selection of detail and incident convey this tone? Would you say that her attitude is overly romantic? Why or why not?

5. Which paragraphs constitute the essay's conclusion? What evidence does the writer provide to support her conclusion?

Responding in Writing

6. Write a personal essay about the most unusual place your have encountered. What made it unusual? Try to capture the uniqueness of this place with vivid description.

7. Write a careful analysis of Dillard's style in this essay, especially her diction and descriptive talents. How does she harness the "poetry" of language to convey both an impression of a faraway location and a meditation on our place in the world?

8. Dillard asserts that since we "are on the planet only once," we should "get a feel for the place" (paragraph 9). Is it necessary to go to some out-of-the-way place to obtain this uncorrupted feel for our planet? Answer this question in a meditative essay.

Networking

9. In small groups, discuss the value of retreating to unspoiled nature to learn something about our life on this planet. Share with group members any experience of nature that you have had that is similar to Dillard's.

10. On the basis of outside reading and library or online research, write an essay in which you compare Dillard's experience in this essay to Henry David Thoreau's experience in *Walden*.

Digging Up the Roots

JANE GOODALL | British naturalist Jane Goodall, born in London in 1934, has spent much of her adult life in the jungles of Tanzania engaged in the study of chimpanzees. Fascinated by animals since childhood, Goodall, after graduating from school, traveled to Kenya to work with the famed paleontologist Louis Leakey, serving as his assistant on fossil-gathering trips to the Olduvai Gorge region. In 1960, at Leakey's urging, Goodall started a new project studying wild chimpanzees in the Gombe Stream Chimpanzee Reserve in Tanzania. In 1965, Cambridge University awarded Goodall a Ph.D. degree based on her thesis growing out of five years of research in the Gombe Reserve; she was only the eighth person in the university's history to earn a doctorate without having earned an undergraduate degree. Goodall has received dozens of major international awards from conservation societies and environmental groups, including the Albert Schweitzer Award, two Franklin Burr awards from the National Geographic Society, and numerous honorary doctorates from universities around the world. Among her many books are the widely read *In the Shadow of Man* (1971), *The Chimpanzees of Gombe: Patterns of Behavior* (1986), and a two-volume autobiography in letters, *Africa in My Blood* (2000) and *Beyond Innocence* (2001). She also has written books for children and participated in media productions based on her work. This essay from the winter 1994 issue of *Orion* reflects one of Goodall's core beliefs—that animals "have their own needs, emotions, and feelings—they matter."

Before Reading

Goodall says that "animals are like us." Do you agree or disagree, and why?

When we lose something that was very precious to us, whatever its na- 1
ture, we grieve. Our grief may be short-lived sorrow or lead to a lengthy period of mourning. The depth of our grief depends on the nature of the relationship that we had with what we have lost, not on who or what that person or thing actually was. We might grieve more for the loss of a dog or a cat than a person—it simply depends on the relative contributions made by each to our physical and spiritual well-being.

I have deeply loved several dogs and grieved correspondingly deeply 2
when they died. Just a few weeks ago at our family home in the U.K. we lost Cider, the dog who has shared our lives for the past thirteen years. I hate the thought of walking where she and I walked together. When I sit on "her" couch I feel a lump in my throat, and when the doorbell rings, and there are no fierce barks, it is not easy to go and let the caller in. I miss

her snoring beside my bed at night. I am not ashamed to weep for her, as I wept for the other dogs who gave me so much.

The nature of my relationship with the Gombe chimpanzees is very different from that with my dogs. For one thing, dogs are utterly dependent on humans; for another, they become part of the household. From them I receive comfort when sad, and I can give comfort in return. With them I can share joy and excitement. With the chimpanzees it is different. They are free and independent. It is true that I have impinged on their lives, but only as an observer. (I speak here of the wild chimpanzees—relations can be very different with captive individuals.) The wild apes tolerate my presence. But they show no pleasure when they see me after an absence—they accept my goings and comings without comment. And this is as it should be since we are trying to study their natural lives. Moreover, the chimpanzees, unlike my dogs, do not depend on me for food or comfort. My relationship with them can best be described as one of mutual trust.

Nevertheless there have been Gombe chimpanzees whom I have most truly loved—even though they did not reciprocate that love. One of these was old Flo. I shall never forget seeing her body as it lay at the edge of the fast-flowing Kakombe stream. I stayed close by for the better part of three days, to record the reactions of the other chimps. As I sat there I thought back over the hours we had spent together, that old female and I. I thought of all I had learned from her about maternal behavior, and family relationships. I thought of her fearless, indomitable character. And I mourned her passing. Just as I grieved for old McGregor whom we had to shoot after polio paralyzed both legs and he dislocated one arm as he dragged his body up a tree. And I was devastated when little Getty died. He had been everyone's favorite, loved by humans and even, I would swear, by the chimpanzees themselves. It was a long time before I could watch other infants without resentment, without asking the meaningless question: Why did it have to be him?

Of course, I was also very close to David Greybeard, the first chimpanzee who ever let me approach. And I missed him very much when we finally realized he must have died. But we never knew exactly when this was, for we never found his body. Thus there was no sudden realization of his passing, no moment in time when grieving could begin.

Of all the Gombe chimpanzees I have known over the years, it was Melissa whose death affected me the most, for I was there at the very end. I wrote about it in my last book, *Through a Window.*

> By evening, Melissa was alone. One foot hung down from her nest and every so often her toes moved. I stayed there, sitting on the forest floor. . . . Occasionally I spoke. I don't know if she knew I was there or,

if she did, whether it made any difference. But I wanted to be with her as night fell: I didn't want her to be completely alone. . . . There was a distant pant-hoot far across the valley, but Melissa was silent. Never again would I hear her distinctive hoarse call. Never again would I wander with her from one patch of food to the next, waiting, at one with life of the forest, as she rested or groomed with one of her offspring. The stars were suddenly blurred and I wept for the passing of an old friend. Even now, seven years later, when I pass the tree where she died, I pause for a moment to remember her.

The nature of the grief I feel when a loved dog dies has one component 7 that is lacking from the sorrow caused by the death of one of my wild chimpanzee friends. Because dogs depend on us for food and comfort and help in sickness, there has always been an element of guilt in my grief for their passing. In their dog-minds, did I not let them down—however hard I tried to help? And could I, perhaps, have done more than I did? This nagging guilt, which we usually feel when a loved human companion passes away, has no place in my grieving for chimpanzee friends who have died. For they had no expectations of help.

The emotions triggered by the death of a chimpanzee I have loved are 8 different again from those that overwhelm me whenever I think of the vanishing wildlife of the world, of animals shot by hunters, snared by poachers, starved by the encroachment of farmers into their feeding grounds. I am angered, as well as saddened, when I think of their suffering, depressed when I think how hard it is to help them. The sight of a rhino killed for his horn is horribly distressing. It brings tears to my eyes, but the tears are part rage because we seem unable to stop the slaughter. True mourning, I believe, can only follow the death of an individual we have known and loved, whose life for a while has been linked with ours.

I have always had a great passion for trees, for woods and forests. Often I lay my hand on the trunk of a tree, feeling the texture of its bark and imagining the sap coursing up the trunk, taking life to the leaves far above. Some trees seem to have characters of their own: the slim and elegant individual, rustling soft songs in the breeze; the helpful one, with wide branches and dense foliage, providing shade; and the strong and comforting tree with a friendly overhanging trunk to protect one from the rain. When I was a child I used sometimes to lie looking up at the blue sky through the leaves of a birch tree in the garden. I specially loved that tree in the moonlight, when the white trunk was bright and ghostly and the leaves were black with glinting silver where the soft light caught them. And when it died, like so many other birch trees in the drought of 1977, when no leaves burst out in the spring, I felt great sadness, and also a sense of nostalgia. In sorrowing for the tree, was I also grieving for my lost youth?

A little while ago I drove along a road in Tanzania that once ran 10
through miles of forest. Twenty years ago there were lions and elephants,
leopards and wild dogs, and a myriad of birds. But now the trees are gone
and the road guided us relentlessly, mile after mile, through hot, dusty
country, where crops were withered under the glare of the sun and there
was no shade. I felt a great melancholy, and also anger. This anger was not
directed against the poor farmers who were trying to eke out a livelihood
from the now inhospitable land, but against mankind in general. We mul-
tiply and we destroy, chopping and killing. Now, in this desecrated area,
the women searching for firewood must dig up the roots of the trees they
have long since cut down to make space for crops.

Gombe National Park is, today, like an island of forest and wildlife set 11
in a desert of human habitation. During a recent visit I climbed to the top
of the rift escarpment and looked to the east, the north, the south. In 1980
I could look out from the same place, and there was chimpanzee habitat
stretched as far as I could see. Now the steep slopes are bare of trees and
have become increasingly barren and rocky, more and more of the precious
top soil washed away with every heavy rain. And the chimpanzees, along
with most of the other wild animals, have gone. But at least the little oasis
of the park is safe, and in its ancient forests I can for a while take refuge
from the problems of the world outside. If Gombe was destroyed I should
know inconsolable grief. For Gombe, with all its vivid and unique chimpanzee characters, with all its tumbling memories, has been an integral part
of my life for more than thirty years. It is, I have always said, paradise on
earth. And who would not mourn expulsion from paradise?

Thinking About the Essay

1. How do you interpret the author's title in light of your reading of this essay? What "roots," in particular, does she seek to dig up?

2. Explain the tone of this essay. Do you find Goodall to be sentimental, overly romantic, or nostalgic for some vanished world? Why or why not? How does she create a certain mood, and how would you define it? How does her decision to insert the "I" point of view serve to strengthen tone and mood?

3. What comparisons does the author draw between human beings, dogs, and chimpanzees? How does she organize her essay around these subjects?

4. What, exactly, is this essay about, and what is Goodall's thesis? Does she state it in one sentence or a series of sentences, or does she imply it?

5. The last section of the essay focuses on trees. How does this last section capture and reinforce what the author wants to tell us about ourselves and the natural world?

Responding in Writing

6. Argue for or against the proposition that Goodall in this essay succeeds in getting to the "roots" of the human and nonhuman condition.

7. Write a personal essay in which you narrate and describe what you have learned from a family pet or from the natural world.

8. Goodall speaks of both the joy and grief that the natural world presents to us. Reread the essay, and explain in a brief paper which of these two emotions tends to dominate the other for the author.

Networking

9. Divide into groups of three and four and list examples of the destruction of natural habitats in the United States and around the world. Present your list to the class along with other groups.

10. Go online with another classmate and find out about the Gombe Stream Research Center and/or the Jane Goodall Institute. Share your findings in class discussion.

In Defense of Nature, Human and Non-human

Francis Fukuyama

Francis Fukuyama was born in 1952 in Chicago, Illinois; he studied at Cornell University (B.A., 1974), Yale University, and Harvard University (Ph.D., 1981). Fukuyama gained worldwide attention in 1989 with the publication in *National Interest* of his essay "The End of History?" In that sixteen-page inquiry, Fukuyama contends that history has reached its logical conclusion, which is liberal democracy. He expanded his thesis into the book *The End of History and the Last Man* (1992), which has been translated into more than a dozen languages. A clear, engaging prose stylist who makes political and economic ideas comprehensible to ordinary readers, Fukuyama is willing to present provocative and debatable theses for consideration both by specialists and by the public. Long associated with the RAND Corporation, Fukuyama today is Bernard Schwartz Professor of International Political Economy at the Johns Hopkins University School of Advanced International Studies. Among his books are *Trust: The Social Virtues and the Creation of Prosperity* (1995), *The Great*

Disruption: Human Nature and the Reconstitution of the Social Order (1999), and *Our Posthuman Future: Consequences of the Biotechnology Revolution* (2002). Fukuyama also writes frequently for magazines and journals. In this essay, from the July/August issue of *Worldwatch,* he poses an important argument about the connection between the defense of human and non-human nature.

Before Reading

What connections do you see between the need to defend nature against technological exploitation and the drive to limit experimentation in human genetics?

People who have not been paying close attention to the debate on hu-   1
man biotechnology might think that the chief issue in this debate is about abortion, since the most outspoken opponents of cloning to date have been right-to-lifers who oppose the destruction of embryos. But there are important reasons why cloning and the genetic technologies that will follow upon it should be of concern to all people, religious or secular, and above all to those who are concerned with protecting the natural environment. For the attempt to master human nature through biotechnology will be even more dangerous and consequential than the efforts of industrial societies to master non-human nature through earlier generations of technology.

If there is one thing that the environmental movement has taught us   2
in the past couple of generations, it is that nature is a complex whole. The different parts of an ecosystem are mutually interdependent in ways that we often fail to understand; human efforts to manipulate certain parts of it will produce a host of unintended consequences that will come back to haunt us.

Watching one of the movies made in the 1930s about the construction   3
of Hoover Dam or the Tennessee Valley Authority is today a strange experience: the films are at the same time naive and vaguely Stalinist, celebrating the human conquest of nature and boasting of the replacement of natural spaces with steel, concrete, and electricity. This victory over nature was short-lived: in the past generation, no developed country has undertaken a new large hydroelectric project, precisely because we now understand the devastating ecological and social consequences that such undertakings produce. Indeed, the environmental movement has been active in trying to persuade China to desist from pursuing the enormously destructive Three Gorges Dam.

If the problem of unintended consequences is severe in the case of non-   4
human ecosystems, it will be far worse in the realm of human genetics. The
human genome has in fact been likened to an ecosystem in the complex
way that genes interact and influence one another. It is now estimated that
there are only about 30,000 genes in the human genome, far fewer than the
100,000 believed to exist until recently. This is not terribly many more than
the 14,000 in a fruitfly or the 19,000 in a nematode, and indicates that
many higher human capabilities and behaviors are controlled by the complex interworking of multiple genes. A single gene will have multiple effects,
while in other cases several genes need to work together to produce a single
effect, along causal pathways that will be extremely difficult to untangle.

The first targets of genetic therapy will be relatively simple single gene   5
disorders like Huntington's disease or Tay Sachs disease. Many geneticists
believe that the genetic causality of higher-order behaviors and characteristics like personality, intelligence, or even height is so complex that we will
never be able to manipulate it. But this is precisely where the danger lies:
we will be constantly tempted to think that we understand this causality
better than we really do, and will face even nastier surprises than we did
when we tried to conquer the non-human natural environment. In this
case, the victim of a failed experiment will not be an ecosystem, but a human child whose parents, seeking to give her greater intelligence, will sad-
dle her with a greater propensity for cancer, or prolonged debility in old
age, or some other completely unexpected side effect that may emerge only
after the experimenters have passed from the scene.

Listening to people in the biotech industry talk about the opportunities   6
opening up with the completion of the sequencing of the human genome is
eerily like watching those propaganda films about Hoover Dam: there is a
hubristic confidence that biotechnology and scientific cleverness will correct the defects of human nature, abolish disease, and perhaps even allow
human beings to achieve immortality some day. We will come out the other
end a superior species because we understand how imperfect and limited
our nature is.

I believe that human beings are, to an even greater degree than ecosys-   7
tems, complex, coherent natural wholes, whose evolutionary provenance
we do not even begin to understand. More than that, we possess human
rights because of that specifically human nature: as Thomas Jefferson said
at the end of his life, Americans enjoy equal political rights because nature
has not arranged for certain human beings to be born with saddles on their
backs, ready to be ridden by their betters. A biotechnology that seeks to
manipulate human nature not only risks unforeseen consequences, but can
undermine the very basis of equal democratic rights as well.

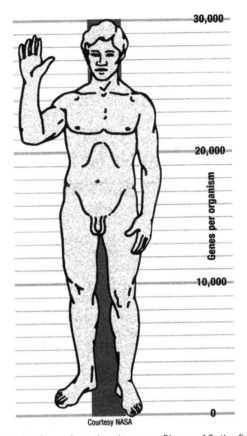

Courtesy NASA

A rendering of man from the plaque on Pioneer 10, the first man-made object to escape the solar system, and the number of genes in the human body. Although scientists initially expected the human genome to consist of 100,000 genes, it takes in fact only 30,000 genes to make up the human genetic code. The plaque on Pioneer 10 was accompanied by a disk of music and languages from around the world; is there something greater than the genome that makes up what it means to be "human"?

So how do we defend human nature? The tools are essentially the same 8 as in the case of protecting non-human nature: we try to shape norms through discussion and dialogue, and we use the power of the state to regulate the way in which technology is developed and deployed by the private sector and the scientific research community. Biomedicine is, of course, heavily regulated today, but there are huge gaps in the jurisdiction of those federal agencies with authority over biotechnology. The U.S. Food and Drug

Administration can only regulate food, drugs, and medical products on the basis of safety and efficacy. It is enjoined from making decisions on the basis of ethical considerations, and it has weak to nonexistent jurisdiction over medical procedures like cloning, preimplantation genetic diagnosis (where embryos are screened for genetic characteristics before being implanted in a womb), and germline engineering (where an embryo's genes are manipulated in ways that are inherited by future generations). The National Institutes of Health (NIH) make numerous rules covering human experimentation and other aspects of scientific research, but their authority extends only to federally funded research and leaves unregulated the private biotech industry. The latter, in U.S. biotech firms alone, spends over $10 billion annually on research, and employs some 150,000 people.

Other countries are striving to put legislation in place to regulate human   9
biotechnology. One of the oldest legislative arrangements is that of Britain, which established the Human Fertilisation and Embryology Agency more than ten years ago to regulate experimentation with embryos. Twenty-four countries have banned reproductive cloning, including Germany, France, India, Japan, Argentina, Brazil, South Africa, and the United Kingdom. In 1998, the Council of Europe approved an Additional Protocol to its Convention on Human Rights and Dignity With Regard to Biomedicine banning human reproductive cloning, a document that has been signed by 24 of the council's 43 member states. Germany and France have proposed that the United Nations draft a global convention to ban reproductive cloning.

One of the early efforts to police a specific genetic technology, recombi-   10
nant DNA experiments, was the 1975 Asilomar Conference in California, which led to the establishment under the NIH of the Recombinant DNA Advisory Committee (RAC). The RAC was supposed to approve all recombinant experiments in which genes of different individuals and sometimes species were spliced together, initially in agricultural biotechnology and later in areas like human gene therapy. A conference held in 2000 on the 25th anniversary of Asilomar led to a general consensus that, whatever the virtues of the RAC a generation ago, it had outlived its usefulness. The RAC has no enforcement powers, does not oversee the private sector, and does not have the institutional capability to even monitor effectively what is happening in the U.S. biotech industry, much less globally. Clearly, new regulatory institutions are needed to deal with the upcoming generation of new biotechnologies.

Anyone who feels strongly about defending non-human nature from   11
technological manipulation should feel equally strongly about defending human nature as well. In Europe, the environmental movement is more firmly opposed to biotechnology than is its counterpart in the United States, and has managed to stop the proliferation of genetically modified foods there dead in its tracks. But genetically modified organisms are

ultimately only an opening shot in a longer revolution, and far less consequential than the human biotechnologies now coming on line. Some people believe that, given the depredations of humans on non-human nature, the latter deserves more vigilant protection. But in the end, they are part of the same whole. Altering the genes of plants affects only what we eat and grow; altering our own genes affects who we are. Nature—both the natural environment around us, and our own—deserves an approach based on respect and stewardship, not domination and mastery.

Thinking About the Essay

1. What is the author's thesis or claim? Is it stated or implied? Explain.

2. How does Fukuyama structure his argument? What are his minor propositions? Where does he provide evidence to support his claims and assertions?

3. Does the author make any value judgments, or is he strictly logical and objective? Justify your answer by reference to the text.

4. Explain the comparative design of this essay. How does the author achieve both balance and unity in creating this comparative approach to his subject?

5. Describe the conclusion of this essay. How does it grow from the middle section? In what way does it reinforce the author's thesis? What is the final tone?

Responding in Writing

6. Argue for or against the proposition that a person who supports environmental causes should also oppose all forms of "a biotechnology that seeks to manipulate human nature" (paragraph 7).

7. Write an essay in which you explain whether or not you found Fukuyama's essay to be convincing.

8. Present your views on human cloning in a brief essay.

Networking

9. Form small groups and jot down all objections members have heard about biotechnological experimentation. Then develop a second list of positive outcomes to biotechnology research. Share your lists in class discussion.

10. Fukuyama refers to the Three Gorges Dam in China (paragraph 3). Conduct online research into this huge development project, and write a brief paper about its supporters and opponents.

A Hole in the World

JONATHAN SCHELL

Jonathan Schell was born in New York City in 1943. Following graduate study in Far Eastern history at Harvard University and additional study in Tokyo, Schell accompanied an American forces operation in South Vietnam in the winter and spring of 1967 that resulted in the evacuation of an entire village after "pacification" failed. He wrote a graphic description of the destruction of Vietnamese villages in *The Village of Ben Suc* (1967) and *The Military Half: An Account of Destruction in Quang Ngai and Quang Tin* (1968). Just as his first two books excoriated the American presence in Vietnam, Schell in his third book, *The Time of Illusion* (1976), offered a critique of the Nixon administration and the Watergate scandal. Schell's next book, *The Fate of the Earth* (1982), still one of the most persuasive treatments of the dangers of nuclear war, became a bestseller. Schell returned to the subject of nuclear proliferation in *The Gift of Time: The Case for Abolishing Nuclear Weapons* (1998). He currently is the peace and disarmament correspondent for *The Nation* and Harold Willens Peace Fellow at the Nation Institute. In the following essay, published in *The Nation* on October 1, 2001, Schell uses the events of 9/11 to raise the even more frightening specter of nuclear destruction.

Before Reading

How has 9/11 made you more aware of the dangers posed by weapons of mass destruction? Do you carry this awareness with you, or does the prospect of an attack with a weapon of mass destruction seem remote and unthreatening? Explain your response.

On Tuesday morning, a piece was torn out of our world. A patch of blue   1
sky that should not have been there opened up in the New York skyline. In my neighborhood—I live eight blocks from the World Trade Center—the heavens were raining human beings. Our city was changed forever. Our country was changed forever. Our world was changed forever.

It will take months merely to know what happened, far longer to feel   2
so much grief, longer still to understand its meaning. It's already clear, however, that one aspect of the catastrophe is of supreme importance for the future: the danger of the use of weapons of mass destruction, and especially

the use of nuclear weapons. This danger includes their use by a terrorist group but is by no means restricted to it. It is part of a larger danger that has been for the most part ignored since the end of the cold war.

Among the small number who have been concerned with nuclear arms in recent years—they have pretty much all known one another by their first names—it was commonly heard that the world would not return its attention to this subject until a nuclear weapon was again set off somewhere in the world. Then, the tiny club said to itself, the world would awaken to its danger. Many of the ingredients of the catastrophe were obvious. The repeated suicide-homicides of the bombers in Israel made it obvious that there were people so possessed by their cause that, in an exaltation of hatred, they would do anything in its name. Many reports—most recently an article in the *New York Times* on the very morning of the attack—reminded the public that the world was awash in nuclear materials and the wherewithal for other weapons of mass destruction. Russia is bursting at the seams with these materials. The suicide bombers and the market in nuclear materials was that two-plus-two that points toward the proverbial necessary four. But history is a trickster. The fates came up with a horror that was unforeseen. No one had identified the civilian airliner as a weapon of mass destruction, but it occurred to the diabolical imagination of those who conceived Tuesday's attack that it could be one. The invention illumined the nature of terrorism in modern times. These terrorists carried no bombs—only knives, if initial reports are to be believed. In short, they turned the tremendous forces inherent in modern technical society—in this case, Boeing 767s brimming with jet fuel—against itself.

So it is also with the more commonly recognized weapons of mass destruction. Their materials can be built the hard way, from scratch, as Iraq came within an ace of doing until stopped by the Gulf War and as Pakistan and India have done, or they can be diverted from Russian, or for that matter American or English or French or Chinese, stockpiles. In the one case, it is nuclear know-how that is turned against its inventors, in the other it is their hardware. Either way, it is "blowback"—the use of a technical capacity against its creator—and, as such, represents the pronounced suicidal tendencies of modern society.

This suicidal bent—nicely captured in the name of the still current nuclear policy "mutual assured destruction"—of course exists in forms even more devastating than possible terrorist attacks. India and Pakistan, which both possess nuclear weapons and have recently engaged in one of their many hot wars, are the likeliest candidates. Most important—and most forgotten—are the some 30,000 nuclear weapons that remain in the arsenals of Russia and the United States. The Bush Administration has announced its intention of breaking out of the antiballistic missile treaty of 1972, which bans antinuclear defenses, and the Russians have answered that if this treaty is abandoned the whole framework of nuclear arms control built up over thirty years may collapse. There is no quarrel between the United States and Russia that suggests a nuclear exchange between them, but accidents are another matter, and, as Tuesday's attack has shown, the mood and even the structure of the international order can change overnight.

What should be done? Should the terrorists who carried out Tuesday's 6
attacks be brought to justice and punished, as the President wants to do? Of course. Who should be punished if not people who would hurl a cargo of innocent human beings against a fixed target of other innocent human beings? (When weighing the efficiency—as distinct from the satisfaction— of punishment, however, it is well to remember that the immediate attackers have administered the supposed supreme punishment of death to themselves.) Should further steps be taken to protect the country and the world from terrorism, including nuclear terrorism? They should. And yet even as we do these things, we must hold, as if to life itself, to a fundamental truth that has been known to all thoughtful people since the destruction of Hiroshima: There is no technical solution to the vulnerability of modern populations to weapons of mass destruction. After the attack, Secretary of Defense Rumsfeld placed US forces on the highest state of alert and ordered destroyers and aircraft carriers to take up positions up and down the coasts of the United States. But none of these measures can repeal the vulnerability of modern society to its own inventions, revealed by that heart-breaking gap in the New York skyline. This, obviously, holds equally true for that other Maginot line, the proposed system of national missile defense. Thirty billion dollars is being spent on intelligence annually. We can assume that some portion of that was devoted to protecting the World Trade Center after it was first bombed in 1993. There may have been mistakes—maybe we'll find out—but the truth is that no one on earth can demonstrate that the expenditure of even ten times that amount can prevent a terrorist attack on the United States or any other country. The combination of the extraordinary power of modern technology, the universal and instantaneous spread of information in the information age and the mobility inherent in a globalized economy prevents it.

Man, however, is not merely a technical animal. Aristotle pointed out 7
that we are also a political animal, and it is to politics that we must return for the solutions that hold promise. That means returning to the treaties that the United States has recently been discarding like so much old newspaper—the one dealing, for example, with an International Criminal Court

(useful for tracking down terrorists and bringing them to justice), with global warming and, above all, of course, with nuclear arms and the other weapons of mass destruction, biological and chemical. The United States and seven other countries now rely for their national security on the retaliatory execution of destruction a millionfold greater than the Tuesday attacks. The exit from this folly, by which we endanger ourselves as much as others, must be found. Rediscovering ourselves as political animals also means understanding the sources of the hatred that the United States has incurred in a decade of neglect and, worse, neglect of international affairs—a task that is highly unwelcome to many in current circumstances but nevertheless is indispensable to the future safety of the United States and the world.

It would be disrespectful of the dead to in any way minimize the catas- 8 trophe that has overtaken New York. Yet at the same time we must keep room in our minds for the fact that it could have been worse. To lose two huge buildings and the people in them is one thing; to lose all of Manhattan—or much, much more—is another. The emptiness in the sky can spread. We have been warned.

Thinking About the Essay

1. This essay appeared less than a month after the 9/11 disaster. Do you think that the writer exploited the catastrophe, or is his purpose valid? Explain your response.

2. Schell's credentials as a specialist on nuclear proliferation are impressive. Is this essay geared to a highly intelligent audience or a more general one? Cite internal evidence to support your response.

3. How is the essay organized? Where does the introduction begin and end? What paragraphs constitute the body? Where is the conclusion? What markers assisted you in establishing these stages of essay development?

4. Reduce the logical structure of Schell's argument to a set of major and minor propositions. Is his conclusion valid in light of the underlying reasons? Explain.

5. What assertion in the essay do you most agree with, and why? Which assertion do you find dubious or unsupported, and why?

Responding in Writing

6. Write an essay in which you agree or disagree with Schell's statement that the danger of the use of weapons of mass destruction is "of supreme importance for the future" (paragraph 2).

7. Schell asserts that the United States has neglected its role in international affairs, including its abandonment of international treaties, thereby endangering the nation's security. Argue for or against his claim.

8. Write an analysis of Schell's style in this essay. Begin with the title itself and how it resonates throughout the essay. Discuss the impact of such graphic uses of language as "the heavens were raining human beings" (paragraph 1). Identify those stylistic techniques the author uses to persuade us to accept the logic of his position.

Networking

9. Divide into groups of between three and five, and create a simulation game whereby a specific city is threatened by a weapon of mass destruction. Imagine the steps taken to thwart the attack, and determine if these steps would be successful or not. Present your scenario to the class.

10. Using an Internet search engine, locate information on nuclear disarmament. Using the information retrieved, write a report on what various groups, agencies, and governments are doing to reduce and prevent the spread of nuclear weapons.

A Casebook on the Contemporary Middle East: Why Does It Matter?

No region preoccupies world citizens more these days than the Middle East. Indeed, many of the major themes of this book resonate in this turbulent region and are heightened by events there. The rise of Al Qaeda and its complicity in the 9/11 attacks, the occupations of Afghanistan and Iraq by American and coalition forces, the seemingly intractable Israeli-Palestinian conflict, and the politics of oil make the region arguably *the* story of our time. Internal political, religious, cultural, and economic conflicts also roil the region, with these conflicts frequently spilling over to other regions of the world. The Middle East calls for—indeed demands—our attention and our understanding.

Yet the complexity of the region makes it difficult for us in the West to grasp the various arguments or appreciate the profound historical reach of the conflicts. The many cultures, civilizations, and languages of the Middle East are not reflected fully in the Western media and can seem impenetrable from a Western perspective. Often the region is simplified by the Western media, ignoring the many divisions and distinctions between Shiites, Sunnis, Jews, and Christians. There are also Persians, Turks, Kurds, Arabs, and Afghanis. The Middle East vibrates with five thousand years of history—a legacy of past greatness and haunting cultural memory that creates conflicts between tradition and modernity, between democracy and absolutism, between the pull of family and tribe and the push of modernization and globalization. How can we in the West even begin to understand and appreciate the nuances and complexities of this area?

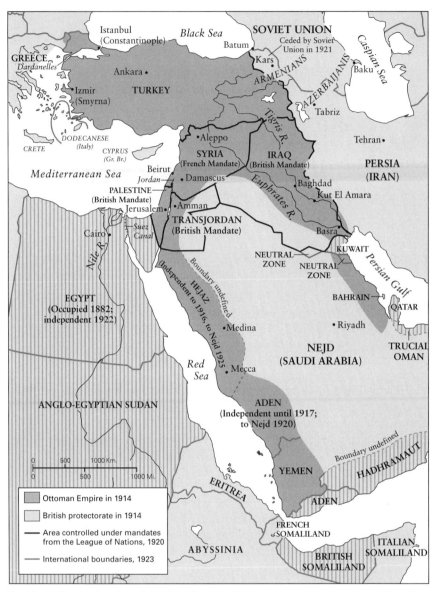

The Middle East during the height of the Ottoman Empire.

One useful way to appreciate this historically rich but conflicted region is through the voices of Middle Eastern writers. Of course, many Western writers and commentators—such as Thomas Friedman, whom you already have encountered—can provide insights into the area. However, a person whose birth or ancestry is in the Middle East (even when he or she might have immigrated to the West) often has a distinct appreciation of the region as well as a certain authority in writing about it. Such writers offer us in the

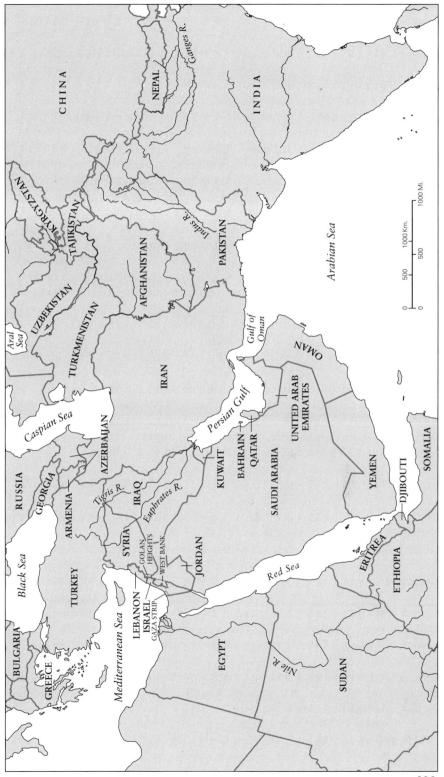

The contemporary Middle East.

West a chance to explore and begin to comprehend the contemporary Middle Eastern situation from a special perspective. They try to reveal and explain parts of their region for Western readers.

We must acknowledge that this region we call the "Middle East" was in fact an invention of the Western mind. It was Westerners, looking eastward, who designated the region as the "middle" East, located between the West and the Far East. Even as the inhabitants of this region have come to accept this construct of the Western imagination, the term obscures rather than enlightens us about the dynamics of the area. Today the region, which historically has had elastic boundaries, consists of disparate and often clashing cultures: the Fertile Crescent nations (Iraq, Syria, Jordan, and Lebanon); other Arab countries, including Saudi Arabia, Kuwait, the Gulf Emirates, and Egypt; and such non-Arab countries as Iran, Turkey, Afghanistan, and Israel.

From a geopolitical perspective, the modern Middle East was an invention of the Western powers, notably England and France. In the aftermath of the First World War and the collapse of the Ottoman Empire that had ruled the greater Middle East since 1453, England and France in 1918 began a process of regional dismemberment that resulted in the creation of nation states. The Ottoman Empire had imposed Islamic rule over provinces that stretched from the lower Balkans to the Persian Gulf. Under the Ottomans, national borders had been unknown. England, which already effectively controlled Egypt and the Persian Gulf, carved boundaries for Iraq, Kuwait, and Saudi Arabia. (It also gained control over Palestine and Transjordan under a mandate granted by the League of Nations.) Similarly, France already had colonial control over Morocco, Tunisia, and Algeria and was granted powers of mandate over Greater Syria, consisting of Syria, Lebanon, Palestine, and Jordan.

These new national borders, a patchwork quilt of Western invention, were not based on indigenous ethnic, tribal, linguistic, or cultural characteristics but instead on the political and economic strategic interests of the Great Powers. (Thus it is not coincidence that Iraq today consists of Kurds in the north, Sunnis in the middle, and Shiites in the south.) In fact, it could be argued that these nation-state divisions, which were augmented by the partition of Palestine and the creation of Israel in 1948, were designed to perpetuate political conflict and confrontation in the region. Moreover, as historian Daniel Yergin describes in *The Prize*, uppermost in the minds of the British army that captured Baghdad in 1917 was control of Mesopotamian and Persian oil supplies, for the West in the aftermath of the First World War suffered from what both American and European companies acknowledged was a gasoline famine. The quest of Western powers to guarantee a continuing flow of oil to their economies remains a geopolitical consideration to this day, and in fact is a major reason Middle Eastern peoples are suspicious of Western intentions toward the region.

By the early 1970's, Great Britain had permitted self-determination for its Middle Eastern entities and, when it turned its base in Bahrain over to the Americans in 1971, effectively ceded nominal control of the Persian Gulf to the United States. The ascendancy of the United States as the driving Western force in the Middle East—and the increasing focus of anti-Western sentiment on America—thus ushered in a new era. In effect, the United States by default became the protector of such pro-Western nations as Saudi Arabia and Iran (until the Iranian revolution of 1979), as well as the guarantor of Israel's survival. In the process, it became the lightning rod for pan-Arab nationalists, Islamists, Palestinian resistance groups, and radical intellectuals, among others, who questioned America's imperial role in the region and throughout the world.

The Iranian Revolution of 1978–1979 and the 1991 Gulf War, which was caused by Iraq's invasion of Kuwait and the U.S. military response, constitute a watershed in the dynamics of the Middle East. On the one hand, the ascendancy in Iran of Ayatollah Khomeini, the occupation of the American Embassy in Tehran, and the creation of the Islamic Republic of Iran arguably gave impetus to the militant Islamic revival we see throughout the world today. On the other hand, with the concurrent end of the cold war and the emergence of the United States as the world's superpower, serving as the arbiter of law and order in the international community, the rules of the game in the Middle East changed drastically. The invasion of Afghanistan to root out Osama bin Laden and the Taliban, and the far murkier motivations underlying the invasion of Iraq, signal the latest episodes of American incursions into the region.

Today, with Western forces on its soil in several nations, the Middle East faces multiple challenges. Across the region there are conflicts between authoritarian regimes and disillusioned populations, between secularists and religious groups, between advocates of conflict and those of cooperation, and between apostles of tradition and those of modernity. Caught once again in this dynamic, in this new phase in Middle Eastern history, are the Western powers and notably the United States. The writers in this casebook, all of Middle Eastern origin, offer provocative and compelling insights into the ways they view their homelands and their relationship to the West.

The Storyteller's Daughter

SAIRA SHAH

Saira Shah was born in London, the daughter of a prestigious Afghan family. Her father, Idries Shah, was a writer renowned for his Sufi fables. Shah first visited Afghanistan when she was twenty-one, spending three years there as a freelance journalist covering the guerrilla war against the Soviet occupation. Subsequently she worked for Britain's Channel Four News, covering conflicts in Algeria, Kosovo, Baghdad, and other parts of the Middle East. Inspired by her family's aristocratic history and their status as *sayeds* (people who trace their ancestry to the prophet Muhammad), Shah returned to Afghanistan to record the devastation caused by the rise of the Taliban. Covering herself from head to foot in a *burqa*, Shah traveled throughout Afghanistan, discovering family members, reliving Afghan myths, and tracking the horrors perpetrated by the Taliban and other warring groups. One result was the acclaimed documentary *Beneath the Veil,* recording the devastation of women's lives caused by the Taliban and broadcast on CNN. Shah writes about her experience in Afghanistan in *The Storyteller's Daughter* (2003); the following episode vividly captures the beauty, horror, and paradox of Afghan life.

From the Northern Alliance post at Ai Khanom, close to the Tajik border, you could look down past a wide, lazy river into a valley where, six weeks ago, it was rumoured, a massacre had taken place.   1

The river was called the Koksha. Down on its banks was a cluster of four villages, caught between the Taliban and Northern Alliance lines. The valley was bursting with almond blossoms, and with blossoms of artillery smoke, too. From this distance, you could not tell them apart. In January, the Taliban had pushed forward briefly and had taken the villages. As they withdrew—almost as an afterthought, the locals claimed—they had shot a dozen or so civilians in each.   2

A young Northern Alliance fighter called Usman agreed to take us down to one of the four villages, a place called Mawmaii. He was young, good-looking and—as far as was humanly possible for an opposition soldier trapped on the front line—he was cooler than cool. When we met him, he was trying to shoot down Taliban jets with a Russian sniper rifle. This seemed physically impossible, but it looked good and he knew it.   3

He begged us for Madonna tapes and bottles of whisky. In another universe, he would have been a spoilt rich kid—mobile phone, fast car, lots of girls. He seemed to realize, through some holistic intuition, that he had been robbed.   4

The closest he had ever come to the debauchery he craved was at medical school in the Tajik capital, Dushanbe, a haven of Western sophistication. "There were girls in my class," he said. "I used to talk to them." Once, he even went to a disco. He had to drop out after just one year: he was needed at the front.   5

One evening, Usman posed strategically on top of a tank, and sang a soulful, catchy song about the bitterness of war. The setting sun highlighted his chiselled Uzbek cheekbones and his dark, almond eyes. When I complimented his voice and his leading-man good looks, he said: "Yes. If it was not for the war, I would have been a great star."   6

The road to Mawmaii lay across an implausibly green plain, ringed with white-wisped mountains and dotted with sheep. I stood in the open back of the truck and inhaled its loveliness.   7

For years, beauty salons were oases of community and friendship for Afghani women. Forced to operate secretly and in great danger under the Taliban, beauty salons are now making a comeback in Afghanistan. This woman is learning to style hair at the Kabul Beauty School—which is kept safe by armed guards.

There was a swooping, singing beauty about this place. The light had a 8
marvellous golden translucency I have only ever come across in Afghanistan.
Shepherd girls waved from the side of the road. Their dresses were emerald,
ruby, turquoise, amethyst—living, sparkling jewels. Every tree was bursting
with blossom. A grey-bearded mullah with a white turban trotted past us on
his donkey; his disciple walked respectfully behind.

How can I explain the beauty of this place? It was beautiful, like a song 9 that makes you want to weep. There was magic in the fields and the mountains and the people and the trees.

Once, when we were flying over Córdoba, a Spanish friend of mine 10 said: "Welcome to my beautiful country." I felt a pang of anguish, because I had no country to be proud of. Now I felt a surge of joy. I hugged myself and whispered: "Welcome to my beautiful country." The words were like a caress on my tongue.

Usman was pretending that Afghanistan was at peace and we were on 11 a pleasure tour. When he had shown us where to cross the Koksha, out of sight of the Taliban guns, and had warned us about the landmines on the bank, he said: "Isn't it lovely?" And it was. The Koksha sparkled with spring sunlight, and was as clear as melted snow.

"This river is famous for its delicious fish," said Usman, like a proper 12 tour guide.

"Let's have some for lunch." 13

"All right," he agreed. "If we have time, we'll go and pick up some 14 grenades and throw them in to catch them."

It was not just my knowledge that was fragmentary, I thought. Despite its 15 physical beauty, the structure of Afghanistan was crumbling under my feet.

We crossed the Koksha river on a raft of goatskins. On the far bank, 16 the elders of Mawmaii were clustered, waiting for us. They were waving pieces of paper. In the painstaking handwriting of the barely literate, they had compiled lists of those who had died, and those who had disappeared. "United Nations!" they cried, as we landed. "At last you have come!"

We walked in a solemn procession up to the hill where their sons and 17 fathers had lain, dotted like sheep on the soft grass. When they left Mawmaii, the Taliban had taken fifty-one men away in trucks as hostages. There was no space for the last seven, so they had shot them.

It was clear that when the villagers looked at the hill, they still saw the 18 bodies lying there. A man with expressive eyes took off his turban to show us how they had found them. His friend, an ugly man with a pockmarked face, used it to tie his hands behind his back. Standing, bound and weeping, in the field, he said: "And I said 'Spare me—for I have not yet lived my life.' But the Taliban commander said: 'No. I do not understand your language.' Then he shot me." He rolled over on to his side, into the exact place where his brother's body had lain. The other men gathered him in a *puttu* and began to carry him away. "You can still see the blood," they said.

Of course, I thought, the blood had been washed away: it belonged to 19 the dead past, the past in which they were living. But as they told me their tale, I imagined that I, too, could see the places where the bodies had lain, curled up foetally upon the slope. And when I looked closely, sure enough, there were little mirrors and cigarette packets, fallen from pockets, and here a spent Kalashnikov round.

Then I discerned what they were trying to show me. In every depression   20
there was an outline of darker, harder earth and greener grass, where blood had nourished the soil.

"It has snowed several times since then," they said, "but the blood has   21
left a mark. Blood is very strong."

As they escorted us down the hill, one of the men turned to me. "The   22
Taliban who did this cannot have been Afghans," he said. "They must have been Pakistanis."

The elders led us to a house in the village. As we stepped into the court-   23
yard, we knew that something bad had happened there. We all felt it. It had left a residue, as tangible as a smell that you can't get rid of—a kick of ammonia. It sent us reeling.

In the courtyard there was a girl. Her face was turned to the wall. She   24
was rocking on her haunches, hunched and silent. In another spot, a second girl was frozen in the same posture of grief. They did not try to comfort each other. An old man was staring into space. His faded blue eyes gazed at some other world, as if the things he saw consumed him, sapping his dignity, his self-respect, his desire to live.

The old man said his daughters had been like this for weeks—ever since   25
the Taliban had come to their home. "I was not here when the men came," he said, as if this was an explanation. "They had taken me prisoner."

A third girl, in a blue veil, came out of the house. She began to speak in   26
Uzbek, a language I could not understand. Her voice was clear and full of cadences, like a flute. There was something indescribably pure about it.

Usman translated what she said: "The Taliban came to our house, and   27
said: 'We are going to make this place our headquarters.' They told my mother and us children to leave. It was snowing, and my mother said: 'Where will I go in the snow with my children?' Without hesitating even for a moment, a Talib lifted his Kalashnikov and shot her, just there, in the courtyard."

I was sure that something had happened to them after their mother was   28
killed, but I couldn't bring myself to broach the subject. I asked the girl who had spoken for her name. It was Fairuza, which means turquoise, the colour of her veil. How old was she? She was twelve. Her elder sister, Amina, was fifteen and her younger sister, Fawzia, was nine.

Sitting in a row, hunched in their veils—pink, yellow and blue—the   29
girls looked like broken birds. All I could see of them was their huge dark eyes. Slowly, from the corner of one eye a tear appeared and quivered for a moment before it burst and flowed. I could not even imagine from what deep well of suffering this single drop had escaped.

How long did the men stay in the house with them, while their mother's   30
body lay in the yard? The old man turned away. No other Afghan father
would have allowed me to ask such a question. But he was impotent: he
had not been there when the soldiers came.

The men had stayed alone with the girls for two days.   31

What did the soldiers do to them during that time? At this point, the   32
eldest girl, Amina, covered her face and began to weep.

Fairuza had an unquenchable spirit. She looked at her sister, then tilted her   33
chin at me and said, in that clear voice: "They asked for food and water. What
could we do? Our mother was dead. We had to do whatever they told us."

Exploring the Writer's World

1. Why does Shah emphasize the beauty of the countryside in this northern
   part of Afghanistan? What is her purpose in murmuring, "Welcome to my
   beautiful country" (paragraph 10)? How do you respond to this careful attention to natural scenery? How does the beauty of the landscape set the
   stage for subsequent discoveries and observations by the writer?

2. How does Shah reveal the lure of the West for otherwise ordinary Afghanis
   who are unfortunately trapped in the madness of war? Why does she focus
   on her guide, the young Afghan fighter Usman? Why does Usman "pretend"
   that Afghanistan is at peace and that they are merely on a "pleasure tour"
   (paragraph 11)? What is the effect?

3. Explain your response to the record of atrocities at the village of Mawmaii.
   How and why does the writer create this response? Why does Shah end the
   episode by focusing on the three girls?

4. With the class, view the documentary film that Shah risked her life to produce, *Beneath the Veil*. What does the film reveal about the author,
   Afghanistan, and the episode at Mawmaii? Why do you think Shah received
   numerous e-mails from people asking about the three girls and volunteering
   to adopt them?

5. In groups of four or five, find out more about the period Shah describes in
   this episode. Focus your research on the Northern Alliance, the Taliban,
   and the role of other Middle Eastern nations and the United States during
   this period. Appoint one member from your group to participate in a panel
   discussion of your findings.

Villages and Compounds

TAMIM ANSARY | Tamim Ansary was born in Kabul, Afghanistan, in
1948, the son of an Afghan father and American
mother. At the age of sixteen he left Afghanistan for the
United States and attended Reed College, where he

received his B.A. degree in 1970. Today he is a San Francisco–based columnist, author, and lecturer. After 9/11, Ansary visited Afghan refugee camps in Pakistan and traveled to Kabul. His memoir, *West of Kabul, East of New York: An Afghan American Story* (2002), captures family history against the backdrop of recent events in that war-torn Middle Eastern nation. Ansary also has written dozens of nonfiction children's books and educational comic books, as well as columns for Microsoft's learning site *Encarta*. He has appeared on the *News Hour with Jim Lehrer* and the *Oprah Winfrey Show,* and on numerous Public Broadcasting System programs. In this selection from his memoir, Ansary captures certain aspects of Afghan culture that contrast sharply with American attitudes toward family life.

In 1948, when I was born, most of Afghanistan might as well have been   1
living in Neolithic times. It was a world of walled villages, each one inhabited by a few large families, themselves linked in countless ways through intermarriages stretching into the dim historical memories of the eldest elders. These villages had no cars, no carts even, no wheeled vehicles at all; no stores, no shops, no electricity, no postal service, and no media except rumors, storytelling, and the word of travelers passing through. Virtually all the men were farmers. Virtually all the women ran the households and raised the children. Virtually all boys grew up to be like their fathers and all girls like their mothers. The broad patterns of life never changed, never had as far as any living generation could remember, and presumably never would. People lived pretty much as they had eight thousand years ago.

That was the countryside. The big cities, such as Kandahar and Mazar-   2
i-Sharif, were living in the fifteenth century or so. And the biggest city, Kabul, where my family lived, had made it to the twentieth century, but just barely. Cars were few, roads were unpaved, and public transportation consisted mostly of *gadis*—horse-drawn two-wheeled carriages. Electricity was scarce, too. Most of us used kerosene lanterns at night. There was no running water. We all had wells. There was no garbage service. We didn't produce any garbage. Hundreds of thousands of people lived in the city, but the houses had no numbers and the streets had no names. If you didn't know where you were going, you probably had no business going there. A postal service existed, but it didn't deliver to private homes unless the mailman felt like it, and he felt like it only if he knew you or had heard of you. Yet even with hundreds of thousands of people in the city, the postman very possibly had heard of you. Oh, not *you* in particular; you were just a leaf, a bud. He'd know the branch, the trunk, the tree itself: your people.

Everybody in the city lived in a compound, a yard surrounded by walls   3
that divided the world into a public and a private realm. That's the main
fact I want to get across about the lost world I grew up in: It was not divided into a men's world and a women's world; the division was between
public and private. Visitors never really knew us, because they never saw
the hidden world inside our compounds. Those who came from the West
didn't even know our private universe existed, or that life inside it was
warm and sweet. And in a way, we Afghans didn't know we had this realm
either, because we didn't know it was possible not to have it.

In the compounds, people spent all their time with the group. As far as   4
I can tell, none of my Afghan relatives was ever alone or ever wanted to be.
And that's so different from my life today, here in the West. Because I write
for a living, I spend most of my waking hours alone in my basement office.
Oh, I jog, do errands, see people I know—but mostly, it's just a man and
his thoughts in a blur of urban landscape. If I'm too much with other people, I need to balance it with some downtime. Most of the people I know
are like this. We need solitude, because when we're alone, we're free from
obligations, we don't need to put on a show, and we can hear our own
thoughts.

My Afghan relatives achieved this same state by being with one another.   5
Being at home with the group gave them the satisfactions we associate with
solitude—ease, comfort, and the freedom to let down one's guard. The reason for this is hard to convey, but I'm going to try. Namely, our group self
was just as real as our individual selves, perhaps more so.

I don't know what term properly applies to this type of group. *Family*   6
doesn't cover it. Even *extended family* feels too small. *Tribe*, however, is
too big. I'm inclined to hijack the term *clan* from anthropology, although
even that is not quite right, because the type of group I'm talking about was
not a formal entity, had no organization, no name, no recognized chief, and
no exact boundaries. It was more like a loose network of extended families
tied together by a mutual sense of having descended from a great someone
in the past—or a string of great someones.

Our group, for example, looked back to Sa'aduddin, a landowner who   7
lived in the nineteenth century and wrote mystical poetry under the pen
name Shuri Ishq—"Turmoil of Love." He was my great-great-grandfather.
Of course, Americans too might have a sense of identity based on a famous
ancestor, but the Afghan experience differs from the American one, because
Afghans prefer to marry their relatives. In America, hardly anyone actually
seeks to date their kin, but in Afghanistan, the ideal marriage is between
first cousins. Therefore, in Afghanistan, the lines of descent from an important man tend to keep curling back toward the center, endlessly weav-
ing a coherent entity through intermarriage. And that's the entity I'll call a

"clan" from now on, because "network of extended families descended from a great someone" is too cumbersome.

We tended to feel more at home with others of our own large group 8 than we did with strangers, and the Afghan tradition of living in compounds deepened this tendency. Once we stepped into one of our compounds in those days, each of us had a different name from the one we used outside. These names were called *luqubs* and were all constructed of the same few words—*flower, lion, sugar, lord, lady, sweet,* and so on, combined with *uncle, aunt, papa, mama,* and the like. My mother's name, for example, was Khanim Gul, meaning "Lady Flower."

In a compound, the old, young, and middle-aged—men, women, girls, 9 and boys—all shared the same space. Living quarters weren't divided into your space and his space and my space. People didn't have places to keep their possessions—few, in fact, had much in the way of possessions: It wasn't a thing-centered world. By day, thin mattresses arranged along the perimeters of the rooms served as furniture. At night, blankets were pulled out of closets and those same mattresses were rearranged in the center of the floor as beds.

At mealtime, any room could become the dining room. A tablecloth 10 would be spread on the floor. Everyone would wash their hands thoroughly and eat with them from a common platter, packed together so tightly around the food on the tablecloth that their oneness was a physical experience, a circle of people who were all touching.

Instead of television, we had genealogy. The elders, the white-headed 11 ones, spent endless hours with one another or with us youngsters, tracing connections. So-and-so married so-and-so, and then their progeny got sorted into these other branches through marriage, so actually your cousin Saliq is your second cousin through Sweet Daddy—and so on. It might not sound exciting, but remember that genealogy was the warp and family stories the woof of the fabric that made us one entity.

We didn't spend much time pondering Islam. We didn't have to. Islam 12 permeated the life of the compound like the custard that binds a casserole together, hardly separable from ordinary daily life. Five times a day, some of us did our ablutions and moved into the prayer ritual, one by one, at our own pace. Prayer divided a day into five parts and gave a sort of rhythm to the household, like breathing in, holding for quiet, and then breathing out, releasing back into noise and activity. There was no Ministry of Vice and Virtue. No one was under the gun to pray; it was not an obligation, just a custom and a way of life. At prayer call, those who didn't pray lowered their speaking voices out of respect for those who did, and we youngsters learned not to be doing our naughtiness near a person who was praying, so that we wouldn't embarrass them by seeing the undignified sight they presented when they got on their hands and knees and touched their forehead to the floor.

In winter, the intervals were shorter; in summer, longer. Some men went 13 to the mosque on Fridays, but that wasn't the locus of Islam in old Afghanistan: It was everywhere. The rhythm of prayer suffused the city, the whole society, all the villages, all the world, as far as we were aware. With so many people praying at once, at home, in the courtyards, in public buildings, five times daily, prayer became the respiration of a whole society calming down at intervals in a rhythm set not by any clock but by the light of nature.

Exploring the Writer's World

1. Consider this essay in relation to the selection about Afghanistan by Saira Shah. What similarities and differences do you see? Why is Ansary's remembrance and explanation of Afghan family life in the late 1940s made even more poignant by your reading of Shah's narrative of life during a time of persistent war?

2. Ansary, who has lived in Afghanistan and the United States, makes interesting observations about the two cultures. What are some of the features of these two worlds that he presents? Does he prefer one to the other? Explain.

3. At a time when many people are concerned about the role of Islam in world affairs, the writer offers a positive perspective on this religion. What do you learn from his treatment of the subject? Do you agree or disagree with his benign presentation of Islam, and why?

4. The day after 9/11, Ansary wrote a now famous e-mail to friends and associates about Afghanistan that rapidly became the most widely circulated letter of its kind in Internet history. Locate this letter and some of the exchanges it prompted, and report your findings to the class.

5. In groups of four or five, find out more about the history of Afghanistan from the nineteenth century to the present. Then construct a timeline that highlights the major events of this period. Be certain to include the role of England, the Soviet Union, and the United States in this timeline. Then enter into a class discussion on what the future might hold for both the Afghan people and the United States and its allies.

Blind Imperial Arrogance

EDWARD SAID | Edward W. Said was born in 1935 in Jerusalem, Palestine, and grew up in Egypt. His family moved to the United States in 1951. Educated at Princeton University (B.A., 1957) and Harvard University (Ph.D., 1964), Said was an influential literary and cultural critic and a noted supporter of the Palestinian cause. University Professor of English and comparative literature at Columbia, Said was best known to the general public as a commentator on radio and television on Middle Eastern affairs. Perceived as a public intellectual, Said for decades advocated Palestinian rights even as he criticized Palestinian policies and leadership. His books *The Question of Palestine* (1979), *Covering Islam* (1981), *The Politics of Dispossession: The Struggle for Palestinian Self-Determination* (1994), *Peace and Its Discontents* (1995), and *The End of the Peace Process: Oslo and After* (2000) offer penetrating analyses of this troubled region. Said also was a distinguished literary critic, the author of the groundbreaking study *Orientalism* (1978), *Culture and Imperialism* (1993), and other books and collections of essays. In the early 1990s Said was diagnosed with leukemia; his illness prompted him to write an autobiography, *Out of Place: A Memoir* (1999), tracing his life and journeys as an exile. Said died in 2003. In the following essay, published in the *Los Angeles Times* on July 20, 2003, Said predicts years of turmoil for the United States in the Middle East.

The great modern empires have never been held together only by military power. Britain ruled the vast territories of India with only a few thousand colonial officers and a few more thousand troops, many of them Indian. France did the same in North Africa and Indochina, the Dutch in Indonesia, the Portuguese and Belgians in Africa. The key element was imperial perspective, that way of looking at a distant foreign reality by subordinating it in one's gaze, constructing its history from one's own point of view, seeing its people as subjects whose fate can be decided by what distant administrators think is best for them. From such willful perspectives ideas develop, including the theory that imperialism is a benign and necessary thing.

For a while this worked, as many local leaders believed—mistakenly—that cooperating with the imperial authority was the only way. But because the dialectic between the imperial perspective and the local one is adversarial and impermanent, at some point the conflict between ruler and ruled becomes uncontainable and breaks out into colonial war, as happened in Algeria and India. We are still a long way from that moment in American rule over the Arab and Muslim world because, over the last century, pacification through unpopular local rulers has so far worked.

At least since World War II, American strategic interests in the Middle   3
East have been, first, to ensure supplies of oil and, second, to guarantee at
enormous cost the strength and domination of Israel over its neighbors.

Every empire, however, tells itself and the world that it is unlike all   4
other empires, that its mission is not to plunder and control but to educate
and liberate. These ideas are by no means shared by the people who inhabit
that empire, but that hasn't prevented the U.S. propaganda and policy apparatus from imposing its imperial perspective on Americans, whose
sources of information about Arabs and Islam are woefully inadequate.

Several generations of Americans have come to see the Arab world   5
mainly as a dangerous place, where terrorism and religious fanaticism are
spawned and where a gratuitous anti-Americanism is inculcated in the
young by evil clerics who are anti-democratic and virulently anti-Semitic.

In the U.S., "Arabists" are under attack. Simply to speak Arabic or to   6
have some sympathetic acquaintance with the vast Arab cultural tradition
has been made to seem a threat to Israel. The media runs the vilest racist
stereotypes about Arabs—see, for example, a piece by Cynthia Ozick in the
Wall Street Journal in which she speaks of Palestinians as having "reared
children unlike any other children, removed from ordinary norms and behaviors" and of Palestinian culture as "the life force traduced, cultism
raised to a sinister spiritualism."

Americans are sufficiently blind that when a Middle Eastern leader   7
emerges whom our leaders like—the shah of Iran or Anwar Sadat—it is assumed that he is a visionary who does things our way not because he understands the game of imperial power (which is to survive by humoring the
regnant authority) but because he is moved by principles that we share.

Almost a quarter of a century after his assassination, Sadat is a forgot-   8
ten and unpopular man in his own country because most Egyptians regard
him as having served the U.S. first, not Egypt. The same is true of the shah
in Iran. That Sadat and the shah were followed in power by rulers who are
less palatable to the U.S. indicates not that Arabs are fanatics, but that the
distortions of imperialism produce further distortions, inducing extreme
forms of resistance and political self-assertion.

The Palestinians are considered to have reformed themselves by allow-   9
ing Mahmoud Abbas, rather than the terrible Yasser Arafat, to be their
leader. But "reform" is a matter of imperial interpretation. Israel and the
U.S. regard Arafat as an obstacle to the settlement they wish to impose on
the Palestinians, a settlement that would obliterate Palestinian demands
and allow Israel to claim, falsely, that it has atoned for its "original sin."

Never mind that Arafat—whom I have criticized for years in the Ara-   10
bic and Western media—is still universally regarded as the legitimate Pales-

tinian leader. He was legally elected and has a level of popular support that no other Palestinian approaches, least of all Abbas, a bureaucrat and long-time Arafat subordinate. And never mind that there is now a coherent Palestinian opposition, the Independent National Initiative; it gets no attention because the U.S. and the Israeli establishment wish for a compliant interlocutor who is in no position to make trouble. As to whether the Abbas arrangement can work, that is put off to another day. This is short-sightedness indeed—the blind arrogance of the imperial gaze. The same pattern is repeated in the official U.S. view of Iraq, Saudi Arabia, Egypt and the other Arab states.

Underlying this perspective is a long-standing view—the Orientalist 11 view—that denies Arabs their right to national self-determination because they are considered incapable of logic, unable to tell the truth and fundamentally murderous.

Since Napoleon's invasion of Egypt in 1798, there has been an uninter- 12 rupted imperial presence based on these premises throughout the Arab world, producing untold misery—and some benefits, it is true. But so accustomed have Americans become to their own ignorance and the blandishments of U.S. advisors like Bernard Lewis and Fouad Ajami, who have directed their venom against the Arabs in every possible way, that we somehow think that what we do is correct because "that's the way the Arabs are." That this happens also to be an Israeli dogma shared uncritically by the neo-conservatives who are at the heart of the Bush administration simply adds fuel to the fire.

We are in for many more years of turmoil and misery in the Middle 13 East, where one of the main problems is, to put it as plainly as possible, U.S. power. What the U.S. refuses to see clearly it can hardly hope to remedy.

Exploring the Writer's World

1. Describe the tone of this essay. How might Said's experience as a Palestinian exile (and perhaps even his terminal illness) condition the tone? Do you think the tone is appropriate to the subject? Why or why not?

2. Said asserts that the United States is an imperial power—hence the essay's title, "Blind Imperial Arrogance." Do you agree or disagree with Said's claim, and why? Why would many people in the Middle East, and especially in Palestine where Said was born, accept his thesis and his thumbnail sketch of the history of Western imperialism? Do you? Do you accept or reject Said's conclusion? Justify your response.

3. Said states that Americans, including those in the media, stereotype Arabs and "Arabists." For example, how do you respond to his reference

to Cynthia Ozick, a noted novelist and essayist, in paragraph 6? Do you think, as Said asserts, that Ozick is guilty of stereotyping? Why are we predisposed to engage in such stereotyping? Do you think that people in the Middle East also stereotype us? Can stereotyping reveal the truth about people or a situation, or is it always a form of discrimination or abuse?

4. Reread Said's article on Andalusia that begins on page 292. Compare and contrast the two essays. Would you say that the history of Andalusia also reveals the sort of imperial ambitions that Said criticizes in this essay? Why or why not?

5. Locate online the essay by Ozick in the *Wall Street Journal* that Said mentions in paragraph 6. Then decide if Said is fair in his criticism of her. Report and defend your decision in class.

"We Have Done the Gruntwork of Peace"

AMOS OZ

Amos Oz, born Amos Klausner in Jerusalem, Israel, in 1939, is an internationally acclaimed writer of fiction and a peace activist. Educated at Hebrew University of Jerusalem and St. Cross College, Oxford, Oz fought in the tank corps in Sinai during the Six Day War in 1967 and in the Golan Heights in 1973 during the Yom Kippur War (called the Ramazan War by Arabs). He has been a visiting professor and writer-in-residence at universities in Israel, England, and the United States, including the University of California at Berkeley and Princeton University; since 1987, he has been a professor at Ben-Gurion University of the Negev. Among his many works, written in Hebrew and translated into more than a dozen languages, are the novels *My Michael* (1972), *Elsewhere, Perhaps* (1973), *A Perfect Peace* (1985), *Fima* (1993), and *Don't Call It Night* (1996) and several short story collections. *The Same Sea*, his extraordinary lyric novel, written in fiction and poetry, was published in 2001. Of Israel, Oz says: "It's my thing and my place, and my addiction." Oz is a persistent critic of Israeli policies toward the Palestinians, but also a defender of Israel's right to exist. In the following essay, published in the *Manchester Guardian* on October 17, 2003, Oz recounts the efforts of Israelis and Palestinians to hammer out a declaration of principles that could lead to peace.

Palestinian schoolgirls walk past Israeli soldiers in Hebron, one of the most contested and violent cities of the West Bank, a region jointly controlled by Israel and the Palestinian Authority. The tomb of Abraham, considered the patriarch of both Judaism and Islam, is located in Hebron; rivalries here extend for millennia.

I went to the Israeli-Palestinian conference in Jordan in a sceptical frame   1
of mind. I estimated that, as so often in the past, we might succeed in drafting a joint declaration of principles about the need to make peace, to halt terror, to end the occupation and oppression, to mutually recognise each other's rights, and to live as neighbours in two states for two peoples. We have done all that many times before, at all kinds of conferences and gatherings and with agreements and public statements and what have you. At many points in the past 10 years we have been in striking distance of peace, only to slide again into the abyss of violence and despair.

The same old points of dispute would, I feared, trip us up again: "the   2
right of return" or a solution to the refugee problem? "Return to the 1967 borders" or a logical map that also takes the present into account, and not just history? Open and explicit recognition of the national rights of the Jewish and Palestinian peoples to live each in its own country, or just some equivocating platitude about "peaceful coexistence"? Explicit Palestinian assent to finally and absolutely renounce any additional future claims, or "black holes" that would permit an eventual renewal of conflict and violence?

In previous agreements, including the Oslo agreement, the two sides   3
were very careful not to get caught in the "radioactive core" of the conflict.
Refugees, Jerusalem, end of the conflict, permanent borders—all these
minefields were marked off by white ribbons and their resolution put off
to a better future. The Camp David conference collapsed, after all, the
minute it trod on those mines.

A Two-Family House, Not a Double Bed

On the first evening, the members of the two groups meet for an opening talk.   4
It is a few days after the murder of families and children at the Maxim restaurant in Haifa, a few hours after the killing of several innocent Palestinians in
Rafiah, children also among them. A strange ambience pervades the room.
Here and there someone tries to crack a joke, perhaps in order to mask the
mixture of emotion, resentment, suspicion, and goodwill. Colonel Shaul
Arieli, former commander of the Israel Defence Forces in the Gaza Strip, sits
facing Samir Rantisi, a cousin of Hamas leader Abd al-Aziz Rantisi. The son
of the late Faisal Husseini, Abd al-Qader al-Husseini (named after his grandfather, who in my childhood was referred to as the commander of the Arab
gangs, and who was killed in 1948 in a battle with Israeli forces) sits facing
Brigadier General Shlomo Brom, a former deputy commander of the Israeli
army's strategic planning division. Next to David Kimche, formerly senior
Mossad official and director-general of Israel's foreign ministry, sits Fares
Kadura, a leader of the Tanzim, a Palestinian militant guerrilla group.

Through the window, beyond the Dead Sea, we can see the small clus-   5
ter of lights that marks Kibbutz Kalia, which the Geneva document would
transfer to Palestinian control. We also see the large dome of lights marking Ma'aleh Adumim, the Jerusalem suburb along the road to Jericho that,
according to the same document, would become an inalienable part of the
State of Israel.

We talk and debate (in fluent Hebrew) until after midnight with   6
Hisham Abd al-Raziq, who spent 21 years—half his life—in Israeli prisons.
Now he serves as the country's minister for prisoners' affairs. He is almost
certainly the world's only cabinet minister for prisoners' affairs. But our
own minister-prisoner, Natan Scharansky, is apparently the only person in
the entire world who bears the title "minister for diaspora affairs." Some
day, Palestine will most likely have a minister for diaspora affairs instead
of a minister for prisoners' affairs. There is a certain intimacy at such meetings: the Israelis and Palestinians are enemies, but not strangers. The Swiss
observer at the conference was certainly astonished to see the frequent
switches that took place here, in the rooms and in the corridors, between
anger and back-slapping and between jabs as sharp as slivers of glass and

simultaneous outbursts of laughter. (Nervous but liberating laughter was brought on by unintentional double-entendres, such as when an Israeli said, "Could I detain you for a moment?" and when a Palestinian said "I'll blow up the meeting on this point.")

When the day comes to sit down with the Syrians, faces will be rigid and   7 stern on both sides of the negotiating table. So the Palestinians are, they say, with the Saudis. But here, in the hotel on the Dead Sea shore (Israeli Knesset member Chaim Oron and former Palestinian cabinet minister Yasir Abd-Rabbo walk around in sandals and shorts) we are more like a long-married couple in their divorce attorney's waiting room. They and we can joke together, shout, mock, accuse, interrupt, place a hand on a shoulder or waist, throw invective at each other, and once or twice even shed a tear.

Because we and they have experienced 36 years of intimacy. Yes, a vio-   8 lent, bitter, warped intimacy, but intimacy, because only they and we, not the Jordanians and not the Egyptians and certainly not the Swiss, know exactly what a roadblock looks like and what a car-bomb sounds like and exactly what the extremists on both sides will say about us. Because since the Six Day War, we are as close to the Palestinians as a jailer is to the prisoner handcuffed to him. A jailer cuffing his wrist to that of a prisoner for an hour or two is a matter of routine. But a jailer who cuffs himself to his prisoner for 36 long years is himself no longer a free man. The occupation has also robbed us of freedom.

This conference was not meant to inaugurate a honeymoon between the   9 two nations. Quite the opposite—it was aimed at, finally, attenuating this warped intimacy. At drafting a fair divorce agreement. A painful, complicated divorce, but also one that unlocks the handcuffs. They will live in their home and we will live in ours. The Land of Israel will no longer be a prison, or a double bed. It will be a two-family house. The handcuffed link between the jailer and his prisoner will become a connection between neighbours who share a stairwell.

A Common Memorial

Nabil Qasis, a former president of Bir-Zeit University and the Palestinian 10 Authority's minister of planning, is a polite, introverted, melancholy man. He is also a tough negotiator. He is perhaps the only member of the Palestinian group who has no inclination to jest or trade mild jabs with the Israelis. He stops me by the bathroom door to say: "Try, please, to understand: for me, giving up the right of return to the cities and villages we lost in 1948 is to change my identity from here on out."

I really do "try to understand." What the words mean is that Qasis's 11 identity is conditional on the eradication of my identity.

Afterwards, during a discussion in the meeting room, Nabil Qasis raises   12
his voice and demands that the word "return" appear in the document. In exchange, he and his associates will consent to the word being accompanied by
reservations. Avraham Burg, a religious Labor member of the Knesset and its
former speaker, also raises his voice. He, too, is angry: let Nabil Qasis give up
part of his national identity just as I, Avraham Burg, hereby relinquish no less
than a part of my religious faith, inasmuch as I am prepared to agree, with a
broken heart, to Palestinian sovereignty on the Temple Mount.

For my part, I say that as far as I'm concerned, "return" is a code name   13
for the destruction of Israel and the establishment of two Palestinian states
on its ruins. If there's return, there's no agreement. Furthermore, I will be
a party only to a document that contains explicit recognition of the Jewish
people's national right to their own country.

This was one of any number of difficult moments of crisis during the   14
conference. In the end, neither the term "right of return" nor the word "return" appear[s] anywhere in the document. It speaks of a comprehensive
solution of the entire Palestinian refugee problem, outside the borders of
the State of Israel. Moreover, the document we signed, the Geneva Initiative, recognises, unequivocally, the right of the Jewish people to their own
country, alongside the state of the Palestinian people.

As far as I am aware, we have never heard from any representative   15
Palestinian actor the words "the Jewish people," and we have certainly not
heard any word of recognition of the Jewish people's national right to establish an independent state in the Land of Israel.

At 2:30am, over the 15th cup of coffee, in a break between argument   16
and drafting and between discussion and bargaining, I tell Yasir Abd-
Rabbo and several of his associates: some day we will have to erect a joint
memorial to horrible folly, yours and ours. After all, you could have been
a free people 55 years ago, five or six wars ago, tens of thousands of dead
ago—our dead and your dead—had you signed a document similar to this
one in 1948. And we Israelis could have long ago lived in peace and security had we offered the Palestinian people in 1967 what this document offers them now. Had we not been inebriated with victory after the conquests
of the Six Day War.

We'll Even Bear Sharon on Our Shoulders

There is no point at all to the hysteria that the document's opponents are now   17
encouraging. Its authors know very well that Sharon and his cabinet are the
legal government of Israel. They also knew that their initiative, which is the
fruit of an intense series of meetings between the parties, conducted in strict
secrecy during a period of two years, is no more than an exercise. The goal of

the exercise is solely to present the Israeli and Palestinian publics with a window through which they can view a different landscape—no more car bombs and suicide bombers and occupation and oppression and expropriation, no more endless war and hatred. Instead, here is a detailed, cautious solution that does not circumvent any one of the fundamental questions.

Its fundamental principle is: we end the occupation and the Palestinians 18 end their war against Israel. We give up the dream of Greater Israel and they give up the dream of Greater Palestine. We surrender sovereignty in parts of the Land of Israel where our hearts lie, and they do the same. The problem of the 1948 refugees, which is really the heart of our national security predicament, is resolved comprehensively, completely, and absolutely outside the borders of the State of Israel and with broad international assistance. If this initiative is put into action, not a single Palestinian refugee camp, afflicted with despair, neglect, hatred, and fanaticism, will remain in the Middle East. In the document we have in hand, the Palestinian side accepts contractually, finally, and irrevocably that it does not have and will never have any future claims against Israel.

At the end of the conference, after the signing of the Geneva initiative, 19 a representative of the Tanzim told us that we now perhaps see on the horizon the end of the 100-year war between the Jews and the Palestinians. It will be replaced, he said, by a bitter struggle between those on both sides who promote compromise and peace, and a fanatical coalition of Israeli and Palestinian extremists.

That struggle is now in full force. Sharon opened it even before the 20 Geneva initiative was published, and the leaders of Hamas and Islamic Jihad rushed to support him, using the very same vocabulary of vituperation.

What does the Geneva initiative document not have? It has no teeth. It 21 is no more than 50 pages of paper. But if the people on both sides accept it, tomorrow or the day after, they will find that the gruntwork of making peace has already been done. Almost to the last detail. If Sharon and Arafat want to use this paper as a basis for an agreement, its authors will not insist on their copyright. What if Sharon presents a different, better, more intricate, more patriotic plan that is also accepted by the other side? Let him do it. We'll congratulate him. Even though Sharon, as everyone knows, is a weighty personage, my friends and I will bear him on our shoulders.

Exploring the Writer's World

1. Oz in this essay provides a poignant narrative of meetings that resulted in the Geneva Initiative, a plan for peace developed by Israelis and Palestinians over two years. Explain the basic details of the plan, and why or why not it seems practical to you. Oz has been a persistent critic of both Israeli

and Palestinian policies and personalities, and especially sharp in his attacks on such leaders as Ariel Sharon and Yasser Arafat. Based on this hostility, do you think that the current Israeli and Palestinian leadership would accept the plan for peace outlined in this article? Why or why not?

2. Oz is a distinguished novelist and uses his literary talent to re-create the mood of the meetings, some of the characters involved, and the conflicts that prevailed and were resolved. He also employs figurative language and other stylistic devices, including a mordant sense of humor, to make his narrative compelling. Point to these stylistic details and strategies that animate the essay and make the subject compelling.

3. After his introduction, Oz presents his essay in three parts, each with a subtitle. How do the subtitles capture the substance of each section? How does the structure resemble a three-act play? Why would a playlike structure be especially appropriate to the subject?

4. Go online and see if you can locate the entire fifty-page document that presents the Geneva principles. Scan this document and summarize its main points.

5. In small groups, construct a timeline on the Arab-Israeli conflict, beginning with the Balfour Declaration—the 1917 British communiqué that called for the creation of a Jewish homeland in the Holy Land.

The Veiled Threat

AZAR NAFISI

Azar Nafisi was born in Iran. She completed graduate study in the United States at the University of Oklahoma, where she received a Ph.D. degree in English in 1979. Nafisi was a professor of English at the University of Tehran, the Free Islamic University, and Allameh Tabatabai University. She was fired from all three institutions for criticism of the Islamic regime, including her refusal to wear the veil. Subsequently she held a literature class for a small group of her former female students in her home, a narrative recounted in her book *Reading Lolita in Tehran: A Memoir in Books* (2003). Nafisi left Iran in 1997 and now teaches at Johns Hopkins University. She has published articles in the *New York Times* and the *Washington Post* and has appeared as a radio and television commentator on Iranian affairs. In the following essay, which appeared in *The New Republic* in 1999, Nafisi explains how the Islamic regime in Iran, while attempting to suppress women, has paradoxically invested them with authority and power.

Iwould like to begin with a painting. It is Edgar Degas's *Dancers Practic-* 1
ing at the Barre, as reproduced in an artbook recently published in the
Islamic Republic of Iran. Under the heading "Spatial Organization," the
book gives a two-paragraph explanation of Degas's placement of the ballerinas: "The two major forms are crowded into the upper right quadrant
of the painting, leaving the rest of the canvas as openspace. . . ."

So far, everything seems normal. But, like most things in Iran today, it 2
is not. Upon closer inspection, there is something disturbingly wrong with
the illustration accompanying this description, something that makes both
the painting and the serious tone of its discussion absurdly unreal: the ballerinas, you see, have been airbrushed out. Instead, what meet the eye are
an empty space, the floor, the blank wall, and the bar. Like so many other
images of women in Iran, the ballerinas have been censored.

Of course, the irony is that, by removing the dancers, the censors have 3
succeeded only in making them the focus of our attention. Through their
absence, the dancers are rendered glaringly present. In this way, Degas's
painting is emblematic of a basic paradox of life in Iran, on the eve of the
twentieth anniversary of the 1979 Islamic Revolution. On the one hand,
the ruling Islamic regime has succeeded in completely repressing Iranian
women. Women are forbidden to go out in public unless they are covered
by clothing that conceals everything but their hands and faces. At all government institutions, universities, and airports, there are separate entrances
for women, where they are searched for lipstick and other weapons of mass
destruction. No infraction is too small to escape notice. At the university
where I used to teach, one woman was penalized for "laughter of a giggling
kind." And, just recently, a female professor was expelled because her wrist
had shown from under her sleeve while she was writing on the blackboard.

Yet, while these measures are meant to render women invisible and 4
powerless, they are paradoxically making women tremendously visible and
powerful. By attempting to control and shape every aspect of women's
lives—and by staking its legitimacy on the Iranian people's supposed desire
for this control—the regime has unwittingly handed women a powerful
weapon: every private act or gesture in defiance of official rules is now a
strong political statement. Meanwhile, because the regime's extreme regulation of women's lives necessarily intrudes on the private lives of men as
well (whose every interaction with women is closely governed), the regime
has alienated not just women but many men who initially supported the
revolution.

This tension between the Islamic ruling elite and Iranian society at large 5
has been vastly underestimated by Western observers of Iran. In part this is
because, over the past 20 years, American analysts and academics, as well as

Edgar Degas, *Dancers Practicing at the Barre,* 1877. The original painting, with its practicing ballerinas.

the Iranian exile community, have had little or no access to Iran. Thus they have relied unduly on the image presented by Iran's ruling clerics.

At present that image is one of increased openness—as symbolized by the   6
election of the moderate cleric Mohammed Khatami to the presidency back in 1997. Recently, for example, CNN cheerfully informed us that, after 20 years, the Islamic Republic has begun to show Hollywood movies. What CNN failed to mention was that Iranian television's version of, for example, *Mary Poppins* showed less than 45 minutes of the actual film. All portions featuring women dancing or singing were cut out and instead described by an Iranian narrator. In *Popeye,* all scenes involving Olive Oyl, whose person and whose relationship with Popeye are considered lewd, were excised from the cartoon. Meanwhile, even as the regime purports to have softened its hostile stance toward the United States, it has not softened the punishment meted out to Iranians who dare show an interest in American culture. In fact, soon after he was appointed, Khatami's new education minister issued a new directive forbidding students to bring material bearing the Latin alphabet or other "decadent Western symbols" to class.

Reproduction of *Dancers Practicing at the Barre,* from an art book published in Iran. The censored version reflects what Nafisi calls a "basic paradox of life in Iran."

However, these are just the mildest examples of the many ways in which 7
the new openness that characterizes Khatami's rule has been accompanied by
increased repression. The brief spring that followed his victory—during
which freedom of speech flourished in public demonstrations and new newspapers—was brought to an end with an abrupt crackdown. The government
has since banned most of the new papers and harassed or jailed their editors.
(They have since been released.) Many of the progressive clergymen who
took advantage of the opening to protest the current legal system were also
arrested and, in one case, defrocked. The regime has also taken the opportunity to clamp down on members of Iran's Bahai minority.

Meanwhile, the parliament has passed two of the most reactionary 8
laws on women in the republic's history. The first requires that all medical facilities be segregated by sex. The second effectively bans publication of women's pictures on the cover of magazines as well as any form
of writing that "creates conflict between the sexes and is opposed to the
Islamic laws."

This past fall, two nationalist opposition leaders, Daryush and Par- 9
vaneh Forouhar, were murdered, and three prominent writers disappeared.
All three were later found dead. Many Iranians were outraged, and tens of

thousands attended the Forouhars' funeral in a tacit protest. The government's initial response gave these Iranians some reason for hope. President Khatami condemned the killings and set up a committee to investigate them. The committee's first conclusion was that those responsible were members of the Information Ministry. However, within days, the committee was proffering a different story, alleging that, on second thought, the murderers were just part of a rogue group within the ministry and that the killings were not political. The committee also has yet to name the killers—much less bring them to justice. Furious, Iranians have flooded the progressive newspapers with angry calls and letters.

To the extent that the Western media have taken note of such incidents, 10 they have mainly cast them as the symptoms of a struggle between the moderate Khatami and his reactionary fellow clerics. More often than not, the media portray acts of repression as measures taken by the hard-liners against Khatami—as if he, and not the people who were actually murdered or oppressed, was the real victim.

This simplistic portrayal of Khatami versus the hard-liners completely 11 misunderstands the current situation in Iran. Khatami does not represent the opposition in Iran—and he cannot. True, in order to win a popular mandate he had to present an agenda for tearing down some of the fundamental pillars of the Islamic Republic. But in order to even be eligible for election he had to have impeccable political and religious credentials. In other words, he had to be, and clearly is, committed to upholding the very ideology his constituents so vehemently oppose.

Khatami's tenure, then, has revealed the key dilemma facing the Islamic 12 regime. In order to maintain the people's support, the government must reform, but it cannot reform without negating itself. The result has been a kind of chaos, a period marked by the arbitrariness of its events. One day a new freedom is granted; the next day an old freedom is rescinded. Both events are symptoms of the deep struggle under way in Iran today, not just between Khatami and the reactionary clerics, but between the people of Iran and all representatives of the government. And at the center of this struggle is the battle over women's rights.

A second image comes to mind—a woman from the past, Dr. 13 Farokhroo Parsa. Like the ballerinas, her presence is felt through her absence. I try to conjure her in my mind's eye. Parsa had given up her medical practice to become the principal of the girls' school in Tehran I attended as a teenager. Slowly her pudgy, stern face looms before me, just as it did when she used to stand outside the school inspecting the students as we entered the building. Her smile was always accompanied by the shadow of a frown, as if she were afraid that we would take advantage of that smile and betray the vision she had created for her school. That vision, her life's goal, was for us, her girls, to be "truly" educated. Under the Shah, Parsa rose to become one of the first Iranian women to be elected to the Iranian parliament, and then, in 1968, she became Iran's first female Cabinet minister, in charge of higher education. In that post Parsa tried not only to raise the quality of education but to purge the school textbooks of sexist images of women.

When the Shah was ousted in 1979 by a diverse group of opposition 14 figures that included Muslim clerics, leftists, and nationalists, Parsa was one of the many high functionaries of the previous government whom the revolutionaries summarily tried and executed. At her trial she was charged with "corruption on earth," "warring against God," and "expansion of prostitution." She was allowed no defense attorney and was sentenced by hooded judges.

At the time, the new revolutionary regime took a great deal of pride in its 15 executions, even advertising them and printing pictures of its victims in the newspapers afterward. But Parsa's photograph was never published. Even more exceptional, in that exceptional time, was the manner of her death. Before being killed she was put in a sack. The only logic behind such an act could be the claim that Islam forbade a man to touch the body of a woman, even during her death. There is some debate about the method of her execution. Some say she was beaten, others that she was stoned, still others that she was machine-gunned. Nonetheless, the central image of her murder remains the same: that of a living, breathing woman made shapeless, formless, in order to preserve the "virtue" and "dignity" of her executioners.

I had not thought of Parsa for many years until the news of her execu- 16 tion resurrected her in my memory. Since then, time and again, I have tried to imagine her moment of death. But, while I can see her living face with its smile and frown, I cannot envision her features at the specific moment when that smile and frown forever disappeared in that dark sack. Could she have divined how, not long afterward, her students and her students' students would also be made shapeless and invisible not in death but in life?

For this, on a broader scale, is precisely what the clerics have done to 17 all Iranian women. Almost immediately upon seizing power, Ayatollah Khomeini began taking back women's hard-won rights. He justified his actions by claiming that he was actually restoring women's dignity and rescuing them from the degrading and dangerous ideas that had been imposed on them by Western imperialists and their agents, among which he included the Shah.

In making this claim, the Islamic regime not only robbed Iran's women 18 of their rights; it robbed them of their history. For the true story of women's liberation in Iran is not that of an outside imperialist force imposing alien ideas, or—as even some opponents of the Islamic regime contend—that of a benevolent Shah bestowing rights upon his passive female subjects. No, the advent of women's liberation in Iran was the result of a homegrown struggle on the part of Iranian women themselves for the creation of a modern nation—a fight that reached back more than a century. At every step of the way, scores of women, unassuming, without much sense of the magnitude of their pioneering roles, had created new spaces, the spaces my generation and I had taken for granted. This is not to say that Iranian women—including those of my own generation—never made mistakes, never wavered in their commitment to freedom. But the fact that Iran's women were fallible does not change the fact that so many of them were vital leaders in Iran's long struggle for modernization.

Probably the first of these leaders was a poet who lived in the middle of   19
the last century, a woman named Tahereh who was said to be stunningly beautiful. At the time, Iran was ruled by the despotic and semi-feudal Qajar dynasty, whose reign was supported by fundamentalist Muslim clerics. The alliance between the mullahs and the despotic regime prompted various groups to begin questioning the basic tenets of Islam. One such group were the Babis—a dissident movement of Islamic thinkers who were the precursors to the Bahais—who eventually broke with Islam to create a new religion, and who are the victims of vicious persecution by the Iranian government to this day. Tahereh was one of the Babis' most effective leaders. She was among the first to demand that religion be modernized. She debated her ideas with men and took the unprecedented step of leaving her husband and children in order to tour the country preaching her ideas. Tahereh was also the first woman to unveil publicly. Perhaps not surprisingly, she paid for her views with her life. In 1852, she was secretly taken to a garden and strangled. Her body was thrown into a well. She was 36.

As Iran began to have increasing contact with the West, many sectors   20
of the population—intellectuals, minorities, clerics, and even ordinary people—became increasingly aware of their nation's backwardness as compared to the West. From the mid-nineteenth century these forces continually struggled with Iran's rulers over the degree to which Iran should close the gap by modernizing itself. By 1908, this struggle had come to a head, with the ruling Shah threatening to undermine the constitution that the modernizers had forced his predecessor to agree to accept in 1906. The new Shah soon began bombarding the parliament.

Once again, women were at the forefront. Many of them actually   21
fought in the violent skirmishes that ensued, sometimes disguised as men. They even marched to the parliament, carrying weapons under their veils

and, once inside, demanded that the men holed up there hand over the jobs if they could not protect the constitution.

The constitutionalists prevailed, and, although the constitution con- 22 tained no language advancing women's rights, the next 20 years saw significant progress in this area thanks to the determined efforts of countless women. Leafing through the books about the women's movements from this era, one is amazed at their members' courage and daring. So many names and images crowd the pages of these books. I pick one at random: Sediqeh Dowlatabadi, daughter of a learned and religious man from an old and highly respected family, who was the editor of a monthly journal for women. In the 1910s she was beaten and detained for three months for establishing a girls' school in Isfahan. One can only guess the degree of her rage and resentment against her adversaries by her will, in which she proclaimed: "I will never forgive women who visit my grave veiled." It was only appropriate that those who murdered Farokhroo Parsa should also not tolerate Dowlatabadi, even in her death. In August 1980, Islamic vigilantes demolished her tomb and the tombs of her father and brother who, although men of religion, had supported her activities.

It was an American, Morgan Shuster, who best appreciated the efforts 23 of Iranian women during Dowlatabadi's period. "The Persian women since 1907 had become almost at a bound the most progressive, not to say radical, in the world," he wrote in his 1912 book *The Strangling of Persia*. "That this statement upsets the ideas of centuries makes no difference. It is the fact."

As part of their push toward modernization, the women of Iran also 24 supported a general movement in favor of greater cultural pluralism. Writers and poets led heated and exciting debates on the need to change the old modes of artistic and literary expression, with many calling for a "democratization" of the Persian language. New literary and artistic forms were introduced to Iran.

The reactionary elements in the clerical ranks and other supporters of 25 despotism rightly recognized that the ideas in these cultural products represented a threat to their dominance and immediately attacked them as "poisonous vapors" coming from the West to destroy the minds of Iranian youth. To the mullahs the idea of women's rights fell in the same category—and they opposed them in the same breath. Two prominent clerics, Sheikh Fazolah Nuri and Sayyid 'Ali Shushtari—mentors of Ayatollah Khomeini—even issued a fatwa against women's education.

But the charge that Iran's women's rights activists—and the moderniz- 26 ers in general—were agents of the West is patently unjust. To be sure, they were keenly interested in bringing in Western ideas. But this desire

stemmed from their acute awareness of Iran's shortcomings and their belief that Iran's road to independence and prosperity lay in understanding
and internalizing the best of the Western systems of government and
thought. It also meant fighting back when the Western nations began brutally exploiting Iran's wealth and natural resources. And Iranian women
were at the forefront of this battle—for instance, organizing a large-scale
boycott of foreign textiles in favor of Iranian-manufactured products and
frequently demonstrating in support of national independence. In fact, it is
safe to say that, more than any other group, women, the same women who
were several decades later demonized as the agents of imperialism, symbolized the nationalistic and antiimperialist mood of those times.

Over the ensuing years, the modernizers gained ground. Whatever else 27
might be said about him, Shah Reza Pahlevi, who came to power in 1925,
was a committed modernizer who in 1936 even attempted to mandate that
all women cease wearing veils. When this failed due to popular outrage, he
worked to encourage unveiling in other ways. His son, Shah Muhammad
Reza, who was in power at the time of the 1979 revolution, continued in
this tradition—for example, granting women the right to vote in 1963. (Of
course, it should be remembered that, contrary to the claims of both the
Shahs and the clerics who opposed them, these actions merely ratified the
progress that had been achieved by Iranian women themselves. Long before the mandatory unveiling law was imposed and long after that law was
annulled, scores of Iranian women chose to throw off their veils of their
own volition.)

By 1979, women were active in all areas of life in Iran. The number of 28
girls attending schools was on the rise. The number of female candidates
for the universities had risen sevenfold during the first half of the 1970s.
Women were encouraged to participate in areas normally closed to them
through a quota system that gave preferential treatment to eligible girls.
Women were scholars, police officers, judges, pilots, and engineers—active
in every field except the clergy. In 1978, 333 of 1,660 candidates for local
councils were women. Twenty-two were elected to the parliament; two to
the Senate. There were one female Cabinet minister, three subCabinet un-
dersecretaries (including the second-highest ranking officials in the Min-
istries of Labor and Mines and Industries), one governor, one ambassador,
and five mayors.

That Khomeini ousted them by resorting to the clergy's old tactic of ac- 29
cusing them of betraying Iranian culture and tradition was not surprising.
What was surprising was that the leftist members of his revolutionary
coalition went along. The leftists had traditionally appeared to support
women's rights. However, this support never ran very deep. The leftists op-

erated under a totalitarian mindset that was ultimately far more at ease with the rigid rules espoused by the reactionary clerics than with the pluralistic approach favored by the women's movement. Thus, when the Ayatollah began his crackdown, he had the leftists' full support.

Most Iranian women, on the other hand, were not so pliant. Another image surfaces—this one a photograph that appeared in an American magazine, I can't remember which. I found it recently among the scraps I had kept from the early days of the revolution. It was taken on a snowy day in March 1979 and reveals tens of thousands of shouting women massed into one of Tehran's wide avenues. Their expressions are arresting, but that is not what is most striking about this photo. No, what draws my attention is how, in contrast to today's pictures of women in Iran—depressing images of drab figures cloaked in black cloth—this photograph is filled with color! The women are dressed in different shades—vibrant reds, bright blues—almost as if they had purposely tried to make themselves stand out as much as possible. In fact, perhaps this was their objective, because, on that March day, these women had gathered to express their resistance to—and their outrage at— Ayatollah Khomeini's attempt to make them invisible. 30

Some days prior, the Ayatollah had launched the first phase of his clampdown on women's rights. First, he had announced the annulment of the Family Protection Law that had, since 1967, helped women work outside the home and given them more rights in their marriages. In its place, the traditional Islamic law, known as Sharia, would apply. In one fell swoop the Ayatollah had set Iran back nearly a century. Under the new system, the age of consent for girls has been changed from 18 to nine. Yet no woman no matter what age can marry for the first time without the consent of her father, and no married woman can leave the country without her husband's written and notarized consent. Adultery is punishable by stoning. On the witness stand it takes the testimony of two women to equal that of one man. If a Muslim man kills a Muslim woman and is then sentenced to death, her family must first pay him compensation for his life. As if all this were not enough, Khomeini also announced the reimposition of the veil— decreeing that no woman could go to work unless she is fully covered. 31

The March 8 demonstration began as a commemoration of the International Day of the Woman. But, as hundreds of women poured into the streets of Tehran, its character spontaneously changed into a full-fledged protest march against the new regime's measures. "Freedom is neither Eastern nor Western; it is global," the women shouted. "Down with the reactionaries! Tyranny in any form is condemned!" 32

The March 8 event led to further protests. On the third day, a huge demonstration took place in front of the Ministry of Justice. Declarations 33 of support from different associations and organizations were read, and an eight-point manifesto was issued. Among other things, it called for gender equality in all areas of public and private life as well as a guarantee of fundamental freedoms for both men and women. It also demanded that "the decision over women's clothing, which is determined by custom and the exigencies of geographical location, should be left to women."

In the face of such widespread protest, the Ayatollah backed down. His **34** son-in-law emerged to say that Khomeini had merely meant to encourage women to dress "respectably" in the workplace. But the Ayatollah's retreat proved only temporary. Even as he was officially relenting on his proclamation on the veil, his vigilantes continued to attack unveiled women in public—often by throwing acid at them. And the Ayatollah soon proceeded to reinstate the veiling laws—this time taking care to move step by step. In the summer of 1980, his regime made the veil mandatory in government offices. Later, it prohibited women from shopping without a veil. As they had before, many women resisted and protested these acts. And, once again, they were attacked and beaten by government goons and denounced by the leftist "progressive" forces. Later, the veil was made mandatory for all women regardless of their religion, creed, or nationality. By the early '80s, and after much violence, the regime had succeeded in making the veil the uniform of all Iranian women.

Yet, even as it enabled the regime to consolidate its control over every **35** aspect of its subjects' lives, this act firmly established the separation between the regime and the Iranian population. In order to implement its new laws, the regime created special vice squads that patrol the cities on the lookout for any citizen guilty of a "moral offense." The guards are allowed to raid not just public places but private homes, in search of alcoholic drinks, "decadent" music or videos, people playing cards, sexually mixed parties or unveiled women. Those arrested go to special courts and jails. The result was that ordinary Iranian citizens—both men and women—immediately began to feel the presence and intervention of the state in their most private daily affairs. These officers were not there to arrest criminals who threatened the lives or safety of the populace; they were there to control the populace, to take people away, and to flog and imprison them. Bazaars and shopping malls were surrounded and raided; young girls and boys were arrested for walking together in the streets, for not wearing the proper clothing. Nail polish and Reebok shoes were treated as lethal weapons. Young girls were subjected to virginity tests. Soon, even people who originally supported the regime began to question it.

The government had claimed that only a handful of "Westernized" **36** women had opposed its laws, but now, 20 years after the revolution, its most outspoken and daring opponents are the very children of revolution, many of whom were the most active members of Islamic students' associations. To cite just one statistic, of the 802 men and women the vice squads detained in Tehran in July 1993, 80 percent were under the age of 20. The suppression of culture in the name of defending against the West's "cultural invasion" and the attempts at coercive "Islamization" have made these youths almost obsessed with the culture they are being deprived of.

The regime has also succeeded in alienating many of the traditionalist 37 women who had initially supported it. Committed religious believers, these women had long felt uncomfortable with the modernization and secularization that had taken place in Iran during the century leading up to the revolution. So, when Ayatollah Khomeini first arrived on the scene, they welcomed him with open arms. So powerful an ally were they that Khomeini, who had vehemently protested when women were granted the right to vote in 1963, decided against repealing it so that he could rely on these women's votes.

After the revolution, these women began to venture into the work- 38 place—which they now deemed sufficiently hospitable to their traditionalist lifestyle. There they encountered those secular women who had not been a part of the Shah's government and who had therefore been allowed to remain in their jobs so that the regime could benefit from their know-how. As time went by, the traditionalist women began to find that they actually had quite a lot in common with their secular counterparts, who they had previously criticized as Westernized. The line between "us" and "them" gradually blurred.

One issue that solidified this bond was the law. For some traditional 39 women, the imposition of the veil was an affront to their religiosity— changing what had been a freely chosen expression of religious faith into a rote act imposed on them by the state. My grandmother was one such woman. An intensely religious woman who never parted with her chador, she was nonetheless outraged at those who had defiled her religion by using violence to impose their interpretation of it on her grandchildren. "This is not Islam!" she would insist.

Meanwhile, other traditional women felt alienated by some of the 40 more draconian aspects of Sharia. The debate around the Islamic laws inevitably led to a critical reappraisal of the basic tenets that had created them. It also led to a discussion of more fundamental issues pertaining to the nature of male-female relations as well as public and private spaces. The regime had changed the laws, claiming that they were unjust, that they were products of alien rule and exploitation. Now that the "alien rulers" were gone, these claims were being tested. Iranian women from all walks of life were discovering that the biggest affront to them was the law itself. It did not protect the most basic rights of women; it violated them. As Zahra Rahnavard, the wife of the last Iranian Prime Minister Mir Hossein Musavi and an ardent Islamist, has lamented to the Iranian press: "The Islamic government has lost the war on the hejab [veil]. . . . The Islamic values have failed to protect women and to win their support."

The incompatibility of these laws with the reality of modern Iran thus 41 became apparent to the more openminded elements that had previously supported the regime. Many of them distanced themselves from the official policies and joined ranks with those on the "other" side. The transformation of the editor and part of the staff of an official women's journal, *Zan-e Rooz,* is a good example. They left office in the mid-'80s and created a new magazine, *Zanan,* sharply critical of many government policies and practices. They invited secular women to participate in the publication of their journal. Some from the ranks of clergy joined them in criticizing the existing laws on women. Such transformations have frightened the hardliners into passing even more reactionary laws, further suppressing the progressive elements working for creation of a civil society and, in the process, fueling a vicious cycle.

The consequence has been that the regime has become far more de- 42 pendent on women for its survival than women are on the regime. The regime can make all sorts of deals with the imperialist powers, even with the Great Satan itself, but it cannot allow its women to change the public image imposed on them; since the regime's legitimacy rests so heavily on the notion that its rules represent the will of the Iranian people, the presence of even one unveiled woman in the streets has become more dangerous than the grenades of an underground opposition. And Iranian women appear to have taken notice. Young girls in particular have turned the veil into an instrument of protest. They wear it in attractive and provocative ways. They leave part of their hair showing from under their scarves or allow colorful clothing to show underneath their uniforms. They walk in a defiant manner. And in doing so they have become a constant reminder to the ruling elite that it is fighting a losing battle.

I would like to end with a final image—this one a joyous one that negates 43 the other mutilated half-images of women I have described. It happened in 1997, when the Iranian soccer team defeated Australia in the World Cup qualifying tournament. The government had repeatedly warned against any secular-style celebrations. But, as soon as the game was over, millions of Iranians spilled into the streets, dancing and singing to loud music. They called it the "football revolution." The most striking feature of this "revolution" was the presence of thousands of women who broke through police barricades to enter the football stadium, from which they are normally banned. Some even celebrated by taking off their veils. Time and again I replay not the actions but the atmosphere of jubilation and defiance surrounding this event. The Iranian nation, having no political or national symbols or events to celebrate as its own, chose the most nonpolitical of all events, soccer, and turned it into a strong political statement.

As usual, the Western press described these events as a message to the hard-liners from Khatami's supporters. But the main addressees of the football revolution's message were not the hard-liners; they had heard the message many times before and had ignored it. If anyone were to learn any lessons from this event it should have been the more "moderate" faction. It was clear then, and it has become clearer since thanks to subsequent demonstrations, protest meetings, and publications, that the majority of Iranians see the current Islamic regime as the main obstacle to the creation of a civil society. 44

It is this problem that faces President Khatami today. He has impressed the West by proclaiming himself a man who stands for the rule of law. But the law in the Islamic Republic is what most Iranians today are protesting against. In reaction the hard-liners have become increasingly repressive; the small openings and freedoms enjoyed by the Iranian people at the start of President Khatami's victory have come with arbitrary crackdowns in which ordinary citizens are stoned for adultery; writers and prominent members of the opposition are not only jailed but murdered; Bahais are deprived of their most basic human rights; and the revolutionary guards and morality police treat the Iranian citizens as strictly as ever. 45

But these actions are taken from a position of weakness, not strength. Unlike in the past, repressive measures have failed to quell the protests. Side by side with the daily struggle that has turned the business of living into a protracted war, there are public debates, protest meetings, and demonstrations, reminders of those sunny-snowy days 20 years ago. And, just as in those days past, women are once again playing a decisive role. 46

In fact, there is an almost artistic symmetry to the way Iranian women at the end of the twentieth century, as at its beginning, are at the center of the larger struggle for the creation of an open and pluralistic society in Iran. The future twists and turns of this struggle are uncertain, but of one thing I am sure: a time will come when the Degas ballerinas return to their rightful place. 47

Exploring the Writer's World

1. While focusing on Iranian women, Nafisi goes beyond this subject to provide an overview of Iranian history and politics from the nineteenth century to the present. What do you learn about Iranian history and culture from her presentation? Where do Iranian women fit in?

2. Saira Shah, in the selection from *The Storyteller's Daughter,* focuses like Nafisi on the lives of women. Are these women's lives similar, or is it necessary to make distinctions between them? Justify your response.

3. How does Nafisi's hostility toward the current Iranian regime surface in this essay? Does she present a convincing argument, or, as a woman who has experienced difficulty at clerical hands, is she too opinionated or biased? Explain with reference to the text.

4. In *Reading Lolita in Tehran,* Nafisi presents a list of novels, including Nabokov's *Lolita* and F. Scott Fitzgerald's *The Great Gatsby,* that she taught to her seven female students. What do you think her motivation was? Why didn't she teach Persian literature? Why did she select, of all novels she might have taught, *Lolita,* which is (at one literal level of this complex masterpiece) about an older man who seduces a teenaged girl?

5. With three other students, go online and find out more about the lives of women in Iran today. Share your findings in class discussion.

Stranger in the Arab-Muslim World

Fouad Ajami

Fouad Ajami was born in Lebanon in 1946 and immigrated to the United States in 1964. He was raised as a Shiite Muslim. A political scientist with a doctorate from the University of Washington, Ajami has taught at Princeton University and, since 1980, at Johns Hopkins University, where today he is Majid Khadduri Professor of Islamic studies and director of Middle Eastern studies. He also is a contributing editor to *U.S. News & World Report* and a consultant to *CBS News.* Ajami received a prestigious MacArthur Fellowship in 1982 for his work on Middle Eastern politics and culture. His work includes *The Vanished Imam: Musa al Sadr and the Shia of Lebanon* (1986), *Beirut: City of Regrets* (1988), *The Arab Predicament* (1981, revised edition 1992), and *The Dream Palace of the Arabs* (1998). In the following essay, published in *The Wilson Quarterly* in spring 2001, Ajami argues that the chroniclers of Arab-Islamic history must come to terms with the spread of American pop culture and a rising trend of anti-Americanism.

That wily, flamboyant Egyptian ruler Anwar al-Sadat contracted an af- [1] fection for things and people American when he dominated his land in the 1970s. In the distant, powerful United States, which had ventured into Egypt, he saw salvation for his country—a way out of the pan-Arab captivity, the wars with Israel, and the drab austerity of a command economy.

But Sadat was struck down in October 1981. The following year Sherif Hetata, a distinguished Egyptian man of letters, published a novel called *alShabaka* (*The net*), into which he poured the heartbreak and unease of his political breed (the secular Left) at America's new role in Egypt.

It is not a brilliant novel. The fiction is merely a vehicle for Hetata's radical politics. A net (an American net) is cast over Egypt and drags the old, burdened land into a bewildering new world. The protagonist of the novel, Khalil Mansour Khalil, is an educated Egyptian who works for the public sector in the pharmaceutical industry and has known the setbacks and the accomplishments of the Nasser years. The Six-Day War shattered the peace and promise of his world in 1967, but vindication came six years later, in October 1973, when Egyptian armor crossed the Suez Canal. "We lived through a period of great enthusiasm, but it did not last." American diplomacy changed things, "weaned" Egypt away from its old commitments.

Khalil feels the new world's temptations when Ruth Harrison, a mysterious American woman with some command of Arabic, enters his life. Glamorous and alluring, Harrison offers him a contract with an American multinational, and Khalil's drab world and marriage to Amina Tewfic, a woman with "roots deep in the ground," are set against the dazzle of Harrison's world: "Amina always faced me with the facts, laid bare the contradictions in my life; perhaps that is why I kept running away from her. But Ruth was different. She exercised an attraction I found difficult to resist. Was it just the fascination of the unknown, of visiting another world where everything is there for the asking?"

Khalil throws over his life and is doomed. Harrison is a spy come to this new American sphere of influence to decimate the Egyptian Left. Predictably, the affair ends in disaster. Harrison is murdered, and Khalil, insisting on his innocence, is put to death. American spies and tricksters and the Egyptians who fall under their sway dismantle the old world and erect in its place a world of betrayal. Egypt wades beyond its depth and barters time-honored truths for glitter, grief, and ruin, the chroniclers of Arab-Islamic history since the mid-1970s must come to terms with two especially puzzling developments: the spread of American pop culture through vast stretches of the Arab world, and the concomitant spread of a furious anti-Americanism. Thus, even as Egypt was incorporated into the American imperium, a relentless anti-Americanism animated Egyptian Islamists and secularists alike. It flowed freely through Egyptian letters and cinema and seemed to be the daily staple of the official and semiofficial organs of the regime. A similar situation now prevails throughout the Arabian Peninsula and the Persian Gulf, where an addiction to things American co-exists with an obligatory hostility to the power whose shadow lies across the landscape.

Historians who take note of these developments will not explain them   5
adequately if they believe that the anti-Americanism at play in the Muslim
world merely reflects the anti-Americanism now visible in France or Russia or India, or among a certain segment of the Latin American intelli-
gentsia. America's primacy in the world since the defeat of communism has
whipped up a powerful strain of resentment. Envy was the predictable response of many societies to the astonishing American economic performance in the 1990s—the unprecedented bull run, the "New Economy," the
wild valuations in American equities, the triumphant claims that America
had discovered a new economic world, free of the market's discipline and
of the business cycle itself.

This global resentment inevitably made its way to Arab and Muslim   6
shores. But the Muslim world was a case apart for Pax Americana and sui
generis in the kind of anti-Americanism it nurtured. José Bové, the provo-
cateur attacking the spread of McDonald's outlets in France, is not to be
compared with Osama bin Laden, the Saudi-born financier suspected of
bankrolling a deadly campaign of terror against American embassies and
military barracks. The essayists of *Le Monde Diplomatique* may rail
against mondialisation American-style (the business schools, the bad food,
the unsentimental capitalism of a Wall Street–U.S. Treasury alliance). But
a wholly different wind blows through Arab lands, where a young boy
drove a Mercedes truck loaded with TNT into an American military compound in Beirut in October 1983; where terrorists targeted a housing complex for the American military in Saudi Arabia in June 1996; where two
men in a skiff crippled an American destroyer on a re-fueling stop in Aden,
Yemen. Grim, defining episodes of that sort, and many others like them,
mark the American presence in Arab-Muslim domains.

In the aftermath of the October 1973 war, the Arab and Iranian heart-   7
land slipped under American sway, and America acquired a kind of Muslim imperium. The development gained momentum from the needs of both
the rulers and the social elites who had taken to American ways. The
poorer states (read Egypt) needed sustenance; the wealthier states (read the
states of the Arabian Peninsula and the Persian Gulf), protection against
the covetous poorer states. A monarch in Iran, at once imperious and possessed of a neurotic sense of dependency on American judgment, effectively
brought down his own regime. The order he had put together became inseparable in the popular psyche from the American presence in Iran. And
they were torched together. The tribune of the revolution, Ayatollah Ruhol-
lah Khomeini, was particularly skilled at turning the foreign power into the
demon he needed. Iran alternated between falling for the foreigner's ways
and loathing itself for surrendering to the foreigner's seduction. It swung

A public display of anti-American sentiment in Tehran.

wildly, from the embrace of the foreigner into a faith in the authority of the ancients and the reign of a clerical redeemer.

In the years to come, there would be no respite for America. Khomeini 8 had shown the way. There would be tributaries of his revolution and emulators aplenty. A world had flung wide its own floodgates. It let the foreigner in and lost broad segments of its young to the hip, freewheeling culture of America. By violent reaction the seduction could be covered up, or undone.

Consider Osama bin Laden's description of America, as reported by a 9 young Sudanese follower of bin Laden who defected and turned witness for American authorities: "The snake is America, and we have to stop them. We have to cut off the head of the snake. We cannot let the American army in our area. We have to do something. We have to fight them."

The American military force that troubles Osama bin Laden, that hovers over his Saudi homeland and reaches the ports of his ancestral land in Yemen, is there because the rulers of those lands acquiesced in its presence, even sought it. Bin Laden and his followers cannot overturn the ruling order in the Arabian Peninsula and the Persian Gulf–entrenched dynasties that have mastered the art of governing and struck workable social contracts with the governed. But the rebels cannot concede that harsh truth. Better to hack at the foreign power. More flattering to the cause to say that the political orders in the region would fall of their own weight were it not for the armadas of the Americans and the military installations and weapons they have stored in the ports of the Persian Gulf and the Arabian Peninsula. Pax Americana may insist on its innocence, but, inevitably, it is caught in the crossfire between the powers that be and the insurgents who have taken up arms against them and who seek nothing less than the extirpation of America's presence from Muslim lands. 10

In fact, as Muslim societies become involved in a global economy they can neither master nor ignore, both rulers and insurgents have no choice but to confront the American presence. America has become part of the uneven, painful "modernity" of the Islamic world. Even American embassies have acquired an ambivalent symbolic character: they are targeted by terrorists and besieged by visa seekers—professionals who have given up on failed economies and a restricted way of life; the half-educated and the urban poor, who in earlier times would never have sought opportunity and a new life in a distant land. 11

Denial is at the heart of the relationship between the Arab and Muslim worlds and America. There can be no written praise of America, no acknowledgment of its tolerance or hospitality, or of the yearnings America has stirred in Karachi and Teheran, Cairo and Beirut, and in the streets of Ramallah. In November 2000, America extended a special gift to Jordan: a free-trade agreement between the two nations. Jordan was only the fourth country to be so favored, after Canada, Mexico, and Israel. The agreement was an investment in peace, a tribute to the late Jordanian ruler, King Hussein, and an admission of America's stake in the reign of his young heir, Abdullah II. But it did not dampen the anti-Americanism among professionals and intellectuals in Jordan. 12

There, as elsewhere, no intellectual can speak kindly of America. The attraction has to be hidden, or never fully owned up to. From Afghanistan to the Mediterranean, from Karachi to Cairo, human traffic moves toward America while anti-American demonstrations supply the familiar spectacle of American flags set to the torch. I know of no serious work of commentary in Arab lands in recent years that has spoken of the American political ex- 13 perience or the American cultural landscape with any appreciation. The anti-Americanism is automatic, unexamined, innate. To self-styled "liberals," America is the upholder of reaction; to Islamists, a defiling presence; to pan-Arabists, the backer of a Zionist project to dominate the region.

In the pan-Arab imagination, there would be a measure of Arab unity 14 had America not aborted it. There would be a "balance" of wealth and some harmony between the sparsely populated Arab oil states and the poorer, more populous Arab lands of the Levant had America not driven a wedge between them. There would be wealth for things that matter had those oil states not been tricked into weapons deals and joint military exercises they neither need nor can afford. "I hate America," a young Palestinian boy in the streets of Gaza said late last year to Michael Finkel, an American reporter who had come to cover the "Second Intifada" for the *New York Times Magazine.* But the matter is hardly that simple. Like the larger world to which he belongs, the boy hates America and is drawn to it. His world wants American things without having to partake of American ways. It has beckoned America, and then bloodied America.

America entered Arab lands on particular terms. The lands were, in the 15 main, authoritarian societies, and such middle classes as existed in them were excluded from meaningful political power. Monarchs and rulers of national states claimed the political world, and it was precisely through their good graces that America came on the scene. Pax Americana took to this transaction. It neither knew nor trusted the civil associations, the professional classes, the opposition. America had good reasons to suspect that the ground was not fertile for democratic undertakings. It was satisfied that Egypt's military rulers kept the peace. Why bother engaging those who opposed the regime, even the fragile bourgeois opposition that emerged in the late 1970s? Similarly, the only traffic to be had with Morocco was through its autocratic ruler, Hassan II. The man was harsh and merciless (his son, and successor, Mohammad VI, has all but admitted that), but he kept order, was "our man" in North Africa, and could be relied on to support America's larger purposes.

America extended the same indulgence to Yasir Arafat, the latest, and 16 most dubious, ruler to be incorporated into its designs. In the Palestinian world, the security arrangements and the political arrangements had been struck with Arafat. His American handlers ignored such opposition as had arisen to him. With no real access to the Palestinian world, and precious little knowledge of Arafat's opponents, America seemed to have to choose between the Islamic movement Hamas and Arafat's Palestinian National Authority. An easy call. The Palestinian strongman, in turn, accepted America's patronage but frustrated America's wishes.

The middle classes in the Arab world were mired in the politics of na- 17
tionalism, whereas the rulers always seemed supple and ready to wink at
reality. There was precious little economic life outside the state-dominated
oil sectors, and little business to be done without recourse to the custodi-
ans of the command economies. It was the prudent and, really, inevitable
solution to negotiate American presence and American interests with those
who, as the Arabic expression has it, have eaten the green and the dry and
monopolized the life of the land.

The populations shut out of power fell back on their imaginations 18
and their bitterness. They resented the rulers but could not overthrow
them. It was easier to lash out at American power and question American purposes. And they have been permitted the political space to do so.
They can burn American flags at will, so long as they remember that the
rulers and their prerogatives are beyond scrutiny. The rulers have been
particularly sly in monitoring the political safety valves in their domains.
They know when to indulge the periodic outbursts at American power.
Not a pretty spectacle, but such are the politics in this sphere of American influence.

America's primacy will endure in Arab and Muslim lands, but the for- 19
eign power will have to tread carefully. "England is of Europe, and I am a
friend of the Ingliz, their ally," Ibn Saud, the legendary founder of the Saudi
state, once said of his relationship with the British. "But I will walk with
them only as far as my religion and honor will permit." In Arab and Muslim domains, it is the stranger's fate to walk alone.

Exploring the Writer's World

1. Ajami begins this essay with a detailed summary of a novel, *The Net,* by
   the Egyptian writer Sherif Hetata. What is his purpose? How does his summary of the novel set the stage for the rest of the essay?

2. How successful do you think Ajami is in presenting the paradox that he
   finds at the heart of Middle Eastern life today? What exactly is this paradox? How convincing is Ajami in supporting his claim?

3. This article was written and published before the events of September 11,
   2001, but Ajami does refer to Osama bin Laden and the rise of a virulent
   anti-Americanism among radical Islamists. Why didn't American policymakers listen to voices like Ajami's, who were warning of these dangers? What
   should be the role of public intellectuals like Ajami?

4. Ajami ranges outside the Middle East to present a global sketch of anti-
   Americanism. What are some examples that he provides? What additional
   examples can you think of? What, in your own words, explains this virulent
   anti-Americanism existing in the world today?

5. In groups of three or four, go online and locate an English-language version of a Middle Eastern newspaper. You may also use Arabic newspapers published abroad, notably in London. (You might want to gain entry into this subject through Google.) Scan at least three articles for evidence of anti-American sentiment, and report your findings to the class.

And They Call This Paradise

AMIRA HASS

Amira Hass, the child of Holocaust survivors, was born in Jerusalem in 1956. After studying history at Hebrew University in Jerusalem and the University of Tel Aviv, she taught in several schools and then began a career in journalism in 1989 as a staff editor at *Ha'aretz*. She moved to the Gaza Strip in 1991 and began writing articles about the occupation, covering the crisis from the Palestinian side of the lines separating the two peoples. "To most Israelis, my move seemed outlandish, even crazy, for they believed I was surely putting my life at risk," she writes in *Drinking the Sea at Gaza: Days and Nights in a Land Under Siege* (2001). Nevertheless, she has continued to monitor daily life in the occupied territories, filing her reports to the newspaper despite considerable danger from both militant Israeli and Palestinian groups. Hass received the 2003 World Press Freedom Prize. In the following article, which appeared in *Ha'aretz* on July 22, 2002, Hass offers an account of one Palestinian community and the daily problems its people face.

A group of bearded men was sitting on a sandy footpath by the mosque in Mawasi, waiting in the shade for the muezzin's call. Most of them have been fellahin since they can remember; some are fishermen. All have land in Mawasi—the fertile agricultural hinterland of the southern Gaza Strip cities of Khan Yunis and Rafah. A pleasant breeze was coming off the sea, which is about two or three hundred meters away. A nearby orchard bathed the eye in green. The sweet brown tea that was prepared in honor of the guests bore a scent of sage. Amer al-Astal, 30, a bushy black Herzl-like beard gracing his face, shot a bemused expression at his bearded colleagues, most of whom, like him, wore long galabias. He is well aware of the associations conjured by their outer appearance. Bin Laden, of course. He jokes: "I stopped shaving, 'cause who's got the money to buy shaving cream every few days?'"

It's been two years since he's seen his family, parents and siblings. They   2
live two or three kilometers away, in the city of Khan Yunis, but anyone
who does not officially live in Mawasi is prohibited from entering the area,
even if they have land or family there. His father is 70. His mother is ill.
Until three weeks ago, only men aged 35 and above were permitted to leave
Mawasi. So Amer al-Astal was not able to leave.

About 8,000 Palestinians live in Mawasi, the green farming area in the   3
middle of the Gaza Strip that is situated west of Khan Yunis. It and its
beach always provided a refreshing contrast to the teeming grayness of the
Khan Yunis refugee camp, which it borders. There was a time when many
more than 8,000 individuals earned their livelihood from this tract of land.
There were families with deep roots going way back, which lived in the
cities of Khan Yunis, Rafah and Dir al-Balah. Some of them lived in
Mawasi, others in the cities. Some of them divided their time between town
and country. Gradually, Israeli settlements were built up between their
fields, orchards and homes. The settlements expanded. The area is now
better known as "Gush Katif."

Residents of Mawasi once invested tens of thousands of shekels to build   4
new hothouses, in an attempt to introduce new crops, and enlarge the
guava orchards that are famous in the area for their sweet fruits. But for
the past three years, selling agricultural produce from Mawasi to anywhere
else in the Strip—or beyond—has been mission impossible. "Now I want
to plant something that doesn't cost any money: hot peppers. The seeds
cost me only a few agorot. I'll sell NIS 200 worth, so that I'll have a little
money for the children, that's all," explains Abu Astal. "My whole life is
in a radius of 100 meters: field, house, mosque, field, mosque, house. We
sit in the shade. If the sun comes, we move somewhere else that has shade.
They tell us we are living in paradise, surrounded by all this lush green, and
with the sea and the cool breeze in front of us. But we are closed in here.
Behind that gate."

Fortified Gate

That "gate," next to the settlement of Neveh Dekalim, is known as the Tu-   5
fah Gate. It is highly fortified. Surrounding the gate are no less than three
army garrisons (bulldozers are busily preparing for the expansion of one of
them, which adjoins a heap of ruins—buildings along the outskirts of the
Khan Yunis refugee camp that the Israeli army destroyed), observation
towers, a line of concrete walls, a fenced-off path, a fortified position for
sentries, two revolving gates, barbed wire, a yellow metal gate, an X-ray
device, shaded lean-tos for local residents to wait their turn—on either side
of the gate, and on the southern side—a concrete wall that continues to get
get higher and higher, which encloses the Neveh Dekalim industrial zone.

For the past three years or so, the only local residents permitted in and out of the gate (aside from the workers employed in the settlements) are residents of Mawasi. Two and a half years ago, the army authorities would still accept an address recorded in the ID card. Anyone with a "Mawasi" address was permitted to pass through. Later on, everyone was required to receive a special number written on their ID card. Since April–May 2001, residents of Mawasi have been required to receive a special magnetic card that is issued only to residents. This meant that families were separated from one another, given no choice in the matter. One brother remains behind to run the family shop in the city, lacking a Mawasi resident magnetic card; the other, with a magnetic card, does not leave the family orchard. 6

At the outset, the minimum age for men wanting to pass through the gate was 45. It has gradually been reduced to 35. With the advent of the hudna, and the abatements implemented by the IDF, the fortunes of the men of Mawasi have improved, and the minimum age for passage has been reduced to 30, with the minimum age for women reduced from 30 to 25. However, only married women and children are included. People say a pregnant women at the right age will be allowed to pass through, but that a woman without children will have problems. A 20-year-old woman who has to get her baby to a clinic for inoculations will have problems. The same is true for an unmarried man who is older than the minimum age. Often, the soldiers will not let him pass through. Children aged 12 and below are permitted to pass: they must show their plastic-wrapped birth certificate, but may enter only in the company of parents or on condition that their parents wait at the gate, as addresses are not recorded on the birth certificate. 7

The gate officially opens each morning at 8:00, and the soldiers officially take a lunch break around 1:00 P.M. But last Wednesday, for instance, a team of Physicians for Human Rights arrived at 1:10 P.M., and the gate was still closed. People were waiting on either side, some to exit in the direction of Khan Yunis, others on their way back into Mawasi. 8

It is forbidden to enter or exit by vehicle. Or by wagon or bicycle. Until two months ago, people were not allowed to reenter Mawasi carrying packages in their hands. They were not permitted to bring bread, fruit, or a toy for a grandchild. Now it is permitted (preferably with light-, not dark-colored plastic bags). The transfer of large amounts of goods is only permitted using the "back-to-back" method: truck or pickup on one side, truck or pickup on the other side, with goods unloaded and loaded onto the vehicle on the other side of the gate, under the soldiers' watchful eyes. On Friday and Saturday, this is how the merchandise is brought to the pathetic grocery stores in Mawasi: three trucks on Friday, three trucks on Saturday. The goods must pass through the X-ray machine. On Sundays 9 and Mondays, Mawasi residents are permitted to "export" produce to Khan Yunis without prior appointment. On Tuesday, they are permitted to bring in durable goods such as water pumps, plastic pipes, clothing, etc. A dog sniffs the items, checking for explosives. On Wednesday and Thursday, residents are again permitted to ship agricultural produce out of the zone. Ambulances are not permitted to drive in and out of the area: patients are also transferred "back-to-back" style.

A Month for a Goat

Everything else must be coordinated in advance: bringing in merchandise, 10 bringing in diesel fuel or medication, entry of medical crews or municipal workers to repair water mains or sewage pipes (belonging to the Khan Yunis or Dir al-Balah municipalities). Some local residents claim it can take a month of preliminary coordination to bring in a goat or chicken.

Abdul Rahim Abu Khatab, head of the Palestinian civilian coordination 11 committee in the southern Gaza Strip, does the dirty work of coordination. He sits in an old caravan, a hand-me-down from a settlement or the civil administration, and each week prepares dozens of requests to enter or exit the tract of land that lies 1,500 meters away from him. Sometimes he waits only a single day for an entry permit for a fix-it crew, sometimes it take three days or more. He collates all the requests he has faxed to the Israeli coordination office in a thick binder. Follow-up on the applications is divided into four categories: the first includes those wishing to leave Mawasi—in other words, those who are under the minimum age: a municipal worker that lives in Mawasi "requests to exit for work purposes," another "requests to exit for dental treatment," a third "requests to exit for ear treatment." Someone "requests to visit his parents in Khan Yunis." And the permits are not always granted.

A second category includes those requesting to enter Mawasi. Mainly 12 these are family members wishing to attend weddings. The third category are those "stuck," who are under the permitted age: individuals below the minimum age, for instance university students and people who needed medical care and left Mawasi after having coordinated their exit, but whom the soldiers at the "gate" did not allow to return to their homes. Why? No special reason. Go to "Abu Hassan" (Abu Khatab), the soldiers say to the members of this third category. These individuals are sometimes stuck for three weeks or more, a kilometer from home.

The fourth category comprises those who are stuck, and are above the 13 approved age. For instance, on July 6, a list of adults who were not permitted back into Mawasi was sent to the Israeli coordination office. It included T., born in 1949, who left Mawasi on June 16. He was not allowed back in until July 6. Last Wednesday, July 16, the Israeli coordination office had still not found the time to consider his case. Z., born in 1965, left his home in Mawasi on June 14. A., born in 1949, left her home on June 24. She is stuck outside. T., born in 1963, is a teacher in Mawasi. He left on May 30, and has been stuck—a kilometer and a half away from home and school.

Abu Khatab continues to carry on his exhausting negotiations with Israeli clerk/soldiers over the right of hundreds of people to return home each week. The fear of being stuck outside makes people try not to leave Mawasi, even those who are above the minimum age. People delay medical exams and treatments until the problem worsens. The doctor from Médicins Sans Frontières and two local doctors with very basic clinics in Mawasi are helpless in the face of people's stubborn insistence not to be exiled from their own homes. Parents who are below the "permitted" age cannot escort their children to the doctor's office. Abu Khatab sometimes struggles for days to enable a 20-year-old mother to take her baby to Khan Yunis for an inoculation. There is no opportunity to refrigerate vaccines and other drugs in Mawasi. Since 1967, Israel has forbidden the hookup of Palestinian homes in Mawasi (which are shouting distance from the well-lit settlements) to the electricity grid, and the private generators operate only a few hours a day.

Al-Astal, a man of permissible age, is afraid to leave, lest he too be stuck outside. "To whom can we complain if not to Allah? We pray each day for the gate to be opened. We hope for death every day."

Seeking the Delicate Balance

The brigade commander of the region is in constant and direct contact with the mukhtars of Mawasi, military sources said in response yesterday. He tries to answer their needs as far as possible while keeping a balance between security needs and humanitarian considerations. Some of the residents of the region have participated in terror attacks against Israeli settlers and IDF soldiers, the sources said.

In principle, they added, the roadblock is open from half an hour after sunrise until half an hour before sunset, and sometimes even later. Meanwhile, the age limit for women who want to cross has been lowered to 20. The reason that children are forced to be accompanied by adults is that a terrorist masquerading as a 14-year-old entered Mawasi.

As for not permitting certain residents to return to Mawasi, this is a decision made by the Shin Bet security services and "even the military sources do not understand it." The process of investigating and lifting a ban, in which the brigade commander is often involved, takes time, they said.

Exploring the Writer's World

1. Imagine that you are a resident of Mawasi. What would your attitude toward Israel be? Conversely, imagine that you are an Israeli living under the constant threat of suicide attacks. Why would you want to have a town like Mawasi under tight control?

2. Were you surprised to encounter an Israeli writer reporting sympathetically from the Gaza Strip about the conditions Palestinians live under? Why does she do this? Do you think she is undermining her nation's official policies by filing such reports? Justify your answer.

3. Consider the title of this article and the way the essay begins. What is Hass's purpose? How does she try to convince the reader that something is drastically wrong in the Israel's policy of occupation and control in Mawasi?

4. Three of the writers in this casebook—Said, Oz, and Hass—were born in Jerusalem. Compare and contrast their vision of life in the Middle East, and their thoughts about the possibility for reconciliation among peoples there.

5. With another class member, go to the Web and locate additional articles by Hass. Download and print one article, summarize it, and present your findings to the class.

The Neo-Con Triumph

HASSAN NAFAA | Hassan Nafaa was born in Egypt in 1947. He received a B.A. degree from Alexandria University in Egypt and then pursued graduate studies in France, receiving a doctorate in political science from the University of Paris in 1977. Hafaa has published more than forty scholarly essays in Arabic on the Middle East, Europe, and the United Nations. He is professor and chair of the Political Science Department at Cairo University. Nafaa writes frequently for *Al-Ahram*, Egypt's main newspaper, and for *Al-Ahram Weekly*, where the following article appeared in July 2003.

Many in the Arab world are under the impression that, since 11 September 2001, the US has come to treat Arabs and Muslims differently from other people. This is not true. Washington does not base its policies on ethnic, cultural, or religious grounds, but on its interests and global vision.

Few would argue the point that the United States has two main inter-ests in the Middle East. One is the Zionist project related to the establish-ment of a Jewish state in Palestine; the other is oil. The interest of the United States in the Zionist project and its support for Israel dates back to the Balfour Declaration. As for oil, US companies were scrambling to ob-tain exploration and production franchises in the region long before World War II underlined the strategic importance of oil. US interest in controlling world oil supplies has never ebbed. So following the end of World War II, when the US threw itself headlong into superpower rivalry, it had two key interests in the region, Israel and oil.

Which poses an obvious dilemma: How can the US guarantee its oil in-terests, which are in mainly Arab hands, while embracing the Zionist proj-ect to the letter? Somehow the US developed a pragmatic foreign policy that contained this dilemma with a fair degree of success.

Until the mid-1960s the US saw the Soviet Union as the main threat to its interests in the world and the Middle East. By stressing this threat it managed to rally the support of conservative and Islamic-based regimes. Meanwhile the US maintained ties with the pan-Arab movement, led by Gamal Abdel-Nasser. Although Arab nationalists had close ties with the Soviet Union they mostly shied away from Marxist ideas, which was good news for the US.

When the pan-Arab movement gained sufficient momentum that it posed a clear threat to US interests in the region, and as it became more deeply involved with the Soviets, the US began to rely increasingly on conservative and Islamic forces in the region, giving them the green light to resist the mostly secular nationalist movement. Not so publicly the US also gave Israel a green light to attack Abdel-Nasser; the result was the 1967 war.

When the Islamic revolution occurred in Iran, the US did not hesitate to use the nationalist movement, or part thereof, to wage a counter-attack. Saddam Hussein, in his eagerness to fill the vacuum created by Abdel-Nasser's death in 1970 and Egypt's disappearance from the military con-flict with Israel in 1978, was the right man for the job. However, when Saddam went beyond what was expected of him and invaded Kuwait, the US exploited his mistake.

The Arab world was aware of the schemes hatched against it, but it kept fulminating, and thus helped to tighten the noose the US had wrapped around its neck. Arab attitudes towards the US were as paradoxical as they were ineffective. The Arabs failed to address the world in one voice, or as a cohesive regional group with common interests to defend. The US, through its bilateral ties with individual Arab countries, became acutely aware of the contradictions in the Arab world; the disparity between words and deeds, the rivalry among individual leaders, and the distrust between rich and poor, radicals and conservatives and nationalists and Islamists, to mention just a few.

Relations between the US and individual Arab states were dominated by bilateral, not pan-Arab concerns. Of course, pan-Arab concerns were an integral part of the domestic agenda of most individual Arab states. But, being a superpower, the US was in a position to ignore such concerns.   8

Every now and then the US would find itself in a position where it had to take sides, for tactical reasons, with the Arabs. This happened twice. The first time was during the 1956 Suez war when Egypt, under Abdel-Nasser, was the spearhead of a vital and promising nationalist movement. The second time was in 1973, when close cooperation between Egypt, Syria, and Saudi Arabia produced extraordinary military and economic results. In both cases the Arab system was able to force the US into making temporary concessions. Yet, the inability of the Arab system to maintain its cohesion, through collective or single-state leadership, gave the US the opportunity to regain the initiative and turn matters to its own advantage in the long run. Even in a bipolar international system the US was able to give Israel a green light to attack Abdel-Nasser's Egypt in 1967 and thus deal a powerful blow to the nationalist movement. And since 1973 Washington has been intent on separating oil from the Arab-Israeli conflict and early made contingency plans to occupy oil fields if necessary.   9

A sea change occurred in US policy towards the Arab world as a result of two developments. First, the most conservative wing of the Republican Party came to power in 2000. Second, the attacks of 11 September 2001 took place.   10

The extreme right-wing came to power in Washington, after eight years of the Clinton administration, fully convinced that the strategy followed by President Reagan succeeded in bringing down the Soviet bloc. The neo-conservatives were incensed that the Clinton administration had wasted a golden opportunity to reformulate the world order according to their vision, and were determined not to let the opportunity slip away. In their new vision of the world the neo-conservatives did not feel the need to have Arab friends of any persuasion. The Arab nationalist project had been defeated, and the Soviet Union, which lent support to this project, was no more.   11

The neo-conservatives have a vision for world domination, and this vision entails Israeli domination of the Arab region. This is why it made sense for the US administration to blame the Palestinian Authority for the failure   12 of US efforts to reach a regional political settlement, and to give Israel the go-ahead to stamp out the Intifada. As part of this new regional approach the US prioritised the destruction of the Iraqi regime, finishing the job left undone during the liberation of Kuwait.

The September 2001 events gave the neo-conservatives an extraordinary opportunity to formulate a cohesive ideological vision through which to redraw the map of the Middle East. The new US administration saw the terror that hit their shores in September 2001 as the outcome of the conflict between corrupt Arab leaders and the disgruntled Arab masses. This conflict, once it struck the heart of the US, became an American issue. The US began blaming Arab regimes, to varying degrees, for what the terrorists had done, the argument being that Arab regimes tolerate political views that malign America, Israel, and the West. It soon became common practice for US pundits to opine that Arab youths, having been deprived freedom in their despotic countries, take out their anger against the US. According to the US administration there is a massive cultural problem in the Arab world, one that cannot be radically addressed except through a major modernisation process imposed by the outside world.

It was in this context that the neo-conservatives began propagating the idea that an attack on Iraq would pave the way for a much-needed modernisation of the Arab world and for reconstituting the region's political, economic, social, and cultural parameters in a manner that would accelerate the pace of transformation. Iraq is a major Arab country with every potential for economic revival, and its ethnic plurality makes it a candidate for the kind of democratic transformation that would be hard to achieve in any other Arab country of comparable stature, went the argument. Once the US had overthrown Saddam's despotic regime and employed Iraq's immense resources to create a pluralistic system, the neo-conservatives claimed, the wheels of change would start turning in the Arab world, and the bandwagon would race to its final destination, ridding the region of hotbeds of corruption, tyranny, and terror.

The main thrust of the above analysis is that the US addresses the Arab world through the prism of its own interests and global ambitions. For the past half century the US has acted in a pragmatic manner, realising that the Arab world is full of contradictions and that these contradictions, if well used, could facilitate US oil interests without harming its policy towards Israel. Not all Arabs are the same, the Americans discovered. The US administration has always maintained Arab friends, particularly among the ruling elites, and provided them with due protection. The US has for long played its cards cautiously. It had to, for the

world was bipolar and the Arab nationalist movement had a few fine   16
moments.

Caution is no longer necessary. The Socialist Bloc has fallen apart, as
has the Arab collective system, first when Egypt bailed out from the military conflict with Israel and then when Iraq came under occupation. As it
is, the US no longer needs to protect any Arab regime, or even listen to it,
regardless of its stature or willingness to cooperate. The US expects everyone in this region to change, to learn how to take orders. It is also convinced that there are enough Arabs ready to offer their services with a
smile. And it is not far off the mark. In time, however, Washington will discover that its regional vision is short-sighted, based on mistaken assumptions, and formulated by people who are more faithful to Israeli interests
than US ones. The neo-conservative approach is not in America's long-term
interest.

Exploring the Writer's World

1. Nafaa is a scholar and expert on the Middle East and the Arab world.
   Would you say that the style of this essay is "scholarly," or does the style
   suggest that he writes for a broader audience than scholarly specialists?
   Point to examples in the essay to support your response. Also evaluate the
   tone of this piece. Is Nafaa objective or subjective in his point of view? How
   do you know?

2. Explain in your own words the nature of Nafaa's claim. What are his minor
   propositions, and what evidence does he provide? Where do you agree
   and/or disagree with him, and why?

3. Does Nafaa ever define a "neo-conservative"? Why or why not? What is
   your definition of this type of American policymaker?

4. Compare and contrast Nafaa's essay with Said's in this casebook. Do they
   share the same attitudes and visions concerning the Middle East and the
   United States, or are there subtle differences and focal points in their respective approaches? Search both essays for evidence to support your response.

5. *Al-Ahram Weekly* has a site in English on the Net. Locate the site and read
   the current edition. Take notes, and share your findings in a group of four.
   Then in class discussion see if other groups share your impressions of this
   newspaper or not.

Awarding of Nobel Peace Prize to Iranian Female Judge Provokes Controversy

MARJANE SATRAPI

Marjane Satrapi was born in Rasht, Iran, in 1969. Her grandfather was the last Qajar Shah of Iran; her own parents, wealthy Marxists involved in the intellectual and artistic community of Teheran. As a child, instead of fairy tales, her father gave her comic books on the history of Marxism to read. She grew up in Tehran, where she studied at the Lycée Francais. After the Revolution of 1979, fearing for their lives under the repressive Islamic regime, Satrapi's parents sent her—alone, at the age of 14—to Vienna, Austria. She spent several vagabond years in Europe, eventually studying illustration in Strasbourg, France.

In the West, Satrapi encountered anti-Iranian prejudice and an ignorance of her culture. In an interview with the French photojournalist Chris Kutschera, she recalled, "I encountered many people who said to me: 'Do you speak Arabic?' Most people didn't know the difference between Arabs and Iranians. They knew nothing of our culture. People have a super-short memory: they think that our country has always been a country of fundamentalists, that women never had a place in our society, and that all Iranian women are hysterical crows."

Satrapi settled in Paris, where she lives with her husband and children and works as an illustrator and an author of children's books. Her graphic novel *Persepolis: The Story of a Childhood,* published in 2002, is an autobiography that reveals a side of Iranian life—especially the lives of women—that has been mysterious to many people in the West. Asked why she chose to tell her story in the form of a graphic novel, she observed that "the pictures, they say always more than the words can say. Also, in pictures, they help me to have the distance without becoming cynical, and be able to describe a part of the story with humor—which I couldn't do otherwise."

Exploring the Writer's World

1. Satrapi has said that the graphic novel can "say always more than the words can say." What story is told, or information revealed, by Satrapi's deceptively simple images in the *cartoon* on page 482? Do her images of Iranian men and women challenge the usual media depictions of Iranians? In what way?

2. Read Shirin Ebadi's lecture upon acceptance of the Nobel Peace Prize (p. 484). How does Satrapi's cartoon complement, or enhance, your understanding of Ebadi's achievement?

3. What does Marjane Satrapi think of the media? How can you tell?

4. Describe the many conflicts—among men and women, between cultures, within Satrapi's own self—that are suggested by this cartoon. Does Satrapi at all hint toward a resolution of any of those conflicts? What advice might Shirin Ebadi give?

For Iranian Women, a Controversial Victory

SHIRIN EBADI

Shirin Ebadi, an Iranian lawyer and human rights activist, was born in Tehran in 1947. She received a law degree from the University of Tehran and subsequently served as president of the city court and as one of the country's first female judges. After the Iranian revolution of 1979, Ebadi was forced to resign her judgeship; more recently, she was imprisoned for supporting the rights of students and other activists protesting the policies of the clerical regime. Teaching today at the University of Tehran, Ebadi continues to serve as a human rights lawyer, defending the rights of women and children, refugees, religious minorities, students and intellectuals, and political prisoners. She has written several books, including *The Rights of the Child: A Study of Legal Aspects of Children's Rights in Iran* (1994), and *History and Documentation of Human Rights in Iran* (2000). Ebadi received the Nobel Peace Prize in 2003; she was the first Iranian and the first Muslim woman to receive the award. In her acceptance speech, delivered in Oslo on December 10, 2003, Ebadi takes both the West and the Muslim world to task for their failures, while offering an essentially humanistic vision of what is needed to achieve global peace.

In the name of the God of Creation and Wisdom.

Your Majesty, Your Royal Highnesses, Honourable Members of the Norwegian Nobel Committee, Excellencies, Ladies and Gentlemen,

I feel extremely honoured that today my voice is reaching the people of   1
the world from this distinguished venue. This great honour has been bestowed upon me by the Norwegian Nobel Committee. I salute the spirit of Alfred Nobel and hail all true followers of his path.

This year, the Nobel Peace Prize has been awarded to a woman from   2
Iran, a Muslim country in the Middle East.

Undoubtedly, my selection will be an inspiration to the masses of   3
women who are striving to realize their rights, not only in Iran but throughout the region—rights taken away from them through the passage of history. This selection will make women in Iran, and much further afield, believe in themselves. Women constitute half of the population of every country. To disregard women and bar them from active participation in political, social, economic and cultural life would in fact be tantamount to depriving the entire population of every society of half its capability. The patriarchal culture and the discrimination against women, particularly in the Islamic countries, cannot continue forever.

Honourable members of the Norwegian Nobel Committee! As you are   4
aware, the honour and blessing of this prize will have a positive and farreaching impact on the humanitarian and genuine endeavours of the people of Iran and the region. The magnitude of this blessing will embrace every freedom-loving and peace-seeking individual, whether they are women or men.

I thank the Norwegian Nobel Committee for this honour that has been   5
bestowed upon me and for the blessing of this honour for the peace-loving people of my country.

Today coincides with the 55th anniversary of the adoption of the Uni-   6
versal Declaration of Human Rights; a declaration which begins with the recognition of the inherent dignity and the equal and inalienable rights of all members of the human family, as the guarantor of freedom, justice and peace. And it promises a world in which human beings shall enjoy freedom of expression and opinion, and be safeguarded and protected against fear and poverty.

Unfortunately, however, this year's report by the United Nations De-   7
velopment Programme (UNDP), as in the previous years, spells out the rise of a disaster which distances mankind from the idealistic world of the authors of the Universal Declaration of Human Rights. In 2002, almost 1.2 billion human beings lived in glaring poverty, earning less than one dollar a day. Over 50 countries were caught up in war or natural disasters. AIDS

has so far claimed the lives of 22 million individuals, and turned 13 million children into orphans.

At the same time, in the past two years, some states have violated the 8 universal principles and laws of human rights by using the events of 11 September and the war on international terrorism as a pretext. The United Nations General Assembly Resolution 57/219, of 18 December 2002, the United Nations Security Council Resolution 1456, of 20 January 2003, and the United Nations Commission on Human Rights Resolution 2003/68, of 25 April 2003, set out and underline that all states must ensure that any measures taken to combat terrorism must comply with all their obligations under international law, in particular international human rights and humanitarian law. However, regulations restricting human rights and basic freedoms, special bodies and extraordinary courts, which make fair adjudication difficult and at times impossible, have been justified and given legitimacy under the cloak of the war on terrorism.

The concerns of human rights' advocates increase when they observe that 9 international human rights laws are breached not only by their recognized opponents under the pretext of cultural relativity, but that these principles are also violated in Western democracies, in other words, countries which were themselves among the initial codifiers of the United Nations Charter and the Universal Declaration of Human Rights. It is in this framework that, for months, hundreds of individuals who were arrested in the course of military conflicts have been imprisoned in Guantanamo U.S. base in [Cuba], without the benefit of the rights stipulated under the international Geneva conventions, the Universal Declaration of Human Rights and the [United Nations] International Covenant on Civil and Political Rights.

Moreover, a question which millions of citizens in the international civil 10 society have been asking themselves for the past few years, particularly in recent months, and continue to ask, is this: why is it that some decisions and resolutions of the UN Security Council are binding, while some other resolutions of the council have no binding force? Why is it that in the past 35 years, dozens of UN resolutions concerning the occupation of the Palestinian territories by the state of Israel have not been implemented promptly, yet, in the past 12 years, the state and people of Iraq, once on the recommendation of the Security Council, and the second time, in spite of UN Security Council opposition, were subjected to attack, military assault, economic sanctions, and, ultimately, military occupation?

Ladies and Gentlemen,

Allow me to say a little about my country, region, culture and faith. 11

I am an Iranian. A descendent of Cyrus The Great. The very emperor 12 who proclaimed at the pinnacle of power 2500 years ago that ". . . he would not reign over the people if they did not wish it." And [he] promised not to force any person to change his religion and faith and guaranteed freedom for all. The Charter of Cyrus the Great is one of the most important documents that should be studied in the history of human rights.

I am a Muslim. In the Koran, the Prophet of Islam has been cited as saying: "Thou shalt believe in thine faith and I in my religion". That same divine book sees the mission of all prophets as that of inviting all human beings to uphold justice. Since the advent of Islam, too, Iran's civilization and culture has become imbued and infused with humanitarianism, respect for the life, belief and faith of others, propagation of tolerance, and compromise and avoidance of violence, bloodshed and war. The luminaries of Iranian literature, in particular our Gnostic literature, from Hafiz, Mowlavi [better known in the West as Rumi] and Attar to Saadi, Sanaei, Naser Khosrow and Nezami, are emissaries of this humanitarian culture. Their message manifests itself in this poem by Saadi: 13

> The sons of Adam are limbs of one another
> Having been created of one essence.
> When the calamity of time afflicts one limb
> The other limbs cannot remain at rest.

The people of Iran have been battling against consecutive conflicts between tradition and modernity for over 100 years. By resorting to ancient traditions, some have tried and are trying to see the world through the eyes of their predecessors and to deal with the problems and difficulties of the existing world by virtue of the values of the ancients. But, many others, while respecting their historical and cultural past and their religion and faith, seek to go forth in step with world developments and not lag behind the caravan of civilization, development and progress. The people of Iran, particularly in the recent years, have shown that they deem participation in public affairs to be their right, and that they want to be masters of their own destiny.   14

This conflict is observed not merely in Iran, but also in many Muslim states. Some Muslims, under the pretext that democracy and human rights are not compatible with Islamic teachings and the traditional structure of Islamic societies, have justified despotic governments, and continue to do so. In fact, it is not so easy to rule over a people who are aware of their rights, using traditional, patriarchal and paternalistic methods.   15

Islam is a religion whose first sermon to the Prophet begins with the word "Recite!" The Koran swears by the pen and what it writes. Such a sermon and message cannot be in conflict with awareness, knowledge, wisdom, freedom of opinion and expression and cultural pluralism.   16

The discriminatory plight of women in Islamic states, too, whether in 17 the sphere of civil law or in the realm of social, political and cultural justice, has its roots in the patriarchal and male-dominated culture prevailing in these societies, not in Islam. This culture does not tolerate freedom and democracy, just as it does not believe in the equal rights of men and women, and the liberation of women from male domination (fathers, husbands, brothers . . .), because it would threaten the historical and traditional position of the rulers and guardians of that culture.

One has to say to those who have mooted the idea of a clash of civi- 18 lizations, or prescribed war and military intervention for this region, and resorted to social, cultural, economic and political sluggishness of the South in a bid to justify their actions and opinions, that if you consider international human rights laws, including the nations' right to determine their own destinies, to be universal, and if you believe in the priority and superiority of parliamentary democracy over other political systems, then you cannot think only of your own security and comfort, selfishly and contemptuously. A quest for new means and ideas to enable the countries of the South, too, to enjoy human rights and democracy, while maintaining their political independence and territorial integrity of their respective countries, must be given top priority by the United Nations in respect of future developments and international relations.

The decision by the Nobel Peace Committee to award the 2003 prize to 19 me, as the first Iranian and the first woman from a Muslim country, inspires me and millions of Iranians and nationals of Islamic states with the hope that our efforts, endeavours and struggles toward the realization of human rights and the establishment of democracy in our respective countries enjoy the support, backing and solidarity of international civil society. This prize belongs to the people of Iran. It belongs to the people of the Islamic states, and the people of the South for establishing human rights and democracy.

Ladies and Gentlemen, in the introduction to my speech, I spoke of hu- 20 man rights as a guarantor of freedom, justice and peace. If human rights fail to be manifested in codified laws or put into effect by states, then, as rendered in the preamble of the Universal Declaration of Human Rights, human beings will be left with no choice other than staging a "rebellion against tyranny and oppression." A human being divested of all dignity, a human being deprived of human rights, a human being gripped by starvation, a human being beaten by famine, war and illness, a humiliated human being and a plundered human being is not in any position or state to recover the rights he or she has lost.

If the 21st century wishes to free itself from the cycle of violence, 21 acts of terror and war, and avoid repetition of the experience of the 20th century—that most disaster-ridden century of humankind, there is no other way except by understanding and putting into practice every human right for all mankind, irrespective of race, gender, faith, nationality or social status.

In anticipation of that day.
With much gratitude,
Shirin Ebadi

Exploring the Writer's World

1. Why would the Nobel Peace Prize committee select a relatively unknown figure for its premier award, especially in a year when commentators thought several more famous figures living in the West would receive it? What message, if any, did the Nobel committee wish to convey, and to what audiences? What current events might have influenced the committee members? Why is it especially appropriate that a Muslim woman received the prize in 2003? Who were the members of this committee? (Check the Internet to obtain this information.) What can you conclude?

2. Ebadi begins her speech with the phrase, "In the name of the God of Creation and Wisdom." Where do these words originate? What do they signify? What is their importance? How do these words both create a persona for the speaker and prepare the audience for the substance of her lecture?

3. Ebadi is a practicing Muslim as well as a secular lawyer defending the rights of various groups that have been discriminated against in Iran. How does she manage to blend religious and secular issues in her speech? What topic does she touch on? Why does she provide snapshots of Iranian history culture from the time of Cyrus the Great to the present?

4. Ebadi offers criticism of the West, especially the United States, and the Muslim world. List some of her complaints. What is her tone? Do you think that she is fair and balanced in her presentation, or biased? Justify your response.

5. Go online and find out more about Shirin Ebadi and the controversy in Iran surrounding her selection as the winner of the 2003 Nobel Prize for Peace. Collaborating with other members of the class, compose a letter to Ebadi in which you express the group's thoughts and sentiments about her award. Find her e-mail address or website and forward the letter to her.

Conducting Research in the Global Era

Introduction

The *doing* of research is as important a process as the *writing* of a research paper. When scholars, professors, scientists, journalists, and students *do* research, they ask questions, solve problems, follow leads, and track down sources. The process of research as well as the writing of the research paper has changed radically over the last ten years, as the Internet now makes a whole world of resources instantly available to anyone. Skillfully navigating your way through this wealth of resources, evaluating and synthesizing information as you solve problems and answer questions, enhances your critical thinking and writing abilities and develops the tools you will need for professional success.

A research paper incorporates the ideas, discoveries, and observations of other writers. The information provided by these scholars, thinkers, and observers helps to support your own original thesis or claim about a topic. Learning how to evaluate, adapt, synthesize, and correctly acknowledge these sources in your research protects you from charges of plagiarism (discussed below). More importantly, it demonstrates to you how knowledge is expanded and created. Research, and research writing, are the cornerstone not only of the university but of our global information society.

The research paper is the final product of a process of inquiry and discovery. The topics and readings in this book bring together voices from all over the world, discussing and debating issues of universal importance. As you develop a topic, work toward a thesis, and discover sources and evidence, you will use the Internet to bring international perspectives to your writing. More immediately, your teacher will probably ask you to work in peer groups as you refine your topics, suggest resources to each other, and evaluate preliminary drafts of your final research paper. Although the primary—and ultimate—audience for your research paper is your teacher, thinking of your work as a process of discovery and a contribution to a larger global conversation will keep your perspective fresh and your interest engaged.

The Research Process

A research paper is the final result of a series of tasks, some small and others quite time consuming. Be sure to allow yourself plenty of time for each stage of the research process, working with your teacher or a peer group to develop a schedule that breaks down specific tasks.

The four broad stages of the research process are

1. Choosing a topic
2. Establishing a thesis
3. Finding, evaluating, and organizing evidence
4. Writing your paper

Stage One: Choosing a Topic

Reading and discussing the often urgent issues addressed in this book may have already given you an idea about a topic you would like to explore further. Your attention may also have been engaged by a television news report, an international website that presented an unexpected viewpoint, or a speaker who visited your campus. Even if your teacher assigns a specific topic area to you, finding—and nurturing—a genuine curiosity and concern about that topic will make the research process much more involving and satisfying. Some topics are too broad, too controversial (or not controversial enough), too current, or too obscure for an effective research paper.

Determining an Appropriate Research Topic

Ask yourself the following questions about possible topics for your research paper:

- Am I genuinely curious about this topic? Will I want to live with it for the next few weeks?
- What do I already know about this topic? What more do I want to find out?
- Does the topic fit the general guidelines my teacher has suggested?
- Can I readily locate the sources I will need for further research on this topic?

Exercise: Freewriting

Review your work for this class so far, taking note of any readings in the text that particularly appealed to you or any writing assignments that you especially enjoyed. Open a new folder on your computer, labeling it "Research Paper."

Open a new document, and title it "Freewriting." Then write, without stopping, everything that intrigued you originally about that reading or that assignment. Use the questions on page 490 to prompt your thinking.

Browsing

Having identified a general topic area of interest, begin exploring that area by *browsing*. When you browse, you take a broad and casual survey of the existing information and resources about your topic. There are many resources to consult as you begin to dig deeper into your topic, nearly all of which can be found at your campus library. Begin at the reference desk by asking for a guide to the library's reference collection.

- *General Reference Texts.* These include encyclopedias, almanacs, specialized dictionaries, and statistical information.
- *Periodical Index.* Both in-print and online versions of periodical indices now exist (the electronic versions are often subscription-only and available only through academic and some public libraries). A periodical index lists subjects, authors, and titles of articles in newspapers, journals, and magazines. Some electronic versions include both abstracts (brief summaries) and full-text versions of the articles.
- *Library Catalog.* Your library's catalog probably exists both online and as a "card catalog"—an alphabetized record organized by author, title, and subject—in which each book has its own paper card in a file. Begin your catalog browsing with a subject or keyword search. Identify the *call number* that appears most frequently for the books you are most likely to use—that number will point you to the library shelves where you'll find the most useful books for your topic.

Making a Global Connection

Unless you read another language, the information you find in books is not likely to be as international or immediate in perspective as that which you will find in periodicals and online. The information you find through the card catalog will direct you toward books that provide in-depth background information and context, but for the most up-to-date information as well as a perspective from the nation or countries involved in your topic, your online and periodical research will probably be most useful.

- *Search Engines.* For the most current and broadest overview of a research topic, a search engine such as Google, Altavista, or Yahoo can provide you with an ever-changing—and dauntingly vast—range of perspectives. Many search engines, including these three, have international sites (allowing you to search in specific regions or countries) as well as basic translation services. At the browsing stage, spending time online can both stimulate your interest and help you to focus your topic. Because websites change so quickly, however, be sure to print out a page from any site you think might be useful in the later stages of your research—that way, you'll have hard copy of the site's URL (uniform resource locator, or web address). (If you're working on your own computer, create a new folder under "favorites" or "bookmarks" entitled "Research Project," and file bookmarks for interesting sites there.)

International English-Language News Sites

http://news.bbc.co.uk/ The British Broadcasting Corporation's website, with streaming audio and video, with breaking news and in-depth features from all over the world.

http://www.cbc.ca/ The Canadian Broadcasting Corporation's website, with streaming audio and video and in-depth archives, provides a viewpoint that is at once North American and not "American" at all.

http://home.kyodo.co.jp/ Kyodo News Service of Japan offers in-depth and breaking news coverage of East Asia.

http://www.efenews.com/ This news agency, based in Miami, Florida, covers issues around the Spanish-speaking globe.

http://allafrica.com/ A collective effort of hundreds of global and regional news and media organizations provides multilingual streaming content, a particularly rich article database, as well as breaking news about the continent of Africa.

http://english.aljazeera.netenglish/ Satellite television news channel based in Qatar, covering breaking news as well as features throughout the Arab world.

Stage Two: Establishing a Thesis

Moving from a general area of interest to a specific *thesis*—a claim you wish to make, an area of information you wish to explore, a question you intend to answer, or a solution to a problem you want to propose—requires thinking critically about your topic. You have already begun to focus on what *specifically* interests you about this topic in the freewriting exercise on page 491. The next step in refining your topic and establishing a thesis is to determine your audience and purpose for writing.

Determining Your Audience and Purpose

- Where have you found, through your browsing, the most interesting or compelling information about your topic? Who was the audience for that information? Do you consider yourself to be a part of that audience? Define the characteristics of that audience (e.g., concerned about the environment, interested in global economics, experienced at traveling abroad).
- *Why* are you most interested in this topic? Do you want to encourage someone (a friend, a politician) to take a specific course of action? Do you want to shed some light on an issue or event that not many people are familiar with?
- Try a little imaginative role playing. Imagine yourself researching this topic as a professional in a specific field. For example, if your topic is environmental preservation, imagine yourself as a pharmaceuticals researcher. What would your compelling interest in the topic be? What if you were an adventure traveler seeking new destinations—how would your approach to the topic of environmental preservation change?
- If you could have the undivided attention of anyone, other than your teacher, with whom you could share your knowledge about this topic, who would that person be and why?

Moving from a Topic to a Thesis Statement

Although choosing a topic is the beginning of the research *process,* it is not the beginning of your research *paper.* The course that your research will take, and the shape that your final paper will assume, are based on your *thesis statement.* A thesis statement is the answer to whatever question originally prompted your research. To narrow your topic and arrive at a thesis statement, ask yourself specific questions about the topic.

Using Questions to Create a Thesis Statement

General Topic	More Specific Topic	Question	Thesis Statement
Preserving the global environment	Preserving the rain forest	What is a creative way in which people could try to preserve the rain forest?	Ecotourism, when properly managed, can help the rain forest by creating economic incentives for the people who live there.

(continued)

General Topic	More Specific Topic	Question	Thesis Statement
Economic security for women in the developing world	Creating economic opportunities for women in the developing world	What approaches could help women in the developing world establish economic security for themselves and their communities?	Microloans are a creative and empowering way of redistributing wealth that allows individual women to develop their own economic security.
AIDS in Africa	The incidence of AIDS in African women	How are international organizations working to stop the spread of AIDS among African women?	Improving literacy and educational opportunities for African girls and women will help to stem the spread of AIDS.
Dating and courtship between people of different religions	Dating behavior among second-generation American Hindu or Muslim teenagers	How are kids from conservative cultural or religious backgrounds negotiating between their family's beliefs and the pressures of American popular culture?	Encouraging multicultural events helps teenagers learn about each others' cultures and beliefs.

Stage Three: Finding, Evaluating, and Organizing Evidence

Developing a Working Bibliography

A working bibliography is a record of every source you consult as you conduct your research. Although not every source you use may end up cited in your paper, having a consolidated and organized record of *everything* you looked at will make drafting the paper as well as preparing the Works Cited page much easier. Some people use their computers for keeping a Works Cited list (especially if you do much of your research using online databases, which automatically create citations). But for most people—even if many of your sources are online—4 × 6 index cards are much more portable and efficient. Index cards allow you to easily rearrange the order of your sources (according to priority, for example, or sources that you need to double-check); they let you jot down notes or summaries; and they slip into your bookbag for a quick trip to the library.

Whether your working bibliography is on a computer or on index cards, always record the same information for each source you consult.

Checklists for Working Bibliographies

Information for a book:

- ❏ Author name(s), first and last
- ❏ Book title
- ❏ Place of publication
- ❏ Publisher's name
- ❏ Date of publication
- ❏ Library call number
- ❏ Page numbers (for specific information or quotes you'll want to consult later)

Information for an article in a journal or magazine:

- ❏ Author name(s), first and last
- ❏ Article title
- ❏ Magazine or journal title
- ❏ Volume and/or issue number
- ❏ Date of publication
- ❏ Page numbers
- ❏ Library call number

Information for online sources:

- ❏ Author (if there is one)
- ❏ Web page title, or title of an article or graphic on the web page
- ❏ URL (website address)
- ❏ Date of your online access

- *Some sites include information on how they prefer to be cited. You'll notice this information at the bottom of a main or "splash" page of a cite, or you'll see a link to a "citation" page.*

Sample working bibliography note: Article

Honey, Martha. "Protecting the Environment: Setting Green Standards for the Tourism Industry." <u>Environment</u> July/August 2003:8–21.

Sample working bibliography note: Online source

World Tourism Association. "Global Code of Ethics for Tourism." <http:www.//world-tourism.org/projects/ethics/principles.html>.

Consulting Experts and Professionals

In the course of your research you may discover someone whose work is so timely, or opinions so relevant, that a personal interview would provide even more (and unique) information for your paper. Look beyond the university faculty for such experts—for example, if your topic is ecotourism, a local travel agent who specializes in ecotourism might be able to give you firsthand accounts of such locales and voyages. If your topic is second-generation teenagers balancing conservative backgrounds with American popular culture, hanging out with a group of such kids and talking with them about their lives will give you the kind of first-person anecdote that makes research writing genuinely fresh and original. Think of "expertise" as being about *experience*—not just a title or a degree.

Checklist for Arranging and Conducting Interviews

❑ Be certain that the person you wish to speak to will offer a completely unique, even undocumented, perspective on your topic. Interviewing someone who has already published widely on your topic is not the best use of your research time, as you can just as easily consult that person's published work.

❑ E-mail, telephone (at a business number, if possible), or write to your subject well in advance of your paper deadline. Explain clearly that you are a student writing a research paper, the topic of your paper, and the specific subject(s) you wish to discuss.

❑ An interview can be conducted via e-mail or over the telephone as well as in person. Instant messaging, because it can't be easily documented and doesn't lend itself to longer responses, is not a good choice.

❑ Write out your questions in advance!

Conducting Field Research

Field research involves traveling to a specific place to observe and document a specific occurrence or phenomenon. For example, if you were writing about the challenges and opportunities of a highly diverse immigrant community (such as Elmhurst, Queens; see the photo on page 76), you might arrange to spend a day at a local school, park, or coffee shop. Bring a notebook, a digital camera, a tape recorder—anything that will help you capture and record observations. Although your task as a field researcher is to be *unbiased*—to objectively observe what is happening, keeping an open mind as well as open eyes—you'll want to always keep your working thesis in mind, too. For example, if your thesis is

> Allowing students in highly diverse American communities to create events that celebrate and respect their own cultural traditions within the general American popular culture helps to create understanding between teenagers and their immigrant parents

your field research might take you to a high school in an immigrant community to observe the interactions among teenagers. You'll want to record everything—both positive and negative, both expected and surprising—that you observe and overhear, but you won't want to get distracted by a teacher's mentioning the difficulties of coping with many different languages in the classroom. That's fascinating, but it's another topic altogether.

Checklist for Arranging and Conducting Field Research

❏ If your field research involves crossing a private boundary or property line—a school, church, hospital, restaurant, etc.—be sure to contact the institution first to confirm that it's appropriate for you to visit. As with the guidelines for conducting a personal interview, inform the person with whom you arrange the visit that you are a student conducting field research and that your research is for a classroom paper.

❏ Respect personal boundaries. Some people might not want to be photographed, and others might be uneasy if they think you are taking notes on their conversation or behavior. If you sense that your presence is making someone uncomfortable, apologize and explain what you are doing. If they are still uncomfortable, back off.

❏ When you use examples and observations from your field research in your research paper, do not use the first person as part of the citation. Simply describe what was observed, and under what circumstances.

Not recommended: When I visited the dog park to see how the personalities of dogs reflect those of their owners, I was especially attracted to the owner of a bulldog named Max. When I introduced myself to Max's owner, George T., and explained my project to him, George agreed with my thesis and pointed out that the owners of large, athletic dogs like Rottweilers tended to be young men, and the owners of more sedentary dogs (like Max) seemed to be a little mellower.

Recommended: A visit to a local dog park revealed the ways in which the personalities of dogs reflect those of their owners. George T., the owner of a bulldog named Max, pointed out that the younger men at the park were accompanied by large, athletic dogs like Rottweilers, while more sedentary people (like George) tended to have mellower breeds such as bulldogs.

Assessing the Credibility of Sources

After browsing, searching, observing, and conversing, you will by now have collected a mass of sources and data. The next step is to evaluate those sources critically, using your working bibliography as a road map back to all the sources you have consulted to date. This critical evaluation will help you to determine which sources have the relevance, credibility, and authority expected of academic research.

Checklist for Assessing Source Credibility

❏ Do the table of contents and index of a book include keywords and subjects relevant to your topic? Does the abstract of a journal article include keywords relevant to your topic and thesis? Does a website indicate through a menu (or from your using the "search" command) that it contains content relevant to your topic and thesis?

❏ How current is the source? Check the date of the magazine or journal and the copyright date of the book (the original copyright date, not the dates of reprints). Has the website been updated recently, and are its links current and functioning?

❏ How authoritative is the source? Is the author credentialed in his or her field? Do other authors refer to this writer (or website) in their work?

❏ Who sponsors a website? Is it the site of a major media group, a government agency, a political think tank, or a special-interest group? If you are unsure, print out the home page of the site and ask your teacher or a reference librarian.

Taking Notes

Now that you have determined which sources are most relevant and useful, you can begin to read them with greater attention to detail. This is *active reading*—annotating, responding to, and taking notes on what you are reading. Taking careful notes will help you to build the structure of your paper and will ensure accurate documentation later. As with the working bibliography, you can take notes either on your computer or on 4 × 6 index cards. For online sources, you can cut and paste blocks of text into a separate word processing document on your computer; just be certain to include the original URL and to indicate that what you have cut and pasted is a *direct quote* (which you might later paraphrase or summarize). Some researchers cut and paste material in a font or color that is completely different from their own writing, just to remind them of where specific words and concepts came from (and as protection against inadvertent plagiarism).

There are three kinds of notes you will take as you explore your resources:

- *Summaries* give you the broad overview of a source's perspective or information and serve as reminders of a source's content should you wish to revisit later for more specific information or direct quotes.
- *Paraphrases* express a source's ideas and information in your own language.

- *Direct quotations* are best for when an author or subject expresses a thought or concept in language that is so striking, important, or original that to paraphrase it would be to lose some of its importance. Direct quotations are *exact* copies of an author's own words and are always enclosed in quotation marks.

Checklist for Taking Notes

❑ Take just one note (paraphrase, summary, or analysis) on each index card. Be sure to note the complete source information for the quote on the card (see the Checklists for Working Bibliographies on page 495 for what information is required).

❑ Cross-check your note-taking cards against your working bibliography. Be sure that every source on which you take notes has a corresponding entry in the working bibliography.

❑ Write a subtopic on top of each card, preferably in a brightly colored ink. Keep a running list of all of your subtopics. This will enable you to group together related pieces of information and determine the structure of your outline.

Sample note: Summary

Subtopic	Indigenous peoples and ecotourism
Author/title	Mastny, "Ecotourist trap"
Page numbers	94
Summary	The Kainamaro people of Guyana are actively involved with the development of ecotourism in their lands, ensuring that their cultural integrity takes precedence over financial gain.

Sample note: Paraphrase

Subtopic	Indigenous peoples and ecotourism
Author/title	Mastny, "Ecotourist trap"
Page numbers	94
Paraphrase	Actively involving indigenous peoples in ecotourism arrangements is important. A representative for the Kainamaro people of Guyana, Claudette Fleming, says that although this community first worried about maintaining their cultural integrity, they came to see that ecotourism would be a more beneficial way to increase their income and at the same time control their lands and culture than other industries such as logging.

Sample note: Direct quotation

Subtopic	Indigenous peoples and ecotourism
Author/title	Mastny, "Ecotourist trap"

Page numbers   94

Direct quotation   "The Kainamaro are content to share their culture and creativity with outsiders—as long as they remain in control of their futures and the pace of cultural change."

Understanding Plagiarism, Intellectual Property, and Academic Ethics

- *Plagiarism.* Plagiarism is the passing off of someone else's words, ideas, images, or concepts as your own. Plagiarism can be as subtle and accidental as forgetting to add an in-text citation, or as blatant as "borrowing" a friend's paper or handing in something from a website with your own name on it. Most schools and colleges have explicit, detailed policies about what constitutes plagiarism, and the consequences of being caught are not pretty—you may risk anything from failure on a particular assignment to expulsion from the institution. There are two basic ways to avoid plagiarism: (1) don't wait until the last minute to write your paper (which will tempt you to take shortcuts); (2) give an in-text citation (see page 505) for absolutely everything you include in your research paper that didn't come out of your own head. It's better to be safe and over-cite than to be accused of plagiarism. For a straightforward discussion of plagiarism, go to http://www.georgetown.edu/honor/plagiarism.html.
- *Intellectual Property.* If you've ever considered wiping your hard disk clean of free downloaded music files out of the fear of being arrested, then you've wrestled with the issue of intellectual property. Intellectual property includes works of art, music, animation, and literature—as well as research concepts, computer programs, even fashion. Intellectual property rights for visual, musical, and verbal works are protected by *copyright law*. When you download, for free, a music track from the Internet, you are violating copyright law—the artist who created that work receives no credit or royalties for your enjoyment and use of his or her work. When you cut and paste blocks of a website into your own research paper without giving credit, you are also violating copyright law. To respect the intellectual property rights of anyone (or anything) you cite in your research paper, you carefully *cite* the source of the information. Using quotes from another writer, or images from another artist, in your own academic paper is legally defined as "fair use"—*if* you make it clear where the original material comes from.
- *Ethics and the Academic Researcher.* As you enter an academic conversation about your research topic, your audience—even if it's only your teacher—expects you to conduct yourself in an ethical fashion. Your *ethos,* literally, means "where you stand"—what you believe, how you express those beliefs, and how thoughtfully and considerately you relate to the "stances" of others in your academic community. In the professional academy, researchers in fields from medieval poetry through cell biology are expected to adhere to a code of ethics about their research. Working with the ideas and discoveries of others in their academic communities, they are

careful to always acknowledge the work of their peers and the contributions that work has made to their own research. You should do the same. When you leave school, these basic ethical tenets remain the same. You wouldn't hand in another rep's marketing report as your own; you wouldn't claim credit for the successful recovery of another doctor's patient; and you wouldn't put your name on top of another reporter's story. To violate professional ethics is to break the trust that holds an academic or professional community together.

Stage Four: Organizing and Outlining Your Information

Now that you have gathered and evaluated a mass of information, the next step is to begin giving some shape and order to what you have discovered. Writing an outline helps you to think through and organize your evidence, determine the strengths and weaknesses of your argument, and visualize the shape of your final paper. Some instructors will require you to hand in an outline along with your research paper. Even if an outline isn't formally required, it is such a useful and valuable step toward moving from a pile of index cards to a logical, coherent draft that you should plan to create one.

Checklist for Organizing Your Information

❑ Gather up all of your note cards and print out any notes you have taken on your computer. Double-check all of your notes to make sure that they include accurate citation information.

❑ Using your list of subtopics, group your notes according to those subtopics. Are some piles of cards enormous, while other topics have only a card or two? See if subtopics can be combined—or if any subtopics could be further refined and made more specific.

❑ Set aside any note cards that don't seem to "fit" in any particular pile.

❑ Find your thesis statement and copy it out on a blank index card. Go through the cards in each subtopic. Can you immediately see a connection between each note card and your thesis statement? (If not, set that note card aside for now.)

❑ Do not throw away any of the note cards, even if they don't seem to "fit" into your current research plan. You probably won't use every single note card in your paper, but it's good to have a continuing record of your work.

Basic Outlining

Many word processing programs include an "outline" function, and your instructor may ask you to follow a specific format for your outline. An outline is a kind of road map for your thought processes, a list of the pieces of information you are going to discuss in your paper and how you are going to connect those pieces of information to each other as well as back to your original thesis. You can begin the outlining process by using the note cards you have divided into subtopics:

> I. Most compelling, important subtopic
>   A. Supporting fact, quote, or illustration
>   B. Another interesting piece of evidence that supports or illustrates the subtopic
>   1. A direct quotation that further illustrates point B
>   2. Another supporting point
>   a. Minor, but still relevant, points

Another useful outlining strategy is to assign each subtopic a working "topic sentence" or "main idea." As you move into the drafting process, you can return to those topic sentences/main ideas to begin each paragraph.

The Writing Process

A research paper is more than a collection of strung-together facts. No matter how interesting and relevant each individual piece of information may be, your reader is not responsible for seeing how the parts make up a whole. Connecting the evidence, demonstrating the relationships between concepts and ideas, and proving how all of it supports your thesis is entirely up to you.

Drafting

The shape of your outline and your subdivided piles of index cards provide the framework for your rough draft. As you begin to write your essay, think about "connecting the dots" between each piece of evidence, gradually filling in the shape of your argument. Expect your arrangement of individual note cards or whole subtopics to change as you draft.

Remember that you are not drafting a final paper, and certainly not a perfect paper. The goal of drafting is to *organize* your evidence, to get a sense of your argument's strengths and weaknesses, to test the accuracy of your thesis and revise it if necessary. Drafting is as much a thinking process as it is a writing process.

If you get "stuck" as you draft, abandon whatever subtopic you are working on and begin with another. Working at the paragraph level first— using the evidence on a subtopic's note cards to support and illustrate the topic sentence or main idea of the subtopic—is a much less intimidating way to approach drafting a research paper.

Finally, as you draft, be sure that you include either an in-text citation (see page 505) or some other indication of *precisely* where each piece of information came from. This will save you time when you begin revising and preparing the final draft as well as the Works Cited list.

Incorporating Sources

As you draft, you will build connections between different pieces of evidence, different perspectives, and different authors. Learning how to smoothly integrate all those different sources into your own work, without breaking the flow of your own argument and voice, takes some practice. The most important thing to remember is to accurately indicate the source of every piece of information as soon as you cite it.

One way to smoothly integrate sources into your paper is through paraphrase. For example:

The educational benefits of ecotourism can help future generations to respect the environment. "Helping people learn to love the earth is a high calling and one that can be carried out through ecotourism. Ecotourism avoids much of the counterproductive baggage that often accompanies standard education" (Kimmel 41).

In revision, this writer used paraphrase to move more gracefully from her main point to the perspective provided by her source:

Teachers like James R. Kimmel have called the ecotourism experience a "nirvana" for educating their students. "Helping people learn to love the earth is a high calling and one that can be carried out through ecotourism," he observes, noting that the "counterproductive baggage" such as testing and grading are left behind (Kimmel 41).

This system of indicating where exactly an idea, quote, or paraphrase comes from is called *parenthetical citation*. In MLA and APA style, which are required by most academic disciplines (see pages 505–506), these in-text citations take the place of footnotes or endnotes.

Using Transition Verbs Between Your Writing and a Source

Using conversation verbs as transitions between your own writing and a direct quote can enliven the style of your paper. In the revised example above, the writer uses "observes" rather than just "states" or "writes." Other useful transitions include:

Arundhati Roy argues that . . .

Peter Carey mourns that . . .

Amy Tan remembers that . . .

Barbara Ehrenreich and Annette Fuentes compare the results of . . .

Ann Grace Mojtabai admits that . . .

Naomi Shihab Nye insists that . . .

Pico Iyer vividly describes . . .

Revising and Polishing

The drafting process clarified your ideas and gave structure to your argument. In the revision process, you rewrite and rethink your paper, strengthening the connections between your main points, your evidence, and your thesis. Sharing your essay draft with a classmate, with your instructor, or with a tutor at your campus writing center will give you an invaluable objective perspective on your paper's strengths and weaknesses.

Checklist for Your Final Draft

❑ Have I provided parenthetical citations for every source I used?

❑ Do all of those parenthetical citations correspond to an item on my Works Cited list?

❑ Does my essay's title clearly and specifically state my topic?

❑ Is my thesis statement identifiable, clear, and interesting?

❑ Does each body paragraph include a topic sentence that clearly connects to my thesis?

❑ Do I make graceful transitions between my own writing and the sources I incorporate?

❑ When I shared my paper with another reader, was I able to answer any questions about my evidence or my argument using sources already at hand? Or do I need to go back to the library or online to "fill in" any questionable areas in my research?

❑ Does my conclusion clearly echo and support my thesis statement and concisely sum up how all of my evidence supports that thesis?

❑ Have I proofread for clarity, grammar, accuracy, and style?

❑ Is my paper formatted according to my instructor's guidelines? Do I have a backup copy on disk, and more than one printed copy?

Documentation

From the beginning of your research, when you were browsing in the library and online, you have been documenting your sources. To document a source simply means to make a clear, accurate record of where exactly a piece of information, a quote, an idea, or a concept comes from, so that future readers of your paper can go back to that original source and learn more. As we have seen, careful attention to documentation is the best way to protect yourself against inadvertent plagiarism. There are two ways you document your sources in your paper: within the text itself (*in-text* or *parenthetical* citation), and in the Works Cited list at the end of your paper.

What Do I Need to Document?

- Anything I didn't know before I began my research
- Direct quotations
- Paraphrases
- Summaries
- Specific numerical data, such as charts and graphs
- Any image, text, or animation from a website
- Any audio or video
- Any information gathered during a personal interview

Parenthetical (in-text) Citation

The Modern Language Association (MLA) style for documentation is most commonly used in the humanities and is the format discussed here. Keep in mind that different academic disciplines have their own documentation guidelines and styles, as do some organizations (many newspapers, for example, have their own "style guides"). An in-text citation identifies the source of a piece of information as part of your own sentence or within parentheses. In MLA style, the parenthetical information includes the author's name and the page number (if appropriate) on which the information can be found in the original source. If your readers want to know more, they can then turn to your Works Cited page to find the author's name and the full bibliographic information for that source. Always place the in-text or parenthetical citation as close to the incorporated source material as possible—preferably within the same sentence.

Guidelines for Parenthetical (in-text) Citation

Page numbers for a book

The end of the Second World War began Samuel Beckett's greatest period of
   creativity, which he referred to as "the siege in the room" (Bair 346).

Bair describes the period immediately after the Second World War as a time of great
   creativity for Samuel Beckett (346).

In the first parenthetical citation, the author is not named within the student writer's text, so the parentheses include both the source author's name and the page number on which the information can be found. In the second example, the source author (Bair) is mentioned by name, so there is no need to repeat that name within the parentheses—only the page number is needed.

Page numbers for an article in a magazine or journal

Wheatley argues that "America has embraced values that cannot create a sustainable
   society and world" (25).

Page numbers for a newspaper article

Cite both the section letter (or description of the section) and the page.

Camera phones are leading to new questions about the invasion of privacy (Harmon 4-3).

A spokesperson for the National Institutes of Health has described obesity as the greatest potential danger to the average American's health (Watts B3).

Website

Arts and Letters Daily includes links to opinions and essays on current events from English-language media worldwide.

Article 2 of the proposed Global Code of Ethics for Tourism describes tourism "as a vehicle for individual and collective fulfillment" (world-tourism).

When an online source does not give specific "page," screen, or paragraph numbers, your parenthetical citation must include the name of the site.

Works Cited List

Gather your working bibliography cards, and be sure that every source you cite in your paper has a corresponding card. To construct the Works Cited list, you simply arrange these cards in alphabetical order, by author. The Works Cited page is a separate, double-spaced page at the end of your paper (see page 519 for an illustration).

Formatting Your Works Cited List

- Center the title, Works Cited, at the top of a new page. Do not underline it, italicize it, or place it in quotation marks.
- Alphabetize according to the author's name, or according to the title (for works, such as websites, that do not have an author). Ignore words such as *the, and,* and *a* when alphabetizing.
- Begin each entry at the left margin. After the first line, indent all other lines of the entry by five spaces (one stroke of the "tab" key).
- Double-space every line.
- Place a period after the author, the title, and the publishing information.
- Underline book and web page titles. Titles of articles, stories, poems, and parts of entire works in other media are placed in quotation marks.

Guidelines for Works Cited List

Book by One Author

Bair, Deirdre. <u>Samuel Beckett: A Biography</u>. New York: Simon and
    Schuster, 1978.

Multiple Books by the Same Author

List the author's name for the first entry. For each entry that follows, replace
the author's name with three hyphens.

Thomas, Lewis. <u>The Medusa and the Snail: More Notes of a Biology Watcher</u>. New
    York: Viking Press, 1979.

—. <u>Late Night Thoughts on Listening to Mahler's Ninth Symphony</u>. New York: Viking
    Press, 1983.

Book with Two or Three Authors/Editors

Moore-Gilbert, Bart, Gareth Stanton, and Willy Maley, eds. <u>Postcolonial Criticism</u>.
    London and New York: Addison Wesley Longman, 1997.

Book with More Than Three Authors/Editors

Nordhus, Inger, Gary R. VandenBos, Stig Berg, and Pia Fromholt, eds. <u>Clinical
    Geropsychology</u>. Washington: APA, 1998.

Book or Publication with Group or Organization as Author

National PTA. <u>National Standards for Parent/Family Involvement Programs</u>. Chicago:
    National PTA, 1997.

Book or Publication Without an Author

<u>The New York Public Library Desk Reference</u>. New York: Prentice Hall, 1989.

Work in an Anthology of Pieces All by the Same Author

Thomas, Lewis. "The Youngest and Brightest Thing Around." <u>The Medusa and the
    Snail: More Notes of a Biology Watcher</u>. New York: Viking Press, 1979.

Work in an Anthology of Different Authors

Graver, Elizabeth. "The Body Shop." <u>The Best American Short Stories 1991</u>. Boston:
    Houghton Mifflin, 1991.

Work Translated from Another Language

Cocteau, Jean. The Difficulty of Being. Trans. Elizabeth Sprigge. New York: Da Capo
    Press, 1995.

Entry from a Reference Volume

For dictionaries and encyclopedias, simply note the edition and its date. No
page numbers are necessary for references organized alphabetically, such as
encyclopedias (and, obviously, dictionaries).

"Turner, Nat." Encyclopedia Americana: International Edition. 1996 ed.

"Carriera, Rosalba." The Oxford Companion to Western Art. Ed. Hugh Brigstoke.
    Oxford: Oxford University Press, 2001.

Article from a Journal with Pagination Continued Through Each Volume

Enoch, Jessica. "Resisting the Script of Indian Education: Zitkala Sa and the Carlisle
    Indian School." College English 65 (2002): 117–141.

Do not include the issue number for journals paginated continuously.

Article from a Journal Paginated for Each Issue

Follow the same procedure for a journal with continued pagination, placing
a period and the issue number after the volume number.

Article from a Weekly or Biweekly Periodical

Baum, Dan. "Jake Leg." New Yorker 15 Sept. 2003: 50–57.

Article from a Monthly or Bimonthly Periodical

Perlin, John. "Solar Power: The Slow Revolution." Invention and Technology Summer
    2002: 20–25.

Article from a Daily Newspaper

Brody, Jane E. "A Pregame Ritual: Doctors Averting Disasters." New York Times 14
    Oct. 2003: F7.

If the newspaper article goes on for more than one page, add a + sign to the
first page number.

Newspaper or Periodical Article with No Author

"Groups Lose Sole Authority on Chaplains for Muslims." New York Times 14 Oct.
    2003: A15.

Unsigned Editorial in a Newspaper or Periodical

"The Iraqi Weapons Puzzle." Editorial. <u>New York Times</u> 12 Oct. 2003, 4.10.

Letter to the Editor of a Newspaper or Periodical

Capasso, Chris. Letter. "Mountain Madness." <u>Outside</u> May 2003: 20.

Film, Video, DVD

If you are writing about a specific actor's performance or a specific director, use that person's name as the beginning of the citation. Otherwise, begin with the title of the work. Specify the media of the recording (film, video, DVD, etc.)

<u>Princess Mononoke</u>. Dir. Hayao Miyazaki. Prod. Studio Ghibli, 1999. Videocassette.
    Miramax Films, 2001.

Eames, Charles and Ray. <u>The Films of Charles and Ray Eames, Volume 1: Powers of
    Ten</u>. 1978. Videocassette. Pyramid Home Video, 1984.

Television or Radio Broadcast

"Alone on the Ice." <u>The American Experience</u>. PBS. KRMA, Denver. 8 Feb. 1999.

Arnold, Elizabeth. "The Birds of the Boreal." <u>National Geographic Radio Expeditions</u>.
    NPR. WNYC, New York. 14 Oct. 2003.

CD or Other Recording

Identify the format if the recording is not on a compact disc.

Bukkene Bruse. "Wedding March from Osterdalen." <u>Nordic Roots 2</u>.
    Northside, 2000.

Personal Interview

Give the name of the person you interviewed, how the interview was conducted (phone, e-mail, etc.), and the date of the interview.

Reed, Lou. Telephone interview. 12 Sept. 1998.

Dean, Howard. E-mail interview. 8 Aug. 2003.

Online Sources

Because websites are constantly changing, and "publication" information about a site varies so widely, think about documenting your site accurately enough so that a curious reader of your paper could find the website. When a URL is very long, give just enough information for readers to find their way to the site and then navigate to the specific page or image from there.

Web Page/Internet Site

Give the site title, the name of the site's editor (if there is one), electronic publication information, your own date of access, and the site's URL. (If some of this information is not available, just cite what you can.)

Arts & Letters Daily. Ed. Denis Dutton. 2003. 2 Sept. 2003 <http://aldaily.com/>.

Document or Article from an Internet Site

Include the author's name, document title, information about a print version (if applicable), information about the electronic version, access information, and URL.

Brooks, David. "The Organization Kid." The Atlantic Monthly April 2001: 40–54. 25

Aug. 2003 <http://www.theatlantic.com/issues/2001/04/brooks-p1.htm>.

Book Available Online

The citation is similar to the format for a print book, but include as much information as you can about the website as well as the date of your access to it.

Einstein, Albert. Relativity: The Special and General Theory. Trans. Robert W.

Lawson. New York: Henry Holt, 1920. Bartleby.Com: Great Books Online. Ed.

Steven van Leeuwen. 2003. 6 Sept. 2003 <http://bartelby.com/173/>.

Wheatley, Phillis. Poems on Various Subjects, Religious and Moral. Project Gutenberg.

Ed. Michael S. Hart. 2003. 6 Sept. 2003 <http://ibiblio.org/pub/docs/books/

gutenberg/etext96/whtly10.txt>.

Database Available Online

Bartleby Library. Ed. Steven van Leeuwen. 2003. 28 Sept. 2003 <http://bartleby.com>.

Source from a Library Subscription Database

Academic and most public libraries offer to their members access to subscription-only databases that provide electronic access to publications not otherwise available on free-access websites. When you cite a book, article, or other source that you have retrieved from such a database, add to your citation the name of the service and the institution that provided the access.

Mastny, Lisa. "Ecotourist Trap." Foreign Policy Nov.–Dec. 2002: 94+. *Questia*. 10

Oct. 2003 <http://www.questia.com/>.

Rossant, John. "The Real War Is France vs. France." <u>Business Week</u> 6 Oct. 2003: 68.

    <u>MasterFile Premier</u>. EBSCO. Maplewood Memorial Library, Maplewood, NJ.

    13 Oct. 2003 <http://0-web24.epnet.com.catalog.maplewoodlibrary.org/>.

Newspaper Article Online

Zernike, Kate. "Fight Against Fat Shifts to the Workplace." <u>New York Times</u> 12 Oct.

    2003. 12 Oct. 2003 <http://nytimes.com/2003/10/12/national/12OBES.html>.

Journal Article Online

Salkeld, Duncan. "Making Sense of Differences: Postmodern History, Philosophy

    and Shakespeare's Prostitutes." <u>Chronicon: An Electronic History Journal</u> 3 (1999).

    5 Apr. 2003 <http://www.ucc.ie/chronicon/salkfra.htm>.

E-mail

Give the writer's name, the subject line (if any) enclosed in quotation marks, and the date of the message.

Stanford, Myles. "Johnson manuscripts online." E-mail to the author. 12 July 2003.

Electronic Posting to an Online Forum

Many online media sources conduct forums in which readers can respond to breaking news or ongoing issues. Citing from such forums is difficult because many people prefer to post anonymously; if the author's username is too silly or inappropriate, use the title of the post or the title of the forum to begin your citation and determine its place in the alphabetical order of your Works Cited list.

Berman, Piotr. Online posting. 6 Oct. 2003. Is Middle East Peace Impossible? 13 Oct.

    2003 <http://tabletalk.salon.com/webx?13@@.596c5554>.

Sample Student Research Paper

Double-space the entire paper. Set one-inch margins on top and bottom, left and right. Indent first line of paragraphs five spaces or one-half inch

Number each page with your last name and page number, one-half inch from top of page and flush right

Title is centered; do not underline title

Title clearly states topic and problem-solving approach

Evidence from several different sources highlights problem suggested by title

---

Casaundra Wiggins   Wiggins 1

Professor Ellen Judge

Expository Writing

June 3, 2004

Ecotourism: Preserving or Polluting the Planet?

 As international travel becomes more attainable to   1
more people, and developing nations struggle to
maintain economic stability in demanding times, some
tourism officials and native communities around the
world have begun to cooperate in creating a new kind of
travel called "ecotourism" (or, alternatively, "sustainable
tourism"). The United Nations declared 2002 the "International Year of Ecotourism," both to call attention to
the environmental and economic opportunities provided
by ecotourism as well as to sound a warning about the
perils native communities and fragile environments face
as they become popular tourism spots (Mastny). The
Ecotourism Society defines ecotourism as "purposeful
travel to natural areas to understand the culture and
natural history of the environment, taking care not to
alter the integrity of the ecosystem, while producing
economic opportunities that make the conservation of
natural resources beneficial to local people"
(Tenenbaum). As the popularity of "ecotourism"
continues to grow by 15–25% each year (Ewert and

Wiggins 2

Thesis statement offers solution to defined problem

Shultis), the role of education in the sustainable practice of ecotourism becomes increasingly important.

Because of its boom in popularity, the very term "ecotourism" has, in some quarters, become suspect (Zurick). Some activists and conservationists are concerned that irresponsibly managed tourism, prepackaged with the consumer-friendly label "ecotourism," does just as much damage to the environment as regular tourism. To address this growing problem, several studies and much field research have demonstrated that when local communities, nongovernmental organizations (NGOs), and tourism facilitators cooperate, ecotourism can indeed achieve its goals of providing economic benefits to a fragile community, preserving and protecting the local environment, and promoting a "sustainable" lifestyle to those tourists who visit.

Online sources often do not have "page" numbers; parenthetical citation includes source author only

After fully spelling out term, Casaundra gives abbreviation for future reference

2

Each paragraph begins with clear topic sentence

Arriving at an ethical universal standard for "ecotourism" has been the goal of many nonprofit and NGO groups working to clarify guidelines for sustainable tourism. At the seventh session of the Commission on Sustainable Development in 1999, delegates created a "Global Code of Ethics for Tourism" (worldtourism.org). This Code of Ethics, along with other codes and qualifiers for evaluating ecotourism (see Kimmel 42), makes it quite clear that "ecotourism" involves much more than staying in a posh beach resort eating vegetarian food, or riding on tour buses into the remote jungle to stare at villagers. Especially important in the code are principles that uphold the rights and empowerment of native peoples; six of the ten articles of the code are founded in the idea that "stakeholders in

3

Complete URL is too long for parenthetical citation; this is an accurate and useful abbreviation

Wiggins 3

tourism development and tourists themselves should observe the social and cultural traditions and practices of all peoples, including those of minorities and indigenous peoples and to recognize their worth" (world-tourism.org).

Topic sentence signals that differing perspectives will be compared

Many activists point out the ironic dangers of "ecotourism" in nations and regions already fragile from years of economic and environmental exploitation. Randy Hayes, president of the environmental activist group Rainforest Action Network, notes that in the Amazon "indigenous people's use of the forest for firewood, meat, and agriculture sometimes comes in conflict with tourists' wishes to keep the land pristine" ("Is Ecotourism Good for the Planet?" 108). Stripped by government officials—and private groups that benefit directly from tourist dollars—indigenous peoples feel that they are "left with no alternatives but impoverish-ment and resentment" ("Is Ecotourism Good for the Planet?" 108). The tourists themselves might remain completely ignorant of these tensions; observing wildlife and photographing rare orchids, they overlook the simmering poverty that the "preservation" of the environment is causing to the very people who depend on the forest to make their living.

4

Transition verb "laments" smoothly connects Casaundra's writing with quoted source

Another region of growing tensions among "ecotourism" outfitters, government officials who benefit financially, and indigenous peoples whose lives are disrupted is the South Pacific. Helu-Thaman laments the move from a land-based, ecologically aware native economy in many Pacific Island nations to an economy (and people) "tenuously based on such touristically

5

salable aspects of their culture as song, dance, and hand-icrafts, rather than on the more productive environment-based aspects" (104). In the island nation of Fiji, for example, tourism is the main industry; with 260,000 visitors each year, the island is "the leading tourist desti-nation" in the region (Zurick). However, as Zurick reports, while tourism accounts for 75% of Fiji's foreign-exchange earnings, it is also linked to "loss of ecological values, loss of fisheries, coastal damage by resort construction . . . and the disruption of traditional environmental activities." More problematic is the movement of Fijian tourists away from established resort areas to "underdeveloped sites" as part of "ecotourism programs" (Zurick); these sites are espe-cially vulnerable to degradation.

Some vacations labeled "ecotourism" strictly for advertising purposes, or "green appeal," may or may not have detrimental effects on their destinations. While Hashimoto argues that there is some benefit to keeping travelers restricted to controllable environments like resorts or cruise ships, minimizing their impact on fragile environments (82), a 1999 study by the nonprofit group Conservation International found that, in 1994, only ten percent of sewage generated by Caribbean cruise ships received any kind of treatment. The report notes that "poor sewage treatment can lead to pollution of ground and surface water, bacterial growth, the smothering of corals, the accumulation of toxins in aquatic and marine organisms, and algal blooms, which reduce oxygen available to other organisms and can cause biologically dead areas" (Tenenbaum).

6

Another transition verb ("argues") integrates quoted source material with Casaundra's own opinions

The author has already been named, so the parenthetical citation need only include the page number

Wiggins 5

Tenenbaum goes on to cite a study by the Annals of Tourism Research that finds environmental degradation *caused by* resorts and cruise ships eventually leads tourists to abandon a region, leaving the indigenous peoples in even greater economic and environmental disrepair.

To promote responsible ecotourism, NGOs and regional groups are beginning to work together to uphold the "Global Code of Ethics for Tourism." For example, the nonprofit environmental group Sierra Club has developed a program of "Service Outings," in which tourists participate in ecologically conscious projects that raise their appreciation of the natural environment while upholding the principles of Article 3 of the code, including the goal that "tourism infrastructure should be designed and tourism activities programmed in such a way as to protect the natural heritage composed of ecosystems and biodiversity and to preserve endangered species of wildlife" (world-tourism.org). On one such "service outing," tourists in Maui helped in a study of humpback whales, which led to a new law in Hawaii protecting whale calving grounds (Sierra).

Another example of mutually beneficial cooperation between organizers of "ecotourism" journeys and indigenous peoples is in Guyana, where the local Kainamaro people at first resisted incursions into their lands. As described by Claudette Fleming, an activist and representative for a small Kainamaro community, families at first resisted their "loss of isolation," but gradually came to realize that by becoming "stakeholders" in ecotourism efforts, they could preserve their way of life and earn

For article without author, parenthetical citation uses only article title

Topic sentence establishes connection between preceding paragraph and this one

Claudette Fleming is quoted within Mastny's article, so the in-text citation refers to Mastny

7

8

Wiggins 6

financial resources in ways that other choices, such as logging or gold mining, would not allow for. "The Kainamaro are content to share their culture and creativity with outsiders," she writes, "—as long as they remain in control of their futures and the pace of cultural change. For example, the Kainamaro limit the number of visitors to their community and require that all outsiders be briefed on cultural sensitivities, such as not wandering into neighboring villages uninvited" (Mastny).

According to Orams and Hill, this kind of thoughtful, careful educating of participants in ecotourism programs is critical to a sustainable and beneficial experience. "Education has received much attention in the ecotourism field and is viewed by some as a critical component of ecotourism experiences," they note in their study of how "ecotourists" in Australia were educated on how to interact with wild dolphins. A resort on Australia's Moreton Island had become well known for the crowds of wild bottle-nosed dolphins that would swim close to shore each evening to be fed. Scientists were concerned about the long-term effects of dolphin-human contact, especially as many resort guests were irresistibly tempted to pet or stroke the dolphins as they were feeding. In a 1994 experiment, a "Dolphin Education Centre" was constructed at the resort, and visitors who wished to feed the dolphins first had to visit the Education Centre to learn more about the biology of the animals, their behavior, and efforts at preserving their health. During the education program, visitors also learned *why* it was important that they not try to touch the dolphins. In follow-up studies, incidents

Wiggins 7

of visitors who tried to touch the dolphins (or otherwise behave inappropriately in the water near the animals) plummeted.

Final 3 paragraphs each provides evidence to support Casaundra's thesis and her solution to described problem

In his article "Ecotourism as Environmental 10 Learning," science educator James R. Kimmel makes it poetically clear that seeing ecotourism as a *learning* experience is the best way to promote sensitivity and sustainability among adventurous travelers. "Helping people learn to love the earth is a high calling and one that can be carried out through ecotourism," he optimistically writes. "People participate out of choice, there are no tests or grades, the sites are exciting and often exotic, and participants expect to learn in an enjoyable manner" (Kimmel 41). Whether it is learning about and respecting the cultures of indigenous peoples like the Kainamaro, or deliberately leaving as little impact or trace of human activity on a fragile ecosystem, travelers from the industrialized Western world can experience "ecotourism" not as an expensive fad but as a way to genuinely enhance their appreciation of—and concern for—the planet.

Works Cited

"Essential Guide to Ecotourism." <u>Geographical</u> June 2000:
78. Questia. 10 Oct. 2003 <http://www.questia.com/>.

Ewert, Alan, and John Shultis. "Resource-Based
Tourism: An Emerging Trend in Tourism
Experiences. <u>Parks and Recreation</u> 32.9 (Sept.
1997): 94+. EBSCO. 12 Oct. 2003 <http://
www.maplewoodlibrary.org/databases.html>.

Hashimoto, Atsuko. "In Pursuit of Paradise: Tourism
and Development." <u>Harvard International Review</u>
24.3 (2002): 82+. Questia. 10 Oct. 2003
<http://www.questia.com/>.

Helu-Thaman, Konai. "Beyond Hula, Hotels, and Hand-
icrafts: A Pacific Islander's Perspective of Tourism
Development." <u>Contemporary Pacific</u> 5.1 (1993):
103–131.

"Is Ecotourism Good for the Planet?" <u>Sierra</u> Mar. 1999:
108. Questia. 10 Oct. 2003 <http://www.questia.com/>.

Kimmel, James R. "Ecotourism as Environmental
Learning." <u>Journal of Environmental Education</u> 30.2
(1999): 40–44.

Mastny, Lisa. "Ecotourist Trap." <u>Foreign Policy</u>
Nov.–Dec. 2002: 94+. Questia. 10 Oct. 2003
<http://www.questia.com/>.

Orams, Mark B., and Greg J. E. Hill. "Controlling the
Ecotourist in a Wild Dolphin Feeding Program: Is
Education the Answer?" Questia. 10 Oct. 2003
<http://www.questia.com/>. <u>Journal of Environ-
mental Education</u> 29.3 (1998): 33–38.

Center heading; every entry is double-spaced; second and following lines of each entry are indented five spaces

If a URL must be divided between two lines, break it only after a slash; do not introduce a hyphen at the break or allow your word-processing program to do so. Indent the turnover line 5 spaces.

Tenenbaum, David J. "Trampling Paradise." <u>Environ-mental Health Perspectives</u> 108.5 (2000). Questia. 10 Oct. 2003 <http://www.questia.com>.

World Tourism Organization. "Global Code of Ethics for Tourism". <http://www.world-tourism.org/projects/ethics/principles.html>.

Zurick, David N. "Preserving paradise." <u>Geographical Review</u> 85.2 (1995): 157+. Questia. 10 Oct. 2003 <http://www.questia.com/>.

Glossary of Rhetorical Terms

allusion A reference to a familiar concept, person, or thing.

analytical essay An essay that defines and describes an issue by breaking it down into separate components and carefully considering each component.

annotation Marking up a text as you read by writing comments, questions, and ideas in the margins.

argument A *rhetorical strategy* that involves using *persuasion* to gain a reader's support for the writer's position.

assertion A statement that a writer claims is true without necessarily providing objective support for the *claim.*

audience The assumed readers of a text.

brainstorming An idea-generation strategy. Write your topic, a key word, or *thesis* at the top of a blank piece of paper or computer screen, and for ten or fifteen minutes just write down everything you associate with, think of, or know about that topic.

cause and effect/causal analysis A *rhetorical strategy* that examines the relationships between events or conditions and their consequences.

claim In *argument,* a statement that the author intends to support through the use of *reasons, evidence,* and appeals.

classification A *rhetorical strategy* that divides a subject into categories and then analyzes the characteristics of each category. See also *division.*

cognitive styles Different and individual approaches to thinking and understanding, especially in regard to how we process language and text.

coherence A characteristic of effective writing, achieved through careful organization of ideas and the skillful use of *transitions.*

colloquial language Informal language not usually found in an academic essay but appropriate in some cases for purposes of *illustration.*

comparison and **contrast** Two strategies that are often used to complement one another in the same essay. Comparison examines the similarities between two or more like subjects; contrast examines the differences between those subjects.

composing process The work of writing, moving from notes and ideas through multiple *drafts* to a "final" essay. All writers develop their own composing process as they become more comfortable with writing.

conflict A struggle between two opposing forces that creates suspense, tension, and interest in a *narrative*.

conventions The expectations general readers have of specific kinds of writing.

deduction An *argument* that begins with a clearly stated *claim*, and then uses selected evidence to support that claim. See also *induction*.

definition/extended definition A writing strategy that describes the nature of an abstract or concrete subject. Extended definition is a kind of essay based on that definition, expanding its scope by considering larger issues related to the subject (for example, the different ways in which different groups of people might define a term like *freedom*).

description A kind of writing based on sensory observations (sight, hearing, smell, touch) that allows readers to imaginatively re-create an experience.

diction The "style" of language, either written or spoken, from which inferences about the speaker's education, background, and origins can be made. Your choice of diction in a piece of writing depends on your intended *audience* and your *purpose*.

discourse Dialogue or conversation. In the study of rhetoric, *discourse* refers to the ways a specific group of people, organization, or institution speaks to and about itself.

division A *rhetorical strategy* that breaks a subject down into smaller parts and analyzes their relationship to the overall subject.

drafting Moving from notes and an outline to the general shape and form of a "final" essay. Writers often go through multiple "drafts" of an essay, moving ideas around, tinkering with the language, and double-checking facts.

editorialize An "editorial" in a newspaper offers the collective opinion of the newspaper's management on a *topical* issue. Writers "editorialize" when they offer opinions on a subject of topical interest. Unlike the approach of an *argument*, editorializing writers do not always consider the viewpoints of their opponents.

evidence In an *argument*, the facts and expert opinions used to support a *claim*.

exemplification See *illustration*.

expository essay An essay that seeks to explain something by combining different *rhetorical strategies*, such as *classification* and *description*.

extended definition See *definition*.

figurative language Imaginative language that compares one thing to another in ways that are not necessarily logical but that are nevertheless striking, original, and "true." Examples of figurative language are *metaphor, simile,* and *allusion*.

illustration Also called *exemplification*. The use of examples to support an essay's main idea. A successful illustrative essay uses several compelling examples to support its *thesis*.

imagery Descriptive writing that draws on vivid sensory descriptions and *figurative language* to re-create an experience for a reader.

induction In *argument*, a strategy that uses compelling evidence to lead an *audience* to an inevitable conclusion. See also *deduction*.

invective Angry or hostile language directed at a specific person (or persons).

irony A *rhetorical strategy* that uses language to suggest the opposite of what is actually being stated. Irony is used frequently in works of *satire* and works of humor.

major proposition See *claim*. In *argument*, the position a writer goes on to defend through *reasons* and *evidence*.

metaphor The comparison of two unlike things to one another for *figurative* effect.

minor proposition *In argument*, the position a writer goes on to defend through *reasons* and *evidence*. See also *claim*.

motif A simple theme (often a phrase or an image) that is repeated throughout a *narrative* to give it a deeper sense of *unity* and to underscore its basic idea.

narration/narrative A type of writing that tells a story. In an essay, narration is often used to describe what happened to a person or place over a certain period of time.

op-ed style Named for the "opinion and editorial" pages of newspapers, "op-ed style" describes brief *arguments* written for a general *audience* that are supported by *evidence* commonly accepted as "true" or "expert."

paraphrase Stating another author's opinions, ideas, or observations in your own words. When you paraphrase, you still give full credit (through in-text citation) to the original author.

persona The voice of the author of an essay or story, even if that voice never uses the first person or gives any further details about its "self." Your persona, in an academic essay, might be that of a concerned citizen, a sociological researcher, or a literary critic.

personal essay An essay written in the first person (the "I" point of view) that uses personal experience to illustrate a larger point.

persuasion A *rhetorical strategy*, often used in *argument*, that seeks to move readers to take a course of action or to change their minds about an issue.

point of view The perspective and attitude of a writer or narrator toward the subject.

précis A *summary* of the relevant facts, statements, and *evidence* offered by an essay, especially an *argument*.

prewriting Any idea-generation strategy that gets you "warmed up" for drafting an essay.

process analysis A kind of essay that describes, in chronological order, each step or stage of the performing of an action (a "how-to" essay).

prologue A brief statement or introduction to a longer work (originally, the introduction to a play spoken by one of the actors).

proposition A *thesis* statement, or *claim,* that suggests a specific action to take and seeks the support of readers to take that action. A proposition is supported by *evidence* demonstrating why this course of action is the best to take. See also *major proposition* and *minor proposition.*

purpose The reason a writer takes on a subject as well as the goal the writer hopes to achieve.

reader response theory Loosely defined, the idea that every reader brings an individual approach and background of knowledge to a text and responds to a text in a unique way.

reasons In *argument, evidence* you offer that your reader will accept as legitimate support for your *claim.* See also *minor proposition.*

rebuttal In *argument,* a considered response to an opposing point of view.

reflective essay An essay in which you examine and evaluate your own actions or beliefs, learning more about yourself in the process.

refutation In *argument,* proof that someone (usually the opposition) is incorrect.

revision The stage in the writing process in which you revisit your draft, reading and rewriting for clarity and *purpose,* adding or subtracting relevant *evidence,* and perhaps sharing your essay with additional readers for comment.

rhetoric The deliberate and formal use of language, usually in writing, to illustrate an idea or demonstrate a truth. The writer of rhetoric always has in mind an *audience* and a *purpose.*

rhetorical strategies Key patterns that writers employ to organize and clarify their ideas and opinions in an essay.

satire Writing that uses humor, often mocking, to call attention to stupidity or injustice and inspire social change. Satirists call attention to the foibles of groups, institutions, and bureaucracies rather than of individual people.

sensory detail Details based on the five senses (touch, sight, smell, taste, sound) that enhance descriptive writing.

simile A style of *figurative language* that compares two unlike things using *like* or *as.* See also *metaphor.*

stipulative definition Creating, based on your own experience and opinions, a definition of a term (generally an abstract term, such as *globalization*) for the purposes of your own *argument.*

style A writer's own unique sense for, and use of, language, *imagery,* and *rhetoric.* Some writers are immediately recognizable by their style; other times, a writer needs to consider *audience* and *purpose* when developing an appropriate style for a particular rhetorical task.

summary As a critical reading strategy, the brief restating (in your own words) of an essay's *thesis,* main points, and *evidence.* Summarizing can help you better understand the logic of a writer's argument and the way an essay is organized. See also *précis*.

symbol Something that stands for, or represents, something else. All numbers and letters are symbols, in that they stand for concepts and sounds.

thesis In an essay, a brief statement that concisely states the writer's subject and opinion on that subject.

tone The writer's "voice" in an essay that, through the use of *diction* and *figurative language,* as well as other *rhetorical strategies,* conveys the writer's feelings about the subject.

topical Relating to an issue or subject drawn from current events or that is of immediate interest to the *audience.*

topic sentence The sentence encapsulating the focus, or main idea, of each paragraph of an essay.

transition The language used to connect one idea to the next in an essay. Skillful use of transitions helps to give an essay *coherence,* allowing the reader to smoothly follow the writer's train of thoughts as well as to clearly see the connections between those thoughts and supporting *evidence.*

unity A quality of good writing that goes beyond *coherence* to an overall sense of completion. A writer achieves unity when the reader feels that not a word need be added to (or taken away from) the essay.

usage In rhetorical studies, the ways in which language is commonly used in speaking and writing.

visual texts Anything that conveys an idea without necessarily using language (photographs, advertisements, cartoons, graffiti, etc.).

voice See *tone.*

warrant In *argument,* a plausible *assertion* that a reader must agree with in order to accept the *claim.*

APPENDIX C

Glossary of Globalization Terms

acculturation The adoption by one *culture* of features from another, often as a result of conquest or colonialization—for example, the use of French as a primary language in many former French colonies in Africa.

anarchy The absence of any authority; total individual freedom.

assimilation The adoption of a society's *culture* and customs by immigrants to that society. At both an individual and a group level, the process is gradual and often reciprocal.

balkanization (From the breakup of the countries of the Balkan Peninsula, in Europe, into hostile and frequently warring nations after World War I.) To break apart into smaller, hostile nations or entities, as in the division of the former Yugoslavia and the breakup of the former Soviet Union.

bilingualism/multilingualism Functional literatcy in two or more languages; policies that promote the acquisition of more than one language.

biotechnology The application of science, especially genetic engineering, to living organisms in order to effect beneficial changes.

borderless economy Through alliances such as *NAFTA* and the European Union, the movement toward the *free trade* of goods and services across national borders.

capital The resources (money, land, raw material, labor, etc.) used to produce goods and services for the open market.

capitalism Economic system based on the ownership and exchange of goods and services by private individuals, and through which individual accumulation of resources is relatively unchecked by governmental regulations.

caste An ancient Indian system of social hierarchy, now much in decline, that held that social status was inherited and could not be changed. The term is more broadly used to indicate a class of people who cannot move up the social hierarchy.

centrist Politically inclined toward moderation and compromise.

civil liberties Guarantees of certain rights, such as freedom of speech and right of assembly. In the United States, these rights are upheld by the Constitution (although they are also frequently challenged in society as well as in the courts).

cold war From 1945 to 1991, a period of tensions and hostilities between the Soviet Union and its Warsaw Pact allies and the United States and its *NATO* allies. The era was marked by massive arms proliferation and mutual paranoia and distrust.

collectivity The sharing of resources and responsibilities among a community or social group, rather than dividing and accumulating individually.

colonialism/postcolonial From the sixteenth through the mid-twentieth century, the conquest and ruling of peoples in Asia, Africa, and South America by European nations.

commercialization The transformation of a concept or idea into something that can be marketed, bought, and sold.

communism Political *ideology* based on the public ownership of resources and centralized planning of the economy. Based on the philosophy of Karl Marx (1818–1883), who sought alternatives to what he saw as the exploitation of the working classes by the rise of *industrialization.*

conservative In the United States, referring to a political *ideology* that supports individual liberties and minimal governmental involvement in the economy. Also, a social inclination toward traditional morals and values and a resistance to change.

consumerism Until recently, policies and practices meant to protect consumers from bad business practices. Has come to mean a lifestyle focused on the accumulation of material goods at the expense of other values.

Creole Refers to both languages and peoples, with different specific implications depending on the geographical region discussed. Generally, refers to a people or language that is the result of a mingling of *cultures, races,* and *ethnicities,* often due to colonization.

culture The shared customs, traditions, and beliefs of a group of people. These shared values are learned by members of the group from each other, and members of a specific culture share, create, contribute to, and preserve their culture for future generations.

democracy A political system through which *enfranchised* citizens (people who are acknowledged by the state as citizens and have been granted the right to vote) determine governmental courses of action through elections.

developing world Nations, especially those formerly colonized or under *imperialist* domination, now moving toward *industrialization* and economic and political stability.

diaspora Originally applied to Jewish people living outside of Israel; now applied to groups of people "dispersed" or widely scattered from their original homelands.

disarmament Originally a *cold war* term used to describe ongoing negotiations between the *superpowers* to limit and eventually dismantle weapons systems; now describes the diplomatic work of convincing nations to stop or reverse the production of weapons (especially nuclear).

disenfranchised See *enfranchisement.*

ecosystem The fragile web of relationships between living beings and their environment.

emigration Leaving one country for another. See also *immigration*.

enfranchisement The granting of the right to vote to an individual or a group. To be "disenfranchised" is to have no vote, and by extension no voice in determining your own or your community's governance.

ethnic/ethnicity Referring to a shared sense of common religion, *race*, national, and/or *cultural* identity.

ethnic cleansing An organized effort to force or coerce an *ethnic* group from a region. In recent history, efforts at ethnic cleansing in places like Rwanda and Serbia has led to *genocide*.

ethnocentrism The belief that one's own *culture* or *ethnic* identification is superior to that of others.

ethnology The anthropological study of *cultures*.

Eurocentric/Eurocentrism A worldview that believes European or Western values to be superior.

expatriate Someone who lives in a country where he or she is not a citizen.

fascism An extremely repressive political *ideology* that exercises complete control over individual and *civil liberties* through the use of force.

feminism The theory that women should have the same political, economic, and social rights as men.

free-market economy An economic system in which individuals, acting in their own self-interest, make decisions about their finances, employment, and consumption of goods and services. In a free-market economy, the government provides and regulates common services such as defense, education, and transportation.

free trade Unrestricted trade of goods and services between countries, free from tariffs (which artificially inflate the prices of imported goods) and quotas (which limit the importation of certain goods in order to protect a country's own industries).

fundamentalism Reactionary movement to establish traditional religious values and texts as the primary and/or governing *ideology* in a society.

genocide The organized destruction of a group of people because of their *race*, religion, or *ethnicity*.

global village Term coined in the 1960s by media critic Marshall McLuhan to describe the ability of new communications technologies to bring peoples together.

global warming A gradual increase in global temperature and resulting changes in global climate, caused by the accumulation of "greenhouse gases" from the burning of fossil fuels and the deterioration of the ozone layer (which shields the earth from ultraviolet rays).

globalization The consolidation of societies around the world due to international trade, economic interdependence, the reach of *information technologies*, and the possible resulting loss of local traditions, languages, values, and resources.

GMO (genetically modified organism) A living entity (plant, animal, or microbe) that has been altered in some way through the intervention of genetic engineering.

hegemony The domination of one state, entity, or social group over another.

homogenous Referring to a society or *culture* of very limited diversity whose citizens share very similar racial and/or *ethnic* backgrounds.

human rights The Universal Declaration of Human Rights ratified by the United Nations in 1948 seeks to guarantee that all human beings have a fundamental dignity and basic rights of self-determination.

ideology A belief system that determines and guides the structure of a government and its relation to its citizens.

immigration The movement of people from their homeland to a new nation. See also *emigration*.

imperialism/empire The economic and cultural influence, and occasionally domination, of nations or peoples by stronger nations. The motives of "imperialist" nations are usually economic (the seeking of raw resources, the opening of new markets for trade) and/or *ideological* (e.g., in the nineteenth century, the British imperialist idea that England had a "duty" to bring "civilization" to other parts of the globe).

indigenous Referring to peoples understood to be "natives" or original inhabitants of lands now threatened by *urbanization* or other factors. Opponents of *globalization* argue that the *cultures* of indigenous peoples are under particular threat from the forces of *globalization*.

industrialization The transformation of an economy from agricultural to industrial, often followed by *urbanization*.

information age Term coined by media scholar Marshall McLuhan in 1964 to discuss the rapidly expanding reach (at the time, through television, radio, and print) of technologies that spread information.

information technology Any electronic technology that enhances the production and dissemination of textual, visual, and auditory content, such as computers and cellular telephones.

liberal Implying a political and social tolerance of different views and lifestyles. In the United States, applies to a political preference for increased governmental involvement, especially in matters of social welfare.

Luddite From an early-nineteenth-century anti*industrialization* movement in England; now describes a person who is opposed to technological progress because of its possible dehumanizing effects.

marginalization The effects of social and governmental policies that leave some members of a society *disenfranchised,* unable to seek or participate in common resources (such as education and health care) and/or unable to freely express themselves and their views.

Marxism A philosophy based on the work of political economist Karl Marx (1818–1883) and from which *socialism* and *communism* are derived. Marxist political thought focuses on the relationships between economic resources, power, and *ideology*, with the goal of redistributing resources equitably.

mestizo A Hispanic American of mixed European and *indigenous* ancestry.

monocultural Referring to a *culture* that is *homogenous* and resists diversification.

multiculturalism The belief that all *cultures* have intrinsic worth and that the diversity of *cultures* within a society is to be encouraged and celebrated.

multilateralism Cooperation between two or more nations on international issues.

NAFTA (North American Free Trade Agreement) An agreement between the United States, Canada, and Mexico that reduces governmental intervention in trade and investment between these countries.

nationalism Personal and communal feelings of loyalty to a nation; patriotism.

NATO (North Atlantic Treaty Organization) Defense alliance originally created in 1949 to counter the potential threat of the Soviet Union and its Warsaw Pact allies; now includes some of those former enemies in its membership.

naturalization The granting of citizenship, with its rights and privileges, to an immigrant.

NGO (nongovernmental organization) Organizations such as the International Red Cross, Doctors Without Borders, and the International Olympic Committee that provide aid or promote international cooperation without the specific involvement or oversight of governments.

patriarchy A society or worldview that subordinates women.

pluralism Encouragement by a society of competing and divergent political viewpoints.

political asylum Protection guaranteed by a government to refugees fleeing persecution in their own country because of their political beliefs or activism.

polygamy In some *cultures,* the practice of marrying more than one wife.

polyglot A person who speaks several languages, or referring to a community or *culture* in which several languages are spoken.

pop culture Values, traditions, and shared customs and references generated by the mass media, as opposed to values based on religion or *ideology.*

privatization The sale and transfer of formerly government-owned assets (such as utilities) to private corporations.

progressive Referring to a political inclination toward active reform, especially in *social justice.*

protectionism A government's efforts to protect its own agricultural and manufacturing industries from international competition. See also *free trade.*

race A group of people who have ancestry, physical characteristics, and *cultural* traditions in common. There is no genetic or "scientific" basis for the defining or classifying of an individual's "race."

rogue state A controversial term coined by the United States to describe states that act irrationally and that pose particular dangers to the United States and its allies. During the Clinton administration, the term was briefly replaced with "state of concern." Some opponents of *globalization* describe the United States itself as a "rogue state" for taking military, economic, and environmental actions without the participation or consideration of other states.

social justice A popular movement to redistribute wealth, resources, and political power more equitably among the members of a society.

socialism A political *ideology* based on considerable governmental involvement in the economy and other social institutions.

sovereignty The power of a state to govern itself and to defend its own interests.

Stalinism Referring to the methods of Joseph Stalin, general secretary of the Communist Party of the USSR and ruler of the Soviet Union from 1922 to 1953. A brutal dictator, his economic policies of forcing rapid *industrialization* and collectivization of agriculture resulted in massive suffering.

superpower During the *cold war*, term used to describe both the United States and the Soviet Union.

terrorism The use of random violence, especially against civilian targets, by ideologically motivated groups or individuals in an attempt to create social upheaval and to achieve recognition of their agenda.

Third World Term generally applied to nations moving toward *industrialization* and economic stabilization; the term *developing world* is now more commonly used.

totalitarianism An extremely repressive political system that attempts to completely control every aspect of a society through the use of force.

transnational A corporation or entity that conducts business and policy across national borders and has interests in several different nations.

urbanization The massive shift of a nation's peoples from rural, agrarian communities to large urban areas, usually as a result of *industrialization*.

utopia An idealized, speculative nation or system of government.

welfare state A nation that assumes primary governmental responsibility for the health, education, and social security of its citizens, often in exchange for heavy individual tax burdens.

Credits

Photo Credits

Chapter 1
P. 2: © AP Photo/Hussein Malla

Chapter 2
P. 30: © Steve Kelley/The Times-Picayune

Chapter 3
P. 76: © AP Photo/Robert Mecea

Chapter 4
P. 118: © NYTimes. P. 152: © SIPA Press

Chapter 5
P. 162: © AP Photo/D. Ross Cameron. P. 189: © David Horsey/Tribune Media Services

Chapter 6
P. 212: © AP Photo/ Christophe Ena

Chapter 7
P. 264: © AP Photo/ Santiago Llanquin. P. 294: © Christie's Images. P. 295: © Thonig/Mauritius. P. 296: © Thonig/Mauritius. P. 296: © Christie's Images. P. 299: © Brown Brothers, Inc.

Chapter 8
P. 308: © AP Photo/Prakash Hatvaine. P. 309: © AP Photo/Ernesto Mora

Chapter 9
P. 346: © AP Photo/Kamran Jebreili. P. 418: Courtesy NASA

Chapter 10
P. 390: © Still Pictures/Peter Arnold, Inc.

Casebook
P. 433: © Jonathan Becker. P. 445: © AP Photo/Amit Shabi. P. 452: © Metropolitan Museum of Art. P. 453: xml:namespace prefix = o ns = "urn: schemas-microsoft com:office:office" / Black and white photo enlargement of drawn original. Courtesy of the artist and Darren Knight Gallery, Sydney. P. 467: © Michael S. Yamashita/Corbis. P. 481: © Marjane Satrapi

Insert
P. 2: © AP Photo/Enric Marti. P. 3: © Joe McNally. P. 4: © Bob Krist. P. 5: © Joe McNally. P. 6: © AP Photo/Ramon Espinosa. P. 7: © AP Photo/Eric Draper. P. 8: © Michael Benanav

Text Credits

Chapter 1

P. 9: From "Love and Race" by Nicholas B. Kristof, *New York Times,*
December 6, 2002. Originally published in *The New York Times, 2002.*
Reprinted by permission of The New York Times Co. P. 16: From "The
Ladybugs," by Ray Gonzalez, in *September 11, 2001: American Writers
Respond,* edited by William Heyen, copyright 2003, published by Etruscan Press.
Reprinted by permission of Ray Gonzalez. P. 24: From "At Muslim Prom, It's
Girls-Only Night," by Patricia Leigh-Brown, *New York Times,* June 6, 2003.
Originally published in *The New York Times, 2003.* Reprinted by permission
of The New York Times Co.

Chapter 2

P. 31: Introduction from *The Way to Rainy Mountain* by N. Scott Momaday.
Copyright © 1969. Reprinted by permission of The University of New Mexico
Press. P. 38: From *Writin' Is Fightin'* by Ishmael Reed, Copyright © 2004 by
Houghton Mifflin Company. Permission granted by Lowenstein-Yost Associates,
Inc. P. 43: From "Our Rainbow Underclass" by Mortimer B. Zuckerman, *U.S.
News & World Report,* 9/23/02, p. 118. Copyright 2002 U.S. News & World
Report, L.P. Reprinted with permission. P. 46: From *Strangers from a Different
Shore* by Ronald Takaki. Copyright © 1989, 1998 by Ronald Takaki. By
permission of Little, Brown and Company, (Inc.). "You Spoke Japanese," by
Richard Oyama. Reprinted by permission of the author. P. 47: "Breaking
Silences" by Janice Mirikitani. Reprinted by permission of the author. P. 49:
From Kazuo Ito, *Issei: A History of Japanese Immigrants in North America.*
Copyright © 1973. P. 50: "From a Heart of Straw" in Nellie Wong, *Dreams in
Harrison Railroad Park.* Copyright © 1977. Reprinted by permission of Kelsey
Street Press. P. 53: From Kazuo Ito, *Issei: A History of Japanese Immigrants in
North America.* Copyright © 1973. P. 55: "American Dreamer" Copyright
© 1997 by Bharati Mukherjee. Used with the permission of the author and
Janklow & Nesbit. P. 62: From "The Cult of Ethnicity" by Arthur M.
Schlesinger, Jr., *Time,* July 8, 1991. © 1991 TIME Inc. reprinted by permission.
P. 65: From "Go North, Young Man" by Richard Rodriguez. Copyright © 1995
by Richard Rodriguez. First appeared in *Mother Jones.* Reprinted by permission
of Georges Borchardt, Inc., for the author.

Chapter 3

P. 77: Copyright © 1990 by Amy Tan. First appeared in *The Threepenny Review.*
Reprinted by permission of the author and the Sandra Dijkstra Literary Agency.
P. 84: Copyright © 1996 The *New York Times.* Reprinted by permission. P. 88:
Spanglish from "Spanish Spoken Here?" by Janice Castro, Dan Cook, and
Cristina Garcia, *Time,* July 11, 1988. © 1988 TIME Inc. reprinted by
permission. P. 91: From "If Black English Isn't a Language, Then Tell Me, What
Is?" by James Baldwin, *New York Times,* July 29, 1979. Originally published in
The New York Times, 1979. Reprinted by permission of The New York Times
Co. P. 96: Pages 1-10 from *Spanglish* by Ilan Stavans. Copyright © 2003 by Ilan
Stavans. Reprinted by permission of HarperCollins Publishers, Inc. P. 104: From

to Anti-Americanism Abroad" by Michael Medved, *The National Interest,* Summer 2002, pp. 5–14. Reprinted by permission of the author. **P. 243:** "The Culture of Liberty," by Mario Vargas Llosa, as appeared in *Foreign Policy,* January 1, 2001, pg. 66. Reprinted with permission. **P. 251:** From Paul Cantor, *Gilligan Unbound: Pop Culture in the Age of Globalization,* pp. 90–100 and 229–231. Copyright © 2001. Reprinted by permission of Rowman & Littlefield.

Chapter 7

P. 265: "Shooting an Elephant" from *Shooting an Elephant and Other Essays* by George Orwell, copyright 1950 by Sonia Brownell Orwell and renewed 1978 by Sonia Pitt-Rivers, reprinted by permission of Harcourt, Inc. **P. 273:** Copyright © 2001 *The New York Times.* Reprinted by permission. **P. 276:** From *What's So Great About America* by Dinesh D'Souza. Copyright © 2002 by Henry Regnery Publishing. All rights reserved. Reprinted by special permission of Regnery Publishing Inc., Washington, D.C., and the author. **P. 279:** "American Dream Boat" by K. Oanh Ha, *Modern Maturity,* May–June 2002, pp. 45–47, 84. Reprinted by permission of the author. **P. 284:** From "The West and the Rest: Intercivilizational Issues." Abridged with permission of Simon & Schuster Adult Publishing Group from *The Clash of Civilizations and the Remaking of World Order* by Samuel P. Huntington. Copyright © 1996 by Samuel P. Huntington. **P. 289:** Copyright © 2001 *The New York Times.* Reprinted by permission. **P. 292:** "Andalusia's Journey" by Edward Said, *Travel & Leisure,* December 2002, pp. 178–194. © 2002 by Edward Said printed with the permission of the Wylie Agency Inc.

Chapter 8

P. 310: "To Any Would-Be Terrorists," by Naomi Shihab Nye. Appeared in *September 11, 2001: American Writers Respond,* edited by William Heyen. Reprinted by permission of the author. **P. 315:** Reprinted by permission of International Creative Management, Inc. Copyright © 2002 by Anna Quindlen. First appeared in *Newsweek.* **P. 318:** "And Our Flag Was Still There" Copyright © 2001 by Barbara Kingsolver from *Small Wonder: Essays* by Barbara Kingsolver. Copyright © 2002 by Barbara Kingsolver. Reprinted by permission of HarperCollins Publishers Inc. **P. 322:** "Letter From New York" by Peter Carey, *The Observer,* September 23, 2001. Copyright © 2001 Peter Carey. Reproduced by permission of the author c/o Rogers, Coleridge & White Ltd., 20 Powis Mews, London W11 1JN. **P. 329:** "Bad Luck: Why Americans Exaggerate the Terrorist Threat" by Jeffrey Rosen, *The New Republic,* November 5, 2001, p. 21. Reprinted by permission of *The New Republic,* © 2001 The New Republic, LLC. **P. 333:** "Blaming America First" by Todd Gitlin, *Mother Jones,* Jan./Feb. 2002, pp. 22–25. © 2002, Foundation for National Progress. Reprinted by permission. **P. 339:** Copyright © 2001 Arundhati Roy. Reprinted from Arundhati Roy, "The Algebra of Infinite Justice," *The Progressive,* Volume 65, Number 12 (December 2001), pp. 28–31. Online at: http://www.progressive.org/0901/roy1201.html. A full version of this essay appears in Arundhati Roy, *Power Politics,* 2nd. ed. (Cambridge: South End Press, 2001), pp. 105–24.

Chapter 9

P. 347: "The Electronic Gap" by Paul Kennedy, *UNESCO Courier,* December 2001, p. 48. Reprinted by permission of the author. P. 350: "A Map of the Network Society" by Esther Dyson, *New Perspectives Quarterly*, Vol. 14, No. 2, March 22, 1997, pp. 25–28. Reprinted by permission of Blackwell Publishing Ltd. P. 356: From *What Just Happened* by James Gleick, Copyright © 2002 by James Gleick. Used by permission of Pantheon Books, a division of Random House, Inc. P. 364: "Webbed, Wired, and Worried" from "Columns: After" section in Thomas Friedman, *Longitudes and Attitudes: America in the Age of Terrorism,* 2002, pp. 259–261. Copyright © 2002 by The New York Times Co. Reprinted with permission. P. 367: Copyright © 2001 by The New York Times Co. Reprinted with permission. P. 372: From *Silicon Snake Oil* by Clifford Stoll, Copyright © 1995 by Clifford Stoll. Used by permission of Doubleday, a division of Random House, Inc. P. 381: "The Digital Revolution and the New Reformation" by Ali Mazrui and Alamin Mazrui, *Harvard International Review*, Spring 2001, pp. 52–55. Reprinted by permission of the authors.

Chapter 10

P. 391: "The Obligation to Endure" from *Silent Spring* by Rachel Carson. Copyright © 1962 by Rachel L. Carson, renewed 1990 by Roger Christie. Reprinted by permission of Houghton Mifflin Company. All rights reserved. P. 398: "Talking Trash" by Andy Rooney, *Diversion,* September 2002. Copyright, 2002, Tribune Media Services. Reprinted with permission. P. 401: Copyright 2001 *Christian Century*. Reprinted with permission from the 5/16, 2001, issue of the *Christian Century*. P. 405: "In the Jungle" from *Teaching a Stone to Talk: Expeditions and Encounters* by Annie Dillard. Copyright © 1982 by Annie Dillard. Reprinted by permission of HarperCollins Publishers Inc. P. 410: "Digging Up the Roots" by Jane Goodall, as appeared in *Orion*, Winter 1994. Copyright © 1994. Reprinted with permission. P. 415: Source: Worldwatch Institute, *World Watch*, Vol. 15, No. 4, copyright 2002, www.worldwatch.org. P. 421: "A Hole in the World" by Jonathan Schell. Reprinted with permission from the October 1, 2001, issue of *The Nation.* For subscription information, call 1-800-333-8536. Portions of each week's Nation magazine can be accessed at http://www.thenation.com.

Casebook

P. 431: From *The Storyteller's Daughter* by Saira Shah, copyright © 2003 by Saira Shah. Used by permission of Alfred A. Knopf, a division of Random House, Inc. P. 436: Excerpt from "Villages and Compounds" from *West of Kabul, East of New York* by Tamim Ansary. Copyright © 2002 by Tamim Ansary. Reprinted by permission of Farrar, Straus and Giroux, LLC. P. 440: "Blind Imperial Arrogance" by Edward Said, *Los Angeles Times*, July 20, 2003 (Op-Ed Section). © 2003 by Edward Said, reprinted with the permission of The Wylie Agency, Inc. P. 444: "We Have Done the Gruntwork of Peace" by Amos Oz, *The Guardian*, October 17, 2003, p. 6. Reprinted by permission of Deborah Owen Ltd. P. 450: "The Veiled Threat" by Azar Nafisi, *The New Republic,*

Index